Medieval Heresy

D1190811

To my wife

Medieval Heresy

Popular Movements from the Gregorian Reform to the Reformation

Second Edition

MALCOLM LAMBERT

BLACKWELL
Oxford UK & Cambridge USA

First edition published in 1977 by Edward Arnold as *Medieval Heresy: Popular
Movements from Bogomil to Hus*
Second edition first published 1992
Reprinted 1994, 1995, 1996, 1997, 1999, 2000

Blackwell Publishers Ltd
108 Cowley Road, Oxford OX4 1JF, UK

Blackwell Publishers Inc
350 Main Street, Malden, Massachusetts 02148, USA

British Library Cataloguing in Publication Data
A CIP catalogue record for this book is available from the British Library

Library of Congress Cataloging in Publication Data
Lambert, Malcolm (Malcolm D.)
Medieval heresy: popular movements from the Gregorian reform to
the Reformation / Malcolm Lambert.
p. cm.
Includes bibliographical references and index.
ISBN 0–631–17431–1 — ISBN 0–631–17432–X (pbk)
1. Heresies, Christian—History—Middle Ages, 600–1500.
I. Title.
BT1319.L35 1992 91–29539
273'.6—dc20 CIP

Typeset in Baskerville on 9.5/11pt
by Hope Services (Abingdon) Ltd
Printed and bound in Great Britain by T. J. Press Ltd, Padstow, Cornwall

This book is printed on acid-free paper

Contents

List of maps

List of illustrations

Acknowledgements

I owe the idea of writing about medieval heresy to Professor N. Cantor. For the opportunity of studying at the Monumenta Germaniae Historica I am indebted to the Alexander von Humboldt Stiftung, whose generosity to its beneficiaries extends beyond academic interests. For hospitality and guidance I am grateful to the late Professor H. Grundmann; for bibliographical advice I am indebted to Dr H. Lietzmann, and for help to Dr M. Polock, Professors J. M. Bak, S. Ćirković, J. Šidak and the late Mr D. Bethell. I am grateful also to the seminars of Professor E. Werner at Leipzig and Professor B. Töpfer in East Berlin for stimulus, even where I disagreed, and to the late Professor D. C. Douglas and Mr W. K. Ford for encouragement. I received from the Colston Research Fund a welcome grant.

Miss S. Rainey worked on proofs and index of the first and second editions; Dr J. V. Fearns and Dr J. Fines gave me access to their theses.

I am indebted to a series of scholars for commenting on chapters and correcting errors. Professor J. B. Russell read drafts on eleventh-century heresy, Mr R. I. Moore on the Cathars, Miss B. Bolton on Innocent III and the Free Spirit, Dr J. A. F. Thomson and the late Mr J. W. Sherborne on the Lollards, Professor F. Seibt and Dr A. V. Antonovics on the Hussites, Dr A. V. Antonovics also on introductory material on the late Middle Ages. Professor R. E. Lerner read an early draft of the whole; Mr A. Murray and Professor C. N. L. Brooke read a more recent version and gave me many hints. Professor W. L. Wakefield commented fully on the first seven chapters, and showed me the Cathar sites near Toulouse.

My father first interested me in historical research and commented shrewdly to the end of his life on all I wrote. It is my keenest regret that he did not live to see publication.

For the second edition, as for the first, I owe a debt to the staff of Bristol University Library, especially Mr J. Edwards, and Mrs Bradford and her team in Inter-Library Loans. Mrs Jones, assistant secretary in the Department of Theology, University of Bristol, and Mrs Perry of Eastcombe have typed for me. Professor W. Eberhard has advised on the Hussites and Dr P. Biller on the Waldensians. To Dr D. Turner, head of the Department of Theology at Bristol University 1986–9, and his colleagues, I owe the happiest years of my university career.

To my wife I owe comment, encouragement and assistance at every stage. The dedication is but a poor return for her unfailing support. In a real sense she has been a co-author and I do not think I would have finished this book or its second version without her.

M.D.L.
The Yews
Eastcombe
Stroud
Gloucestershire GL6 7DN

Preface

This book is a working synthesis of the state of research on popular heretical movements in Western Europe from the Gregorian reform to the Reformation, intended both for the undergraduate reader who needs a one-volume introduction and for the scholar working in one portion of this vast field who wants a handbook for quick reference on the subject as a whole. 'Popular' has been taken to mean movements with a substantial following amongst laymen. Individual heretical episodes involving small numbers may only be included in so far as they reveal a stage in the growth of a movement on a larger scale. Intellectual heresy would make another book; it has not been studied here, except in those cases where it gave a direct impetus to a popular heresy. Thus the case of Abelard, despite the general interest it aroused, is excluded; Wyclif, on the other hand, because of his effect on the Lollards, is given a chapter, and space is devoted to learned disputes about Wyclif and his teaching in the University of Prague because they are essential to the understanding of the Hussite revolt, which was a popular movement.

The history of medieval heresy is a history of failure, for none of the movements surveyed succeeded either in imposing their views on the Western Church or in gaining toleration for their opinions and practices. Condemnation of their beliefs as heretical by the papacy, whatever the time-lag or the vicissitudes on the way, led either to effective repression and so to extinction, as in the case of the Cathars, or to an underground, often precarious, survival, as in the case of the Lollards or the Waldensians. Substantial doctrinal unity in the Church was maintained partly by force, and partly by a continuing public commitment to the cause of orthodoxy; when this broke down, and beliefs condemned as heretical maintained themselves successfully against all efforts at repression, the Middle Ages was at an end.

I have written as a historian, not a theologian. I have taken heresy to mean whatever the papacy explicitly or implicitly condemned during the period. It has to be recognized, of course, that the growth of heresies and the failure of local authorities to deal effectively with them was one factor in the extension of papal power in the Church, and that it was some time before a clear legal concept of heresy emerged from the uncertainties of the eleventh and twelfth centuries: nevertheless, this definition will be a convenient working tool. It may incidentally lead to criticism in relation to the Hussites: some historians, not without reason, regard the moderate wing of the Hussites as reformers rather than heretics, and note that the condemnation of Hus was the work of a council that itself had unorthodox views of the papacy. Yet Hus denied the medieval doctrine of the papacy, and even the moderate Utraquists received papal condemnation. I have therefore, with consistency, treated the Hussite movement as heretical. Where Byzantine heresy is concerned, I have followed the decisions of the patriarchate of Constantinople; for early heresy, I have followed the decisions of the great councils of the undivided Church.

When dealing with certain Western heresies, I have felt justified in making a distinction between 'real' heresies, that involved a major distortion of orthodox belief or practice, and 'artificial' heresies, which as an ensemble in a living context did not exist, as in the case of the Free Spirit of the late Middle Ages. The case of the poverty of Christ and the heresy of the *fraticelli* occupies a curious position. A real heresy was present, it seems to me, and predated the counteractions of authority. The distortions of the ideal of poverty involved threatened to overturn the balance of Christian ethics; yet the actual decisions, whereby the pope of the time condemned them and tried to uproot the basis of their ideas in the Franciscan order, were in fact based on technical issues, and may fairly be called 'artificial'. The concept of 'artificial' heresy also enables me to give attention to the cases in which unpopular groups or individuals were smeared with slanderous charges by authority at various levels or by local opinion and to allude, but no more, to the closely allied subject of witchcraft.

Allocation of space has been dictated by consideration of the intrinsic importance of a particular movement and by the availability of secondary literature. Catharism and its antecedents has been given substantial space, justified by the importance of the counteraction which it inspired in the Church and by the lack of summaries in English. Both Joachimism and the problems of the Franciscans have already been given extensive up-to-date treatment in English: the accounts of these, therefore, are cut short. Lollardy post-1414, well recorded in English from the point of view of prosecutions, is studied at a length greater than the importance of its adherents alone would deserve because it affords us a valuable body of information from a limited area about the conduct of heretics under persecution. Hussitism is given the largest space of all because of its significance as the movement which had the greatest potential to destroy the doctrinal supremacy of the Roman Church. Politics in this case is inextricably intertwined with the growth of heresy, so that any meaningful account must be a long one.

Advances have been made since the first edition of this book, using the techniques of anthropology and sociology, in understanding the origins of the revival of heresy in the West in the eleventh century. I used to believe that the Byzantine dualist heresy of Bogomilism began to touch the West in that epoch. Fresh work, especially on the heresy at Orléans and on the significance of the Peace of God movement in Aquitaine, has caused me to retreat from that view. I have rewritten the chapter, focusing on a limited number of heretical episodes, in order to provide a better synthesis and to give the reader a picture early on in the book of the awkward, prejudiced character of so much of the source material for heresy.

My general survey has become more 'Western' in its emphasis, and gives less attention to the Byzantine Church and its fringe areas. A chapter on the Bogomils has been excised, as has been a section on the problem of the Bosnian Church. Bogomils still mattered for the rise and development of the Western heresy of Catharism and fresh, significant work has been done on Bosnia. But I hope to come back to these themes in a forthcoming book on the Cathars. For this reason, the revised edition does not go into the fine new work on Catharism in any depth. I am indebted to Emeritus Professor W. L. Wakefield for the gift of certain unpublished chapters on Catharism and the inquisition in the south of France, where he is a master, they will be used in the new book.

The study of Waldensianism as an underground movement, especially in German-speaking lands, in the centuries following the Waldensian Conference of Bergamo in 1218 has made great strides since the first edition. A definitive answer on outstanding problems, especially about differing Waldensian groups and their teaching, has not been reached; none the less the outline of a consensus is discernible and has led me to recast entirely the chapter on the Waldensians after 1218.

The first edition ended with the reconciliation of the Hussites with the Church at Jihlava in 1436 and the return of their hated king, Sigismund. It certainly marked the end of an epoch in the struggles of the Bohemians, but a review by the late Professor A. Molnár and the reading of two volumes by Professor W. Eberhard on late Hussitism and the formation of confessions convinced me that I was wrong to stop the Hussite narrative at that point. I have added a new chapter, taking the story of the Utraquists and the *Unitas Fratrum* up to the decree of toleration of Kutná Hora of 1485 and examined the fate of Hussitism in the epoch of the Reformation in another chapter, replacing a slim epilogue on medieval heresy and the Reformation in the first edition.

In this new chapter only three movements are looked at in any detail: the Waldensians, the Lollards and the Hussites (including with the Utraquists the *Unitas Fratrum*). That has the advantage of giving English readers introduction to the high scholarship of Dr G. Audisio on the Waldensians in the Luberon and the strange episode of the payment by the Waldensians of the Valleys for the French translation of the Bible by Olivétan in a language few could understand. The Lollards stand in the centre of the vivid debate among scholars about the nature of popular response in England to the entry of Reform ideas from the Continent. The Utraquists in the sixteenth century have been underestimated and the work of Eberhard is not well known to English readers.

The chapter on the English Lollards has needed more change than most because of the major work of editing and analysis by Professor A. Hudson. All study of medieval heresy is weakened because of the lack of original source material from the condemned heretics themselves. In the case of the Lollards, that is much less the case than in the past because of Professor Hudson's uncovering of much scholarly literary material written by Wyclif supporters, and her work has imposed some reassessment of the potential menace presented by the heresy in the years before Oldcastle's revolt.

Professor Norman Cohn has so effectively revised his work *The Pursuit of the Millennium* as to knock out the criticisms I expressed in the first edition and I have simply excised them. I am only sorry that knowledge of his revision had not then reached me. Subsequently he has put all historians of popular religion in his debt by a survey of Satanism and religious slander in his *Europe's Inner Demons*.

Every historian of heresy must encounter the conflict of emphasis between the supporters of religious and of socio-economic factors as prime movers in the genesis of heresy. It dates back at least as far as the still-living work of G. Volpe, and it has received fresh impetus by political divisions amongst scholars since the war. To my mind, the late Professor H. Grundmann is the best single guide to popular medieval heresy; like him, I believe that the first necessity for the historian of heresy is to examine the religious and intellectual climate of orthodoxy in order to understand deviations from it. On the other hand, supporters of the 'religious' view, among whom I am to be numbered, have not always been ready enough to visualize the concrete situation in which heresy arises, and have been too easily satisfied with merely negative refutations of the most simplified socio-economic views. I am convinced that there is more to be said on this side and that detailed analysis of individual cases of heresy, or heresy-bearing localities will continue to advance understanding in the future.

Two books published after my first edition went to press demonstrate how detailed investigation brings progress. One is Le Roy Ladurie's *Montaillou*, which, in the context of a remote Pyrenean village, puts before us the blend of motives which sustained heresy there: the influence of peasant fatalism, of the wandering life of the shepherd, of family power and tradition, of a doubt and materialism that sometimes has a surprisingly modern ring, of wavering consciences, and of the search for salvation. The other is R. I. Moore's *Origins of European Dissent*, which, breaking down such phrases as 'Gregorian reform' and clarifying the effects of religion on communities, marriage and legal judgements, shows us case by case through the refracting mirror of the chroniclers what made the heretical leaders of the early centuries of dissent effective.

The format of a one-volume introduction necessarily tends to put greatest emphasis on the religious aspect; as I write, I have been conscious that I have been able to say less about the often subtle social and economic background to these movements than I could have wished. The maps showing the distribution of heresy which I have included, none the less, may do something to rectify that deficiency. They are sketches, and in most cases they are necessarily incomplete; for they tell us, not about the total distribution of heresy in a locality, but about the distribution of detected heresy, which may be a very different matter; they are subject to all the idiosyncrasies of evidence which attach to underground movements, yet I hope that they will act as a stimulus to further and fuller investigation of the reasons why heresy settled in certain localities. The map of the Waldensians in Austria, taken from Dr M. Nickson's work, shows how a heresy may be embedded in the countryside; so, too, does the map of Cathars in the Lauragais, derived from Dr Y. Dossat's work, which, combined with his evidence of the incidence of certain punishments in the inquisition held there in 1245–6, gives a clue to the numbers then involved in heresy. The map of the spread of the Waldensians from the original nucleus at Lyons in the first century of their existence, taken from the work of Dr J. V. Fearns, shows the variety of environments in which heresy could take hold; a new map, drawn from Professor A. Patschovsky's edition of sources for inquisitions in Bohemia in the fourteenth century, illustrates the remarkable spread of heresy there before the coming of Hussitism. The map of Lollardy underground, based on the work on prosecutions by Dr J. A. F. Thomson and Dr J. Fines, shows how heresy may fan out in villages and hamlets from the effects of a preacher's activity, and illustrates the relationship which existed in late Lollardy between heresy and textile areas. A further map, based on an analysis of Foxe's *Martyrs*, plots for contrast with Lollardy the places of origin and of burning of the Marian martyrs. One other map, that of the dualist Churches and the spread of conflict among the heretics, is not concerned with geographical distribution or social origin of heresy, but rather is designed to recall to the reader the degree to which late twelfth-century Catharism was dependent on the dualists of the Balkans and Byzantium.

The pioneer of the study of medieval heresy in modern times for the English reader was H. C. Lea, the historian of the inquisition; his work, in three volumes,[1] seriously outdated on many aspects, remains the most comprehensive treatment of the subject, and may still be used with profit. Lea wrote with a powerful indignation. He hated the Middle Ages and its Church, and he lacked any sympathetic understanding of the persecuting churchmen and their ideals. Yet the reader who disagrees with Lea and his lack of perspective while admiring his detailed scholarship, must still be reminded that the history of medieval heresy is a terrible story – one of persecution of men and women for their religious opinions.

---

[1] H. C. Lea, *A History of the Inquisition of the Middle Ages* (New York, 1888); review: J. Dahlberg-Acton, *EHR* III (1888), pp. 773–88.

Part I

The beginnings

I

The problem of heresy

Heresy, and the horror it inspires, intertwines with the history of the Church itself. Jesus warned his disciples against the false prophets who would take His name and the Epistle to Titus states that a heretic, after a first and second abomination, must be rejected. But Paul, writing to the Corinthians, said, 'Oportet esse haereses', as the Latin Vulgate translated his phrase – 'there must be heresies, that they which are proved may be manifest among you'[1] – and it was understood by medieval churchmen that they must expect to be afflicted by heresies.

Heresy was of great importance in the early centuries in forcing the Church progressively to define its doctrines and to anathematize deviant theological opinions. At times, in the great movements such as Arianism and Gnosticism, heresy seemed to overshadow the Church altogether. Knowledge of the individual heresies and of the definitions which condemned them became a part of the equipment of the learned Christian; the writings of the Fathers wrestled with these deviations, and lists of heresies and handbooks assimilated this experience of the early centuries and handed it on to the Middle Ages.

Events after Christianity became the official religion of the Empire also shaped the assumptions with which the Church of the Middle Ages met heresy. After Constantine's conversion, Christians in effect held the power of the State and, despite some hesitations, they used it to impose a uniformity of belief. Both in the eastern and in the western portions of the Empire it became the law that pertinacious heretics were subject to the punishments of exile, branding, confiscation of goods, or death. These regulations survived the fall

---

[1] Titus 3: 10; 1 Cor. 11: 19. H. Grundmann, 'Oportet et haereses esse: Das Problem der Ketzerei im Spiegel der mittelalterlichen Bibelexegese', *AKG* xlv (1963), pp. 129–64. For the meaning of the Greek term from which 'heresy' is derived in Titus and other early sources, see L. Goppelt, *Apostolic and Post-Apostolic Times*, tr. R. A. Guelich (London, 1970), pp. 165–77. I owe this reference to Mr W. K. Ford.

of the Empire, and so did the assumption that it was the right of the Church to call on the State to put down heresy.

Heresy was not thought to be the product of the individual speculative intelligence, or of devout men and women seeking a higher ethical life – still less of oppressed lower classes demanding better conditions and masking their economic objectives in the outwardly religious forms of their age. All these interpretations have been put forward by modern historians of medieval heresy, but they are quite alien to the assumptions of churchmen, whether of the Middle Ages or of the early centuries of the Church. They believed that heresy was the work of the devil. Descriptions of heretics were couched in sets of favourite adjectives and texts, passed on from author to author, and only too often imposed with scant discrimination on the heretics, their beliefs and practices.[2] Some were an inheritance passed on to the Middle Ages from the age of the Fathers; others were developed in the Middle Ages themselves. The descriptions served primarily to develop a set of conventional characteristics of the type-figure of the heretic: his pride, which must be a feature, for he has set himself up against the teaching of the Church; his superficial appearance of piety, which must be intended to deceive, and cannot be real, since he is in fact the enemy of the faith; and his secrecy, which is contrasted to the openness of Catholic preaching. He may well be described as unlettered (even if this is not entirely true), since *a priori* he lacks the equipment of the orthodox churchman; he may be accused of counterfeiting piety while actually indulging in libertinism – an accusation which strangely repeats those made by pagan writers against early Christians, and sometimes appears to feed on the same material. His beliefs may be crudely assimilated to the heresies of the patristic age, even when they are quite unrelated, though this tendency fades as more accurate knowledge of actual medieval heresy penetrates the conventions. The bulk of sources emanate from the repressing forces or the chroniclers on the Catholic side, and their descriptions are thus shaped by these conventions. Surviving work of the heretics, in which we can see for ourselves the nature of their teaching, is very much less, either because the heresy was conveyed more often by word of mouth than by writing, or because repression has destroyed documents.

The historian thus faces acute problems of evidence when he wishes to study the behaviour, motives and beliefs of the medieval heretic. He is dealing much of the time with underground movements existing behind a barrier of secrecy – and because Church and State are most often combined against them, they are willy nilly secret opposition movements hostile to authority. As a modern historian, he must elucidate motives from sources which are very rarely concerned with them, and scrape off layers of convention and prejudice from his originals in order to reach a true delineament of the heretics.

The subject is also two-sided. It takes two to create a heresy: the heretic,

[2] H. Grundmann, 'Der Typus des Ketzers in mittelalterlicher Anschauung', *Kultur- und Universalgeschichte Festschrift für Walter Goetz* (Leipzig and Berlin, 1927), pp. 91–107 (fundamental for approach to sources); for a collection of his articles, of fundamental importance, see *Ausgewählte Aufsätze* I: *Religiöse Bewegungen* (Stuttgart, 1976), II: *Joachim von Fiore* (Stuttgart, 1977), III: *Bildung und Sprache* (Stuttgart, 1978); obituary assessment: A. Borst in I, pp. 1–25, bibliography: H. Lietzmann, I, pp. 26–37. I owe gifts of these volumes to Dr Lietzmann. P. Biller, 'Topos und Wirklichkeit des Ketzers als 'Illiteratus', ' *Religiöse Laienbildung und Ketzerabwehr im Mittelalter*, ed. D. Harmening, Würzburg, 1994 (forthcoming). A Patschovsky, 'Der Ketzer als Teüfelsdiener', *Papsttum. Kirche und Recht im Mittelalter*, ed. H. Mordek, Tübingen, 1991, pp. 317–34.

with his dissident beliefs and practices; and the Church, to condemn his views and to define what is orthodox doctrine. It was in the persistent resistance to the teaching of the Church that heresy consisted: error became heresy when, shown his deviation, the obstinate refused to obey and retract. In the thirteenth century Robert Grosseteste's definition stated that 'a heresy is an opinion chosen by human perception contrary to holy Scripture, publicly avowed and obstinately defended'. The Church, confronted from the twelfth century onwards with a challenge from hostile sects, was forced, step by step, to recognize how these sects differed from those of late antiquity, and to take new measures to deal with them. A machinery was created both for defining doctrine and for uncovering and putting down those who refused to accept the decisions of authority.[3] Not all of these developments have been fully studied by medievalists, for, although we have known much since Lea of the origins and workings of one of the instruments of repression, the inquisition, much more needs to be known about the doctrinal decision-making of ecclesiastical authority and the way in which the medieval concept of heresy was built up. Moreover, the search for understanding of the motives of the heretic will take the historian into the study of medieval societies and economic changes and into the issues of the morale of the faithful, the conditions in regional Churches and the effect of abuse in stimulating heresies. All are subjects open to investigation, where often enough no final word, even within the limitations of our sources, has yet been said.

In view of these difficulties, both of the multifarious nature of the subject and of the problematic, sometimes prejudiced, sources, it is hardly surprising that the study of medieval heresies has tended to lag behind research on other facets of medieval history. Yet heresies are an integral part of the medieval scene in a number of countries, and their growth is a phenomenon which runs side by side with, often directly influencing, such well-known developments as the rise of papal power, the growth of the canon law, the emergence of religious orders and the development of the crusading ideal. The need for detection and repression of heresy shaped the Western Church for the future for good and ill, and in political history was occasionally of decisive importance, as for example the Albigensian crusades in French history and the Hussite crisis for the lands of the Bohemian crown. The heretical movements of the Middle Ages failed in their purpose, but they nevertheless left their imprint on the course of events.

Comparative neglect has in recent years given way to an upsurge of interest among scholars; a number of discoveries have enlarged the store of works written by heretics themselves, or have enabled us at least to get closer to their ideas and to shake off some of the distortions of the Catholic source material. The time is ripe for a summary in English, to survey the whole field, and to give a guide to recent progress – bearing in mind always that fresh research in a subject in rapid flux is bound to change current generalizations, and that the

[3] On the medieval notion of heresy, see *MBPH*, pp. 1–7 and *The Concept of Heresy in the Middle Ages (11th–13th C.)* Medievalia Lovaniensia Series I, Studia IV, ed. W. Lourdaux and D. Verhelst (Leuven and The Hague, 1976). See also prologue to G. Leff, *Heresy in the Later Middle Ages: The Relation of Heterodoxy to Dissent c. 1250–c. 1450* (Manchester, 1967), 2 vols (survey stressing intellectual factors); reviews: H. S. Offler, in *EHR* LXXXIV (1969), pp. 572–6; M. D. Lambert, in *History* LV (1970), pp. 75–9.

refracting mirror of medieval assumptions about heresy and the scarcity of the
requisite type of sources will always tend to inhibit our vision of the truth.

Not only the existence of the assumption that State and Church have a duty
to persecute and the emergence of a machinery to detect and examine
religious dissidents, shaped the conditions of existence of the medieval heretic.
He was also subject to one basic principle of medieval Christianity generally:
that the heretic who wilfully persisted in his error was condemned to the pains
of hell for eternity. The persistent dissident was thus not only defying a visible
authority – and, as we shall see, that authority was not always very clearly in
evidence, or actively pursuing heretics; he was also challenging the fear of
damnation, and backing his own judgement or that of his group against a
spiritual authority with the power to decide his eternal future. That groups of
men and women in medieval society were prepared to make this defiance is
one of the striking facts to record, and one major theme of this book will be the
examination, where possible, of the motives which led them to do it. Second
only in interest to this question is that of the failure of all medieval heretical
movements that made this defiance to survive in the long term. Why, we may
ask, having once challenged authority, were these heretics severally unable to
maintain the independence of their beliefs?

The search for salvation, coupled with the conviction that the Church no
longer channelled the means of salvation or had distorted the teaching of
Christ or was temporarily in the hands of evil men, was the most important
single factor impelling the leaders of heretical movements to challenge
ecclesiastical authority. Conviction that their reading or hearing of Scripture
or an inner illumination or the instruction of a holy man and the conferring of
a valid sacrament where the Church's sacraments had become valueless,
overrode the decisions of priests, bishops or popes.

The search for salvation moved the rank and file of such movements as well
as the leaders: we have a vivid demonstration of this in the battle for souls at
the deathbed between the Cathar *consolamentum* and the Catholic last rites, and
the wavering of the sick and their relatives between rival claims.

Eloquence could change lives – briefly or permanently. If the preacher
could fuse through his exhortation social and economic grievance and a
religious exaltation, extraordinary events became possible. For a moment at
Le Mans in 1116, Henry the Monk, blending Lenten revivalism with
anticlerical emotions, broke down social barriers, brought prostitutes to
repentance and induced young men to marry them; on a far wider scale
in Bohemia three centuries later, radical Hussite preachers led peasant
families to go *en masse* on pilgrimage to the hills, joining large-scale preachings
and celebrations of communion in both kinds, breaching the normal barriers
of society and creating the manpower for the most effective of Hussite
armies.

The appeal of the great heresies, Cathar, Waldensian, Lollard, was
perennial, supra-regional and transcended the personalities of their leaders.
Given that this was so, it is necessary to look at local and regional conditions
in order to understand why a heretical movement survived or even prospered
in one area rather than another; to explain this, the political, social or

economic circumstances of a region will be decisive.[4] Northern Italy was the land of heresy *par excellence* because of its social pressures and its intellectual vitality, and above all because its cities prized their independence so highly that they preferred to tolerate heretics rather than surrender to the demands of their bishops or of popes. Parts of Languedoc were a seed-ground for Catharism because of its chronic political anarchy, which deterred secular authority from repression of religious dissidence, and because of a certain casual, meridional tradition of tolerance, which gave time for its missionaries to gain recruits and build up their Churches. The city of Rome's material grievances gave Arnold of Brescia a political and religious platform for his teaching on poverty and the disendowment of the Church. It was no accident that Milan was at one and the same time a fast-growing industrial centre and the cradle of proliferating heretical groups. The clash of Czech and German speakers in Prague and the social tensions of the New Town account for much in the history of Hussitism.

And yet, however much the fate of the movements with mass support rested on these varying terrestrial circumstances, the actions of the dedicated heretic were dictated far more by conscience and his conviction that he was doing the will of God as he braved persecution. Some historians have been inclined to see in the chroniclers' accounts of heretics accepting their fate with equanimity, even with joy, literary *topoi* with an insecure basis in fact. Not so: better-recorded narratives of the bearing of dedicated men and women before the fire, and some modern medical information, make these stories wholly credible. The stake was the last and fiercest test; the courage of the heretical missionaries and the strongest of their supporters developed over the years made them ready, when all opportunities of escape failed, to face a cruel death. Their religious convictions account for the longevity of the movements for which they sacrificed their days.

Defiance none the less ended either in destruction or at least in the cowing and marginalizing of these movements. Repression makes martyrs, but, efficiently conducted, it is also largely successful. In a sufficient number of cases, orthodoxy commanded the services of the secular arm, the emperors, kings and aristocrats with military and economic power. Studies devoted to the analysis of medieval heresies may often unwittingly conceal this point, because they are concerned with the exceptions, the occasions when repression was ineffective or not even attempted. At most times and in most places orthodoxy had support, and not only the support of the leadership in society, but of rank and file too. In the Albigensian Crusade, for example, volunteers repeatedly came to serve in the south of France in order to repress heresy, and although some came in the expectation of winning land, others came out of religious conviction and served the time needful to gain the crusading indulgence, then went home. In the long history of Lollardy, the bulk of the English populace remained indifferent to the heresy. Some were

[4] Anthropology shows itself fruitful; for general comments, see J. L. Nelson, 'Society, theodicy and the origins of heresy: towards a reassessment of the medieval evidence', in *SCH* IX, pp. 65–77; another view: T. Asad, 'Medieval heresy: an anthropological view', *Social History* XI (1986), pp. 354–62; survey of hypotheses: J. B. Russell, 'Interpretations of the origins of medieval heresy', *MS* XXV (1963), pp. 26–53. The latest historiography is in G. G. Merlo, *Eretici ed Eresie Medievali nella Storiografia Contemporanea*, Torre Pellice, 1994 (see esp. P. Biller's report, pp. 39–63).

positively hostile, as is demonstrated by the grim evidence of the will of a London goldsmith, bequeathing money to buy faggots for the burning of heretics.

Both heresy and the defence of orthodoxy stirred deep emotions, and struggles over heresy had a major impact on the course of events in the Middle Ages.

2

The revival of heresy in the West:
the eleventh century

Heresy and politics at Orléans

Sometime after a fire in the year 1078 Paul, a monk of the community of St Père de Chartres, celebrating the memory of Aréfast, a Norman aristocrat, benefactor and former member of the community, inserted in the cartulary which he was compiling a vivid account of the startling events in which his hero had been involved some sixty years previously.[1] His narrative has circumstantial details which suggest the evidence of an eye-witness, conceivably Aréfast himself; or Paul may have had a *libellus* in front of him, written by an Aréfast supporter much closer to the events to edify and to praise his achievement. We shall never know exactly from where Paul got his information; what we have from the *excursus* in his cartulary is a moral tale, the spiritual odyssey of a layman, who set out on a chivalrous quest[2] on behalf of

[1] *Gesta Synodi Aurelianensis* in Bouquet, x, pp. 536–9; tr. *WEH* (largest collection of translated texts, with historical sketch, pp. 1–55), pp. 76–81, also *MBPH*, pp. 10–15 (working selection of translated texts up to triumph of Catharism; introduction to medieval attitudes, pp. 1–7). I am indebted for information to Professor W. L. Wakefield and Mr R. I. Moore. Paul of St Père remains the prime source. He had access to the recollections of the contemporary eye-witness Aréfast, gives concrete detail and sometimes appears to echo the words of the accused in the trial. In all points derived from Aréfast or the trial, he may be taken as accurate. As we have it, the source is, admittedly, a very late one. B. Stock, *The Implications of Literacy: Written Language and Models of Interpretation in the Eleventh and Twelfth Centuries* (Princeton, 1983), as part of his illuminating analysis of chroniclers' thought-world, develops the hypothesis that Paul was using an earlier *libellus* (below, p. 13, n. 10). That would explain the ring of authenticity in his account. The story of the orgy and the viaticum from a dead child has literary antecedents and should be excised as a legendary digression. For other sources see appendix to my *Medieval Heresy*, 1st edn (London, 1977), pp. 343–7, abandoning my hypothesis of Bogomil infiltration and noting that the heading 'rejection of flesh eating' for Jean of Fleury (p. 344) should be enlarged in the light of the essential revision made in R. H. Bautier, 'L'hérésie d'Orléans et le mouvement intellectuelle au début du xie siècle', *Actes du 95e Congrès National des Sociétés savantes (Rheims, 1970): Section philologique et historique* (Paris, 1975), i, pp. 63–88; *libellus* and analysis of Paul: pp. 67–9, 76–7; H. Fichtenau, *Ketzer und Professoren Häresie und Vernunftglaube im Hochmittelalter*, Munich, 1992, pp. 33–43 (parallel discussion of popular heresy, culminating in Cathars, and academic developments; numerous facts and insights, though it is hard to bring together the two sections, as the author desired).

[2] Stock, *Literacy*, p. 109.

the Church, survived the trials and dangers of a heretical circle and played a major part, when the efforts of the natural authorities, king and bishops, were in danger of foundering, in unmasking an evil sect.

These events have been freshly analysed by R. H. Bautier in a publication of 1975.[3] In the narrative which follows, Paul's exposition has been put side by side with the facts about the political and ecclesiastical allegiances of the protagonists, as Bautier has elucidated them.

Orléans was a centre of education, and of critical importance in a long-running battle for power between Robert the Pious, king of France, and his rival, Eudes II, Count of Blois, who needed the city to establish links between his holdings in the Sancerrois and his counties of Blois, Chartres and Tours. He who controlled the bishopric was a fair way towards controlling the city and its surrounding territory. Robert imposed on the chapter his candidate, Thierry, a protegé of his queen, Constance. The disappointed rival, Odalric, was a nephew of the bishop of Beauvais and, probably, of Eudes II: in any case, he was Eudes' man. Robert's intervention was controversial, but he got his way. Some of the chapter appealed for assistance to the honoured figure of Fulbert, bishop of Chartres, who condemned Robert's intervention and declined to take part in the consecration of Thierry. Some years passed. Suddenly, most likely late in 1022, Thierry was displaced. Odalric reigned in his place and Thierry took flight, first to his former monastery, St Pierre-le-Vif at Sens, and then to Rome. He died on the way.

Thierry's departure was a major defeat for Robert the Pious's party. At Christmas 1022 Robert journeyed with Queen Constance to Orléans to preside over a synod of bishops. A scandal had been uncovered in Orléans and the backlash from it had led to a shift of power. The bishops proceeded to interrogate a distinguished group of clergy, its core lying in the canons of the church of Holy Cross. The total may have been as many as twenty, including, as well as the canons, nuns and other women, clergy, members of the nobility and Stephen, one-time confessor to Queen Constance. Aréfast, who was of the lineage of the dukes of Normandy and vassal to Duke Richard II, a member of the alliance of Eudes II of Blois, had got wind of heresy through his chaplain, Heribert, who had studied in Orléans and had learnt heresy in the house of Stephen, the queen's confessor, and Lisois, a canon of Holy Cross. Aréfast took action. When Heribert tried to ensnare him, he contacted his duke, who alerted King Robert. A trap was set. Posing as a potential convert, Aréfast set out for Orléans, turning in by the way to consult Fulbert, bishop of Chartres, the opponent of Thierry and a natural supporter of Eudes II. In Fulbert's absence, he took advice from Evrard, sacristan of Chartres, who recommended him to dissimulate, to listen and in due course to expose, while all the time availing himself of the protection afforded by Christ and the Church, praying, making the sign of the cross and doing what would have been unusual in a layman of the time, receiving holy communion every day.

It turned out to be a thoroughgoing heresy, traces of which in Orléans apparently went back to about 1015. The core of the heretics' beliefs lay in a *gnosis*, entry to which was conferred by a ceremony of laying-on of hands.

[3] Bautier, *Actes du 95e Congrès*.

Initiates, relieved of the stain of all sin, were filled by the gift of the Holy Spirit, which gave them full understanding of Scripture. Orthodox doctrines connected with Christ's possession of a human body were denied in the group: 'Christ was not born of the Virgin Mary. He did not suffer for men. He was not really buried in the sepulchre and was not raised from the dead.'[4] There was wholesale denial of the validity of the sacraments of the Church. 'In baptism there was no washing away of sins.' Ordination was rejected, as was the mass. 'There is no sacrament', it was reported to be their belief, 'in the consecration by a priest of the body and blood of Christ.' Penance was also rejected. The initiate who had gained inner illumination was superior to these things, having entered on another level of being where he fed on heavenly food and saw angelic visions. Priesthood and Church were thus demoted by the experience of illumination. The 'heavenly food' Paul interpreted as meaning a devilish viaticum made of the ashes of a murdered baby, the child of the group's secret and nocturnal orgies, in which each of the men 'grabbed whatever woman came to hand'.

King, queen and bishops assembled. The heretics were captured, then interrogated in the church of Holy Cross. Aréfast, in chains with the rest, revealed himself. It was essential in such cases to have a confession, and Aréfast's inner knowledge finally secured that. As the heretics attempted to hide their true beliefs behind cloudy phrases, he challenged them to reveal the nature of the teaching they had given him. Then, when Bishop Guarin of Beauvais questioned Stephen and Lisois, they turned on him, admitting Aréfast's accusations and explaining their denial of orthodoxy in terms of a blend of scepticism and an other-worldly rejection of earthly things. To the bishop's exposition of the reality of Christ's suffering and resurrection, they replied, 'We were not there, and we cannot believe that to be true', and to his question on the Virgin Birth, 'What nature denies is always out of harmony with the Creator'. When he asked them whether they believed in the doctrine of creation by the Father through the Son, they defied him, contrasting their knowledge of the Law written on the heart by the Holy Spirit and derived directly from the Creator with the bishop's teaching, fit to be related to 'those who have earthly wisdom and believe the fictions of carnal men, scribbled upon animal skins'. 'Do with us what you will', they concluded. 'Now we see our king reigning in heaven, He will raise us to His right hand in triumph.' The assembly argued with them, trying to persuade them to recant; they resisted 'with the obstinacy of iron'. The clergy were then vested, solemnly stripped of their vestments by the bishops, and condemned. The queen, at the king's command, stood before the door of the church 'to prevent the common people from killing them inside the church', and as Stephen, her former confessor, passed, struck out his eye with a staff. One clerk and a nun recanted; the rest were burnt in a cottage outside the walls of Orléans.

With the living, Paul tells us, were burned the 'evil ashes', the diabolical viaticum that issued from the nocturnal orgies. Punishment extended to the dead; after the executions, Odalric the bishop exhumed the body of the dead cantor, Theodatus, who had once been a member of the heretical circle, and

---

[4] These and subsequent quotations are from *MBPH*; another tr.: *WEH*, pp. 76–81.

threw it on waste ground.[5] Every trace of heresy was to be destroyed or removed, lest it imperil souls and damage the kingdom.

No-one can say exactly what was in the mind of the king when he condemned the heretics to burn, for he had no near precedent for imitation of any kind.[6] No Capetian king of France had ever burned heretics, and there had been no capital punishment for heresy in the West for centuries, since the execution of Priscillian of Avila in 383. Priscillian was suspect of the dualist heresy of Manichaeism, which excited fear and anger among both Christians and pagans; but in fact the official reason for burning him was witchcraft.

Had Robert been influenced by the popular custom of burning for sorcery? Or did the memory linger on among his councillors of the punishment for burning in Roman law for certain kinds of heretics? To the Romans, sorcery and religious deviation alike were political offences: both damaged the order and welfare of the State. The offence of heresy came to be assimilated to that of *lèse-majesté*, and punishment reached beyond the grave: hence, perhaps, at Orléans the exhumation of the dead cantor. Or was the dominant influence the notion that fire purged, and would most completely rid his kingdom of the taint of the heretical? Robert, an insecure ruler, could not afford to tolerate a heresy whose adherents openly defied orthodoxy: he was taking up the traditional Carolingian role of corrector and protector of the Church, destroying its enemies. A proper order was to be restored in society by the utter destruction of the heresy – even though that proceeding would bring damage to the king's immediate political interests.

And so it did. Thierry had had to go. A blow had been struck at the king and at the queen, whose marriage originally had been to the detriment of the Blois interest.[7] The heresy had come dangerously close to the court circle, since Lisois had been on close terms with the king, who was said to have admired his sanctity, and Stephen, revealed as a master in the heresy, had been the queen's confessor. The queen, a resourceful virago, distanced herself from the danger when she assaulted Stephen, repudiating his beliefs and no doubt giving vent to her own anger at the damage done by his folly. The king by his sentence could not have repudiated the heresy more emphatically.[8]

Aréfast, when he reported his suspicions to Duke Richard, was putting a powerful weapon into the hands of the duke and the party of Eudes II of Blois, and by his dangerous role as spy ensured that it was effectively used. None the less, Aréfast's weapon would not have worked had not a genuine horror of heresy been present among clergy and people. Heresy in this episode stirred the common man: the crowd wanted to lynch the guilty, moved no doubt by their drastic denials of orthodoxy and by the conviction that they were (as the chroniclers said) servants of Satan, who should be eliminated from the earth.

[5] Adémar of Chabannes, *Chronique* III.lix, ed. J. Chavanon (Paris, 1897), pp. 184–5; *WEH*, p. 75. On Adémar as source, see Stock, *Literacy*, pp. 97, 115–17 and see below n. 36. New edns by J. France, N. Bulst and P. Reynolds (1989), G. Cavallo and G. Orlandi (1989).

[6] R. Gorre, *Die ersten Ketzer im 11. Jahrhundert: Religiöse Eiferer -Soziale Rebellen?* Konstanzer Dissertationen 3 (Constance, 1985 edn) (analysis, with fine bibliography, of cases of Leutard, Orléans, Arras, Monteforte), pp. 102–16; burning: p. 274, n. 133.

[7] R. I. Moore, *The Origins of European Dissent* (London, 1977, Oxford, 1985; references are all to 1985 edn) (forceful, well-written analysis from c.1000 to early Cathars, with use of anthropology, sociology; classic introduction); summary on Bautier, Stock and Orléans: pp. 285–9, this reference: p. 287.

[8] For some of the reactions which followed, see Bautier, *Actes du 95e Congrès*, p. 79; Fichtenau, *Ketzer*, p. 35, stresses Robert's desire for publicity as a Catholic ruler acting decisively – hence the unusual punishment of burning.

Was a real heresy at work in Orléans, or had heresy accusations been artificially confected in the interests of a conspiracy? Bautier's analysis of the power-struggle over the bishopric which accompanied the scandal of heresy might suggest the latter:[9] the discrediting and condemnation of clergy close to the king and queen was convenient and excitable accusations had been made before. No-one would now accept that there was any genuine basis, for example, for accusations of heresy against Gerbert of Aurillac, the pioneer scholar, yet they were made. On this interpretation, Odalric, when he exhumed the body of the dead cantor and threw it on to waste ground, was exercising revenge on the plea of heresy on a former chapter member who had worked against his candidature.

Paul, or his source, was unaware of any conspiracy. He does not name the bishops who were present, or allude to the crisis over the episcopal election: his focus is solely on the battle between Aréfast, advised by Evrard the sacristan (a possible author for a *libellus* on the episode), and the heretics.[10] The assumption of Paul, which runs through his narrative, is that heresy must be of diabolical inspiration, and his *excursus* displays much of the prejudice and typecasting of heretics which bedevils most eleventh-century sources. Heresy, for Paul, is 'depravity', 'poison', 'the path of error', 'depths of wickedness', 'madness and devilish error'. The heretics are 'enemies of all truth', 'doomed and wretched'. Heribert is 'intoxicated with a deadly draught of evil'. There is an analogy with sickness: the heresy is described as 'the disease that was lurking in his [i.e. Robert's] kingdom'. These are heavily emotive, dehumanizing terms: R. I. Moore has shown us the effect which terms relating to medical disorders are liable to have.[11] They arouse fear, demand urgent remedies, conjure up frightening images and distract the observer from reporting or explaining.

When Paul reaches the climax of his story and the bishop of Beauvais at last, given the lead by Aréfast, elucidates the real views of the heretics, he shows himself quite uninterested in explaining how the heretical ideas had reached the guilty men, precisely the questions which intrigue the modern historian. There is an inner logic about this. If heresy is the work of the devil, it does not matter greatly what instruments he chances to use.

For Paul, the magical ash made from the dead baby had a well-nigh irresistible force: 'whoever', he says, 'had partaken of no matter how small a portion . . . was scarcely ever afterward able to direct his mind away from heresy'. A logical confutation – which was attempted in vain by the bishops – was no answer. What was effective was the superior power of Christ in the Host, protecting Aréfast. This ash was so dangerous, it had to be destroyed along with the recalcitrant in the cottage outside the walls.[12]

[9] R. I. Moore, *The Formation of a Persecuting Society* (Oxford, 1987), p. 16, comes close to rejecting an authentic heresy, calling the Orléans episode: 'precursor of sensational intrigues such as those . . . at the French, English and papal courts around the beginning of the fourteenth century'; burning of Priscillian: pp. 12–13.

[10] For illuminating analysis, see Stock, *Literacy*, pp. 108–15 (focusing on chronicler); for Stock's general contribution, see R. I. Moore, 'New sects and secret meetings', *SCH* xxiii, pp. 47–68 at pp. 52, 59.

[11] R. I. Moore, 'Heresy as disease', *Concept*, ed. Lourdaux and Verhelst, pp. 1–11 (stressing twelfth century).

[12] On ashes, Gorre, *Ketzer*, pp. 64–7; on burning generally, Fichtenau, *Ketzer*, p. 35.

The heretical group, in Paul's account, behaved exactly as heretics in the medieval stereotype were expected to behave, deceiving their judges about their beliefs, concealing them 'behind a shield of words'. Paul compares the respondents evading questions to a serpent 'which the more easily eludes the grasp the more tightly it is held in the hands'.[13] Only Aréfast's painstakingly acquired inner knowledge forced the guilty into confession. The trial did not, apparently, elucidate the secret libertinism of the adepts of the sect: Paul throws this in by way of explanation and admonition 'so that Christians should beware'. The link with the diabolical is explicit: only with the descent of a demon 'in the guise of some wild beast' are the lights extinguished and the orgy begun, the effects of which lead first to a birth and then to 'the test of the flames after the manner of the ancient pagans' of the baby, and the confecting of the diabolical ash-viaticum, the counterpart of the orthodox last rite.

Gnostics of the early centuries sometimes were libertines. Epiphanius's shamefaced yet circumstantial account of a sect he knew in the fourth century, man and woman copulating, then taking the man's sperm in their hands and looking up to heaven, has a ring of truth,[14] which Paul's account does not. At this point in his narrative, his concern with the diabolical has entirely detached him from the realities of the eleventh century – an impression reinforced by the discovery of a close and incongruous correspondence between Paul's orgy narrative and the work of the Christian apologist Justin Martyr, describing slanderous accusations by pagans against early Christian communities.[15]

For a modern observer, the combination of Paul's account of the secret orgy with his prejudices, and implicit evidence for conspiracy springing from the electoral conflict, might well lead to the conclusion that his testimony (albeit sincere) is fatally biased, and that a true group heresy at Orléans never existed.

The issue is complicated by the existence of five other chronicles of varying dates, which describe the doctrines of the Orléans group, sometimes in terms corresponding to those of Paul, sometimes not – and one of these, the letter by Jean de Fleury, was written only months after the synod.[16]

And yet, for all Paul's emotive terminology, his description of the manner in which the leaders of the Orléans circle carried Aréfast step by step towards their inner secrets corresponds so well to the technique of a Gnostic, illuminist sect, in which the core of doctrine is only revealed to a select few, taken on 'from the Charybdis of false belief' until illumination is attained and the

---

[13] I here follow *WEH*, p. 80.

[14] G. Filoramo, *A History of Gnosticism* (Oxford, 1990; *L'attesa della fine: Storia della gnosi*, tr. A. Alcock), p. 184.

[15] R. L. Poole, *Illustrations of the History of Medieval Thought and Learning* (repr. New York, 1960), p. 85; N. Cohn, *Europe's Inner Demons* (London, 1975). Did the heretics' views on marriage provide a starting-point for the orgy story? (Duby's hypothesis.) Andreas of Fleury (see his *Vie de Gauzlin, Abbé de Fleury*, ed. R. H. Bautier and G. Labory (Paris, 1969) attributed to them the view that 'marriages do not need blessing; let every man take any woman he likes, whoever she is'. For controversy on sacralization of marriage, see below, p. 24, n. 52.

[16] See appendix to my *Medieval Heresy*, 1st edn. Bautier, using Jean and Andreas of Fleury as his supports, argues for a neo-Pelagian heresy.

neophyte has begun 'to open his eyes to the light of the true faith'.[17] The approach is well known, both from the history of the Gnostic sects of the early centuries and that of the Cathar movement in the twelfth and thirteenth centuries in the West. No other source has the telling details of Aréfast's search, his consultation with Evrard, the challenge to his erstwhile colleagues or the assault by the queen on her confessor. The physical details have an authenticity: should we dismiss, by contrast, *all* the exposition of doctrine contained in the same source? Paul, or his source, casts the narrative of the synod in the form of a dialogue between interrogators and heretics, in which the latter are finally pushed into revealing their beliefs; at the end of his drama we have the sentence of defiance to the bishop: 'You may spin stories in that way to those who have earthly wisdom and believe the fictions of carnal men, scribbled on animal skins.' It has all the idiosyncratic character of *ipsissima verba*. The trial ended in recalcitrance: the little group, with a leadership of trained minds, refused to recant and make an orthodox profession of faith, as they could have done. Death followed. There is no suggestion in the sources of torture or private mental pressure to elicit designed responses, as in later heresy trials in the Middle Ages.[18] The accused in the end were defiant; according to one source they 'laughed as they were bound to the pyre':[19] probably the effect of a strange state of exaltation which, as modern medical investigations suggest, confers immunity to pain and fear.

Few heresy accusations were ever launched out of pure concern for purity of doctrine; in this case the occasion for the unmasking of the heretics was political – but the heresy itself was real. It had spread from clergy to laity and embraced, as well as the intellectual core, members of the nobility. Heribert's attempt on Aréfast shows that they were ready to missionize. The fire extinguished them and there is no record of any subsequent tradition in Orléans. Authority had cut them off.

The heresy was *sui generis*, probably an amalgam of neoplatonic speculation and of inferences made from the search, familiar to biblical scholars of the time, for an inner meaning beneath the literal surface of the text of Scripture 'written on animal skins'.[20] The radical nature of the denials of the adherents, of the doctrines of incarnation and resurrection, have led some historians to argue that the heresy was imported, to some degree ready-made, and that it represents a fragmentary influence from the developed heretical tradition of the movement of the Bogomils, then spreading from its cradle-land in Bulgaria into other parts of the Byzantine Empire.[21] Like the Orléans group,

---

[17] Key passages: *MBPH*, pp. 11–12.

[18] See e.g. the case of the Templars, below, pp. 180–1.

[19] Adémar: *WEH*, p. 76.

[20] B. Smalley, reviewing Moore, *Origins, EHR* xciii (1978), pp. 853–6 at p. 855; books gave confirmation of pre-existing beliefs, in Fichtenau's view (*Ketzer*, p. 34).

[21] As I have done: *Medieval Heresy*, 1st edn, pp. 26–7, 31–3; for arguments against Bogomil infiltration, see Moore, *Origins*, pp. 26–8; interpretation of Orléans heresy: pp. 25–39, 40–4, 285–9. For debate between supporters of a Bogomil and a Western interpretation, see *RB* (classic interpretation of medieval heresy), pp. 476–83; Ilarino da Milano, 'Le Eresie popolari del secolo xi nell' Europa occidentale', *Studi Gregoriani*, ed. G. B. Borino, ii (Rome, 1947), pp. 43–89; for the most exclusively Western interpretation, see R. Morghen, *Medievo cristiano* (Bari, 1953), from *ADRSP* lxvii (1944), pp. 97–151, arousing controversy in A. Dondaine, 'L'Origine de l'hérésie médiévale', *RSCI* vi (1952), pp. 43–78; further work

Bogomils taught Docetism, believed that the body of Christ was an illusion, rejected a bodily resurrection and were led by an elite of specially trained initiates, admitted after careful instruction by a ceremony of laying-on of hands.[22] But the absence of any external evidence of Bogomil missionizing at this time and a wider realization of the number of factors in Western society which fostered dissidence in the eleventh century, entirely distinct from imported Bogomilism, have caused the theory to lose support. What seems most likely is that the heresy was intellectual in origin and a facet of the reawakening of learning in the late tenth and early eleventh centuries.[23] Gerbert of Aurillac, dogged by accusations of heresy and necromancy, had felt himself compelled to issue a declaration of orthodoxy derived from the fifth-century *Statuta Ecclesiae antiqua*, a declaration aimed, among other items, at dualist heresy on the legitimacy of marriage and the eating of meat. Liery, archbishop of Sens who took part in the synod at Orléans, had been involved earlier in the century in eucharistic controversy and, when he changed the words of consecration in the mass, had received a letter from Robert the Pious threatening him with deposition. Odorannus, a protégé of Thierry at St Pierre-le-Vif, was persecuted on grounds of heresy in the aftermath of the Orléans affair.

Fears of heresy were aroused by the work of scholars and their discussions; accusations circulated, could be, and were, used in politico-ecclesiastical battles. The suspects of Orléans, however, in the hot-house atmosphere of their little circle had incubated a heresy of their own and through Heribert had begun to missionize. Challenged, they were defiant. The first burning in the West was a burning of true heretics.

Heresy at Monteforte

So was the second, at Milan about 1028. Archbishop Aribert of Milan, accompanied by some of his clergy and *capitanei*,[24] the leading class of Milan and its *contado*, had embarked on a pastoral tour of his suffragan dioceses,

by Morghen in *HS*, bibliography and pp. 121–38 (see esp. Delaruelle's quotation, p. 137; facts in C. Thouzellier, 'Tradition et résurgence dans l'hérésie médiévale', *HS*, pp. 105–20; for the fullest exposition, see J. B. Russell, *Dissent and Reform in the Early Middle Ages* (Berkeley and Los Angeles, 1965) (central theme of Western generation of heresy but with added dimension of pre-1000 heresy); for a succinct account, accepting partial Bogomilism, see A. Borst, *Die Katharer* (Stuttgart, 1953) (classic account of Catharism, with emphasis on doctrine), pp. 71–80; for criticism of Bogomil interpretation, see H. C. Puech, 'Catharisme médiévale et Bogomilisme', *Oriente ed Occidente nel Medio Evo* (Rome, 1957), pp. 84–104; E. Werner, 'Häresie und Gesellschaft im 11. Jahrhundert', *SSAWL, Philologischhistorische Klasse* cxvii, v (1975), pp. 5–83; for Bogomil influence based on subtle dogmatic analysis, formerly used by me, see J. V. Fearns, 'Peter von Bruis und die religöse Bewegung des 12 Jahrhunderts', *AKG* xlvii (1966), pp. 311–35. I am indebted to Dr Fearns. Helpful surveys in C. N. L. Brooke, 'Heresy and religious sentiment: 1000–1250', *BIHR* xli (1968), pp. 115–31, repr. C. N. L. Brooke, *Medieval Church and Society* (London, 1971), pp. 139–61; G. Cracco, 'Riforma ed Eresia in momenti della cultura Europa tra x e xi secolo', *Rivista di storia e letteratura religiosa* vii (1971), pp. 411–77.

[22] D. Obolensky, *The Bogomils* (Cambridge, 1948); for a subtle account of doctrines in analysis of Cosmas the Priest, see H. C. Puech and A. Vaillant, *Le Traité contre les Bogomils de Cosmas le Prêtre* (Paris, 1945); survey: M. Loos, *Dualist Heresy in the Middle Ages* (Prague, 1974); summary: Lambert, *Medieval Heresy*, 1st edn, pp. 12–23.

[23] For argument and examples which follow, see Bautier, *Actes du 95e Congrès*, pp. 82–6.

[24] *Capitanei* rather than 'a troop of brave knights' (*WEH*, p. 86): Gorre, *Ketzer*, p. 184 and p. 312, n. 5.

designed to knit them more closely to the see of St Ambrose, when in the diocese of Turin he received news of a suspected heresy at the castle of Monteforte, in the diocese of Asti, three days' journey from the city.[25] Their leader, Gerard, was brought to Turin to be interrogated. It is not clear whether he was a layman or a cleric. He had certainly undergone some intellectual training and, unlike the Orléans leadership, did not wish to conceal his views from authority. Indeed, in the account given by Landulf Senior, a reputable Milanese historian, writing some seventy-five years after the event, but apparently with some record of Aribert's investigation in front of him, Gerard responded to the archbishop with all the bright confidence of an adept. 'To God Omnipotent . . .', Landulf reports him as saying, 'I give boundless thanks that you take the pains to examine me so carefully. And may He who knew you from the beginning in the loins of Adam grant that you live unto Him and die unto Him and be glorified.'[26]

He then proceeded to expound the group's belief and inner discipline. It was austere indeed. Sexual intercourse was prohibited as wrong in itself. Virgins were expected to preserve virginity, married men to treat their wives as though they were their mothers or sisters. The group never ate meat, allowed no private property, and fasted. Gerard mentioned elders ('majores') who took turns in praying, night and day, 'that no hour may pass without prayer', and a single leader ('major noster') who gave 'permission' for those who had lost their virginity to observe perpetual chastity. In a mysterious phrase he said: 'None of us ends his life without torments, that we may thus avoid eternal torments.' His conclusion sounded conventional. 'We believe in and confess', he said, 'the Father, Son and Holy Spirit. We believe truly that we are bound and loosed by those who have the power of binding and loosing. We hold to both the Old and New Testament and to the holy canons, and we read them daily.' Apart from the oddity of the 'torments', Gerard's group sounded like an ascetic monastic community, exactly of the kind then spreading in Italy, albeit with the important qualification that Gerard and his group's teaching made the celibate, monastic way of life compulsory for all.

Aribert scented heresy: 'recognizing his astuteness and evil genius from certain phrases', he pressed Gerard on the Trinity. Gerard's replies, which to a modern historian suggest Neoplatonism from Eriguena or Augustine,[27] almost certainly appeared to Aribert and his companions to be heretical definitions of the Persons of the Trinity. 'The Father', he said, 'is the eternal God, who created everything in the beginning and in whom all things exist. The Son is the spirit of man ['animus hominis'], beloved by God. The Holy Spirit is the understanding of divine matters ['intellectus divinarum scientiarum'] by

---

[25] *Landulphi senioris Mediolanensis historiae* . . . , ed. A. Cutolo, Muratori IV, 2, pp. 67–9, tr. *WEH*, pp. 86–9; *MBPH* (using *MGH* edn) pp. 19–21; C. Violante, *La Società Milanese nell'eta precommunale* (Bari, 1953), pp. 176–86, Stock, *Literacy*, pp. 174–215, esp. pp. 188–9 on portrait of Aribert; H. E. J. Cowdrey, 'Archbishop Aribert', *History* LI (1967), pp. 1–15; dating of episode from R. Glauber, from his allusion to crowning of Conrad II. Glaber, Burgundian Cluniac, unreliable on doctrines, provides factual material. Stock, *Literacy*, p. 139, rejects attempts to reconcile Glaber and Landulf. On Glaber and class of heretics ('miles'), see Gorre, *Ketzer*, p. 218; geographical setting: pp. 212–13.

[26] *WEH*, p. 87, for this and the following four quotations.

[27] Gorre, *Ketzer*, pp. 185–204; Fichtenau, *Ketzer*, p. 46, doubts a diffusion of Eriguena, preferring neo-platonism via Augustine.

which individual things are governed.'[28] Aribert probed further: 'What do you say of Christ, the Word of God, born of a virgin?' Had Gerard clung to the kind of accepted ecclesiastical formulae which underlay Aribert's questioning, he might yet have saved himself, but he chose not to. He replied, 'The Jesus of whom you speak is the spirit, born sensibly ['sensualiter'] from the Virgin, that is the understanding of sacred scripture.' The phrases are reminiscent of Eriguena's commentary on St John's Gospel, where he uses a mode of discussion of the doctrine of the Trinity based on analogies rather than definitions, and there are echoes in Gerard's replies of Eriguena's double similitudes.[29] But Aribert is likely to have seen nothing other than a denial of the existence of Christ as a historical person, and a voiding of orthodox doctrine.

A question followed about the implications of Gerard's views on marriage for procreation and the future of humanity. Gerard answered that if the human race agreed 'not to experience corruption' (i.e. engage in sexual intercourse) it would then be begotten 'without coition, like bees'. This was another intellectual reminiscence, for Ambrose, Isidore of Seville and Alcuin had all used the bees as an image of purity.[30] 'In whom', Aribert went on, 'is absolution of our sins – in the Pope, in a bishop or in any priest?' Gerard in reply dismissed all the hierarchy in favour of the direct experience of the Spirit. 'We do not have that Roman pontiff, but another who daily visits our brothers, scattered throughout the world, and when he brings God to us, pardon is granted.' Aribert asked how life ended 'in torments'. The answer implied murder. 'If we expire through torments inflicted upon us by the wicked, we rejoice, but if nature at any time brings us near death, the one nearest us kills us in some way ['quoquo modo'] before we yield up our soul.' A last question in Landulf's account was a catch-all, covering the faith of the Roman Church, the nature of Christ, 'truly the Son of God, who was born of the Virgin Mary according to the flesh', and the validity of the sacrament of the body and blood of Christ, as administered by a Catholic priest 'though a sinner'. The reference to the priesthood only elicited a repetition of Gerard's denial of papal authority. 'There is no other pontiff beside our Pontiff, though he is without tonsure of the head or any sacred mystery.'

Heresy was manifest. Aribert sent a strong force to arrest the heretics of the castle and bring them to Milan. Landulf describes them as 'milites', rough men, castellans, often engaged in local war. The haul included both men and women, among whom was a countess. The attempt was made to convert them to orthodoxy, but without success; on the contrary, Landulf says, 'those most wicked persons, who had come into Italy from some unknown part of the world' missionized among curious peasants who had come into the city from the countryside.

The *capitanei* acted, in Landulf's interpretation against the wishes of Aribert,[31] and forced the heretics to choose between a pyre and a cross. Some

[28] Tr. in Stock, *Literacy*, p. 142, preferred to *WEH*; my capitals.

[29] Gorre, *Ketzer*, as above; see esp. pp. 198–9; H. Taviani, 'Naissance d'une hérésie en Italie du nord au xie siècle', *Annales* xxix (1974), pp. 1224–52; criticism: Gorre, *Ketzer*, p. 318, n. 54.

[30] Moore, *Origins*, p. 14; pungent account of Monteforte: pp. 31–5.

[31] Gorre, *Ketzer*, p. 226, is sceptical about this; Moore, *Origins*, p. 35, is not.

chose the cross and recanted; 'many, covering their faces with their hands, leaped into the flames'. Landulf, like Paul of St Père for the Orléans affair, described a duel between good and evil, in which heresy is disclosed and punished; his hero is an archbishop, not a devout layman, penetrating the true nature of the heresy where his companions could not. It forms part of Landulf's depiction of a faithful spiritual leader, the repression of a heresy being one of the multifarious duties of his position, successfully carried out. For the chronicler heresy is wickedness, but Landulf's account lacks the demonological overtones of Paul.

The heresies were in each case illuminist: the experience of the group or the leader overrode the teaching of the Church. At Orléans, at first reluctantly, and then openly in the final exchanges with the bishop of Beauvais, and at Monteforte without shame from the outset, a spokesman for the accused rejected the Church. Gerard expounded his Trinitarian views wholly in personal terms. A threefold 'dixi' in Landulf's narrative, 'What I called the Father', 'What I called the Son', 'What I called the Holy Spirit', makes plain where Gerard's authority lay – in his own inner understanding. In both cases the spur to heresy seems to have been intellectual, in a neoplatonist tradition; but how and where Gerard acquired his knowledge remains unknown. Perhaps even the 'torments' of the group, which Landulf and Aribert found so strange, owe their origins to a strained understanding of Eriguena's exposition of Paul's saying in Galatians about being crucified with Christ.[32]

Puzzles remain. The 'torments' set up echoes in the mind of a reference to remission of sins through the 'martyrdom' of the sect, contained in an abjuration of heresy from Moissac in the early days of Catharism in the south of France.[33] Did dualist, as well as neoplatonic, influences play on Gerard's group? At the core of the inner discipline lay an exasperated asceticism, perhaps derived from Western monastic tradition, or perhaps from the Messalian heresy, a feature of Byzantine monasticism.[34] A Byzantine colony still existed in the south of Italy, a possible source of contacts.

What clearly differentiates the Monteforte group from the circle uncovered at Orléans is the degree of lay participation. The heretics at Orléans were churchmen, with a certain overspill into the lay world at a high level; it is a membership wholly compatible with an intellectual heresy, developed secretly among scholars in a closed study circle. At Monteforte there is no certain clerical membership at all, and the core of the incipient movement lay in the *milites* and their dependants.[35] The heresy reached as high as a countess, and could also touch peasants (taking Landulf's *rustici* in its most literal sense) from the *contado* of Milan. Landulf, who appreciated diligence, recorded an unceasing activity on the part of the heretics, 'who behaved as though they were good priests, and daily spread false teachings wrenched from the scriptures'. It was a threat to souls and to stability of authority in the *contado*; on that the *capitanei* acted.

[32] Gorre, *Ketzer*, p. 201.

[33] Below, pp. 57–8.

[34] Moore, *Origins*, pp. 31–4.

[35] Gorre argues that poverty and isolation predisposed to a life of renunciation, *Ketzer*, p. 225; I am not convinced.

Heresy and the Peace of God in Aquitaine

In Aquitaine in the same epoch the chronicler Adémar of Chabannes recorded a heretical movement on a scale dwarfing the episodes at Orléans and Monteforte. He gave his movement a label, recalling one of the most infamous names in the constellation of ideas of medieval churchmen, that of the third-century heretical preacher, Mani. 'Shortly thereafter', he wrote, 'Manichees arose throughout Aquitaine seducing the promiscuous populace, negating holy baptism and the power of the cross, the Church and the Redeemer of the World, marriage and the eating of meat – whatever was sound doctrine. Abstaining from food, they seemed like monks and faked chastity. But in fact among themselves they practised every depravity and were the messengers of the Antichrist; and they turned many simple people from the faith.'[36] In the earliest extant manuscript Adémar's account of the rise of the Manichees follows on the heels of a tragedy at the shrine of St Martial in the basilica at Limoges, in which fifty-two men and women were accidentally trampled to death in a panic before dawn in mid-Lent 1028. In that manuscript he wrote at the beginning of his Manichee sentences 'e vestigio' (translated above as 'shortly thereafter'), a phrase which elsewhere in his chronicle carries an element of causality. He changed his mind about linking the basilica tragedy to the Manichees and in two subsequent versions replaced 'e vestigio' by 'paulo post', which has no hint of causality, and introduced material after the account of the trampling, separating it from the story of the Manichees, and so concealing any connection.[37] Why did he come to do this?

One hypothesis is that he came to see the episode as discreditable to the shrine of St Martial and its reputation on which he had spent so much effort. A very late tradition had it that Abbot Geoffrey II attempted to molest a woman in the basilica, and that the scandal turned to panic amongst a great crowd.[38] The tragedy, at a critical point in the febrile history of religious revival in Aquitaine, caused a breakdown in confidence between excited masses and the monastic and ecclesiastical establishment. The rise, perhaps, better, the popularizing of a 'Manichee' movement outside the Church, was the result. 'They seemed like monks', Adémar wrote of the heretics. Disillusioned with official monasticism, they turned to a fiercely ascetic monasticism of their own outside the Church. Popular enthusiasm, in sum, outran the leadership of churchmen.

That deep passions were aroused by St Martial emerges from Adémar's description, for the panic took place at nocturnal vigils, that is before dawn, and the numbers at this early hour must have been great to issue in so many

[36] Edn of Adémar, as above, n. 5; R. Landes, 'The dynamics of heresy and reform in Limoges: a study of popular participation in the "Peace of God" (994–1033)' in *Essays on the Peace of God: The Church and the People in Eleventh Century France*, ed. T. Head and R. Landes, *Historical Reflections/Réflexions Historiques* xiv, 3 (1987), pp. 467–511 at p. 499, translates a conflated version of three texts of the chronicle. See also p. 502, n. 118. Landes's article provides a fundamental reinterpretation of Adémar's discussion of Manichees. See also R. I. Moore, 'Heresy, repression and social change in the age of the Gregorian reform', *Medieval Christendom and its discontents*, ed. S. J. Waugh, P. Diehl, Cambridge, 1996. I owe a copy of his work to Professor Landes.

[37] Landes, in *Essays*, ed. Head and Landes, pp. 501–3.

[38] Ibid., p. 502, n. 120; in a forthcoming article ('La vie apostolique . . .') Landes notes a new document and stresses the significance of *apostolica vita* and independent lay action.

deaths. Hagiographers, Adémar prominent among them, had so developed the cult of Martial that he came for a time to be accepted in Aquitaine as an apostle, one who held the towel for Jesus at the Last Supper. The bubble burst in 1029, on the very day on which the saint's remains were to be translated and an apostolic liturgy sung in his honour. Adémar, challenged by a speaker, the Lombard Benedict of Chiusa, on the accuracy of Martial's claim to apostolic status in the presence of listening crowds, could not make a convincing defence. Support for Martial's apostolicity vanished. It was a sign that the adherence of the masses could not be taken for granted – they could listen to arguments, exercise choice and accept or reject religious leadership.[39]

So in the Peace movement as a whole. Born, probably, at the Council of Le Puy under Bishop Guy in 975 with oath-taking from the assembled laity to preserve peace, protect Church property and the poor, the Peace of God had some of its most effective life in Aquitaine under the patronage of William v, duke 990–1031, who with the bishops and the magnates commanded a remarkable response from the mass of the laity.[40] Adémar described the scene at the Council of Limoges under the duke in 994 in the presence of the relics of the saints, with solemn oath-taking to keep the peace and the threat of excommunication and interdict to enforce compliance, and 'a huge crowd of people filling all the places to twelve miles around the city, rejoicing under open, brilliant skies'.[41] Eschatological expectations heightened enthusiasm at the millennium of Christ's birth in the year 1000 and again at the millennium of the crucifixion in 1033.[42] The sacral power of the saints was used to enforce peace and break the habit of brigandage and private war on the part of *milites* profiting by the weakness of royal power and the breakdown of Carolingian structures of authority in the south of France. Councils roused fervour, in which for a time duke, magnates and the 'pauperes', those without a share in power,[43] were united in common endeavour. To an unusual degree a wide social alliance, which included the common people, was forged by religious zeal. Unarmed crowds played a significant part. Miracle stories at the time of the councils emerged from among the common people.[44]

But inner tensions whittled away this unity, and brittle enthusiasm turned among some to dissent and heresy. When Abbot Geoffrey's death occurred, the bishop, who was his nephew, declined to consecrate his successor as abbot and kept the abbot's revenues for himself for two years and, although public opinion compelled the bishop to take action and consecrate, it was the kind of episode which weakened the alliance between churchmen and the masses.

[39] Ibid., pp. 495–7; illuminating comment on crowd behaviour.

[40] F. S. Paxton, 'The Peace of God in modern historiography: perspectives and trends', in *Essays*, ed. Head and Landes, pp. 385–404; B. Töpfer, *Volk und Kirche zur Zeit des beginnenden Gottesfriedensbewegung in Frankreich* (Berlin, 1957); H. E. J. Cowdrey, 'The Peace and the Truce of God in the eleventh century', *PP* XLVI (1970), pp. 42–67; outline: J.-P. Poly and E. Bournazel, *La Mutation Féodale x–xiie Siècles* (Paris, 1980), pp. 234–50, maps: pp. 241, 243; heresy: p. 390.

[41] Landes, in *Essays*, ed. Head and Landes, p. 467.

[42] For Glaber as chronicler and the millennium, see Stock, *Literacy*, pp. 466–72; G. Duby, *L'An mil* (Paris, 1967). See *The Peace of God. Social violence and religious response in France around the year 1000*, ed. T. Head, R. Landes, Ithaca, London (forthcoming); postscript by R. I. Moore, pp. 308–26.

[43] For this interpretation of 'pauperes', see R. I. Moore, 'Family, community and cult on the eve of the Gregorian Reform', *TRHS*, 5th ser. XXX (1980), pp. 49–69.

[44] Landes, in *Essays*, ed. Head and Landes, p. 488.

Adémar's challenger, who worsted him in public debate about St Martial, claimed openly that the monks pursued the cult of the saint out of pride, arrogance and the desire for money. In the 1020s the effectiveness of ⸺⸺⸺⸺⸺ ⸺⸺ ⸺⸺⸺, ⸺⸺ ⸺⸺ ⸺⸺ ⸺⸺⸺⸺, ⸺⸺⸺⸺ ⸺⸺⸺ of breaking down. If some did turn against their ecclesiastical leaders, the very meetings of enthusiastic crowds in the open air which accompanied the Peace could point the way to a heresy, of the type of the alleged Manichees, which dispensed with hierarchy, buildings and religious apparatus.[45]

Temporal factors also mattered. The Peace of God offered a vision of unity, peace and order from which all would benefit. In practice the rewards were not available for those without power. Lords, churches, monasteries, not the small men gained from the upheavals then taking place in the south, whether connected or not with the Peace.[46] There was disillusionment. Towards the end of his life Duke William seems to have accepted that the Peace was no longer a mass-movement – or perhaps he no longer wished that it should be so in his Duchy. Its law-enforcing function continued, with the pact and the oaths; but directed by the magnates. St Martial was still honoured. Great crowds were present at the consecration of a new basilica in his honour, and the duke came to venerate his relics in 1028. But the intimate link between the Peace and widespread religious enthusiasm had frayed. At about the same time as the translation of St Martial and the consecrating of the basilica the duke determined on action against the 'Manichees' and summoned a council of bishops and abbots at Charroux 'to wipe out the heresies which the Manichees had been spreading among the people'.[47]

The trial at Arras

In 1025 a group of heretics was seized at Arras; Bishop Gerard of the diocese of Cambrai and Arras, most probably on a pastoral visitation, got wind of their presence and had them imprisoned. He wrote to his fellow bishop Roger I of Châlons, upbraiding him for being deceived by them and failing to act effectively when warned of the presence of 'wicked men, bewitched by the spirit of error', whose missionaries, he claimed, came to spread their errors in Arras.[48] Report said they came from Italy and they acknowledged a master, Gundolfo, who was not captured. Gerard kept them in prison for three days, where they may have been tortured, and ordered a day's fast by the monks

---

[45] Ibid., pp. 505 (bishop and revenues), 495 (monks' motives), 506 (open-air meetings).

[46] G. Duby, *The Three Orders: Feudal Society Imagined* (London, 1980), pp. 147–66. I owe the reference to Mr R. I. Moore.

[47] *MBPH*, p. 10; Landes, in *Essays*, ed. Head and Landes, pp. 507–8. The Peace of God had popular vitality elsewhere, as Landes explains.

[48] *Acta Synodi Atrebatensis*, orig. ed. Luc d'Achery, *Spicilegium* (Paris, 1677), pp. 1–63; see Migne, *PL* CXLII; for the following quotations, see *MBPH*, pp. 15–19; tr. extracts synodal proceedings: *WEH*, pp. 82–5; E. van Mingroot, 'Acta Synodi Atrebatensis (1025): problèmes de critique de provenance', *Studia Gratiana* XX (1976), pp. 202–30, for dating, and identification of Gerard's addressee as Roger I of Châlons, eliminating doubts of J. B. Russell, 'A propos de synode d'Arras en 1025', *RHE* LVII (1962), pp. 66–87; Gorre, *Ketzer*, p. 276, n. 2, p. 310, n. 164 (diocesan history); analysis of sources: J. B. Russell, *Dissent*, pp. 21–7, Stock, *Literacy*, pp. 120–39, Moore, *Origins*, pp. 9–18, Gorre, *Ketzer*, pp. 132–62 (dissects influences on bishop's speech); Lambert, *Medieval Heresy*, 1st edn, p. 27, n. 16, is superseded. Evidence for the torture of the suspects lies in the term 'supplicia' used by the bishop in his letter to Roger I.

and clergy of his diocese in hopes that the heretics might be restored to orthodoxy. On the third day, a Sunday in January, the bishop, in the majesty of his office, processed with his archdeacons carrying crosses and copies of the gospels and 'a great throng of all the clergy and people' to a formal hearing in church.

It must have lasted at least a day. As the report of the synod describes it, the heretics were interrogated by the bishop, revealed their beliefs and their dependence on Gundolfo, 'by whom they had been instructed in the precepts of the Gospels and of the apostles', and, with the assembled clergy and people, the archdeacons, abbots and monks seated in order of rank, were treated to a long exposition of orthodoxy by the bishop.

The report was written up, no doubt by order of Gerard, some time after the event; the bishop's sermon, almost 20,000 words in length,[49] cannot all have been delivered as it stands: it was enlarged, probably greatly enlarged, and then published. The reproachful letter to Roger of Châlons promised him a *libellus* on the heresy, and this was very likely it. To one modern historian, the bishop's statement reads like a summary from some handbook for the education of priests, deploying, though not acknowledging, for example, the Carolingian theologians Radbert and Hrabanus Maurus, to refute at length the heretics' views on baptism.[50]

A veteran imperialist bishop with traditionalist views, the enemy of the Peace of God movement, which he regarded as subverting the order of society, he seized the opportunity to launch a defence of the sacramental system of the Church, aimed as much at the instruction of the assembled orthodox audience, and especially the monks and clergy, as at the heretics themselves. A phrase in the synod's report which may well go back to the sermon actually preached, gives a clue to the bishop's intentions. 'The day was now wearing to a close and the lord bishop said . . . "There are other things, brothers, which I ought to say to strengthen you in your faith, but in case I oppress you with a great burden of words let that suffice." '[51] The brothers ('fratres') can only be the monks and clerks in the bishop's audience.

Gerard believed that the accused heretics rejected the legitimacy of marriage. They may, in fact, not have done so, but the bishop put forward a defence of matrimony in which he is breaking a lance in a long controversy over the status of marriage, which troubled the eleventh-century Church. On the one hand, ecclesiastical authority wished to enforce celibacy on the clergy – and this was widely resisted. On the other, authority wished to eliminate concubinage amongst the laity and enforce monogamy. That, too, was widely resisted, partly on the ground that sexual union was not the business of the Church. Gerard was as grudging as contemporary churchmen generally were on marriage. 'God is not pleased', he wrote, 'by marriages that incite men to sensuality and pleasure as if they were beasts.' But, none the less he was quite clear that a total rejection of marriage, a dualist, Manichaean view, was to be avoided: 'anyone who uses marriage so that, in the fear of God, its intent is the

---

[49] Moore's estimate: *MBPH*, p. 15.

[50] Gorre, *Ketzer*, pp. 133, 163; I have not accepted Gorre's view, p. 169, that the Arras group were not heretics.

[51] *MBPH*, p. 17.

love of children rather than the satisfaction of the flesh, cannot, merely for the
fault ['culpa'] of marriage, be excluded from the community of the faithful'.[52]

What the accused at Arras seem to have inculcated was, simply, the
restraint of the flesh 'from carnal longings', not necessarily the same thing as a
rejection of marriage *per se*, though that inference cannot be excluded.
Accusations of dualism and the total rejection of the legitimacy of matrimony,
however, were in the air, and Bishop Gerard is not likely to have been careful
to pinpoint exactly what the heretics before him believed.

The safest entry-point to their teachings lies early on in the report of the
synod, where the bishop interrogated them. Their answers to his queries put
Scripture first – in the interpretation by Gundolfo of 'the precepts of the
Gospels and of the apostles'. 'They accepted no other Scripture than this',
says the report. The bishop had heard that they rejected the sacraments,
baptism, the mass, confession and penance and 'legitimate matrimony'. He
cited Christ's words to Nicodemus about being born again of water and the
Spirit, as a proof text out of Scripture that they so valued, for the necessity of
baptism, and they replied summarizing their way of life, which they insisted to
be in accord with Scripture. Their 'law and doctrine' was 'to abandon the
world, to restrain our flesh from carnal longings, to earn our bread by the
labour of our hands, to wish harm to none, to show loving-kindness to all who
are gripped by zeal for our way of life'.[53] The practice of this moral life, which
they described as *justitia*, the way of righteousness, did away with any
necessity for baptism. If *justitia* was observed, they argued, baptism was
superfluous; if not, it could not save. Anticlerical feeling and insistence on
individual responsibility influenced them against baptism in a way that was to
become familiar in the twelfth century in the West. It was invalid because of
the evil life of its ministrants, the certainty that sins renounced in it would be
repeated in later life and the impossibility of an adult making renunciations on
behalf of a child.

Gerard brought the power of his office to bear – although, interestingly
enough, he was prepared to argue texts with them, and that at length. He
made plain in the body of his sermon that the right interpretation lay with the
priest and not the layman, and expounded what *justitia* consisted in. At the
end, the synod report described the heretics as 'stupefied'. They were
illiterate. Their master Gundolfo was not with them. They submitted. Bishop

---

[52] G. Duby, *The Knight, the Lady and the Priest* (London, 1984); review: J. B. Gillingham, *JEH* xxxviii
(1987), pp. 275–7; see ch. 6; quotations: p. 114; comment: p. 116 – 'The Latin discourse expanded in the
Libellus was not addressed to the unlettered inhabitants of Cambrai [*sic*] but to the priests.' The
controversy over the Church's role in marriage may lie behind statements attributed to the Orléans
heretics by certain chroniclers. Andreas of Fleury's witness is the key point (p. 111); see also above, p. 14
and n. 15.

[53] I have preferred *WEH*, p. 84, at this point to *MBPH*, p. 17. Did the Arras group reject marriage,
either for themselves or for all believers on the lines of Monteforte group? Their will to restraint from
'carnal longings' runs side by side with the will to abandon the world: it is therefore likely that they were a
quasi-monastic group, as Monteforte was. There is no evidence that they, as opposed to Bishop Gerard,
had any concern with the debate about the sacralization of marriage. The bishop assumed that they did
condemn matrimony *per se* (perhaps in his view, as part of the wholesale rejection of sacraments, their
characteristic feature): I agree with Moore, Stock and Gorre in thinking his speech is not evidence either
way. On the bishop's motives, see Moore, *Origins*, p. 15.

and clergy made a declaration of orthodoxy in Latin, including the sentence 'The Lord and his disciples and the apostle of the gentiles gave licence for marriage and ordained it to be observed by those to whom it is permitted'.[54] The heretics asked for translation into the vernacular, then put their cross against an attestation of faith and were allowed to go home unpunished, for they had submitted.

Early Western heresy

Heresy had reappeared in the West after a long gap. The effects of the barbarian invasions in Western Europe had provided a kind of *tabula rasa* for orthodoxy. Catholicism under the pope at Rome came to win almost total victory in the territories under his jurisdiction.[55] Arianism, the fourth-century heresy which denied the true divinity of Christ, brought to central German tribes by the preaching of Wulfilas, had for a time hindered the achievement of uniformity but was finally overcome. Events had altered the environment in which the heresies of the early centuries had once spread. Churchmen were occupied with the needs of defence and the spread of the gospel among the heathen barbarians. There was no longer a cultivated laity. The centuries following the fall of Rome were filled with warfare. Heresy of the old pattern virtually ceased to exist, its place being taken by the resistance to Christianity of paganism and superstition.[56]

Such outbreaks of doctrinal dissidence that did occur were treated mildly by the authorities, presumably because they presented no significant challenge to the Church:[57] they tend either to be the work of individual theologians who develop a real heresy but gather no movement, or that of rustic preachers who hold crowds in their hands but are themselves hardly more than isolated rebels and eccentrics. Four such episodes, dating from the eighth and early ninth centuries, a time of greater order and tranquillity, may be taken to illustrate the point.

One is the case of the ascetics whom Boniface met in Germany, some being abstainers from foods 'ordained by God for our use', others men who lived on milk and honey, perhaps recalling God's promises for the land of Canaan or adapting John the Baptist's diet of locusts and wild honey.[58] Two others are rural preachers. Aldebert, from Boniface's time, who first emerged in the region of Soissons, declared himself a saint, distributed his hair clippings and nail parings to followers, and, claiming to lead the apostolic life, travelled round preaching to large crowds. Theuda in the ninth century followed a similar career in the villages round Mainz, claiming a special revelation and a

---

[54] *MBPH*, p. 18. On the submission of the Arras group, "R. I. Moore, 'Literacy and the making of heresy, c.1000–c.1150'", P. Biller, A. Hudson, *Heresy and Literacy 1000–1530*, Cambridge, 1994, pp. 19–37 at p. 32.

[55] H. I. Marrou, 'L'héritage de la Chrétienté', *HS*, pp. 51–4, at p. 53 (see *HS* for wide-ranging articles on heresies and society and pages of accompanying discussion from original colloquy at Royaumont).

[56] A. Giesztor, 'Mouvements para-hérétiques en Europe centrale et orientale du 9e au 11e siècle: apostasies', *HS*, pp. 159–67.

[57] For early Western heresy, see Russell, *Dissent*, esp. pp. 251–2. I am indebted to Professor Russell for helpful comment and free use of his maps – the more generous in view of our difference of academic judgement.

[58] The latter is Russell's suggestion (ibid., p. 11); for the episode see ibid., pp. 10–11, and further his 'St Boniface and the Eccentrics', *CH* XXXIII (1964), pp. 3–15.

knowledge of the date of the imminent end of the world.[59] A fourth and very different case is that of Claudius, bishop of Turin, one-time master of a school in Aquitaine, who was appointed to his see by the favour of Louis the Pious between 81 [and 82 [60] He denounced the use of images in Christian worship, and ordered them to be removed from his diocese. The cult of the cross excited his disapproval: in a *reductio ad absurdum* he asked why, if the cross was venerated, all virgin girls should not on similar grounds be paid reverence, since Christ was nine months in the womb of a virgin and only six hours on the cross. He rejected the cult of the saints, and questioned the value of pilgrimages. The pope's authority was put in doubt on the grounds that Peter's primacy was personal to him and ceased at his death; apostolic authority rested on good life rather than any institutional position. Thus uncannily a ninth-century theologian anticipated a part of the English Lollard heresy of the fifteenth century.[61]

Of the four, Theuda was an eccentric prophetess of a kind recurrent at all periods of the Church's history. Aldebert had a little more positive doctrinal content in his preaching – a rejection of wealth seems implicit in his simple costume and his claim to the apostolic life. The German ascetics are hard to place. It is natural to assume a scriptural basis for their behaviour but, unless they were arguing that their diet was necessary for all Christians, they were not strictly heretics. All differ from Claudius, who was giving vent to a dogmatic heresy, if not a very profound one; he, however, left no following and no tradition.

At this stage popular impulses to dissidence are not combining with doctrinal heresy to form movements against the Church. The Adoptionism taught by Felix of Urgel in the eighth century in his diocese of Toledo, though it reached the people, hardly qualifies as an exception. There, as elsewhere in this period, we do not meet the dedicated sectary with doctrinal apparatus and organization, of the kind that existed in the early centuries and was still to be found in Byzantium. Heresy in the West at this time remains rare, sporadic and formless.

In the renewed period of disorder which followed the death of Louis the Pious and the breakdown of the Carolingian Empire, we meet no recorded cases of heresy at all in the West for a period of one hundred years.[62] Western churchmen used the traditional texts of the Fathers and the councils of the early centuries in which heresy is denounced and categorized, and continued to believe that it was a deadly sin and a principal weapon of the devil against the Church; but by the late tenth century there was no-one among them with any personal experience of a living heresy.

Challenge and response

Then in the eleventh century dogmatic heresy with both lay and clerical support, missionizing, with some spectacular deviations from orthodoxy,

---

[59] Russell, *Dissent*, pp. 102–8.
[60] Ibid., pp. 13–17.
[61] See below, ch. 14.
[62] Russell, *Dissent*, pp. 17–18.

reappeared in sporadic outbreaks. There was a violent and hostile response. Recalcitrant heretics from Orléans and Monteforte were burnt to death. The group at Arras escaped because they made a full submission. At Goslar in 1051 the Emperor Henry III hanged heretics who had been brought to the imperial court for judgement by Godfrey II, duke of Upper Lorraine. The accused, required to kill a chicken, had refused; apparently their refusal led to conviction and execution, presumably on the ground that their attitude implied a dualist-type belief in the transmigration of souls through the animal kingdom.[63] Both Adémar of Chabannes and Raoul Glaber, a Cluniac chronicler who also had a passionate interest in the Peace of God movement, allude to acts of violence against heretics elsewhere, sometimes by official tribunals, sometimes by popular action.[64] Anselm of Liège reported that among the French pallor had come to be seen as a sign of heresy (presumably because pallor would be produced by the extravagant fastings of the 'Manichees') and that because of this innocent Catholics had been put to death.[65] There was a flurry of fear and repression.

Leading laity were as active as the clergy in imposing violent punishment. At Orléans the king gave the order, the queen struck out her confessor's eye, the mob wanted to lynch the convicted; at Milan the *capitanei* took the heretics from Monteforte to the pyre to choose their fate; at Goslar the emperor hanged heretics probably after interrogation by Godfrey of Upper Lorraine.

The clergy assented to capital sentences, although Aribert at Milan was apparently reluctant. Where a properly constituted tribunal was at work, they must have been the authorities to make the decision as to whether heresy was present. It was the bishop's right and duty to recognize heresy, confute it and put it down. The tribunal of bishops exercised that right at Orléans, as did Archbishop Aribert of Milan and Gerard, bishop of Arras. One voice was raised against violence: that of Wazo, bishop of Liège. Let the wheat grow with the tares till the time of harvest, he said.[66] It was advice which went unheeded in the Middle Ages.

Fear was part of the impulse to violence. Authority assumed that heresy and rebellion went together. There was a fear of the laity *en masse*, the *rustici* of the chroniclers, and what they might do under a leadership hostile to churchmen. At Milan the impact of dedicated preachers on the common people coming in from the countryside was the decisive event, leading the *capitanei* to destroy the group from Monteforte with the threat and the reality of death. The monks of St Martial, a central point in the initially orthodox movement of enthusiasm for the Peace of God, wished for a wide participation of the laity in the prayers of the Church. Gerard of Arras would have no truck with this approach. His *libellus* made plain what he thought: that the peasant should work and the priest and monk should pray. The growth of lay literacy

[63] Ibid., p. 42; Borst, *Katharer*, p. 79, dating: n. 23; for references on Goslar, see *MBPH*, p. 21; for tr. of Anselm of Liège, with Bishop Wazo's reflections on this episode, see *MBPH*, pp. 21–4; form of test derived from Augustine (Fichtenau, *Ketzer*, p. 103); Godfrey was exiled from Upper Lorraine; heretics, probably from elsewhere, were brought to him because of his linguistic skill for interrogation (*op. cit.*, p. 31); correction on Goslar, Fichtenau, *Ketzer*, p. 31.

[64] Landes, in *Essays*, ed. Head and Landes, p. 500, n. 112, and references given.

[65] *MBPH*, p. 24. Anselm of Liège, reporting Wazo's attempt to stop violence against heresy, recalled St Martin of Tours, opposing Priscillian's execution, and the use of pallor (allegedly produced by abstinence from meat) as a sign of heresy.

[66] Ibid., p. 23.

and a widening society gave new opportunities to the inquiring layman. Not all would be content with the passive role indicated for them by Gerard.

Beside fear there was care for souls in a hierarchical and paternalist Church. Scabby sheep could not be left to infect the flock. The group detected at Arras, when they put their cross to an affirmation of faith, were being given both a protection and a warning. 'Each of them made a certain mark in the form of a cross . . . so that if they held to this faith this sign might be presented for them at the Last Judgement for their salvation, but if they should violate it, it would bring about their confusion.'[67] At Orléans, in Milan for the Monteforte group and at Arras authority wrestled with the accused in order to secure submission to orthodoxy and save them from the power of Satan.

Behind the heresies lay a challenge to the Church. The clergy at Orléans and the leader of the Monteforte group preferred their own inner understanding to the decisions of bishops or the formal declarations of faith inherited from the past. At Arras the accused based themselves on Gundolfo and his interpretation of Scripture: the text as he expounded it to them, together with their group experience of the way of righteousness seemed to them to be sufficient without the intervention of the priesthood as ministers of the sacraments. They seemed surprised when this was challenged. 'Anyone who chooses to examine carefully our law and doctrine', they are reported as saying, 'which we have learned from our master, sees it to be contrary neither to evangelical principles nor to apostolic sanctions.'[68] Adémar of Chabannes's Manichees rejected the externals of contemporary religion, the cross, baptism, the Church itself, to follow their own way. Apostolicity was sought, not in monasteries, shrines or churches, but in the shared experience of their own communities outside the Church.

The eleventh century in the West was the age of the formation of communities *par excellence* – ascetic groupings in abundance leading to the formation of new orders, often with a stress on the eremitical aspect of monasticism; guilds in towns; communes; new villages, the product of the drive to colonize the waste lands. Heretical communities run parallel to this widespread process and are another facet of a fast-changing society. A new ability to read and understand texts; the emergence of charismatic interpreters, a Gundolfo at Arras, a Gerard at Monteforte; the fall-out from the brittle enthusiasm of the Peace of God movement in Aquitaine; the incubation of a heresy in the secret circle of illuminist clergy at Orléans; all played a part in the emergence of these new and alarming communities.

Social and economic changes also had a role: developing economic life created routes for trade which aided the diffusion of heretical ideas. Texts, preached from, repeated, studied in small groups, brought into being what Brian Stock has called 'textual communities',[69] within which the allegiance to the group or the leader came to transcend every other kind of allegiance. A nexus of thought and action was created, revolving round a number of sentiments or quotations, written or unwritten, with a transforming power, leading an association's members into resistance to authority, even willing

---

[67] Ibid., p. 19.
[68] *WEH*, p. 84; see also *MBPH*, p. 17.
[69] Stock, *Literacy*, p. 90.

death. Sporadic doubts about aspects of the Church's teaching or the conduct of its priests which touched individuals in earlier epochs could be taken up and incorporated in the teaching of a group, which thus gave them durability. Burchard of Worms in his canon law collection at the beginning of the eleventh century had felt it needful to include a penance for those who held the Donatist view that sacraments administered by unworthy priests were not valid.[70] It must have been widespread enough to have justified a set penance in Burchard, but without the teaching and companionship of a heretical group to sustain such beliefs they remain transient and individual, without major effects on Church life.

Other heresies were reported. Raoul Glaber wrote of the grammarian Vilgard of Ravenna who 'began to preach many things contrary to the faith', notably that 'the words of the poets [i.e. classical authors] ought to be believed in all cases';[71] Glaber said that he gained supporters in Sardinia, Italy and Spain and violence was used to suppress them. This seems improbable.

He also described the career of the peasant Leutard from the village of Vertus in the diocese of Châlons-sur-Marne who, after being tormented in a dream by bees who entered his body through his private parts, stinging him as they made their way out through his mouth with a loud noise, then 'bidding him to do things impossible to men', went home from the fields.[72] He dismissed his wife 'as though he affected the separation by command of the gospel' ('quasi ex precepto evangelico'), went to the village church and broke the crucifix and thereafter gathered a hearing for his views among the peasants – aided no doubt by his welcome belief that it was not necessary to pay tithes. Part of his appeal was based on Scripture, used selectively: he is said to have taught 'that the prophets had set forth some useful things, and some not to be believed'. The bishop exposed the weaknesses of this rustic agitator who committed suicide by throwing himself into a well; his following lingered on for years after his death. Historians have suggested at various times that he was an isolated rural fanatic,[73] that he had been affected by fragments of Bogomil belief,[74] or was a victim of ergotism, the symptoms of which may include the sensation of burning in the genitals.[75] It has been wisely noted that the diocese of Châlons-sur-Marne was struck three times by heresy, once in the case of Leutard, once more *c*.1025, when Bishop Roger I failed to deal satisfactorily with heretics who sent their emissaries on to Arras, and for a third time when a successor of Roger wrote to Wazo of Liège in the 1040s asking for advice about peasants who 'followed the perverse teaching of the Manichees'. In each instance, whatever the exact nature and motivation of the heresy, it was marked by a rigorous concern for personal purity.[76]

[70] On the absence of specific rulings on heresy, see Moore, *Origins*, p. 252.

[71] *WEH*, p. 73; Moore, *Origins*, p. 24; pungent comment, Russell, *Dissent*, p. 111.

[72] Raoul Glaber, *Les Cinq livres de ses histoires (900–1044)*, ed. M. Prou, I (Paris, 1886), pp. 49–50; *WEH*, pp. 72–3.

[73] P. Alphandéry, 'De quelques faits de prophétisme dans les sectes latines anterieures au Joachimisme', *RHR* LII (1905), pp. 177–218, esp. p. 185.

[74] Borst, *Katharer*, p. 73.

[75] Moore, *Origins*, p. 36.

[76] Ibid., pp. 36–8.

But the stories of Leutard and Vilgard lie buried beneath the assumptions of the chronicler. Glaber wrote at a distance from the episodes he describes, and he is unlikely to have had anything other than oral report to guide him. He placed the Vilgard affair c.970 and Leutard c.1000. the episodes formed a pair of heresies lying at the extremes, one a learned, the other a peasant heresy, twin menaces to the Church in the millennial epoch.[77] Glaber's symbolism enfolds the Leutard story. The bees, often seen as symbols of purity, or treated by Bede as symbols of the Fathers themselves, interpreters of Scripture who make the honey of the spiritual understanding of the Word of God, in the growth of heresy have their good functions reversed.[78] They become messengers of evil and they enter the body of Leutard through a shameful gate, just as a party of demons, who had left Orléans after the trial, attempted in a vision of a monk to enter the monastery of Fleury via the latrines, till they were stopped by the relic of the staff of St Benedict from coming up into the cloisters.[79] Once inside Leutard, the bees drive him to a false understanding of Scripture, dividing the message of the Prophets where orthodoxy would see all their teaching as a unity.

Literary contamination also affects a strange text embedded in a collection made up by the monks of St Germain d'Auxerre in the eleventh century, including St Augustine's classic work on heresies and a ninth-century treatise on the legitimacy of receiving tithes and offerings – an all-purpose compilation designed to defend monks against all their enemies. It takes the form of a letter by a monk, Heribert, addressed to all Christians at the four points of the compass, denouncing a heresy in Périgord whose adepts claimed to follow the apostolic life, eating no meat, drinking no wine beyond a measure every third day, refusing to handle money and making a hundred genuflections daily. They rejected the veneration of the cross and denounced liturgical chant as a vain invention. Some of these pseudo-apostles might chant the mass as a means of deception, throwing down the Host beside the altar or thrusting it into a missal. The devil gave them supernatural powers. Heribert was witness to strange feats in which the adepts, bound with iron shackles and put overnight in a wine tun turned bottom up, escaped, Houdini-like, by morning. A full analysis of the provenance of these tales has not been made. Perhaps Périgord and St Germain were affected by heresy; or perhaps we have before us a propaganda piece put together from old sources to smear the opponents of the monks.[80]

Heribert's letter did not mention Manichees explicitly. But the reader catches a whiff of it. The accusation of Manichaeism is a demonstration by the chroniclers of their lack of equipment for dealing satisfactorily with the revival

[77] Landes, in *Essays*, ed. Head and Landes, p. 500, n. 110.

[78] Gorre, *Ketzer*, p. 23.

[79] T. Head, 'Andrew of Fleury and the Peace League of Bourges', in *Essays*, ed. Head and Landes, p. 522. For the association between demons and excrement, see E. Le Roy Ladurie, *Montaillou*, tr. B. Bray (London, 1978), p. 472, n. 1.

[80] G. Lobrichon, 'Le clair-obscur de l'hérésie au début du xıe siècle en Aquitaine: une lettre d'Auxerre', in *Essays*, ed. Head and Landes, pp. 422–44 (an elegant redating and reinterpretation of a source, re-used by monasteries in the twelfth century); tr.: *WEH*, pp. 138–9; dating: *WEH*; Lambert, *Medieval Heresy*, 1st edn, pp. 62–3, should be corrected. For minor reports of heresy, see Russell, *Dissent*; for Gerard of Csanád, see Lambert, *Medieval Heresy*, 1st edn, p. 35.

of heresy.[81] It must be false, for Manichaeism had died out in the West some five centuries earlier, and there is no trace of their distinctive doctrines and organization in these outbreaks. Adémar used the term energetically, Landulf applied it to the Monteforte sectaries, another chronicler applied it to the accused from Upper Lorraine and a bishop of Châlons-sur-Marne, in his letter to Wazo of Liège, damaged his account of heretics in his diocese by recording that they believed that Mani was the Holy Spirit.[82] It is not likely that these dissidents had ever heard of Mani.

Writers smelt dualism, and Manichaeism was the most famous form of dualism because of the experience of St Augustine. What is common to the heresies, which the chroniclers were inclined to put down as Manichaeism, is a stress on flight from the world, a will to purity, a positive repugnance, it would seem, for material objects, and for human flesh and its desires.

Stress on renunciation is plainly related to the existence of the monastic reform movement, which was at this time beginning to stir the laity. Starting with the foundations of Cluny and Gorze in the previous century, a revival of monasticism was purging moribund houses over Western Europe, and by a natural overspill affecting the lay world as well. Increasingly, the desire for reform made itself felt in the secular Church, with a call to greater purity and devotion among the clergy. Monks were often instigators of reform and their ideals most widely diffused, with a concomitant tendency to consider the world of little worth. A radical pessimism about the natural order is a strong feature of this reform.[83] So, too, is the contrast preached by reformers between the Church of the apostles as evidenced in Scripture, and the state of the contemporary priesthood and hierarchy.

These two features help to account for the reaction in these heresies against the material world, towards an ascetic withdrawal, and also for the appeal which they made, however confusedly, to Scripture as against the contemporary Church and its practices. In a sense, a segment of the lay world in the more advanced countries of the West was experiencing a conversion in the eleventh century. The fortress Christianity of the Dark Ages was giving way, in the more propitious social circumstances of the age, to a religion which could touch the intellect of the layman. There are signs of this in some of the outbreaks: it is especially marked at Arras, with the insistence on adult responsibility in the refusal of infant baptism.

Heresy did not last. Only in the diocese of Châlons-sur-Marne and Liège, as far as our records run, does it appear more than once in any given site. It seems to have been snuffed out by repression, extinguishing heretical circles once they are discovered, without leaving a remnant of proselytizers to revive their heresy when publicity was over. After the hanging of the accused from Upper Lorraine in 1051 silence descends.

The heresies themselves are individual compositions – in a sense collectors' pieces – with features not repeated later. Reconstruction is made difficult by the brevity and prejudice of many of the reports, and by the capacity of some

[81] Russell, *Dissent*, p. 208.
[82] *MBPH*, p. 22.
[83] Background in Moore, *Origins*, ch. 2; Russell reminds me of some hard sayings in the Fathers about sexual activity. R. Bultot, *La Doctrine du mépris du monde* (Louvain and Paris, 1963), is informative.

churchmen for outright slander. Heresy in this century will always remain particularly obscure and tantalizing.

Perhaps the reason lies not only in the inadequacy of the literary equipment of the age, or the inexperience of the interrogators; it may also lie in the lack of developed, logical understanding of their own beliefs by the heretics themselves, innocent, ill-equipped seekers after purity. Unable to explain themselves adequately, they leave a blurred imprint on the sources.

Heresy thus reappears in the West after a gap of a hundred years, creates alarm in the 1020s, fades, then disappears as mysteriously as it had come.

Part II

The twelfth century

3

Orthodox reform and heresy

The nature of twelfth-century heresy

Early in the twelfth century half a century's silence in the history of Western heresy was broken. A new rhythm becomes apparent:[1] heretical episodes occur more frequently. Heresy changes character. The heretical groups of the eleventh century sought a flight from the world to practise their austerities. They were generally content with a personal abnegation and a set of idiosyncratic views to be discussed within the closed circle of the chosen. The new breed of heretics are aggressive reformers who insist on changes in the Church that will bring Catholicism into line with their own ideas. The eleventh-century groups spread their views quietly, through personal contacts; in the best-documented example, at Orléans, a heretical group among the clergy existed secretly, expanding through quiet missionizing for years before attracting notice from authority. Twelfth-century heretics have other assumptions. Heresy is spread more by open and aggressive preaching. Hearers are stimulated to positive action. It may be that crosses are torn down and burnt, that women give up their jewellery, or, as in the case of Henry the monk at Le Mans, a whole town rebels against its overlord. Heresiarchs are not afraid to use physical force: Eon de l'Étoile mobilizes a peasant force to rob churches in Brittany; Arnold of Brescia allies himself with the forces of republicanism to hold Rome against the pope; Tanchelm of Antwerp, whether suspect reformer or heretic leader, uses a bodyguard of soldiers.

The heretics and their supporters demand that the Church as a whole shall hear them and stir itself to follow. There is a new concern for the social

---

[1] Borst, *Katharer*, p. 83; H. Grundmann, *Ketzergeschichte des Mittelalters, Die Kirche in ihrer Geschichte: Ein Handbuch* ed. K. D. Schmidt and E. Wolf, II, G. pt I (Göttingen, 1963), pp. 15–20; his 'Neue Beiträge zur Geschichte der religiösen Bewegungen im Mittelalter', *AKG* XXXVII (1955), pp. 129–68 (research report) also in *Relazioni* III, pp. 357–402, *RB*, pp. 487–524 (2nd edn only); Moore, *Origins*, esp. ch. 3; A. Vauchez, *Les Laics au moyen age Pratiques et expériences religieuses*, Paris, 1987, illuminates the effects of Gregorian reform.

implications of the gospel, or a desire for radical changes among the clergy and in the relations between the Church and society.

We will not have far to seek the reasons for this change. An orthodox reform movement, first issuing from monks and from inferior strata in the hierarchy, then taken up vigorously by the papacy, had begun to stir the consciences of the laity at large.[2] Pamphlet and preaching warfare between the imperial and papal parties had taken discussion of the rightful place of the Church in the world into circles hitherto unaffected by such matters. Under Gregory VII the papacy had been led by a dominating personality prepared to open issues of principle to general discussion and to offer support for enthusiasts in rebellion against a simoniacal clergy.

The case of the lay movement of the Pataria in Milan, whose origins pre-dated the investiture controversies, is especially illuminating for the forces stirred by the reform movement.[3] The preaching of the deacon Ariald unleashed a formidable rebellion against the power of a simoniacal and unchaste upper clergy. Social tensions played a part as humbler citizens[4] attacked the power of a feudal nobility allied with the cathedral clergy, who lived an unregenerate life hardly distinguishable from that of their fellow nobles. Other cross-currents were the patriotism of a city and archbishopric with a distinguished past, and the rival interests of pope and emperor. Held together by an oath like a communal movement, the Pataria continued their inflammatory agitation from 1057 to 1075, and carried their influence into the cities of Brescia, Piacenza and Cremona. From Florence and the reform movement of St John Gualbert they drew uncorrupt priests to serve their needs in Milan.[5]

Lay participation was considerable, though lower clergy as well came to support the agitation, and two laymen, the knight Erlembald and his brother Landulf, notary of the Milan church, were leaders. In the fiercest language unworthy clergy were attacked, their houses were plundered, and the sacraments which they administered were boycotted. Landulf was quoted as saying that the people should think of their masses as if they were dogs' dung, and their churches as if they were cattle sheds; layman as he was, he preached, it would seem, without specific authorization, and was attacked by a chronicler for doing so. Accusations of heresy were flung about, the conservatives in Milan accusing the reformers of being heretics, while

[2] G.Volpe, *Movimenti religiosi e sette ereticali nella società medievale Italiana (secoli XI–XIV)* (Florence, 1926) (a stimulating survey, still of use); *RB*, pp. 13–16.

[3] C. Violante, *La Pataria milanese e la riforma ecclesiastica* I: *Le Premesse (1045–57)* (Rome, 1955) (the standard work); H. E. J. Cowdrey, 'The papacy, the Patarenes and the Church of Milan', *TRHS*, 5th ser. XVIII (1968), pp. 25–48; G. Miccoli, 'Per la storia della pataria milanese', *BISIAM* LXX (1958), pp. 43–123; E. Werner, *Pauperes Christi* (Leipzig, 1956), pp. 114–64 (Marxist survey with hypothesis of Bogomil influence which I do not accept); comment in E. Dupré Theseider, *Introduzione alle eresie medievali* (Bologna, 1953), pp. 77–94; Stock, *Literacy*, pp. 151–240 (fresh analysis with comparison to heresies in early eleventh century); Moore, *Origins*, pp. 55–62, 266–8; note comment on sources: p. 77, references: p. 296, n. 13. C. Thouzellier, *Hérésie et hérétiques* (Rome, 1969), pp. 204–21.

[4] It used to be thought that the names Pataria and Patarene were derived from the rag-market. G. Cracco, 'Pataria: *opus* e *nomen*', *RSCI* XXVIII (1974), pp. 357–87 at pp. 357–62, argues that this is not so.

[5] C. Violante, 'Hérésies urbaines et hérésies rurales en Italie du 11e au 13e siècle', *HS*, pp. 171–98 (individual hypothesis on the social reasons for Italy's fertility in heresy) at p. 177.

distinguished members of the reform party in Rome in the same period made free with the word 'heresy' as a term of abuse for moral faults in the clergy.[6] The reformers wrote as controversialists at a time when scant attention had been given to setting a strict and technical boundary between heresy and orthodoxy; nevertheless the use of the word was important. If simony in the clergy was to be equated with heresy, extreme action to bring it to an end might seem justified. At the end of his career Erlembald went close to usurping a clerical function for himself, when he made a decision about the administration of baptism. To avoid use of chrism consecrated by the unworthy, he had a chrism made and administered by a Patarene priest.

Strictly, no action of the Paterenes went beyond the lines authorized by orthodox reformers in the Easter synod at Rome in 1059, which forbade laymen to hear the masses of married priests. They were not heretics: they lacked the will to proceed against the sacramental and doctrinal system of the Catholic Church.[7] But the reservations which even that most radical reformer St Peter Damiani expressed about the actions of the Pataria had some justification, for their reforming zeal tended to shake all Church authority, and set forces in motion whose direction could not be foreseen. This did not check the support which Gregory VII gave to the movement before and during his pontificate: influenced by him, Alexander II had given a banner to Erlembald, making him a kind of *gonfalonier* of the Roman Church. When Erlembald was killed in street fighting in 1075, Gregory honoured him as a martyr. The same public justification for action against unreformed clergy and the boycott of their sacraments was explicit in Gregory's rehabilitation of Ramihrdus, a priest in Cambrai burnt as a heretic after refusing to receive the sacrament from the hands of unworthy clergy. Ramihrdus roused a movement in Cambrai and its region that had affinities with the Pataria, burnt by a bishop, supporter of Henry IV, making an example of a Gregorian.[8] Yet the line was perilously thin between the boycott of the masses of unreformed clergy and the heresy, to which we may refer for convenience as Donatist, that the masses of unworthy clergy were invalid, and in the atmosphere of reform, with preaching and pamphlets stressing the vices of the unreformed clergy, the step into that heresy was easy to take. By calling on him to take action against unworthy clergy, the Gregorian movement demanded from the layman a certain personal responsibility. This, a relatively new sentiment in the West, was to be fateful for the future development of heresy.

Church reform and heresy have important links. The revolutionary programme of the Gregorians set before the Church ideals which could never be wholly realized, and gave to some clergy and numbers of laymen a vision of a free Church that, in the social and political circumstances of the time, could never be expected to be wholly realized. At first, the Gregorians, as in the Pataria and elsewhere, could work with popular lay movements: thus the zeal of the common man who had been awakened to reform in the more advanced centres of Western Europe found an orthodox channel. That fact will explain

---

[6] J. Leclercq, 'Simoniaca haeresis', in *Studi Gregoriani* I, pp. 523–30. I owe the reference to the late Mr D. Bethell.

[7] Dupré Theseider, *Introduzione*, p. 77.

[8] Russell, *Dissent*, pp. 43–4; *MBPH*, pp. 24–6; Moore, *Origins*, pp. 62–3, 260; Fichtenau, *Ketzer*, p. 51.

the relative absence of heresy in the half century that lay between the
executions at Goslar and the reappearance of popular heresy.[9]

But in time the direction of papal reform tended to change, and its aims
became more narrowly clerical and juridical. At worst, it might separate
clergy from laity without necessarily raising the devotion and efficiency of the
former. The momentous question of the freedom of the Church and the
worthiness of candidates for bishoprics tended to contract into the lesser issue
of the right to deliver to the bishop the sybmols of his sacred office; and, as
compromise was reached on this at the Concordat of Worms in 1122, it might
well be felt that some of the early call to purification had failed in its effect,
and that the orthodox reform movement was turning into disputes over
minutiae. Before Worms, reform in its most immediate impact on the lay
world was beginning to run into the sands, and as this happened the number
of heretical episodes began to rise. A first cause for the recrudescence of heresy
in the West lay in the expectations roused by Gregorian reform and its failure
to fulfil them.

Where the papacy scored its most lasting popular success was in the
crusades. Here Urban ii and his successors aroused a genuine popular
enthusiasm, the driving force which outlasted so many military and political
failures, and found expression in such obviously spontaneous and unrehearsed
movements as the crusade of Peter the Hermit, which preceded the first
crusade proper, or the children's crusade of the thirteenth century. How deep
into the popular consciousness the crusades had penetrated is apparent from
the belief of the inhabitants of the primitive region of western France on the
borders of Brittany, Anjou and Maine, that the hermits of the woods who
emerged as wandering preachers in shaggy attire were Saracens who had
arrived by a concealed tunnel from their own land to betray the West from
within.[10]

Crusade preaching stirred millennial enthusiasms. The Holy Land was
represented as being literally a land flowing with milk and honey; the success
of the crusade would, it was believed, issue in the new kingdom at Jerusalem
that would reconcile men's quarrels, and usher in the era of plenty that would
precede the End. The crusades aroused a deep popular feeling for the
sufferings of Christ at the crucifixion and a corresponding hatred for the Jews:
pogroms accompanied the summons to the crusade in a number of towns, and
aided the spread of a mood of eschatological enthusiasm, in which the
slaughter of the enemies of Christ was expected to lead to the events preceding
the end of the world. A mood of religious enthusiasm was created that could
lead to the rise of extravagant leaders and might easily run into unorthodox
channels.[11]

[9] *RB*, p. 483; Brooke, in *BIHR* xli (1968), p. 119. I have not examined the history of the followers of
Berengar of Tours in the eleventh century, which might modify generalizations about the absence of
heresy after 1051. I owe comment to Dr M. Gibson.

[10] Bernard of Tiron, *Vita* (*PL* clxxii, col. 1409b).

[11] On aberrations linked to the crusades, see N. Cohn, *The Pursuit of the Millennium* (London, 1957), tr.
into German, 1961, French, 1962, Italian, 1965; reviews: M. E. Reeves, in *MA* xxviii (1959), pp. 225–9;
B. Smalley, in *EHR* lxxiv (1959), pp. 101–3; E. Winter, in *DLZ* lxxxiii (1962), cols 998–1001, H. Grundmann, in *HZ* cxcvi (1963), pp. 661–6; R. Manselli, in *RSLR* iii (1967), pp. 532–8. See summary of Cohn's

The machinery of the crusades and the setting up of crusaders' kingdoms in Palestine that was their most obvious result, led to a renewed contact with Eastern heresy. Direct contact of crusaders with heresy is hardly recorded. In only one instance do we have such information, and that was when they came across a *castrum* inhabited by heretics, most probably Paulicians. The crusaders' reaction was to destroy the place and its inhabitants.[12] Yet the crusades were an important link in the chain binding closer the peoples of western Europe to Byzantium and the Balkans,[13] and the increased commercial activity stimulated, in part, by the existence of the crusader States would no doubt have facilitated formal and informal contacts with underground Bogomil churches in Constantinople, Asia Minor and the Balkans.

Nevertheless, dualism would never have made its re-entry into the West had not the soil been well prepared for the reception of heresy. A reaction against orthodoxy, an undogmatic dissatisfaction with the Church, was the necessary first stage if dissentient circles were ever to be able to accept, *en masse* and for a long period of time, elements of drastically ascetic religion well on the margins of Catholicism. This dissatisfaction was the product of a reform that for some had gone sour, or the effects of a rigidity and conservatism in the Church that was unable to accept new interpretations of the Christian life.

Most of a century was required before ecclesiastical authority was able to adapt its outlook and establish a coherent policy; in the doubts and hesitations, in the reaction to crude and sweeping condemnations, themselves the products of the uncertainty of authority, heretical groups found occasion to cut themselves off from the Church. The long, simmering crisis found for the first time the outline of a solution in the hands of Innocent III in the early thirteenth century. Till then, the anxieties of churchmen about the spread of heresy were not unjustified, for the Church of the twelfth century as a whole did not understand the forces at work behind the popular heretical movements, and had no effective answer to them.

Orthodox wandering preachers

What made the heresy of the twelfth century insidious was its relatively unformed nature, its lack (at least until Catharism began to solidify towards the end of the century) of concise dogmatic positions, and its close relationship

theory and definition of terms in his 'Medieval millenarism: its bearing on the comparative study of millenarian movements', in *Millennial Dreams in Action*, ed. S. L. Thrupp (The Hague, 1962), pp. 31–43. Cohn's second edition of *The Pursuit of the Millennium* (London, 1970) offers a profound revision of his first, which occasions me to withdraw my first-edition criticism, pp. 47–8; he no longer adopts a stress so exclusively urban; revolutionary millenarianism, he says (p. 281), appealed most to peasants who were not 'firmly integrated in the life of village or manor' or to artisans who were not 'firmly integrated in their guilds'. It appealed to those on the margins, whether in town or country.

[12] N. Garsoïan, *The Paulician Heresy* (The Hague and Paris), p. 15, n. 9; Lambert, *Medieval Heresy*, 1st edn, pp. 23, 34.

[13] C. Thouzellier, 'Hérésie et croisade au XIIe siècle', *RHE* XLIX (1954), pp. 855–72 (hypothesis linking development of heretical doctrine to crusaders from second crusade; for its weakness, see A. Borst, *DA* XI (1954–5), pp. 617–18, R. Manselli, in *BISIAM* LXVII (1955), p. 221n., S. Runciman, in *JEH* XVIII (1967), pp. 89–90; see now revised version of Thouzellier's article in her *Hérésie et hérétiques*, pp. 17–37 (note diagram on p. 37).

to the ideals and preoccupations of orthodox piety. Most popular heresies are initiated, before the rise of the printing press, by a period of spontaneous wandering preaching. Those of the twelfth century were no exception. But the preaching, which stirred the populace and unconsciously helped to make them ready for the reception of the principal 'evangelical' and dualistic heresies of the century, often had an orthodox origin. We have seen it in operation in the Milan Pataria. In France it was carried on by wandering hermits well known in Catholic history as the founders of religious congregations. It was not a work of planned missionizing by some organized sect. Its aim was the entirely orthodox one of the preaching of penance, the call of clergy and people to reform. Here we have a kind of spontaneous overspill of the fierce asceticism of the woods of western France, the work of reformers and monks who had not found full satisfaction in the normal outlets of cloister, canons or life among the secular clergy. Their work of preaching was not disapproved by the Church; some could show a papal permission for wandering preaching, analogous to the permission given to preach for the first and second crusades; but the preachers themselves were fiery and idiosyncratic and their preaching tours had consequences that were not always comfortable.

The earliest to be discussed by Johannes von Walter in his pioneer work on the wandering preachers of France was Robert of Arbrissel, and the case was typical for the reaction against the conventional ways of religion.[14] Robert was once in the household of the bishop of Rennes, and had been a participant in the Gregorian reform movement, but he threw up a conventional career in the Church for the life of a hermit in the great wood of Craon, where he attracted followers and set out on preaching tours. Another case of reaction against a customary pattern of religious life is that of his follower Bernard of Tiron, who had become a monk, then prior of St Savin-sur-Gartempe where he came into conflict over the simony issue with Abbot Gervasius, then again abbot of St Cyprian near Poitiers, where he clashed with his monks who did not want to accept reforms. After an unsuccessful dispute with Cluny, he was forced to leave. His solution was to turn his back on the unprofitable world of monastic communities and suits at Rome, and flee to the woods at Craon.

Another of the wandering preachers, Vitalis of Savigny, had been chaplain to Count Robert of Mortain and canon of the church of St Ebrulf at Mortain; but a love of poverty drove him into the waste and made him a hermit at Dompierre, east of Mortain, for seventeen years. The best known of von Walter's group was Norbert of Xanten, who had found the work of reform in circles of canons insufficient and took to the roads as a wandering preacher. As with the others, his zeal was not easy to incorporate into existing religious structures – an early attempt to make him leader of a group of Augustinian canons in Laon failed because of the canons' resistance to his reforms and he

---

[14] *Die ersten Wanderprediger Frankreichs* (Leipzig, 1903–6), 2 vols. An ingenious but basically unsuccessful attack by H. Böhmer is in *TLZ* XXIX (1904), pp. 330–4, with reply from von Walter, *Wanderprediger* II, pp. 169–79. Full modern exposition by J. Becquet, 'L'érémitisme clérical et laie dans l'ouest de la France', in *L'Eremitismo nei secoli XI e XII* (Milan, 1965), pp. 182–211; and his 'Érémitisme et hérésie au moyen age', in *HS*, pp. 139–45; H. Leyser, *Hermits and the New Monasticism: A Study of Religious Communities in Western Europe, 1000–1150* (London, 1984).

was led, in co-operation with the bishop of Laon, to found a new association which flowered into the Premonstratensians.

Though the backgrounds might differ, there are similarities within the group of wandering preachers which bear witness to some interesting new strands in popular piety. Their love of poverty is striking. Robert appeared on the preaching tours in rags almost to the point of indecency, with a beard and a grey cowl, going barefoot; Bernard of Tiron in shaggy attire, barefoot or riding on a donkey as a sign of humility. In the woods they lived on fruits and berries or on the product of rough manual labour, like turning, or the products of simple gardens, worked by themselves without any lay brothers or hired labour. There were eccentricities: Robert of Arbrissel had a special calling for the religious care of women, and was accused by an opponent of undue intimacies – which in fact reflected no more than a characteristic lack of discretion. Bernard wept continually in his reflections on the sufferings of Christ all through the mass, and went about with his shoulders perpetually damp from his tears.

The audiences that these idiosyncratic figures drew on their preaching tours are a tribute, not only to their preaching power, but also to a diffused reverence for extreme asceticism and poverty. Poverty and preaching were closely linked: the lack of a stipend and the complete dependence of the preacher on the spontaneous offerings of his hearers were a guarantee of the preacher's independence and sincerity. Followers were speedily attracted, partly in the normal fashion, as the hermit who flees to the woods is seldom long there without attracting some visitors who come to seek a holy man's blessing and advice,[15] partly as mixed bodies of men and women attached themselves to the preachers as they travelled round the countryside. The denunciations of a married clergy and the general abuses of the pre-Gregorian world which were so much part of Robert's sermons probably drew to him the cast-off wives of reformed clergy, which a reformer might well describe as prostitutes.[16]

These mixed bodies created some not wholly unjustified alarm on the part of authority. There were questions about the permission to preach; Norbert, for example, was queried in 1119 about the legitimacy of his wandering tours. Influence was brought to bear on the preachers to cause their followers to settle down and choose a stable form of religious life in community. Thus, partly out of a normal zeal, partly at the instance of a reforming diocesan concerned for the spiritual benefit of his own locality – as in the case of Hermann of Laon,[17] and partly out of the pressure of anxious authorities, wandering preachers became founders of monasteries and orders.

The idiosyncracy prevailed, however, here: the foundations were not of a conventional kind. Some, like Robert, revived the long disused idea of the double monastery. All were distinguished by a special care for poverty and a rejection of certain kinds of property. The foundations contributed to the variety of religious life in the first half of the twelfth century. Prémontré

[15] H. Grundmann, 'Zur Vita S. Gerlaci eremitae', *DA* XVIII (1962), pp. 539–54; economic interpretation of hermit movement in Werner, *Pauperes Christi*, pp. 25–52.
[16] Böhmer, in *TLZ* XXIX (1904), pp. 330–4.
[17] C. Dereine, 'Les origines de Prémontré', *RHE* XLII (1947), pp. 352–78.

developed on the Slav frontier a missionary aim. But this was the exception. Robert of Arbrissel's foundation at Fontevrault, beginning as a pioneering monk, with an unusual care for the status of women, ended as a religious house for the daughters and widows of the French court and nobility. Despite certain original features, the apostolic life, as interpreted in terms of wandering preaching and poverty, could not be realized within these monasteries. That life was replaced for the followers of the preachers by withdrawal from the world in a stable pattern of life under vows.

It is striking how the sources, both for heretical movements and for the wandering preachers, speak of the apostolic life as a mark of these spontaneous phenomena. The clothing of the preachers amounted to a special uniform, with bare feet, minimal clothing and the donkey as the sign of the special humility of those practising the apostolic life. The noteworthy feature is that the apostolic life is no longer being interpreted exclusively along traditional lines, as the life of the monk or nun in community according to the pattern of the early Christians at Jerusalem, who held their goods in common and continued a life of prayer and charity to those in need. A new understanding of the apostolic life has come into being – based on the texts in Matthew and Luke about Christ sending out the Seventy to wander preaching through the villages, having neither scrip nor purse nor shoes and taking no money with them.[18]

The older view formed the scriptural justification for the life of the monks; it was very ancient and continued to hold considerable sway in the twelfth century, a period of vigorous development in new forms of monastic life.

But the spread of the reforms of the canonical life encouraged the development of the second, modern view of the apostolic life. The great stress on poverty in this interpretation is partly explained by the ascetic roots of these movements, with a strong semi-monastic tinge, partly by the post-Gregorian reaction against an over-endowed Church. That poverty had extraordinary popularity is apparent, for example, from the existence of an order like the Grandmontines, with its frail constitution and overwhelming emphasis on renunciation of worldly goods. A few entered to share the austerities; many more in the world remained outside to admire.

The poverty movements represented a reaction against the wealthy Church and a developing bourgeoisie in a time of rapid economic growth.[19] Wealth was notably concrete and visible, displayed in the finery of a merchant and his family. Behind the criticism of the Church as over-wealthy lay also an increasing popular rationalism, capable in a groping way of making comparisons with a new historical sense between the simple Church of the apostles and the elaborate hierarchical Church of the twelfth century. What a leader and prophet of the Church in St Bernard of Clairvaux might set down

[18] C. Dereine, 'Chanoines', in *DHGE*; 'La problème de la vie commune chez les canonistes, d'Anselm de Lucques à Gratien', *Studi Gregoriani* III, pp. 287–98. M. D. Chenu, 'Moines, clercs, laïcs au carrefour de la vie évangélique (XIIe siècle)', *RHE* XLIX (1954), pp. 59–89, comment in Leyser, *Hermits*, pp. 26–8.

[19] Outline by H. Grundmann, 'Soziale Wandlungen-Kaufleute, Bürger, Städte', in *Über die Welt des Mittelalters: Propyläen Weltgeschichte, Summa historica* (Berlin, 1965), pp. 435–42. M. Mollat, 'La notion de la pauvreté au moyen âge: position de problèmes', *Revue d' histoire del' église de France* LII (1966), pp. 6–23.

for the pope in the *De consideratione*, urging on him the example of the simplicity of the early Church, might also be understood in a cruder way at more popular levels, and, mishandled, turn towards heresy. A historian describing an encounter he had with a heretic at Bonn in the first half of the century described his scorn for the members of the Church hierarchy who lived so wrongfully (*irrationabiliter*) – the word is illuminating for the forces which operated below the surface against a traditional, conservative-minded hierarchy.[20]

Against this diffused advance in understanding, the dissemination of a new logic at more popular levels, the Church had relatively slight defences. The great crowds which turned out for a popular preacher expressed the need for more coherent instruction, which the Church was in substance not meeting at the lower levels. As is well known, proposals to set up training centres for the clergy and to use cathedrals as foci for a popular theology broke down. Before the coming of the friars standards of training remained low. Systematic instruction of the laity was rare. Contemporary descriptions reveal sometimes in a flash the nature of the situation in the growing towns, against which reformers had to contend. A startling example is the new industrial town of Antwerp in the early twelfth century in the time of Tanchelm, where the only church for the entire town was allegedly served by a simoniac who lived in sin with his niece. Only relatively slowly did the Church begin to cope with the problems caused by the lack of a developed cure of souls within the towns.[21]

Here lay, in outline, the opportunities for the heretics – in the existence of much popular zeal, which reacted against a conservative Church still much in need of reform, a kind of primitive rationalism no longer satisfied with the fortress Church of the barbarian age, a new understanding of certain texts of Scripture, which had entered the popular consciousness[22] and could not be brought into accord with the ecclesiastical practices that the zealous few saw around them and, again among the few, a rejection of a still coarse and bloodstained age, with its crude materialism. Their yearning for a new way of apostolic life becomes explicable when set against this background. A preacher of skill, who came out of an ascetic background and denounced abuses, was sure of a hearing, and this remained true whether his views were essentially within the bounds of orthodox reform or not. These facts explain the success of the wandering preachers of France – but also the success of the heretical preachers nearly contemporary with them.

[20] Morghen, *Medioevo Cristiano*, p. 253; Ekbert of Schönau, *PL* cxcv, col. 88. *Ratio* can mean 'right'; Morghen argues for the meaning of illogicality implicit here as well as of moral fault. I owe comment to Professor C. N. L. Brooke.

[21] Russell, *Dissent*, pp. 60, 283; colourful anecdotes of moral failure generally in Lea, *Inquisition* i, pp. 1–56; sketch of more subtle approach to relation between heresy and pastoral deficiencies in C. N. L. Brooke, 'The Church in the towns, 1000–1250', in *SCH* vi, pp. 59–83, esp. p. 79; fuller discussion below, pp. 85–7.

[22] Morghen, *Medioevo Cristiano*, pp. 204–81 *passim*.

4

Heretical preachers and the rise of Catharism

Henry the Monk and Peter of Bruis

Henry the Monk provides a good example of a development in one wandering preacher from the ideas of drastic reform, largely still on the lines of the Gregorians, to a theological heresy, in which, nevertheless, issues of practical conduct still held first place.[1] In this he was typical of the theologically unformed protest of the twelfth century, in contradistinction to the more developed ideas of the thirteenth.

His origins are unknown. His success as a preacher in French-speaking areas suggests strongly that he himself was born somewhere in France or in a French-speaking part of the Empire. Henry was an apostate monk, probably also a priest, who had taken to the roads as a preacher of penance. The first detailed account of his activities comes from Le Mans, where he entered the city in 1116 preceded by two disciples carrying a cross on an iron-tipped staff, bearded, barefoot, and with poor clothing. He was at first welcomed by the bishop, who unwisely left him in freedom there while he set off for Rome. On his return he found that the city had been turned upside down, the clergy

---

[1] My principal source for the first edn was J. V. Fearns, 'The Contra Petrobrusianos of Peter the Venerable' (PhD thesis, University of Liverpool, 1963), pt I, ch. 3, 'Peter of Bruis and Henry of Lausanne'; some conclusions are in *AKG* XLVIII (1966), pp. 311–35. I am indebted to Dr Fearns for generously putting his thesis at my disposal. Early work in von Walter, *Wanderprediger* II, pp. 130–40; new text with commentary in R. Manselli, 'Il monaco Enrico e la sua eresia', *BISIAM* LXV (1953), pp. 1–63; see his *Studi sulle eresie del secolo XII* (Rome, 1953), pp. 45–67 (survey linking evangelical heresies of Henry, Peter of Bruis, Valdes; critique: Ilarino da Milano, *RSCI* IX (1955), pp. 424–31); for preachers, see R. B. Brooke, *The Coming of the Friars* (London, 1975). Social context finely re-created by R. I. Moore, *SCH* XXIII, pp. 54–7, *Origins*, pp. 82–101, comments on source: pp. 86–9; for the following quotation I use Moore's tr., *SCH* XXIII, p. 54, and follow his views on pollution and prostitutes, and dowries. Reflections in E. Werner and M. Erbstösser, *Ketzer und Heilige: Das religiöse Leben im Hochmittelalter* (Berlin, 1986), pp. 233–71.

denounced, boycotted by shopkeepers and stripped of all reverence among the people, who were brought to repentance by Henry's extraordinary eloquence.

Henry was at this stage a radical Gregorian reformer, full of scathing denunciation for the sins of the clergy. But he showed some particular social concern and in Le Mans he had an eminently suitable milieu, both for that and for clerical denunciation. It was a town which had failed in its attempt to set up a commune in 1070 and it was dominated by the clergy. It lacked men of substance. The commerce or industry which might have enabled the citizens to wrest a degree of independence from bishop and clergy were wanting.

A long resentment accounts for the violent espousal of Henry's leadership and the ferocity to the clergy which accompanied it. Hildebert the bishop was a reforming Gregorian and, it is likely, imposed the orthodox reformers' novel rules on the prohibited degrees of marriage, insisted that marriage was a sacrament of the Church and required clerical control of it. Later Henry in controversy attacked that view and said that 'the consent of the persons alone makes a marriage'. The rules were onerous and Henry gained support by rejecting them. In a meeting he vividly set forth his programme for the reform of marriage procedures, linking his ideas on Christian marriage with the need to rescue the prostitutes of the city. 'He proclaimed the new dogma', the chronicler said, 'that women who had not lived chastely must, naked before everyone, burn their clothes and their hair. Nobody should accept any gold or silver or goods or wedding gifts with his wife, or receive any dowry with her: the naked should marry the naked, the sick marry the sick and the poor marry the poor, without bothering about whether they married chastely or incestuously.'[2] 'Incestuously' for the chronicler meant within the prohibited degrees. In the exhilaration of emotional revivalism the hair and clothes of the prostitutes, polluted by their calling, were burnt, a collection was taken up to buy new clothes, and young men came forward to marry them. The chronicler might grumble that the prostitutes went back to their old ways, but, for a moment, in the fire of Henry's eloquence and the city's repentance, old social barriers, the dowries and the novel Gregorian rules were swept away. Such a breaking of the social code was rare, but while it lasted it had great potency: three centuries later it occurred with such force on a wider scale as to mould Bohemian peasants into the victorious fighting forces of Hussitism.

Henry was an individualist: in appearance he resembled other preachers of repentance, but he was, as we have seen, a marriage reformer rather than a preacher of celibacy. He stressed poverty and sponsored the burning of ornaments, but he did not give the same emphasis as other preachers did to asceticism, particularly in diet. As a preacher he had a long career, reappearing to move the populace against the clergy at various times in Lausanne, Poitiers and Bordeaux, as well as Le Mans, before moving into the lands of the count of Toulouse, where his traces are lost after 1145. An attempt was made to divert him from heresy at the Council of Pisa in 1135, where he promised to enter a monastery and give up wandering preaching, the council handling him relatively mildly and denouncing only three tenets.

---

[2] Tr. of original text, the *Actus pontificum Cennomannis*, in *WEH*, pp. 108–14, *MBPH*, pp. 33–8 (this tr.).

This restrained treatment by the council, at a time when churchmen were not specially disposed to leniency towards heresy, suggests that at this time he was still rather a wild radical preacher than a heretic proper.[3] We know from a refutation of Henry's teaching by an unknown monk William that nevertheless in the end he did become a heretic of a dangerous kind.[4] The keynote of his heresy was its radical anticlericalism. Henry rejected the medieval role of the clergy as the dispensers of God's grace in favour of the responsibility of the individual.[5] This was carried to extreme lengths, involving Pelagianism.[6] Original sin was rejected: the individual fell by his own act, not by any taint from Adam. Baptism was a personal act of responsibility and could not thus be conferred on infants without under-standing. In a similar way, prayers for the dead had no value, for this would cut across their own responsibility in life for their acts.

These two denials were of themselves not so significant, for they accompanied the normal reaction of an awakening laity to their responsibilities in the twelfth century. But what impresses in Henry is his denial of any useful part to the clergy. The sacramental life of the Church, as administered by an ordained priesthood, simply ceased to exist. The sacrifice of the mass was repudiated, the eucharist rejected, the power of binding and loosing denied to the priests, and sacerdotal confession replaced by a reciprocal confession of sins among the laity. In matrimony the consent of the individuals concerned was adequate: no place at all was left for any intervention by the clergy.

Behind these denials lay a burning desire for simplicity. Church buildings were unnecessary. All the accretions, as Henry saw them, which had grown up since the days of the New Testament were to be cast aside. The clergy were to hold neither money nor honours – an extreme, but not heretical view. Worship was to be simplified in accord with the text of the New Testament. Chrism and oil in baptism, having no warrant in Scripture, were to be eliminated, as were the ring, the mitre and the pastoral staff. A fervent acceptance of the New Testament, not for the first or last time, led to a wholesale rejection of practices which appeared to have no explicit scriptural warrant.

Henry's ideal was a poor wandering clergy, without sacramental functions, but with a vital preaching and exhorting role, wholly without institutional backing and apparatus, and he took such ideas to their most dramatic conclusion. While the orthodox reformers stressed the need to reform clerical morals, Henry cut the knot simply by removing the special functions of the clergy altogether. No doubt he began by taking up the very common heretical position, that it was the unworthiness of the clergy which invalidated the sacraments, especially the mass administered by them. But he proceeded to the unusual position of eliminating the mass altogether. Could he have arrived at this position out of reflections on the Gregorian ideal and his own

[3] Fearns's argument is in 'Contra Petrobrusianos', p. lxxxvii. Tr. of text: *WEH*, pp. 114–15; *MBPH*, p. 39.

[4] See below, p. 47, n. 10; text ed. Manselli, in *BISIAM* LXV (1953), pp. 36–62, tr. *WEH*, pp. 115–17; *MBPH*, pp. 46–60. Possibly William was William of St Thierry.

[5] For this exposition I am much indebted to Fearns, 'Contra Petrobrusianos'.

[6] See Manselli's comments (*Studi*, pp. 57–9); on Peter the Venerable's attitude to heretics, see J-P. Torrell and D. Bouthillier, *Pierre le Vénérable et sa vision du monde: Sa vie-son oeuvre-l'homme et le demon* (Louvain, 1986).

experience? Certainly this is a possibility. Nevertheless it is tempting to see an outside hand influencing his steps. J. V. Fearns suggests that the final step from radical preacher to heretic was facilitated by the influence of Peter of Bruis, the heretic leader from the mountains of the Embrun region, who, like Bogomil, began his career as a village priest.

Peter the Venerable, the abbot of Cluny and our prime source on the views and career of Peter of Bruis, believed when he wrote his tract against the sect, the *Contra Petrobrusianos*, that Henry was a faithful member of Peter's sect.[7] Later, when he wrote his introductory letter to the tract, he had learnt more of Henry and had come to give him a greater independence. He saw that Henry had had an independent career as wandering agitator before he encountered Peter of Bruis. A comparison of views of the two men confirms the dependence of Henry on Peter, but also his eclecticism. On a number of points they coincided, perhaps most strikingly in the total rejection of the eucharist, but also in the attacks on Church tradition, on offerings for the dead, and in the rejection of church buildings. The contemporary source, the *Actus pontificum Cennomannis*, says that, after Henry received permission to leave the synod of Pisa, he took up a new course with a fresh sect.[8] This can hardly be anything other than the Petrobrusians. Yet he did so with significant variations.

Despite Henry's zeal for the simplicities of the New Testament, he never followed Peter of Bruis in his rejection of the Old Testament or in his repudiation of the veneration of the cross. Henry began his career in the evangelical, post-Gregorian tradition of reform and, though aided across the frontiers of orthodoxy by the more dogmatic heretic Peter, he and his followers always remained closer than the Petrobrusians to the tradition of evangelical heresy.[9] This is revealed by his attitude to poverty and the *apostolica vita*. For Henry, in the tradition of the wandering preachers, the poor life was a vital prerequisite for the clerical state; for Peter and his followers this played no special part. The right to preach freely mattered for Henry as it did for his orthodox predecessors. Like some of them, he claimed it from Christ's command to preach the gospel to all creatures. We hear little of this in the Petrobrusians.

The *Actus*, if we accept the identification of the new sect with the Petrobrusians, places the crucial meeting of Peter and Henry after the Synod of Pisa in 1135.[10] This would fit well with the career of Peter, who had long preached heresy in obscurity in the mountains; but, it would seem, shortly before the *Contra Petrobrusianos* was written, extended his activities to the prosperous lands of Languedoc. Henry returning from Italy could readily have met him, then commenced his career as an agitator in southern France.

The setting for the preaching of the two heretics is significant. When Peter,

---

[7] Ed. J. V. Fearns in *Corpus Christianorum, Continuatio mediaevalis* x (Turnhout, 1968); for dating, see Fearns, 'Contra Petrobrusianos', ch. 4.

[8] Ed. J. Mabillon in *Vetera Analecta* (Paris, 1723), col. 323A; Fearns, 'Contra Petrobrusianos', p. lxxxviii; *WEH*, p. 115. Introductory letter, subsequent to Peter's tract, ed. Fearns, *Corpus Christianorum* x, pp. 3–6; it should be dated *c.*1139–40 (see *MBPH*, p. 60; tr. ibid., pp. 60–2; *WEH*, pp. 118–21).

[9] Fearns, 'Contra Petrobrusianos', p. xcii.

[10] I have preferred Fearns's dating (ibid., p. lxxxvii) to that of Manselli in *BISIAM* LXV (1953), pp. 1–63: the date of appearance of the refutation by William the Monk is the crucial point.

the Cluniac mountain priest, came to extend his range, he roved through the prosperous towns of south-western France addressing great gatherings. At the time Peter the Venerable wrote, the heresy had spread into the province of Narbonne, westwards to Toulouse and the surrounding plain, and finally, by the time he had completed his prefatory letter, into the diocese of Arles and into Gascony.[11] At St Gilles, Peter ended his career with a violent death.

Henry was taken by the archbishop of Arles to the Synod of Pisa, and thus may be presumed to have been active as a preacher in his province. After his return from Pisa, he began a second career in Languedoc, reaching the end of his tours in Toulouse, where St Bernard, if we believe his panegyrist, robbed Henry of his hold on the populace.[12] But the damage had been done. It can hardly be accidental that the area of Peter and Henry's success in the third decade of the century bears some similarity to that infiltrated by Catharism in the latter half of the century, where the Church had to face its greatest crisis. Peter and Henry deserve to be remembered, not only as founders of heretical groups in the age of rebirth of heresy, but also as forerunners of the Cathar success in Languedoc.[13]

The origins of Peter's heresy raise problems. Peter began as a parish priest, and then was ejected from his cure. Probably after this he began a career as a heretical agitator which lasted some twenty years, from about 1119 to his death in approximately 1139–40. Bruis was a small village in the canton of Rosans in the Hautes-Alpes; it was either Peter's birthplace or his parish. Peter's early years of preaching were spent in the mountainous regions of Embrun, Gap and Die. What surprises us is the geographical origins of this heresy: the Hautes-Alpes one would expect to be a backward area, a possible fount for heathen survivals, but not for a 'modern' heresy in the twelfth century. Of course, Peter could himself have incubated his own heresy. He is too shadowy a figure in our sources for us to be able to come to any useful conclusions on his personality and capacities. A clue, however, on a possible source is to be found in the geography of Bruis. It lies on one of the Alpine routes to Italy. Here would be a passage-way to the mountain villages for novel heretical ideas, disseminated by travellers to and from that part of western Europe that was most open to external influences.[14]

Peter's theology was more interesting and idiosyncratic than Henry's, since only a part of his teaching resembled the common ideas of earlier and contemporary twelfth-century sects. The teaching of the sect was radical and violent. Views were conveyed by vigorous practical demonstration, and it was in the course of one of these, while inciting the people at St Gilles to make a bonfire of their crucifixes, that Peter met his end, being pushed in himself and burnt by his opponents. At other times he and his followers would drag monks

[11] Fearns, 'Contra Petrobrusianos', p. xliv; tr. of Peter the Venerable's letter, in *WEH*, pp. 118–21; geographical references in text and introductory letter, ed. Fearns, *Corpus Christianorum*, pp. 3, 10.

[12] See texts tr. *WEH*, pp. 122–6; *MBPH*, pp. 39–46. The *Vita prima* of St Bernard (*PL* CLXXXV, col. 313) says Henry was captured and brought to the bishop in chains. This may have been in 1145; see *WEH*, p. 680.

[13] E. Griffe, *Les Débuts de l'aventure cathare en Languedoc (1140–1190)* (Paris, 1969) (survey of early Midi Cathars with strong feeling for locality), pp. 21–48.

[14] Fearns, in *AKG* XLVIII (1966), p. 329, n. 92; on possible contact with Bogomil-infected regions, cf. p. 332 and n. 100.

from their monasteries and force them to marry or, in a ceremony which foreshadows some actions of the radical group of Lollards at Norwich in the fifteenth century, would eat meat on Good Friday.[15]

Beneath their various tenets lay a belief in the Church as the spiritual unity of the congregation of the faithful.[16] The accretions of later ages are all stripped away to reveal the underlying true nature of the Church. The keynote, as among the Henricians they influenced, was a rejection of all external forms. The negative tenets of the sect, which naturally enough form the staple of Peter the Venerable's attack, are the repudiation of the authority of the Old Testament, of the Fathers and all the traditions of the Church, the rejection of infant baptism, of the doctrine of the eucharist and the sacrifice of the mass and of prayers for the dead. The use of church buildings was condemned, as was the veneration of the cross and the practice of singing in church. But behind the denials lay some varied strands of thought, not all readily reconcilable with the common ferment of popular religious ideas of Peter's own time. The rejection of so many of the externals of worship springs from the desire for a de-materialization of worship. The formal objects of veneration – buildings, crosses, altars – are seen as positive incumbrances to true religion, and violently cast aside.

Behind the rejection of the eucharist, as celebrated in the contemporary Church, and the practice of infant baptism, lay the literal appeal to the gospels. The eucharistic denial did not spring from the usual rejection of the unworthiness of the ministers of the sacrament, but from an extremely literal reading of Scripture. As they understood the gospels, the transformation of the bread and wine into the Body and Blood took place once only at the Last Supper, and was a miracle never since performed by anyone else. Christ had no intention of instituting a rite to be repeated on the altars of the Church; not even a symbolic rendering of the act was open to consideration in their group. This is an exceptionally radical viewpoint, not easy to parallel: it will not fit with the dualism either of the Bogomils earlier, or of the Cathars later, for the Petrobrusians were not denying that Christ did offer his body and blood in the Upper Room. They were not forced by a rejection of matter, as among the Bogomils, to interpret Christ's actions on that occasion purely figuratively. The likelihood seems, as Fearns suggests, that on this issue Peter made a personal contribution to heresy.[17] He was not a dualist, but he did act as a kind of John the Baptist to the organized dualist churches of the second half of the century, preparing a way for them among the people.

In one other outbreak, two peasants, Clement and Ebrard, from the village of Bucy-le-Long near Soissons in about 1114, preached a heresy which appeared to have dualist undertones.[18] Christ did not in reality take on flesh; the bread and wine were not really transformed into the Body and Blood; the mouth of the priest was the opening of hell. They spoke of themselves as followers of the apostolic life and lived in a rigid asceticism. The mention of

---

[15] Below, p. 272.

[16] Fearns, 'Contra Petrobrusianos', p. xlvii; for dynamism unleashed by town life, Fichtenau, *Ketzer*, p. 63.

[17] Ibid., pp. lvii–lix.

[18] Borst, *Katharer*, p. 84; another interpretation in Russell, *Dissent*, pp. 78–81 (note the comment on Bishop Joscelin's creed); source in *WEH*, pp. 102–4. I assume the story of the orgy is not authentic.

the *vita apostolica* and the denunciation of the unworthy priesthood place them in the Western stream of heresy; but the Docetism is not common in spontaneous Western heresy. Especially significant is the nature of their renunciations. They refused everything that had been procreated as a result of sexual intercourse. Clement was subjected to the ordeal and failed it; when he was thrown into the vat and 'floated like a stick' there was rejoicing, perhaps because of his link with a 'rapacious' count, John of Soissons. The bishop did not carry out sentence on the basis of the verdict of the ordeal but went to seek advice. The crowd broke into the prison and burnt Clement and Ebrard.[19]

In another rural setting at the village of Ivoy in the first quarter of the century, a group of heretics met secretly and taught their followers to reject the eucharist and the baptism of infants.[20] The case may be taken as typical of the episodes in which the sources are inadequate to reveal fully the nature of the heresy. We catch only a gleam of the popular concern for the individual's religious responsibility – the usual motive for the rejection of infant baptism.

Tanchelm and Arnold of Brescia

Tanchelm of Antwerp and Arnold of Brescia, well separated in time – one in the Netherlands, the other in Italy – show how the ferment of reform ideals in the post-Gregorian age could lead to heresy.[21] According to the traditional account, Tanchelm owed his rise to the glaring neglect of the Church authorities for the developing town of Antwerp.[22] Disgusted by the state of the Church, Tanchelm began his preaching, soon held a dominance over the religious life of the town and carried his preaching into Flanders, Zeeland and Brabant. His hearers came from the lower classes, but the success of his sermons in Zeeland must prove that they were far from exclusively drawn from townsmen, for this remained economically a relatively undeveloped land of fishermen and farmers. Tanchelm totally rejected the Church and its sacraments, and said that the Church had become a brothel. The best-known source, a letter of the cathedral chapter at Utrecht, describes some fantastic scenes as Tanchelm declared himself God, entered into a symbolic marriage with a statue of Mary, and, accompanied by a former priest and a smith, made his way through Antwerp dressed in golden robes and with an armed guard.[23] The common people revered him as God, and drank his bathwater. But the interlude of fantasy came to an end after only three years, in 1115, when he was struck down by a priest.

Tanchelm had a gift for self-projection.[24] The size of following which he drew to him ensured the continuation of his preaching tours for years unmolested: it would have been too dangerous to put him down by force.

[19] R. I. Moore, 'Popular violence and popular heresy in Western Europe *c.*1000–1179', *SCH* xxi (1984), pp. 43–50 at p. 49.
[20] Russell, *Dissent*, pp. 54–6; source in *WEH*, pp. 105–7.
[21] Discussion by Grundmann, in *HZ* cxcvi (1963), pp. 661–6.
[22] For a hypothesis based on reaction to industrial conditions, see Cohn, *Millennium*, 1st edn, pp. 35–8.
[23] Tr. in *WEH*, pp. 96–100; *MBPH*, pp. 28–31.
[24] Moore, *Origins*, p. 64 ('talent for manipulation').

The odd episode of the bathwater has been variously interpreted, as a sign of the overwhelming reverence of credulous followers or as a misunderstanding by the writer, who had not understood Tanchelm's distribution to his followers of a watered wine;[25] connoisseurs of the twilight of popular cults may recall in favour of the first hypothesis that Garibaldi's servant found a good sale, all unknown to his master, for his bathwater. But other features in the usual description are not quite convincing. Why, if Tanchelm's original platform was the wickedness of the orthodox Church and the immorality of its priesthood, was he a libertine, who used his sway over women to satisfy his sexual needs?[26] Libertinism is almost an automatic accusation for a popular heretic who influences his women hearers. The principal source emanates from the enemies of Tanchelm in the chapter of Utrecht who sought to denounce him in 1112 to Frederick, archbishop of Cologne, and might be expected to press any possible hostile rumour on Tanchelm into service. Not everything in the case meets the eye. Behind the accusations of heresy could well lie an episode in the Gregorian–anti-Gregorian contest, much as accusations of heresy without much cause had been bandied about in the affairs of the Pataria in Milan and Ramihrdus in Cambrai, and were again to be in the case of Lambert le Bègue in Liège.[27] Such an interpretation is made more plausible by the evidence of direct borrowing of detail in the letter from Utrecht from the sixth-century chronicler Gregory of Tours.[28]

Pirenne brought some light when he inferred that Tanchelm was an agent of Count Robert II of Flanders, a supporter of the Gregorians, who wanted to use his party support in order to gain for the Flemish bishopric of Tournai a part of the bishopric of Utrecht, then in the hands of the imperialist party.[29] Tanchelm, on this view, played the part of the demagogue, stirring the populace against a lax imperialist clergy, and making manifest the need for a Gregorian reform in this area, which in turn might facilitate the diocesan rearrangements which the count desired. Pirenne made the connection too close: he was mistaken in thinking that Tanchelm was a layman, and a one-time notary of the count.

It now appears that Tanchelm is to be numbered among the heretical leaders who sprang from the clergy. But was he already a Gregorian when he appealed to the count for aid? Much rests on timing.[30] The letter of Utrecht can be read not as a hostile and discrediting account of a popular preacher with Gnostic undertones, but as a collection of slanders which wilfully distort Tanchelm's reforming activities. The letter might enable us to conclude that

---

[25] Borst, *Katharer*, p. 85, n. 13.
[26] Ibid.; Russell, *Dissent*, p. 65 (the best account of sources and dating, pp. 265–9, 282–3).
[27] Ibid., pp. 90–6; on Lambert, see *MBPH*, pp. 101–11; L. K. Little, *Religious Poverty and the Profit Economy in Medieval Europe* (London, 1978), p. 129.
[28] W. Mohr, 'Tanchelm von Antwerpen, eine nochmalige Überprüfung der Quellenlage', *Annales Universitatis Saraviensis* III (1954), pp. 234–47; rejected by Werner (*Pauperes Christi*, pp. 205–7); Moore, *Origins*, is inclined to accept an element of extravagance as part of Tanchelm's technique to attract followers.
[29] H. Pirenne, 'Tanchelin et le projèt de démembrement du diocèse d'Utrecht vers 1100', *ARBB*, 5th ser. XIII (1927), pp. 112–19; see further, Russell, *Dissent*, pp. 265–9.
[30] I follow Russell (*Dissent*, p. 282).

Tanchelm was first active in Zeeland,[31] not in Antwerp, and that he was active there in the first instance because this was the area which it was intended should be taken from the bishopric of Utrecht. The letter says that Tanchelm rejected the Church, for that one might understand the local Church, tainted by immorality and its imperialist connections. The rejection of Transubstantiation one might read as a rejection of the ministrations of unworthy priests, and the alleged union with God supposed to give Tanchelm divine powers one might read as an orthodox exhortation to mystical union with Christ. The betrothal with Mary, using rings, might be a version of a campaign to persuade women to give up luxuries and bestow their rings on a statue of Mary. Difficulties remain, even if this revision is accepted; there is still a hostile tradition, not necessarily dependent on the Utrecht letter, in other sources. The truth will never be quite clear, but we are on secure ground if we assume that there was much less heresy and excess than the sources suggest, and that we are probably right if we think of Tanchelm as a Gregorian who, especially at the end, slipped into Donatism.[32]

In the case of Arnold of Brescia the sources are not obscure, although they lack the confirmation of the direct words or writing of the heresiarch himself. Arnold first showed his hand when ruling a community of canons regular in his native city of Brescia, once influenced by the Pataria agitation, and in the 1130s the scene of a struggle for the bishopric between Villano and Manfred, supporters of the rival claims to the papal tiara of Anacletus II and Innocent II.[33] In the absence of Manfred, the successful candidate, from his city, Arnold allied himself with the supporters of a commune, and used the opportunity to set about a drastic reform of the clergy. Manfred incurred Arnold's hostility, not because he was some idle nobleman in episcopal orders, but simply because his moderate reforming plans, which had already come up against the hostility of the local clergy, did not go far enough. For Arnold the pattern of apostolic life was realized in the lives of strict canons regular, and the solution to the problems of wealthy, simoniacal and unchaste clergy was to impose on them *tout court* what was in effect the life of canons regular.

Arnold's movement, though it loosely resembled the Pataria and the agitation of Ramihrdus of Cambrai, went beyond their ideas in some respects. Nor did Innocent II give Arnold the support Gregory VII had once given to the Pataria. Condemned in 1139, Arnold was forced to leave Italy and make for Paris, where he had formerly studied under Peter Abelard. There his attacks on the clergy and, surprisingly, on St Bernard of Clairvaux earned him a condemnation at the Council of Sens in 1140, somewhat rhetorically associated as pupil with the ruin of his master Abelard. In flight, he was befriended by Guy, papal legate to Bohemia, who persuaded him to submit and accept penance. Misguidedly, Pope Eugenius III invited him to Rome to

---

[31] Not first aroused by clerical deficiency (as Borst, *Katharer*, p. 84); correction by Russell (p. 283).

[32] Russell (p. 64) goes farther in attributing heresy than I, partly on the analogy of the eccentric backwoods prophet Aldebert in the eighth century. I am more impressed by the possibilities of slander, and think excess more likely in a man of Aldebert's than Tanchelm's background.

[33] A. Frugoni, *Arnaldo da Brescia nelle fonti del secolo XII* (Rome, 1954) (stresses influence of gospel on Arnold in Morghen tradition); review: Ilarino da Milano, *RSCI* IX (1955), pp. 417–33; comment: Dupré Theseider, *Introduzione*, pp. 134–7; Violante, *HS*, p. 177, discusses relative absence of heresy in Italy before Arnold.

keep him under his eye, only to discover that the spectacle of abuses of the curia and the involvement of the papacy in temporal affairs caused a revival of his agitation in a fiercer form. 'The pope himself', he came to believe, 'was not what he professed to be an apostolic man and shepherd of souls – but a man of blood who maintained his authority by fire and sword.'[34] The grievances of Rome's citizens offered him a better platform than the communal movement at Brescia, and with their aid he expelled the pope and declared the independence of the city, where he attempted to realize his ideal of the poor clergy – preaching, administering the sacraments, wholly unencumbered by possessions or political power. For a time his views, especially his rejection of the Donation of Constantine and his belief that the emperor should receive his crown from the citizens of Rome rather than the pope, recommended him to the imperial party. The pope, though he returned with the aid of military force, was again expelled in 1150. But Arnold's reform plans of that year revealed what a radical he was, and he could only retain his place through a conspiracy of faithful followers of the inferior class and without further aid from the nobles. The logic of his own radical religious positions led him into an extreme democratic position in politics. It was as a revolutionary holding on to power with limited numerical support that he was finally hunted down under Pope Hadrian IV and executed in 1155.

His eloquence and appeal to the crowds assimilate him to the inspired wandering preachers of France, and he is fully in accord with the ideas of the time in his stress on the overwhelming value of poverty. But he differed from the wandering preachers in his readiness to use political force to gain his ends, and in the fact that he offered a programme, not merely for the salvation of the individual, but also for the Church at large – a programme he was prepared to enforce with the sword. Its fundamental tenet was that clergy and monks who had possessions could not be saved. There were other, sacramental errors in his beliefs, which linked with the central position on poverty. The sacraments were not denied in themselves, but there was a sweeping application of the common post-Gregorian position, that the sacraments had become invalid through the unworthiness of ministers. As one might expect from the pragmatic nature of Arnold, there was no deep dogmatic difference with orthodoxy, and in fact he was never formally arraigned for heresy.[35] The spiritual power of Rome was denied because of its involvement with the things of this world. Preaching was open to all, and depended, not on a particular training or authorization, but simply on the life of the preacher.

In practice nearly all shrank from the drastic renunciations which Arnold demanded of the hierarchy. He was too radical to be at ease with reformers within the Church. The sympathy of Guy, the cardinal legate in Bohemia, and his earlier readiness to repent showed that initially he was not far from the Church. But the emotional experience of contact with the darker side of Rome and his own temperament carried him beyond reconciliation.

The Arnoldists as an organized force never again played a significant part in Italy, for their power was broken by the events which followed the

[34] John of Salisbury, *Historia Pontificalis*, tr. M. Chibnall (London, 1956) (under 1149); and *WEH*, p. 148. See also texts tr. in *MBPH*, pp. 66–71.
[35] Grundmann, *Ketzergeschichte*, p. 20; see A. Frugoni, 'Filii Arnaldi', *BISIAM* lx (1958), 521–4.

re-establishment of the commune in 1150. Arnold, however, was one of those dissident leaders whose power is derived, not from any great originality of thought, but from their ability to focus widespread discontents, and these long outlived his movement. The numbers of Arnoldists were thought worthy of refutation by Bonacursus of Milan in his polemical work, the *Manifestatio haeresis Catharorum*, written between 1176 and 1190, which included a section attacking the belief that evangelical poverty was obligatory, that laymen who practised it had full rights of preaching, and that their sins incapacitated priests and hierarchy from administering the sacraments and holding the power of binding and loosing.[36] Though at that date Arnoldism may well have represented a current of thought rather than a sect, the name passed into the catalogue of heresies to be periodically denounced by popes, continuing to exist in bulls, though surely not in reality, down to 1511.[37]

Eon (or Eudo) de l'Etoile

The case of Eon carries us back to the wild rural agitators, Aldebert, Theuda and Leutard.[38] Though lettered and probably a younger son of the Breton nobility, Eon's following consisted exclusively of credulous peasants. The sources say that he gathered his followers to pray in secluded places, that he was opposed to church buildings, and with his followers attacked them and stripped them of ornaments. He believed himself the Son of God, and persuaded his followers into believing that he was 'eum' of the Latin phrase probably known to him from the formula of an exorcism: Jesus Christ who would return in glory – 'per eum qui venturus est cum gloria judicare vivos et mortuos et seculum per ignem'.[39] His disciples he called by the names of angels, prophets and apostles. His staff was, as it were, a sceptre shaped in the form of a Y – as long as the Y pointed upwards, two-thirds of the world belonged to God the Father, one to Eon; if he inverted the fork, the position would be reversed. The Council of Rheims in 1148 heard these revelations with laughter, and banished Eon to prison, where he soon died.

Some commentators have, reasonably, thought that he was mad; others have noted apparently Gnostic elements.[40] Werner notes the deep superstitions of Brittany, which had established so strong a hold that in the seventeenth century part needed in effect to be freshly converted by the Jesuits.[41] Russell depicts him as sincere but deranged. Mad, or only 'mad north north west', with an eye to church plunder and escaping the death sentence at Rheims, one

[36] Ilarino da Milano, 'La "Manifestatio heresis catarorum"', *Aevum* XII (1938), pp. 281–333 (see third section of treatise); Arnoldists discussed in his *L'Eresia di Ugo Speroni nella confutazione del Maestro Vacario* (Vatican, 1945), pp. 444–52. Note warning by W. L. Wakefield, *WEH*, p. 146, that the links between Arnold and the Arnoldists are not wholly assured.

[37] D. Kurze, 'Die festländischen Lollarden', *AKG* XLVII (1965), p. 68, n. 1. (article important for terminology and study of popular religion).

[38] Russell, *Dissent*, pp. 118–24; note discussion of his name: pp. 120–1, 289.

[39] Borst, *Katharer*, p. 87n. Or derivation from 'per eundem dominum nostrum Jesum Christum' (Russell, *Dissent*, p. 120). Sources tr. in *WEH*, pp. 141–6; *MBPH*, pp. 62–6. Did he take on a new name, like a novice entering monastic life (*Fichtenau*, Ketzer, p. 54)?

[40] References in *WEH*, pp. 685–6; Russell, *Dissent*, p. 120 and n. I agree with Russell in thinking there is little in this.

[41] *Pauperes Christi*, p. 180.

certain feature of the case is the pitiable condition of the followers of Eon. Their heresy was manifestly based on a profound ignorance.

The early Cathars

Heresy in the first three decades of the century tended to depend heavily on the personality of one preacher; his influence removed, the following he collected falls back into obscurity, or disappears completely. In Eon's time (the 1140s), the first signs appear that this phase in the history of Western dissent is coming to an end as writers and chroniclers describe the stirrings of a fully international movement, named differently in different countries, but having distinctive elements of belief and organization in common.[42] These betray a connection with the Bogomils of Byzantium and the Balkans.

The anonymity of the new heresy alarmed some orthodox observers. St Bernard, on hearing of it, exclaimed at the contrast between it and the heresies of the early Church, named after their founders, Mani and the Manichees, Sabellius and the Sabellians, Arius and the Arians.[43] Events bore out his fears, as over the following two decades this Bogomil-influenced heresy spread widely in the West.

The first outbreak to be recorded took place in the Rhineland, where in 1143–4 the Premonstratensian provost Everwin of Steinfeld described to St Bernard of Clairvaux the traits of a heresy detected at Cologne which had its own bishop and organization.[44] There were three ranks of adherents – auditors, believers and elect, entry from the lowest category to that of believers, and from believers to elect, being gained by a ceremony of laying-on of hands and a process of testing. The baptism thus obtained through the laying-on of hands 'in fire and the Spirit' was contrasted with the baptism by water of John the Baptist. The group refused to drink milk or consume anything produced as a result of coition, and rejected marriage. At daily meals, Everwin reported, they 'consecrated' their food and drink with the *Pater Noster*. They claimed their belief went back to the time of the martyrs, and that they had fellow adherents in 'Greece' (i.e. Byzantium) and 'certain other lands'. The bishop, his assistant and some others stood their ground in debate, and when they refused to recant were burnt by the people.

The distinctions among adherents, the existence of a category of adepts, the elect, the double initiation ceremony with the laying-on of hands, like the *baptisma* and the *teleiosis* known in Byzantium to the orthodox twelfth-century writer Euthymius Zigabenus, the contrast between this and the baptism in water of John, the rejection of milk, the products of coition and the repudiation of marriage, and finally the belief in the existence of co-religionists in Byzantium – all are good evidence of an infiltration of the Balkan and

[42] Borst, *Katharer*, pp. 89–96; perceptive comments in B. Hamilton, 'Wisdom from the East: the reception by the Cathars of eastern dualist texts', Biller, Hudson, *Literacy*, pp. 38–60.

[43] *Sermo* 66, *PL* CLXXXIII, col. 1094; *RB*, p. 50n.; for discussion of long-term effect of orthodox realization of the appearance of a rival Church inside Christendom, see P. Biller, 'Words and the medieval notion of religion', *JEH* XXXVI (1985), pp. 351–69; note p. 363.

[44] *PL* CLXXXII, cols 676–80; tr. in *WEH*, pp. 127–32; on this correspondence, see Manselli, *Studi*, pp. 89–109; *MBPH*, pp. 74–8; comment on punishment by the people, in Moore, *SCH* XXI, pp. 47, 48.

Byzantine heresy of Bogomilism.[45] Bogomil himself was a tenth-century Bulgarian village priest (his name, 'worthy of the pity of God' was probably a pseudonym) who organized and gave new shape to dualist ideas floating in his backward country, newly and shakily converted from paganism. He gave a voice to a peasantry oppressed by its Byzantine conquerors, its alien Byzantine priesthood and the Bulgarian aristocracy. So far from being weeded out in Bulgaria, the heresy developed and spread into Byzantium proper and Constantinople, carried forward by the strong, superficial attractions of the dualist interpretation of the world with its initial simplicity and its apparent solutions to the problem of the presence of evil in a world created by a good God. At the centre of the Bogomils' experience was the conviction that what is seen is evil: flesh itself is the creation of a fallen angel, Satan, given over to evil. What is unseen is spiritual. Initiates, who might appear like the most ascetic of Byzantine monks, lived a life as far removed from the fleshly world as was conceivable, eschewing eggs, milk, cheese, meat, all the products of coition, remaining celibate and fasting ruthlessly. Supporters venerated the initiates, gave them the opportunity to continue their renunciations and listened to their preaching, but were under no obligation themselves to renounce the products of coition, marriage or parenthood. A high ideal existed for the few; the many had very limited commitments.

The Bogomil ascetic ideal appealed in the West in the age of St Bernard and the Cistercians, when asceticism was given so high a value. Everwin's description tells us why Bogomil enthusiasts gained converts – they followed the pattern of the poor, wandering preacher. The Cologne heretics claimed, he said, that 'theirs alone is the Church, inasmuch as only they follow in the footsteps of Christ. They continue to be the true imitators of the apostolic life, seeking not those things which are of the world, possessing no house, or lands, even as Christ had no property . . . "You, however," they say to us, "add house to house, field to field, and seek the things that are of this world. You do this to the point that they who are considered the most perfect among you, such as monks and canons regular, although owning nothing of their own and holding everything in common, nevertheless possess all these things." Of themselves they say, "We, the poor of Christ, who have no fixed abode and flee from city to city like sheep amidst wolves, are persecuted as were the apostles and the martyrs." '[46]

Apostolic life had been the turning-point.[47] Where authority claimed apostolicity for the Church because of the succession of its bishops from the

---

[45] H. C. Puech and A. Vaillant, *Le Traité contre les Bogomiles de Cosmas le Prêtre* (Paris, 1945) (subtle account, with analysis of Bogomils); D. Obolensky, *The Bogomils* (Cambridge, 1948); E. Werner, 'Bogomil – eine literarische Fiktion?', *FF* XXXIII (1959), pp. 24–38, followed on Bogomil's historicity, not on derivation of name; I. Dujčev, 'I Bogomili nei paesi slavi e loro storia', *Medioevo Bizantino-Slavo* I (Rome, 1965), pp. 251–82; H. I. Marrou, 'Un Ange déchu, un Ange pourtant', *Satan* (*EC* XXVII (1948)), pp. 28–43; E. Turdeanu, 'Apocryphes bogomiles et pseudo-bogomiles', *RHR* CXXXVIII (1950), pp. 22–52, 176–218; for *apocryphon: Interrogation of John*, see *Le Livre secret des Cathares, Interrogatio Johannis, Apocryphe d'origine bogomile*, ed. E. Bozóky (Paris, 1980); for summary, see Lambert, *Medieval Heresy*, 1st edn, pp. 12–23 and references; M. Dando, *Les Origines du catharisme* (Paris, 1967) (hypothesis on pedigree of Catharism). B. Hamilton, 'Wisdom from the east: the reception by the Cathars of eastern dualist texts', *Heresy and Literacy 1000–1530, Cambridge Studies in Medieval Literature XXIII*, Cambridge, 1994, ed. P. Biller, A. Hudson, (forthcoming), will discuss Bogomil influence. G. Rottenwöhrer, *Der Katharismus* III, *Die Herkunft der Katharer nach Theologie und Geschichte*, Bad Honnef, 1990, elucidates the relationship to Bogomilism.
[46] *WEH*, p. 129.
[47] *RB*, pp. 18–27.

apostles and the tradition of its doctrine from the early Church, the heretics bypassed that claim by their plea for realization of the apostolic life. It is conceived by the heretics, and plainly also by their hearers, as the wandering insecure life of the disciples on the pattern of the sending of the Seventy. Orthodox Gregorian preachers, of whom the hermits of western France are the best-known examples, helped to create a demand for this pattern of apostolic life. Through conservatism this demand was never met by orthodoxy in this period. The heretics were the beneficiaries.

Not all of the Cologne heretics accepted the Bogomil influence, however. Another group described by Everwin had beliefs of a 'Western' type, rigorist in morality, pleading for a simple spiritual Church free of the tainted Catholic clergy and putting weight on the response of the individual conscience. They denied the validity of Catholic masses, Everwin said, 'because no priests of the Church are validly ordained. For, they say, the apostolic office has been corrupted through involvement in secular business . . . he who sits in the chair of Peter has lost the power to ordain which was bestowed upon Peter. And because the apostolic see does not have this power, the archbishops and bishops, who lead worldly lives within the Church, cannot receive from that see the power to ordain anyone.' They accepted the baptism of adults, 'baptized by Christ, no matter who may actually administer the sacrament', but rejected infant baptism as not in accord with Scripture. Texts again buttressed their idiosyncratic doctrine that only marriage between virgins was lawful, and also their rejection of purgatory. Penance they found unnecessary, 'because, on whatever day the sinner shall have lamented his sins, all are forgiven'.[48] Only observances established by Christ or the apostles were acceptable.

Alike in their ethical concern and their attacks on the clergy, the groups thus diverged markedly in their more positive beliefs. Dissension between them led to their discovery.

In 1145 St Bernard of Clairvaux, engaged on his few days' preaching against the followers of Henry the Monk in Toulouse, may have brushed another heresy, described in an imprecise phrase apparently as that of 'weavers and Arians'.[49] At Liège a group was discovered with its own hierarchy and with a division among its adherents between initiates, called 'believers', and 'auditors', who were neophytes in the heresy. They rejected wholesale the sacraments, including marriage.[50]

A profession of faith and formula for abjuration amongst the manuscripts of the abbey of Moissac in the south of France dating from mid-century implies the existence of a heresy rejecting baptism, the eucharist, marriage and meat eating, which included among its beliefs the view that remission of sins could

[48] *WEH*, pp. 130–1.

[49] *PL* CLXXXV, col. 411; Manselli, 'Una designazione dell'eresia Catara "Arriana Haeresis"', *BISIAM* LXVIII (1956), pp. 233–46; Griffe, *Débuts*, pp. 33–7. R. I. Moore ('St Bernard's mission to the Languedoc in 1145', *BIHR* XLVII (1974), pp. 1–10) argues that Bernard did not meet the type of heresy of the first Cologne group there, as is sometimes alleged.

[50] *WEH*, pp. 139–41; *MBPH*, pp. 78–9. I have preferred H. Silvestre, in *RHE* LVIII (1963), pp. 979–80; P. Bonenfant, in *LMA* LXIX (1963), pp. 278–9, on dating to J. B. Russell ('Les Cathares de 1048–54 à Liège', *BSAHDL* XLII (1961), pp. 1–8) who places the source, a letter from the faithful of Liège to the pope 'L', in the pontificate of Leo IX (1048–54).

only be obtained through the imposition of hands, or the 'martyrdom' of their sect.[51]

In the Rhineland a trial at Cologne in 1163[52] showed that the burnings two decades earlier had been ineffective; a Western-type heresy still existed there, but it had, according to the description of the prime source, Ekbert, later Benedictine abbot of Schönau, blended with the Bogomil-influenced group.[53] Amongst their errors, some held the belief that only marriage between virgins was legitimate – a sign that the 'Western' heresy still had its influence. But dissension between the groups seemed to have disappeared, and the 'Westerners' now existed as an outer circle, taught dissenting evangelical beliefs, while an inner circle of adepts had a secret doctrine which included belief in a Docetic Christology, transmigration of souls, and the creation of the world by an evil god. Initiation to the circle of adepts was obtained in a secret ceremony by the laying-on of hands. Ekbert believed that the heresy had an international character. In Flanders, whence the heretics had come, he said, they were called 'Piphles', in France 'Texerant' because of their weaving, and in Germany 'the Cathars', a Greek term meaning the 'pure ones'.[54] The latter has been taken most widely by modern writers as a term for the new heresy of the twelfth century, formed by the coalescence of Western evangelical heresy and Bogomil influences from the East.

Ekbert's sermons in one way represented a step forward in the progress of the Church's polemic against heresy, for they attempted to expound in full the dogmatic basis on which the Cologne heresy rested. Yet, progressive as this attitude was by contrast with that of the mass of writers hitherto, content with fleeting and superficial notices of denials of orthodoxy, Ekbert's work was largely vitiated by his fatal penchant for transferring bodily the doctrines of the Manichees of the fourth century, attacked by Augustine, to the account of the Cologne sectaries.[55] His description of the teachings of the adepts, with their thoroughgoing dualism, must be treated with scepticism: it is possible to infer merely that the first group at Cologne described in the 1140s by Everwin had survived, that it had dualist beliefs and, further, that rationalist propaganda was being used to attract followers. Although the true basis for the rejection of the mass lay in their rejection of bread and wine as part of an evil creation, the heretics used a primitive logic. Christ's body, they said, must have been as big as a mountain to feed the faithful for so long.[56]

Two years after the Cologne outbreak, a conference held at Lombers, a

---

[51] Manselli, in *BISIAM* LXVII (1955), pp. 212–34; for a summary see Manselli, *L'Eresia del Male* (Naples, 1963), pp. 165–8. I have not been able to see the 2nd edn of 1980.

[52] For discussion of this trial and others in the dioceses of Cologne, Trier, Liège, with analysis of major source, Ekbert, see Moore, *Origins*, pp. 175–82.

[53] *Adversus Catharos*, *PL* CXCV, cols 11–102; extract tr. in *MBPH*, pp. 88–94; reconstruction of events in Russell, *Dissent*, pp. 220–4.

[54] 'Hos nostra Germania Catharos, Flandria Piphles, Gallia Texerant ab usu texendi appellat', *PL* CXCIII, col. 193; terminology for heretics generally in *RB*, pp. 29–38. But I think Grundmann underestimates the significance of references here and elsewhere to weaving; see below, p. 113. The term 'Cathar' should strictly only be applied to the leading class in the heresy; I have used the term as a generic one for the sect because it is so well established. Fichtenau, *Katharer*, pp. 95–6, discusses the role of cellars.

[55] Borst, *Katharer*, pp. 6–7; Manselli, *Eresia*, pp. 163–4.

[56] Noticed by Manselli, *Eresia*, p. 164.

castle near Albi, in the south of France, revealed the relative freedom of Cathar heretics on a favourable terrain.[57] Local heretical leaders, known as 'the good men', debated with their opponents before a distinguished gathering which included, as well as William, the diocesan, the archbishop of Narbonne, other bishops, the viscount of Béziers, in whose lands Lombers lay, and Constance, countess of Toulouse and sister of the king of France.

The representatives of orthodoxy had to restrict their exposition so as to cite proof-texts only from the New Testament, since the heretics did not recognize the Old. The 'good men' stressed the evils of the way of living of churchmen, and their own superiority in this sphere. 'They said also', the record of the assembly runs, 'that Paul stated in his Epistle what kind of bishops and priests were to be ordained in the churches, and that, if the men ordained were not such as Paul had specified, they were not bishops and priests, but ravening wolves, hypocrites and seducers, lovers of salutations in the market place . . . desirous of being called rabbis and masters contrary to the command of Christ, wearers of albs and gleaming raiment, displaying bejewelled gold rings on their fingers, which their Master Jesus did not command.'[58] The ecclesiastics tried to draw their opponents on to the fields of dogma, in order to expose their deviations from orthodoxy. But the heretics were not to be drawn. They are reported as saying that they did not want to be forced to reply about their faith. Eventually, as the bishops seemed to be getting the better of it, the 'good men' appealed to the people, and made a declaration which sounded quite Catholic. But they refused to swear to it since, following texts in James and the gospels, they held that all oaths were unlawful. In any case they had said enough to be convicted of heresy, though the bishops never penetrated to the core of their beliefs.

The debate, it is plausibly argued, was intended to be a kind of legal pleading in the presence of eminent laity, in which the fact that the 'good men' were preaching heresy should be made manifest, and the secular authority consequently moved to action.[59] At Cologne there had been formal trial, which led instantly to punishment; at Lombers adjudication against the beliefs of the 'good men' had no effect at all.

A similar demonstration of the strength and independence of Catharism in the Midi took place some two years after Lombers in the international council of dualists held at the village of Saint Félix in the Lauragais, at which the territory most affected by Catharism was divided up into bishoprics, delimited territorially on the Catholic pattern.[60] In Lombardy a Cathar mission established itself in the fifth, or early in the sixth, decade of the century. A narrative, probably based on oral tradition, recounted a century later by the inquisitor Anselm of Alessandria, described how a party of heretics from northern France made their way into northern Italy, and converted a gravedigger called Mark from the Milan area who became the apostle of Cathar Italy, and with his friends John Judeus, a weaver, and Joseph, a smith,

---

[57] Bouquet, xiv, pp. 431–4; tr. *WEH*, pp. 190–4; *MBPH*, pp. 94–8; the best analysis is by Griffe, *Débuts*, pp. 59–67.

[58] Tr. in *WEH*, p. 191.

[59] Griffe, *Débuts*, pp. 60–1.

[60] See below, pp. 126–8.

established a base for mission at Concorezzo near his birthplace.[61] Fragments of later information on the spread of Byzantine heresy through the French conquerors of Constantinople in 1204,[62] and on the flight of Cathars from the Midi before the inquisition to the area of Como in the thirteenth century, jostle each other in this semi-legendary account.[63] But we may retain from it the fact, elsewhere attested, that Catharism reached Lombardy and established its hold before 1167 and, less certainly but with high probability, the surprising conclusion that stimulus to it was given by missionaries from northern France. Under Mark's leadership the heresy spread in Lombardy and thence into the March of Treviso and Tuscany.

In addition to these established examples, other outbreaks imperfectly recorded, such as the case of the clerk Jonas in Cambrai,[64] an episode in Vézelay in 1167,[65] or that of the party of strangers from either the Rhineland or Flanders who landed in England, only to be branded at the Council of Oxford in 1166 and turned adrift to starve,[66] have the smell of Catharism, and may well have formed part of the same movement.[67] There is evidence, but no details, of a strong Cathar following being established early on in northern France.[68]

The greatest strength of the movement lay in its ethical appeal to populations who had been sufficiently affected by the religious sentiment of the age to value poverty and self-sacrifice, yet lacked orthodox instruction. The key figures were a number of highly dedicated missionaries whose fiercely ascetic way of life had an immediate impact, and whose courage before the fire impressed the Catholic chroniclers. Their distinctive rites, their total opposition to the Church, which was yet coupled with considerable skill in the arts of evasion, gave a new stiffening to pre-existing movements of dissent, some of whose tenets they shared. Writers on the Catholic side still lacked the skill fully to penetrate the inner beliefs of the movement; probably ethics remained for some time more important than dogma, even to the adepts.

---

[61] A. Dondaine, 'La hiérarchie cathare en Italie', *AFP* xix (1949), pp. 282–312; xx (1950), pp. 234–324 (ms discoveries with analysis, lists of heretical bishops, important for internal history of Italian Cathars). Discussion of Anselm in *AFP* xx (1950), pp. 259–62; this portion of Anselm's text is in *TDH*, pp. 308–9; tr. in *WEH*, pp. 168–70. See below, p. 125; A. Dondaine, *Les Hérésies et l'inquisition xiie–xiiie siècles* (Aldershot, 1990) (coll. papers).

[62] This seems to me the plain meaning of 'postea francigene iverunt Constantinopolim ut subiugarent terram et invenerunt istam secta, et multiplicati fecerunt episcopum, qui dicitur episcopus latinorum' (*sic*) (*AFP* xx (1950), p. 308). I reject Dondaine's supposition that this could mean the second crusade (ibid., p. 240).

[63] E. Dupré Theseider, 'Le Catharisme languedocien et l'Italie', *CF* iii, pp. 299–316 at p. 300.

[64] Russell, *Dissent*, pp. 217–18.

[65] H. Maisonneuve, *Etudes sur les origines de l'inquisition* (Paris, 1960), pp. 115–16 (account of legislative aspect of inquisition, with survey of heresy).

[66] Russell, *Dissent*, pp. 224–6; for dating and sources, see ibid., pp. 309–10; tr. in *WEH*, pp. 245–7. See A. Morey and C. N. L. Brooke, *Gilbert Foliot and his Letters* (Cambridge, 1965), pp. 241–3.

[67] I suspect that the sect described by Gerhoh of Reichersberg in his work on Antichrist of 1161–2 is solely of literary provenance. For text, see K. Heisig, 'Eine gnostische Sekte im abendländischen Mittelalter', *ZRG* xvi (1964), pp. 271–4.

[68] Evidence of Anselm of Alessandria (*AFP* xx (1950), p. 308), on foundation of a bishopric of northern France; for hypothesis of siting in diocese of Châlons-sur-Marne at Montwimers, alias Mont-Aimé, see Borst, *Katharer*, pp. 91, 93 and cf. pp. 123n., 231. The issue is complicated by the uncertain dating of the Liège letter mentioning Montwimers. Borst opts for 1144–5.

In roughly two decades from the undoubted appearance of Bogomil influence at Cologne, the new heresy was disseminated from the Rhine to the Pyrenees, and into the Italian peninsula [69]

[69] Borst, *Katharer*, p. 92.

5

The Waldensians and the
deepening crisis

In the last thirty years of the twelfth century Catharism was the heresy which preoccupied authority. It was not put down: in northern and central Italy and in Languedoc it actually succeeded in increasing its hold. At the same time, the other currents of heresy maintained themselves and, within the evangelical tradition, two new groups emerged: the Humiliati and the Waldensians, simple gospel-based movements whose members desired the right to exhort their fellow Christians. Both fell foul of authority on the issue of the right to preach; both, though at the outset apparently untainted by heresy, passed after their experience of rejection from disobedience into unorthodoxy. The papacy under Lucius III made a more strenuous and broader-based attempt to grapple with the problem of efficient repression of heresy, but could not find a solution;[1] at the end of the century there was more heresy than ever before. The zeal of the Humiliati and Waldensians had been lost to the Church, and in the two most dangerous regions in Italy and Languedoc heretical teachers were able to spread their ideas almost in freedom.

The Waldensians and the Humiliati

The Waldensians, the last and the most tenacious of the twelfth-century wandering-preacher movements, are the classic example of the would-be reform movement drawn into heresy by the inadequacies of ecclesiastical authority. Valdes, the founder,[2] was a rich businessman of Lyons who was

---

[1] See the discussion of *Ad abolendam* below, pp. 66–8. Survey on papal policy in B. Bolton, 'Tradition and temerity: papal attitudes to deviants, 1159–1216', in *SCH* IX, pp. 79–91; see *RB*, pp. 50–69.

[2] K. V. Selge, *Die ersten Waldenser* I: *Untersuchung und Darstellung*; II: *Der Liber antiheresis des Durandus von Osca* (Berlin, 1967) (summary on Valdes and early history, ch. 3; see Lambert, *Medieval Heresy*, 1st edn, pp. 353–5; review: H. Grundmann, *DA* XXIV (1968), pp. 572–3; French version in Selge's 'Caractéristiques du

touched by a jongleur's version of the life of St Alexius, the penitent son of a rich man who rejected a bride and went away to live in poverty, returning after many years to die unrecognized, destitute in his father's house. The sequel was that Valdes, after consulting a master of theology, decided to give up his wealth and the world. There was a Franciscan touch in his religious passion, throwing money on the street, rejecting the usurious business methods that had brought him wealth, insisting on receiving his food from others and having to be forced by the archbishop to eat with his wife: He made provision for his wife, endowed his daughters so that they might enter Fontevrault, but did not himself enter a monastery. From the outset Valdes showed an individualist, pragmatic streak. For more than two months in the famine of 1176 he operated a soup-kitchen. His aim was the apostolic life of poverty and preaching on the lines of the gospel texts of the sending of the Seventy.[3] What distinguishes him from earlier wandering preachers, however, is his concern as a layman for self-instruction through vernacular translations of Scripture and the Fathers. Etienne de Bourbon, who supplements the edifying account of his conversion in the anonymous chronicle of Laon, tells us that he 'was not well-educated, but on hearing the gospels was anxious to learn more precisely what was in them',[4] set about commissioning translations, then drew followers. He desired to preach, and he and his followers set about doing so.

Soon he came into conflict with authority. The traditional interpretation of orders in the Church gave the right of preaching and of the cure of souls to the pope and the bishops, as successors of Peter and the Twelve, and to the priests, as successors of the Seventy.[5] Canon law restricted preaching to the clergy, and there were few exceptions.[6] Valdes's movement was a popular success, likely to arouse both the fears and the jealousies of the local clergy. From a controversial local situation the group appealed to the pope,[7] and sent representatives to the third Lateran Council in 1179 at Rome, showing their translations, and asking for his authorization of preaching. The response,

premier mouvement vaudois et crises au cours de son expansion', in *CF* II, pp. 110–42; sources given in *EFV* (standard collection of Waldensian sources), and analysis by G. Gonnet in his 'La figure et l'oeuvre de Vaudès dans la tradition historique et selon les dernières recherches', in *CF* II, pp. 87–109; H. Böhmer, 'Die Waldenser', in *RPTK* xx, cols 799–840 (partly outdated by MS discoveries, but still valuable); reflections: G. G. Merlo, 'Le mouvement vaudois des origines à la fin du XIIIe siècle', in *Les Vaudois des origines à leur fin (XIIe–XVIe siècles)*, ed. G. Audisio (Turin, 1990) (surveys, with lively, informal debates by Merlo, P. Biller, G. Audisio, J. F. Gilmont; recent bibliography), pp. 15–35; I owe a copy to Dr Biller's kindness.

[3] Matt. 10: 7–13. *Chronicon universale anonymi Laudunensis*, ed. G. Waitz, in *MGH Scriptores* xxvi, p. 447; *WEH*, pp. 200–2; *MBPH*, pp. 111–13; conversion 1173 (Laon), 1176 (Böhmer, in *RPTK* xx, col. 806); 1176 preferred; on soup-kitchen, see P. Biller, in *SCH* xix, pp. 55–77 at p. 58; re topoi in Anonymous of Laon, Biller (in *Vaudois*, ed. Audisio, pp. 39–40) notes topoi do not necessarily mean falsification – see bibliography, ibid, p. 67.

[4] A. Lecoy de la Marche, *Anecdotes historiques, Légendes et Apologues tirées du Recueil inédit d'Etienne de Bourbon, Dominicain du xiiie siècle*, SHF Publications CLXXXV (Paris, 1887), p. 291; *WEH*, p. 209. On the language of the translation commissioned (that of the region of Grenoble), see M. Carrières, 'Sur la langue de la Bible de Valdo', *BSSV* LXXXV (1946), pp. 28–34.

[5] *RB*, p. 63; A. Dondaine, 'Aux origines de Valdéisme: une profession de foi de Valdès', *AFP* xvi (1946), pp. 191–235 (document and survey of background); see below, pp. 64–5.

[6] Selge, *Waldenser* I, pp. 22n., 23n. and references.

[7] Ibid., p. 23; see discussion, pp. 21–35, 243–59.

according to Walter Map, the chronicler and servant of Henry II, was a theological examination designed to show their fitness to preach, in which that worldly cleric exposed their weaknesses by asking them in turn whether they believed in God the Father, the Son, the Holy Spirit and then the mother of Christ. To each question they replied, 'We do', only to be laughed at when they gave the same response to the question about Mary, whether through their naïvety in seeming to put Mary on equality with the Trinity, or because of Nestorian implications in their answer. They withdrew, Map said, in confusion.

Map need not be taken seriously. He intended to make fun of the Waldensians, just as he deliberately garbled his account of the Cathars immediately preceding this anecdote.[8] But we may infer from him at least that there was some examination, and that no full, blanket permission to preach was then given to the group. The Laon chronicler says that Pope Alexander III embraced Valdes, 'approving his vow of voluntary poverty, but forbidding preaching by either himself or his followers unless welcomed by the local priests'.[9] Local clergy were not welcoming, and so the pope's decision in practice was the near-equivalent of total refusal.

The approval of the vow of poverty coupled with the grave caution about preaching are characteristic of the traditional attitude. The practice of a dedicated way of life, in or on the margins of monasticism, was applauded; preaching remained the proper function of the clergy. Map's account recalls another facet of the situation – the clergy's fear of the consequences of any breach of their exclusive position. After describing the way of life of the Waldensians – going about two by two, barefoot, clad in woollen garments, owning nothing, holding all things common like the apostles, naked, following a naked Christ – he added the sharp observation, 'They are making their first moves now in the humblest manner because they cannot launch an attack. If we admit them, we shall be driven out.'[10]

The following year Valdes and his followers were still in the Church. The papal legate Henri de Marcy, a leading Cistercian who had become the principal in high-level attempts to check the growth of Catharism in the Midi, presided over a diocesan council at Lyons in which Valdes assented to a profession of orthodox faith.[11] The great fear of authority, it would seem from this document, was that Waldensian enthusiasm would be infiltrated by the Cathar heresy. The profession was prophylactic, intended to alert Valdes to the dangers, and secure his specific rejection of a number of dualist tenets, taken either from twelfth-century experience in the field or derived from a

[8] W. Map, *De nugis curialium*, ed. M. R. James (Oxford, 1914), pp. 60–2; tr. in *WEH*, pp. 202–4. I owe the interpretation to Professor C. N. L. Brooke.

[9] *Chronicon universale*, ed. Waitz, p. 449, tr. in *WEH*, p. 203. On problems of chronology, see Gonne in *CF* II, pp. 94–7.

[10] *De nugis*, in *WEH*, p. 204.

[11] Text by Dondaine in *AFP* XVI (1946), pp. 231–2, Selge, *Waldenser* II, pp. 3–6, Gonnet, in *EFV*, pp. 31–6; analysis in C. Thouzellier, *Catharisme et Valdéisme en Languedoc*, 2nd edn (Louvain and Paris, 1969), pp. 27–36 (see esp. for deep analysis of contemporary controversial literature), tr. *WEH*, pp. 204–8; dating: p. 709, n. 1. Either 1180 or 1181 is possible. Gonnet (*Vaudois*, ed. Audisio, p. 11) notes that Valdes's early actions recorded in Anonymous of Laon correspond to the *propositum*, vital at the end of a profession of faith.

profession of faith compiled in the fifth century and formerly used in the consecration of bishops under the Gallican rite. Other, non-dualist tenets, such as the Donatist rejection of sacraments administered by evil priests, common coin among quite varied twelfth-century groups, may well also have stemmed from experience of Cathars in the Midi. There was in addition a careful enumeration of the sacraments to be accepted, one or two other errors, probably unrelated to Catharism, to be repudiated, and a conclusion relating specifically to the Waldensians, in which Valdes declared his intention to renounce the world, to be poor and take no thought for the morrow, to accept neither gold nor silver, and to accept the precepts of the gospel as commands. It was a programme derived from the sending of the Seventy – but there was a total and significant silence on the right to preach. Valdes showed his will to obedience and orthodoxy by making the profession of faith; in return, as it were, he was able to state the intention of his group.

Trouble again came out of local conditions. At the end of the profession Valdes had repudiated unorthodox zealots who took the name of his association; perhaps he had not in the event been able to prevent their infiltration. Étienne de Bourbon sourly describes the indiscriminate preaching which aroused hostility, of those 'stupid and uneducated' persons who 'wandered through the villages, entered homes, preached in the squares and even in the churches'.[12] John of Canterbury, archbishop of Lyons, possibly after a vain attempt to bring them under control through the appointment of a provost, prohibited their preaching; they refused, and were excommunicated and driven from the lands where the archbishop held temporal power.[13]

For the disobedience a number of factors were responsible. One, to judge by later Waldensian writing, was the sense that Valdes had a direct mission from God; another was the state of the Church, and feeling against unworthy clergy; another may well have been the ambiguous language of the profession of faith, in which Valdes declared his resolve to follow the precepts of the gospel as commands. Had not the Saviour enjoined his disciples to preach, in the same passage in which they were told to take neither gold nor silver, to carry neither scrip nor staff? The disciples, whom the Waldensians imitated, had been told to preach the gospel to every creature, and Peter before the Sanhedrin had appealed to a higher obligation when he said that one should obey God rather than men. Fidelity to Scripture and the divine call seemed to require preaching. So the association was carried into schism.

Similar forces were at work among the Humiliati of northern Italy.[14] Like other penitential associations, they aimed to lead a purer ethical life in the world in accord with the gospels without renouncing marriage. In reaction to

[12] Lecoy de la Marche, *Anecdotes*, p. 291; *WEH*, p. 209.

[13] Also known as Bellesmains: see P. Pouzet, *L'anglais dit John Bellesmains* (Lyon, 1927), pp. 7–9, C. T. Clay, in *Yorkshire Archaeological Journal* xxxv (1940–3), pp. 11–19. I owe these references to Professor C. N. L. Brooke. Events and Waldensian motives given by Selge, *Waldenser* i, pp. 76, 84, 184–5, 254–9 (dating 1181–2; Gonnet, *CF* ii, p. 97, prefers 1182 or 1183); texts on Waldensians generally and tr. in J. B. Russell, *Religious Dissent in the Middle Ages* (New York, 1971), pp. 41–53.

[14] B. Bolton, 'Innocent iii's treatment of the Humiliati', in *SCH* viii, pp. 73–82. Documents in G. Tiraboschi, *Vetera Humiliatorum Monumenta* i–iii (Milan, 1766–8); L. Zanoni, *Gli Umiliati* (Milan, 1911); older summary in E. S. Davison, *Forerunners of St Francis* (New York, 1927), ch. 5; F. Vernet, 'Humiliés', in *DTC* vii, cols 313–21; *RB*, pp. 157–61; K. V. Selge, 'Humiliaten', *TRE* xv, cols 691–6.

the commercial life of Italy, free from the temptations of usury, they earned their bread in a number of Lombard towns by simple manual work, largely in the wool industry. As a sign of their humility they wore garments of undyed wool, and received their name either because of their way of life or their dress. A strict and literal interpretation of the gospels led them to reject oaths as well as lies, and the practice of litigation. Though a few individual, leading figures were well-connected citizens, most Humiliati stemmed from a social level well below that, although they were not, as Zanoni once alleged, members of the proletariat: they included clergy. They repudiated the accumulation of wealth, and gave away all superfluity in alms.[15]

The impulse to apostolic life here had another outlet, which did not include wandering begging, but did include a demand to preach and the wish to exercise a ministry with the direction of souls. First of all the orthodox groups in the Church, they seem to have hit on the idea of preaching to refute heresy, while themselves following an interpretation of the gospels and apostolic life no less strict than that of the leading heretics.[16] Once again there was an attempt to cross the line which divided the practice of a better moral life, whether in or out of monasticism, from the right to a cure of souls; and it received the same rebuff as had the Waldensians. Alexander III heard and rejected their request to be allowed to preach. Like the Waldensians, they insisted on continuing and fell under the ban of the Church.

The Waldensians and the Humiliati came under consideration at Verona in 1184. In one sense, the legislation which issued as a by-product of the reconciliation between pope and emperor after their long disputes represented a step forward in the Church's battle against heresy. The bull *Ad abolendam*, which involved the active co-operation of the emperor Frederick Barbarossa, is the first attempt in the whole century to try to deal with the challenge of heresy from a supra-national point of view. Hitherto the onus of action had lain heavily on the individual bishop, exercising his duty as successor of the apostles to act as guardian of orthodoxy and to repress heresy, little aided from above. He had reacted to the presence of heresy in his diocese in very different ways, according to his own predilections.[17] Some bishops were quite inactive; others who did act were uncertain what procedure to follow. In the case of the peasant brothers suspect of heresy at Bucy-le-Long, discussed above, the bishop of Soissons had first applied the primitive procedure of the ordeal by water, found that one of his suspects failed the test and, uncertain what to do next, went off to seek advice; while he was away the mob burst into the prison and burnt the suspects.[18] A council at Rheims in 1157 had specifically mentioned a duty of the laity to aid the bishop in reporting cases of heresy, but still no detailed procedure was laid down.[19]

[15] B. Bolton, 'The poverty of the Humiliati', in *Poverty in the Middle Ages*, ed. D. Flood, *FFor* xxvii (1975), pp. 52–9.

[16] *RB*, p. 65.

[17] Ibid., pp. 51–2; also Maisonneuve, *Etudes*, ch. 2; C. Thouzellier, 'La répression de l'hérésie et les débuts de l'Inquisition', in *Histoire de l'église*, ed. A. Fliche and V. Martin, x (Paris, 1950), pp. 291–340.

[18] Above, p. 50, n. 19; defending, Moore argues (*SCH* xxi, p. 49), the right of community judgement in the ordeal.

[19] Maisonneuve, *Etudes*, pp. 108–11.

The papacy gave vacillating direction. In the case of Flemish townsmen accused of heresy who came to appeal to Alexander III, the pope first attempted to send them back with letters to the archbishop of Rheims from whom they had appealed and, then, when they demurred, decided to confer further with the archbishop, Louis VII of France and others. His letter to the archbishop urged restraint rather than strictness, but offered no direction as to how that prelate was to set about establishing whether or not the townsmen really were heretics.[20]

The one locality which concerned the popes over generations, and where they repeatedly exhorted against heresy, was Languedoc – and not only its heartland (where the problem ultimately became acute) but Gascony and Provence as well.[21] From the time of the Council of Toulouse in 1119, a scattering of provincial councils under papal presidency warned against the presence of heresy, and urged local secular leaders not to give heretics protection. Evidently it was the toleration of heresy by lords which created anxiety.

Ad abolendam attempted more than provincial legislation for the Midi, for it surveyed the field of heresy generally, not merely in the south of France, and it attempted to invigorate and systematize the bishops' pursuit of heresy.[22] It dealt seriously with heresy in Italy, the place of origin of a good proportion of the sects condemned. In the Church at large all exemption from the bishops' jurisdiction in matters of heresy was abolished; the bishop or his representatives were required to visit the parishes where heresy was believed to exist once or twice a year, and impose oaths on local inhabitants who would then declare any knowledge they might have of heresy in the locality. Secular authorities were to assist this inquisition under pain of penalties both secular and ecclesiastical. Maximum publicity was to be given by higher ecclesiastics to these regulations.

These decisions failed, however, to sway the situation to the Church's advantage. Discovery of heresy was still dependent on the accidents of popular denunciations – effective enough where there was general feeling against heresy, as in northern France, of little use in areas such as the regions of Languedoc or northern Italy, where there was more inertia or toleration. Procedure for proving or disproving the existence of heresy in formal trial remained primitive: it still included the oath and the ordeal, and did not impose the appropriate solution, i.e. the interrogation of suspects by experienced theologians. The bull of Lucius III reorganized the episcopal inquisition, but provided no means for ensuring that bishops in fact observed their duty to maintain it. Finally, and most deleteriously, *Ad abolendam* offered no solution to the problem of recognition and classification of heresy. A series

---

[20] *RB*, pp. 55–7.

[21] Ibid., pp. 52–5; on definition of Languedoc, see below, p. 81, n. 62. The county of Provence lay in imperial territory.

[22] Mansi, xxii, cols 476–8; Maisonneuve, *Etudes*, pp. 151–6. On the changing attitude to repression of heresy 1179–84, see R. Manselli, 'De la "persuasio" à la "coercitio"', in *CF* VI, pp. 175–97; for a discussion, see A. Kolmer, *Ad Capiendas Vulpes: Die Ketzerbekämpfung im Südfrankreich in der ersten Hälfte des 13. Jahrhunderts und die Ausbildung des Inquisitionsverfahrens* (Bonn, 1982) (precise investigation of development of techniques of repression, investigation in Languedoc), p. 29, n. 21; review: J. L. Biget, *Annales* XLII (1987), pp. 137–40.

of groups were named and anathematized – 'the Cathars and the Patarenes, and those who falsely call themselves the Humiliati or Poor of Lyons, the Passagini, the Josephini, the Arnoldists . . .';[23] the only distinction made was that between those who preached without authority and those who preached actual error. The Waldensians and Humiliati were in the first category – linked in the Latin by *vel*, not necessarily because they had joined forces, but because, in an abusive word-play, they are linked together as liars, falsely taking to themselves the name of 'the humble' or 'the poor' without justification for the title.[24] For the author of the document, neither the humility nor the poverty could be genuine, because it was unaccompanied by a saving obedience to the Church's authority; in a common anathema they are lumped together with the profound heresy of the Cathars, to which they were bitterly opposed. The faithful are merely informed how heretics may be recognized by their unauthorized preaching, by their errors against the sacraments, or by declarations made by the bishops. This is a crude labelling technique; we have no word about the inner core of false doctrine that has led the sectaries into their denials of the sacraments or their preaching, and no encouragement to the churchmen who might wish to distinguish more subtly between the recalcitrant and those who could be led more gently back to the Church.

So *Ad abolendam* completed the rejection of the Waldensians. There followed an equivocal phase, in which the edict was only partially effective.[25] In practice, Waldensianism as an enemy took second or third place to the Cathars, and the general inefficiency of repression helped to preserve them. The penalty of expulsion, often the most serious punishment applied, did no more than disseminate their influence more widely. The sequel to the decisions of 1184 was, moreover, muffled. In Languedoc the archbishop of Narbonne, Bernard-Gaucelin, made an enquiry into Waldensian beliefs and issued a condemnation, probably between 1185 and 1187. But it was not effective. The populace approved their moral life; some lower clergy regarded them as auxiliaries and were sympathetic. Their preachers moved about freely, and were even invited to participate in debates which allowed expression to heretical and orthodox points of view. Only in Montpellier, where Count William VIII was hostile, does there seem to have been effective counteraction. In Aragon, Alfonso II in 1194 and Pedro II in 1198 issued edicts against Waldensians, the latter imposing the death penalty for obstinacy. Perhaps these edicts were aimed as much at conditions in the fiefs of the kings of Aragon on the French side of the Pyrenees as in the kingdom itself: in neither area do they appear seriously to have handicapped the preachers. To the north of Languedoc in Lorraine and in the border lands between France and the Empire, Waldensian missions gained success, although in Toul in

[23] Mansi, XXII, col. 477. On Passagians, see *WEH*, pp. 173–85, Manselli, 'I Passagini', *BISIAM* LXXV (1963), pp. 189–210; on Josephini, *WEH*, p. 31.

[24] *RB*, p. 67, n. 120, comments: pp. 68–9; Selge, *Waldenser* I, p. 177, n. 151.

[25] For this phase and examples given below, see Thouzellier, *Catharisme et Valdéisme*, pp. 50–1, 133–8; Selge, *Waldenser* I, pp. 131n., 279–81, 287, 290–1; M. H. Vicaire, *Saint Dominic and his Times* (orig. *Histoire de Saint Dominique* (Paris, 1957), tr. K. Pond (London, 1964), the standard biography), p. 75; Innocent III, *Epistolae* xii, 17, (*PL* CCXVI, col. 29f.) on school in Milan.

1192 the bishop ordered the rounding-up of 'Wadoys'. In Metz at the end of the century the authorities were so ill-informed that, when they came across laymen reading the Scriptures in unauthorized gatherings, they failed to realize that they were Waldensians. In Italy the inability of the hierarchy to get on top of heresy in the cities meant that the Waldensians shared in the general atmosphere of liberty. Only in the period 1196–1206, for example, was the archbishop of Milan able to enforce the destruction of a school that they had long held undisturbed in the city.

Much the same applied to the Humiliati,[26] who spread in the cities, sometimes also in the *contado* where some of their groups had originated. They appealed to industrial workers and artisans or to peasants lately come to the towns; their workshops and houses were usually found in the *faubourgs* where artisans lived.

The Waldensians, spreading through the zeal to preach the gospel, their mission expedited rather than hampered by the expulsion from Lyons following the excommunication by Archbishop John, found a home in the anticlerical atmosphere of Lombardy and became more radical in consequence.[27]

In Languedoc they seem to have been attracted by the frailty of the hierarchy's control of the religious scene, which enabled them to preach without interference in many places, and showed themselves eager to take advantage of the opportunity to show both the injustice of their excommunication and the orthodoxy of their beliefs by preaching against the Cathars and opposing them in debates. From Lyons they passed over to north-east France and into the German-speaking regions on the Rhine and beyond.[28]

Their appeal at first cut across class divisions. In the early days, companions of Valdes are described as giving up their goods and bestowing them on the poor, a fact which shows they were of some substance. Laymen formed a majority, but there were also fugitive monks and nuns, and some priests and *litterati*. Some support came from higher ranks in society, though it was less than the Cathars enjoyed; members of the class of *ministeriales*, lesser nobility in the service of the Empire, were noticed, for example, as adherents in the diocese of Metz.[29] The influence which preaching had on women was observed with a hostile eye by Catholic writers. Women thought suitable had the right to preach on terms of equality with the men, which may well have made the movement seem attractive to certain temperaments, dissatisfied with the circumscribed opportunities for religious service for women within orthodoxy.[30]

[26] Above, p. 65, n. 14; suggestions on class by Bolton, in *SCH* VII, pp. 79–80; note on workshops by Violante, in *HS*, p. 179.

[27] Selge, *Waldenser* I, pp. 259–63, 284–8.

[28] Ibid., pp. 288–93.

[29] *RB*, pp. 161–4, Selge, *Waldenser* I, pp. 266–9, Böhmer, in *RPTK* xx, col. 809. G. Koch, *Frauenfrage und Ketzertum im Mittelalter* (Berlin, 1962) (Marxist survey, not always conventional, underestimated in the West; review by E. Delaruelle in *RHE* LX (1965), pp. 159–61), pp. 156–7. Koch is one-sided on class, but notes shortage of early sources. I express here my regret at Dr Koch's tragically early death. For class structure post-1250, see below, p. 170.

[30] Koch, *Frauenfrage*, pp. 158–9.

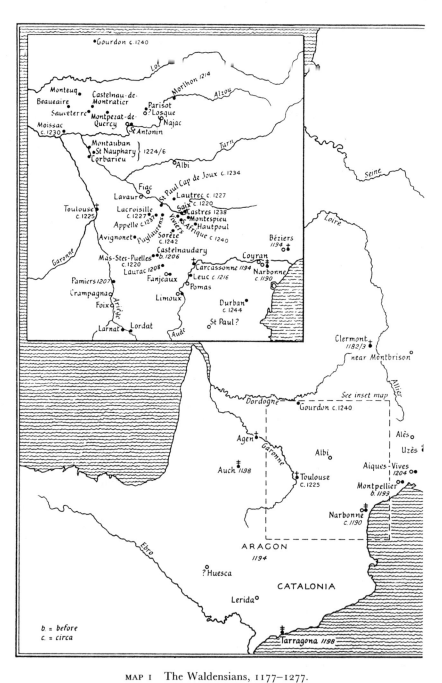

MAP I   The Waldensians, 1177–1277.

Source: Map by J. V. Fearns, from Herder's *Atlas zur Kirchengeschichte* (Freiburg-im-Breisgau, 1970), no. 56B.

Note: The Waldensians of Austria, detected in an inquisition of *c*.1266, will be found on Map 4.

M.V

? Liège 1202/3

Rhine

Mainz 1233

Main

? Trier 1231

Moselle

Meuse

† Metz 1199/1200

? Schwäbisch Hall 1248

Regensburg c.1262

‡ Toul 1192

Danube

? Strasburg 1211/2

Jonvelle c.1218

Rhine

Inn

‡ Besançon 1248

Saône

Rhône

Dongo

Gruaro

Lyon 1177

?Seregno

Bergamo 1218

Verona 1199

‡ Vienne 1198

Legnano

Milan b.1206

Valence c.1235

Pavia

Ronco

Cerea b.1203

Montélimar

† Turin 1210

Piacenza c.1192/7

Po

Rhône

Pinerolo 1220?

Modena

Bollène

‡ Embrun 1198

Faenza 1206

Bagnols

‡ Genoa

Orange

Sisteron

Carpentras

† Florence 1206

Avignon

Nîmes c.1204

† Antibes

‡ Arles 1198

‡ Aix 1198

? Ramatuelle

Rome 1179

0   250 Miles

0   400 Km

o   *Places of origin of Waldensians*   ‡ *Seat of Archbishop*

•   *Places of residence of Waldensians*   † *Seat of Bishop*

1206 *Earliest dated evidence of the appearance of Waldensians before 1218*

1237 *Earliest dated evidence of the appearance of Waldensians after 1218*

The development of Waldensian organization and tenets

No rule for the new association has come down to us from the hand of Valdes or his contemporaries, but the regulations of the Poor Catholics, the group of reconciled Waldensians who carried on their way of life with the approval of the Church in the early thirteenth century, combined with incidental references by both Waldensians and their opponents, are sufficient to provide a reconstruction of the life of the group as it developed over the decades following *Ad abolendam*.[31] The leaders in the movement were the preachers, known as the *pauperes spiritu, fratres, sorores*, and later in Lombardy and German-speaking lands, *magistri, magistrae*, 'apostles', 'lords' (*Herren*); they travelled two by two in accord with the gospel texts, wearing simple, apostolic dress, at first apparently barefoot, but seen in sandals of a particular sort that came to serve as a sign of their special status. The granting of the right to wear the sandals accompanied the right to preach. Catholic writers sometimes called them the *Insabbatati* (from the word *sabot*) because of this.[32] Like Valdes, they had to renounce the world and give up their goods before they could become preachers. But though authentically part of the twelfth-century movement of wandering preachers, poverty did not have the same passionate force among them that it had had among the hermits of western France, or that it was to have in the future among the Franciscans. Valdes, after making a similar break with the world of property as St Francis of Assisi, and influenced like him by the tension between the Christian conscience and the business world, thereafter did not feel the same need to strive perpetually for the highest possible form of renunciation.[33] Austerity rather than destitution was the keynote of the Waldensians.

Preaching consisted of simple exhortation, the call to repentance, and the criticism of sins, both in the individual and in the Church, together with the repetition of many texts of Scripture, learned by heart in the schools of the movement, often in astonishing quantities.[34] The training necessary for the preacher, which on the French side of the Alps came later to be some five or six years, and on the Lombard side one or two,[35] was particularly devoted to the direct study and memorization of the bare text of Scripture in vernacular translation. Only after selection and training, together with the renunciation of goods and of marriage, could the preacher begin his mission. Thus, in a sense, he was as marked off from the rest of society as any Catholic priest. The difference was that in the association no episcopal ordination was considered necessary; women might be granted the right to preach; and no distinction was made between those who happened to be in priest's orders and the others who were laymen.

Preaching helped to recruit more members for the office of preacher. Moved by exhortations, the hearer might then receive spiritual counsel to go and undo the injustices that he had committed and from this he might progress to

---

[31] Böhmer, in *RPTK* xx, cols 811–12; survey of life and ideas on cols 811–19.
[32] Ibid., cols 806, 812, 813; Selge, *Waldenser* I, p. 270, n. 118.
[33] For my dissent from Selge on the poverty issue, see Lambert, *Medieval Heresy*, 1st edn, pp. 353–5.
[34] Böhmer, in *RPTK* xx, col. 814.
[35] Ibid., col. 812.

the status of the 'recently converted', who in a kind of novitiate were tested and instructed in preparation for mission.[36] Others remained in the world, and were known as 'friends' (*amici*), who supported the preachers by their alms and participated in the study of the vernacular Scriptures. Their task was to see to the bodily needs of the preachers, to collect a kind of tax among the supporters, later known as the *talea* in Italy, and to maintain the schools of the association, generally held in private houses.[37] Like the preachers, their knowledge of the Bible was often remarkable. Children began to learn the gospels and the epistles. It was not unknown for an illiterate supporter to know forty Sunday gospels by heart, and in Austria in the thirteenth century a relatively objective Catholic observer, the Passau Anonymous, recorded the case of a member who knew all the book of Job by heart.[38]

Attitudes of churchmen towards vernacular translations (in so far as they were to be used by the common people) tended to be hostile partly because of the use made of them in practice by heretical preachers. When the bishop of Metz wrote to Innocent III in 1199 denouncing laymen and women who had commissioned vernacular translations of Scripture and relied on them for debating about their contents in secret gatherings and for preaching, the pope was slow to authorize repression.

His chief concern lay with the unauthorized preaching. He asked the bishop to find out about the author of the translation, his intention and the quality of faith of those who used it – and about their attitude to the papacy and the Church. His reply to the bishop's renewed complaint that some of them had been disobedient to Innocent's requirements, alleging that they owed obedience only to God, was to commission three Cistercian abbots to go to Metz to investigate further and correct the laity where necessary. It is not known what happened, though a later Cistercian chronicle speaks of abbots burning translations in Metz. It was a likely outcome.

Clearly Innocent was suspicious of an over-hasty bishop and anxious not to extinguish enthusiasm. He said that the 'desire for understanding the Holy Scriptures and a zeal for preaching what is in the Scriptures is something not to be reprimanded but rather to be encouraged', and it is significant that at the end of his pontificate, when he drew up constitutions for the fourth Lateran Council of 1215, he did not include in them any blanket prohibition of translations of Scripture. Nevertheless he also explained that 'the secret mysteries of the faith ought not . . . to be explained to all men in all places . . . For such is the depth of divine Scripture, that not only the simple and illiterate but even the prudent and learned are not fully sufficient to try to understand it.'[39] Here lay the nub of the matter. The study of Scripture demanded

---

[36] Preaching in Selge, *Waldenser* I, pp. 95–127, 142–7; relation to confession (using Durand of Huesca), pp. 95–8.

[37] Böhmer, in *RPTK* XX, cols 815, 829–30 (assuming later practice reflected earlier; evidence of the *talea* ibid., col. 830).

[38] Ibid., col. 815 and references; on Passau Anonymous, see below, p. 149.

[39] *Epistolae* (*PL* CCXIV, cols 695–9); work on this by M. Deanesly, *The Lollard Bible* (Cambridge, 1920), p. 31 (surveys attitudes to Bible-reading in the West; ch. 2 has an introduction on the Waldensians), superseded by L. E. Boyle, 'Innocent III and vernacular versions of Scripture', *The Bible in the Medieval World*, ed. K. Walsh and D. Wood, *SCH* Subsidia IV (Oxford, 1985), pp. 97–107, using *Die Register*

training and skill; the use of it formed a part of the Church's teaching and could not be divorced from it. If the use of translations came to be associated with something hostile to, or contemptuous of the priesthood, as was the case in Metz, then the translations were likely to be casualties. Repression of translations as well as of heretical preachers was the simple disciplinary solution, especially when local prelates had narrow horizons.

Scripture was to be mediated, as it were, to the faithful through authorized preachers; the bare text was not to be put into the hands of anyone who might misuse and misunderstand it. The Waldensians naturally rejected this viewpoint and were inclined to think that the authorities and the learned created needless obfuscation. They stressed the literal understanding of the text and the direct fulfilment in their own lives of Christ's demands.

There was a gradual slide deeper into heresy; as the original moderation of Valdes and the Lyons group was breached, the Waldensians spread and developed their teaching in fresh circumstances, and the split from the Church took a psychological toll. The process can be traced in the years between *Ad abolendam* and 1205, the time at which the French and Lombard wings of the movement divided.

Valdes's own influence was always exerted in favour of moderation, with an eye to the ultimate reconciliation with Rome that he seems never finally to have ruled out. He was supported by some of the clerical converts, for whom Durand of Huesca, the former priest, active in Languedoc against the Cathars, is the best spokesman. His *Liber antiheresis*, composed in the late 1180s or early 1190s, a handbook designed to equip former clergy who read Latin for controversy with both Catholics and Cathars, is proof of the surviving will to orthodoxy in some sections some years after the condemnation of *Ad abolendam*.[40]

Durand was fighting a battle on two fronts: against the orthodox controversialists, who objected that the Waldensians had no right to preach, and that they parasitically lived off their hearers when they ought to have earned their bread by their labour; and against the Cathars, with their own claim to observe the apostolic life, who objected that the Waldensians were not members of the Church because, unlike themselves, they did not have the orders of bishops, priests and deacons. In justifying Waldensians and arming his readers for attack on the weak points of Catharism, its dualism and the lack of austerity of its believer class, Durand keeps free of heresy for most of the time. The root of the matter, of course, was the right to preach, even after authority had prohibited it, and the appeal which Durand makes to God's call to Valdes as justifying it. Here there was a direct challenge to Church authority. But Durand, a practical controversialist with a missionary aim, does not use the issues as a springboard for a developed heretical theology. He does slip into Pelagianism in his eagerness to refute Cathar teaching on

Innozenz III 2: *Pontifikatsjahr 1199–1200*, ed. O. Hageneder, W. Maleczek and A. A. Strnad (Rome, 1979), pp. 271–6, 432–4; see Böhmer, in *RPTK* xx, col. 815.

[40] Above, p. 62, n. 2; dating: Selge, *Waldenser* ii, pp. xvii–xviii; purpose, ibid., i, p. 45; Thouzellier, *Catharisme et Valdéisme*, pp. 60, 271. The name is Durand of Huesca (Aragon) and not Osca (ibid., pp. 213–14 of 2nd edn, correcting theory of Dossat).

predestination but as a whole, the simple biblically based piety of the *Liber antiheresis* is orthodox.[41]

Some made more radical inferences from the common Waldensian thesis of the prime responsibility of the individual for his destiny, and denied Catholic belief in the value of prayers for the dead, or went farther and rejected purgatory altogether. Others, setting out from the Waldensian desire for fidelity to the texts of the gospels, argued that the sayings of Jesus, such as His injunction, 'swear not at all', were to be taken literally, and that in consequence of this principle, all lies were to be treated as mortal sins, and oaths and shedding of blood forbidden in all circumstances. One group in Languedoc carried rigorism so far that they claimed that, as true disciples of Christ, they alone could baptize where neither the Cathars nor the Catholic clergy could. Valdes repudiated them about 1200, whereupon they seem to have formed themselves into a Church of their own, with a hierarchy of bishop, priests and deacons.[42]

There were many pressures working against early orthodoxy. Awareness of the moral need of the Church, which was a mainspring of the movement, easily inclined preachers to move on from a criticism of fallen clergy to a rejection of their sacraments. The study of the vernacular Scriptures could rouse fresh questions about contemporary belief in the minds of idealists. Initially, Scripture-reading was buttressed and restrained by a concomitant study of the Church Fathers – Valdes's initial stock of translations included patristic texts[43] – but there were many simple men in the association, and the battle with the hierarchy over the legitimacy of their preaching constantly led Waldensians to appeal to the text of Scripture. From this the way led to a more clearly Biblicist attitude, in which whatever was not justified in the text of Scripture alone was not legitimate. The battle with the Cathars also tended to move them away from orthodoxy because it put pressure on them, as they wrestled for the souls of the people, not to seem less faithful to the words of Scripture than their opponents and not to appear mere collaborators with the stained Catholic Church. The Cathars wholly rejected lies, oaths and the shedding of blood: could the Waldensians afford to seem less Biblicist on these issues than the Cathars were? The stress on doing penance in the movement led to an increased use of confession which could hardly be met by clergy accustomed to hearing confessions at most once a year. Low estimates of the character of the Catholic priesthood also inhibited recourse to them, and so confession to laymen within the Waldensian circle emerged as a substitute. A similar motive, of concern for the pastoral needs of their adherents, led the Waldensians to celebrate the eucharist themselves in regions where it was not readily available from the hands of Catholic priests.[44] When the former

[41] Prologue to *Liber*, Selge, *Waldenser* II, 8; discussion, ibid., I, ch. 1; for Durand on predestination, see Thouzellier, *Catharisme et Valdéisme*, p. 75; K. V. Selge, 'Discussions sur l'apostolicité entre Vaudois, Catholiques, et Cathares', in *CF* II, pp. 143–62.

[42] For this paragraph, see Selge, *Waldenser* I, ch. 2; comment by Grundmann in *DA* XXIV (1968), pp. 572–3.

[43] Etienne de Bourbon in Lecoy de la Marche, *Anecdotes Historiques*, p. 290; Selge, *Waldenser* I, p. 152, n. 73.

[44] Selge, *Waldenser* I, pp. 155–7 (reaction to Cathars), 146–9 (confession), 159–63 (eucharist).

Waldensian, Bernard Prim, was received back into the Church in 1210, it was conceded that honourable motives were at work among Waldensians who did this.[45] But the move was dangerous because it opened the way to a rival Church and organization, with its own 'pure' sacraments, in contrast to the 'impure' ones of the sinful priests in the Church.

Spontaneous moves farther from the Roman Church were aided by the geographical diffusion of the movement away from its original nucleus. More radical views emerge among the Waldensians found at Metz in 1199. Though not yet formally Donatist, they are highly critical of the clergy, and tend to be exclusive in their attitudes to their own preachers and translations: they give the impression of a group on the verge of forming a counter-church.[46] The Waldensians who crossed the Alps to Italy grew more extreme. Ardizzo's report on them in Piacenza in the last decade of the century describes how they broke up marriages in gaining recruits, took nuns from nunneries, and taught that only with them was salvation to be found.[47] The Humiliati affected the newcomers in another way, influencing them to adopt their own static life of manual labour, even for preachers, in place of the primitive wandering. To Valdes this was quite unacceptable: the gospel texts were mandatory for the preacher class, who were obliged to live from their hearers rather than by their own efforts.

Another source of dissension lay in the Lombard group's selection of ministers for the duty of administering the sacraments, in contrast to the purely temporary *ad hoc* arrangements normal on the French side of the Alps. The decision had a symbolic importance: where Valdes still thought in terms of reconciliation with Rome, and he and those like him saw a Waldensian administration of the sacraments as merely an occasional bowing to necessity, the Lombards wanted to make a permanent arrangement, and were indifferent to the effects that this might have on their relations with Rome.

A third factor precipitating crisis was the election of John de Ronco as provost, opposed bitterly by Valdes on the grounds that the only leader of the association could be Christ. Personalities played some part. The Lombards detected despotic tendencies in Valdes; John de Ronco seems to have been a raw personality, and a later report from the Catholic controversialist Salvo Burci accused him of being unlettered.[48] The election brought about a split in 1205; despite attempts at reunion, it was never healed, and the Waldensians for the rest of the Middle Ages remained divided into the Lyonist group, who remained faithful to Valdes, and the Poor Lombards,[49] as they were called, with their stronghold in northern Italy. After 1205 the latter drew away still further, and became more explicitly Donatist.

The Italian split was one element in a general process of alienation of Waldensians from the Church. From the first refusal of the prohibition of

[45] Ibid., p. 159; Innocent III, *Epistolae* xiii, 94 (*PL* CCXVI, col. 291); on Prim, see Thouzellier, *Catharisme et Valdéisme*, pp. 232–7, 262–7.

[46] *PL* CCXIV, cols 695–9 (above, p. 73, n. 39); Selge, *Waldenser* I, pp. 290–3.

[47] Letter of Ardizzo, bishop of Piacenza, ed. A. Dondaine, in 'Durand de Huesca et la polémique anti-Cathare', *AFP* XXIX (1959), pp. 273–4.

[48] *WEH*, p. 273.

[49] For the causes of the split, see Selge, *Waldenser* I, pp. 172–88; for prime source, see below, pp. 93–4.

preaching at Lyons in the early 1180s there had been a gradual decline from schism to heresy proper. The authorities had had the worst of both worlds, for prohibition had not greatly inhibited the spread of the movement yet it had contributed to its deterioration. The hope of reconciliation could not be deferred too long; even ineffective persecution increased Waldensian hostility to the Church; the breach from Catholic instruction and aid inevitably opened the way to popular heresies inside the movement. A natural impression is that the papacy and the bishops had wholly underestimated the strength of feeling which lay behind the Waldensian demands, and that a heresy had emerged largely out of the attitudes of the Church.

The Speronists

While the Waldensians slipped out of orthodoxy into the world of the sects, another heretical group was forming in Lombardy, the Speronists.[50] They resemble the Waldensians in one thing: they were a group founded by a layman – something for which we have no earlier precedent, if we except the followers of Eon de l'Étoile as too like a robber band to be properly discussed.

Speroni was a jurist, a one-time friend of the great legal authority Vacarius, to whose refutation of Speroni's heresy we owe nearly all our information about the sect. Consul in Piacenza in 1164, 1165 and 1171, Speroni between the years 1177 and 1185 fomented a movement against the Church which lasted fifty years. Piacenza was and remained its centre. A probable starting-point can be seen in Speroni's involvement in the long conflict over the rights of the monastery of S. Giulia in Piacenza, in which he and other protagonists of Piacenza met papal opposition.

The heresy represented an extreme rejection of all Church authority, which spread well in Piacenza because the anticlerical spirit of the town favoured any movement of opposition to the Church. Priesthood itself was jettisoned. Here Speroni differed in approach from Arnold of Brescia, whose denial of the place of the priesthood sprang from a rejection of their vices: because they had sinned so deeply, their acts had lost validity; and because the Roman Church had become involved in property, it had lost its right to confer sacramental powers. Speroni was much more radical. No doubt his views were born out of a reaction against a power-loving priesthood, but his understanding of religion left no place for a priesthood *ab initio* and on principle. They simply had no function left, for Speroni condemned all the sacraments – especially baptism, the mass and penance – as their stupid inventions. All formal acts of worship and exterior observances represented an idolatrous materialization of spiritual religion; they were quite simply an obstacle. Arnoldists, or followers of the wandering preachers, might well have broken into overt acts of violence – Petrobrusians, for example, felt so deeply about the distortions of the contemporary Church that they rejected them in dramatic scenes, burning crosses or eating meat ostentatiously at forbidden times. For the Speronists all

---

[50] Ilarino da Milano, *L'Eresia di Ugo Speroni nella confutazione del Maestro Vacario, Studi e Testi* cxv (Vatican, 1945); analysis of heresy and Vacarius's polemic: text, pp. 483–583; see esp. on Speroni (pp. 37–75) reconstruction of core of heresy (pp. 411–22); place on Italian scene (pp. 423–69); extract in *WEH*, pp. 152–8.

this was unnecessary. Their members had already the consciousness of union with the Word; in Speroni's phrases, they had the Holy Spirit, the Spirit of Jesus and of wisdom, and were in union of faith and love with Jesus. They could therefore quietly attend mass while their minds were elsewhere, pursuing the interior calm and justice that lay at the heart of their beliefs, *alieno mente*.

The centre of their religion was a kind of interior baptism, a spiritual communion with God. It was not an ascetic movement, and had nothing in common with the twelfth-century striving after apostolic life[51] – on the contrary, Speroni and his followers rejected ascetic practices, the good works and moral activity of the individual, in favour of a total devotion to interior sanctification. All that mattered was the inner life of the individual. Speroni denied that there was original sin, but argued for two categories of humanity, the predestined and the foreknown. The foreknown were doomed to damnation; by contrast the predestined soul remained holy even when, from the point of view of exterior justice, it was leading a life of sin.

Such a theology could hardly be the basis of an effective organization, and Speroni had no predilection for preaching. Yet his following lasted. One major reason, we may assume, was the Speronists' consciousness of their predestination. Speroni's liking was for a ministry of the written word, and we may suspect that he drew a following from the better educated. Certainly they outlasted his death, though they never became a dynamic feature on the Italian scene. The *Liber supra stella*, written by Salvo Burci in 1235, also a citizen of Piacenza, is evidence that some fifty years later they were still in existence.[52]

The crisis areas

The Speronists were odd men out in their century, but not in their locality. Lombardy, and to a lesser extent, central Italy in these decades was rapidly attaining the distinction of being the land of heresy *par excellence*, rivalled only by Languedoc. The causes were embedded in the development, economic, social and political, of all those regions where the semi-independent commune had established itself as a determining factor. A burgeoning economic life, in advance of developments anywhere else in Europe, put everything into the melting pot. There was an extraordinary mobility of classes, with peasants from the *contado* moving into the towns or transferring from one part of the *contado* to another, lords from the countryside coming into the towns and joining in the social struggles within them, while fortunes were made from commerce and industry. New classes of artisans, notaries and petty businessmen were formed, and the communes defied outside authority and started to battle for control of their own regions. Social change and mobility, Violante has suggested, made men ready to break with tradition in religion

[51] Ilarino da Milano, *Eresia*, p. 435.
[52] Ilarino da Milano, 'Il "Liber supra stella" del piacentino Salvo Burci contro i Catari e altre correnti ereticali', *Aevum* XVI (1942), pp. 272–319; XVII (1943), pp. 90–146; XIX (1945), pp. 218–341; see his *Eresia*, p. 42.

and opened their minds to unorthodox ideas.[53] The vivid economic life of Italy fostered reaction against the business world and the practice of usury bound up with it, and led some idealists into the heretical groups who practised poverty, or stimulated them into violent reaction against a hierarchy who officially denounced usury and were leaders of a Church based on a gospel which called for renunciation, yet were themselves deeply involved in moneymaking. The continuance of a lay educational tradition in Italy, and the intellectual agility sustained by the commercial life and political intensity within the communes, opened the way to protests against a bureaucratic Church with a limited place for its laity, and aided the growth of heretical groups which gave a place to the laity for preaching, Scripture reading and spiritual direction. The same agility and the questing spirit which accompanied it was also a seed-ground for those elements of plain disbelief which intertwined with other causes of dissent to create heresy. Orthodox enthusiasms, like the flight to eremitism or the increase of itinerant preachers, blended with economic forces to create a flux which shook the power of traditional ecclesiastical forms and organization to hold the faithful. Exchanges of view were facilitated by the heterogeneous character of the travellers, not so much on the great international routes, but on the lesser roads where the pace was less hot, and lower clergy, pedlars, itinerant artisans and pilgrims were thrown into informal contact.[54] The geographical position of Italy and the opening of routes through commerce facilitated both the entry of missionaries and the flight of refugees from persecution elsewhere. Movement itself created a psychological climate in which it was easier to step outside orthodoxy.

The politics of communal struggles aided heresy because they weakened the authority of the natural guardians of faith, the bishops, and confused the context between orthodoxy and heresy with the battle for independence of the communes from episcopal and papal power. The investiture controversies had destroyed the control of the bishop over his town. He remained a considerable figure because of his high birth and connections with ruling families, as well as the lands and rights of his bishopric; but his interest had become only one political force among a series of others, and he had no power any more to ensure that the rule of faith was maintained and heresies put down by force. So heretical groups might be tolerated in communes, not because they had a hold on a major portion of the populace, but because they demonstrated independence from episcopal control.

Similar effects flowed from the popes' struggle against the temporal claims of the emperors in Italy. There was a natural alliance between heretics and the Ghibellines, the factions which existed in the cities based on local and family groupings and interests, but owning a general allegiance to the Empire. Heresy was a stick with which imperial supporters could beat the papacy, disliked for its political rather than its religious claims. Ghibellinism, then, provided the favourable milieu in which heretics could swim. At the same time the efforts which popes made to raise money, levy troops and exert pressure in these contests made them easy targets for the classic contrast

---

[53] *HS*, pp. 171–98; Italian background in Volpe, *Movimenti religiosi*; attempted refutation by Morghen in *Medioevo Cristiano*, pp. 204–81.

[54] Violante, *La Pataria Milanese* I (Rome, 1955), pp. 103–25.

drawn by the preacher between a worldly and wealthy Church involved in the infighting of Italian politics and the simple band of apostles gathered round Jesus or depicted in action in the Acts of the Apostles.[55] Too often the clergy in Italy appeared in the guise of politicians, tax gatherers or warriors rather than as pastors. It is the political involvement of the *popuo in Italy* which explains the apparent paradox that in the Middle Ages heresy flourished most readily in lands that lay closest to the seat of the papacy.

An upward movement in the graph of heresy over all Western Europe, placed by Wakefield about mid-century,[56] was followed in the 1160s by an intense struggle between Alexander III and the emperor Frederick Barbarossa over Italy. This had the effect of distracting the popes from the problem of heresy, and of delaying attempts to grapple with it. *Ad abolendam* followed on the reconciliation of pope and emperor and was a first fruit of the new peace. While the contest was on, there was much destruction in Italy; the fighting and schism in the papacy fomented by Barbarossa disrupted religious life, and contributed to the weakness of ecclesiastical authority on which Italian heresy flourished. Most suggestive is the transmutation which took place in the term 'Patarene' between its origin in the eleventh century, as a term for supporters of the orthodox if radical reform in Milan favoured by the papacy, and its reappearance in the third Lateran Council of 1179, and then in *Ad abolendam*, long after the Pataria had died away, as a technical term for Italian heretics, most often applied to the Cathars.[57] It was an indication of the loss by later twelfth-century popes of the leadership of popular religious sentiment, now tending to flow out of the Church rather than into it.

Two examples, one of partial success, the other of defeat for the forces of orthodoxy in the last decades of the century, may suffice to show how the situation then lay in Italy. In Milan St Galdinus, consecrated archbishop in exile during Barbarossa's wars, began in 1167 to restore the fortunes of his see and, towards the end of his pontificate, to preach against the Cathars who were then spreading in the city.[58] His *Vita* attributes much success to his efforts, and to the effects of his campaign we may perhaps assign the conversion of the heretical teacher Bonacursus, who proceeded in his *Manifestatio* to describe the heresy he had left.[59] The significant feature of the *Vita* is the vagueness with which the heresy is mentioned, a sign that at this time Catholics were not very well informed about their enemy, and the fact that St Galdinus had no other weapon but exhortation. Evidently he could not coerce the citizens to drop Catharism. He checked the rise of heresy, but only temporarily. In the first decade of the thirteenth century James of Vitry said, with a moralist's exaggeration, that Milan was a pit of heretics.[60] In fact they were minorities, divided and disputing among themselves, but they were

---

[55] Volpe, *Movimenti religiosi*, pp. 38–48, Morghen, *Medioevo Cristiano*, pp. 275–81.

[56] *WEH*, p. 28.

[57] See above, p. 36, n. 4; for heretical nomenclature, see Thouzellier, *Hérésie et hérétiques*; and on Patarines, pp. 204–21.

[58] *Acta sanctorum*, 18 April, II, p. 591; *WEH*, p. 151.

[59] Ilarino da Milano, 'La manifestatio heresis catarorum quam fecit Bonacursus', *Aevum* XII (1938), pp. 281–333; *WEH*, pp. 170–3.

[60] *Lettres de Jacques de Vitry*, ed. R. B. C. Huygens (Leiden, 1960), pp. 72–3; comment: G. G. Merlo, *Studi Storici. Valdesi e Valdismi Medievali: Itinerari e proposte di ricerca* (Turin, 1984), p. 18.

energetic, and each group seems to have had more supporters there than anywhere else.

The other example is that of Orvieto where Catharism first appeared a little after mid-century, to make but modest progress till about 1170, when the arrival of two preachers from Florence began to raise the temperature. In the end a territorial dispute with the papacy caused Innocent III to put Orvieto under interdict; the bishop withdrew, Catharism made inroads in his absence. Innocent's action had an effect opposite to the one intended: while the city still lay under the ban, an heretical teacher from Viterbo began to preach and drew many after him.[61] When the Catholics of the town rallied and appointed Pietro Parenzo to restore order, he was assassinated. In the reaction and the proliferation of miracles which followed on instant popular veneration of the dead Pietro, Catharism went underground. But it still survived, and the story had lessons, *mutatis mutandis*, for the treatment of heresy in all the Italy of the communes. Catharism and the evangelical heresies, some of which had been in part stimulated into existence by the menace of the Cathars, had made a place for themselves within many of the towns. Responsibility for their progress or repression lay heavily with the laity, as the case of Orvieto shows. The popes and the bishops could not count on support to put them down. This loss of authority over heresy and the evident failure of *Ad abolendam* produced in Italy a state very like crisis by the end of the century.

In the other major area of disquiet, Languedoc, the conditions which fostered heresy were unlike those in Italy,[62] though the end result in the emergence of small but tenacious heretical minorities, and a loss of power by churchmen to control them, was much the same. The resistant forces were not primarily the towns, which were smaller than those of northern Italy and lacked their independence, but elements of the petty nobility in the countryside. St Gilles and Toulouse had international trade connections, and there were common linguistic and cultural links along the Mediterranean littoral into northern Italy; yet commerce in the Midi was smaller in scale than in Lombardy. Industry produced for a regional market, by and large, and was stable. The flux in social classes which followed on the exceptional economic vitality of Italy, as well as the intellectual agility and the higher standards of lay education, were missing.

The precondition for the success of heresy in the affected regions of Languedoc was the chronic political anarchy caused by the gradual decomposition of the authority of the counts of Toulouse since the time of the journey to the first crusade of Count Raymond IV,[63] and the disequilibrium created by the rival, undecided claims to suzerainty of three powers, the kings

---

[61] V. Natalini, *S. Pietro Parenzo: La leggenda scritta dal maestro Giovanni canonico di Orvieto* (Rome, 1936), pp. 155–6; quoted in Manselli, *Eresia*, p. 186. See *MBPH*, pp. 127–32.

[62] W. L. Wakefield, *Heresy, Crusade and Inquisition in Southern France 1100–1250* (London, 1974) (concise survey with translation of documents), ch. 3 and bibliography; P. Wolff *et al.*, *Histoire du Languedoc* (Toulouse, 1967); J. R. Strayer, *The Albigensian Crusades* (New York, 1971) (lucid on politics and war, but out of date on heresy); P. Wolff, 'France du Nord, France du Midi: Les Luttes sociales dans les villes du Midi français', *Annales* II (1947), pp. 443–54. Definition of Languedoc and other geographical terms in Wakefield, *Heresy, Crusade*, p. 50, Strayer, *Albigensian Crusades*, ch. 1.

[63] A. Dupont, *Les Cités de la Narbonnaise première depuis les invasions germaniques jusqu'a l'Apparition du Consulat* (Nîmes, 1942), pp. 686–7.

of France, the kings of England and the counts of Barcelona, followed by their heirs the kings of Aragon. Local conditions also militated against the establishment of any one overriding political authority; the existence of partible inheritance by females created a fatal subdivision of rights in land, and hampered the raising of armies by feudal means. Mercenaries were widely employed in consequence; and churchmen, denouncing the spread of heresy, simultaneously deplored the ravages of these *routiers*.[64] Chronic war disrupted Church life and handicapped bishops who might be interested in an active oversight of the rural parishes where heresy first established itself. It also created a condition of lawlessness, with plundering of Church property by secular lords and much petty friction, which tended to devalue the influence of churchmen in purely religious matters, and correspondingly increase the popularity of a profoundly anticlerical heresy which rejected all Church authority. Disorder inhibited the great local lords when the call came to put down heresy: they lacked the power to do so, and in the uncertain conditions could not afford to alienate any subjects.

The petty nobility in the rural areas enjoyed a large measure of independence from their suzerains, but no very secure economic position. The subdivision of inheritance led to the appearance of large numbers of knights, with resources insufficient to support them and little outlet but in waging of war. Usurpation of tithes by these men was widespread. Rural clergy were poor for this reason, and heavily dependent on local nobles; the latter had a commitment against doing justice to the legitimate claims of churchmen, and a predilection for anticlerical heresy which taught that the payment of tithes could not rightly be demanded by the Church from the laity. As in Italy, anticlericalism formed the favourable ambience for heresy proper, but it was an anticlericalism focused more closely on local rights and less concerned with high political claims. Within this anticlerical atmosphere, men in the early stages were more often patrons, fautors of heresy or fringe members, the women the true converts. As they joined the ranks of Cathar perfect or gave wholehearted support to their preachers, the heresy began to settle in. In a second generation more menfolk made the renunciations demanded for admission to the leading class of perfect or, at least, became believers; under the umbrella of noble protection the heresy was preached to lower classes. Both then and earlier the heresy made its impact in some of the towns, especially Toulouse, where it secured some men of influence, though the surest support for it always remained in the countryside.[65]

The clergy of the Midi lacked the will, the ability and the resources to put

---

[64] Griffe, *Débuts*, pp. 7–14, 117–24; M-H. Vicaire, '"L'affaire de paix et de foi" du Midi de la France', in *CF* IV, pp. 102–27.

[65] Griffe, *Débuts*, ch. 7 (comment, p. 182, n. 14). For social context, see C. P. Bru, 'Eléments pour une interprétation sociologique du Catharisme occitan', in *Spiritualité de l'hérésie: Le Catharisme*, ed. R. Nelli (Paris, 1953), pp. 23–59 (clarifying survey, arguing that Catharism was not specifically urban, p. 36). Koch, *Frauenfrage*, ch. 1, s. 1, overstresses towns and textile workers (but pp. 26–8 presages Griffe's hypothesis; see discussion of motivation, p. 31); J. H. Mundy, *Europe in the High Middle Ages* (London, 1973), pp. 534–49, is perceptive. M. Roquebert, in private conversation, notes that he believes both Griffe and Dossat tended a little to underestimate the rank and wealth of Cathar adherents. I hope to investigate this.

effective obstacles in the way of the heretical preachers.[66] The higher clergy were also affected by the disorders, and were often not on good terms with their secular counterparts. They had their share of unworthy prelates – the archbishop of Narbonne from 1190 to 1212 was an ineffectual absentee – and the best of them were competent rather than inspiring. Before Fulk of Toulouse (appointed in 1206), who launched a drive with aristocratic support against both heresy and usury, none of them was able to inspire the laity in their charge to fervour against the heresy. Clergy most in contact with the heretics were hampered by poverty which, because it was not voluntary, had no spiritual benefit, and was merely a handicap. As far as we know, the lower clergy were no worse morally, than, say, the lower clergy of Normandy, where there was no heresy;[67] but they were poorly educated and demoralized by their treatment at the hands of the laity. They made a feeble showing in contrast to the dedicated ascetics who represented the heresy, and they lived in a region not distinguished for the quality of Catholic intellectual development.[68]

The Midi's achievement in the cultural sphere lay in the study of Roman law and its troubadour literature, sponsored by the courts of leading aristocrats and especially by noblewomen. It was not heretical, though it did share in the prevailing anticlerical atmosphere; its influence was confined to a small class, and it was irrelevant to the heresy question.[69] In the religious sphere the land was underdeveloped: it lacked the schools which gave lustre to northern France and provided the sinews for intellectual defence against heresy and, though there had been orthodox preaching missions and a special association with the crusading ideal, no major reforms had affected Church life. As elsewhere, a demand for apostolic life in poor wandering preaching was met, not by the orthodox, but by heretics.

One feature of the region was its toleration of different views and races. Jews were well treated,[70] so were heretics; Waldensians as well as Cathars moved freely.[71] Given the inability of local forces to contain the situation, intervention from outside the Midi might well seem the only answer; it was attempted, following an appeal to Louis VII of France and a letter to the Cistercians sent by Raymond V, count of Toulouse, in 1177, but it was not

---

[66] Y. Dossat, 'Le clergé méridional à la veille de la croisade albigeoise', *RHL* I (1944), pp. 263–78, 'La répression de l'hérésie par les évêques', in *CF* VI, pp. 217–51; H. Vidal, *Episcopatus et pouvoir épiscopal à Béziers à la veille de la croisade albigeoise, 1152–1209* (Montpellier, 1951); R. W. Emery, *Heresy and Inquisition in Narbonne* (New York, 1941); E. Delaruelle, 'Le Catharisme en Languedoc vers 1200: une enquête', *AM* LXXII (1960), pp. 149–67 (stimulating set of queries); review of C. E. Smith, *The University of Toulouse in the Middle Ages* (Milwaukee, 1958), in *AM* LXXIII (1961), pp. 234–5; on learning, see *CF* V; Wakefield, *Heresy, Crusade*, ch. 4 (surveys Church; discussion of numbers of heretics, pp. 68–71); on relation of reform to heresy, cf. Griffe, *Débuts*, pp. 16–19, correcting Fliche, in *Histoire de l'Eglise*, ed. Fliche and Martin, IX, p. 91. See below, p. 97, n. 22.

[67] Strayer, *Albigensian Crusades*, p. 18.

[68] Bibliography in P. Ourliac, 'La société languedocienne du XIIIe siècle et le droit romain', *CF* VI, pp. 199–216.

[69] D. Zorzi, *Valori religiosi nella Letteratura provenzale: La Spiritualità trinitaria* (Milan, 1954); Koch, *Frauenfrage*, pp. 139–44.

[70] B. Smalley, reviewing the 2nd edn of Thouzellier, *Catharisme et Valdéisme* (*JEH* XXI (1970), pp. 184–6).

[71] Above, p. 69.

pressed home, and the results were superficial.[72] A projected expedition by the kings of France and England came to nothing. A legatine mission scored some ᴊᴜᴄᴄᴇꜱꜱ by securing condemnation of a rich heretic, Pierre Maurand, in Toulouse and bringing two leaders of heresy, one probably the Cathar bishop of Toulouse, to a public discussion in the city. But the two came under safe conduct, and left freely at the end, excommunicate but not otherwise punished.[73] In 1181 an armed expedition to Lavaur put pressure on the Trencavel viscount of Béziers, implicated with heresy, and enforced the handing over of the two heretics who had gone free in 1178. They duly confessed.[74] But such short-term expeditions only scratched the problem, and were handicapped by lack of local knowledge.

There was a vicious circle here. Churchmen in the Midi were not tackling the problem; churchmen outside could not well understand the area. More lay below the surface, probably, than the legates understood. Raymond v's appeal may be interpreted as an attempt to call in fresh forces in the ancient quarrel with the viscounts of Béziers.[75] There is a suspicion that Maurand's emergence as the major suspect in Toulouse owed something to social tensions there and his own successful career in business.[76]

The legates did what they could. Of Henri de Marcy, the conscientious Cistercian who was member of the first mission and leader of the second, one could not reasonably expect that he be another Bernard of Clairvaux. He did not greatly like the Midi, and turned down an offer of the bishopric of Toulouse.[77] After he left the scene this phase of intervention ended. Alexander III especially had given attention to the problem after the easing of the crisis with the Empire. From the fall of Jerusalem in 1187, however, the papacy was preoccupied elsewhere. For the cure of the affected region of Languedoc, probably some lever was needed against the aristocrats who declined to use force against heresy; what was certainly necessary was prolonged preaching by churchmen who knew the language and the locality, and this the region did not have.

In the absence of fresh intervention, the situation grew worse rather than better. Not all of the south was seriously affected. The heresy noticed in Gascony did not become a problem. The Mediterranean seaboard was scantily affected. The crucial region lay, rather, to the west and inland, in the eastern Toulousain, the Carcassès and the eastern Albigeois and in their leading towns.[78] In certain places within these lands, because of the attitudes of some members of the nobility, by the end of the century the Cathars had

---

[72] Gervase of Canterbury, *Chronicon*, ed. W. Stubbs, LXXIII, i (*RS*) (London, 1879), pp. 270–1; date of Raymond's appeal, Thouzellier, *Catharisme et Valdéisme*, 2nd edn, p. 19, n. 23; letters, *PL* CCIV, cols 235–42; CXCIX cols 1120–4.

[73] Sources, tr. of Roger of Hoveden, *WEH*, pp. 194–200; similar text tr., *MBPH*, pp. 113–16.

[74] Narrative 1173–81, Griffe, *Débuts*, chs 4 and 5; on Lavaur, see pp. 126–32.

[75] Wakefield, *Heresy, Crusade*, p. 83.

[76] J. H. Mundy, *Liberty and Political Power in Toulouse, 1050–1230* (New York, 1954), pp. 60–2 (links between heresy and social tension, pp. 74–84); his *Europe*, p. 304; and his *The Repression of Catharism at Toulouse: The Royal Diploma of 1279* (Toronto, 1985), pp. 12–13; survey on early history of repression, pp. 7–26; P. Hordern, in *EHR* CIII (1988), pp. 477–8, suspends judgement on Mundy's early datings.

[77] Griffe, *Débuts*, pp. 113–14, 137–9.

[78] Ibid., pp. 176–7 (see also map on endpapers).

come near to displacing the Catholic Church, rendering parish clergy impotent, preventing the administration of the sacraments and securing in practice a right of open preaching for themselves In Toulouse and other towns they were a known but unmolested minority, and included men of influence. The leading aristocracy were still not effective persecutors and Raymond VI, who succeeded his father as count of Toulouse in 1194, was more equivocal in his attitude to heresy than his predecessor.[79] In many *castra*, the fortified settlements of the countryside, the Cathars' leading class was installed in houses, directing men and women in austere lives, preaching and giving counsel, even receiving the payments normally due to the parish clergy. Waldensians, officially under the ban of the Church, were in practice little hampered.

Conclusion

To survey the regions of Italy and Languedoc, where the Church's authority to impose submission to its doctrines had broken down, makes a fitting conclusion to a chapter on heresy in the twelfth century, because it is a story of lost opportunities and of only partially successful repression: by the end of the century the balance in the battle between heretical minorities and ecclesiastical authority had definitely swung against the Church. One should be chary of giving literal credence to the preachers and reformers who so loudly proclaimed the sins and weakness of the Church; the medieval Church retained great vitality together with its scandals and defects, and was ever capable of comprehending in one organization extremes of devotion and of wickedness. Nowhere could one justly speak of a mass apostasy, and only the ambiguous character of the anticlerical ambience in which heresy proper moved could lead one to think it was likely to happen. The will to heresy has to be distinguished from faint-hearted orthodoxy and a desire to impede any increase in the secular power of the Church; and the number of committed heretics, by all indications, was still not very great.

None the less an anxious situation did exist, the more so because the hierarchy seemed not to have ideas for meeting the challenge. The tragedy had been that so much enthusiasm had already slipped away, condemned to the twilight world of the sects. With few exceptions, the heretical groups of the century were still not mounting a profound doctrinal challenge to the Church. Their appeal was emphatically to Christian life, and they drew converts above all because of the attractive power of the earnest and dedicated lives of many of their teachers and the force of their exhortation to moral living in their hearers.

No doubt because of the utterly changed circumstances in which the heresies of the high Middle Ages expanded as contrasted with those of the late Roman world, we miss the intellectual heresy based on the teaching of some distinguished mind that formed the stuff of the classical heresies condemned in the early centuries. The intellectual appeal of the heretical leaders in the twelfth century is very limited and, though they are often men in orders, they

---

[79] Ibid., p. 207.

do not include anyone of strong academic background. The common ground
between many of them was the appeal to an apostolic life based on wandering
preaching in poverty and, where this was practised, crowds could be drawn to
listen and follow.

Sometimes it seems almost a matter of chance whether the following
collected will remain orthodox or form a sect. Instruction was not adequate to
guard the faithful against deviations of belief, and the situation remained
fluid. Leaders of heretical groups were not always clear themselves where
their ideas were leading them. In these circumstances, the decisions of
authority were particularly potent: elements within the dissident religious
movements were susceptible to a recall to the Church, provided outlets could
be found for their enthusiasms. The desire to hear preaching and to preach
was a recurrent theme. So was the yearning for simplicity, sometimes an
illusory simplicity of the romanticized early Church and an impatience with
sophisticated explanations. Certain texts from the gospels struck their leaders,
and demanded a direct and literal observance. There was a will to understand
directly what lay in the gospels. Asceticism had an appeal *per se*, irrespective of
the motivation and the doctrinal substructure. Anticlericalism was generally
the stimulus for heresy, as well as being its protection. The most common
heretical tenets were concerned with the powers of the priesthood and the
demands of conscience. – with the validity of sacraments administered by
unworthy clergy and the value of infant baptism, as opposed to the willing
acceptance of belief by the adult. Involved with the deviations from orthodoxy
were social tensions hinted at rather than clearly revealed in the sources,
associated with the lack of outlets for religious women, struggles for power in
the towns, poverty and wealth.

That reform in the lives of the clergy would have taken much of the sting
out of twelfth-century heresy is a commonplace. Part of the difficulty lay in the
rising expectations of the laity and the stimulus imparted by Gregorian
reforms. The corollary of the way of thinking that laid such stress on the
sacred character of the priest's office was that the priest's life must be worthy
of so high a calling. The solution, given the problems of the recruitment or
supervision of clergy, their training, and the standards of the higher clergy in
many areas, remained bafflingly difficult.

What was clear was, that to meet the challenge of heresy, it would not be
enough to maintain the old ways. On the lowest level, the episcopal
inquisition was not adequate for the searching out of offenders, and its
operations were too dependent on the energy, or lack of it, of the individual
diocesan. Understanding of the tenets of the heretics, though it had grown
through the century, especially with the appearance of full-scale summaries of
unorthodox beliefs after 1160, still had far to go. Parts of Languedoc and
much of northern and central Italy plainly presented peculiar difficulties
because of the widespread fautorship and patronage of heresy. At a higher
level, the demands and enthusiasms of the popular movement for preaching
and the apostolic life, though they conflicted with much precedent and canon
law and upset interested parties, were not of themselves heretical at all. Doors
closed at Lyons and Verona could be reopened. More could be done to
separate off misled enthusiasm from the recalcitrant elements, to bring into

focus the alien inspiration of Catharism, and draw away from it adherents unaware of the implications of dualism. The lines between heresy and orthodoxy altogether could be drawn more clearly.

There was not much time. The sects had grown since the beginning of the century in cohesion and durability. In the early decades they barely outlast the deaths of their founders, and are obviously profoundly dependent on the force of the individual charismatic personality. Then Catharism develops, a supranational heresy, no longer nearly so dependent for its existence on individual personalities, important though they may be, and capable of lasting because of its developed ritual and organization and the dogmatic envelope it gave to dissent. As the century wore on, the evangelical heresies seem also to last better, and Waldensianism appears, the culmination of the previous wandering preacher movements, strengthened by the novel element of vernacular translations of Scripture.

By the end of the century there was more heresy, it was more firmly embedded, and two crisis areas had emerged. It was this sombre scene which confronted the young Pope Innocent III on his elevation to the papacy in 1198.

Part III

Heresy and the Church

6

The counter-attack: Innocent III to Innocent IV

With the advent of Innocent III the papacy was for the first time occupied by a churchman who made the treatment of heresy and the religious movement associated with it one of the prime occupations of his pontificate.[1] In the previous century Alexander III and Lucius III had both taken steps to deal with the problem; but in comparison to Innocent's subtle handling of the difficulties their solutions appear fumbling and incomplete. Moreover, Innocent was followed by three popes, Honorius III, Gregory IX and Innocent IV, who all gave attention to the counter-attack on heresy. The work of two saints, Dominic and Francis, and the emergence of the orders of mendicant friars, encouraged by Innocent and aided by his successors, had a powerful effect on thirteenth-century religious life, and provided trained personnel to preach against heresy and to pursue its recalcitrant adherents. More study of heresy and the application of scholastic methods to its refutation brought forth fruit in treatises and handbooks that classified heretical tenets, and made clearer where precisely the boundary between heresy and orthodoxy lay.[2] Under Gregory IX use of the overriding authority of the papacy brought into being a papal inquisition to supply the deficiencies of the episcopal prosecution of heresy, and to give new energy to the tracking and examining of offenders. By the mid thirteenth century the guiding principles of the Church's counteraction were settled, and most of the machinery requisite for repression was in action, not to be altered in essentials for the rest of the Middle Ages.

   Innocent's part in this upswing of orthodox fortunes was that of the initiator who set out the principles for future action. His approach was two-sided: he

---

[1] *RB*, pp. 70–156; comment by E. Jordan in *RHE* xxxii (1936), pp. 968–72. Cf. A. C. Shannon, *The Popes and Heresy in the Thirteenth Century* (Villanova, Pa, 1949). For another facet of Innocent III, see B. Bolton, *Innocent III: A Token for Good* (Oxford, forthcoming).

[2] Borst, *Katharer*, pp. 6–21.

offered to enthusiasts who had strayed a means of returning to the Church,
and diminished the dangers in the movement for wandering preaching in
poverty by welcoming this form of apostolic life under safeguards within the
Church; and at the same time he attempted to make the use of force against
fautors and obstinate heretics more effective. His metaphor was that of the
farmer who distinguishes carefully between wheat and tares in his field, taking
precautions against uprooting the one with the other.[3] Proper handling of the
heresy problem demanded precise and careful examination of what heretics
believed and, above all, of their attitudes to authority. If they were willing to
submit, then arrangements might be made to meet the needs of enthusiasts
wherever they did not conflict directly with orthodox doctrine. If they were
recalcitrant, then every kind of measure might be employed to bring them to
justice and force those who patronized them to relinquish their support.

Innocent explored all the resources of canon law to find a place for popular
religious associations that had hitherto lain on the margin of orthodoxy or
beyond, welcoming their representatives to the curia and obtaining from them
proposita, short statements of intent, tending to stabilize their position.
Humiliati who wished for recognition were accepted, and given regulations
that allowed the continuance of three branches with separate ways of life: one
clerical, a second consisting of laymen and women living in communities, and
a third consisting of married men living with their families, all according to
existing legal norms.[4] A careful explanation showed them that there were
legitimate occasions when oaths had to be sworn, but they were allowed to
avoid any that were not strictly necessary, and to retain other special features
of their apostolic way of life as they had observed them while under the ban of
the Church. The wholesale refusal of the right to preach that had helped the
Humiliati into heresy after the third Lateran Council was breached with a fine
distinction: members of the third, the married group, who were 'wise in faith
and expert in religion', might preach, provided that they confined themselves
to moral exhortation and eschewed the preaching of doctrine – that was
properly the province of the clergy.[5]

Durand of Huesca, converted after a colloquy with the representatives of
orthodoxy at Pamiers in 1207, was given, together with the colleagues who
came over with him, the right to lead a life of wandering preaching without
property, engaging in mission against heresy, exactly as he had done while a
Waldensian, provided that he accepted Catholic authority and repudiated
errors such as Donatism, which had been current among some Waldensians.
He and his group were given the technical status of penitents in the Church,
living under three vows of poverty, chastity and obedience, and styled 'the

[3] *PL* ccxiv, cols 788–9, p. 74, n. 5. Cp. *PL* ccxv, cols 1246–8; and Bolton, in *SCH* ix, p. 86.

[4] M. Maccarrone, 'Riforma e sviluppo della vita religiosa con Innocenzo iii', *RSCI* xvi (1962), pp. 29–72; and Bolton, in *SCH* viii, p. 78.

[5] Tiraboschi, *Vetera monumenta* ii, pp. 133–4; *RB*, p. 81, n. 24, tr. of phrase, Bolton in *SCH* viii, p. 77. But would they stop short at moral exhortation, in fact? (Miss Bolton, in a private letter, noting their rate of literacy.) For aristocratic Humiliati, see Bolton, in *SCH* viii, p. 79; B. Bolton, *The Medieval Reformation* (London, 1983) (concise, wide-ranging survey; Humiliati: pp. 63–6); K. V. Selge, 'Humiliaten', *TRE* xv (Berlin and New York, 1987), pp. 691–6. I owe a copy to the author. On poverty as the mark of the 'new man' in the twelfth century, see B. Bolton, '*Paupertas Christi*: old wealth and new poverty in the twelfth century', *SCH* xiv, pp. 95–103.

Catholic poor'.[6] Bernard Prim, also a Waldensian from Languedoc who came over in 1210, was given similarly sympathetic treatment. As with Durand's group, the basis for his reconciliation with the Church was the profession of faith which Henri de Marcy had imposed on Valdes, with the addition of certain points on the sacraments and the repudiation of the right of women to preach.[7] The important difference with the case of Valdes was that, the repudiation of errors once completed, preaching was permitted. Durand and Prim, after they had submitted, were allowed to continue essentially the same way of life as poor wandering preachers.

These decisions in effect detached a small group of moderates from the movement of Waldensian preachers and rescued many Humiliati for the Church. For a moment it might well have seemed that Innocent's policy was going to have more far-reaching effects, as a hundred Waldensian preachers in Italy after Durand's conversion asked, under conditions, for acceptance by the Church;[8] but we do not know what happened to them, and after 1212 we hear no more of such requests. Innocent's sympathetic approach could only work if reconciling moves came from the Waldensians themselves: the bulk of the movement made no further approaches to Rome, but attempted to recover unity amongst themselves.

At first, in the aftermath of the Waldensian split of 1205,[9] the situation remained confused. Donatist views gained ground amongst the Poor Lombards, who were in a strong majority in Italy; yet members of the Lyonist wing, who were faithful to the tradition of Valdes, did not disappear altogether. A reaction amongst some of the Italian membership in the direction of moderation took place after a council of the Lombards in the period 1208–9, when a hen upset the chalice as John de Ronco celebrated the eucharist, and women trampled on the spilt wine. There was a split. Some indignant brothers declared, in reaction against such disorder, that the sacrament should only be administered by Roman priests.[10]

Contacts between Lombards and Lyonists over the Alps were not totally severed. In time the deaths of John de Ronco and Valdes appeared to remove personal obstacles to reunion, and a last attempt, possibly emanating from the Waldensians then feeling the effects of persecution in Languedoc, was made to bring the two wings together. Six representatives from each side met in conference near Bergamo in 1218 to thrash out their differences. The Lyonists were ready to make generous concessions on the issues which had kept them apart, allowing provosts and ministers for the sacrament to be appointed for life if the Lombards insisted, and dropping Valdes's rigid opposition to their arrangements on manual labour. The conference broke on the Lombards' Donatism, and the issue, subordinate but of high emotional significance, of

---

[6] *EFV*, pp. 129–36; *WEH*, pp. 222–6, Selge, *Waldenser* I, pp.193–225; Thouzellier, *Catharisme et Valdéisme*, 2nd edn, pp. 215–26; for status, cf. Maccarrone, in *RSCI* XVI (1962), pp. 29–72.

[7] *EFV*, pp. 136–40; Thouzellier, *Catharisme et Valdéisme*, pp. 232–7; Selge, *Waldenser* I, pp. 188–93.

[8] Ibid., pp. 204–5. Pou y Marti argues for a disturbing effect of Poor Catholics in Catalonia in H. E. Lee, M. Reeves and G. Silano, ed., *Western Mediterranean Prophecy: The School of Joachim of Fiore and the Fourteenth-Century Breviloquium* (Toronto, 1989).

[9] Above, p. 76.

[10] Selge, *Waldenser* I, p. 307.

FIGURE I   Pope Innocent III, from a thirteenth-century fresco at the Sacro Speco, Subiaco.
Photograph: Deutsche Fotothek, Dresden.

the salvation of Valdes and his companion Vivet. The Lyonists insisted that they were in paradise; the Lombards answered coldly that they would be if they had satisfied God for their sins before their deaths. Eucharistic beliefs formed the doctrinal breaking-point, the Lombards making merit, not office, the crucial questions for the validity of the sacrament and, in our source for the conference, a letter of information to adherents of the Poor Lombards in Germany, massing authorities in Scripture and the Fathers for their point of view, their opponents standing on the Catholic belief that the sacrament was valid only if the celebrant were a priest, whatever his life might be.[11]

Two rival traditions had evolved. The Lyonist wing supporting Valdes in 1218 had still not broken irrevocably with the Church. They stood firm on the

[11] *EFV*, pp. 169–83, tr. *WEH*, pp. 278–89; Selge, *Waldenser* I, pp. 305–12, Böhmer, in *RPTK* xx, cols 810–11. I accept Germany as the destination, on the evidence of the title subsequently added to the document. Text in A. Patschovsky and K. V. Selge, ed., *Quellen zur Geschichte der Waldenser* (Gütersloh, 1973), pp. 30–43 (definitive edn).

belief that their preachers had a direct mission from God, and they rejected the Church's excommunication. They did not press on, as the Lombards did, to subject all practices of the Church to stern examination in the light of Scripture and the pattern of the early Church. If critical of the Roman hierarchy and priesthood, they had still not unchurched them. The Lombards had, and pressed the others to do the same.

The wings never came together again after the failure at Bergamo, though some sporadic and not wholly hostile relations between them continued, aided perhaps by the fact that the missionary endeavours of the two wings tended to lie in different regions.[12] The moderates did not return to the Church, and voluntary reconciliations, such as those of Durand and Prim, are not recorded again; instead, persecution encouraged more out-and-out opposition. The chance of reunion with the Church seemed to have disappeared.

The success of the Waldensian groups who returned to the Church was partial. Prim's group brought to the service of the Church an apostolate based on a poor life, with exhortation and some recourse to manual labour; the Poor Catholics under Durand pursued a more learned mission, with a hospital at Elne in Roussillon which also formed a centre for the production of antiheretical writings. The hospital had fifty beds and catered for 'those in distress, the poor, the sick, abandoned children, poor women in childbirth and the provision of clothing in winter'. There was a division of function between those who preached and the converted laity who looked after the sick.[13] Durand, a precise polemist who painstakingly followed the convolutions of developing dualist doctrine and over-matched his opponents in knowledge of Scripture, worked on, growing in stature between his Waldensian *Liber antiheresis* and his Catholic *Contra Manicheos*.[14] Both groups had the advantage over heretics of realizing in their own persons the apostolic life of poor preaching; but they were unable to break down the hostility of the bishops or to gain a major popular success, and in the perspective of thirteenth-century Church history they appear as imperfect sketches of the successful mendicant orders. The reconciled Humiliati earned the praise of James of Vitry in 1216 for their preaching against heresy in Milan; he knew of some 150 houses of theirs.[15] Their success was of its time; the Humiliati remained exclusively Italian, and they did not go on to form an order of first-class importance. The breakthrough for the harnessing of the apostolic life of poor, wandering preaching to the mission of the Church came only when two saints were able to make use of the fertile climate of opinion and Innocent's will to experiment.

[12] Böhmer, *RPTK* xx, col. 811.

[13] Elne, in Roussillon, then ruled by the kings of Aragon, diocese in province of Narbonne. On the school, see Thouzellier, *Catharisme et Valdéisme*, pp. 269–84 and references; for the quotation and information on the hospital, see Biller, in *SCH* xix, p. 60.

[14] *Liber*, text: Selge, *Waldenser* ii; analysis: Thouzellier, pp. 60–79, implications: Selge, *Waldenser* i, ch. 1; *Contra Manicheos*, in Thouzellier, *Un Somme anti-Cathare: Le 'Liber contra Manicheos' de Durand de Huesca* (Louvain, 1964); reviewed by J. Jolivet in *RHR* clxix (1966), pp. 77–80; analysis in Thouzellier, *Catharisme et Valdéisme*, pp. 303–73 (authorities cited on pp. 375–424). Pioneer study, including other themes, A. Dondaine, 'Durand de Huesca et la polémique anti-Cathare', *AFP* xxix (1959), pp. 228–76. R. H. and M. A. Rouse, 'The Schools and the Waldensians: a new work of Durand of Huesca', in S. Waugh, ed., *Christendom and its Discontents* (forthcoming) illustrates Durand's high contacts and readiness to use new techniques. I am indebted to Professor Rouse.

[15] *Lettres*, ed. Huygens, p. 73 ('cl congregationes conventuales').

In Languedoc in 1206, when a mission of Cistercians, earnest but hampered by official status and entourage, failed to make progress in a preaching drive, the Castilian bishop Diego of Osma and his subprior Dominic hit on the idea of preaching in poverty in accord with the gospel texts, and on terms of equality with their enemies the Cathars. Dominic, constantly encouraged and aided by Innocent, established himself in Fanjeaux, in the centre of the Cathar country, and founded a house nearby at Prouille for women and girls rescued from the Cathars.[16] In 1215 he moved to Toulouse; in 1216–17 he obtained recognition for his order of preachers, known to history as Dominican friars – in effect a special development of the way of life of the Augustinian canons to whom Dominic belonged. Meeting a widespread demand, they rapidly grew into a large international order dedicated to the preaching of the faith, and including in its aims the confutation of heresy.[17] They affected the whole religious landscape, setting new standards in preaching, entering the universities and playing a major part in the development of scholasticism, bringing their piety and zeal to bear on the towns short of pastoral care, where heresy found adherents, and deploying against Cathars and Waldensians the silent but most effective argument of their own observance of apostolic life. Determined papal support, good planning by Dominic and his successors, and the Languedoc emergency all helped the young order to avoid suffocation by conservatism, though opposition by the secular clergy to the rights of the friars to preach, to hear confessions and to intervene in the parishes long remained a factor in Church life.

Five years before the fourth Lateran Council, at which St Dominic's plans were discussed, St Francis of Assisi, with eleven companions, asked at Rome for confirmation of a way of life of the most extreme poverty blended with preaching based on the gospels, especially the account of the sending of the Seventy.[18] Francis's first rule consisted largely of texts, and was not based on an existing rule at all; moreover, the renunciations he asked for seemed beyond human powers. The pope seems to have hesitated, but was persuaded by the argument that to turn down Francis's request would be tantamount to saying that the gospel itself could not be observed. He met the request by the unprecedented course of giving Francis's way of life an oral confirmation; a right to preach was granted to Francis, and through him to his followers, on terms resembling those given to the Humiliati. The group, at first a lay association, was allowed to preach penance – to engage in moral exhortation rather than the preaching of doctrine that was reserved to clergy. Rapid growth in numbers, contemporary needs and papal policies soon turned them into a great international order of friars, clerical and often learned, with full rights of preaching, and many resemblances to the Dominicans.

St Francis himself hardly referred to heresy at all. His Testament has an observation on binding suspect members of the order so as to bring them

---

[16] Vicaire, *St Dominic*; *CF* i; J. Guiraud, *Cartulaire de Notre Dame de Prouille, précédé d'une étude sur l'Albigéisme languedocien au xiie et xiiie siècles* i–ii (Paris, 1907). M-H. Vicaire, *Dominique et ses prêcheurs* (Paris and Fribourg, 1977).

[17] For introduction, see D. Knowles, *Religious Orders in England* i (Cambridge, 1950), pp. 146–62.

[18] Ibid., pp. 114–26; Matt. 10: 7–13. See below, ch. 11.

safely to the cardinal protector. Etienne de Bourbon records a meeting with a heretic who complained to him of the misdeeds of a concubinary priest. Francis's response was simply to kiss the priest's hand in token of reverence for his office.[19] Preaching for him was a spontaneous overflow of the interior life; unlike Dominic, he had no aim of confuting heresy specifically, but thought of his order as auxiliaries to the priesthood, preaching penance and thereby, no doubt, recalling men from error. Circumstances changed this, and the Franciscans came to play an important part directly against heresy through preaching, the intellectual refutation of error, the writing of treatises, and a full apostolate in the towns, made more effective through the institution of the third order. But their most distinctive contribution lay in the revolution they helped to bring about in popular piety through their stress on the incidents of Christ's life and His sufferings, and their acceptance of the created world and joy in nature. It was the indirect answer to Cathar rejection of the world and their non-human Jesus.[20]

In the problem area of Languedoc, the centres of heresy once discerned, Innocent characteristically began seeking solutions at two levels simultaneously. One was the fostering of religious revival through preaching, as shown in his advice to his Cistercian legates 'to proceed in such a way that the simplicity of your attitude is clear to the eyes of all',[21] and in his encouragement of the mission of Diego and St Dominic; the other was the application of pressure to the unwilling episcopate of the region and the leading nobles who would not put heresy down. The second came to dominate the first after his legate, Pierre de Castelnau, was assassinated in 1208 in circumstances which threw suspicion on Count Raymond VI of Toulouse. Innocent called a crusade, and so put into the field north French barons eager for Raymond's lands.[22] At the end of the pontificate Raymond stood dispossessed of nearly all his holdings apart from those in Provence, and the bulk of the episcopate had been deposed and replaced by others who, Innocent hoped, would be more fervent against heresy. Yet the effects of the war were to ally, for the moment, local patriotism and interests entirely with the cause of heresy. Innocent gave a full legal justification for the crusade, based especially on his own decretal of 1199, *Vergentis in senium*, with its assimilation of heresy to the crime in Roman law of *lèse-majesté*, with

[19] L. Lemmens, *Testimonia Minora s.xiii de S. Francisco Assisi* (Quaracchi, 1926), pp. 93–4. I owe the reference to Dr R. B. Brooke.

[20] E. Delaruelle, 'L'influence de saint François d'Assise sur la piété populaire', in *Relazioni* III, pp. 449–66; Manselli, *Eresia*, p. 270.

[21] *PL* CCXV, col. 360; tr. Vicaire, *St Dominic*, p. 87.

[22] M. Julien, 'Pierre de Castelnau: un Légat autoritaire', *CEC* IX (1958–9), pp. 195–202, Wakefield *Heresy, Crusade*, ch. 6, and bibliography, Strayer, *Albigensian Crusades*; P. Belperron, *La Croisade contre les Albigeois et l'Union du Languedoc á la France (1209–1249)* (Paris, 1942) (north French bias); A. P. Evans, 'The Albigensian Crusade', in K. M. Setton, *A History of the Crusades* II: *The Later Crusades, 1189–1311*, ed. R. L. Wolff and H. W. Hazard (Philadelphia, 1962), pp. 277–324; *CF* IV (esp. for ideas); comment in Thouzellier, *Catharisme et Valdéisme*, p. 269, n. 1, B. Hamilton, *The Albigensian Crusade* (London, 1974) (Historical Association pamphlet G. 85); J. Sumption, *The Albigensian Crusade* (London, 1978) (vivid account; ch, 2 is outdated); M. Roquebert, *L'Epopée Cathare* I: *L'Invasion* (Toulouse, 1970), II: *La Dépossession* (1977), III: *Les Lys et la croix* (1986), IV: *Mourir à Montségur* (1989); *La Nuit des Amis de Dieu* (forthcoming).

concomitant penalties of confiscation of goods;[23] but he was unable to keep control once the crusade was launched, or to maintain canonical procedure. The lands of Raymond VI were confiscated without any trial taking place, and other southern nobles were arbitrarily dispossessed. The war had its own momentum. The champion of the Church, Simon de Montfort, was a fine general who lacked the gifts of a politician. Innocent was not master of the spirits he had conjured up.

In the long term the crusade helped to create a new political situation dominated by the north French, in which effective persecution became possible. But there were side-effects. Crusade was a blunt instrument. When it was used again to eradicate dualists in Bosnia in the pontificate of Gregory IX, it actually increased their security in the land.[24] The bishop of Bremen called a crusade in 1234 against the *Stedinger*, peasants who opposed his rule and refused tithes, as though they were heretics, and in so doing showed how easily the mechanism could be corrupted.[25] Moreover, it will always be open to doubt whether such an application of force to the situation in Languedoc was required, and whether Innocent, distant from the scene, was misled on the true character and extent of heresy in the Midi, especially by the authoritarian Pierre de Castelnau.[26] Not many years were given to preaching. Dominic had few helpers and only the one religious house at Prouille in the early days.

The active pontificate of Innocent III left a body of case-law, precedent and legislation for dealing with heresy which supplemented and improved, but did not fundamentally change, the episcopal inquisition as prescribed by *Ad abolendam*. The influence of the bishops was weighty at the council and tended to conservatism. Exhortation, the use of legates with overriding powers – even deposition of unworthy bishops, as in Languedoc – gingered up episcopal prosecution of heresy, or alternatively tempered its crudities. For the Patrimony Innocent decreed in 1207 that all the goods of heretics should be confiscated and their homes destroyed. At the end, in the fourth Lateran Council canons summed up existing legislation, and a dogmatic constitution, mainly anti-Cathar and based closely on the profession of faith presented by Henri de Marcy to Valdes, gave a concise picture of the errors to be suppressed. The pope's own use of procedure *per inquisitionem*, in which the responsible judge carried on both investigation and judgement, and started an inquiry on the basis of mere *fama*, was part of his passionate will to correct the abuses of churchmen. Simplicity of procedure aimed at short-circuiting the delays of the accusatorial process, and the use of *fama* at breaking through

---

[23] Maisonneuve, *Etudes*, pp. 156–8, R. Foreville, 'Innocent III et la Croisade des Albigeois', in *CF* IV, pp. 184–217, Thouzellier, *Catharisme et Valdéisme*, pp. 136, 146, 155–6; Kolmer, *Vulpes*, pp. 35–41, noting how Innocent's decision on confiscation outruns Gratian; see influence of fourth century *Lex quisquis*; correction of Ullmann, p. 40, n. 27; events, Sumption, *Albigensian Crusade*. I have not been able to use H. Roscher, *Papst Innozenz III und die Kreuzzüge* (Göttingen, 1969).

[24] Lambert, *Medieval Heresy*, 1st edn, pp. 142–50; J. V. A. Fine, Jr, *The Bosnian Church: A New Interpretation* (Boulder, 1975) (full analysis; hypothesis that the Church itself was not heretical).

[25] Grundmann, *Ketzergeschichte*, p. 39; Lea, *Inquisition* III, pp. 182–6.

[26] Delaruelle, in *AM* LXXII (1960), pp. 149–67; contrast contemporary plea for force in treatise attributed to Ermengaud de Béziers, ed. Dondaine, *AFP* XXIX (1959), p. 271, *WEH*, pp. 230–5; analysis, Thouzellier, *Catharisme et Valdéisme*, pp. 284–92.

barriers of secrecy in clerical corporations. But, though its aim was to detect simony and moral failing, not heresy, the utility of the procedure was manifest for heresy cases. Innocent's moral investigations marked a stage on the road to the development of the inquisition commissions of Gregory IX.[27]

An intellectual heresy, the trinitarian views of a Calabrian abbot, Joachim of Fiore, was also condemned at the council, albeit with a stress on Joachim's own submission to the papacy in his lifetime.[28] Joachim's error was contained in a *libellus*, now lost, in which he attacked the trinitarian teaching of Peter Lombard, author of the authoritative textbook, the 'Sentences', and a leading influence at the Paris theological school, to which Innocent himself had belonged. Joachim's own major literary activity, in which he applied traditional methods of exegesis to Scripture in order to understand the patterns of history and to foresee the future, was not condemned, although, amongst much that was orthodox, it contained a potentially subversive notion of a coming third age of the Holy Spirit, that would in some sense supersede the arrangements of the present Age of the Son.[29] A group of supporters of Amaury of Bène, a Paris master who died in about 1206, had been condemned in 1210, some to death, others to perpetual imprisonment; another master, Godin, was burnt about two years later.[30] Amaury's corpse was exhumed from consecrated ground; the sect was virtually annihilated.

Amaury, a brilliant speculator, had been influenced in a pantheistic direction by his reading of John Scotus Eriguena, the ninth-century theologian, and elements in his teaching had created scandal during his lifetime. His followers, often intellectuals themselves, seem to have taken his views further. They were accused of holding an amalgam of heretical beliefs, pantheist, antinomian, gnostic, libertine. A bowdlerization of the *Pater Noster* was attributed to them, designed to play down phrases awkward to their tenets.[31] They were said to believe in their own sinlessness and to have

[27] Mansi, XXII, col. 982, *EFV*, pp. 158–63; tr. in *DTC* I, p. 683–6; Dondaine, in *AFP* XVI (1946), pp. 191–235; Innocent's policy: Kolmer, *Vulpes*, pp. 35–63; inquisitorial procedure: pp. 56–63.

[28] Mansi, XXII, cols 982–6, M. Reeves, *The Influence of Prophecy in the later Middle Ages: A Study in Joachimism* (Oxford, 1969) (the fundamental study of Joachim and his influence), pp. 28–36;B. McGinn, *The Calabrian Abbot: Joachim of Fiore in the History of Western Thought* (New York and London, 1985) (valuable in relating Joachim to the body of Christian exegesis and apocalyptic; summary on historical context, pp. 1–47); extracts: B. McGinn, *Visions of the End: Apocalyptic Traditions in the Middle Ages* (New York, 1979), pp. 126–41; K. V. Selge, 'L'origine delle opere di Gioacchino dà Fiore', *L'Attesa della fine dei tempi nel medioevo*, ed. O. Capitanei and J. Miethke (Bologna, 1990), pp. 87–130 (establishes sequence of works).

[29] Definitive exposition is in Reeves, *Prophecy*, pp. 16–27, 135–44; cf. an illuminating analysis by the same writer, 'The *Liber Figurarum* of Joachim of Fiore', *MRS* II (1950), pp. 57–81; M. W. Bloomfield, 'Recent scholarship on Joachim of Fiore and his influence', *Prophecy and Millenarianism*, ed. A. Williams (Harlow, 1980), pp. 21–52 at p. 27, notes how Joachim gives the New Testament 'an inner future spiritual dimension'.

[30] *RB*, pp. 355–73, M. Th. d'Alverny, 'Un fragment du procès des Amauriciens', *AHDLMA* XXVI (1951), pp. 325–36, sources tr. in *WEH*, pp. 258–63. Bène (sometimes Bènes or Bena) was a parish in the diocese of Chartres. All previous work is superseded by G. Dickson, 'The burning of the Amalricians', *JEH* XL (1989), pp. 347–69.

[31] 'Beau Pere qui estes in celz et en la terre, confermez vestre nom en nos cors; denez nes vostre regne; vestre volente seit faite en terre si come au cel; denez nos que mesters nos est a chascun et chascun jer aus armes; pardonez nos nos mesfez si com nos pardonom a austrui; gardez nos des enginz au de de (able?); delivrez nos de toz maus.' D'Alverny, *AHDLMA* XXVI. Here we may detect a pantheistic note ('in celz et en la terre'), the replacement of material bread by vague needs, the transformation of Evil into accidental evils.

rejected the sacraments – which was all the more troubling to ecclesiastical authority then concerned with the sacramental life of the Church and anxious to popularize the practice of confession.[32] The crisis of Amaury's death and the loss of his leadership seems to have galvanized them into becoming an active missionary sect. Perhaps at the same time, they became convinced that an Age of the Spirit was at hand, of which they were the forerunners, when all men would become 'spiritual', as they were: it sounds like a crude version of Joachim's Age of the Spirit.[33]

The pantheistic views of Amaury were condemned in the same canon of the council as Joachim's trinitarian exposition; on some other occasion in the pontificate Ortlieb of Strasburg was also condemned for having taught that man must keep himself from all external things and only follow the Spirit in him,[34] and in 1210 a work of David Dinant imbued with pantheism was also burnt. From the evidence we have there appears to have been some efflorescence of 'spiritualizing' heresy cut short under Innocent. Of Joachim, however, more was to be heard.[35]

Innocent's successor, Honorius III, at once less resolute and less original, nevertheless continued to build up antiheretical legislation by ensuring that laws on the duties of secular powers to repress heresy and aid Church authorities were made part of secular codes. The Emperor Frederick II made such laws part of imperial legislation – it was originally his *quid pro quo* for coronation by the pope – and made burning the punishment for the recalcitrant.[36]

But the major innovation came under Gregory IX when, after some experiments with various procedures and after realizing the inadequacies of episcopal inquisitions, he resorted to special agents equipped with full powers from the papacy to hunt out heretics. In 1231 he issued a general commission to the Dominican prior of Regensburg, and in 1233–4 made arrangements for a staff of such agents to be given powers in Languedoc   They showed themselves so much more efficient than the bishops that their inquisition became the normal means of extirpating heresy. The episcopal inquisition tended in most lands affected by heresy to become of secondary significance. So the papal inquisition of the Middle Ages was born.

It was the last move required to implement all the existing laws against heresy. The agents so appointed supplied the deficiencies of the bishops, for

[32] A point made by Dickson, *JEH* XL, p. 361; p. 355 corrects d'Alverny on intellectual level.

[33] Grundmann's judgement in *RB*, p. 365, and *Ketzergeschichte*, p. 43. I follow Dickson's judgement (above, n. 30) on the likely link between the aftermath of Amaury's death and the development of the idea of the new age.

[34] W. Preger, *Geschichte der deutschen Mystik* I (Leipzig, 1874), p. 468, l. 78. On Ortliebians, see A. Fössel, *Die Ortlieber. Eine Spiritualistische Ketzergruppe im 13. Jahrhundert*, Hanover, 1993. See Leff, *Heresy* II, p. 309; on all these episodes, cf. Grundmann, *Ketzergeschichte*, pp. 41–2; Neoplatonic background in G. Leff, *Medieval Thought* (London, 1958).

[35] Below, pp. 194–205.

[36] Maisonneuve, *Etudes*, pp. 243–57.

[37] Y. Dossat, *Les Crises de l'inquisition toulousaine au XIIIe siècle (1233–1273)* (Bordeaux, 1959), ch. 5, see review: B. Guillemain, *AM* LXXIII (1961), pp. 106–111; Lea, *Inquisition* I, ch. 7 *et passim* (still of value); chs 7–14 repr., with introduction by W. Ullmann, in H. C. Lea, *The Inquisition of the Middle Ages: Its Organization and Operation* (London, 1963). B. Hamilton, *The Medieval Inquisition* (London, 1981) (surveys fundamental assumptions; relationship between role of confessor and inquisitor should be noted, pp. 49–59); survey of literature in Kolmer, *Vulpes*, pp. 13–22. Further bibliography below, p. 176, n. 1.

they were appointed for the one purpose of putting down heresy, and were not distracted by other business. Their commissions to act as Inquisitors were of long duration; appointees could thus build up knowledge and gain a professional's expertise. Most commonly Dominicans were appointed to the office by arrangement with their superiors: they brought to the task the dedication of men under vows belonging to a highly trained order with a special vocation against heresy. Franciscans, more rarely appointed, had similar dedication. Continuity of record was established. Each inquisitor kept registers, with the depositions of suspects, which could be handed on to his successors or used as a basis for further inquiries at a later date. The records were a threat to everyone who had once been interrogated, and even to the relatives and descendants of suspects, against whom a record of conviction or complicity could be invoked. With such data at his disposal a medieval inquisitor had resources comparable to that of a modern police officer, ever ready to check and cross-check information. One full confession by a heretic of wide acquaintance could uncover a multiplicity of leads to his fellows; the practice of granting a period of grace at the beginning of an inquisition in which punishments were waived for those who gave information, and the insistence that only full confession of all available facts gave proof of repentance were calculated to produce a free flow of incriminating details. An international body, the inquisition could link up actions against heresy in different lands, and try to prevent the escape of refugees; flight at an early stage of proceedings or while awaiting trial remained one of the few effective means of avoiding successful prosecution.

As the customs and procedures of the inquisitors developed, so in time a class of writing often known as 'inquisitors' handbooks' came into existence, assembling past experience on heretics and their beliefs, and giving information on the customs inquisitors used and the regulations under which they worked.[38] In Languedoc a working knowledge of Catharism under a few simple heads had become the common knowledge of clergy habitually in contact with the heretics, and this knowledge passed over to the thirteenth-century inquisitors; in Italy, ever more sophisticated, inquisitors tended to have a more speculative interest in the origins and nature of the heresies they were dealing with. There was in any case a general rise in the number and standards of the treatises which described and refuted heresy, a product of the new scholasticism and of the concern of churchmen over the problem; these contributed to the pool of information available to the inquisition; in turn, further treatises were also influenced by the habits of mind of the inquisitors themselves.

The inquisitor was the heir to the body of legislation against heretics and their supporters which reached back to *Ad abolendam* as well as to the enactments passed after 1231 in his favour. It was a formidable structure. Ecclesiastical law on heresy was keeping pace with developments in civil law,

---

[38] A. Dondaine, 'Le manuel de l'inquisiteur (1230–1330)', *AFP* xvii (1947), pp. 85–194, Borst, *Katharer*, pp. 21–7. Polemical literature (see below, pp. 177–8) in Dondaine, 'Nouvelles sources de l'histoire doctrinale du Néo-Manichéisme au Moyen Age', *RSPT* xxviii (1939), pp. 465–88; W. L. Wakefield, 'Notes on some antiheretical writings of the thirteenth century', *FS* xxvii (1967), pp. 285–321 (demonstrates extent of casual plagiarizing). On origins and working of the inquisition, see P. Segl, *Die Anfänge der Inquisition im Mittelalter*, Köln, Weimar, Wien, 1993 (conference articles).

where there was also a strong trend to the use of the inquisitorial rather than the accusatorial procedure. That procedure was ideally suited for the uncovering of heresy, which was an elusive crime. Under it any suspect could be summoned and put under oath to declare his participation in forbidden rites and meetings, his contacts with heretics, or any relevant information at all about his beliefs and his movements; from 1252 by a decision of Innocent IV, who improved the detailed workings of the inquisition, torture might be used on him.[39] It was intended that the instruments should be applied by the secular power, and not the inquisitor's staff; but four years after Innocent's bull his successor, Alexander IV, permitted inquisitors to evade the restriction. The subject could thus be compelled to incriminate himself. Heavy penalties compelled suspects or witnesses to appear and to answer; others enforced the aid of the secular power, whenever required, to ensure his attendance and to assist with, or be responsible for his or her punishment if convicted. Rights to the property of convicted heretics also helped to secure the willing support of the secular power. Fautorship of heresy was a grave crime, and penalties could be incurred by a mere obstruction of the inquisitor in his duty.

In the determination that nothing should stand in the way of speedy and efficient action against heresy, the checks designed in canon law to ensure fair trial, the validity of evidence, and the impartiality of the judge were all set aside. In the last resort the inquisitor, who combined the role of judge and of priest dealing with a penitent, held near-unfettered powers over the suspects who came before him. At his discretion – and the scrutiny of his sentences required under the regulations tended to be slight and formal – was an array of penalties stretching from fines, pilgrimages and the wearing of yellow crosses on the clothing, to imprisonment up to and including life and burning, as well as sentences of confiscation, destruction of dwellings, and attendant disqualifications from office-holding affecting descendants.[40]

If the clergy and secular authorities did give wholehearted support to the inquisition, and its agents were given time to conduct thorough and repeated investigations, it was difficult to see that, armed with these powers, they could fail to eliminate a popular heresy.

The innovations of these decades permanently altered the circumstances under which the Church met the challenge of heresy. The initiative passed to the Church. The enclaves of orthodox Europe, where in practice heresy had enjoyed a measure of toleration through ecclesiastical inertia or the anticlericalism of the secular power, were gradually eliminated. The decisions taken early in the century marked an end for the view, still sporadically expressed earlier on, that gave precedence to peaceful conversion and counter-preaching over repression. It was accepted that force was the correct answer, to be applied vigorously, and an apparatus was now in existence that

---

[39] Maisonneuve, *Etudes*, p. 312. Use of torture in secular courts, mentioned by Innocent IV to justify use by inquisition, developed as the ordeal became discredited, R. C. Van Caenegem, *La Preuve dans le Droit du Moyen Age occidental: Rapport de Synthèse* (Brussels, 1965) (*Recueils de la Société Jean Bodin* XVII), p. 739 and n. I owe the reference to Mr A. Murray; E. Peters, *Torture* (Oxford, 1985), pp. 64–5.

[40] See Lea, *Inquisition* I, chs 12, 13; Dossat, *Crises*, pp. 247–68; articles in *CF* VI. I have been unable to consult W. Ullmann, 'The defence of the accused in the medieval inquisition', *Irish Ecclesiastical Record*, 5th ser. LXXIII (1950), pp. 481–9; on it, however, see Wakefield, *Heresy, Crusade*, p. 192.

legitimized its use and defined the offences against which it was to be employed. The phase of uncertainty that had characterized the eleventh and twelfth centuries now finally came to an end.

The counteraction of the Church affected the manifestations of heresy. In place of the open preaching and agitation of the twelfth century, we meet more secret missionizing and underground conspiracy. The emergence of the friars met for a time the demand for poverty and wandering preaching in an orthodox context. The development of theology and the diffusion of information about heresy enabled the seeker after truth to know better where he stood. The distinction between heretical sects and Catholic orders grew clearer.

Yet all was not progress: counter-attack against heresy was not the same thing as fundamental reform. Innocent III had always stressed the intimate connection between heresy and the failings of the clergy, and in some ways it was easier to welcome innovations in the religious life and to legislate for more efficient repression of heresy than to make reform prevail against deep-seated abuses or deficiencies in the Church. Grave problems connected with the numbers, selection and training of the clergy remained. The difficulty of the wealth of the Church continued, and was basic. The reforms initiated at the fourth Lateran Council had but limited success; response to legislation varied widely in different lands, stretching all the way from the English Church, where the council was the prelude to something of a golden age with a plethora of scholars and saints on the episcopal bench, to the churches of Spain, obsessed with the crusade in the Iberian peninsula, where the effect was non-existent. Innocent's own will to experiment with forms of dedicated life met an apparent check in canon thirteen of the council, which forbade new religious orders. Although its meaning was less restrictive than has been assumed,[41] nevertheless, given episcopal conservatism and the decisions of later popes and councils, the net effect was to make it harder for the Church to accept fresh religious movements in the future, and Innocent's immediate notion of communities of clergy for preaching and ministry under the direction of bishops was stillborn.

In the political sphere, Innocent's design for a settlement of the old problem of papal–imperial relations and the security of papal lands in Italy failed to hold: a subsequent struggle for power with Frederick II overshadowed the pontificates of Gregory IX and Innocent IV, began to tarnish a traditional focus for lay piety through the misuse of crusades launched against the Hohenstaufen, and led the very popes who did much to raise the efficiency of prosecution of heresy, as we have seen, to restrain their agents wherever disturbances caused by the pursuit of heretics led to the risk of losing allies against Frederick.

The heavy conflict with the Cathars was not brought to a successful conclusion until the early fourteenth century.[42] Friars, inquisition, lay confraternities, the development of Catholic piety, and rising standards of education, together with the internal dissensions of the heretics, combined to bring them down, but only after great efforts had been expended. The Waldensians, though by and large less hard pressed than the Cathars, came

[41] Leff, *Heresy* I, p. 15, needs to be modified by Maccarrone, in *RSCI* XVI (1962), pp. 29–72.
[42] Below, pp. 125–46.

under heavy fire in the lands of their origin on each side of the Alps, but compensated in some degree for their losses by wide extension of missions in German-speaking lands to the east and by finding refuge from persecution, both geographically and psychologically, through the erection of a camouflage of subterfuge.[43] These heretics lasted beyond the thirteenth century into the age of the Reformation. Cathars and Waldensians, the most notable of the surviving twelfth-century heretics, now demand separate treatment, and will be discussed in chapters of their own, with the intention of showing both the attractions of their life and beliefs that gave them vitality and drew in recruits, and also how each of the heresies fared under the stiffer pressures of a resurgent Catholicism.

New developments in Church life did not, however, bring a final solution to the problem of heresy. Reform by means of centralization and the growth of canon law raised standards in the Church; but, carried on against a background of inadequate communications and central bureaucracy, coupled with the strain of papal taxation and the Italian conflicts, it created simultaneously a ground swell of opposition, the potential seedbed of heresy. Above all, stress on law, when it was unfertilized by religious sentiment, aided the growth of formalism. It was no chance that 'spiritualizing' heresies, with varied roots but having in common a claim that their adherents were more 'spiritual' than their fellows, and a desire for escape from the routine of the medieval Church, its hierarchy and sacraments, grew more common as the thirteenth century wore on. What is noteworthy is that the heresies sprang more commonly from inner circles of Church life, and were not the heresies of 'outsiders', as were those of the Cathars and Waldensians.[44]

The very instruments of the Catholic resurgence that won back the initiative for the Church began to create heresy. The Franciscan friars, subjected to great pressures in their swift development from a small brotherhood to a large and powerful order with a leading intellectual role, fell into difficulties, growing in intensity from the time of the Council of Lyons in 1274 and issuing, first, in internal rebellion and then in true heresy, which was spread to the laity through the third order.[45] The inquisition's techniques, directed by the papacy and higher churchmen, could and did make heresy where none existed, imposing beliefs on victims who did not hold them, or, through interrogations under torture, exaggerating and distorting the unorthodox views they in fact held. So some disquieting features in lay mysticism and the views of a few deviant individuals, handled with prejudice, were blown up into the supposed heresy of the Free Spirit in the early fourteenth century.[46]

How these new heresies came into existence or were artificially created will be discussed after an analysis of the position of the Cathars and Waldensians.

---

[43] Below, ch. 8.

[44] Compare the analysis of social class among Cathar adherents below (pp. 111–17) and among the Waldensians (pp. 168–71). There were few clergy among the Cathars, and hardly any of high rank. From the later thirteenth century Waldensianism is pre-eminently the religion of the small man.

[45] Below, ch. 11.

[46] Below, pp. 181–8.

7

The Cathars

Catharism appeared to be the most powerful heresy of the thirteenth century.[1] Reaction against it by leading churchmen helped to change patterns of Church life. More than any other group, the Cathar heretics inspired alarm and hostility, and they stimulated the development of the inquisition; not only bishops, but also popular movements that were themselves under suspicion, the Waldensians and the Humiliati, felt the need to check their influence. A description has already been given of the factors in twelfth-century popular religion that favoured the rise of Catharism, and of the means whereby their early teachers found a platform for spreading their beliefs, blending their ascetic life with an existing movement for wandering preaching in poverty. A narrative account of twelfth-century heresy has described, in effect, the

---

[1] The traditional and substantial survey is Borst, *Katharer*, with historiography to 1950, pp. 1–58 (reviews: H. Grundmann, *HZ*cliii (1955), pp. 541–6), E. Dupré Theseider, *RSI* lxvii (1955), pp. 574–81, H. Sproemberg, *DLZ* Jhrg. 78, xii (1957), pp. 1095–104, R. W. Emery, *Speculum* xxix (1954), pp.537–8), E. Werner, *Byzantinoslavica* xvi (1955), pp. 135–44, and W. Ullman, *JEH* vii (1956), pp. 103–4); doctrinal analysis from standpoint of comparative religion in H. Söderberg, *La Religion des Cathares: Etudes sur le gnosticisme de la basse antiquité et du Moyen Age* (Uppsala, 1949) (a pioneer work, still with valuable historical references); bibliography to 1963 in Grundmann, *Ketzergeschichte*, pp. 22–8; reviews and articles in *Heresis* (publication of Centre National d'Etudes Cathares, Carcassonne); speculative survey in Manselli, *Eresia*; general account with Balkan and Byzantine heresy, M. Loos, *Dualist Heresy in the Middle Ages* (Prague, 1974); J. Duvernoy, *Le Catharisme* i: *La Religion des Cathares* (Toulouse, 1976), ii: *L'Histoire des Cathares* (1979), review of vol. i, C. Thouzellier, *RHR* cxciii (1978), pp. 218–25 (rejects hypothesis on origins); in ii, see esp. pt 3 on Midi, pp. 195–333, map, p. 233, with knowledge of mss, terrain; succinct survey on Italy, pp. 165–92 (viewpoint sympathetic to Catharism, more suspicious than Borst of orthodox sources); crisp, popular account, in sympathy with Duvernoy's style of interpretation. A. Brenon, *Le Vrai Visage du Catharisme* (Portet-sur-Garonne, 1988); many documents (badly edited) in I. von Döllinger, *Beiträge zur Sektengeschichte* (Munich, 1890), ii; translations from good texts in *WEH*, with analysis (the best single achievement of the book), summary, pp. 41–50. I am indebted to Dr Brenon for gifts of books and for advice. For work up to 1976, see *Historiographie du Catharisme*, *CF* xiv (1979). On Bogomils and Cathars, see Fichtenau, *Ketzer*, ch. 3, 6. G. Rottenwöhrer, *Der Katharismus* iv, 1–3, *Glaube and Theologie der Katharer*, Bad Honnef, 1993 is the definitive study of Cathar doctrine. L. Albaret, *Recherche sur l'Historiographie du Catharisme depuis 1970* (MA thesis; close analysis) is available at the Centre National, as above. I am grateful to the author for a copy. Y. Stoyanov, *The hidden tradition in Europe*, London, 1994, surveys beliefs and legends. M. Hanssler, *Katharismus in Südfraukreich*, Regensburg, 1991, re-examines statistics for late Catharism. M. D. Lambert. *The Cathars*, Oxford, 1998, forthcoming (comprehensive account).

external reasons for the growth of the heresy of Catharism. It should now be
balanced by an analytic account, intended to examine more closely internal
reasons for its success, taking evidence without strict attention to chronology
from varying points in time after the end of the first missionary phase in the
early 1160s. Italy and Languedoc will be the prime sources for examples, since
they were the regions where Catharism was most strongly established and
where evidence is readily available; though it should not be forgotten that
Cathars were apparently well represented in Germany until the persecutions
there in the 1220s and 1230s.

THE APPEAL OF CATHARISM

The status of the 'perfect' and the rites of the sect

Any attempt to explain the attractions of Catharism must take the 'perfect' as
a central theme. Numerically, these men and women, the adepts, were a small
elite. Although in the time of prosperity for the Cathars in parts of Languedoc,
when whole families became deeply committed and young adolescents
adopted the status, there would be quite heavy concentrations of the perfect,
as for example at Mirepoix, where there were said to be fifty houses of them,[2]
it was still true that the perfect were few in comparison with the other classes
of adherents, the believers and the more loosely attached sympathizers. On
this small body of the perfect in normal health the drawing power of the
movement depended and, when they fell both in numbers and in calibre, it
was doomed.

Entry to the status was conferred by the ceremony known as the
consolamentum,[3] which derived from the rite whereby the Bogomils admitted
their adepts.[4] A first part of the ritual, the delivery of the prayer, possibly once
corresponding to the *baptisma* of the Byzantine Bogomils, granted the
candidate the right to say the Lord's Prayer, the rank and file supporter, being

---

[2] Griffe, *Le Languedoc*, p. 150. 'usque ad quinquaginta' – a rhetorical phrase.

[3] For the *consolamentum* and other rituals, see Borst, *Katharer*, pp. 190–202, Söderberg, *Religion*, pp. 218–37, 250–6 (standpoint of comparative religion, not fully critical of individual sources); M. Cazeaux-Varagnac, 'Exposé sur la doctrine des Cathares', *Revue de Synthèse*, n.s. XXII, XXIII (1948), pp. 9–14 (underlying principles); introduction to J. Guiraud, *Cartulaire* I (lucid and still helpful, safer to use than his hurriedly written *Histoire de l'inquisition* I–II (Paris, 1935); on the distractions of Guiraud's career, see Y. Dossat's commemoration address (*CF* II, pp. 275–89). Latin text of *consolamentum* in A. Dondaine, *Un Traité neo-manichéen du XIIIe siècle: Le Liber de duobus principiis, suivi d'un fragment de rituel cathare* (Rome, 1939), pp. 151–65; Provençal in L. Clédat, *Le Nouveau Testament traduit au XIIIe siècle en langue provençale, suivi d'un rituel cathare* (Paris, 1887), pp. ix–xxvi; comparison in Dondaine, *Un Traité*, pp. 34–9, tr. with other rites in *WEH*, pp. 465–96; for a full and scholarly account of rituals, sources, criticisms of Church by Cathars, see G. Rottenwöhrer, *Der Katharismus* I (in 2), II (in 2) (Bad Honnef, 1982) (note value of MSS and printed references); G. Schmitz-Valckenberg, *Grundlehren katharischen Sekten des 13. Jahrhunderts* (Munich, Paderborn and Vienna, 1971) (concentrates on Moneta of Cremona); on contemporary terms for the perfect, see M.-H. Vicaire in A. Brenon and N. Gouzy eds., *Christianisme médiéval, mouvements dissidents et novateurs*, *Heresis* XIII, XIV (Villegly, Aude, 1989); Y. Hagman, 'Catharism, a medieval echo of Manichaeism or of primitive Christianity?' (Ph.D. Department of History of Religions, Lund, 1988) is esp. helpful on the rituals. I am indebted to the author. For up-to-date survey, with bibliography, D. Müller, 'Katharer', *TRE* XVIII (Berlin and New York, 1988); on history of dualism, G. Rottenwöhrer, *Unde malum*, Bad Honnef, 1986. See dating of Latin ritual in Rottenwöhrer, *Katharismus* IV (1), pp. 35–42; doctrine, pp. 42–67; correction of Borst, p. 63.

[4] Above, p. 56, n. 45; Lambert, *Medieval Heresy*, 1st edn, pp. 12–23.

still in the domain of Satan, having no right to call his God 'Father' at all. A second part of the ritual (or separate rite),[5] corresponding to the Byzantine *teleiosis*, forgave the candidate's sins, and did away with the consequences for him or her of the fall of the angels from heaven and their imprisonment in bodies by Satan. At the Fall, it was believed, the angel that formed the soul of a man had left behind his spirit in heaven; with the *consolamentum* soul and spirit were reunited, and the soul passed out of the power of Satan.

The preliminaries to attaining the status were usually arduous. The candidate had to be approved by other perfect and have shown fitness to undertake the life by a year's probation, in which he fulfilled the fasts of the perfect on every Monday, Wednesday and Friday as well as during three penitential seasons – all on bread and water – and at all times observed the prohibition of the products of coition: meat, milk, eggs, cheese. In effect both candidate and perfect observed the dietary regime, made more rigorous by days and weeks of bread and water, of the modern vegan who declines any aid to life from the animal kingdom at all. The one exception to the rigour of this rule was the consumption of fish, which the Cathars, in common with many orthodox, believed to be the product, not of coition, but of water itself.[6] Naturally all sexual contact was forbidden and, especially in the last days of the movement, even the most harmless physical contact between man and woman was rigorously excluded.[7] If married, a candidate had to abandon his or her parter; if not, lifelong celibacy was the rule.

Sexuality formed part of Satan's creation. The angels imprisoned were sexless; in one of the most affecting of the dualist myths they wept when they found that the bodies in which Satan had thrust them were sexually differentiated.[8]

Once having received the *consolamentum* – or, in the contemporary phrase, 'having been consoled' – the newly fledged perfect faced a lifetime of rigid observance of the precepts of his life, made more exacting than the analogous life of the most ascetic orders in Catholicism by the incongruity with Cathar theology of any device for meeting lapses, such as the Catholic confession, contrition and penance. Every month the perfect of a community or locality held a meeting for the public confession of sins amongst themselves, the *apparellamentum*;[9] but this was reserved for minor faults, such as failure to say the requisite number of *Pater Nosters*, and was an occasion for mutual encouragement in the tense battle for perfection in their way of life. It was not used for breaches of the code of abstinence which formed the backbone of Cathar morality. These all ranked the same: it was equally serious, say, to fall by eating an egg as to indulge in theft or commit a murder;[10] any breach of the code involved the sinner once more in Satan's world, and lost him the

---

[5] *WEH*, pp. 465, 776, n. 4.

[6] Borst, *Katharer*, p. 184.

[7] Koch, *Frauenfrage*, pp. 108–9.

[8] *Interrogatio Johannis* (originally Bogomil), in R. Reitzenstein, *Die Vorgeschichte der christlichen Taufe* (Leipzig and Berlin, 1929), pp. 297–311; tr. *WEH*, pp. 458–65 at p. 460; see edn and analysis, Bozóky, *Le Livre secret des Cathares*, review: M. D. Lambert, *JTS* xxxix (1988), pp. 285–6.

[9] *WEH*, p. 466; Borst, *Katharer*, pp. 199–200.

[10] Sacconi's *Summa* ii; Dondaine, *Un Traité*, pp. 64–78, D. Kniewald, in *Rad Jugoslavenske akademije znanosti i umjetnosti* cclxx (1949), p. 104ff.; *WEH*, pp. 329–46 at p. 320; *MBPH*, pp. 132–45.

consolamentum. It is not quite clear what did happen in the early days to one who had lapsed. Later a form was used for re-consoling a sinner, but it was a ceremony held in private, without the presence of the mass of supporters, and it was only allowed after substantial penance.[11] Standards were long maintained. Pseudo-Capelli, an anonymous controversialist from Milan, carries conviction when he describes the short shrift given to a fornicating perfect: either he was ejected, or only re-consoled after a heavy penance.[12]

Breach of the code entailed loss of the *consolamentum* both for the sinner and for all those who had in turn been consoled by the sinning perfect. One fall could entail a chain-reaction. Sacconi comments, 'all Cathars labour under very great doubt and danger of soul'.[13] The reason was that no one could tell if a minister of the *consolamentum* had committed a secret sin. There was, in consequence, much anxious re-consoling as rumours of faults of these men reached their followers. All in all, the perfect in the heyday of Catharism walked a tightrope, carefully, even obsessively, maintaining a way of life that was intended as far as possible to eliminate outlets for the natural instincts, taking care not to eat the forbidden grease, ensuring that the proper gulf was maintained between the sexes,[14] repeating over and over his chains of *Pater Nosters*, the prayer of the sect.

Yet this harsh way of life had its attractions. There was the sense of common endeavour among the perfect of a community. Capelli writes of the spirit which prevailed among the deacons of the sect in Italy and the Cathars who came to their hospices 'linked to each other by a bond of affection'.[15] There was, too, the appeal of being able to carry the burden; the analogy is with the monks of the Egyptian desert, competing like athletes of Christ in their austerities. There was the appeal of exclusiveness itself. Only the *consolamentum* saved; it was the sole means of escape from Satan's power. The perfect had received it, and, provided that he could maintain his footing on the tightrope and the minister who had given it to him did not lapse, he was assured of his return at death to heaven, or at least of progress on the chain of being towards it.

In the world, moreover, there were immediate compensations. The perfect, except in time of persecution, seem never to have been withdrawn from society. If he held office he was continually on the move, preaching, administering the *consolamentum*, encouraging his fellow perfect. Thinness and pallor through fasting, the black robe put on at the *consolamentum*, were the outward signs and the uniform of his state of perfection; they revealed him pubicly as it were for the admiration of all. If he or she did not hold office, then a house would be their normal seat, where sympathizers would visit them, for at least as long as the time of security for the perfect lasted. Their struggle for perfection was played out against a background of public respect and adoration; even in the underground years after the inquisition had got a hold,

[11] Borst, *Katharer*, pp. 178–96.
[12] *WEH*, pp. 301–6 (tr. and comment) at p. 305. I have not consulted the original text, ed. D. Bazzocchi (1920), but as amended in *WEH*.
[13] Dondaine, *Un Traité*, pp. 69–70; *WEH*, pp. 329–46 at p. 336.
[14] Manselli, *Eresia*, pp. 226–31.
[15] *WEH*, p. 303.

as perfect moved about secretly, they were still sustained by the devotion of a believer class who saw in them a race of restored angels, the one tangible presence of the divine in Satan's world.

Ritual and instructions for daily living brought perfect and adherents into contact on terms which highlighted the status of the former. The *melioramentum*, the greeting to the perfect which was often the first overt sign of involvement in Catharism and which the inquisition called 'adoration', conveyed the gulf between the categories and the aspiration of the adherent to be one day consoled. It was supposed to be given on all occasions of meeting, at services, or on entry to a house of perfect. Threefold genuflections and greetings to the perfect with replies culminated in the exchange – from the adherent, 'Pray God for me, a sinner, that he may make me a good Christian and lead me to a good end', and from the perfect, 'May God be prayed that he may make you a good Christian.'[16] This had special meaning; to be a good Christian, or a Christian at all, in Cathar belief was to become a perfect. To come to a good end was to die in possession of the *consolamentum*, not having forfeited it by lapse. In the exchange and the genuflection perfect and adherent reminded each other of their status, the one waiting, not yet freed from Satan, the other outside his power, in a unique position.

The breaking of bread, the ceremony preceding a meal, again gave the key-role to the perfect. The senior present held bread, wrapped in a white cloth, while the *Pater Noster* was said, blessed it and distributed it to all. Variously explained as an allegory recalling the supersubstantial bread of the Cathar version of the *Pater Noster* or as an imitation of the Catholic *eulogia*, a distribution of blessed bread, the act served to bring perfect and adherents together.[17] The bread was a reminder to the rank and file of the presence of the perfect; in time of persecution the fragments of the blessed bread were carefully preserved by adherents for later use.

Instructions for the saying of the *Pater Noster* kept the gulf between adherent and perfect. The Provençal ritual, one of the two texts of their ceremonies to emanate from the Cathars, refuses all place to the rank and file adherent: 'The office . . . of saying the Prayer should not be confided to a layman', it says.[18] Their role was quite passive; they would merely listen as the perfect said the *Pater Noster*. So the formal ceremonies supported the perfect in his way of life: entry to the status was hard, and preserving it inviolate harder still; but the consciousness of a unique position in mankind, reinforced by the attention of the outer supporters of his sect, would often hold him to his austerities.

The appeal of the position of an adherent in the sect was of a quite different type. The great majority of the ordinary sympathizers would never go forward to receive the *consolamentum* in full health and so endure the *abstinentia*, the period of probation, or the restrictions of the perfect's life, though these were features which attracted them to the sect in the first place. Their attachment to Catharism was marked by attendance at sermons and by the performance of the *melioramentum*. A little deeper attachment might involve attendance at

---

[16] Borst, *Katharer*. p. 198 and references given. I follow Borst's version; compare the exchange in Bernard Gui, *Manuel de l'inquisiteur*, ed. G. Mollat, 1 (Paris, 1926), p. 20.

[17] Ibid., p. 201 (*eulogia*); Manselli, *Eresia*, p. 233 (allegory).

[18] *WEH*, p. 491, Clédat, *Nouveau Testament*, p. xxi.

the breaking of bread and a more active share in the maintenance of the perfect.

The status of believer was something more. It is still not clear whether a formal ceremony was needed to attain the status. The Provençal ritual speaks of a believer who has had the Prayer administered to him, and the rite which precedes the administration of the *consolamentum* proper is styled the ministration of the Prayer. Was the believer, the *credens* of the inquisition sources, one who had passed through special training and had the right to say the *Pater Noster* though he had not yet received the *consolamentum* and was not one of the perfect, or was he or she simply a heavily involved supporter of the sect?[19] In the dark days for Catharism the inquisition classed believers according to their functions: of collectors, for the expenses of the perfect, of receivers, who gave them refuge, or of the guides, for the perfect making their way over the country in secrecy.[20] The matter is not clear.

But whatever the truth of the position with regard to the believer, it is apparent that all who were not perfect, whether fringe sympathizer or committed believer, had very limited functions in the sect, and could not have more so long as they were still attached to Satan's creation. In practice they seem to have lived in no way greatly different from their orthodox contemporaries, were married, engaged in war, and worked in various ways for their living. Logically, however, Catharism had no morality for them at all so long as they remained without the *consolamentum*. From this probably sprang the assumption of most Catholic polemists that their morals were low, especially that they tended to sexual depravity and had usurers among them, who were unrestrained by Cathar teaching. Accusations of sexual failings tend to be commonplace abuse; evidence about usury is more equivocal. There may have been point in Fulk of Toulouse's drive against both heresy and usury in Toulouse, and investigation of the evidence for confiscations for heresy affecting Toulouse families has shown a significant minority of the patrician and wealthy class there were involved in Catharism. There does not seem to have been much appeal to the poor in the city. In general, some Cathars did retain wealth even as perfect. On the other hand, the practice of usury straddled the religious divide and leading businessmen were often firmly orthodox.[21]

All accusations of sexual depravity in the Middle Ages need to be treated with care. Like any other group whose activities were secret, Cathars tended

[19] Clédat, *Nouveau Testament*, pp. xi, xxi; *WEH*, pp. 485, 491. I am indebted to Professor W. L. Wakefield for information.

[20] Y. Dossat, 'Les Cathares d'après les documents de l'inquisition', in *CF* III, pp. 71–104 (concise survey) at p. 89.

[21] Compare Borst, *Katharer*, pp. 105–6, and R. W. Emery's review in *Speculum* XXIX (1954), pp. 537–8. 'Catharism in southern France . . . cut across class lines. But in so far as we can identify the followers of the sect, they appear to have been rather significantly concentrated outside of the more advanced districts economically . . . usurers themselves were – we must suppose – relatively hard-headed men, little likely to risk everything by identifying themselves with an outlaw and suspected group' (Professor Emery in a private letter). J. H. Mundy, *The Repression of Catharism at Toulouse: The Royal Diploma of 1279* (Toronto, 1985) discusses class adherence, pp. 54–61, usury, p. 58, with some modification of views contained in his standard work, *Liberty and Political Power in Toulouse, 1050–1230* (New York, 1954). For sexual accusations, see Wakefield in *WEH*, pp. 46–7; Manselli, *Eresia*, p. 201; cf. Borst, *Katharer*, pp. 180–3. On sexual morality of perfect, see below, pp. 130–1.

to he the butt of accusations that meetings were occasions for orgies, even when, in the case of the perfect, it seems least probable. So, *mutatis mutandis*, with the adherents. No doubt it was logical for them, sharing Cathar beliefs, to regard any sexual activity that did not issue in procreation as at least one stage better than bringing more souls into the power of Satan through childbirth: whether in fact they acted on their assumption on this point has yet to be proved. They may well have lived like the Catholics – or better.

One action was crucial for all categories of adherents: the reception of the *consolamentum*. The Provençal ritual, a late thirteenth-century text as it stands, includes a formula for consoling the sick.[22] The ministers are to inquire how the candidate has behaved to the Church and whether he owes it money; he is to be clothed and helped to sit up in bed. The rites of the delivery of the Prayer and the laying-on of hands are there, but shortened and run together; all that the sick man or woman has to do is to make the responses and promise abstinence; the absolute minimum is to be conscious enough to say the *Pater Noster*. It became part of the art of the ministers of the sect to time the administration well, so that the candidate could speak, but death would soon follow.[23] If there was recovery, the Provençal ritual required another administration of the *consolamentum*. For the dying the austerities they promised were of little moment; the reward in escape from Satan was no less great than that of the perfect who were consoled in full health. Many more received the *consolamentum* in this way than through the ceremony reserved for those who had passed through the period of probation. The austerities of the way of life of the perfect were so great that it could never have been undertaken by the mass of the membership, and the deathbed *consolamentum* was the solution to the problem.

The social context

Certain social factors intertwined with the religious influences to keep the elite in being and to draw in sympathizers. These can most easily be studied in Languedoc because there a systematic investigation by the inquisition from the fourth decade of the thirteenth century onwards elicited series of confessions[24] from most of the key affected areas which go right back to the decades before the Albigensian Crusade when the heresy settled in. Italy is more problematical because really effective action by the inquisition came so

---

[22] Clédat, *Nouveau Testament*, pp. xxii–xxvi; *WEH*, pp. 492–4.

[23] Dossat, in *CF* III, p. 83.

[24] Esp. used by E. Griffe, *Le Languedoc cathare de 1190 à 1210* (Paris, 1971). See also M. Roquebert, *L'Epopée cathare, 1198–1212: l'Invasion* (Toulouse, 1970); earlier summary by C. P. Bru, 'Eléments pour une interpretation sociologique du Catharisme occitan', in *Spiritualité de l'hérésie: le Catharisme*, ed. R. Nelli (Paris, 1953), pp. 23–59; M. D. Lambert, 'The motives of the Cathars: some reflections', *SCH* xv, pp. 45–59; A. Cazenave, 'Hérésie et société', in *Christianisme*, ed. Brenon and Gouzy, pp. 7–61, suggests occitanian interactions between heresy and society (see esp. pp. 22, 34, 52–3; note A. Vauchez, p. 61). Brenon, p. 60, notes relevance of a 'familiarité' and 'solidarité' in occitan feudal caste, aiding oral diffusion. A. Brenon, 'Les Cathares: bons Chrétiens et hérétiques', *Christianisme*, ed. Brenon and Gouzy, pp. 115–70 (with debate) argues that interpretations by Dondaine and Borst are outdated (p. 121); I do not agree. But none the less, her article seems to me to convey peculiarly well the nature of the appeal of Catharism, esp. in the Midi.

much later in most cities, and thus the evidence does not relate in the same
way to the time of the implanting of heresy in the last thirty years of the
twelfth century. Moreover, the history of heresy in Italy tends to be more
disparate. Each city has its own story.[25] Nevertheless, certain generalizations
emerge for Italy and may be used as points of contrast.

In Languedoc favour by the rural nobility provided the matrix for
Catharism. In the first generation of the implantation period men were more
often the patrons, while their womenfolk seem to have been drawn towards
the position of perfect in rather larger numbers. In the Niort family,[26] for
example, the men began as patrons, and took to the *consolamentum* only in the
course of the thirteenth century. A comparatively small number of supporters
and actual perfect high in the social categories gave prestige to the movement;
lesser nobility were thickly involved, and all classes participated. Certain
areas of the countryside were most heavily affected but there was no gulf
between town and country and movements of population carried heresy from
one to the other and vice versa. Family influence is the most important single
social factor, and here the initial impact of the Cathar missionaries on women
in the *castra* of the countryside was decisive. Inquisition records build up a
vivid picture of houses of women perfect, often only with a mere handful of
inmates, but densely distributed across the affected regions in many of the
villages where candidates for the *consolamentum* were trained, sermons were
delivered to any of the locality who were willing to hear and common meals
were held. From them the deacons and officers of the sect went out on their
pastoral duties. A widow might receive the *consolamentum* and then be joined by
others in her own house, which thus became a natural centre for the sect, or a
single woman might be aided by her family; in other cases women left their
husbands to undergo the probation. A good example of a noble lady setting up
as a perfect is the case of Blanche de Laurac, whose husband Sicard had been
one of the major figures in the rural nobility.[27] She received the *consolamentum*,
and made her home a house of perfect; one boy and four daughters were
brought up in heresy, three daughters marrying and thus diffusing Catharism
at the adherents' level; another became a perfect and the son, after first
supporting Simon de Montfort, went to defend his sister at Lavaur and was
hanged for breaking faith with the crusaders. Blanche's grandson remembered
living with her and eating bread blessed by the perfect. In about the year 1200
almost all the population of Laurac turned out to hear preaching and give the
melioramentum to the perfect.

Houses of men perfect were formed in the same way, as in the case of the
knight Pierre Raymond de Cuq, who was consoled in his house at Auriac and
lived there with other men perfect.[28] But, although the houses for men were
also of some importance, one may suspect that the quiet diffusion and
implanting of heresy in families was naturally a woman's work, and that men
perfect played their most effective role as the mobile ministers of the sect,

[25] E. Dupré Theseider, 'Gli eretici nel mondo comunale Italiano', *BSSV* LXXIII (1963), pp. 3–23.

[26] W. L. Wakefield, 'The family of Niort in the Albigensian Crusade and before the inquisition', *Names*
XVIII (1970), pp. 97–117, 286–303; prosecution: Kolmer, *Vulpes*, pp. 82–104.

[27] Griffe, *Languedoc*, pp.109–13; Roquebert, *Epopée*, p. 114.

[28] Griffe, *Languedoc*, p. 99.

bishops, bishops' auxiliaries, deacons, preaching, visiting, administering the *consolamentum* and, above all, calling on the dying to administer their *consolamentum*, which came to take the place of the Catholic extreme unction.[29] A territorial basis existed for their organization. Bishops took titles in an impudent imitation of Catholicism, but in Languedoc resided at rural places where they were sure of the protection of the local nobility, and not in the towns of their title. The *filius maior* and the *filius minor* were vicars of the bishops, and succeeded them at their deaths; deacons had their spheres of influence and regular residences. But all these ministers must often have been on the move.

Noble or humble, a perfect lived cheaply, for the way of life demanded so little expenditure. But whereas the noble woman could live on her own money, together with gifts of adherents or family, those lower in society had to work, and so some houses of perfect engaged in cottage industry or trade: at Mirepoix they had a shoemaker's shop, at Les Cassès and Montmaur they made shirts and footwear.[30] Heretical influence was then diffused at the place of work or, as in the case of Pierre de Gramazie, who went to work in his childhood in workshops owned by the heretics at Fanjeaux, imbibed with apprenticeship.[31]

The influence of heretics on children helped to make Catharism part of the background of life; Bernard Mir remembered as a child going in to a house of perfect at Saint-Martin-la-Lande and being given nuts to eat and taught to bend his knees to ask for a blessing, so being trained in the *melioramentum*.[32] Hospitality made contacts. At Puylaurens the mother of Sicard de Puylaurens lived with two of her sisters and another noble lady, all perfect, and men and women came and ate fruit from their hands. Families tolerated widely different views. In the Arrufat family at Castelnaudary the head of the household left his wife free to welcome both Cathars and Waldensians. Pelfort de Rabastens, lord of the settlement there, had a mother and sister who had been consoled. A witness described the easy contact between the family and its heretical members, as Pelfort's wife visited the heretic ladies; yet the same noble house produced Raymond de Rabastens, archdeacon of Agen and, briefly, bishop of Toulouse.

In a few places Cathar influence reached a peak. At Cambiac, for example, the curé complained that he considered all his parishioners bar four to be Cathar believers,[33] at Caraman, Lanta and Verfeil about 1215 few died without the *consolamentum*, although as well as the heavily affected villages there were others where Cathars were a minority. The perfect often enough occupied in practice the position of the Roman clergy, being exempt from certain impositions and receiving goods at the death of their faithful. The

[29] Dossat, in *CF* II, pp. 71–104; correcting and supplementing Guiraud, *Inquisition*, esp. I, ch. 7.

[30] Griffe, *Languedoc*, p. 189. For example at Cordes, see Koch, *Frauenfrage*, p. 18n., correcting Grundmann in *Relazioni* III, p. 399n., C. Schmidt, *Histoire et doctrine de la secte des Cathares ou Albigeois* I (Paris, 1849), p. 289.

[31] Griffe, *Languedoc*, p. 189; on low status of weaving, Fichtenau, *Ketzer*, p. 95 and n.

[32] Ibid., pp. 125–6 and following references: pp. 95 (Puylaurens), 122–3 (Castelnaudary), 65–8 (Rabastens).

[33] Ibid., p. 91, and following references (Caraman, Lanta, Verfeil). On numbers, see Wakefield, *Heresy, Crusade*, pp. 68–70.

creation of an atmosphere in which adherence to heresy was nothing abnormal, in which custom reinforced devotion, was a considerable achievement, and its effects were long lasting.

We may ask how far non-religious factors were at work in producing this result. Koch, the East German Marxist historian, puts his finger on one factor when he describes the social and economic forces influencing the women in Languedoc. The houses of women perfect, Koch points out, occupied the place of beguinages elsewhere in Western Europe, providing outlets more cheaply than nunneries for widows and other surplus women.[34] Poor girls were left with perfect women. Jordan of Saxony, the Dominican, complained of the way in which parents put daughters into these houses of the perfect to be supported – and so, inevitably, to be drawn into heresy. It was a natural consequence of the acceptance of Catharism in certain localities. There were factors more specific to Languedoc. For the nobility, Roman laws of inheritance gave a place to women that they did not have in many other parts of Europe, and so made it easier for widows and heiresses to set up houses of the perfect. The life of the perfect might give meaning to the surplus woman's existence, just because of its rigid duties of prayer and fasting; so might the use of her residence as a focus for missionary work and hospitality.

In ritual and status, Catharism offered certain advantages to women not to be found in Catholicism. No position in Catholicism, not even that of abbess, offered the status which accrued to a woman who received the *consolamentum*. The woman perfect, no less than the man, possessed the Spirit. If she was debarred by her sex from holding office and could never be deacon or bishop, she took precedence in any gathering over all supporters who were not perfect, whether man or woman. If no man perfect was present, she would lead the prayers. She was entitled to the *melioramentum* from all. It would seem that members of the nobility tended to avoid giving it to a woman, but no doubt those lower in the social scale did not.

Status might attract; the teaching about marriage and procreation on the other hand might, and sometimes did, repel women. The wife of William Viguier of Cambiac resisted her husband's pressure to make her an adherent because she had reacted against the Cathar teaching that pregnancy was from the devil. A mother, Sybil Peter of Arques in the days of Pierre Autier's revival, was told by a perfect not to feed her sick infant daughter Jacoba any more after she had been given the *consolamentum*, but when the perfect and her husband had left, she gave Jacoba the breast, to the subsequent anger of her husband. Humanity prevailed over Cathar belief. Careful statistical analysis from the inquisition evidence of the proportion of women adherents of Languedocian Catharism has thrown up the fact that men were more often *credentes* than women. That does not seem to be the position in Waldensianism. It may be that the utter denial of the value of carnal affection and family life which, masked as it often was in the day-to-day contacts between perfect and supporters, none the less lay at the heart of Cathar teaching, worked against the movement for many women.[35]

---

[34] *Frauenfrage*, chs 1, 3; comments on motives, pp. 14, 31; following refs, Jordan of Saxony: p. 28 (see *Libellus de principiis ordinis praedicatorum* in *MOPH* xvi (Rome, 1935), p. 39); ritual: *Frauenfrage*, ch. 7.

[35] P. Biller, 'The common woman in the Western Church in the thirteenth and early fourteenth

Sometimes a religious passion is the only possible explanation for a woman maintaining the perfect's life, as in the case of Furneria, wife of Guillaume-Roger de Mirepoix, who apparently left her husband to live in a house of perfect women, went to Lavelanet, returned to take her daughter away, induced her to be consoled and finally fled before the crusaders to the fortress of Montségur.[36]

In Italy family links were still of crucial importance, though all our early generalizations are weakened by a lack of broad-based evidence for the years of initial infiltration. Certainly there Catharism had a less firmly territorial base. Whereas in Languedoc the historian can draw a line on the map – say from Marmande in the Agenais in the north down to the foothills of the Pyrenees in the south, and from Toulouse in the west to Béziers in the east – and be sure that he has included much the greatest part of the heretical activity in the Midi, and that all the heaviest concentrations within the outline are directly contiguous to each other,[37] in Italy Catharism had its supporters scattered in a multitude of cities, especially Milan, Piacenza, Cremona, Brescia, Bergamo, Vicenza, Verona, Ferrara, Rimini, Florence and Orvieto, in the countryside and along the routes which led from southern France to Lombardy.[38] Bishops, deacons and supporters kept in touch with each other through the network of communications established in the developed areas in the north and centre where Catharism largely settled, but the nexus was, in geographical terms, much looser than in Languedoc. Bishoprics, which in Languedoc were delimited territorially, in Italy generally were not. Instead, the dividing lines were differences of belief, which sprang out of Italian contentiousness and ingenuity and the greater proximity of Italy to the cradles of dualism in the East.[39] Personalities counted for more, and disputes were exacerbated by them. Bishops and deacons ruled adherents scattered over sprawling territories, with duplicate organizations at enmity with each other exercising oversight in the same cities.

Mobility was a keynote of the lives of many of those involved in Catharism, more so in Italy than in Languedoc. The merchant class, of greater weight because of the Italian economic development, was of its nature given to travel. Catharism had a hold amongst them and, to judge by the statistics of the goods confiscated by the inquisition in the course of the thirteenth century,

centuries', *SCH* xxix, pp. 127–57, examples at p. 155 from Guiraud, *Inquisition* I, p. 92n; *Registre d'Inquisition de Jacques Fournier, évêque de Pamiers (1318–25)*, ed. J. Duvernoy (=Fournier, *Inquisition*) II (Toulouse, 1965), pp. 414–15; R. Abels and E. Harrison, 'The participation of women in Languedocian Catharism', *MS* xli (1979), pp. 215–51; J. H. Mundy, *Men and Women at Toulouse in the Age of the Cathars* (Toronto, 1990), pp. 43–4 (discussion on the role of women underestimates the significance of houses of *perfectae*); review: J. Duvernoy, *Heresis* xv (1990), pp. 136–9; J. H. Mundy, 'Le mariage et les femmes à Toulouse au temps des Cathares', *Annales* (1987), pp. 117–34. I owe a photocopy to Dr Biller and comment on the adoration of *perfectae* to Professor W. L. Wakefield. See M. C. Barber, 'Women and Catharism', *Reading Medieval Studies* III (1977); A. Brenon, *Les Femmes cathares* (Paris, 1992) (inquisition evidence; vivid).

[36] Griffe, *Languedoc*, pp. 148–9.
[37] Ibid., pp. 18–22.
[38] Dupré Theseider, in *BSSV* lxxxiii (1963), p. 11.
[39] Below, pp. 125–33.

some wealthy individuals were found among them.[40] Many of the lesser men in the sect, the artisans and pedlars, were also forced to travel by the nature of their occupation, and weavers and other cloth and leather workers were often enough footloose people.[41] Dupré Theseider has uncovered significant links in the late thirteenth century between Catharism and the trade of pursemaking at Bologna.[42] The workers travelled from house to house and town to town making and selling their wares and at the same time making heretical contacts. Inns, workshops and mills were casual meeting places for supporters. At Modena certain mills were known in the late twelfth century as 'the mills of the Patarenes' (which by this time meant Cathars).[43] In other cases certain houses were known to be safe refuges for perfect who travelled about on their pastoral duties. Armanno Pungilupo of Ferrara said that signs were used which made it possible to recognize houses of the Cathars.[44] Evidence given to the inquisitors provides us with glimpses of the blend of family influence and upbringing, casual contact and proselytism in which heresy existed, much on the lines of Languedoc. In Ferrara, for example, a maker of sacks had brought up his son and daughter to be supporters of the sect; they received instructions at home and in a neighbouring house, and were visited by a number of perfect. Aristocratic dwellings in the *contado* of various cities formed safe hiding-places for leading Cathars under pressure in the cities.

Aristocratic patronage was important – the support, based on hostility to the Church, of Ezzelino da Romano and the marquis Oberto Pelavicino, for example, was of great value for the spread of Catharism in the regions of the March of Treviso and the Po valley that they controlled[45] – and developed into deeper involvement in a number of cases, such as those of Stefano Confalonieri in Milan,[46] Conrado da Venosta in the Valtellina,[47] and the Uberti of Florence.[48] But the carrying class, as it were, of Italian Catharism seems to have been the artisans and lesser traders. Two modern authorities, Violante and Dupré Theseider, concur in this generalization. Although Cathars did exist among the major bourgeoisie, by and large the leading businessmen tended, as in Languedoc, to be conventional in religion. Members of the *arti minori*, minor commercial operators and artisans, were those most persuaded by Catharism, and the reserve areas of support in the cities seem to have been the suburban areas between the old walls and the new ring, built to accommodate the population growth of the twelfth and

---

[40] Dupré Theseider, *BSSV* LXXXIII, p. 17n.

[41] C. Violante 'Hérésies urbaines et hérésies rurales en Italie du 11e au 13e siècle', in *HS*, pp. 171–98, s. 3.

[42] 'L'Eresia a Bologna nei tempi di Dante', in *Studi storici in onore di G. Volpe* (Florence, 1958), I, pp. 383–444.

[43] Dupré Theseider, in *BSSV* LXXXIII, p. 16; L. A. Muratori, *Antiquitates Italicae Medii Aevi* v, pp. 86–7.

[44] Violante, in *HS*, p. 186 (see also following references to Ferrara).

[45] Guiraud, *Inquisition* II, pp. 447–51, 472–3, 534–8, 543, 545–50.

[46] For the organizer of the plot against St Peter Martyr, see Guiraud, *Inquisition* II, pp. 496–8, 542–3, and Violante, in *HS*, p. 181 (note survey of Catharism in cities, pp. 179–84).

[47] Violante, in *HS*, p. 181; see Manselli, 'Les hérétiques dans la société italienne du 13e siècle', in *HS*, pp. 199–202.

[48] See J. N. Stephens, 'Heresy in medieval and Renaissance Florence', *PP* LIV (1972), pp. 25–60.

thirteenth centuries. Here the Humiliati and the friars installed themselves, and here, above all, the battle was fought out between heresy and orthodoxy in the thirteenth century.[49] The most insecure and dependent were not members in any great numbers; both perfect and adherent tend to be those who had at least a small competence. The unskilled labourers and the flotsam and jetsam of the cities were not numerically significant. Nor were peasants. Whereas in Languedoc the peasants were early drawn in, albeit in small numbers, by the patronage of the rural nobility, and then became more and more important later in the history of the sect, in Italy this class was missing from the membership, or from the records, throughout.[50] Evidence from the Austrian region, which includes Ivo of Narbonne's story of his wanderings and his long stay in Wiener Neustadt in what was then Styria, and the attacks of the Austrian poet Stricker on specifically Cathar errors, leaves no doubt that Catharism had a presence in this frontier province. Evidence is lacking, however, about the heretics' social background. The most that one can say is that the disturbances in Austria in the first half of the thirteenth century gave a good opportunity for heresy to grow there.[51]

The sect developed some intellectual appeal. Ivo of Narbonne reveals the existence of university aspirations; Alan of Lille knew Cathars who were capable of using scholastic logic; Dominic's work implies that there was a challenge to be met by preaching and reason. Italy presented the greater menace, for Catharism had freedom to evolve over a much longer period of time; intellectual development was cut short by crusade and repression in Languedoc. Polemicists modified traditional assumptions about heretics as *illiterati* in the light of experience.[52]

One may ask how far it was the status of the perfect which appealed to the artisan and to those of lower class generally. The Cathar conception of perfection, attained through a set of tangible measures of abstinence and by repetition of prayers, appealed to the individual's sense of achievement.[53] Ascetic life was not, as in an informed Catholicism, a means to perfection; it was the sole means of salvation. The Cathar teacher could say without reserve to his neophyte, 'Do this; receive the *consolamentum* and you will be saved.' It was a part of the strength of the movement's appeal. How far did the rise in status, achieved by the individual's own efforts at self-mortification, entitling him to the *melioramentum* from members of all social classes and to a veneration from all adherents, appeal to those whose occupation kept them low in the social scale? Was this a factor which helped to hold to the way of life the apostles of Cathar Italy, Mark the gravedigger and his humble companions?

[49] A. Murray, 'Piety and impiety in thirteenth-century Italy', in *SCH* VIII, pp. 83–106 at p. 86.

[50] Violante, in *HS*, pp. 184–5. Materials for class analysis with exposition, brilliantly precise but schematic, on the history of the Cathars, in Borst, *Katharer*.

[51] P. Segl, *Ketzer in Österreich: Untersuchungen über Häresie und Inquisition im Herzogtum Österreich im 13. und beginnenden 14. Jahrhundert* (Paderborn, 1984). Note the Bogomil-type heresy about pregnant women discussed on pp. 228–9.

[52] Comment on lay-controlled schools and education of perfect: Cazenave in *Christianisme*, ed. Brenon and Gouzy, pp. 51–2; use of Scripture and Cathar beliefs: Brenon, *Visage*, pp. 58–72; I owe information to Dr P. Biller, Dr Y. Hagman, Mlle P. Jimenez Sanchez. On Italy see now L. Paolini in Biller, Hudson, *Literacy*, pp. 83–103.

[53] E. Werner, reviewing Borst, in *Byzantinoslavica* XVI (1955), pp. 135–44.

Teaching

In all areas methods of missioning followed the pattern of the Bogomils: there was a pedagogic progression from the generalities, which seemed to blend easily into the contemporary religious environment, to the inner mysteries, reserved for the perfect or for believers of long standing.[54] The approach, natural to all sects influenced by Gnosticism, had the effect of concealing the profoundly heretical nature of Catharism from the neophyte until he was sufficiently detached from the influence of orthodox belief.

Much proselytism was done informally, and in this all the perfect and believers played their part. Formal preaching, whether in houses, on ritual occasions or in the days of prosperity openly in public places in Italian cities and the villages of Languedoc, was more commonly a duty of those who held office in the sect.

But because of the overriding importance of the class of the perfect, from whose number alone the officers could be chosen, no duty was ever reserved entirely to these officers, and rank and file perfect sometimes preached – women among them, though never so much as Waldensian women preachers – their most likely audience being a gathering of adherents, not other perfect.

The nature of these sermons can be gleaned from chronicle and other accounts, from extant Cathar treatises, and to some extent from the text of the rituals. Two principal objectives in the open preaching seem to have been to detach casual sympathizers from the influence of the Church, by playing on the sins of the clergy in contrast to the standards set down for Christian living in the gospels and epistles, and by using a particular Cathar exegesis of Scripture, together with unwelcome natural phenomena, to inculcate the belief that the visible world was evil; thunder, earthquakes, the existence of worms, toads and fleas, for example, were cited to show that the world could not have been the work of a good God.[55] Many of the world-renouncing texts of Scripture were pressed into service to show how the teaching of Christ and his apostles rejected material things. No attention was paid to the rules of exegesis: texts were wrenched out of context, and no hint was given of the precise meaning of 'the world' to the New Testament writers.[56] But the audience for a Cathar sermon would not be familiar with the rules of exegesis, and they would hear what would seem to them an exhortation by good men based on the words of the founder of Christianity and of his followers. Preaching was heavily larded with texts – at least, this seems a fair inference from the surviving Cathar treatises, a good part of which consist of scriptural references and quotations.[57]

---

[54] Manselli, *Eresia*, pp. 223–31; Brenon stresses, rather, use of stories as a pedagogical device and casts doubt on 'inner mysteries', in *Christianisme*, ed. Brenon and Gouzy, pp. 131–40.

[55] Manselli, in *CF* III, p. 169.

[56] See, e.g. C. Thouzellier, *Un Traité cathare inédit du début du xiiie siècle d'après le Liber contra Manicheos de Durand de Huesca* (Louvain, 1961) (review: E. Delaruelle, in *RHE* LX (1965), pp. 524–8), pp. 90–5; *WEH*, pp. 498–500.

[57] (i) Thouzellier, *Traité*; (ii) *Liber de duobus principiis*; first edn. in Dondaine, *Un Traité*; latest edn., intro., tr., in Thouzellier, *Livre des deux Principes* (Paris, 1973), earlier analysed by Borst, *Katharer* (pp. 254–318). Partial tr. of Dondaine text in *WEH*, pp. 511–91; (iii) *A Vindication of the Church of God* and a separate gloss on the *Pater Noster* in T. Venckeleer, 'Un Recueil cathare: le manuscrit A.6.10 de la collection

Much Cathar exhortation was, of itself, wholly orthodox and dwelt on the need for patience under persecution, a moral life and fidelity to Christ. Outwardly, the perfect were not readily to be distinguished from good monks or nuns. In a *cause célèbre* which dragged on until 1301 Armanno Pungilupo, of ascetic reputation, who had been buried with honour in the cathedral of Ferrara in 1269, was finally proved to have been guilty of heresy and posthumously condemned.[58] Near Toulouse in 1234 when an old woman near her end desired the *consolamentum* the Catholic bishop got wind of it: he came in and spoke to her of the contempt of the world and of earthly things. Hearing him, she believed he was a Cathar, and confessed her heresy. The bishop had her burned.[59]

At a number of points orthodoxy and Catharism converged, and the likeness readily deceived the unwary. Some dualist teaching on Satan would have sounded like Catholic doctrine. The *consolamentum* administered to the dying must have seemed like Catholic extreme unction. In orthodoxy, it was not unusual for a dying man to be carried to a monastery before his end, and there take the habit: the practice of taking the dying to a house of perfect, which occurred in Languedoc, would have appeared much the same. The language of orthodox ascetic writers, discussing the nature of the world or the inferiority of the female sex, often came quite close to dualism. Even the practice of the perfect of saying chains of *Pater Nosters* was not unknown to thirteenth-century piety. The perfect honestly thought that they were the only true Christians, that the clergy were servants of Satan's Church; and that Cathar teaching presented a stream of pure underground Christianity, often persecuted, but always surviving and reaching back to the days of the apostles.[60] By a strange chance the rite of the *consolamentum* that appears in the thirteenth-century texts does seem to have been based on a rite for baptism and on practices connected with the catechumenate much earlier than the contemporary Catholic rites of baptism or ordination.[61] The adherent who witnessed these ceremonies was exposed to much that was wholly edifying and orthodox. Little wonder that many in the days of the growth of the sect were deceived.

One other element in proselytism is at first sight surprising in a sect whose inner mysteries made considerable demands on the credulity of followers. This was the appeal to raw scepticism. We have seen this in action in the Rhineland, where Cathars appealed to materialist arguments to deny orthodox views of the mass.[62] Heresy did not create this scepticism, which was of spontaneous growth,[63] but it latched on to it to deny this or that doctrine or practice of the Church. Catharism benefited from doubts cast on the validity of the Church's teaching, just as Bogomilism had done.

vaudoise de Dublin, I: une apologie; II une glose sue le pater', *RBPH* XXXVIII (1960), pp. 820–31; XXXIX (1961), pp. 762–85, tr. *WEH*, pp. 592–606. On *Vindication* as catechism, A. Brenon, 'La Parole cathare': une catéchèse de l'évangile', *Actes du VIII colloque Jean Boisset*, Montpellier, 1995, pp. 99–121.

[58] Guiraud, *Inquisition* II, pp. 587–90.

[59] Dossat, in *CF* III, pp. 101–2.

[60] Dondaine, *Un Traité*, p. 159, II. 22–4; *WEH*, p. 477.

[61] Guiraud, *Cartulaire* I, pp. clxii–clxv; *Inquisition* I, ch. 4.

[62] Above, p. 58.

[63] For the thirteenth century, see Murray, in *SCH* VIII, pp. 83–106; note case cited by Dossat in *CF* III, p. 78. I have benefited from conversation with Professor W. L. Wakefield on this point and from his

Introduction to the hidden revelation of Catharism came after the neophyte had received a grounding in dualism, and through rites and practices had had impressed upon him the vital importance of the *consolamentum*. The period of *abstinentia* before receiving the *consolamentum* was also a period of instruction when, if not earlier, the candidate was given more specific information on positive beliefs of the sect and acquainted with their mythology. Doctrines held in the inner circle of the perfect were sometimes denied altogether, as in the response of two perfect to Bernard de Montesquieu of Puylaurens in 1273, who was told, contrary to fact, that they did not believe that the devil created man's body.[64] For most candidates, entry on the *abstinentia* would have brought an end to this concealment: they could then feel the attractions of the secret revelation, placed, they would believe, in the position of the apostles, to whom Christ had said, 'it is given unto you to know the mysteries of the kingdom of heaven'.[65]

These secrets were concerned pre-eminently with finding explanations for the presence of good in a world which the neophyte had already been taught to regard as evil. How had the soul, which was the work of a good God, found its way into a body created by Satan? Many of the answers given by teachers in the sect followed, with variations, the pattern of the Bogomils.[66] Satan was a good angel, or a son of God, who fell and carried other angels with him, then created the visible world and with it bodies into which he beguiled the fallen angels.

A second set of explanations, however, was based on quite different assumptions: that there was an evil God, co-eternal and of equal powers with the good God, and that the Fall and imprisonment of the angels in bodies was caused by an invasion of heaven, which captured good angels and imprisoned them in bodies of the evil creation against their will. In this version the evil principle and his creation would never come to an end, although the good angels would be released from their prison; in the older Bogomil version, as in orthodoxy, Satan in the end was subject to the power of God; his evil creation would in the Last Days be consumed. The crucial difference between these views – the first moderate dualist, the second radical dualist – lay in the status of evil: did it originate with a fallen spirit or an eternal evil principle? Both views evolved in Balkan and Byzantine dualism, and were then transferred to Western soil. The first was the dualism described in Bulgaria by Cosmas the Priest and, with variations, in Byzantium by Euthymius of Peribleptos and Zigabenus;[67] the exact origins of the second view are still obscure, and all that we know with certainty is that it was brought into the West from Constantinople by Nicetas, the most influential of medieval dualist missionaries, in the late 1160s or a little afterwards.

Despite their profound differences, both views rested on the same

---

unpublished article on records of an inquisition held at Toulouse 1270–3, with evidence of spontaneous scepticism. Compare English Lollardy (below, pp. 280–3).

[64] Dossat, in *CF* III, p. 38.

[65] Matt. 13:11.

[66] Borst, *Katharer*, pp. 143–56; myths discussed in Söderberg, *Religion*; R. Manselli, 'Eglises et théologies cathares', in *CF* III, pp. 129–76 (sketch with psychological insight).

[67] Above, p. 56, n. 45; Lambert, *Medieval Heresy*, 1st edn, pp. 10–23; on psychology of dualism, see Fichtenau, *Ketzer*, pp. 149–50, and Rottenwöhrer, *Katharismus* IV (3), pp. 277–383 (perceptive overall summary).

conviction of the utter incompatibility of the body and soul. Both set the struggle between matter and spirit, good and evil, on which the candidate for the *consolamentum* was already engaged, within a cosmic frame. Belief in the truth of Cathar teaching rested on personal experience of this struggle, and the exemplification of it in the perfect; the myths came to add colour and literary force, to give a sense of space to the daily struggle of the candidate or perfect, and to provide fantastic narratives for the adherents.

The stories

The raw material for the stories about the Fall and its consequences derived from a mixture of scriptural reminiscence, names and anecdotes, with much apocryphal matter, part from Jewish apocalyptic literature, part from ancient extra-canonical Christian legends still circulating in the Middle Ages, combined with the sheer imaginative power of certain teachers. Legendary material played a considerable part in medieval popular religion; thus the use of apocryphal material was nothing strange in itself. Scriptural fragments, incorporated arbitrarily to authenticate the stories, maintained contact with the central Christian tradition. The Apocalypse was a storehouse of images; the story of war in heaven and the fall of Satan[68] was familiar in the orthodox tradition. The teacher embroidered further on these themes with a dualistic bias. One direct importation was the *Interrogation of John*, or Secret Supper, brought from the Bogomils in Bulgaria who composed it by Nazarius, bishop of the Italian church of Concorezzo, about 1190.[69]

What the stories have in common, whether exemplifying moderate or radical dualism, is literary force, a tendency to gross materialization, an interest in sexual themes, and a strong vein of fantasy. The *Interrogation of John*, describing how Satan solved the problem of inducing Adam and Eve, angels imprisoned in clay bodies, to have sexual intercourse, depicts him planting a bed of reeds in Paradise, making a serpent of his own saliva, then entering the serpent and emerging from the reeds to have intercourse with Eve with its tail.[70] The story echoes part of the narrative of Genesis, but embellishes it with some powerful carnal imagery.

The same literary quality and free play of storytelling emerges from stories of the Fall current in a last phase of Catharism in Languedoc. In these[71] Satan stood outside the gate of heaven for thirty-two years hoping to entice the good angels; once inside, he tempted them with the greater joys he said he had to offer in his own kingdom, including a most beautiful woman. Curious to see a woman, something quite unknown to them, the angels fell into Satan's trap, were inflamed with lust, and in crowds followed him out of heaven, until God closed the gap through which they fell. Satan then created a heaven of glass for them; but God broke it and the angels found themselves despoiled of their

---

[68] Rev. 12: 7–9.

[69] Reitzenstein, *Vorgeschichte*, p. 293; *WEH*, p. 465; P. Biller, 'The Cathars of Languedoc and written materials', Biller, Hudson, *Literacy*, pp. 61–82; see also his general survey, pp. 1–18.

[70] Reitzenstein, *Vorgeschichte*, pp. 301–2; *WEH*, p. 460; definitive edn, Bozóky, *Le Livre secret*.

[71] Summary by Söderberg, *Religion*, p. 73, based on versions as related to inquisition ed. Döllinger (*Beiträge* II, pp. 149–51, 173, 176, 186, 203–5, 213–15, etc.).

splendour, and deceived. They repented, and sang songs of Sion; to take away memories of their past, Satan shut them up in human bodies.

In some accounts the battle between Satan and his seduced angels and the forces of the good God in heaven took pride of place;[72] there were vivid descriptions of the flow of blood, the destruction of the seduced angels' bodies, and the fall of their souls from heaven. The sufferings of the children of Israel in Psalm 78 were taken as an allegory of this battle.

Sometimes a wild fantasy takes charge, as in the explanation, cited by St Peter Martyr and probably derived from an Italian group, of the Cathar prohibition of flesh-eating.[73] Beasts and birds, it was said, were of human flesh – the foetuses of pregnant women which fell from heaven on to the earth after they had miscarried during the battle between the forces of God and Satan. The prohibition of eating their flesh thus amounted to a prohibition of cannibalism.

Together with the stories of the Fall in all their variations, there was a vision of heaven not substantially different from that of orthodox popular religion, but sharpened by the utter contrast in dualist belief between earth and the heaven of the good. We have an example of its consolatory power in the case of a perfect from Languedoc related by a witness before the inquisition at Pamiers in 1321, who had been troubled by doubts about Catharism, and was rewarded by a vision, in which he mounted on the shoulder of an angel through the seven heavens to the presence of the Father, who asked him whence he had come. 'From the land of tribulations', was the answer. He wanted to stay, but the Father told him that he could not do so, 'since flesh born of corruption could not remain there', but must descend to the land of tribulations and preach the faith. The vision was of a southerner's heaven. He saw 'great brilliance, many angels, beautiful groves and singing birds . . . most moderate temperatures'.[74] The model for his journey through the heavens was an *apocryphon* of the early Christian centuries, the *Vision of Isaiah*, much used by the Bogomils. Such images were an especial aid in persecution, which was made more tolerable by the certainty of entry to heaven, provided only that a valid *consolamentum* was retained.

The stories obviously played a major role in Catharism, for members of the sect devoted much attention to retailing them and weaving new ones out of the mass of available material; a kaleidoscope of these poetic narratives, continuously developing through the history of the sect, has been bequeathed to us. Variations are accounted for by the different nuances of dualism, stretching all the way from the frail Satan of the Bulgarian *apocryphon*, the *Interrogation of John* (which influenced the moderates), powerless to act except at the will of the Father,[75] to the external evil principle of the Italian teacher John of Lugio.[76] Adjustments in the stories met the needs of different schools of dualism, developed within the Cathar movement by leading personalities.

Flexibility of myth was also a consequence of the sovereign power of the

[72] Borst, *Katharer*, pp. 145–6.

[73] T. Kaeppeli, 'Une somme contre les hérétiques de S. Pierre Martyr(?)', *AFP* XVII (1947), pp. 295–335 at p. 330; Manselli, *Eresia*, pp. 226–7.

[74] Döllinger, *Beiträge* II, pp. 166–7; *WEH*, pp. 456–8. See Vaillant, in *RES* XLII (1963), pp. 109–21.

[75] Reitzenstein, *Vorgeschichte*, p. 300; *WEH*, p. 459.

[76] Below, p. 131.

perfect in the field of religious belief. Inventiveness in the teacher was apparently prized. The language of the stories was that of revelation: Cathars listened to a teacher expounding mysteries that he knew, which were guaranteed by his personality and status, and which they were disposed to accept. The stories evidently met an emotional need – for legendary narrative *per se*; for an expression, it may be, of disgust with organic life registered in the sequences of coarse imagery of the stories; for a transposed sexuality, for an outlet for poetic imagination. Most simply, they met the needs of those who lacked much logical and critical sense, who were satisfied with the flimsy, partial argumentation of Cathars handling sacred texts, and who loved good stories.[77]

The liking for myths was the common possession of radical and moderate dualists alike; but radicals differed so much from all the schools of moderates that it is reasonable to assume that the attractions of Catharism were for them somewhat different, requiring a little separate treatment.[78] Radicals were dualists who were prepared to rewrite the traditional tenets of Bogomilism in order to iron out the logical contradiction they saw in the appearance of good in an evil world. Moderates, they believed, did not solve the problem of the origins of evil by their stories of the fall of Satan and his ordering of the world on the basis of an initial creation by God, but only pushed it, so to speak, one stage further back. The dilemma remained: how was evil compatible with the creation of a good God? To satisfy themselves, they postulated two creations, wholly distinct and equally eternal, and bravely followed out the consequences of their belief – two heavens, two earths, for example, or a life of Christ in another world, judgement already passed, hell identified *tout court* with this earth. There were still confusions, and all was affected by the atmosphere of uncritical myth-making characteristic of the whole movement. The pressures of Catholic teaching and polemic showed up their contradictions, and led them deeper into difficulties, especially on the nature of Christ.[79] But in so far as the radicals were faithful to their principles, there were important differences of psychology and belief between them and the moderates. Radicals had to be determinists. Evil is not born of an act of free will, as the moderates and the orthodox believed. Satan, no longer the officer of God who sins by pride, is the agent of the evil God who penetrates the good creation. The good angels are incapable of sin; Satan deceives or forces them.[80] If radicals still made use of the myth of the seduction of the angels, this was an illogicality, inherited from moderate Bogomilism.

The appropriate myth for the radicals is that of battle in heaven and conquest by Satan. Captured in Satan's bodies, radicals could not tell whether they were the angels conquered by Satan but bound to return to the good creation, or the devils of the evil creation who would stay below in the hell which was earthly existence; only at death would they know. Yet, as is common in such cases, this did not prevent their enthusiastic adherents from

---

[77] See Manselli's comments (*Eresia*, pp. 212–13).

[78] Borst, *Katharer*, pp. 143–74 (fundamental), Manselli, in *CF* III, pp. 129–76.

[79] See Dondaine, introduction to *Un Traité* and extracts from John of Lugio in *WEH*, pp. 511–91; Borst, *Katharer*, p. 122.

[80] *CF* III, p. 147.

sacrificing themselves and clinging zealously to their *consolamentum*. Unconsoled, the angel trapped in the body of a sympathizer moved on in a chain of ⲙⲓⲟⲧⲁⲛⲟⲩ ⲃⲟⲟⲗⲟ ⲱⲁⲛⲇⲟⲧⲟⲇ ⲛⲟⲙ ⲃⲟⲇⲩ ⲧⲟ ⲃⲟⲇⲩ, stretching back to humble creatures and forward to distinguished and noble men, till they arrived at a body of a perfect. If indeed the soul was an angel, then in possession of the valid *consolamentum* after death, it returned at once to the heaven of the good creation. A sympathizer, on the other hand, was in effect rewarded by a step up in the chain; he would next be incarnate in a more attractive being. So, as a stimulant, transmigration of souls had a similar function to the orthodox doctrine of purgatory; penance must yet be done, but there was ultimate hope. Cathars speculated with pleasure on their previous incarnations. In Languedoc a perfect related how he had been a horse, and conveniently found a shoe by the road that he said he had cast in his previous life.[81]

For an evil life, however, there was the penalty of slipping back on the chain to a lower creature. For the devils there was the prospect of endless punishment in different bodies as the evil God and his servant Satan imposed through sexuality their penalty of life on earth. It was a picture of stark force, more gaunt and at the same time more logical than that of the moderates.[82]

It is obvious how deeply Catharism distorted Christian belief, for all the appeal to the Scriptures, made more effective by the vernacular translations kept by the perfect, for all the Christian language of their ritual and the texts which decked their mythology. As Guiraud long ago pointed out,[83] the true affinities of the perfect lay with the ascetic teachers of the East, the bonzes and fakirs of China or India, the adepts of the Orphic mysteries, or the teachers of Gnosticism. Cathar belief, just like Bogomilism, to which it was heir, upset the structure of sacramental life in favour of one rite of supreme importance, the *consolamentum*; replaced a Christian morality by a compulsory asceticism, which made faults consist rather in a soiling by matter than an act of will;[84] eliminated redemption by refusing to admit the saving power of the Crucifixion; and rejected the Trinity in favour of a subordination of two persons to the Father. Cathars could not admit that Christ was God – an angel, perhaps, or a son of God, but still not equal with the Father. Nor could they logically admit that he was man, with a body like that of other men. So the hinge of Christian belief, the incarnation, was destroyed. Radical dualism went still further in its destruction of the pillars of Christian belief, and can hardly be regarded even as extreme Christian heresy. With its belief in two gods and two creations, it might almost be described as another religion altogether.

Yet these distortions of Christian belief would not necessarily repel the uninstructed Catholics, who largely formed the audiences of heretical preachers; the divergences from orthodoxy in all probability would not be apparent to them. The positive drawing power of the heresy lay above all in the life of the perfect and the status of the *consolamentum*; we have seen how the allure of these two drew sympathizers into the heresy or, less reputably, kept

---

[81] Ibid., p. 142.

[82] Emotions best conveyed by Manselli (*CF* iii, pp. 129–76).

[83] *Cartulaire* i, pp. ccxxii–ccxxiii.

[84] As in Bogomilism; see Puech and Vaillant, *Traité*, p. 261.

them in a kind of vacuum waiting for a deathbed *consolamentum*, and how the social context in Languedoc and Italy supported a heretical church organization. Dogmatic instruction followed on a process of assimilation of the sympathizer to the heretic's way of life, which excited his zeal and interest while detaching him from the residual influence of the Church, damned from the start as the Church of Satan. Myths entranced those of poetic imagination and limited critical sense. As churchmen generally complained, a committed Cathar had great immunity to the preaching and teaching which pointed out the difficulties and contradictions of his position. So Cathars were made and retained for their faith.

DIVISIONS AND DECLINE

The fall of Catharism was as dramatic as its rise. From appearing to be a major threat to the Church in the early thirteenth century, it sank to a small, persecuted minority and disappeared altogether in the course of the fourteenth. To account for this we need to bring together the history of the Western Church and the internal development of the sect itself. To some extent this will mean holding up the members of the sect to another kind of mirror to that employed in the previous section in order to show, in place of their attractions, the defects and weaknesses of their position. It will also mean a shift in emphasis amongst the sources, making greater use of Catholic anti-Cathar treatises and summaries in addition to the information from chronicles, inquisitors' interrogations and the works and rituals of the sectaries chiefly used above.

We should look first at the history of organizational and doctrinal dispute within Catharism, which followed speedily on its emergence in the West.

Missionaries, refugees or traders, the dualists of the East who carried their beliefs into the heart of Catholic Europe and began the Cathar movement, also carried with them the religious and personal conflicts which beset them at home.[85] The enterprise which built up Catharism made itself felt in the West in the 1140s; in the 1170s Nicetas, bishop of a radical dualist Church in Constantinople, arrived in Lombardy to confront Mark the gravedigger and the youthful Cathar mission, thus sowing the seed of dissensions there which ended only when the inquisition destroyed the Cathar Churches of Italy. Two sources inform us of the encounter. One is the work of a Catholic observer in Lombardy writing before 1214–15, who had access to details of the doctrinal history of the Italian Cathars,[86] the other is the account of Anselm of Alessandria written some fifty years later, reflecting the tradition of the sect, which reached him in his capacity as inquisitor, no doubt via interrogations.[87] Differing in detail, they agree in the importance they attach to Nicetas's visit.

---

[85] For Eastern dualists, see above, p. 56; D. Obolensky, *Bogomils*; Puech and Vaillant, *Traité* (esp. for nuances of dualism).

[86] *DHC*; *WEH*, pp. 159–67; *MBPH*, pp. 122–7.

[87] *TDH*; *WEH*, pp. 167–70, see also pp. 361–73; *MBPH*, pp. 145–54.

The message of Nicetas to Mark and his friends was quite simple: the Church order on which they based their status was faulty. The earlier source makes extensive use of the Catholic term *ordo*,[88] which seems to mean the authentic tradition both of the *consolamentum* and of the orders of bishop and deacon in the organization, on the analogy of the apostolic succession in the Catholic Church. It was of profound importance, for without the true order Mark's *consolamentum* and that of his group was void, and they were lost. Mark heard the stranger from Constantinople with attention, and decided to accept his order, that of Dragowitsa[89] or Drugonthia,[90] in place of his own, which was that of Bulgaria.[91] The Lombard group were reconsoled, and Mark received the gratification of episcopal orders from the hands of Nicetas, so becoming the first Cathar bishop of Italy.

More was involved in the reconsoling than a change of order. Subsequent history suggests that with the order came the doctrines of radical dualism. The location of Dragowitsa (probably the original of Drugonthia and other forms) is obscure: the name may possibly have derived from the river Dragovitsa in the region of Philippopolis in Thrace, long a stronghold of the Paulicians. Bulgaria is clear enough. This was the cradle of Bogomilism, and its order represented the traditional, early Bogomil belief described in Cosmas and the moderate dualism of the mission phase of Cathar history before Nicetas.

From Italy, Nicetas and Mark passed on to Languedoc. The journey is not mentioned in Italian sources, but the presence of both men is attested in the Cathar record of a great council held at St Félix de Caraman, a village in the Lauragais in 1167.[92] The record as we have it, which begins with the

---

[88] *DHC: AFP* xix (1949), p. 306, l. 5, l. 6, l. 8, l. 9, l. 12, l. 17; p. 306, l. 1; p. 308, l. 9, l. 11; p. 309, l. 1; p. 310, l. 8, l. 10; p. 312, l. 7 (*ordo*); p. 306, l. 16 (*ordo episcopi*); p. 307, l. 1, l. 6 (*episcopalis officio*); p. 308, l. 9 (*episcopatus officium*); p. 308, l. 31 (*ordo episcopatus*). *TDH*, by contrast, though its narrative carries the same implication about the vital role of *ordo* barely uses the term: see *AFP* xx (1950), 'Marchus . . . voluit ire ultra mare ut reciperet ordinem episcopalem ab episcopo de Bulgaria.' For diaconate, see *TDH*, in *AFP* xx (1950), p. 309, l. 2, 'factus est Marchus diaconus'. For vicars of bishops, *filius maior, filius minor*, see Borst, *Katharer*, p. 211.

[89] Identification (hypothetical) and all other Balkan church sites, F. Šanjek, 'Le rassemblement de St-Félix de Caraman et les églises cathares au xiie siècle', *RHE* lxvii (1972), pp. 767–99; map and commentary in M. D. Lambert, 'Die katharischen Bistümer und die Verbreitung des "schismas" von Osten nach Westen', in *Atlas zur Kirchengeschichte: die Christliche Welt in Geschichte und Gegenwart*, ed. H. Jedin, K. S. Latourette and J. Marten (Freiburg im Breisgau, 1970), pp. 56–7.

[90] 'Drugonthia' (*DHC*); 'Drugontia' (*TDH*); 'Drogometia' (acts of council of S. Félix (*Act. Fel.*, below, n. 92)), 'Dugunthia' (Sacconi; see Dondaine, *Un Traité*, p. 70), taken as corruptions of Dragowitsa.

[91] B. Primov, 'Medieval Bulgaria and the dualistic heresies in Western Europe', *Etudes historiques à l'Occasion du xie Congrès International des Sciences Historiques* (Stockholm and Sofia, 1960), pp. 79–102.

[92] All earlier work on this document (*Act. Fel.*) is superseded by B. Hamilton, 'The Cathar Council of S. Félix reconsidered', *AFP* xlviii (1978), pp. 23–53. It is, he believes, a succinct and composite record of three documents: (i) an account of the Council of St Félix, possibly embedded in a more general Cathar history, written by Cathars; (ii) a sermon of Nicetas to the Cathar Church of Toulouse; (iii) an agreement made about boundaries between the Cathar bishoprics of Carcassonne and Toulouse in 1223, the record as a whole being commissioned by Peter Isarn, Cathar bishop of Carcassonne at a time of doctrinal disunity and geographical uncertainty. Hamilton defends authenticity of a controversial source, and has slain an old dragon. Duvernoy, *L'Histoire*, p. 219, argues that Nicetas did not disturb doctrinal unity; see Duvernoy in debate with A. Brenon in *Christianisme*, ed. Brenon and Gouzy, pp. 159–62, and illuminating article by Brenon, 'Les Cathares: bons Chrétiens', ibid., pp. 115–55 (suspicious of emphasis on dualism and dissension in anti-Cathar treatises); Duvernoy and Brenon argue for a Cathar unity imparted by unvaried rite of baptism, pp. 130, 147, 159, more significant than dualist discussions (see also Languedoc

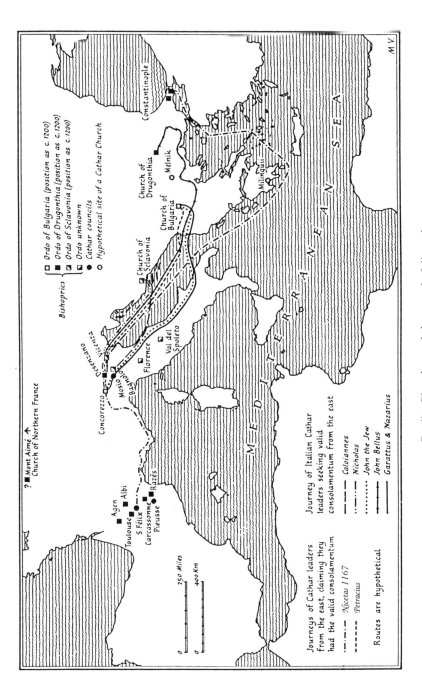

Map of Dualist Churches showing the Mediterranean region with the following labels:

Bishoprics:
- □ Ordo of Bulgaria (position as c.1200)
- ■ Ordo of Drugonthia (position as c.1200)
- ▣ Ordo of Sclavonia (position as c.1200)
- □ Ordo unknown
- ● Cathar councils
- ○ Hypothetical site of a Cathar Church

Locations labelled on the map:
- ? Mont Aimé — Church of Northern France
- Agen
- Albi
- Toulouse
- S. Félix
- Carcassomme
- Pieusse
- Razés
- Comcorezzo
- Desenzano
- Vicenza
- Mosio
- Bagnolo
- Florence
- Val del Spoleto
- Church of Sclavonia
- Church of Bulgaria
- Church of Drugonthia
- Melnik
- Milingui
- Constantinople
- MEDITERRANEAN SEA

Scale: 250 Miles / 400 Km

Journeys of Cathar leaders from the east, claiming they had the valid consolamentum

---- Nicetas 1167
----- Petracius

Routes are hypothetical

Journey of Italian Cathar leaders seeking valid consolamentum from the east

---- Caloiannes
...... Nicholas
.... John the Jew
⊢⊢⊢ John Bellus
——— Garattus & Nazarius

M.V.

MAP 2 Dualist Churches and the spread of dissension.

liturgical formula 'in diebus illis' customary in introducing historical passages read at mass, may well have come from a historical record of Cathars history of the kind which might have been used in the education of the perfect. In summary form it commemorates a mighty gathering, crucial for the history of the Cathars, attended by the chiefs of the movement in the Midi, a 'great multitude' of all their followers and the leader from northern France, Robert de Spernone. The north suffered more persecution than the south, but it had been the source of dualist missions both to southern France and to Lombardy. The gathering covered the lands of Cathar evangelizing in the West. All listened to Nicetas and, we must assume, his attack on the legitimacy of the order of Bulgaria, to which they had hitherto belonged, and were reconsoled under the order of Dragowitsa, including Robert, leader of the mother church.

Only one Cathar bishopric then existed for the Midi, which had the title of Albi, and lay near the site of the open debate of 1165 between Cathar and Catholic representatives at Lombers. Its bishop, Sicard Cellerier, was reconsoled and reconsecrated. His bishopric had most to lose by a subdivision and reorganization which Nicetas proposed to the growing membership in the south, and it was to the Church of Toulouse that Nicetas addressed a sermon, briefly summarized in the record after the description of the great council at St Félix. Nicetas, after referring generally to the customs of the Cathar Churches, went on to speak of the tranquillity, which, he said, prevailed among the dualist churches of Byzantium and the Balkans, and of the virtues of a territorial delimitation between dioceses. The implication was plain: that the Cathars of the south where the heresy was growing should divide up the lands where they had their strength into episcopal units. This they did. In addition to the bishopric at Albi, three more were set up for Toulouse, Carcassonne and, by a plausible modern hypothesis, Agen,[93] with the north French leader as bishop of their Church. After candidates had been elected, they all received their episcopal orders from the hand of Nicetas. In his sermon he had listed the churches of the East, the *Ecclesia Romanae*, Nicetas's own, the New Rome of Constantinople, Drogometia (= Druguntia), Melenguia, the Church of the Milinguii in the Peloponnese, Bulgaria and Dalmatia (elsewhere called Sclavonia). They echoed the churches of Asia of the Apocalypse. With Mark from Lombardy and Robert de Spernone for northern France, the three new bishops in the Midi and Sicard Cellerier at Toulouse, the Cathars of the West had their bishoprics and a symbolism was complete.

No word was said in the text of doctrine but the sporadic evidence of the teaching of the Cathars after this date shows that they were radical dualists

evidence, by Brenon, post St Félix, p. 162). The circumstances of Baptists in modern times offer an analogy which does not support this view. A major doctrinal division exists between Particular and General Baptists, yet it in no way affects the circumstances of their practice of adult baptism: a common rite does not necessarily unite. Rottenwöhrer, *Katharismus* IV (I) is conclusive on doctrinal divisions.

[93] Hamilton, *AFP* XLVIII (1978), pp. 35–6; Y Dossat, 'Remarques sur un prétendu Evêque cathare du Val d'Aran en 1167', in *Bulletin Philogique et Historique du Comité des Travax Historiques et Scientifiques*, Années 1955 et 1956 (Paris, 1957), pp. 339–47; Thouzellier, *Catharisme et Valdéisme*, p. 14, n. 7 (against *Act. Fel.* reading of 'aranensis'); on Albi, see M. Bramel, 'Le Catharisme dans le diocèse d'Albi', in *CF* III, pp. 237–52; Hamilton's comment: *AFP* XLVIII, p. 34. Events in Rottenwöhrer, *Katharismus* III; note correction of Dondaine, p. 542, n. 84; Brenon's view, p. 544. Dating of S. Félix, Rottenwöhrer, pp. 517–22; see A. Jimenez in *Heresis xxii, xxiii.*

accepting the two-god doctrine.[94] Nicetas returned to the East, having achieved a notable victory for his Church and teaching.[95]

After some years another visitor from the East arrived in Italy with disquieting news. Petracius of the Church of Bulgaria came to tell the Lombard Cathars that Simon, who had administered the *consolamentum* to Nicetas (presumably somewhere in the East), had been guilty of moral lapses, including suspect contact with a woman.[96] If this minister of the *consolamentum* fell, so did all he had consoled; and again the Lombard dualists were lost.

This time there was no unified response: some supported Petracius, others vacillated. Accounts differ a little:[97] in Anselm of Alessandria the coming of Petracius shortly preceded the death of Mark, the first bishop, and the succession of Judeus (John the Jew). When Judeus took office, Nicholas of the March, ambitious to be bishop himself, raised a fresh doubt: had Mark himself made a good end? Were the orders of Judeus valid? For the anonymous writer of the early thirteenth century, it was simply Petracius's story that troubled the consciences of the Lombards and resulted in the formation of two parties: that for Judeus and that against him, led by a certain Peter of Florence.

The Cathars yet felt their need of unity, and after a time sought advice from a Cathar bishop outside Italy, who recommended reconciliation by election and the drawing of lots: each party should choose a candidate from the other, and chance should then decide between them.[98] At Mosio, between Mantua and Cremona, they held a council, and Garattus emerged as the bishop accepted by all. But, according to the anonymous writer, just as Garattus was preparing to go in search of an undoubted *consolamentum* from the Church of Bulgaria and collection was being made for his expenses, he was discovered in reprehensible circumstances with a woman.[99] With that, all attempt at unity foundered.

[94] For Languedoc, there is the *Manifestatio* attributed to Ermengaud de Béziers (ed. Dondaine, in *AFP* xxix (1959), pp. 268–71), written before the crusade (radical dualism, but moderate dualism then reappearing: 'Est autem quedam heresis que de novo prosilivit', p. 271; see also Dondaine, in *Miscellanea Giovanni Mercati* v (Rome, 1946), p. 354, and Moore, in *AM* lxxxv (1973), p. 88. For Italy, analyses by contemporaries in *DHC* and *TDH*.

[95] The significance of Nicetas's journey is a key theme of Borst (*Katharer*, pp. 98, 108, 142). It is a victory, Borst believed, with seeds of defeat, for it began a phase of greater concentration on dualism in Catharism, which in the end repelled Western Christians. Compare Dondaine in *Miscellanea* v, p. 354. Would a council of this international calibre have been held only to settle diocesan boundaries? Was not doctrine also involved? (Conversation with M. Roquebert.)

[96] 'inventus in conclavi cum quadam' (*DHC*, in *AFP* xix (1949), p. 306, ll. 13–14).

[97] Compare *DHC*, p. 306; *TDH*, in *AFP* xx (1950), p. 309. *DHC* generally preferred as source nearer to events and more circumstantial on Italian Cathar Churches. It lacks legendary opening on Manes in *TDH* (*AFP* xx (1950), p. 308).

[98] *DHC*, in *AFP* xix (1949), p. 306, l. 22 to p. 307, l. 3. Emissaries are sent 'ad quemdam episcopum ultra montes'. He recommends that the successful candidate should go to Bulgaria to get his episcopal orders ('ut . . . iret in bulgariam ordinem episcopatus suscipere'), i.e. to a moderate dualist Church. If *Act. Fel.* is authentic and Languedoc radical dualist, Moore asks, how is this possible? (*AM* lxxxv (1973), p. 87). Hamilton in *AFP* xlviii (1978), p. 33, resolves the problem by suggesting that the bishop was bishop of northern France, whence came the original mission to Italy, and that his Church had reverted to moderate dualism before the crisis arose.

[99] 'garattus . . . duobus testibus astantibus, reprehensibilis, causa unius mulieris, habitus est' (*DHC*, in *AFP* xix, p. 307, ll. 35–6).

Now others were despatched to find a foolproof *consolamentum*. From the Church of Bagnolo, with its centre in or near Mantua, Caloiannes went to the Church of Sclavonia, a group of moderate dualists in the predominantly Catholic coastal strip of Dalmatia converted to heresy by merchants trading from Constantinople;[100] from Vicenza Nicholas went to the same destination. Judeus, who had humbly resigned office before Mosio to create unity, was next persuaded to take office again as bishop of the Church based on Mark's birthplace at Concorezzo near Milan and to go himself to Bulgaria as a necessary preliminary to get a valid order. Garattus, though at first subdued, remained a force to be reckoned with and later on seems to have made his own pilgrimage to Bulgaria. From the same misty land came the Bogomil *apocryphon*, the *Interrogation of John*, brought to Nazarius of the Church of Concorezzo.[101] Other Churches came into existence at Florence and the Val del Spoleto; here and probably elsewhere local patriotism played a part.

Thus on the ruins of Mark's original mission there emerged six separate Cathar Churches in Italy, with competing adherents scattered widely, but generally linked together by common belief and order; map 2 shows the distribution of their geographical centres as well as the journeys which fostered or accompanied their growth, from East to West the fateful movements of Nicetas and Petracius, from West to East the quest of Western Cathars for the authentic *consolamentum*.

Accounts of the Italian conflicts are retailed to us by hostile witnesses who were not displeased at the discomfiture of the heretics. It is difficult to know what to make of the sexual scandals which punctuate this history. Libertinism was an element in Gnostic heresy; from the tenet that all matter is evil and contact with it, including sexual relations, is to be condemned, it is possible to adopt another position, that for the elect, who have freed themselves from the taint of matter, it has become wholly indifferent whether they engage in sexual relations or not. They are, so to speak, beyond sin, and the rules which must be observed by neophytes no longer apply to them. This was the teaching of the Byzantine heresy of the Messalians, who believed that their initiates, after training and self-denial and the expulsion of the demon in every man's heart, could indulge or not as they pleased, wholly without sin in either case.[102] But there is little sign of libertinism on principle in the Cathars, to judge by the testimony of the inquisition or the evidence of the response to congregations at this stage to news of the fall of this or that perfect. Philip, bishop of Desenzano, was said by Anselm of Alessandria to have disseminated the maxim that there was no sin for man or woman below the girdle, and to have gained followers on the strength of it.[103] The story may have been slander. More significant was the statement of Sacconi from his own experience that perfect regretted not having taken more advantage of the sexual freedom of the believer before they received the *consolamentum*.[104] In the last resort,

---

[100] Identification of Sclavonia in *TDH* (*AFP* xx, p. 308, ll. 11–14; for Prior Suibert of Hungary in 1259, see Gerard of Fracheto, *Vitae Fratrum*, ed. B. M. Reichert (Louvain, 1896), pp. 305–8; literature above, p. 126, n. 89, p. 98, n. 24.

[101] Above, p. 121, n. 69; Duvernoy, *Religion*, p. 108, n. 15 (corrects historians).

[102] Obolensky, *Bogomils*, pp. 48–52.

[103] *TDH*, in *AFP* xx, p. 310, ll. 3–4; cited as hearsay ('dicitur').

[104] Dondaine, *Un Traité*, p. 66.

however, we need assume no more than the commonsense view, that some perfect did fall, as did many among the Catholic clergy, and that the hypersensitivity and rigidity of the Cathars over the *consolamentum* tended to exaggerate any genuine failing, and may even have led to the invention of others. The libertine in the days of vitality of the sect was very much the exception.[105]

Personal conflicts, anxiety over the *consolamentum* and local patriotism all made the Italians a prey to dissensions imported from the East. Their intellectual activity perpetuated the doctrinal divisions and created others; differences of belief continued a disunity, in contrast to the relative stability of the territorially based and less speculative Church of Languedoc.[106] Dossat finds only one instance of an adherent in Languedoc refusing contact with another because of a doctrinal difference.[107]

In Italy the doctrinal quarrels continued after the disintegration into separate Churches, fed by the struggles of leading perfect against each other, and by the pressures of rational reflection or of the example and polemic of the orthodox. The most profound division was that which lay between the radical dualists of Desenzano and the moderates; the Churches which accepted the order of Sclavonia occupied a middle ground between them and the traditional Bogomilism of Bulgaria. Especially significant are the efforts in the thirteenth century of two Cathars on opposite wings of the movement to put their beliefs on a more rational footing. Desiderius, *filius major* of the Church of Concorezzo, tried to do away with the influence of the *apocrypha*, and taught that the texts of Scripture on marriage were to be interpreted literally for the adherents of the sect, so providing them with a conventional sexual framework.[108] He acknowledged that Christ did have a human body. John of Lugio, probably originally of the Church of Desenzano, and his followers took the opposite view and taught that dualism of the moderate kind could not be defended, any more than Catholicism, and that the only logical answer to the problem of evil was a thoroughgoing radical dualism, given philosophical justification in the Book of Two Principles from their school, the most considerable intellectual achievement of any Cathar. Repetitious, ultimately wearying, as its first editor Dondaine justly noted,[109] it was a sign that Italian Cathars were beginning to feel the force of Catholic polemic.

[105] See Capelli's evidence, above, p. 108.

[106] B. Hamilton accepts a conversion to radical dualism after the visit of Nicetas, and believes that there was an attempt by Bartholomew of Carcassonne in the aftermath of the Albigensian Crusade to win back ground for the moderate dualists in the diocese of Agen, but that this was short-lived, and that by 1229 Agen was again radical dualist (*AFP* XLVIII (1978), pp. 44–8). A. Brenon, 'Les Cathares . . .', in *Christianisme*, ed. Brenon and Gouzy, pp. 161–2 (debate), argues against a conversion of the Cathar leadership in Languedoc to radical dualism at the hands of Nicetas, citing the abjurations of moderate dualism by Raimon de Baimiac and his *socius* after the capture of Lavaur (above, p. 84), and accepts, rather, a gradual move to radical dualism as a result of logical reflection (see also pp. 131–40).

[107] *CF* III, 79.

[108] *TDH*, in *AFP* XX, pp. 310–12, tr. in *WEH*, pp. 362–4; *MBPH*, p. 149. Borst, *Katharer*, p. 122.

[109] *Un Traité*, p. 22; on the author, see Thouzellier, *Le Livre* (latest edn, above, p. 118, n. 57), pp. 33–46. A. Reltgen, 'Dissidences et contradictions en Italie', *Christianisme*, ed. Brenon and Gouzy, pp. 89–109 (debate, pp. 110–13), discusses Cathar innovations as sign of weakness in face of vitality of Catholics in thirteenth century; see useful summary on credibility of antiheretical treatises: pp. 92–4; characterizing of all Italian heresies, pp. 104–9, noting inability 'to renew their spirituality'. See also G. Zanella, *Itinerari ereticali : Patari e Catari tra Rimini e Verona* (Rome, 1986), pp. 29–45. Rottenwöhrer, *Katharismus* iv (2) shows *Diprinzipialismus* (preferred term for radical dualism) was dominant in Languedoc.

The evidence suggests that the Cathars began with a stress on evangelical life in the twelfth century, and came in time to devote more and more attention to dualist beliefs, which at first had remained in the background. Catholic counter-attack constantly stressed dualism, aiming to show the wavering faithful that Catharism, so far from being a movement of reform and asceticism, was in fact a heresy which denied fundamental doctrines of Christianity: their polemic forced the Cathars to think more about their dualism, and drew it out of the shadows.[110]

Both John of Lugio and Desiderius were attempting in their different ways to update Catharism in response to new needs and more effective attacks. Neither could impart a new direction to the heresy, though both attracted followers. Desiderius battled against his bishop Nazarius, a weaver of fantasies of the old school, and split the Church of Concorezzo; John of Lugio could not move older adherents but did reach some members of the younger generation of Cathars. The majority of the Italian Cathars were not deeply interested: they liked their *apocrypha* and their myths, for all their internal contradictions.[111] But where Desiderius and John of Lugio and their disciples had been impelled to rethink their position by the force of a revived and better informed Catholicism, we may assume others outside Catharism had been influenced against the movement altogether. Orthodox polemic and the preaching and argument based on it would not necessarily detach existing adherents[112] but it warned others against being drawn into heresy. Borst is surely right to see in the work of these two a symptom of decline.

In the thirteenth century in Languedoc as well as in Italy, a conventional pattern of Church life built up in Catharism; obedience, order and hierarchy came to outweigh the earlier stress on morality. It has been argued the writing of a Latin ritual for the *consolamentum* in Italy in the thirteenth century sacrificed vernacular freshness (seen in the Provençal version) for Latin solemnity. That is unlikely: Latin probably came first.[113] But the development of rituals for lesser occasions may well have been an imitation of the sacramental structure of Catharism,[114] and greater formalism is implicit when it came to be admitted that a perfect who had fallen could be reconsoled, and a procedure for doing so emerged.

The Cathars attempted to prove that they had seven orders, just as the Catholics.[115] The constitutional position could never be quite the same as in Catholicism because of the status of the perfect. In the Latin rite of the *consolamentum*, however, obedience by the candidate to his superiors was given greater emphasis.[116] The rights of election of the whole body of perfect

[110] Vicaire, in *CF* III, pp. 105–28.

[111] On this I prefer Manselli (*Eresia*, p. 272 and n. 41) to Dondaine (*AFP* XX, p. 274).

[112] Implied in Manselli, *Eresia*, ch. 9 (characterization of Cathar supporters, pp. 210–13); compare Vicaire, *CF* III, pp. 122–3. Contemporary polemists and modern historians may have exaggerated the significance of nuances of dualism for rank and file Cathars.

[113] Above, p. 106, n. 3; dating and origin, Rottenwöhrer, *Katharismus* IV (1), pp. 35–7; Hamilton in Biller, Hudson, *Literacy*, pp. 38–60 at p. 48.

[114] Borst, *Katharer*, p. 121.

[115] Ibid., p. 212, n. 34 and references.

[116] Ibid., p. 282.

diminished in practice; it became usual to feel that the bishop could only be consecrated by another bishop, as in Catholic practice. The more the *consolamentum* was administered on the deathbed, the more importance attached to the ministers of the sect, especially the deacons, who undertook this duty. The increasing prominence of the hierarchy tended to depress the status of the women perfect, who were debarred from these offices; myths were affected by practice, Koch believes, and the fundamental early tenet of equality of the sexes after the administration of the *consolamentum* was obscured by narratives which stressed woman's secondary creation or her evil role as a tool of Satan.[117] *Verkirchlichung*, the development of a conventional Church structure and life outlined for us by Borst,[118] represents both a natural stage in the history of religious movements and, especially in Italy, an effect of the peaceful competition with the Church; but it diminished the force of Catharism's challenge to orthodoxy.

Meanwhile, repression of heresy, first in Languedoc, then in Italy, grew more effective. The political situation decided the extent to which legislation against heresy was actually effective. In Languedoc, Innocent III's crusade at first threw the Cathars into disarray and scattered their communities. Numbers of perfect were killed as a by-product of operations, but the organization re-formed and continued to work, albeit with diminished numbers. In 1225, indeed, they held a council at Pieusse and decided to set up a new diocese at Razès.[119] The brutalities of the crusade inhibited the work of re-conversion of Bishop Fulk of Toulouse and St Dominic. Civic patriotism in Toulouse and the attitudes of the Midi generally, with its traditional toleration and penchant for political balancing, weakened the cause of orthodoxy. But the ending of warfare and the surrender of the count of Toulouse at the Treaty of Paris in 1229 opened the way to effective persecution. It descended like a storm on the minority of leading families and their supporters in Toulouse who had been involved in Catharism; between 1229 and 1237 the backbone of heresy in the city was broken; from mid-century Toulouse ceased to be significant in the history of Catharism. The Council of Toulouse in 1229 set the scene for persecution, systematizing existing canonical decisions, giving confirmation to a pre-existing development in the Midi of the synodal witnesses of the *Ad abolendam* era into a form of police specializing in heresy and foreshadowing the mass investigations by inquisitors proper by its injunctions to the gathering of oaths of fidelity to the Church and the making of full lists of parishioners. A network for supervision was to be created, that would easily throw into focus any deviation from Catholic

---

[117] Koch, *Frauenfrage*, pp. 71–8.

[118] A good working hypothesis, which nevertheless cannot be fully secure until we have more exact dating of developments in Cathar rites and practice. Mr R. I. Moore reminds me that Garattus was rehabilitated and that the story of Nicetas's mission shows concern for consecration of bishops by other bishops. The role of women in Autier's revival (below, p. 139) is clearly secondary, but it was natural for this man to wish to build round him a corps of men perfect, physically active and hardy enough for the rigours of relentless, often nocturnal, movement, keeping ahead of persecution.

[119] But note Wakefield's comment (*Heresy, Crusade*, p. 132); sequence of events described in chs 7, 8, 9. Pieusse lies close to Carcassonne on the south. I owe a correction on this to M. Roquebert; for summary on crusade and attitudes, see Mundy, *Repression*, pp. 18–26; interesting example of ostentatious gesture of contempt by a Cathar: p. 24.

MAP 3   Inquisition versus Catharism: the enquiries of 1245–6.
Source: Adapted from Y. Dossat, *Les Crises de l'inquisition toulousaine au xiiie siècle (1233–1273)*
(Bordeaux, 1959), pp. 228–9.

observance. Bailiffs were to be coerced into cooperation.[120] It was not wholly
effective, for Count Raymond vii in the 1230s was still acting equivocally and
his servants gave only partial support to repression. The first commissions of
Gregory ix to Dominicans to exercise authority in 1233 put into action some of

---

[120] On persecution in Toulouse, see Mundy, *Repression*; on Council of Toulouse, see Kolmer, *Vulpes*,
pp. 64–78.

the most formidable instruments of repression; but they were not all at once successful. The Dominicans were even driven out of Toulouse for a time in 1235, and in 1238 Gregory IX, who wished to detach Raymond from support of Frederick II, met the count's wishes and virtually suspended the tribunal based on Toulouse for three years. But time favoured repression, and a mechanism for pursuing heresy grew in efficiency.

In the country the years 1240 to 1243 were the turning-point.[121] Peter Seila, Dominican, former companion of St Dominic, who had campaigned earlier as inquisitor in Quercy with moderate success, achieved much more in a second inquisition of 1241–2, in which more suspects availed themselves of the time of grace at the opening of inquiries to make their confessions of heresy. Fear had grown of the reality of punishment to follow conviction. The tide had begun to turn. Two vain revolts showed the southern nobles that they would never regain independence by force; and the killing of a party of inquisitors at Avignonet aroused determination to scotch the heresy. The murder had been organized from Montségur, a castle in the foothills of the Pyrenees long a refuge for perfect and their supporters; an army under a royal seneschal besieged and took it and handed over to the Church two hundred or more perfect, including the bishops of Toulouse and Razès. The Cathars of the south never recovered from the loss of so many of the elite. At the same time Raymond abandoned his policy of equivocal support, and began to persecute. In 1249, with less discrimination than the inquisitors, he burnt eighty suspects at Agen in one day. His successor Alphonse of Poitiers, brother of King Louis IX and a cold zealot, was unusually energetic in persecution.

In fact, for the majority of the southern higher nobility, the Cathars had always been negotiable. The wars had been fought over the control of the south, not over heresy, and Raymond VII was characteristic of most of the higher nobility in being ready to throw the heretics over when it was politically expedient to do so. Once the struggle for control of Languedoc was decided, the heretics found few important defenders. There were great conspiracies, both of silence and of action, including a plot to steal inquisition records at Carcassonne and the murder of inquisitors' assistants at Caunes.[122] The last Cathar was burnt in Languedoc as late as 1330.[123] Nevertheless, from 1243, the writing was on the wall.

Why, given the final defeat of the indigenous baronage of Languedoc, this should have been so may be illustrated by examining the inquisitors of the region at the top of their form in the inquiries of Bernard de Caux and his aides in the region of the Lauragais and the neighbourhood of Lavaur in 1245–6.[124] In these investigations 5,471 persons in two archdeaconries were interrogated. Suspects brought to light were to an overwhelming degree

---

[121] Wakefield, *Heresy, Crusade*, ch. 10 (bibliography on Montségur, p. 191, n. 3); Raymond, pp. 148–50, Dossat, *Crises*, pp. 271–5; for remarks on Seila's inquisition of 1241–2, see Kolmer, *Vulpes*, pp. 150–62.

[122] Plot at Carcassonne described in Guiraud, *Inquisition* II, ch. 11; and murder at Caunes by Wakefield (*Heresy, Crusade*, p. 187). See also the latter's 'Friar Ferrier, inquisition at Caunes, and escapes from prison at Carcassonne', *CHR* LVIII (1972), pp. 220–37.

[123] Borst, *Katharer*, p. 136.

[124] Dossat, *Crises*, chs 2, 3, pp. 226–44 (map: pp. 228–9; table of sentences: pp. 258–9); for Waldensians, see Y. Dossat, 'Les Vaudois méridionaux d'après les documents de l'inquisition', *CF* II, pp. 207–26 at p. 212.

FIGURE 2   Quéribus (les Corbières), the last fortress of the Cathars, surrendered to royal forces after a short siege in 1255; subsequently a defensive point for the frontier against Aragon.

Photograph: Leonhard von Matt, Buochs/Switzerland.

Cathars; only forty-one references are to be found to Waldensians. Questions were of the police-court type, concerned with the external acts such as adoration, which revealed complicity with heresy; only marginally did they deal with belief. Each adult in the communities shown on map 3 was compelled to answer. If a suspect broke down under interrogation, others would follow; lies were uncovered by cross-checking. Five more inquiries were launched in this region. In 1260 the record of the original investigation was recopied.

TABLE 1   Sentences of Bernard de Caux, 1246

Community	Prison	Crosses and other penances	Community	Prison	Crosses and and penances
Airoux	0	1	Le Mas-Saintes-Puelles	0	8
Auriac	0	4	Les Cassés	1	3
Avignonet	0	11	Montauriol	0	1
Baraigne	0	3	Montégut	0	3
Barelles	3	3	Montesquieu-Lauragais	0	7
Beauteville	0	2	Montgiscard	1	4
Bram	0	3	Montmaur	0	2
Cambiac	1	4	Odars	0	1
Cambon	0	4	Pexiora	0	5
Castelnaudary	0	8	Prunet	0	1
Drémil	0	1	Roumens	1	4
Fanjeaux	3	25	Saint-Germier	0	1
Gaja-le-Selve	0	1	Saint-Julia	0	1
Gibel	0	1	Saint Martin-la-Lande	7	19
Goudourville	1	2	Saint-Paul-Cap-de-Joux	0	1
Juzes	0	2	Saint-Paulet	1	1
Lanta	0	1	Villeneuve-la-Comtal	0	7
Laurac	2	28	Villepinte	0	3
Lavaur	1	5	Villesiscle	0	3
Lavelanet	1	0			

Source: From Y. Dossat, *Les Crises de l'inquisition toulousaine au XIIIe siècle (1233–1273)* (Bordeaux, 1959), pp. 258–90.

The table of sentences, derived from the close study of Dossat, covers those pronounced by Bernard de Caux between 18 March and 22 July 1246, and gives us as fair a picture of the extent of heresy in this region in 1245–6 as we are likely to get. As Dossat warns, it is still not wholly accurate as a picture of heresy uncovered in these enquiries, as the manuscripts on which he based the table are not necessarily comprehensive, but it is unlikely to be gravely misleading. Heretics were a minority, but a tenacious one, and they were widespread, as the thirty-nine localities in the table shows. A wide, if rather thin, scattering seems a fair inference, although we may notice some concentration in the south-west corner of the region, in, for example, Fanjeaux, Laurac and St Martin-la-Lande.

However, tenacity on the part of the heretics was matched by tenacity on the part of the inquisitors. The sequence of enquiries shows that in this region the connections with heresy of the whole population were searched out by blanket interrogation, then rechecked over the years, gradually rooting out the guilty. Sentencing was not unusually harsh. The table lists 207 sentences; twenty-three were of imprisonment, and the rest consisted of lighter penalties, such as compulsory pilgrimages or crosses worn on the clothing. Burning was not included in the records Dossat surveys, but we know from other evidence that its incidence was quite light.[125] The essence of the method was persistence and long memory: terror was maintained as much by the threat as by the reality of prison or fire. No minority religious movement could continue indefinitely in the face of pressure of this kind. Rural Catharism was weakened by the effects of the phase of speedy persecution in Toulouse after the peace of 1229. In Toulouse and elsewhere the friars had some success in raising standards. Peter Seila was able to influence the patriciate; he was more than an efficient inquisitor. At best, the friars could provide examples of idealism to rival the *perfecti* and the growing practice of auricular confession gave new vitality to orthodox spiritual life. In Toulouse the extent of charitable foundations and activities is witness to an orthodox conscience at work. In the country the problem of standards and training of local clergy remained. Force and persuasion worked together to undermine heresy, probably in differing proportions in different places; bitterness over the cruelties of repression, and the defeat of a traditional leadership worked one way; on the other hand, the eventual victory of the north, and of the monarchy offered new opportunities. The fall of Catharism and the decline of the traditional south has complexities.[126]

Signs of decline were apparent from the 1240s onwards. The life of the perfect changed character,[127] and secrecy grew. The black robe was exchanged for a girdle worn next to the skin, and individual perfect moved from houses known to the public to huts and cabins. Chances of proselytism lessened and, as far as the women were concerned, the popularity of Dominic's foundation at Prouille seems to have grown. Women perfect were in retreat, while about mid-century Prouille had fifty nuns. Emigration of Cathars to their colleagues in Italy began.[128] By about 1250 Sacconi calculated that the old Cathar Churches of Toulouse, Albi, Carcassonne and Agen had less than 200 perfect between them;[129] perhaps, though, as an inquisitor and a former perfect he tended to exaggerate the extent of the Church's success by that stage.[130]

---

[125] Wakefield, *Heresy, Crusade*, pp. 184–5, 193, n. 10.

[126] See comments of Biget, reviewing Mundy, *Repression*, in *Annales* XLII (1987), pp. 137–40; on inner contradictions of Catharism as a factor in decline, I remain unconvinced that they had much impact in Languedoc, and on this point differ from Dondaine (*AFP* XX, p. 274) and Borst (*Katharer*, p. 133). I am still moved by Borst's powerful book, but believe he underestimates force, especially in Languedoc, to some degree in Italy, and overestimates the destructive effect of radical dualism.

[127] Koch, *Frauenfrage*, chs 4, 9; Dossat, in *CF* III, p. 74.

[128] Dupré Theseider, in *CF* III, pp. 299–313.

[129] Dondaine, *Un Traité*, p. 70; *WEH*, p. 337.

[130] Comment of Professor C. N. L. Brooke.

Still there was adaptation to circumstances. The range of contacts, which extended as far as a north French immigrant, of the Cathar deacon Pagès in his long career from 1269 to 1284 in Cabardès and neighbouring lands, shows how heresy could live on in these late days.[131] Under pressure, leaders authorized the perfect to shed blood;[132] the *convenenza*, a pact between a perfect who would administer the *consolamentum* and a candidate, to be fulfilled at a moment of necessity when death was at hand and the candidate could no longer speak, was evolved to meet more desperate circumstances. The *endura*, a form of suicide, occasionally by violent means, but usually by taking to bed and refusing food, passing from life secure in the possession of the *consolamentum* on a diet of sugared water, became an occasional feature;[133] it had always been a logical end for those who believed that life itself was an imprisonment under Satan, and a possible psychological effect of the obsessive and perfectionist life of the perfect, but its early incidence is rare and a little ambiguous. Never at all frequent, its incidence increased in late Catharism, when after 1295 one commanding personality, the radical dualist Pierre Autier, a notary of Ax, led a revival in the highlands of Foix.[134]

A professional man in a semi-literate society, he was accustomed to taking a lead. His missionizing splayed out from his family connections; there were few of his relatives who did not see him secretly, aid him, give him refuge or introduce him to candidates to be consoled. Like a good businessman financing a commercial enterprise, he retained deposits, the product of his sale of assets before he left for training in Lombardy: the reserves, coupled with the gifts of adherents, kept him and his little band afloat. Pierre's brother Guillaume, a gentler personality, was prepared tacitly to abandon the rule that a candidate for the *consolamentum*, who through illness was unable to pronounce the *Pater Noster*, could not have the rite administered; Pierre was not. It was he who told Guillem Catalan that she would forfeit her status if she were touched on the naked skin by a man. Such rigorist attitudes fostered the *endura*, for it ensured that the dying slipped safely out of life with all their renunciations intact, and, incidentally, removed dangerous witnesses when the inquisition was on their track.

There were only fourteen perfect at maximum at any one time in the mission. It was too few, and, as repression removed helpers, the survivors were unable to console enough of the requisite calibre to replace losses. For a

---

[131] Guiraud, *Inquisition* II, pp. 277–8.

[132] For this and what follows, see Y. Dossat, 'L'évolution des rituels cathares', *Revue de Synthèse*, n.s. XXII–XXIII (1948), pp. 27–30.

[133] Dossat (*CF* III, pp. 85–7) corrects and supplements C. Molinier, 'L'Endura: coutûme religieuse des derniers sectaires albigeois', *Annales de la Faculté des Lettres de Bourdeaux*, 1r ser. III (1881), pp. 282–99; Brenon, in *Christianisme*, ed. Brenon and Gouzy, p. 149, argues that the *endura* is a semi-legend; on *convenenza*, see Cazenave, ibid., p. 22, relating Cathar practice to meridional contract.

[134] J. M. Vidal, 'Les derniers ministres de l'Albigéisme en Languedoc: leurs doctrines', *RQH* LXXIX (1906), pp. 57–107; 'Doctrine et morale des derniers ministres albigeois', *RQH* LXXXV (1909), pp. 357–409, LXXXVI (1909), pp. 5–48; Koch, *Frauenfrage*, pp. 82, 87–8; differing emphasis by Wakefield in *Heresy, Crusade*, p. 189. A. Pales-Gobilliard, *L'Inquisiteur Geoffroy d'Ablis et les Cathares du Comté de Foix (1308–1309)* (Paris, 1984) (valuable introduction; see also index). *Le Registre d'Inquisition de Jacques Fournier (1318–1325)*, ed. J. Duvernoy, I–III (Toulouse, 1965); E. Griffe, *Le Languedoc cathare et l'inquisition (1229–1329)* (Paris, 1980), esp. chs 8, 9; J. Duvernoy, 'Le catharisme en Languedoc au début du XIVe siècle', *Effacement du Catharisme? (XIII–XIV siècles)*, *CF* XX (1985), pp. 27–56.

time Autier with Guillaume and his devoted missionary son, Jacques, was able to create a new priesthood manifestly austere, with little in the material world to gain from their hunted, underground lives, a replacement for a relaxed, poorly educated Catholic priesthood in the highland villages. Then Pierre at last was captured, kept for twenty months in prison and burnt in 1311. It marked the end of Cathar hopes. Yet Autier's short-lived success was significant. It was proof that the vitality of the old heresy, to which he brought no innovations save perhaps the more extended use of the *endura*, in the right hands and in the right context, had not been extinguished; and that its fall in the highlands of Foix was not due to inner decadence or to the quality of the peaceful competition of Catholicism, but to the determined use of the machinery of repression by a few churchmen.

The Autier brothers appear and disappear in the recollections of the inhabitants of the village of Montaillou, high in the mountains in the Sabartès region in the south of the lands of Foix, near to Catalonia.[135] Catharism probably came nearer to taking over an entire locality in this remote hamlet than anywhere else in Languedoc and the investigations of the Dominican Geoffrey d'Ablis in 1308–9 and then, more spectacularly, of the Cistercian bishop of Pamiers, Jacques Fournier, subsequently Pope Benedict XII, over the years 1318 to 1325 provide an unusual richness of evidence for so small a place. There were only 200–250 inhabitants early in the fourteenth century; in the time of Geoffrey d'Ablis, Cathar households formed a majority in the village; under Fournier, the investigation revealed eleven households of heretics, five of Catholics and a few shifting or dividing, as well as many where some heresy was present.

It was a resilient Catharism. It entered by family relationship. Guillaume Autier was the son-in-law of Arnaud Benet of Ax, whose brother Guillaume was head of a household in Montaillou. It was fostered by a strange circumstance, in which two brothers, Bernard Clergue, the bayle, representing lay power, and Pierre Clergue, the village priest, were sympathetic to Catharism and secretly fostered it. Pierre Clergue, a passionate and vengeful village Napoleon, used his authority to blackmail any Catholic opposition and ward off or manipulate any hostile investigations from the ecclesiastical authority based lower down. He was outwardly diligent, saying mass, hearing confessions, attending synods, and was pleased that his mother had been buried near the altar to the Virgin at Notre Dame de Carnasses, the pilgrimage chapel of Montaillou. Yet he was also prepared to say that his mother's soul would be in heaven because she had sent to the heretics of Montaillou when

[135] See Pales-Gobilliard, *L'Inquisiteur*; Duvernoy, 'Le catharisme'; E. Le Roy Ladurie, *Montaillou: village occitan de 1294 à 1324* (Paris, 1975); tr. (abridged) B. Bray, *Montaillou* (London, 1978); for Clergue brothers, Le Roy Ladurie, ch. 3; on Catharism in the *domus*, pp. 54, 58; Guillaume Autier's claims and evidence of Béatrice de Planisolles, p. 469; the Cathar paradise, p. 611. For Pierre's rigorism, see *Fournier*, ed. Duvernoy, I, pp. 287, 294. I am indebted for anthropological comment to Ms L. S. Davison, kindly forwarded by Dr J. O. Ward, Department of History, University of Sydney. Le Roy Ladurie should now be read in conjunction with L. E. Boyle, 'Montaillou revisited: *mentalité* and methodology', *Pathways to medieval peasants*, ed. J. A. Raftis, Toronto, 1981, pp. 119–40 (witty, penetrating critique) M. Benad, *Domus und Religion in Montaillou*, Tübingen, 1990, focusses on Clergues; excellent literature but problem hypotheses. I owe information to Dr J. Duvernoy. See Duvernoy in *Mediaevistik* iii (1990), 417–8.

they were in prison, and in conversation with his former mistress, he assured her that God alone could forgive sins, and that she had no need to go to confession. He was a determined lecher, prepared to blackmail women at the baths of Ax with the threat of the Inquisition in order to seduce them. Bernard, collecting the tithe, ensured that a portion was left for the Cathar perfect, and that no complaints about heresy reached the central administration.

The perfect came and went secretly and mysteriously: sometimes they disguised visits, passing themselves off as tailors, which gave them opportunities to infiltrate their views in conversations with the womenfolk of Montaillou. They seemed to the inhabitants a race apart, not exacting as orthodox clergy often seemed to be, but living simply and earning their own way. Celibacy, abstinence from meat and extensive fasting set them apart from humdrum mankind and gave them a position of respect. 'They follow the path of the apostles Peter and Paul', one inhabitant said. They had a social function, were witnesses to oaths and helped to integrate a poor, divided society. Catholicism revolved round the church building; Catharism round the household, the *domus* or *ostal*. Here the perfect or their committed followers set to work, instructing informally, talking by the fire, addressing small gatherings, exercising a talent for the storytelling in which the great myths of the war in heaven, the origins of evil and the transmigration of souls could be entertainingly brought over to a peasant audience.

Books played a very minor role in an oral society, in which perhaps only 2 per cent were literate. Guillaume Autier had a Cathar calendar, lost to us, which he lent to Pierre Clergue; it was used as a book for talks. The gospel book, placed on the head of a neophyte at the reception of the *consolamentum*, no doubt added to the drama and solemnity of the occasion in a society in which books were relatively rare.

Illiterate though they were, the villagers were not lacking in interest in the issues of life, death and the hereafter, and their capacity for conversation on these high matters was exploited by the agents of heresy. Heresy moved from household to household, and descended in families. Much was known about the opinions of neighbours, but interrelation and the fear of consequences, as well as the Clergue brothers, inhibited denunciations. Cathars married Cathars.

Occupation was not without influence on religious opinion. Peasants near subsistence in a static settlement naturally tended to fatalism, and this trait opened the way to acceptance of the determinism built into the tradition of radical dualism. The absence of material goods and the wandering, precarious life of the shepherds seem to have given them an affinity for the way of life of the perfect and a distaste for the Catholicism of the plains.

The Catholicism of the village was that of a pre-Gregorian world, unreflective, syncretistic and wholly untouched by the changes in the life of the Church at large, which had taken place since the eleventh century. Friars did not come up to these heights. Side by side with the Catharism and Catholicism, of a sort, was a third force, pagan, folkloric, sceptical – the survivor of a more distant past, but none the less pervasive and influential. On the whole, it worked more for Catharism than against it, providing the basis for a crude materialism about the mass, leading readily to cynicism about the orthodox doctrine of creation. Catholicism lacked potency: the support of the *Aubian* family, rivals of the Clergues, was more a matter of clans and family division and less a matter of ethical commitment. Baptism was customary but it had a predominantly social function. There was little genuine hostility to the heresy: the Catholic households maintained towards the heretical ones a benevolent neutrality.

Where Catharism scored most was at the deathbed. The *consolamentum* gave an assurance of salvation, guaranteed by the calibre of life of the perfect. Guillaume Autier made unqualified claims for the powers of the perfect to absolve which, he said, were equal to those of the apostles Peter and Paul; the Catholic Church, by contrast, had no such power. At the point of death, this supreme confidence, and the respect in which most perfect were held, could work powerfully on the mind. So Béatrice de Planisolles described how a woman of Montaillou grappled with her children to induce them to fetch one of the perfect to console her, despite their fears of punishment. They were anxious about the penalties of confiscation of goods if the hereticating was discovered: she reproached them with preferring her goods to her soul. The Cathar leadership was tolerant of the failings of rank and file members; rigid themselves, with rare exceptions, over sexual matters, they appeared to be, or perhaps had to be, complacent about the activities of villagers who were relatively untouched by Catholic teaching and were driven most of all by care for the family and the security and prosperity of the *domus*. It was an evil world, and sexual activity of any kind was diabolical; but all sins, however deadly, could be forgiven in a moment by the laying-on of hands and the dying promises of renunciation in the *consolamentum*. The reward was instant and unqualified by the pains of the Catholic purgatory – a paradise in which 'each soul will have as much joy and happiness as any other; and all will be one'. So long as the perfect remained in action and sustained their own renunciations the appeal of deathbed consoling kept its power; but the perfect were physically vulnerable, and in Geoffrey d'Ablis, 'a soul without feebleness', they met their match.

The turn of the Italians to suffer persecution came later. When Ivo of Narbonne, fleeing from what he claimed to be an unjust heresy charge, wandered amongst the Cathars of northern Italy in 1214, he found a remarkable degree of freedom and vitality among them, at ease in Como, Milan, Gemona in Friuli and elsewhere, living well, spreading their faith among the merchants at fairs and sending adherents to study logic or theology at Paris, with the aim of overthrowing Catholicism from an inner knowledge.[136] While the Churches of Languedoc crumbled, Italy was a relatively safe place of refuge; during the siege of Montségur a Cathar bishop in Cremona sent through a fraternal letter to the bishop of Toulouse with an offer of asylum, which he refused. Guides and hospices by the way facilitated the emigration of heretics from Languedoc, probably for the sake of secrecy along the most difficult route by the Alpes Maritimes, Nice, the Col de Tende and so via

---

[136] Manselli, *Eresia*, p. 221; Ivo of Narbonne, *WEH*, pp. 185–7; authenticity: Segl, *Österreich*, pp. 76–111.

Roccavione to the plain of Cuneo.[137] A trickle of perfect came back on return missions to give pastoral care or the *consolamentum* to the fragments of the Churches of Languedoc in the dark days, and at Asti the greatest of the exiles, Autier, received his heretical ordination. Bacconi noted that the remains of the north French Church, amounting to some 150 perfect in mid-century, had found refuge in Verona and Lombardy generally.[138] This security was, however, based on no firm foundations, since Cathars in Italy were being tolerated by communal authorities, not so much for their own sake as for the sake of the autonomy of the cities or anticlerical and antipapal feeling, and when, for one reason or another, opinion tilted against the heretics, they had no reliable defenders.

Local sentiment was volatile. As we have seen, Catholic reaction in Orvieto brought Pietro Parenzo into power;[139] his assassination instantly aroused popular feeling in sympathy. Yet in 1239, the Dominican convent in the city was sacked.[140] In Florence there was violence against a Ghibelline *podestà* in 1245 because of his failure to take action against the Cathar Barone del Barone. On the other hand, the inquisitor St Peter Martyr was assassinated in 1252 because of his prosecution of heretics in the country outside Milan, and seven years later there was protest in the city against the work of his subordinate and successor, Sacconi.

So matters swung to and fro. What generally preserved the quasi-immunity of the heretics in the first half of the century was the struggle between Frederick II and the popes. Having secured the promulgation of antiheretical legislation by Frederick II and built up a corpus of law against heresy, the popes were unwilling to exert great pressure on the cities to implement this legislation for fear of losing allies. Suspicion in the communes of central authority was at first enough to prevent general acceptance of statutes of support for the introduction of the inquisition, and the popes lacked the leverage to insist. Frederick's own attitude was opportunist.[141] The reality of his concern was shown by his inaction towards heresy in the Regno: to take effective action would have meant introducing the friars to his kingdom, and he was unwilling to do this on political grounds. But he noticed the reluctance of Gregory IX to press the heresy issue so long as his own political requirements made it inconvenient, and used this as a point of criticism in his propaganda. His successor Manfred was a fautor of heretics.

The Cathars used any support that they could find. A natural conjunction of interest brought them into alliance with the Ghibellines. But the heretics never formed an independent force anywhere in communal politics; they generally tended to receive favour in times of interdict, but they were pawns in a political battle, and when the Ghibelline forces lost they were without support.

---

[137] Guiraud, *Inquisition* II, ch. 9; Dupré Theseider, in *CF* III, pp. 299–316; why did they flee to Italy, and not into Spain? Dr A. Roach of Glasgow University asks this question in his unpublished Oxford D.Phil thesis of 1989, 'The relationship of the Italian and Southern French Cathars, 1170–1320'; see his 'The Cathar economy', *Reading Medieval Studies* XII (1986), pp. 51–71.

[138] Dondaine, *Un Traité*, p. 70; *WEH*, p. 337.

[139] Above, p. 81.

[140] For this and following episodes, see Manselli, *Eresia*, ch. 12, and Guiraud, *Inquisition* II, ch. 8.

[141] Manselli, *Eresia*, pp. 283–4.

Until 1250 the association with Ghibellinism carried the heretics into a blind alley. While Frederick lived, relative security remained. They were not free of the risk of legal proceedings by any means; but they still had numerical strength. Sacconi, trying to reckon up the strength of the various Churches, assessed Concorezzo, the moderate dualists, as greatest with 1,500 perfect; below that came Desenzano with 500 and a series of smaller ones at lower figures: Bagnolo at 200, Florence, Val del Spoleto and Vicenza at 100. The organization outlasted Sacconi, and the lists of bishops for the various Churches go on without interruption into the 1280s.[142]

Nevertheless, the death of Frederick II and the decline of the imperial party in Italy, the victories of the papal champion Charles of Anjou against Frederick's successors, and the success of conservative Guelf parties in the cities tilted the balance against the dualists. Charles of Anjou's system had no room for the heretics; the popes, released from the anxiety over allies, could press the case for persecution. Patrons died, in Verona Oberto Pelavicino was succeeded by the Scaligeri, who were no longer willing to assist heresy.[143] One by one, in a halting sequence which lasted through the rest of the century, cities allowed thorough inquisitorial proceedings. Flight to protectors in the *contado*, movement to other cities, and concealment delayed but could not prevent decline. In Florence a stage in this downward movement is marked by the numbers of perfect who submitted in the inquisition held in 1282 by brother Salomone da Lucca.[144] At Sirmione by Lake Garda an expedition captured 178 perfect, who were burnt in Verona in 1278, and dealt a terrible blow to the Church of Desenzano.[145] The repression still did not go easily; traditional suspicion of the inquisition remained, and some Cathars struck back – in the Valtellina an inquisitor was murdered, Parma sacked its Dominican convent in 1279[146] – but by the end of the century even Milan, the ancient capital of heresy, had been brought to order. The last major series of trials were held in Bologna from 1291 to 1309.[147] Cathar history thereafter is that of a remnant. The last bishop to be reported in western Europe was captured in Tuscany in 1321;[148] survivors continued for a time to find refuge, possibly in the Lombard countryside and in the Alps.[149]

A summary of the history of the inquisition in Italy, however, does not alone explain the decline of the heresy; the peaceful countermeasures of the Church and the internal difficulties of Catharism are also relevant. Inquisitors were not necessarily only policemen. St Peter Martyr, for example, as well as pursuing his legal duties, was the leader in a movement for setting up Catholic

[142] Borst, *Katharer*, pp. 231–9.

[143] Manselli, *Eresia*, p. 285.

[144] Ibid., p. 218; confessions of converted perfect in Languedoc in H. Blaquière and Y. Dossat, 'Les Cathares au jour le jour: confessions inédites de Cathares quercynois', in *CF* III, pp. 259–316, see pp. 259–89.

[145] Guiraud, *Inquisition* II, p. 573.

[146] Ibid., pp. 573 (Valtellina), 575 (Parma).

[147] Dupré Theseider, in *Studi storici in onore di G. Volpe* I, pp. 383–444.

[148] Stephens, in *PP* LIV (1972), p. 30.

[149] Evidence on Catharism in the Alpine valleys in the late Middle Ages may be suspect: see below, pp. 164–5.

confraternities to deepen faith and erect barriers against heresy.[150] The Lombard Alleluia of 1233 and the flagellants of 1260 were popular movements of penance and revival, hostile to heresy The intellectual level was higher than in Languedoc, and it is fair to assume therefore that the intellectual attack on heresy and the effect of the conflicts in Catharism mattered more. Police action was requisite to cut down the recalcitrant. But at the same time a general change in the atmosphere and a revived Catholicism inhibited the flow of recruits on the earlier scale; so the heresy was squeezed into its ultimate oblivion. One can speculate about economic factors, and argue that improvements in conditions drew men's minds from a creed which so relentlessly preached that the world was utterly in the power of Satan; but too many in easy circumstances participated in the heresy, and men's motives for adherence to a religious group are generally too complex for any simple correlation between poverty, injustice and Cathar recruitment, or between economic improvement and Cathar decline, to carry conviction. Catharism was in any case eclectic, a religion that absorbed ideas and practices sponge-like from various quarters, and so catered for varied needs, somewhat at the expense of consistency. Knowledge was expanding in the thirteenth century and, with the development of universities and of medical schools and the expansion of travel, horizons widened. Catharism could not keep up.[151] Two developments on the Catholic side, however, were of especial importance for the change of outlook that inhibited this particular heresy.[152] One was the rise of a new piety, associated especially with the Franciscans, which focused attention on the incidents of Christ's life. The Christmas crib, the vivid preaching about Christ's life, the devotions centred on the crucifixion which led the worshipper to participate in the sufferings of Jesus were the enemy of the dualistic faith. For most adherents the Cathar Christ was a wraith or a visiting angel and not a man; he was venerated above all as the distant founder of a pure Church. He could not survive against the competition of the Catholic Christ, man and God, as realized in the piety of the thirteenth century. The positive sentiment concerning nature and creation had similar effects in dispelling, by experience rather than reason, the Cathar vision of all matter as evil. The pastoral mission of the friars as preachers and confessors together with the development of Third Orders for laymen and women who remained in the world brought a good Christian life within the range of the many – it was no longer reserved for the dedicated few who received the *consolamentum*.

Finally the appearance of Joachimism on the thirteenth-century scene contributed to popular religious feeling a set of myths that rivalled in their appeal the myths of the Cathars, and yet were more optimistic in tone. As in Cathar eschatology, there was to be a profound struggle with evil, but it would issue in a state of bliss here on earth, a foretaste, after spiritual warfare, of the

---

[150] Guiraud, *Inquisition* II, ch. 18; studies by G. G. Meersseman in *AFP* XX (1950), pp. 5–113; XXI (1951), pp. 51–196; XXII (1952), pp. 5–176, cited in Manselli, *Eresia*, p. 268.

[151] I am indebted for information on this to Mr A. Murray.

[152] Manselli, *Eresia*, pp. 270 (Franciscans), 331 (Joachimism). Manselli, 'Evangelisme et mythe dans la foi cathare', *Heresis* v (1985), pp. 9–17: bibliography and obituary: ibid., pp. 5–24 and XII (1989), pp. 79–86 (by J. Duvernoy).

pleasures of paradise. For those who had taste for such things, these myths were more positive: dualist myths of creation and the End faded in competition with them. All was not gain for the Catholics; there were dangers in Joachimism, and heresies fed on it.[153] But it was another factor against Catharism. In a word, Italian dualism was in part eradicated by force and in part simply outgrown.

---

[153] Below, pp. 194–205; comment in Hamilton, *Crusade*, pp. 31–2.

8

The Waldensians after the Conference of Bergamo

Survival and mission in Germany and the East

Only one heresy of the twelfth century survived in unbroken continuity into the sixteenth century to emerge from its hiding-place and link hands with the Protestant Reformation. Where Catharism, which initially created more alarm in the Church, disappeared, Waldensianism outlasted all the persecutions, often, in the end, only in out of the way places, generally in the lower ranks of society, and at the cost of loss of *élan*.[1] But still it lasted, to bequeath to Protestant historiography the memory that even in the depths of the Middle Ages there had been an evangelically based protest against Catholicism, and to leave to the historian the vivid stories of their resistance to persecution and a precious collection of vernacular scriptural commentary and religious literature. The Protestants who investigated the Waldensians of the Italian

---

[1] J. Gonnet and A. Molnár, *Les Vaudois au Moyen Age* (Turin, 1974) (working survey; earlier chs assemble scattered articles of Gonnet; ch. 4 (underground Waldensianism), ch. 8 (theology, by Molnár) demand special attention); H. Böhmer, 'Die Waldenser', *RPTK*, 3rd edn xx (Leipzig, 1908), cols 799–840 (concise perspective, still of value); Leff, *Heresy* ii, pp. 452–85 (based on Haupt with helpful bibliography; overstresses value of organization); sources in *Quellen zur . . . Waldenser*, ed. Patschovsky and Selge; articles by P. Biller (on issues of detail, give valuable glimpses of Waldensian life overall), see '*Curate Infirmos*: the medieval Waldensian practice of medicine', *SCH* xix, pp. 55–77; 'Medieval Waldensian abhorrence of killing pre-1400', *SCH* xx, pp. 129 –46; '*Multum ieiunantes et se castigantes*: medieval Waldensian asceticism', *SCH* xxii, pp. 215–28; '*Thesaurus absconditus*: the hidden treasure of the Waldensians', *SCH* xxiv, pp. 139– 54; 'The oral and the written: the case of the Alpine Waldensians', *BSRS* iv (1986), pp. 19–28; K. V. Selge, 'Die Erforschung der mittelalterlichen Waldensergeschichte', *TR* Neue Folge, 33 Jhrg. iv (1968), pp. 281–343 (historiography). I owe the reference to Professor A. Patschovsky. I express my gratitude for advice and offprints from the late Professor A. Molnár. See below for new work by Merlo (n. 53), Patschovsky (n. 22), Audisio (n. 47); P. Biller, 'Les Vaudois aux xive et xve siècles: le point', *Vaudois*, ed. Audisio, pp. 43–59, analyses research; see esp. discussion of Molnár's theory of late medieval Waldensian history: pp. 43–4, 49, international links of Waldensianism: pp. 56–8, bibliography: 65–75; J. F. Gilmont, 'Sources et critiques des sources', ibid., pp. 105–13. G. Audisio, *Les 'Vaudois': Naissance, vie et mort d'une dissidence (xiie–xvie siècles)* (Turin, 1989), (survey, of calibre, but no footnotes); P. Biller, 'La Storiografia intorno all'eresia medievale negli Stati Uniti e in Gran Bretagna (1945–1992), *Eretici ed Eresie Medievali*, ed. G. G. Merlo, Torre Pellice, 1994 (forthcoming). A Patschovsky, 'The literacy of Waldensianism from Valdes to c. 1400', Biller, Hudson, *Literacy*, pp. 112–36.

Valleys, the principal centres for their ultimate survival, discovered that life
underground had had its deleterious effect in introducing an element of semi-
magical procedure of secrecy and cunning, that the *barbi*, their leaders, were
not well educated and that the movement had, for their taste, retained a little
too much of Catholicism.[2] Yet they could not withhold their respect for the
simple congregations who had retained their beliefs under pressure for so long
and their struggles attracted the attention in later centuries of a series of
historians and travellers, among whom the English have been especially
prominent. They are now the subject of renewed interest among professional
historians, which may be expected before long to issue in an acceptable
synthesis of their story from the time of the failed Conference of Bergamo.

The *Rescriptum*, which is our principal source for the conference, was
addressed 'to the brothers and sisters, *amici* and *amicae*, leading godly lives on
the other side of the Alps'.[3] Another hand has added 'in Germany', and this
fits the facts, for the Germans were represented and would have needed to be
informed. Even in Valdes's time missionaries had jumped the language
barrier and brought German speakers into the movement. The first impetus to
their conversion appears to have come from the frontier with French-speaking
regions, and presumably from the Lyonist wing of the movement; yet by 1218
they stood on the Lombard side, if a shade uncertainly, for the authors of the
Rescriptum felt the need to convince them of the rectitude of their own position.
They were a sister organization and not dependent on the Italians.

Their history in the thirteenth and fourteenth centuries is the success story
of the whole movement.

Political circumstances facilitated the spread of Waldensianism in Germany,
as the papal–imperial conflict moved to its climax under Innocent iv,
distracting the clergy from pastoral duties and the repression of heresy,
encouraging the appointment of unworthy prelates and disturbing Church life
through interdict, schism and warfare.[4] The outbreak of popular unrest in
Schwäbisch-Hall, centring on support of the Emperor Frederick ii, played into
the hands of Waldensian propagandists, for its supporters proclaimed, as a
by-product of the struggle against pro-papal clergy, that their interdicts were
invalid and their exercise of office null through their sins. Even after the death
of Frederick ii a schism continued in the archbishopric of Salzburg, and the
weakness of central power in the long imperial vacancy, together with the
prevalence of political prelates in Germany, did nothing to assist the pursuit of
heresy. One major persecution, the reign of terror of Conrad of Marburg, before
his death in 1233, the Waldensians outlived: Conrad's lack of scruple over
evidence may well have brought as many innocent as guilty to the fire, and still

---

[2] Below, pp. 362–6; on the term *barba* (uncle), pl. *barbi*, see T. Pons, 'Barba, barbi e barbetti nel tempo e
nello spazio', *BSSV* LXXXVIII (1967), pp. 47–66. I owe the reference to Dr P. Biller; see also Audisio, *Luberon*
(below, n. 47), p. 226.

[3] *Quellen zur . . . Waldenser*, ed. Patschovsky and Selge, pp. 20–43; *WEH*, pp. 278–89.

[4] H. Haupt, 'Waldensertum und Inquisition im südöstlichen Deutschland bis zur mitte des 14.
Jahrhunderts', *DZG* II (1889), pp. 285–330, 337–411 (still valuable); synthesis in A. Hauck,
Kirchengeschichte Deutschlands (Berlin and Leipzig, 1954), IV, pp. 896–906; M. Schneider, *Europäisches
Waldensertum im 13. und 14. Jahrhundert* (Berlin and New York, 1981), (concise review of teaching,
organization in major territories), pp. 95–120; reviews: A. Patschovsky, *DA* XXXVIII (1982), pp. 281–2;
M. D. Lambert, *CHR* XX (1984), pp. 287–8.

let heretics, Cathar or Waldensian, escape.[5] They did not merely survive: Waldensianism in Germany gained the support of the comparatively wealthy. In such cities as Strasburg and Augsburg in the late fourteenth century the supporters of the Waldensians included men of substance with wealth from trade in cloth or hides, who had inherited their beliefs from parents, grandparents or even earlier generations. They gave valuable financial aid.[6]

From its base in Germany in the thirteenth century, Waldensianism achieved a remarkable expansion, travelling with the waves of German colonization into Bohemia and lands further east: the uncovering of this extensive undergound network in German-speaking lands has been the achievement of modern historians and it has compelled revision of the traditional assessment of the role of the Waldensians within the spectrum of medieval dissent.

In Austria the movement had embedded itself by mid-thirteenth century. A good source, the Passau Anonymous, a secular priest or Dominican, author of a compilation on Jews, heretics and Antichrist dating from the second half of the thirteenth century, gives us a detailed picture of their life based on his experiences of an inquisition conducted there in about 1266.[7] The forty-two place-names the Anonymous describes as bearing heresy are scattered over villages, farms and market towns in Lower Austria, roughly following today's railway line. The inquiry plainly extended only to the Austrian side of the Danube. It is not likely that the river was a barrier to the passage of heresy; rather, that Austria's ruler, Ottokar II, was the instigator of the investigations, and that they therefore dealt only with heretics in his territories and not in the Duchy of Bavaria on the other bank.[8]

Beyond the demonstration that Waldensianism at this time was a country movement we cannot go: the Anonymous is very sparing with information on the social origins of heretics. He mentions only Henry the glovemaker of Theben, the modern Devin at the confluence of the Danube and the March, who frankly informed the clergy as he was led to execution at some unknown date, that they in turn could expect death at the hands of the Waldensians if ever they came to power.[9] A hierarchy appears little in evidence. The Anonymous mentions a bishop at Anzbach; a certain Neumeister burnt in 1315 in Vienna or at Himberg, near Vienna on its southern side, claimed to

---

[5] R. Kieckhefer, *The Repression of Heresy in Medieval Germany* (Pennsylvania, 1979) (institutional study, with sidelights on beguines and Waldensians); review: M. D. Lambert, *CHR* LXVIII (1982), pp. 294–5; P. Segl, *Ketzer in Österreich: Untersuchungen über Häresie und Inquisition im Herzogtum Österreich im 13. und beginnenden 14.Jahrhundert* (Paderborn, 1984), pp. 47–52; P. Segl, 'Conrad von Marburg, inquisitor', *Neue Deutsche Biographie* XII (Berlin, 1980), pp. 544–6; see A. Patschovsky, in *DA* XXXVII (1981), pp. 641–93.

[6] *SCH* XXIV, p. 147.

[7] M. Nickson, 'The "Pseudo-Reinerius" treatise: the final stage of a thirteenth century work on heresy from the diocese of Passau', *AHDLMA* XXXIV (1967), pp. 255–314; extracts from the text, on heresy in the Passau diocese (pp. 291–303). Note the rustic flavour of the section on causes of heresy (pp. 291–3). The treatise is an abridged version of parts of the Passau Anonymous; on the relationship, see Nickson's introduction (pp. 255–60) and A. Patschovsky, *Der Passauer Anonymus: Ein Sammelwerk über Ketzer, Juden, Antichrist aus der Mitte des 13. Jahrhunderts* (Stuttgart, 1968). Professor Patschovsky is preparing a new edition of the Anonymous for *MGH*.

[8] Segl, *Österreich*, gives a definitive analysis of heresy and its repression in Austria; Ottokar: pp. 153–65; Passau Anonymous and spread of heresy: pp. 165–233; map: p. 169.

[9] Ibid., p. 248.

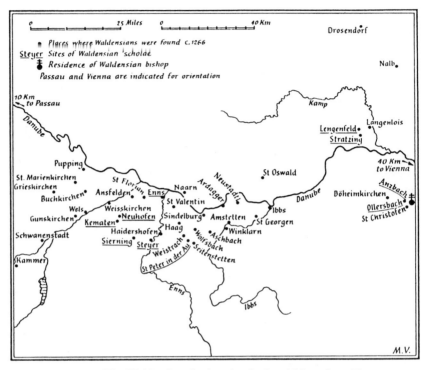

MAP 4   The Waldensians in Austria: the inquisition of *c*.1266.
Source: Adapted from M. Nickson, *Archives d'histoire doctrinale et littéraire du moyen âge* XXXIV (1967),
p. 279.

have been a bishop of the Waldensians for over fifty years, and may have been
the same man.[10] The term may spring from the minds of inquisitors, labelling
a leader of the Waldensians in the manner usual in orthodoxy: his authority
may well have been more a matter of *regimen* than *ordo*.

A special feature of the heretics described by the Passau Anonymous was
the absence of distinctive ranks. All were obliged to preach, women as well as
men, and children were expected to take part in instruction. Ten places
underlined are described as *scholae* – the instructional centres where formal
teaching was given and the Scripture learnt, in a fashion similar to the English
Lollards of the fifteenth century. Sacraments were of the simplest. Catholic
priests were criticized for imposing heavy penances; these Waldensians, by
contrast, remitted sin by the laying on of hands, citing the words of Christ to
the woman taken in adultery: 'Go and sin no more.' They spoke of daily
communion, and rejected the rites of the mass: their communion service is
likely to have been, above all, an expression of the fraternal solidarity of these
Waldensian groups. The words of consecration could, they said, be spoken as
well by a woman as by a man.[11]

[10] Segl, *Österreich*, p. 315.
[11] Solidarity: Schneider, *Waldensertum*, p. 124; Segl, *Österreich*, p. 204 (consecration by women); *scholae*
best analysed in Segl, pp. 193–4.

The Passau Anonymous met with more than one type of Waldensian. The *Runcarii* he alludes to were clearly the heirs of John de Ronco, the leader of the Lombard split in Valdes's movement, and may be taken as a synonym for the Poor Lombards.[12] Lyonists were present as well, but the vigour of the attacks on the Church which he reports suggests a Lombard predominance.

He explains, directly or by implication, the reasons for the durability of the movement. They lay pre-eminently in the faults of the clergy, which he proceeds to enumerate as general causes of all heresy. They form a strange blend of ignorance and superstition, personal, especially sexual, laxity, and excessive claims for themselves and their parishes; the flavour is somewhat rustic and backward, with some pseudo-miracles being claimed and parishioners being told that to go to another church would be adultery. The Host was sometimes dropped, the wine spilled and the confessional abused in a large number of ways. This miscellaneous, sometimes contradictory, list of ecclesiastical abuses shows the roots of Waldensianism amongst simple people: it lay in the contrast between a run of the mill, not too well instructed clergy with their human failings, and the cells of the Waldensian movement, studying the Scripture, a devoted underground elite.[13]

The Anonymous is uninhibited in his description of the tenacity of the heretics. 'All Leonists [i.e. Lyonists],' he says, 'men and women, adult and child, learn and teach unweariedly by day and night, the workman devotes the day to his work, the night to religious instruction; so that little time remains over for prayer; the newly converted after a few days seek others to draw into the sect.'[14] The Anonymous recalled the case of a Waldensian who swam the river Ibbs on a winter's night to make a convert; he noticed, too, that they taught in leper houses. *Scole leprosorum* were held in the village of Neuhofen. A curious passage described the Waldensian approaching wealthier potential converts in the guise of the travelling salesman selling pretty things, rings, scarves and the like, and then, when the customer asked if he had other items for sale, replying that he had much more valuable gems – but would need to be assured that he would not be betrayed to the clergy. There would follow a recitation of some gripping scene from Scripture – the Annunciation, John's account of the Last Supper, or Paul's exhortation in the twelfth chapter of Romans, 'Be not conformed to this world.' Such devices were designed to take the neophyte into a reading circle.[15]

The basis of the vernacular Scriptures was important, most of all because of the potency of Scripture itself, but also because of the opportunity for direct instruction and self-instruction through the plain text afforded by the Waldensian system for the laity in contrast to their passive role at orthodox services.

Oral instruction was a religious outlet open to all, intelligent, partially educated and totally ignorant, and it kept knowledge of the text of Scripture in being. Beliefs lacked the exotic element in Catharism and the way into the sect was relatively easy. Donatism and Biblicism had prevailed and there was

---

[12] Segl, *Österreich*, pp. 218–19, correcting Lambert, *Medieval Heresy*, 1st edn.

[13] Segl, *Österreich*, pp. 233–70.

[14] See Nickson in *AHDLMA* xxxiv (1967), pp. 255–314; for *scole leprosorum*, see Biller, in *SCH* xix, p. 68.

[15] For the above, see Segl, *Österreich*, p. 198.

greater hostility to the Church, as witnessed in the threats to the clergy that
they would have their tithes and possessions removed and be reduced to day
work; later there were not only threats to life but actual cases of murder of
clergy.

Much of the core of Waldensian belief lay in a cutting away of what were
seen to be the excrescences of orthodox belief in purgatory, in images, in
pilgrimages; in an insistence on good living; and in the literal observance of
the texts of Scripture. They would not take oaths, because they believed that
the text 'Swear not at all' must be taken literally; they would not lie; they
would not accept judgements of blood – a belief which had the more
poignancy when executions of heretics took place. What they heard of the
Scriptures, no doubt initially from orthodox instruction, was to be observed to
the letter and not glossed away. The Anonymous said they could be detected
just because they were better than their neighbours. It was, in effect, the
religion of the ordinary layman who had rejected his clergy for ministers of his
own, like him in condition and in devotion and who was sustained by his
scriptural knowledge. Wherever clerical abuse gave a hold to propaganda,
where the need for better vernacular instruction was felt, the way was open to
building congregations.

Investigations in 1311 and 1313–15 based on Steyer, Krems and elsewhere
(including Vienna) showed that the heresy had stayed alive in Lower Austria.
Depositions give a hint as to how it was done: through secrecy and by attending
services to ward off suspicion. Perjury, one said, was not a sin; another had
little vernacular phrases to murmur to himself at mass, denying what was
done. 'Es ist gelogen was man singet' ('It is a lie what one sings'). As in 1266,
membership at all levels was distinguished by much rote knowledge of the
Scriptures in the vernacular. The Church was vehemently attacked and its
sacraments ridiculed. The sacrament of the altar was an artificial god, 'der
gemacht got', and the friars 'Kirchphaffen'. A burgher of Krems, Ulrich
Woller, put on a public spectacle for his guests, using his children to pillory
the sacrament of marriage, himself ostentatiously breaching the Catholic
observance of Good Friday.[16]

A 'master of the heretics', like his predecessors in 1266, foreswore the
penances of the priests and simply enjoined his penitents to kiss the earth – an
action linked to popular superstition, which led the orthodox in south
Germany and Austria when they were in need of the last rites and no priest
was available, to use earth instead of holy oil.[17] Witnesses said that they had
sixteen, or in another account, twelve, apostles who travelled great distances
to care for the believers, and that two of them would go every year to paradise
to receive from Elias and Enoch the power of binding and loosing – evidence
of the crucial role of the leaders, and of a natural process of psychological
compensation in the minds of the rank and file, where these stories had
evolved, for the pressures engendered by their way of life.[18] A woman called

[16] Segl, *Österreich*, pp. 284–341, esp. pp. 309, 310, 303–4.

[17] Ibid., pp. 305–7.

[18] Ibid., pp. 314, 328; M. Erbstösser, *Sozialreligiöse Strömungen im späten Mittelalter* (Berlin, 1970)
(Marxist summary on Flagellants, Waldensians, Free Spirit); see pp. 147–53 for illuminating summary on
masters.

Gysla, when her interrogators asked if she was a virgin, said she was a virgin above ground but not below it – a belief apparently shared by others of the accused.[19] It is as if a curtain twitched back, then closed again, reveals in Austria a coarse, resolutely anti-Church movement, capable of rousing heroic resistance and still trained in scriptural knowledge, embedded, however, in a local vernacular culture with idiosyncratic and superstitious elements.

Waldensianism, transmitted from Germany and Austria, prospered in Bohemia and farther east. Fragments of the record of an inquisition conducted by the Dominican friar Gallus of Neuhaus (Jindřichův Hradec) between 1335 and *c*.1353 reveal astonishing figures for heretics, chiefly Waldensians, interrogated and punished.[20] The fragments that remain witness by implication to an inquisition working over years, achieving numbers of interrogations, condemnations and burnings at a level comparable only with those of the classic tribunals of Languedoc. The existing fragments carry more than 300 names, whether of witnesses or of accused, including some 180 suspect of Waldensianism and eleven accused beguines, and refer incidentally to fifteen burnings, one of them being the burning of an exhumed corpse. The record is arranged under localities; the pagination gives a basis for inferring how many folios at minimum are lost; if those folios are taken into account and the assumption made that they would record similar percentages under other geographical headings for witnesses, accused persons and burnings, then the figures which emerge are astonishing – an involvement one way or another of 4,400 persons, including among them 2,640 Waldensians, 160 beguines, dozens of accused beghards, 580 suspect without any clearly defined allegiance, and the burnings of 220 persons. When Neumeister, the Waldensian bishop, was burnt in Austria in 1315, he told his enemies that the number of believers in Bohemia and Moravia was 'immeasurable'; the record of Gallus's inquisitorial activity suggests much more lay behind Neumeister's claim than defiant hysteria.[21]

They were German speakers. The one frontier that was not crossed was the linguistic one; Czech speakers apparently remained orthodox. 'Pure Bohemians', Jerome of Prague claimed in 1409, were not convicted of heresy. The burgeoning of Bohemian Waldensianism was the fruit of colonization, mission and flight from persecution by German speakers flowing over the frontier from Austria into southern Bohemia. They formed a dense network of relations and friends, above all in the villages but in towns as well, in Prague, Hradec Králové, České Budějovice, Jindřichův Hradec and, in Moravia, in Brno and Znojmo. Of Prachatice, close on the frontier with Austria, it was said that a majority of the population were Waldensians. They moved readily between town and village, to marry, to live with relations or for economic reasons. Most of the accused in Gallus's inquisitions were peasants or craftsmen, but close inspection of their situation in the villages shows them to be either in a leading role or at least of middle rank, the prosperous rather than the

---

[19] Segl, *Österreich*, pp. 309, 330.

[20] A. Patschovsky, ed. (with introduction), *Quellen zur böhmischen Inquisition im 14 Jahrhundert, MGH, Quellen zur Geistesgeschichte des Mittelalters* xi (Weimar, 1979); discoveries made by Patschovsky and I. Hlavacek (p. 13, n. 13); review: T. Scott, *JEH* xxxiii (1982), pp. 129–30.

[21] Ibid., pp. 18–24; for Neumeister, p. 21, n. 33, quoting Annales Matseenses ('numerus infinitus').

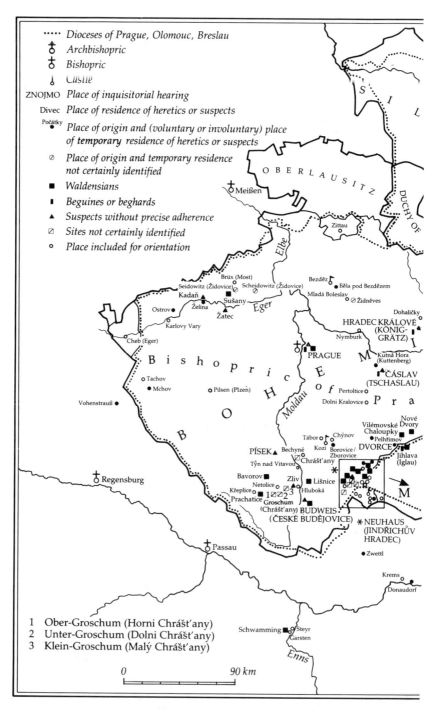

Dioceses of Prague, Olomouc, Breslau
☦ Archbishopric
☦ Bishopric
⚔ Castle
ZNOJMO Place of inquisitorial hearing
Divec Place of residence of heretics or suspects
Počátky Place of origin and (voluntary or involuntary) place
● of **temporary** residence of heretics or suspects
⊘ Place of origin and temporary residence
not certainly identified
■ Waldensians
▮ Beguines or beghards
▲ Suspects without precise adherence
⊠ Sites not certainly identified
○ Place included for orientation

S I L

O B E R L A U S I T Z

DUCHY OF

☦ Meißen

Zittau

Elbe

Brüx (Most)
Seidowitz (Židovice)   Scheidowitz (Židovice)
Kadaň   Bezděz ● Běla pod Bezdězem
Ostrov ●   Želina ▲   Sušany   Mladá Boleslav
Karlovy Vary   Žatec   ⊘ Židněves
                                                          Dohaličky
Cheb (Eger)   HRADEC KRÁLOVÉ
                                            (KÖNIG-
B i s h o p r i c   Nymburk   GRÄTZ)
                    ☦   Kutná Hora
                  PRAGUE   (Kuttenberg)
                              M
○ Tachov   E   ⚔ ČÁSLAV
● Mchov   ○ Pilsen (Plzeň)   o f   (TSCHASLAU)
Vohenstrauß ●   O   Pertoltice○
                                  Dolní Kralovice○ P r a
                     Moldau
                                          Nové
                              Vilémovské Dvory
                                    Chaloupky
B   Tábor○ ● Chýnov   Pelhřimov
                          Kozí Borovice/ DVORCE
PÍSEK ▲ Bechyně   Zborovice   Jihlava
☦ Regensburg   Týn nad Vitavou   Chrášťany (Iglau)
             Bavorov ■   Zliv   *
             Netolice ○   1⊠⊠2   Lišnice   M
Křeplice○   ▲   Hluboká
Prachatice ● 1⊠⊠2 3
            Groschum
            (Chrášťany) BUDWEIS
              (ČESKÉ BUDĚJOVICE) * NEUHAUS
                                  (JINDŘICHŮV
☦ Passau   HRADEC)

                              ● Zwettl

                                      Krems○
                                      Donaudorf

1 Ober-Groschum (Horní Chrášťany)
2 Unter-Groschum (Dolní Chrášťany)   Schwamming ■○ Steyr
3 Klein-Groschum (Malý Chrášťany)   Garsten

                                        Enns

0   90 km

MAP 5   Heretics in Bohemia and Moravia in the fourteenth century: the inquisition of
Prague and Olomouc.

Source: Adapted from *Quellen zur böhmischen Inquisition im 14 Jahrhundert*, ed. A. Patschovsky
(Weimar, 1979).

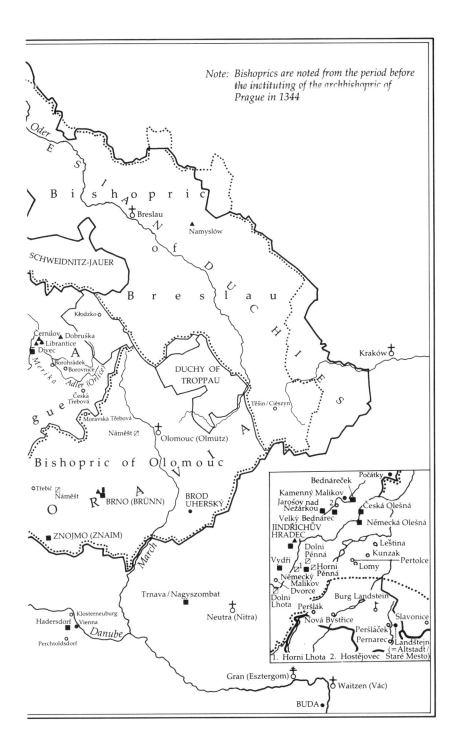

Note: Bishoprics are noted from the period before
the instituting of the archbishopric of
Prague in 1344

Oder

E   S   I

B   i   s   h   o   p   r   i   c

✝ Breslau
○ Breslau

▲ Namyslów

SCHWEIDNITZ-JAUER

A
N

o   f   D   U   C

B   r   e   s   l   a   u

○ Kłodzko

H

Černilov ▲ Dobruška
Librantice
■ Divec

A

I

E

○ Borohrádek
○ Borovnice

Meřika

Adler (Orlice)

Česká
Třebová

DUCHY OF
TROPPAU

S

Kraków ✝
○

gue

▲ Moravská Třebová

Náměšt ▱

○ Těšín / Cieszyn

✝
○ Olomouc (Olmütz)

Bishopric   of   Olomouc

V

○ Třebíč   ▱
Náměšt

A

R

▲▲
■ BRNO (BRÜNN)

A

O

BROD
UHERSKÝ
●

■ ZNOJMO (ZNAIM)

March

Trnava / Nagyszombat
■

○ Klosterneuburg
Hadersdorf ○ Vienna
●
Danube

○ Perchtoldsdorf

Neutra (Nitra)
✝
○

Gran (Esztergom) ✝
○

✝
○ Waitzen (Vác)

BUDA ●

Počátky ●
Bednáreček ●

Kamenný Malikov
Jarošov nad   2 ■
Nežárkou   ■   Česká Olešná
Velký Bednárec
JINDŘICHŮV
HRADEC ▲   ■ Německá Olešná
            Dolni
            Pěnná   ○ Leština
Vydři   ▱   ○ Kunzak
■   ▱ 1 ▱ Horni   Pertolce
            Pěnná   ○ Lomy
      Německý ○
      Malikov
      Dvorce
Dolni   ▱
Lhota   ○ Peršlák   Burg Landstein
      ○ Nová Bystřice   ○
            Peršláček
            Pernarec ○○ Slavonice
            ○ Landštejn
                (=Altstadt /
1. Horni Lhota 2. Hostějovec Staré Mesto)

downtrodden, including village magistrates and heads of households with servants. Their Waldensianism was the self-confident protest of the tolerably prosperous and capable against an orthodox Church they believed, not without reason, to be neglectful. It is likely that a nucleus of Waldensians had existed in Bohemia for about a hundred years before the earliest of the hearings noted in the extant Gallus inquisition protocols. The settlement Gallus uncovered was too thick to have arisen over a short period of time. It may well have been the presence of Waldensians that led Alexander IV to appoint an inquisition for Bohemia in 1257, instigated by the same Ottokar II who gave impetus to the drive against heresy in Austria.[22]

Research elsewhere fills out the picture of an underground Waldensian network spread out across Germany and the colonized German-speaking lands to the east. Their presence has been confirmed in Trier and Heidelberg. They have long been known to have been widespread in Upper Germany. Whole districts of Brandenburg and Pomerania had substantial Waldensian populations and their presence in Schweidnitz has been investigated. R. E. Lerner notes that 'it now seems likely that there were more German-speaking Waldensians in the fourteenth century than there were heretics of any sort whatever from any other language group'.[23]

Defection and inquisition

None the less this Waldensianism was a movement under heavy pressure. In 1368 correspondence between Waldensian masters and the Poor Lombards showed how the movement had suffered blows. Two preachers had defected. The survivors sought comfort from the Lombards and defended their own position against the defectors, demonstrating in their answers competent knowledge of Scripture and the Fathers.[24]

The Waldensians had evolved a version of their own history in order to give themselves a longer and more distinguished pedigree with which to confront the Catholic controversialists. They used a commonplace of the poverty movement of northern Italy, the defection of the Church at the time of Constantine through the acceptance of endowments:[25] as Pope Sylvester accepted the fatal gift, they said, an angel was heard crying, 'To-day is poison poured out in the Church of God'. A companion of Sylvester, however,

---

[22] Geographical and linguistic distribution, Patschovsky, *Quellen zur . . . Inquisition*, pp. 71–87; social analysis, pp. 55–71, suggesting, p. 57, n. 174, some overstressing of peasant character of Waldensianism in Erbstösser, *Strömungen*; comment by T. Scott, *JEH* XXXIII (1982), pp. 129–30, to whom I am indebted for help; on persecution and origins of Waldensianism, Patschovsky, pp. 81–2, correcting his earlier views, *Die Anfänge einer ständigen Inquisition in Böhmen* (New York and Berlin, 1975), p. 45.

[23] *Rapports, Comité international des Sciences Historiques*, XVI *Congrès international des Sciences Historiques* (Stuttgart, 1985), I, pp. 360–2; on Schweidnitz, see A. Patschovsky, 'Waldenserverfolgung in Schweidnitz 1315', *DA* XXXVI (1980), pp. 137–76, arguing inquisition was probably successful.

[24] G. Gonnet, 'I Valdesi d'Austria nella seconda meta del secolo XIV', *BSSV* CXI (1962), pp. 5–41 (summary: pp. 27–9); tr. of letters in E. Comba, *Histoire des Vaudois* I: *De Valdo à la Réforme* (Paris, 1901), pp. 190–205; see Döllinger, *Beiträge* II, 355–62; Kieckhefer, *Repression*, pp. 53–73 ('The crisis of the Waldensians') for the context; Gonnet and Molnár, *Les Vaudois*, pp. 149–52. Dr P. Biller of York plans to publish on this subject.

[25] Gonnet, in *BSSV* CXI, p. 15; the story does not originate with Waldensians (as Leff, *Heresy* I, p. 9, argues). Cf. Bonacursus on Cathars, *WEH*, p. 173.

rejected the gift, was excommunicated and with his fellows endured persecution, thus maintaining through poverty the purity which the Church had once had in the centuries before the Donation of Constantine. So on this showing, there was a Waldensian movement before Valdes, who becomes, not the initiator but, in their words, the 'repairer' of the movement, stimulating it at a time of flagging zeal. Echoes of fact linger in the story that Valdes tried to convince the hierarchy of the justice of his case, but was excommunicated; the venue, however, has become Rome and Valdes himself has suffered an extraordinary change, being described as a priest and given the name Peter.

The Waldensians thus met the question, 'Where were you before Valdes?' by evolving a version of Church history which made them from the outset the true Church and the papal Church a false or malign one from the time of the Donation of Constantine, incidentally overturning the truth about Valdes – that he was a layman who claimed the right to preach – by putting him into priest's orders. The unhistorical name Peter recalls Peter in the gospels and in Acts as leader of the apostles: it forms a kind of counter-claim to the papacy as successor of St Peter and recalls the episode in Acts of Peter confronting the Sanhedrin and declaring that he would obey God rather than men[26] – just as the Waldensians claimed to do, rejecting human traditions and rites in favour of those alone they believed to be of divine origin. A Waldensian version of Church history was a comfort in time of trouble, for it showed alternations of shining life and decadence, like the phases of the moon, in which none the less a faithful remnant survived. In their phrase, although the new moon seemed to come to nothing, 'yet it is always the moon'.[27]

A crisis seems to have afflicted the leadership in the course of the fourteenth century. Others followed the example of the Austrians who defected. A list of twenty masters, nineteen of whom went over to Catholicism, is extant. Five of them subsequently entered the priesthood, and one a monastery.[28] The defection of the dedicated few, the celibates who travelled two by two about the countryside preaching and hearing confessions, was doubly distressing. Under pressure, the movement had become less and less a lay-orientated Church. Confession of one member to another was given up. The elite, selected, trained and put in apprenticeship, were the ones who heard confessions, used books and instructed the faithful – carried out, in a word, the work of an underground priesthood, effective because of their high moral standards. The faith of the rank and file was the more shaken when the preacher class, whom they venerated, defected, and, in some cases, not only defected but set about missionizing amongst their former supporters. From the point of view of security, the damage was still greater, for the preachers alone had a wide-ranging knowledge of the location of their flock and inquisition procedures were such as to encourage, indeed demand, full disclosure of information as a sign of repentance of the sin of heresy.

The consciousness of a high level of danger and the bitterness of abandoned supporters is revealed when Waldensians murdered defectors. Four of the listed masters are said to have been assassinated. At Strasburg, killers were

---

[26] Acts 5: 29.
[27] Döllinger, *Beiträge* II, p. 354.
[28] Kieckhefer, *Repression*, p. 58.

promised fifty pounds for killing a defecting master. It was in crass contradiction to the doctrine repeatedly taught by the masters, the birth of which goes back to the early days of Waldensianism, when reactions against the effects of warfare, massacres of Jews, crusades and the harshness of judicial execution of thieves in times of famine issued in an absolute prohibition of killing under all circumstances.[29] In the Reformation epoch Waldensians were still uneasy about the use of force by the State; but a question by Waldensians to Oecolampadius in 1530 presupposes that there had been acceptance in the past of the legitimacy of putting defectors to death.[30]

The phase of defections merges into a series of large-scale campaigns against Waldensians in southern and eastern German towns in the years 1389–1401; Kieckhefer is inclined to see a connection and speculates that the field for investigation was opened to inquisitors by the revelations of 'supergrasses' among the Waldensians' ranks.[31] No Ottokar II and no John XXII appear to have sparked off these drives and the German bishops have not been shown to be especially concerned with the heresy; though some episcopal inquisitions operated in southern Germany, the major impetus seems to have come from three itinerant inquisitors, Martin of Amberg, Peter Zwicker and Henry Angermeier, who used episcopal authority when they needed it, but appear to have been self-motivated. Papal commissions played virtually no part.[32]

Zwicker, a Celestinian, was one of the great inquisitors. When he turned his attention to the Waldensian network in Brandenburg and Pomerania, he put to use a range of questions, more extensive than was customary, comprising seventy articles. He and his team were very thorough and the answers they elicited enable us to see with clarity the spectrum of Waldensian belief and practice in the field, not schematized, as is often the case in inquisitors' handbooks. Zwicker's penitents were generally small people, drawn from over 120 villages and small towns in Brandenburg and Pomerania. Some had wealth, with their own farms and households; most were of modest rank. No nobles or businessmen were involved.[33]

Rank and file in these prosecutions lacked the capacity to give a justification for their beliefs, which stretched all the way from a borderline position between Waldensianism and Catholicism to wholesale polemic against the Church. The cult of Our Lady was one of the strongest links to orthodox piety.

---

[29] Biller, in *SCH* xx, pp. 129–46; Kieckhefer, *Repression*, p. 58; on importance of Strasburg, see Erbstösser, *Strömungen*, p. 124.

[30] Biller, in *SCH* xx, p. 135; for correspondence with Oecolampadius, see below, p. 362.

[31] *Repression*, pp. 58–9; D. Kurze, 'Zur Ketzergeschichte der Mark Brandenburg und Pommerns vornehmlich im 14 Jahrhundert', *JGMO* xvi–xvii (1968), pp. 50–94 at p. 70.

[32] A major theme of Kieckhefer.

[33] Kurze, in *JGMO* xvi–xvii (excellent trial analysis), esp. pp. 71, 76, 88, 89; geographical orientation, p. 87; Haupt, in *DZG* iii (1890), p. 46; Leff, *Heresy* ii, pp. 478–80; for edn D. Kurze, *Quellen zur Ketzergeschichte Brandenburgs und Pommerns, Veröffentlichungen der Historischen Kommission zu Berlin* xlv, *Quellenwerke* vi (Berlin and New York, 1975); reviews: G. G. Merlo, *Valdesi e Valdismi medievali* (Turin, 1984), pp. 101–5. On Zwicker's treatise, *Cum dormirent*, see P. Biller, 'Les Vaudois dans les territoires de langue allemande vers la fin du xive siècle: le regard d'un inquisiteur', *Mouvements dissidents et novateurs, Heresis* xiii, xiv (1989), pp. 199–200. I owe the reference to Dr A. Brenon. On the quality of fourteenth-century German evidence, see Biller, in *Vaudois*, ed. Audisio, p. 48.

The leadership taught that prayer should only be addressed to God and not to the Virgin, who would thereby be disturbed in the fullness of her heavenly joy; but supporters were reluctant to give up accustomed ways and would pray for her intercession, at least in times of need. One adherent said that a person who died when on pilgrimage would be damned; yet another Waldensian woman went as a pilgrim to Rome, Aachen and Wilsnack. A majority rejected prayers for the dead and one with a characteristic pungency of denunciation said it was as senseless to pray for the dead as to give fodder to a dead horse. For them there were only two ways, to heaven or to hell; purgatory did not exist. Yet others did pray for the dead – whether, as Kurze notes, out of hazy conviction, custom, friendship or out of reluctance to stand against the parish priest. Some rejected wholesale the sacraments and apparatus of the Church, vestments, chants, bells, organs, hierarchy and relics; but baptism was accepted, some arguing that rainwater was as effective as holy water, others using it, falling in with custom or not wanting to make themselves conspicuous.[34] In these ways Catholic custom and the environment of friends and neighbours modified Waldensian practice, as did a natural eclecticism and failure of logic.

The oath was firmly rejected; it was even said that one who swore an oath could not go to heaven. But it was understood that it might be needful to take an oath when in danger of death. Persecution and the need to establish their distinctive role led them easily to believe that only Waldensians could be saved; but that harsh view was mitigated in some cases by the positive sentiment of a membership deeply concerned with the pursuit of a moral life for good works, whoever performed them and whatever the background belief.[35]

What held these Waldensians together was the mobile preacher, coming in secrecy and by night, known only by Christian name, to exhort, instruct and, above all, to hear confessions. Fifteen of them are identifiable in Zwicker's record – Klaus of Brandenburg, Conrad of Saxony, Gottfried of Hungary, Nicholas of Solothurn, Nicholas of Vienna and so on – men who came remarkable distances to care for their people. These Waldensians, like their fellows in Austria, believed that the confessors went to paradise periodically to hear God's voice or to obtain power from him.[36] They came on average once a year, alone or with a pupil, to visit their believers who led them from place to place secretly and cared for them with food, money and necessities. Clearly attitudes to penance differed in different regions and at different times. In the long run the austere watchfulness of the confessor over his own life might well be reflected in the rigour of the penances he imposed.[37] Organization was of the simplest; Waldensianism lived in the family, and the wandering preachers were their essential lifeline. The simplicity of the needs of the movement kept it alive.

Zwicker administered relatively mild punishments; none the less, the great drive he and his fellows led must have marked a cesura in the history of

---

[34] Kieckhefer, *Repression*, pp. 62–3.
[35] Kurze, in *JGMO* xvi–xvii, pp. 83–7.
[36] Ibid., pp. 77–8, 81, 82–3; discussion in Erbstösser, *Strömungen*.
[37] Biller, in *SCH* xxii, p. 226; survival: Erbstösser, *Strömungen*, p. 122.

German Waldensianism. In Brandenburg and Pomerania some of the same
places were still harbouring members of the movement in 1458; but they had
suffered heavy blows.

Prosperity and decline in France[38]

Though excommunicated, the Waldensians of France, the original birthplace
of the movement, were for decades untroubled by any systematic persecution.
In the course of the Albigensian Crusade seven Waldensians were burnt at
Morlhon in Rouergue, but it was an isolated atrocity. The crusade created the
political conditions for persecution in the south, but did not have a major
impact on Waldensians. They were strongest in Lorraine and Burgundy and
on the fringes, rather than in the heartlands of Catharism, in Quercy and
Rouergue and not Toulouse, Albi and the surrounding countryside. In
Quercy they prospered for a time. Montauban was the only place in southern
France where the Waldensians had more supporters than the Cathars, where
they possessed a cemetery and a house and were in demand for their medical
services. In the record of the inquisition by Peter Seila which took place in
Quercy in 1241, and includes earlier material, no less than seventy-four
persons from Montauban, Cathars among them, admitted to asking for
medical help from them.[39] It is possible that they had a hospital. In Quercy
generally, the brothers visited the sick in accordance with Christ's injunction
in the sending of the Seventy, and sometimes stayed with a patient. Rewards
were commonly in kind: 'she gave them wine', one witness recalled, 'since
they would not accept money'.[40] One name, that of Pierre de Valz, recurs in
depositions both because of his preaching and his medical work: he was 'loved
like an angel of God'.[41] In Montauban Waldensians were for years integrated
into a community which tolerated both Cathars and Waldensians, and into
the 1220s permitted preaching in public places. Disputations took place
between adherents of the two movements. Even in the hairdressers a customer
might find himself the object of a Waldensian exhortation. There are
examples of manual work undertaken without charge in a spirit of simple
helpfulness. Support reached across classes, embracing the poor and some
wealthier bourgeois families. Only the nobility were missing: Catharism could
win them, Waldensianism could not.[42] Women preached and there were
houses of Waldensian sisters in Montcuq and Beaucaire, living a common life
in celibacy; their role within the movement in general has been underestimated
by historians.[43] Here and elsewhere they were, in effect, nuns, the counterpart
of the celibate preacher class, the *Meister, fratres* or *barbi*, with a role in some
respects comparable to the second order amongst the mendicant friars. The

---

[38] Summary in Schneider, *Waldensertum*, pp. 7–55.

[39] Biller, in *SCH* xix, pp. 55–77 (general survey of Waldensians' medical care, related to scriptural
precedent; Quercy: pp. 61–6; Seila as inquisitor: p. 61, n. 20 (identified as Selhan, following Dossat);
Wakefield, *Heresy, Crusade* (under Seila), pp. 141–3, 168.

[40] Ibid., p. 65.

[41] Ibid., p. 66.

[42] Social analysis: Schneider, *Waldensertum*, pp. 11–17, 36–9, 41 (before and after the development of
persecution).

[43] Biller, in *SCH* xxii, pp. 219–20; also *SCH* xx, p. 138n.

contemplative element in Waldensian literature may well have been designed with them in mind.

Freedom in Montauban, and to a lesser degree in other localities in Quercy, may well have led casual supporters, patients or witnesses to sermons genuinely to think that the preachers were not heretics. When the Franciscans came and founded houses for their first and second orders in Montauban in 1250 and 1258, clearly exercising similar functions in society, former Waldensian supporters leaned to them. Cases are known of members of families who once had Waldensian connections giving financial support to the new convents or becoming members of them.[44]

As more effective persecution developed in the 1230s, the preacher class was driven into secrecy. For some, the forbidden fruit had its own appeal;[45] but the open tasks which the preachers and their supporters had once been able to undertake had to be given up. A penumbra of casual support faded; the contact between the supporters proper, the *credentes* and their preacher class grew tighter as dangers grew; the essential nub of the movement, as in German-speaking lands, came to be the act of confession behind closed doors and the associated exhortation and instruction of the wandering preacher. By the fourteenth century a hierarchy had developed; persecution appears to have facilitated a process of *Verkirchlichung*, the building of a rigid and stratified Church.

In the long run, Waldensianism in France was a casualty. Its adherents remained faithful to Valdes's wish; they never wholly rejected the sacraments of the Catholic priesthood and they declined to offer the Church the radical challenge of the Poor Lombards. This may have weakened them. Or perhaps persecution was more effective there.[46] Numbers dropped. Bernard Gui, a very active inquisitor in Provence in the early decades of the fourteenth century, found Cathars and Beguins but only rather small batches of Waldensians. In 1492 two *barbi* from the Alps were captured at Oulx; they had been on tour in France and had visited scattered families who retained their ancient allegiance. They were to be found in a wide range of localities, Ardèche, Velay, Auvergne, Burgundy, the Lyonnais, the Valentinois, but they were few.[47] In secrecy, as part of an economically motivated immigration from Piedmont from 1460 onwards, numbers had greatly increased in unpopulated lands in Provence. These groups also existed very quietly. Their purpose was to live on and to maintain the faith of their ancestors.

The communities of Vallouise, l'Argentière, Freissinières, the Valcluson in Dauphiné formed part of the complex of Waldensian survival on both sides of the Alps, and shared characteristics with the mountain heresy of the Piedmontese refuges; as elsewhere, the indifference of religious authorities let the movement grow. Quiet was disturbed by the preaching of St Vincent Ferrier, 1399–1403; bishops became more energetic in the fifteenth century

[44] Schneider, *Waldensertum*, p. 14.
[45] Intriguing example: ibid., pp. 35–6.
[46] Ibid., p. 55.
[47] For survey, see G. Audisio, *Les Vaudois du Luberon: Une minorité en Provence (1460–1560)* (Gap, 1984), review: P. Biller, *JMH* LIX (1987), pp. 853–6 (reconstruction of life of most secret of Waldensian groups, with reflections on *barbi* and adherents, of general validity); summary: Audisio, in *Vaudois*, ed. Audisio, p. 83.

and pursued cases of sorcery among the peasants; an anti-Waldensian crusade, in which some plain rapacity was involved, was launched in 1487–8. Bitter losses followed, with erosion by conversion and emigration; none the less martyrdoms reinforced the determination of survivors and the Waldensians showed their calibre by the manner in which they resisted prosecutions and used the judicial system to enforce in 1509 a rehabilitation of victims unjustly sentenced and a quashing of confiscations. On the eve of the Reformation an interaction between the *barbi* and their communities, led by a small number of committed families, kept the movement in being – not challenging the Church with a radical alternative but sustaining an underground life based on preaching, confessions and penance.[48]

Italy, the Alps and Provençal immigration

The Poor Lombards are the least known of all the heretical movements in Italy of the twelfth and thirteenth centuries. Born of a fusion between Waldensianism from France and the anticlerical ferment of northern Italy, they shared in the anarchic vitality of the Lombard plain. Probably there were other strands in Italian Waldensian life. Merlo has argued that the references in the Conference of Bergamo both to the 'societas ultramontanorum fratrum' and the 'societas Italicorum fratrum' can be read as meaning that the latter should not simply be equated with the Poor Lombards.[49] There were Tortolani, so called from the consecrated bread of the eucharist which was celebrated by one master once a year; another group taught the priesthood of all believers – or at least, of all men believers; another required re-baptism of its members. Both Lyonists and Poor Lombards, divided by ideology, existed in Italy. A heretic from the Lyonists captured in the diocese of Besançon had spent years of study in Milan. Etienne de Bourbon, the Dominican inquisitor, who described the capture, retailed with pleasure information about the burgeoning of differing heretical groups, for it was a sign of the falsity of their opinions in contrast to the unity of the true Church.[50]

The atmosphere of northern Italy ensured that the Poor Lombards retained their hostile attitude to the Roman Church: it was the Whore of the Apocalypse. That view was only reinforced as the Italian cities, one by one, accepted a duty of repression. The Poor Lombards had intended to provide a counter-Church with its own sacraments, but that became more and more difficult to do as persecution became a reality. When it was objected that Waldensian supporters were dying without holy communion because of the exigencies of life underground, a leader of the Lombards referred to Augustine's interpretation of John 6:57, and stressed the inner communion of spirit with Christ.[51]

[48] P. Paravy, 'Les Vaudois du Haut-Dauphiné de la croisade de 1488 à la réforme', *Christianisme*, ed. Brenon, pp. 255–86 (for nicodemism as fruit of original concept of Waldensianism as a movement of awakening, p. 282); on crusade, Cameron, *Reformation*, pp. 25–61; minor survivals in France, geographical survey in Audisio, *Luberon*.

[49] Merlo, *Valdesi*, p. 11; reflections: pp. 143–5; Tortolani: p. 17; see also Merlo, in *BSSV* cxxxvi (1974), pp. 1–30, on Alpine adherents.

[50] *Quellen zur . . . Waldenser*, ed. Patschovsky and Selge, pp. 47–8; Merlo, *Valdesi*, p. 16.

[51] Schneider, *Waldensertum*, pp. 72–3.

FIGURE 3   The ruins of a Waldensian settlement near l'Argentière-la-Bassée at the entry to the valley of Vallouise, illustrating the harshness of the terrain in the refuges of the Haut-Dauphiné.

Photograph: Roger-Viollet, Paris.

In time the old centres of Italian Waldensianism were lost; the movement faded in Lombardy but gained support in certain villages in the Alps and in the south of Italy. They grew strong in Calabria, whither Charles the Lame, king of Naples 1285–1309, called in textile workers from the north, all unconsciously drawing Waldensianism into his kingdom.[52]

The Piedmontese Valleys constitute a special case,[53] for there deep poverty and isolation was the necessary background; a feeling of the distinctiveness of the Valleys as contrasted with the life of the plains may have played a part in sustaining the movement. The hierarchy denounced unorthodoxy, and spasmodic inquisitions revealed some hundreds of suspects, but secular authority was seldom zealous in support, probably for fear of disturbing the local population. If we can believe the reports of the proceedings of inquisitions held in Piedmont at various times in the fourteenth and fifteenth centuries, the Valleys acted as refuge-points for heretics of another cast altogether and formed a crucible for a Cathar–Waldensian syncretism which co-existed with the dominant strand of plain Waldensianism.[54] So we meet, beside the denials of purgatory and the invocation of the saints, the rejection of oaths, Donatism and the belief in the superiority of confession to their own preachers, an idiosyncratic logic that Christ was not true God since God could not die,[55] Cathar teaching on dualism and the *endura*, and the acceptance of sexual licence. We meet the extraordinary figure of Giacomo Bech, interrogated in 1388, who apparently had in his time been an adherent of the *fraticelli*, the Waldensians and the Cathars of the mitigated dualist variety;[56] and Giovanni Freyra, who confessed in the preceding year to having adored the sun and moon, saying the *Pater Noster* and *Ave Maria*.[57] We also meet the hoary old *canard* in the interrogations of 1387–8 and 1451 of the secret sexual orgy, begun after one of the preacher class, the *barbi*, put out the light, saying, 'Qui ama, si tegna!'[58]

The first known source in the medieval West for stories of heretics participating in indiscriminate sexual intercourse in the dark is the account of the Orléans heresy of 1022 by the monk Paul of Saint-Père de Chartres.[59] Such practices were attributed to heretics in the twelfth century by Guibert de Nogent[60]

---

[52] Gonnet and Molnár, *Les Vaudois*, p. 142.

[53] G. G. Merlo, *Eretici e inquisitori nella società piemontese del trecento* (Turin, 1977) (analysis of heretical environment, with stimulating, sometimes controversial hypotheses), reviews: K. V. Selge, *HZ* ccxxxi (1980), pp. 445–7; J. C. Schmitt, *BSRS* iv (1986), pp. 19–20; see also Merlo, *Valdesi* (essays, stressing Waldensian discontinuities).

[54] G. Gonnet, 'Casi di sincretismo ereticale in Piemonte nei secoli xiv e xv', *BSSV* cviii (1960), pp. 3–36; for editions, see footnotes. A partial, faulty edition of 1387–8 proceedings is in Döllinger, *Beiträge* ii, pp. 251–73.

[55] Gonnet, *BSSV* cviii, p. 19; for oddities, see belief in a dragon (ibid., p. 21).

[56] Ibid., pp. 22–4. There is even a fragment of immoralist Free Spirit heresy, p. 34 (for Free Spirit, see below, pp. 181–7). Bech sounds to me like a verbal exhibitionist, and his evidence suspect.

[57] Ibid., p. 17.

[58] Ibid., p. 33. On the *barbi* (or *barbae*), sing. *barba*, see above, n. 2. The term was current in the fifteenth century.

[59] Above, p. 11. Gonnet, *BSSV* cviii, pp. 33–6, accepts charges of immorality. I dissent. Audisio, *Luberon*, pp. 261–4, also accepts libertinism. I do not think this justified.

[60] Guibert de Nogent, *Histoire de sa vie (1053–1124)*, ed. G. Bourgin (Paris, 1907), iii, xvii, pp. 212–13; discussion of orgy stories: M. Barber, 'Propaganda in the Middle Ages: the charges against the Templars', *NMS* xvii (1973), pp. 42–57; see pp. 45–8.

and Walter Map;[61] Gregory IX issued a bull, *Vox in Rama*, describing heretics of his day who so indulged,[62] and interrogators elicited confessions about orgies at various times from Templars and rebellious Franciscans.[63] A starting-point for the attribution of libertinism to the Waldensians may well lie in a phrase sometimes used at the end of a service: 'let him who has grasped (the meaning) retain it'. The congregation who had listened to the preaching would meditate in darkness for a few minutes before leaving.[64] Later medieval Waldensianism had to operate in darkness and secrecy and so came, willy nilly, to conform to the classic controversialist's picture of the insidious heretic. From darkness and secrecy to the slander of the secret orgy was an easy step. *Vox in Rama* was probably based on the fantasies of Conrad of Marburg about the doings of German heretics; receiving papal confirmation gave Conrad's poisonous stories a vogue they might not otherwise have had and helped to popularize accusations of libertinism. The story of the secret orgy, sometimes blended with fantasies about the sacrifice of a baby, has a startlingly long history, investigated by Norman Cohn,[65] reaching back to slanders of the early Christians by Minucius Felix, as Table 2 demonstrates.

The story, it is clear, could be applied to any unpopular movement, and in the fourteenth century the Waldensians were losing ground in public opinion. The story of libertinism is on all fours with a popular slander also in vogue, of a hidden Waldensian treasure that gave the lie to their claims of leading a poor, apostolic life.[66] The most perceptive inquisitors rejected such stories. Zwicker refused belief in the legend of the hidden treasure. David of Augsburg, though he would give credence to doubtful tales about *barbi*, refused orgy stories. By contrast, the inquisitors in the Valleys were not of the highest calibre, and believed in stories of libertinism. Moreover, though many of those who came before them had indeed been involved in heresy, they were often fringe members.[67] What Merlo calls 'heretical syncretisms' floated about the Valleys. In Chieri part of the local aristocracy were under a Cathar-dualist influence; in the Valleys and in land immediately below them Waldensianism was stronger. Folklore played a part just as it did amongst the Cathars of Montaillou.

One of the most frequent tenets was the denial of purgatory, based on the standard Waldensian teaching that there were only two paths to follow, one of which led to heaven and the other to hell. The accused, however, sometimes said that purgatory existed 'in this world'. At Montaillou some believed that

---

[61] *De nugis*, ed. James, I, xxx, p. 47.

[62] *Epistolae saeculi XIII e regestis pontificum Romanorum*, ed. C. Rodenberg (*MGH*, Berlin, 1883), Epistolae I, no. 537, pp. 432–4; tr. by Barber, *NMS* XVII, pp. 45–6.

[63] F. Ehrle, 'Die Spiritualen: ihr Verhältniss zum Franciscanerorden und zu den Fraticellen', in *ALKG* IV, pp. 1–190 at p. 137 (note discussion of *barilotto*; I dissent from Ehrle's judgement that orgies took place, find significant the use of torture on suspects, and consider popular suspicion poor evidence); also Templars in Barber, *NMS* XVII, and below, pp. 180–1.

[64] N. Cohn, *Europe's Inner Demons* (London, 1975) (powerful analysis of demoniac fantasies and witch cult; slanders of Waldensians: pp. 32–42), p. 41 and reference to Amati cited; comment: P. Biller, in *Vaudois*, ed. Audisio, p. 48.

[65] Cohn, *Demons*, chs 1–5.

[66] Biller, '*Thesaurus absconditus* . . .', *SCH* XXIV, pp. 139–54.

[67] Criticisms by Selge, *HZ* CCXXXI, pp. 445–7.

TABLE 2   Accusations of libertinism

Author and date	Target	Reports
Minucius Felix first century	Christians	Worship of donkey's head; orgy; killing of baby
St Augustine	Manichees; the Elect class	Orgy
Paul of St Père de Chartres eleventh century	Heretics at Orléans	Orgy; viaticum from ashes of dead baby
Guibert de Nogent twelfth century	Heretics at Soissons	Baby killed by being passed from hand to hand
Walter Map twelfth century	Heretics	Worship of black cat; orgy
Gregory IX: *Vox in Rama* 1233	Heretics in Germany	Worship of Lucifer in various guises; orgy
Nicholas Eymeric: *Directorium Inquisitorum* 1368	Waldensians	'in the dark it is lawful for any man to mate with any woman'
Antonio di Setto 1387–8	Waldensians in the Alps	Drinking toad excrement; worship of Lucifer; orgy
St John Capistrano (source for Flavio Biondo) 1449	Fraticelli burned at Fabriano	Orgy; baby roasted

the spirits of the dead wandered in the ravines of the Sabartès. In Piedmont and in Montaillou inquisitions thus brought to light ancient, pre-Christian beliefs and practices. Some of the Piedmont heretics preferred to bury their dead in their own fields and gardens, where they would be near to them: in so doing they were asserting their independence of the clergy and their rites.[68]

This is strange evidence, which historians have not found easy to assess, for some of the tenets uncovered in these inquisitions consort uncomfortably with other evidence of the nature of the Waldensianism which survived in the mountain environment. Waldensian literature, with its pastoral message, was written in the dialect of the same mountains and bears no trace of the contaminations elicited by the inquisitors. When the *Unitas Fratrum*, or, later, Reformation missionaries, came into contact with the Valleys, they found that the *barbi* had been marked by their long underground existence; they did not meet the odd, amorphous syncretisms thrown up by these inquiries.[69] A riddle has not been solved.

From Piedmont came a substantial reinforcement for the shattered movement in France – at least in purely numerical terms – as Waldensians blended quietly with waves of emigration from the overcrowded Valleys

---

[68] J. C. Schmitt, in *Annales* XXXV (1980), pp. 309–11.
[69] Selge's exposition, to my mind, carries greatest weight.

between 1460 and the 1520s and settled, often as small landed proprietors, in the Luberon and other parts of Provence,[70] They kept possessions in their ancestral Valleys and returned occasionally for business and personal reasons.

It is hard to believe that the Catholic clergy of the lands of immigration were unaware of their presence; but, as elsewhere, inertia and perhaps humanitarian considerations led them to turn a blind eye. The Waldensians were careful to do nothing to make themselves conspicuous. In many things they did as their Catholic neighbours did. They paid tithes, they participated in observances which implied the existence of purgatory (whatever their private reservations) and they took oaths. Their faith was the faith of a household, just as Catharism had been in the Sabartès. Secrecy was maintained by a careful marriage policy. Waldensians married Waldensians and passed on their faith to their children. The same Christian names recur and recur over the years. Comparison of their wills with those of a predominantly Catholic settlement at Cucuron shows that the Waldensian families were inclined to make more gifts to the poor than the Catholics did – a survival, it may well be, of the stress on poverty and charitable activities going back to Valdes himself.[71] Commemoration of their dead took a more sober form in their bequests than in those of the Catholics. They tended to omit the additional commemorative masses which Catholics founded and made less use of the cross, holy water and torches at burials.[72] At Lourmarin, where there was a substantial Waldensian presence, the records of the parish priest reveal a full observance of Sundays and days of obligation.[73] The Waldensians were contributing without reservation to the support of their Catholic priest, yet at the same time maintaining in secrecy their inner life through contact with wandering preachers, taking what Audisio refers to as a 'homeopathic antidote' to the Catholic observance they followed so fully.

Material from the Luberon, Provence and Piedmont in the later fifteenth and early sixteenth centuries enables us to reconstruct the life and work of the *barbi* in the last phase of Waldensianism before the Reformation.[74] A network of families ran over the Alps, linking Piedmont and Dauphiné to the Luberon and associated areas and it was these families who gave sons to the movement for training as *barbi*. The candidates would be put through two or three years' probation and taught to read and write. Peasants' sons were being recruited to speak to peasants: it was part of the movement's strength that this was so. Initiation had some resemblance to profession in a monastic order. The candidate undertook lifelong celibacy. He underwent apprenticeship and was put under obedience to a senior *barba*, seniority being decided by the time at which ordination took place. The senior provided an example, teaching and control for the junior. There followed a lifetime of wandering, visiting the

---

[70] Audisio, *Luberon, passim*. Biller, in *BSRS* IV (1986), p. 20 calls it a 'masterpiece': so it is, above all because of the quality of scholarship illuminating refractory material.

[71] Audisio, *Luberon*, p. 270.

[72] Ibid., p. 215.

[73] Ibid., p. 220; see Erbstösser, *Strömungen*, p. 142, arguing that parish clergy in Brandenburg and Pomerania must have known of existence of Waldensians.

[74] See Audisio, *Luberon*, pp. 228–43, on occupations and duties of *barbi*; book as sign of office: p. 237; information in Biller, '*Multum ieiunantes . . .*', *SCH* XXII, pp. 215–28, and his comment, 'a mendicant order frozen at a fairly early stage', p. 218.

hidden flocks, operating in one zone for a limited number of years, then changing to another for the sake of security.

Visits to the homes of the underground families followed a regular pattern. Exhortation preceded the invitation to confess. The penitent knelt before the *barba*, made his confession and was absolved, the *barba* laying his hand on the penitent's head and imposing the penance. The penitent gave some small sum as a gift to the *barba*; the *barba* in return gave a little token, such as pins, which seem to have had a symbolic significance. Confession might well mark the entrance of a young person in the family to full membership.

The visits of preachers brought access to books, the sign of their office, the *aides-mémoire* in size comparable to the little pocket-books which friars used for their own itinerant ministry, which thus entered the homes of peasants otherwise unused to books.

On the *barba* hung the security and organization of Waldensianism, even some of the financial arrangements, for *barbi* took collections for the support of brothers. They were, so to speak, members of a mendicant order which had not been allowed an official existence. Persecution kept them, on the whole, from relaxation. Sexual offences were dealt with strictly; riches can hardly have been a temptation. Annual gatherings in August, often in a remote spot in Piedmont, kept them together, enabled collective decision-making and the assembling and disposal of money. Yet over it all hung an odd contradiction. The *barbi* were part of a movement which felt itself to be the salt of the earth. They were devoted to an austere life of exhortation and the hearing of confessions. They were preachers but they could very rarely preach openly in accordance with the instructions of Jesus.[75] They could, and did, sustain Waldensianism, but they would not spread it.

Belief and practice

The literature of the Waldensians was of a character adapted to its membership: it had a predominantly ethical character and was closely linked to Scripture.[76] Many of the texts were written in Alpine dialect, reflecting the influence of the Waldensians' last redoubt on the movement as a whole. Some 200 dialect sermons are extant, other texts were in Latin. It is becoming clear that the Waldensians retained men of some learning in their preacher class who could read Latin and who understood the clerical tradition of the Middle Ages, which they adapted for the use of their simpler colleagues and the benefit of adherents. Letters exchanged between Italian and German-speaking preachers in the 1360s show that the more learned among them understood the rules of composition in Latin and used both Peter Lombard and Gratian's *Decretum*. The *Liber Electorum*, which contained a short history of the Waldensians, was a Latin translation of a work in Alpine dialect, Latin providing a *lingua franca* for the more educated amongst German-speaking preachers. The existence of a Latin confessor's tract bears witness to the

[75] Audisio, *Luberon*, p. 235.

[76] Survey, incidental to the author's purpose, by P. Biller in *BSRS* IV, pp. 19–28 at pp. 21–3, with references to work in progress; Gonnet and Molnár, *Les Vaudois*, pp. 319–69; see also Biller, in *SCH* XXII, pp. 220–3, and in *Vaudois*, ed. Audisio, pp. 53–5, bibliography, pp. 73–5.

importance of penance amongst Waldensians. The Waldensian bestiary is an intriguing example of their willingness to adapt from the orthodox clerical tradition to which they were heirs: Jaco, who translated it into Alpine dialect for some of his pupils, simplified it, no doubt for the use of preachers, and omitted material on heresy and on Mary. A bestiary moralized on the creation and was a natural choice for a missionary elite working amongst peasant adherents, with their animals round them.[77]

Scripture held a dominant place: it was the 'unique norm of teaching and living', and to it appeal on all disputed questions was made. Vernacular translations were a nodal point for the instruction and rote learning which mattered so much to adherents. Waldensian literature proper, or literature taken over by the Waldensians, served the purpose of opening or explaining the Scriptures and of confirming the membership in their ethical life. One of the best-known pieces, the *Nobla leycon*, was a poem of about 1400,[78] which gives a survey of the whole Bible under the headings of the three laws of God: the law of nature, the law of Moses and the law of Christ. There was also simple catechetical material, such as the seven articles of faith, and orthodox extracts, such as a collection of sentences from the Fathers, and a work of Augustine on the virtues and vices, called 'the Thirty Stages'. This type of reading matter was not heretical at all and reveals no trace of syncretism or corruption through the underground existence of the movement. What does betray the clandestine existence of Waldensians are the tiny books, even as small as $2\frac{1}{2} \times 2\frac{1}{4}$ inches, adapted for rapid concealment in the clothing of *barbi* threatened with discovery.[79]

No one man ruled the whole Waldensian movement after Valdes. Amongst the Lombards an important role was played by the general chapters,[80] held once or twice a year, at which the vital decisions were taken about the spending of money, the reception of new brothers and sisters, appointments to office and missionary activity. The chapters held together the Lombards and the Germans in the thirteenth century, as we have seen, although they did so somewhat loosely, for the German representation was slight; by the fourteenth century that direct link had been lost. The adherents or friends formed a supporting class to the preachers, fulfilling a function not unlike that of the *credentes* of the Cathars of Languedoc, who aided the journeys of the perfect and gave financial and other support.

Their manner of life differed in various regions. In Lombardy, where the issue had been so significant at the Conference of Bergamo, they probably joined the workers' associations on the pattern of the Humiliati, with set workplaces which were also centres of instruction and evangelization. The nature of meeting places varied according to the pressures put on the movement, from a regular, known building, like the school which long existed in Milan, to individual houses of supporters.

---

[77] *Bestiario Valdese*, ed. A. M. Raugei, *Biblioteca dell' 'Archivum Romanicum'*, ser. I, vol. CLXXV. The *barbi* used the standard glosses of the medieval clergy on the Bible (*Vaudois*, ed. Audisio, p. 103).

[78] Dating by Biller, in *SCH* XIX, p. 71.

[79] Biller, in *SCH* XXII, p. 221.

[80] Böhmer, in *RPTK*, cols 818, 821. For modern controversy on the degree of unity and continuity in Waldensianism, *Vaudois*, ed. Audisio is esp. valuable; see pp. 62–3.

Women remained important,[81] both as preachers or sisters and as supporters, personally and financially; they were still playing a considerable role in Piedmont in the late fourteenth century, and their preaching, a stumbling-block to the orthodox hierarchy, continued and was observable as late as the fifteenth century. But Koch is probably right when he argues that the position of women tended to deteriorate, conforming more to the general status of women in this period in the world outside, *pari passu* with a loss of impetus in Waldensianism – especially in the south of France, where from the early fourteenth century it became more difficult for them to enter the preacher class. The *De vita et actibus* is witness that in the late thirteenth century they were being excluded from the chapters.[82]

Social origins[83] of both adherents and preachers, where known, tended, after an initial phase stretching from the preaching of Valdes to about the middle of the thirteenth century, to be remarkably uniform. Above all, Waldensianism was the religion of the small man, whether in town or country. At first, preachers both gained recruits higher in society and themselves had been of higher rank: Valdes was a rich businessman, and the same factors which drove him out of his business acted on others of similar station; and a group of former clerics existed among the preachers. Examples of higher adherence or patronage become rarer as persecution began to bite and, though in the later Middle Ages examples exist of well-off townsmen becoming involved in certain south German and Swiss towns, the lasting success of the movement lay lower in society; the core consisted of peasants and artisans. This, of course, does not tell us whether adherents were necessarily poor, for wide variations of wealth were possible in these classes. What seems clear is that much support lay in the countryside, and that there was no sharp division between town and country.

The split between the Lyonists and the Lombards concerned the Waldensians less as persecution affected them all. Though it was not healed, limited relations persisted in individual cases, such as that of the French leader, Joannes Lotaringius, who at the end of the thirteenth century journeyed through Italy.[84] Everywhere pressure welded together the rank and file and transformed the earlier movement of awakening within the Church of Valdes's day into a secret, underground movement.

The nature of the hierarchy of the movement varied between the two wings and fluctuated in the course of time;[85] the situation is also complicated by the possibility that hostile observers did not always grasp the details of the leadership. After the Conference of Bergamo the Lombards rather than the Lyonists were more interested in having leaders for life; yet by the end of the thirteenth century the Lyonists were appointing a *maior minister* who was to

[81] Biller, in *SCH* xxii, pp. 219–20, suggestion of motivation for celibacy: p. 228; also *BSRS* iv, pp. 23–4; Koch, *Frauenfrage*, pp. 156–69.

[82] Koch, *Frauenfrage*, p. 168.

[83] Summary in Grundmann, *Ketzergeschichte*, p. 33; Böhmer, *RPTK*, cols 809 (early years), 824–5 (later Middle Ages); Gonnet and Molnár, *Les Vaudois*, pp. 164–6; helpful social and geographical observations: Biller, in *SCH* xxii, p. 227; Erbstösser, *Strömungen*, pp. 119–31.

[84] Böhmer, *RPTK*, col. 811; Döllinger, *Beiträge* ii, p. 109.

[85] G. Gonnet, 'Nature et limites de l'episcopat vaudois au Moyen Age', *CV* ii (1959), pp. 311–21; Böhmer, *RPTK* cols 816–19, 829–30.

hold office for a lifetime. The threefold orders of bishop, priest and deacon are often witnessed in the sources but were not employed in precisely the manner of the Catholics. Nor are they continually in evidence; congregations held different views, some stressing the priesthood of all believers, others stressing more the distinction between the preacher class and the rest.

Above all, differences flowed from the biblicism of Waldensians; all beliefs and practices were set against the word of Scripture and different groups naturally formed different interpretations.[86] On the eucharist, for example, there were many variations. There were those who took a spiritualizing view; there were those who believed that the validity of the sacrament was conditioned, not only by the worthiness of the celebrant, but also of the communicant; there were Donatists and sacramentalists; there were those who believed that the eucharist should be celebrated once a year on Maundy Thursday and those who believed that it should be celebrated every day during common meals. In Montauban a curiosity was the consumption of a meal of blessed bread and fish on Maundy Thursday.[87]

Erbstösser rightly observes that the passage of time did not tighten Waldensian organization.[88] At Bergamo they were sufficiently close knit for both wings to be able to send representatives. But such a unity did not last. In the fourteenth century Bernard Gui, the Dominican inquisitor long active in the south of France, whose work on the Waldensians is admittedly heavily derivative, described quite an elaborate organization with varied offices.[89] Germany, on the other hand, had no such structure and the congregations of Peter Zwicker's persecution were held together by the simplest means; yet the Germans still had resilience and outlasted a heavy persecution. That fact, coupled with the varieties of organization over the centuries, casts doubt on any hypothesis which lays weight on organization as such as a factor in survival. It was not the offices, or even the chapters, which counted in the last resort; it was the tenacity and mobility of the preachers visiting their flocks, the *barbi* of the Alpine Valleys, the *Meister* in Germany. They kept Waldensianism alive till the Reformation.

---

[86] G. Gonnet, *Le Confessioni di fede valdesi prima della reforma* (Turin, 1967); Gonnet and Molnár, *Les Vaudois*, pp. 371–441; G. Scuderi, 'Il problema del matrimonio nella fede, nella pietà e nella teologia del Valdismo medioevale', *BSSV* CVI (1959), pp. 31–54; analysis under geographical headings in Schneider, *Waldensertum*.

[87] Schneider, *Waldensertum*, pp. 24–5, suggesting a reminiscence of the feeding of the five thousand.

[88] *Strömungen*, p. 133.

[89] Leff, *Heresy* II, pp. 463–4, citing Bernard Gui's *Manuel*, ed. Mollat, I, p. 52; for survey on *barbi* and their arrangements in the western wing of Waldensianism, see *Vaudois*, ed. Audisio, pp. 84–5.

9

Tension and insecurity: Gregory x to John xxii

While the Cathars were being put down by persecution and by peaceful competition from the Church, the popes faced grave problems, not directly connected with doctrinal unorthodoxy.[1] At first the search for security and independence in Italy lay at the heart of their troubles; they had fought for years to defend themselves against the menace of the Hohenstaufen dynasty holding simultaneously the Empire and the Regno, and threatening them in Rome. Under Innocent IV every means, fair and foul, was used to defeat Frederick II, and no small part of the papacy's reputation and sacral quality was sacrificed in the process. Later, in order to prevent Frederick's heirs again menacing the papacy's independence, a papal champion, Charles of Anjou, was employed to take and to defend the Regno. As we have seen, Charles's success had effect throughout the peninsula, and incidentally helped to create the conditions for the determined persecution of Cathars in Lombardy. The papacy achieved a major victory through the Angevin alliance, and eliminated the Hohenstaufen – only to find the power and ambitions of Charles, brother of Louis IX of France, and the strength of the Capetian dynasty to which Charles belonged profoundly disquieting.

The conflict with the Hohenstaufen had important side-effects: it tended to debase papal policy, and the search for a rival champion helped to create parties within the college of cardinals and to increase tensions between national groups. When in turn the dangers of Charles's power became

[1] Summaries and bibliography in B. Moeller, *Spätmittelalter: Die Kirche in ihrer Geschichte*, ed. K. D. Schmidt and E. Wolf, II, pt I (Göttingen, 1966) (exposition from 1250); F. Rapp, *L'Eglise et la vie religieuse en Occident à la fin du Moyen Age* (Paris, 1971) (from 1303); reflections in R. W. Southern, *Western Society and the Church in the Middle Ages* (Harmondsworth, 1966). See J. K. Hyde, *Society and Politics in Medieval Italy* (London, 1973) for Italian background, and G. Barraclough, *The Medieval Papacy* (London, 1968) for papal history; F. Oakley, *The Western Church in the Later Middle Ages* (Ithaca, NY, and London, 1979).

apparent, one of the policies adopted was that of attempting to build up the papal states in central Italy as partial counterbalances by means of nepotistic appointments.[2] Successive popes sought security through promoting relatives; but pontificates were short, and the relatives of one pope might well be the enemies of another. The policy brought no long-term security and damaged papal reputations.

Charles's decline was due, not to papal policy, but the effects of his misgovernment. A revolt in Sicily in 1282, aided by intrigue and bribes from his foreign enemies, gravely weakened his position. The Angevin menace was thereafter effectively removed, but the popes did not jettison the Angevin alliance. Instead, they backed the attempts of Charles and his heir to regain the island of Sicily and, over a period of two decades after the revolt of the Sicilian Vespers, committed papal money and prestige to the Angevin cause, declaring expeditions against their opponents to be crusades. In the end, despite these efforts, defeat had to be accepted at the Peace of Caltabellotta, to which the pope assented in 1303.

This was one beneficent event in the pontificate of Boniface viii, a first-rate canon lawyer and capable diplomat who was also a gross nepotist and ruthless power politician. Under his highly controversial rule, a dispute with the king of France, Philip iv, escalated into a major conflict. Shortly after Boniface had issued the bull *Unam Sanctam* in 1302, the most extreme statement of the temporal claims of the papacy, he was attacked by Philip's servants in his residence at Anagni, and died shortly afterwards of shock. His fate and his doubtful reputation overshadowed the following two pontificates, for Philip used the threat of a charge of heresy against Boniface as a means of applying pressure. Clement v, elected after the short pontificate of Boniface's immediate successor, Gascon-born, settled at Avignon, partly because of his personal predilections, partly because of the convenience of being close at hand for negotiations with Philip. The temporary residence of the papacy there lasted, with one short interruption, until 1377. Temperamentally reluctant to take firm action, Clement, however he might manoeuvre, in the end felt himself compelled to accept Philip's will. At the Council of Vienne in 1312 he suppressed the order of Templars, earlier convicted of wholly imaginary offences at the instigation of Philip, who needed their goods in order to satisfy pressing economic needs. As if to underline the changed position of the clergy *vis-à-vis* the laity, the same council discussed the encroachments of the laity on ecclesiastical goods and jurisdictions without finding any effective defence against them. It was a melancholy contrast to Innocent's fourth Lateran Council a century earlier.

After a prolonged vacancy, John xxii was elected to succeed Clement in 1316. As trenchant as Clement had been vacillating, he at once set about restoring the papal position, and in an eighteen-year pontificate, aided by the waning of France's strength after the death of Philip iv, went far towards recreating independence. In place of his predecessor's debts he built up an unprecedented surplus. The curia was reorganized, and once again the papacy came to occupy a central position in international diplomacy; all

[2] Hyde, *Society*, p. 130.

spheres felt the impress of the pope's personality – energetic, authoritarian, inflexible. On issues of faith and heresy, his instinct was to back authority, to define and condemn, and to give work to the inquisition. The pontificate was marked by a series of definitions and proceedings aimed at suspect theologians and sectaries. Authoritarian methods roused opposition. Obstinate deter mination to make his own will prevail over the choice of emperor aroused a conflict with Lewis of Bavaria, who gave protection to Franciscan rebels and heretics as a weapon against the pope, and John failed to bring him down. At the end, lacking the suppleness of Innocent III and the essential aid of powerful reform movements within the Church and religious orders, he had been unable to stimulate profound or long-lasting changes to the benefit of the Church, and the methods whereby he rebuilt the papal position alienated opinion.

Over the clergy, in contrast to the laity, the papacy exerted an ever-increasing control during these difficult years. Centralization continued apace within the Church, and canonists erected a structure of thought which drew out the implications of the doctrine of the 'fullness of power' inherent in the papal office. A major impetus to centralization was, however, fiscal. Costly wars and foreign policy, and expanding bureaucracy demanded money and the growing papal power within the Church was more often directed towards stopgap solutions of immediate problems than the needs of reform. In form and theory, the place of the papacy within the Church expanded; in reality, popes suffered from a chronic insecurity and inability to match means to ends.

A changing society was becoming less amenable to papal leadership. Damaged by the papacy's own misuse, the attractions of the crusading ideal waned. One stage in its decay was reached by the time that Gregory X, a sincere crusading pope, summoned the Council of Lyons of 1274. It was intended to heal the schism with the Greek Church, counter Charles of Anjou's designs on Byzantium, and act as a launching platform for an expedition to the Holy Land. Gregory's investigations at the time of the council revealed how far interest in crusades had waned; a traditional link between papacy and laity was gradually eroding.

The Empire was far less significant than it once had been: power had passed to the national kingdoms. The events of the pontificates of Boniface VIII and Clement V showed the difficulties which popes had in coming to terms with the shift in temporal power that had taken place.

Educational standards amongst the laity were rising, and new directions in lay piety were beginning to make themselves felt. The mystical way, formerly the preserve of the monastery or nunnery, was being opened to the laity and to the secular clergy, with the aid of the friars and their spirituality. It reflected a developing trend towards individualism in later medieval piety, not of itself hostile to the Church and the sacraments – indeed eucharistic fervour might be a feature of the pursuit of the mystical way – but stressing the soul's experience of God rather than the Church's mediation.

No movement arose on the scale of the Cistercians in the twelfth century or the friars in the early thirteenth to rouse the energies of the devout and give backing to any papal reforming designs; reform impulses were still there, but they found expression in piecemeal, local movements or in the lives of dedicated individuals. The Franciscans, so long a support of the papacy, showed signs of strain; at the Council of Lyons earlier dissensions dating back to St Francis's lifetime began to emerge again in a form so acute as eventually to demand prolonged papal investigation.

Complexity, bureaucracy and worldliness produced a reaction. The popes faced difficulties that were not susceptible of swift, personalized solutions; but their position was rarely considered with sympathy, and from the early years of the fourteenth century we may detect something of the sense of betrayal which Leff rightly distinguishes as characteristic of late medieval opinion about Church leadership.[3]

Abuse of the inquisition's powers, the Free Spirit and the heresy associated with the Spiritual Franciscans, to be discussed in the following chapters, have to be set against this background of centralization, political pressure and change in the years between the Council of Lyons and the death of John xxii in 1334, affecting both the men and women accused of heresy and their repressors.

---

[3] *Heresy* I, p. 29.

10

Inquisition and abuse

THE PROBLEM OF THE INQUISITION

The papal inquisition was founded by Gregory IX, building on the foundations of his predecessors, and the extraordinarily wide powers of investigation and punishment which accrued to inquisitors were granted in order to make an end of heresies already condemned by the Church, most notably Catharism.[1] Naturally new sects and heresies that arose fell within its purview and, equally naturally, the influence of those who were given inquisitorial powers tended to be directed towards the tightening of the Church's law on heresy, in favour of condemnation rather than toleration of doubtful beliefs and practices. The desire of the inquisitor was for clear-cut condemnations and lists of erroneous beliefs that could be incorporated in handbooks and used as a basis for action in the field; his instinct was to widen the scope of his authority and to bring more activities into his sphere. So, for example, inquisitors attempted to bring sorcery under their jurisdiction after application to Alexander IV, whose ambiguous declaration that they might only do so if 'manifest heresy' were involved was used as a starting-point for an ultimate, if long delayed, assumption of authority in this sphere.[2] Higher churchmen who shared the inquisition mentality exercised their influence in similar ways, and were inclined to see heretical tendencies in movements and groups in the Church of which they disapproved. Bishops within their dioceses exercised wide powers and, if zealous, could give scope to their suspicions on the same lines as the

---

[1] Above, pp. 100–2; survey in C. Thouzellier, 'La répression de l'hérésie', in *Histoire de l'église*, ed. A. Fliche and V. Martin, x, pp. 291–340; bibliography in E. van der Vekené, *Bibliographie der Inquisition: ein Versuch* (Hildesheim, 1963); short notes in Wakefield, *Heresy, Crusade*; Kolmer, *Vulpes*, bibliography; orientation in B. Hamilton, *The Medieval Inquisition* (London, 1981). A full account of the inquisition and its distortions is beyond the scope of this book. Proceedings of one of the Bayreuther Historische Kolloquien, in 1992, devoted to the origin and activity of the Inquisition, will be edited by P. Segl. I am indebted to Prof. W. Trusen for a note of his paper.

[2] Lea, *Inquisition* III, p. 434; see J. B. Russell, *Witchcraft in the Middle Ages* (Cornell, 1972); *WEH*, p. 251.

inquisitors. The untramelled power of the inquisitor, the high penalties exacted or exactable for heresy and the opportunities in some cases of enrichment of interested parties in the wake of convictions made it inevitable that the unscrupulous would seek to take advantage of heresy charges to advance their own power, to ruin rivals or to feather their own nests.³ Unjust accusations of heresy were not new, and there is little doubt that zealots with no pertinacious will to unorthodoxy were killed or ruined in the twelfth century, before the development of more advanced techniques of detection and judgement. Confusion, then a major factor, was no longer so prevalent in the late thirteenth century; the new feature was the international character of persecution and its greater sophistication. On the one hand, the development of antiheretical treatises, bulls of definition and inquisitorial handbooks helped to dispel the old ignorance;⁴ on the other, if prejudice did once enter into these sources, they were disseminated much more widely, and the new character of persecution made possible what had not existed earlier – the manufacture of a whole artificial or semi-artificial heresy.

At the lowest level the office of inquisitor exposed its holder to temptation: it was the other side of the coin in the new efficiency of persecution which flowed from the commissions and legislation of Gregory IX and his successors. *Inquisitio* as a legal process confounded in one and the same person the offices of prosecutor and judge. There was also a blurring between the coercion implicit in a penal system and the healing of the soul which lay at the heart of the voluntary system of confession followed by the performance of penance. The secrecy of proceedings, the wide powers of arrest and imprisonment, the lack of any obligation to inform the accused of charges against him or to name witnesses, the absence of defending counsel, and the extreme difficulty of appealing against decisions meant that the preservation of justice rested to a large extent on the integrity of the individual who conducted a case. There was scope for greed, political bias, the malice of neighbours, bullying and sadism. Weight was given to mere *fama*, the ill report of a suspect's orthodoxy in a neighbourhood. Some yielded to the temptations of their authority; others, especially in early days, remained zealous, hard-working bureaucrats, inclined to cut corners in their eagerness to get to grips with heresy, yet not gravely unfair to suspects.⁵

The most important danger, however, lay in misunderstanding and unconscious distortion, either through over-sophisticated questioning or over-rigid adherence to some preconceived pattern of heresy derived from treatise or handbook, then imposed by forceful interrogation on a cowed suspect. Bernard Gui, who completed his manual about 1322–3, gives us an example of the dangers of over-sophistication in his section on tricks of the

³ Lea (*Inquisition* I, chs 7–14) is still of value: see above, p. 100, n. 37.

⁴ Above, p. 101.

⁵ See, e.g. Y. Dossat, 'Une figure d'inquisiteur: Bernard de Caux', in *CF* VI, pp. 253–72. The career of the outrageous Conrad of Marburg (above, p. 148) shows how, even in the earliest days of these free-ranging commissions, power could be abused; see Wakefield, *Heresy, Crusade*, pp. 185–6, for sound comment; on the confusion of penance and punishment, see Hamilton, *Inquisition*, pp. 49–59; see also E. Peters, *Inquisition* (New York and London, 1986) (concise survey, ch. 1 on classical precedent, ch. 2 on Middle Ages).

Waldensians, in turn taken from a thirteenth-century work attributed to David of Augsburg.[6] The inquisitor questions his suspect on the articles of faith. He replies briskly, 'I firmly believe.' The inquisitor asks him about transubstantiation. He replies, 'Ought I not to believe this?' The inquisitor responds, 'I am not asking if you ought to believe it, but if in fact you do', and gets in turn the reply, 'I believe all that you and other good doctors order me to believe.' The inquisitor believes this is an evasion, and goes on, 'Those good doctors which you are willing to believe are the masters of your sect. If I think as they do, you will believe both me and them; if not, not.' So the two continue to wrestle until the wily Waldensian is finally broken down on the sensitive issue of oath-taking.

No doubt life underground did produce the Waldensian heretic experienced in such evasions, equivocating to save himself and his friends, and trying to avoid direct lying; but inquisitors would also meet simple Catholics, untrained on the limits of heresy and orthodoxy, nervously attempting to ingratiate themselves, and falling deeper in the mire. Behind interrogation lay torture, to be applied at the will of the inquisitor, who, if he felt he was never touching rock-bottom belief in his suspect's answers, could use force in such a way as to compel incriminating answers, at least from most of common humanity. Confinement, fear and detachment from family and friends worked in the same way, and might lead to conviction by baseless, or scantily based, confession. The danger of a vicious circle was obvious, for inquisitors believed that in heresy they were fighting the work of the devil and were inclined to think that suspects were more subtle than they really were. Force, and the threat of force, could produce the guilty answers they felt they ought to be getting. The classic example is witchcraft, whose apparent popularity owed so much to the interest of inquisitors.[7]

More subtle distortion might spring from the use of leading questions based on handbooks' summaries of heretical tenets, obliterating an individual's personal variations of belief. Heresies changed, and handbooks did not necessarily keep pace with them; they tended to be based on a stereotype, and did not take adequate account of variations within heretical groups in different areas and times. Or the ethics of heretics might be slandered, and their tenets confused with those of other, more extreme heresies; we have seen the likelihood that this was the case in fourteenth- and fifteenth-century Piedmont.[8]

Each set of records of proceedings and testimony needs to be examined closely, in order to see whether the inquisitor or the bishop's officers have, through their questioning, provided a fair and accurate picture of heresy or a heretical group. Sometimes there are signs of distortion of testimony or blind repetition of predetermined sentiments; sometimes idiosyncratic replies by

[6] *Manuel*, ed. Mollat, I, p. 67; on authorship, see Dondaine, in *AFP* XVII (1947), pp. 93–4, 180–3; Borst, *Katharer*, pp. 22, 25; and for comment, Patschovsky, *Passauer Anonymus*, pp. 135–6; *Bernard Gui et son monde*, *CF* XVI (1981).
[7] Lea, *Inquisition* III, p. 50; the approach tends to differ from that of Russell, *Witchcraft*. Earlier work in H. C. Lea, *Materials toward a History of Witchcraft*, ed. A. C. Howland (Philadelphia, 1939); J. Hansen, *Quellen und Untersuchungen zur Geschichte des Hexenwahns und der Hexenverfolgung im Mittelalter* (Bonn, 1901).
[8] Above, pp. 164–6.

suspects and the flavour of many-faceted heresy as it appears in real life will assure us of the substantial accuracy of what we read; sometimes the signs are that the beliefs of a group have remained fairly static, and our records are doing substantial justice to the accused. The historian making these assessments will take account of deterioration in accuracy and fairness among inquisitors in the later medieval centuries.

In the higher ranks of churchmen manipulation of heresy charges occurred. A grey area is revealed, for example, in the activities of Bernard de Castanet, bishop of Albi, who controlled the workings of the inquisition in his city, damping them down as long as the heresy-infected leading bourgeoisie were on his side in battles of jurisdiction against the king, unleashing them in a famous set of trials of 1299–1300, after leading citizens had broken the alliance, and had come to work with royal officials against his interests.[9] The convicted were indeed heretics, and the bishop, an ultramontane ecclesiastic of the stamp of Boniface VIII, no doubt was in any case little inclined to distinguish between the crime of heresy and attacks on his temporal power, especially when they were the work of the same persons; but the fact remained that those convicted were the partisans of the Albi oligarchy and the king against the bishop, and that the trials followed hard on the heels of another, apparently unsuccessful, attempt in 1297–9 to put pressure on hostile oligarchs through the bishop's temporal jurisdiction. The importance of city politics for the Albi inquisition was obvious.

The development of papalist canon law in the thirteenth century tended to reinforce autocracy, and to encourage the inclination to equate heresy with disobedience to the pope, in the temporal sphere as much as in the spiritual; strangely enough, Frederick II's imperial legislation, *mutatis mutandis*, tended to confound heretics and political offenders in a similar fashion. The vague use of heresy charges ran hand in hand with the debasement of the crusade to attain political ends for the popes within Christendom, the accusations being a part of the propaganda against offending rulers and a justification for military action against them. So the Hohenstaufen were attacked in this way;[10] so Boniface VIII used the charge against his enemies in the Colonna family; so John XXII proclaimed his political enemies in Italy, the Visconti of Milan, the house of Este, the Ghibellines of Umbria, guilty of heresy, and declared the recalcitrant emperor Lewis of Bavaria to be a fautor.[11] As temporal opponents of the popes often favoured or tolerated heretics as pawns in their political game, or refused for reasons of security to allow the inquisition to operate in their lands, accusations of fautorship of heresy were not wholly baseless. But contemporaries recognized that it was concern, not about unorthodoxy, but about papal rights and the balance of power in Italy

[9] J. L. Biget, 'Un procès d'inquisition à Albi en 1300', in *CF* VI, pp. 273–341; G. W. Davis, *The Inquisition at Albi 1299–1300* (New York, 1948). I have accepted Biget's viewpoint.

[10] For this example and others, see Lea, *Inquisition* III, chs 4, 5; Grundmann bibliography in *HS*, pp. 448–50.

[11] F. Bock, 'Studien zum politischen Inquisitionsprozess Johanns XXII', *Quellen und Forschungen aus italienischen Archiven und Bibliotheken* XXVI (1935–6), pp. 21–142; XXVII (1936–7), p. 109–34; 'Der Este-Prozess von 1321', *AFP* VII (1937), pp. 41–111, 'Processi di Giovanni XXII contro i Ghibellini italiani', *ADRSP* LXIII (1940), pp. 129–43.

that motivated these charges. A debasement of the concept of heresy was implicit in this type of action.

The Templars

The loose use of heresy charges could not be expected to remain a monopoly of churchmen, and Philip IV of France and his ministers made the most dramatic and unscrupulous use of them in the entire period in their actions against the Templars (1307–12). They had been preceded by charges against Boniface VIII, scion of a Campagna family, a man of scant tact and of easy manners, whose insensitive actions and pungent remarks brought him many enemies, and provided a fund of disturbing statements that, spiced with exaggeration and hearsay, had formed the pretext for charges of heresy and other malpractices brought by Philip the Fair and his servants.[12] The threat of a formal trial of Boniface acted as a blackmail on the insecure Clement V, and opened the way for the French crown's sudden assault on the Templars in 1307.[13] Novel forces were arrayed against the papacy when an advanced secular monarchy, already blooded in the contest of wills with Boniface VIII, made uninhibited use of inquisitional techniques in order to gain the Templars' wealth. The inquisitor of France was the king's confessor; and the bishops of the kingdom were solid in support of the monarchy's cause; the Templars were a rich, secretive body that seemed to have lost its crusading *raison d'être* when the last foothold of the Christians in the Holy Land at Acre fell in 1291. Disappointment at the failure of Christendom to recover Jerusalem and the search for a scapegoat may have made some of Philip's subjects receptive to charges against the Templars; it does not seem that anyone outside France believed them, and no modern historian of repute will accept them as true. The Templars, it was said, imposed a denial of Christ and blasphemous rejection of the cross on their novices, required them to kiss their receptor's posterior, told them that homosexuality was lawful, adored an idol, and had the custom of not consecrating the Host when priests in the order celebrated mass. To this extraordinary farrago of nonsense were added other variant tales – of eucharistic heresy, worshipping a cat, betraying the cause of Christendom to the Moslems, of laymen in the order hearing confessions and granting absolution, of unlawful gains and sinister secrecy in chapter meetings. Charges were skilfully selected to undermine popular confidence and had more than one echo of accusations customarily made against heretics.[14]

The vicious circle was operating with a set of accusations from tribunals directed by the episcopate and royal servants. Tortured or in other ways subjected to pressure, a sufficient number of Templars confessed, to provide 'evidence' for the case against them. The affair demonstrated that any string

---

[12] T. S. R. Boase, *Boniface VIII* (London, 1933), pp. 355–79; articles in *HS* (Grundmann bibliography), p. 449, nos. 515–18.

[13] Up-to-date account with literature in Barber, *NMS* XVII, pp. 42–57; see also M. Barber, *Trial of the Templars* (Cambridge, 1978), the standard account; P. Partner, *The Murdered Magicians: The Templars and their Myth* (New York, 1982).

[14] Barber, *NMS* XVII, pp. 45–8, 54.

of accusations could be made effective, given the necessary zeal in interrogation and the employment of force; outside France, however, interrogation worked less well in providing evidence, because the necessary drive to produce confessions was lacking. But sufficient had been done to ruin the order's position. Clement was dogged by the threat of Boniface's memory, and too heavily involved to draw back; and at the Council of Vienne in 1312 the order was suppressed, and the French monarchy had gained the resources it urgently needed.

THE FREE SPIRIT AND HERETICAL MYSTICISM

The Templar episode was the most naked case of the use of the machinery of persecution for pure slander; the treatment of the beguines, beghards and mystics in northern Europe was a more subtle case of misunderstanding, in which genuine grounds for disquiet combined with suspicious conservatism and the persecuting mentality to smear pious, unprotected groups.[15]

Beguines were religious women leading lives of chastity, generally grouped in convents, supporting themselves by manual work and engaging in prayer but without any fixed rule, organization or final vows.[16] In the north both *beguinus* and *beghard* as a term for a man was usual. The males frequently lived by begging, but resembled the much more numerous female beguines in leading a religious life without fixed organization. The terms, however, were used rather imprecisely.[17]

The beguine movement in the north was a spontaneous, local outgrowth of the urge to apostolic life which moved zealous Christians in the twelfth century and offered occupation for women, generally in comfortable circumstances, who could not expect to find a husband. One starting-point lay in the appeal of a charismatic preacher to women who wished to lead a holy life without necessarily entering a nunnery; so Lambert le Bègue (the stammerer), a humbly born parish priest and reformer in the diocese of Liège, who died in 1177, drew such a group of women whom he directed, and whose association is sometimes thought of as the first beguinage. Lambert was accused of heresy

---

[15] H. Grundmann, 'Ketzerverhöre des Spätmittelalters als quellenkritisches Problem', *DA* XXI (1965), pp. 519–75 (fundamental reassessment of sources), R. E. Lerner, *The Heresy of the Free Spirit in the Later Middle Ages* (Berkeley, 1972) (the standard critical account for northern lands); R. Guarnieri, 'Il movimento del Libero Spirito', *Archivio Italiano per la storia della pietà* IV (1965), pp. 351–708 (quarry of material, value for work on Porete's *Mirror*); J. C. Schmitt, *Mort d'une hérésie, l'eglise et les clercs face aux beguines et beghards du Rhin supérieur du xive et xve siècle* (Paris, 1978). I am indebted to Professor R. E. Lerner for information, and for his work, extensively used in this section.

[16] Older literature, sometimes superseded, in Grundmann, *Ketzergeschichte*, pp. 52–8 (written before his 1965 article); background in E. W. McDonnell, *The Beguines and Beghards in Medieval Culture, with Special Emphasis on the Belgian Scene* (New Brunswick, 1954); reflections by Southern, *Western Society*, pp. 318–31. *RB* (pp. 170–318) discusses the problem of women and the religious life, and beguines (pp. 319–54), but some conclusions are upset by the important revision, based on German evidence, of J. B. Freed ('Urban development and the *cura monialium* in thirteenth-century Germany', *Viator* III (1972), pp. 312–27). I owe this reference and comment to Miss B. Bolton; see her 'Mulieres sanctae', in *SCH* X, pp. 77–95.

[17] Lerner, *Free Spirit*, pp. 35–7. The Beguins of southern France (below, pp. 205–12) form part of a different movement, linked closely to the Spiritual Franciscans, principally in the Franciscan province of Provence.

by a ruthless opposition, resentful of his fearless criticism of abuses: his letter of defence to Calixtus III shows how honesty and idiosyncracy could give a handle to enemies.[18] The very institutional formlessness of the beguinages may have been an attraction, and their simplicity made foundation easy. Some beguines went on living devout lives of charitable service in their own homes or those of their parents; others entered loosely organized associations, which had a woman superior; others again were cloistered. They fitted naturally into urban life, met a need for women who could not find acceptance in established orders, and so continued an unobtrusive existence in large numbers in certain towns of Flanders, northern France and Germany. They also attracted devout women who preferred the role of the beguine on religious grounds to that of a nun, and women from poorer homes who could not afford the price of entry to a nunnery.

The beguine and beghard occupied an ambiguous position. Rigorous interpretation of canon thirteen of the fourth Lateran Council might put their position in question. In status they lay somewhere between the orders and the parish clergy, subject to neither, and liable to be looked at askance by both.[19] Beghards formed a suspect penumbra to the mendicant orders. Mystical works stimulated the piety of these groups, often aided by confessors and directors from the mendicants and distinguished by a stress, in the style of the friars, on the incidents of the lives of Christ and Mary in the gospels. Because of their lack of established status and organization, they were vulnerable to the accusation of heresy, and popular suspicion seems to have given them their name, beguine being most probably a corruption of Albigensis, the term for a Cathar of southern France. Both beguines and beghards came to enjoy a strangely mixed reputation, sometimes the butt of accusations of sexual immorality on no good grounds, sometimes accused of the hypocritical feigning of virtue but also praised and given patronage by churchmen of influence. James of Vitry, inspired by Marie of Oignies, the pivot of a movement of female piety in the diocese of Liège, gave them help;[20] Fulk, bishop of Toulouse, thought that beguines might be used as a bulwark against Cathar influence;[21] in the mid-thirteenth century Robert Grosseteste placed their way of life, poor but self-supporting through manual labour, on a higher level even than the mendicancy of the friars.[22]

But by the time of the Council of Lyons in 1274, the earlier suspicion that had dogged them had again risen to the surface. It was a time of growing friction and tension in Church life, and beguines and beghards tended to be Aunt Sallies.[23] The mendicants, conscious of their waning popularity, struck out at groups close to them in their attitude yet precarious in status, and made them scapegoats; on the other side, forces hostile to the friars used them as stalking horses for attacks in reality directed against the friars. Self-interested

[18] L. K. Little, *Religious Poverty and the Profit Motive in Medieval Europe* (London, 1978), p. 129; *MBPH*, pp. 103–11.
[19] Lerner, *Free Spirit*, ch. 2, is helpful.
[20] McDonnell, *Beguines*, p. 20.
[21] *RB*, p. 172.
[22] Ibid., p. 322.
[23] Lerner, *Free Spirit*, pp. 45–6.

hostility there had always been, in the resentment of relatives or would-be-husbands at the loss of their women to the beguine life. At the time of Lyons pamphlets appeared against the beguine movement; the Franciscan Gilbert of Tournai complained that beguines had unauthorized vernacular translations of the Scriptures containing heresies (which he did not specify), and that they read these in public places; Bruno of Olmütz proposed bluntly that they should be told to marry or enter one of the established orders. Canon thirteen of the fourth Lateran Council was reiterated and, by the decision of the council, became a barrier *tout court* to all new forms of religious life: no new order was to be founded, and those that had come into existence despite the canon were to be suppressed. Without leading to any direct action, this obviously made the situation of beguines and beghards more precarious. Nothing occurred in the following decades to refurbish their image. Instead, synodal decrees in Germany witnessed to irritation at beghards as unauthorized preachers; arrests for heresy occurred at Colmar and Basle of both beguines and beghards in 1290; and the Franciscan chapter at Colmar, faced with a procession of 300 beghards begging for bread, warned their members against associating with these suspect competitors.

The beguines entered the crucial early decades of the fourteenth century vulnerable, their reputation damaged by accusations against their beliefs and behaviour, although they were not, as yet, the butt of any precise charge of heresy. The mystical movement generally had begun to occasion some suspicion: in an ill-recorded episode, the scholastic Albertus Magnus reported in the 1270s on a set of opinions emanating from the Swabian Ries that contained pantheistic and immoral beliefs – the outflow of speculation, it may be, on the state of mystical adepts.[24] But no evidence connects the mystics of the Ries with the beguines and the opinions, extant only as isolated fragments of testimony, are too inconsistent with each other and too unrelated to a historical or literary context to provide clear evidence of the reality of a heresy in Swabia at that date.

All that can be inferred safely from Albertus's judgement is that anxiety was stirring in the Church in his time about the pursuit of the mystical life. It was a consequence of a growing vogue for mystical reading in the vernacular, made possible by the greater leisure and resources of aristocracy and bourgeoisie and their higher educational standards, and an increased democratization of the mystical way. Once the province of the monk and nun, often in enclosed orders, the mystical way had become more accessible to those outside, to the beguine and to the pious layman. The possible dangers in the pursuit of mysticism, the absence of firm control through an institutional framework over those who now pursued it, and the very fact that profound theological matters were being presented in the vernacular, appeared as an anxiety to authority. The beguines heavily involved in the mystical movement were accused of harbouring a sect of heretical mystics, named as adherents of the Free Spirit.

Soon the popes began to concern themselves with antinomian heresy. In 1296 Boniface VIII issued a bull against a sect who prayed in the nude, and in

[24] Grundmann, *Ketzergeschichte*, pp. 45–6; Lerner, *Free Spirit*, pp. 13–19.

1311 Clement v was writing to the bishop of Cremona to require the uprooting of a sect of the Free Spirit of Italy, claiming freedom of action because of the innocent̶i̶a̶ of the Holy Spirit in them.¹ In 1307 an authoritarian archbishop of Cologne, Henry of Virneburg, included in decrees for his diocese, as well as complaints of a traditional style against beghards (of both sexes; he apparently preferred not to use the term beguine for the females) for defying the canons against new orders, preaching and interrupting friars' sermons, a charge of heretical mysticism. Then, between 1306 and 1308, a beguine named Marguerite Porete of Hainault, one of whose books had already been burnt by the bishop of Cambrai, was arrested for spreading heresy 'among simple people and beghards' through another book, and was sent to Paris. There she refused to respond to interrogation, and was convicted of heresy on the strength of some extracts taken from this book, submitted for judgement to a commission of theologians. Her earlier conviction meant that she was guilty of relapse, and she was burnt in Paris in 1310.

The charge was again heretical mysticism, but in this instance we have the heretic's own work with which to check the veracity of the accusations made against her. By chance, the treatise which caused her conviction and burning, the *Mirror of Simple Souls*, survived, to circulate anonymously in monasteries and nunneries, in the original and in translation, from the fourteenth century to the present.[26] So little obvious was the heresy in it that hardly any of its readers over the centuries questioned its orthodoxy; or if they did they came down eventually on the side of the *Mirror*, like the Middle English translator who felt some disquiet but concluded that it was written of 'high divine maters and of highe goostli felynges and kerningli and ful mystili it is spoken'.[27] Indeed it was, using an extensive vocabulary, and drawing on what was plainly deep personal experience to describe in dialogue form the progress of the soul through seven states of grace, the greater part of it being both traditional and edifying.

The danger lay in the fifth and sixth states, the highest that could be attained in this life, when the 'annihilated' or 'liberated' soul is unified with God. Here, in Lerner's judgement,[28] Marguerite Porete went beyond traditional masters, applying, for example, the similes used by St Bernard of Clairvaux for the state of the soul in paradise to its condition in an advanced mystical state here below. There were some extravagant thoughts: the soul, still in the body, is described as being united with the Trinity, or as finding God in itself without searching. There is much about the soul's farewell to the virtues, which could lead to misunderstanding by those who failed to observe

[25] Ibid., pp. 78–84 (also for Henry of Virneburg); L. Oliger, *De secta spiritus libertatis in Umbria saec. XIV; disquisitio et documenta* (Rome, 1943) (accepts genuineness of accusations).

[26] Lerner, *Free Spirit*, pp. 68–78, text of *Mirror* ed. Guarnieri in *Archivio Italiano per la storia della pietà* IV (1965), pp. 513–635; for account of case, see under appropriate years in her chronology of heresy; tr. of Middle English version in C. Kirchberger, *The Mirror of Simple Souls* (London and New York, 1927). For the way in which suspicion came to play on the mystical language sometimes used in impeccable sources, see R. E. Lerner, 'The image of mixed liquids in late medieval mystical thought', *CH* xxx (1971), pp. 397–411. An account of Middle English texts is given by E. Colledge, 'The treatise of perfection of the sons of God: a fifteenth-century English Ruysbroeck translation', *English Studies* XXIII (1952), pp. 49–66.

[27] Quoted, Lerner, *Free Spirit*, p. 74, from text, ed. M. Doiron, in *Archivio . . . pietà* v (1968), p. 247.

[28] *Free Spirit*, pp. 200–8.

Marguerite's reasons for saying it, that the virtues are always with the liberated soul in any case. Finally, there is something disquieting in Marguerite's description of the passivity of the liberated soul: it 'does not seek God by penance, nor by any sacrament of the Holy Church, nor by thought, words or works'.[29] Marguerite was aware of the dangers of *doubles mots*, and remarked that 'simple minds might misunderstand them at their peril'.[30] She was treating of esoteric matters, and it was not a book for the many, although obviously designed for reading aloud in the vernacular. Two factors seems to have weighed in her condemnation: her pertinacity, shown in the repeated dissemination of her views and her refusal to respond to interrogation, and the alleged publicity given to the *Mirror* among simple people. What might have been possible in an established nunnery, without publicity, appeared not to be allowed to a beguine who wanted to propagate her work. Her views were not fairly represented. The *Mirror* might seem doubtful on the passivity of the liberated soul and on its lack of any need for the sacraments, and presumptuous on the state of union with God in the fifth and sixth states; but it is not libertine. Porete's enemies argued that it was, quoting a phrase of the *Mirror* on the liberated soul, giving 'to nature, without remorse, all that it asks';[31] they omitted Porete's covering explanation, that in the liberated state nature 'does not demand anything prohibited'. A recent authority has argued that Marguerite remained silent because her book, in its dialogue between Love and Reason, which elucidates her controversial distinction between 'Holy Church the Great' and 'Holy Church the Less', had already met all possible objections against its orthodoxy.

Heresy, then, in this case, if it existed at all, was of a specialized character, concerned solely with the condition of mystical adepts at an advanced stage of perfection; there was no advocacy of libertinism and disregard of the moral law for anyone; and the accusations against Porete gave an unfair picture of her views. Doubts about her case are only reinforced when we realize that the inquisitor of France directing the final moves against her was also responsible for accusations against the Templars.

Hard on the heels both of the Porete case and of the statutes of the Council of Mainz in 1310, witnessing to a continuing concern in the Rhineland about beghards and heresy, came the decision of the general Council of Vienne in 1312, in *Ad nostrum*, that there was a heresy of the Free Spirit amongst the beguines and beghards of Germany;[32] it was called an 'abominable sect'. Beliefs were set out in eight clauses. All were concerned with the belief that

[29] Ibid., p. 205; Lerner's translation from Guarnieri text on p. 586.
[30] Lerner, *Free Spirit*, p. 208; Guarnieri text, pp. 533, 537.
[31] Lerner, *Free Spirit*, p. 76; Guarnieri text, p. 527. D. Turner's unpublished analysis reassesses the position of the *Mirror* and gives reasons for the author's silence (see end of para.); the author's survey *The Darkness of God: negativity in western mysticism* (Cambridge, 1995) will shortly be published.
[32] P. Fredericq, *Corpus documentorum inquisitionis haereticae pravitatis Neerlandicae* I (Ghent, 1889), n. 172, pp. 168–9, partial tr. in Leff, *Heresy* I, pp. 314–15 (Leff's exposition of the Free Spirit (ch. 4) cannot be recommended; see Grundmann, in *DA* xxiv (1968), pp. 284–6; Offler, in *EHR* LXXXIV (1969), pp. 572–6; Lerner, *Free Spirit*, p. 8). A. Patschovsky, 'Strassburger Beginenverfolgungen im 14.Jahrhundert', *DA* xxx (1974), pp. 56–198 (clarification of beguine and beghard trials in Strasburg with new MS evidence); see p. 117, n. 153. He regards concern about heresy in the Rhineland episcopate as the major impetus leading to *Ad nostrum*; see also his warning about elements of genuine heresy in some Free Spirit accusations (pp. 98–9). For Council of Mainz, see Patschovsky, *DA* xxx, pp. 96, 141–2.

those who had attained a lofty state of perfection, such as the adepts who reached the fifth and sixth states of the *Mirror of Simple Souls*, could then escape the trammels of ordinary men. The opinions that those in this category had become incapable of sinning or of surpassing their present state of grace, that they did not need to fast or pray since they had obtained such control over their senses that they could afford to them complete freedom, and that they were not subject to obedience, because 'where the spirit of the Lord is, there is liberty',[33] were all condemned. Five other clauses dealt with further consequences or aspects of the condition of sinless freedom, condemning the view that it was possible to attain final blessedness in this life; that the divine light of glory was not needed to enjoy the vision of God; that acts of virtue were only necessary for imperfect men, and that the perfect soul no longer needs them; that sexual intercourse was not a sin when nature demands it; that it was not necessary to rise at the elevation of the Host, since this meant descending from the heights of contemplation. The sect who held these views was to be rooted out.

But did such a sect ever exist? The surprising answer, after so much research has been carried out on a supposed heresy of the Free Spirit, is that in the medieval inquisitor's usual sense it did not. There was no organized sect at all, with a teaching programme hostile to the Church, like the Cathars or the later Waldensians. All that really existed were individual mystics in communication with like-minded friends and followers on an informal basis, some of whom wrote or said some dangerous or extravagant things. *Ad nostrum* took a set of these statements that looked heretical or immoral when quoted out of context, and wove together a heresy and a sect from them.[34]

The Council of Vienne took its decision in an atmosphere of intense hostility to the beguines. We know from another of the bulls decided on at Vienne, *Cum de quibusdam*, that the fathers of the council had seriously considered suppressing the beguines outright.[35] The bull opens by decreeing suppression, and draws back from doing so only in an escape clause at the end, either the fruit of Vienne's second thoughts or of a subsequent revision. The perils of beguines discussing high theological matters, disputing on the Trinity, the divine essence and the sacraments, were mentioned in the bull as ground for suppression.

On top of this general hostility arrived the reports of antinomian heresy abroad in the Church. Much of the documentation of the Council of Vienne has vanished, making exact reconstruction of the historical context of *Ad nostrum* impossible; but Marguerite Porete's *Mirror* gives us an essential clue as to how the council came to attribute antinomian heresy to the mystics, for there we have the opportunity to put side by side some of the charges against a mystical suspect and the actual statements from which they are derived. The

---

[33] 2 Cor. 3: 17.

[34] The central theme of Lerner, *Free Spirit*; compare Grundmann, in *DA* xxi (1965), pp. 519–75; contrast Leff, *Heresy* i, ch. 4 and M. Erbstösser and E. Werner, *Ideologische Probleme des mittelalterlichen Plebejertums: Die freigeistige Häresie und ihre sozialen Wurzeln* (Berlin, 1960), who offer differing explanations of the Free Spirit (see extract tr. by Russell, *Dissent*, pp. 143–7), but are alike in accepting the existence of a sect; discussion on these assumptions also in Erbstösser, *Strömungen*, pp. 84–119.

[35] Fredericq, *Corpus* i, no. 171, pp. 167–8; partial tr. in McDonnell, *Beguines*, p. 524.

Mirror was a quarry for certain suspect statements condemned in *Ad nostrum*: clause six of the bull, on the perfect soul having no need of the virtues, is derived from Porete's work but, significantly, without the justification that the fuller context of the statement in the *Mirror* would give. Other clauses on rising at the elevation of the Host, on attitudes to prayer and fasting, and to sexual intercourse, have analogies to statements in the *Mirror*, or can be derived from misunderstanding of statements there.[36] Mystics, of whom Porete is a fair, though not distinguished, example, were describing rare states and treating great mysteries, that lay near the limits of ordinary language: they used paradoxical, even shocking, phrases in trying to convey their meaning. These were taken up, rawly and literally, by the council, and fashioned into a heresy.

Definitions in *Ad nostrum* helped to create heretics to match the bull. When it was issued early in John xxii's reign, it became part of the apparatus for fashioning interrogations by inquisitors and other churchmen who believed themselves to be on the trail of the Free Spirit. Faced with the suspect beghard or beguine, or what they believed to be a heretical mystic, they took him or her through the clauses of *Ad nostrum*, and in successful cases elicited the appropriate, self-convicting answers. Preliminary questions – Was the suspect 'free in spirit'? Did he believe he was sinless? – answered affirmatively, could open the way to a systematic interrogation based on the clauses of the bull, taken one by one. Answers as given by suspects in the records sometimes reproduce almost word for word the expositions of *Ad nostrum*.[37]

Testimony appeared to show that those who held the views condemned in *Ad nostrum* did practise libertinism. There were stories of orgies, of aberrant sexual practices, outrageous statements like that of Johann Hartmann in 1367, that the free in spirit could have intercourse with sister or mother, even on the altar.[38] It is all suspect; Hartmann was probably a verbal exhibitionist. Other testimony sprang from envious gossip, inquisitorial imagination, or distortion of the paradoxical statements of true mystics.[39] The accusations consort uneasily with the hard evidence of poor, ascetic lives among beguines and other followers of mysticism. Magnetic rogues of the Rasputin variety, combining libertinism and religion, cannot be excluded; but they were surely a small proportion of those interrogated. Similar scepticism should be applied to talk of other breaches of the ethical code, theft, murder, disobedience; such offences have not been proved.

What in fact did the Free Spirit amount to? For a century and a half after *Ad nostrum* cases of the heresy were turned up. Suspicion of the kind that issued in the bull played round other, greater figures. The leaders of the vernacular mystical movement had to exercise vigilance in their teaching to avoid the suggestion of complicity with the Free Spirit. Meister Eckhart himself fell victim of the same Henry of Virneburg who had launched accusations against

---

[36] Lerner, *Free Spirit*, pp. 82–3.

[37] Grundmann first brought out the vital relationship between *Ad nostrum* and the interrogations of suspects (*DA* xxi, pp. 519–75). See esp. the interrogation of Konrad Kannler at Eichstätt in 1381.

[38] Testimony in Erbstösser and Werner, *Ideologische Probleme*, pp. 136–53, comment, Lerner, *Free Spirit*, pp. 135–9.

[39] As above, pp. 184–5.

the Cologne beguines; he was accused of heresy, and had twenty-eight propositions from his work condemned in 1329 after his death. Beguines and beghards went on suffering from suspicion; as a movement they were saved from total shipwreck by the limitation in *Cum de quibusdam*, and in 1318 by John XXII's defence in *Racio recta* of 'good' beguines who led stable lives and did not dispute on high theological matters.[40] But the Free Spirit affair damaged them, and so long as the zeal against the Free Spirit lasted, which seemed to have been for about a century after *Ad nostrum*, they were at peril from investigations.

The beguine movement reached its term in the fourteenth century, after a remarkable efflorescence. In the middle of the century in Cologne there were 169 beguinages and 1,170 beguines: they still met an economic and religious need and were supported by the urban patriciate. In 1452, however, the number of beguinages had fallen to ninety-three and of beguines to 637. In Strasburg there were eighty-five in the fourteenth century; in 1538 they had fallen to seven. Heresy accusations dwindled generally in the fifteenth century but hostility did not; polemics against them on the grounds of idleness, hypocrisy and unjustified begging, never wholly absent, grew in number and intensity and took the place of accusations of heresy. There was a change in the climate of opinion; the negative image of the 'sturdy beggar' took hold; the patriciate, source for the crucial benefactions, turned away from them and beguines declined in number and esteem.[41]

Meanwhile, the Free Spirit investigations trawled up odd cases, usually in the towns of Germany. The sources in the north are resistant to much positive analysis. A thorough sceptical analysis on the lines of Lerner's work has yet to be undertaken for the supposed cases in the southern lands; an analysis may turn out to give different results from the north. But what peeps through the distortions seems to be this. There was a movement of radical mysticism, running *pari passu* with the writings of the best-known masters such as Eckhart, and feared by them. It was not libertinist or immoral, but went at least to the limits of orthodoxy in its views on the possibility of union with God in this life, and was indifferent, if not hostile, to the sacraments and to the mediating role of the Church. Apart from this core of somewhat perilous belief and practice was a miscellaneous assemblage of suspects, suggestible women liable to say what interrogators wanted, some eccentrics, even madmen who might have remained untroubled but for investigating zeal, some religious individualists, perhaps touched by mysticism but having odd views of their own – anti-sacerdotal for example, possibly Amaurian, or rigorist on sexual ethics. Free Spirit suspects were not necessarily beguines or beghards at all, and there was a good deal of slander.[42]

[40] Fredericq, *Corpus* II, no. 44, pp. 72–4, McDonnell, *Beguines*, p. 536; subsequent history, below, pp. 213–14; the literature on Eckhart is substantial, but for a short note see B. McGinn, in *Neoplatonism and Christian Thought*, ed. D. J. O'Meara (Norfolk, Va., 1990).

[41] Schmitt, *Mort*, pp. 47, 148–51, 187–91, 203–4; discussion of terms: pp. 64–70; Małkaw case of 1391 as classic of multiple unjustified heresy accusations: p. 77.

[42] See now D. Müller, 'Les béguines', in *Christianisme*, ed. Brenon and Gouzy, pp. 351–89, on feminine protest in Marguerite Porète, Guglielma, Prous Boneta; A. Vauchez, pp. 385–6, stresses search for the divine in the fourteenth century and inspired women, radical but orthodox, consulted by male Church leaders; notes Boniface VIII's *Periculosum*; for beguine survival and forced marriage, J. Duvernoy, pp. 388–9.

Spiritual Franciscans and heretical Joachimites

The Franciscan problem

The origins of the Franciscan problem run back deep into the thirteenth century and are inseparable from the ideals and personality of St Francis himself.[1] Utterly dedicated to the ideal of poverty which he saw in Christ's commands in the gospels, above all in the account of the sending of the Seventy, Francis bequeathed to his followers the belief that the Franciscan way of life reincarnated that of Christ and the apostles. His way of living was extraordinarily hard, harder to bear than that of the most ascetic monastic orders, for Francis aimed to renounce not only individual but also common property, the normal background of collective security for even the most austere individual monk. Moreover, Francis intended that for many of his followers an extraordinarily harsh standard of poverty should be combined with a pastoral activity in the world. From early days the two objectives tended to run counter to each other; yet the very combination of harsh poverty and pastoral activity gave a spiritual force to the early Franciscans which drew in recruits at a prodigious rate whose presence and needs soon began to

[1] M. D. Lambert, *Franciscan Poverty: The Doctrine of the Absolute Poverty of Christ and the Apostles in the Franciscan Order, 1210–1323* (London, 1961), esp. chs 1 and 2 (new edn forthcoming, with changed text, Bonaventure, NY, 1998). Leff, *Heresy* I, pp. 51–255 (esp. helpful for intellectual aspect and bulls of John XXII), J. R. H. Moorman, *A History of the Franciscan Order from its Origins to the Year 1517* (Oxford, 1968) (comprehensive survey), R. B. Brooke, *Early Franciscan Government, Elias to Bonaventure* (Cambridge, 1959) (constitutional history, personal insights); documents in H. Böhmer, *Analekten zur Geschichte des Franciscus von Assisi*, 3rd edn (Tübingen, 1961); *Scripta Leonis et Angeli Sociorum S. Francisci*, ed. R. B. Brooke (Oxford, 1970) (see introduction), D. Knowles, *Religious Orders in England* I (Cambridge, 1948), ch. II (short introduction), R. B. Brooke, *The Coming of the Friars* (London, 1975) (documents on early Franciscans, background of preachers and heretics, with comment). D. Nimmo, *Reform and Division in the Franciscan Order 1226–1538* (Rome, 1987), introduction and pt I; D. Burr, *Olivi and Franciscan Poverty: The Origins of the Usus Pauper Controversy* (Philadelphia, 1989), ch. I (penetrating observations on Franciscanism); M. A. Habig, ed., *St Francis of Assisi: Omnibus of Sources* (Chicago, 1973) (all texts translated); on the strand of dissidence in Franciscanism, M. Cusato in *Christianisme*, ed. Brenon and Gouzy, pp. 293–321.

distort the original ideal. Troubles occurred in Francis's own lifetime: at the end, after years of semi-eremitical life in resignation from active government of the order, Francis dictated a last Testament in which he looked back with nostalgia to the simple early days of his brotherhood and, by implication or direct statement, condemned many of the developments then taking place which mitigated the old poverty and simplicity, and tended to give his order a privileged place within the Church.[2] It was his deathbed statement, and to this day it cannot be read without emotion. Constitutionally Francis had no right to bind his successors; yet he ordered this Testament to be kept with the rule and read with it, and his command, legally invalid as it was declared to be,[3] carried all the emotional weight of the dying speech of a beloved founder. More than any single document, the Testament was the stimulus to subsequent internal dissension.

The majority of friars were either not fully aware of the distinction between Francis's personal wishes and the existing way of life in the order, or felt that change was positively desirable. Transformation still retained a considerable degree of poverty, more than that of the older monastic orders; yet it enabled the order to fulfil a major role in the life of the Church which would have been impossible if the numbers and conditions of Francis's own time had continued unchanged. Papal policy favoured change, and a series of clarifications of the rule from the popes legitimized the process. How far this adaptation of the order's life was right or wise must always remain controversial; the historian of heresy must observe that the transformation, by deploying so much disinterested zeal in the service of the Church and diffusing Franciscan preaching and piety, went far to aid the defeat of Catharism.

Dissatisfaction with the transformation of the life of the order to fit the needs of a clerical body with a place in the universities, developed techniques of preaching, and privileges to take up all the duties of the secular clergy, and the mitigation of the old poverty which this entailed, found only occasional outlet, both in Francis's lifetime and for years afterwards. The nucleus for this disquiet lay in a body of simple early companions, generally with a taste for the eremitical life, who could not approve of the influx of learning and the great place which the Franciscans gained in the Church: these men handed on the traditions, filtered through their own minds, of Francis's life and sayings especially in the last years, and kept alive the memory of the Testament.

A transformation so great and so rapid imposed strains on tender consciences. Were the friars in fact being faithful to the literal words of the rule which they professed when they followed the mitigated way of life of the bulk of the order? Were they in fact in breach of their vow? Was it honourable to continue to claim the highest poverty and a peculiar fidelity to the life of Christ and the apostles, when in practice they used money, which Francis had forbidden, and enjoyed the fruits of property, which Francis had excluded? Such questions were disturbing, and not only to rigorists. The most passive plea for freedom to follow a primitive observance implied a criticism of the majority's way of life and, as the practitioners of *satyagraha* in Gandhi's

[2] Text and analysis in K. Esser, *Das Testament des heiligen Franziskus von Assisi* (Münster-i-W., 1949); K. (Cajetan) Esser, *Origins of the Franciscan Order* (Chicago, 1970).

[3] By *Quo elongati* (*BF*, Epitome, pp. 229a–231b).

FIGURE 4   The habit of St Francis of Assisi: an authentic relic preserved at the Sacro Convento in Assisi. The Spiritual Franciscans imitated its destitution, sometimes with extravagance.

Photograph: Leonhard von Matt, Buochs/Switzerland

campaign against the salt-tax found, passive disobedience can stimulate violent response. Hence the ferocity of punishment with which recalcitrant rigorists were treated by some superiors, and the casual violence apparent, for example, in the burning of the Testament over the head of a friar by some exasperated minister.[4]

The disputes in the south of France

The dispute over the rightfulness of the observance of poverty in the order had all the makings of a profound conflict. Yet a true crisis did not begin to emerge until the time of the Council of Lyons in 1274 and the following years, the 1290s being the watershed. This was almost certainly due to the fact that friars in considerable numbers would not be moved, so long as the order did maintain the substance of its mitigated way of life. After 1274, though much zeal remained, the Franciscans had passed the peak of their early enthusiasm, and in various provinces were no longer keeping adequately even to the mitigated way of life. Worldliness rather than gross abuse was the problem, together with the difficulty of holding firmly to a rule glossed and 'clarified' in various ways; but it was enough to stimulate a more widespread call to return to an earlier standard. Italian provinces – Umbria, Tuscany and the March of Ancona – were affected, partly because a living tradition of Francis's wishes existed there, and partly because of the existence of a strong eremitical tradition which tended to rigour over poverty, and in the case of Tuscany because of the influence of one teacher, Petrus Johannis Olivi, a native of the south of France and for some years lector in Florence, and of his fervent supporter Ubertino da Casale.[5] In the Franciscan province of Provence, geographically wider than the title would imply and including a substantial part of the Midi, a special situation existed.[6] Subsequent history must lead us to conclude that ministers in that area were both relaxed in their attitudes to poverty and harsh in enforcing discipline. Abuse stimulated rigour, and the province became deeply divided between defenders of the *status quo* (and worse), generally called 'Conventuals', and the rigorist Spirituals.

The situation was made more complicated and more acute by the abilities of Olivi, a friar from the convent of Narbonne; he was the dominating mind among the Spirituals and, independently of the poverty issue, a thinker of the front rank at a time of unusual disturbance and confusion in the history of scholasticism.[7] His achievement for the Spirituals was to work out a doctrine of the *usus pauper*. This firmly associated sustained and serious infringements of austerity in the use of goods with breach of the vow of poverty; repeated and gross deviations without justification, so that the 'use' of goods by a friar was

---

[4] Lambert, *Poverty*, p. 84.

[5] On Olivi, see below, n. 9; on Ubertino, Godefroy, 'Ubertin de Casale', *DTC* xv, cols 2020–34, and, a fine sketch, L. Oliger, 'Spirituels', *DTC* xiv, cols 2522–49.

[6] R. Manselli, *Spirituali e Beghini in Provenza* (Rome, 1959); cf. his *La 'Lectura super Apocalipsim' di Pietro di Giovanni Olivi* (Rome, 1955). D. Burr, *Olivi's Peacable Kingdom*, Philadelphia, 1993 (lucid and definitive; alters Manselli's perspective).

[7] Leff, *Heresy* i, pp. 100–62; Burr, *Olivi*, ch. 2, revises chronology; summary: p. 135, suggesting beginnings of conflict 'around 1279'. His hypothesis of link to *Correctorium* controversy with Dominicans, pp. 148–58, is illuminating.

to be considered rich rather than poor, involved the offender in mortal sin. Friars who became bishops could not be dispensed from this obligation to the 'poor use'. This doctrine focused the order's attention on their actual, day-to-day, observance as opposed to their formal (and often rather hollowly juridical) renunciation of property rights. The years of transformation had issued in a theory of Franciscan poverty whereby the order held no property at all, all rights over the goods they used being by a legal fiction retained by the papacy.[8] Earnest but moderate friars, of whom the greatest was St Bonaventure, minister-general 1257–74, were not satisfied with renunciation of property rights as summing up Franciscan poverty; they accepted the papal ownership, but still struggled against practical relaxation in the use of goods. At a time of deteriorating observance, the Olivi doctrine appeared to strengthen such earnest superiors.

But there were difficulties. No aspect of Franciscan life was so vulnerable to changes as day-to-day poverty; powers of dispensation and the discretion of superiors were needed if Franciscans were to maintain their duties in the world, and consciences were not to be overloaded. The *usus pauper* could be held unduly to infringe these rights of superiors. There were problems in assessing what were necessities and what were not. Controversy over the Franciscan life with the Dominicans created sensitivities. Behind Olivi lay poverty fanatics; it was not clear what they might make of the *usus pauper* as an obligation, so there were some grounds for considering Olivi's doctrine as 'perilous', in the words of one censure.[9] Controversy grew over this issue, strengthened by the Spirituals' honest reaction to abuses in the province, and by the chance that Olivi was a bold speculative thinker who in his scholastic writing threw off views which, in part following the way which led to Ockham, alarmed some other Franciscans.[10] Conflict began as a dispute between Olivi and another Franciscan lector, 'brother Ar.', involved the province, then the minister-general. Often inferior minds did not grasp what Olivi as an academic thinker intended; his views on poverty and points of doubt in his scholastic writing became bound together in an internal struggle in which superiors and other scholastics pressed charges of heresy and error over almost two decades before his death in 1298, and thereafter till the Council of Vienne in 1312, without ever succeeding in pinning a definitive condemnation on him. Much of this was unfair: though at one stage rehabilitated and sent to Florence, Olivi in consequence of the dissensions did not achieve the academic recognition which his talents deserved and ended his career as no more than lector in Narbonne. Academic controversy, with serious undertones springing from the state of the order and the nature of Olivi's influence, had much the same effect on a smaller scale as conflicts at Prague over Wyclif had in the early fifteenth century:[11] issues, too long undecided, roused bitterly divided

[8] Lambert, *Poverty*, chs 3–6.

[9] D. Laberge, 'Fr Petri Joannis Olivi, o.f.m.: tria scripta sui ipsius apologetica annorum 1283 et 1285', *AFH* xxviii (1935), pp. 115–55, 374–407; xxix (1936), pp. 98–141, 365–95; note esp. xxviii, p. 382, ll. 7–8; Burr, *Olivi*, pp. 67–8, 135–58 (helpful comments: pp. 144–5).

[10] Leff, *Heresy* i, pp. 107–11; but see also A. Maier, 'Zu einigen Problemen der Ockhamforschung', *AFH* xlvi (1953), pp. 174–81; Burr, *Olivi*, pp. 41, 44.

[11] Below, pp. 294–300, 303–16.

parties, and turned an academic conflict into a popular fight. Dissension amongst the Franciscans of the first order easily spilled over into the lay world through the institution of the third order: in the Italian provinces this does not seem to have happened on any scale, but in the Midi tertiaries from the towns were drawn in.

One reason lay in the existence of a tradition blending veneration for poverty and Joachimite speculation in a lay circle which went back to Hugues de Digne, Olivi's religious ancestor in the area, who can be glimpsed in mid-century pondering Joachimite prophecy with laymen, notaries and others at Hyères.[12] Olivi himself had magnetic qualities, not fully discernible to us in his extant writings, and endured harassment with courage: he acted as a focus for the religious sentiments of tertiaries under the influence of Spiritual friars who met to hear mass, to be encouraged in their personal life by the hearing of sermons and vernacular treatises in which Spiritual beliefs played a great part, and who became convinced both that Olivi was a martyr to unjust persecution and that the conflicts about poverty in the order were the prelude to the Last Times. Without understanding the academic issues, these tertiaries or more casual sympathizers, known as Beguins, were quite clear in their minds about the practical issues of poverty under discussion, the pressure that Spiritual friars were under, and the heroic virtue of Olivi. Joachimism, misunderstood or adapted for the Franciscan situation, heightened the tension in these Spiritual-directed lay circles, and was the most dangerous single element in an amalgam of doctrines forming in the 1280s and 1290s in the heat of persecution and conflict in the Midi.

Joachimism and the development of heresy

The exact nature of Olivi's influence and of his own thinking about the Last Times remains the most suspect and elusive aspect of his work. One great stimulus to his eschatological interest lay in Joachim of Fiore, the Calabrian prophetic writer who died in Innocent III's pontificate after a lifetime spent pondering the patterns of history discernible through meditation on the Scriptures.[13] Three popes, Lucius III, Urban III and Clement III, had encouraged him in his exegetical writing[14] and, though his influence received a blow in the condemnation of a trinitarian *libellus* at the fourth Lateran Council, his ideas on history and the future were quite uncondemned, and had great potency, directly and indirectly, throughout the thirteenth century.

Joachim's ideas on a coming third age of the Holy Spirit had a special appeal to members of religious orders. Ever scholarly, reluctant to fix

[12] Lambert, *Poverty*, p. 178. For a sidelight on Hugues de Digne and his influence on the fate of the Brethren of the Sack, see K. Elm, 'Ausbreitung, Wirksamkeit und Ende der provençalischen Sackbrüder ... in Deutschland und den Niederlanden', in *Francia: Forschungen zur westeuropäischen Geschichte* 1 (Munich, 1973), pp. 257–324. I owe the reference to Mr A. Murray. Burr, *Olivi*, pp. 18–24, 29–30, subtly analyses Hugues's position on poverty; Hugues cannot simply be classified as a Spiritual but his *Disputatio* provides evidence of tensions over poverty in the south of France and punishment of dissidents by superiors. For Salimbene, who gives evidence on Hyères, see D. C. West Jr, 'The education of Fra Salimbene of Parma: the Joachite influence', in Williams, ed. *Prophecy*, pp. 193–215.

[13] Above, p. 99.

[14] Reeves, *Prophecy*, p. 28.

precisely on a date for the end of the present order of things or to describe closely the conditions of life in the third age of the Spirit, Joachim none the less lived in a state of constant expectancy – 'I suspect all times and all places', he said   and through his writings bequeathed to the clerical world a persuasive set of metaphors, symbols and scriptural parallels for apocalyptic speculation.[15] His diagram of the sequence of history, produced by him personally or under his influence in the *Liber figurarum* (*c.*1200), may better convey the nature of his appeal than a more detailed exposition.[16] In the centre is the trumpet of the Apocalypse ('I was in the Spirit . . . and heard behind me a great voice, as of a trumpet saying, "I am Alpha and Omega . . ."'[17]). It speaks in the third age of the Holy Spirit, given below the trumpet as *tercius status*, and provides the spiritual understanding which characterizes the Age of the Spirit. The history of mankind is flowing into the state of illumination which is the culmination of life on earth. There is a *status* corresponding to the first person of the Trinity, beginning on the far left of the diagram with the *initiatio primi status* marked by Adam, characterized by married men; then a second *status* corresponding to the second person of the Trinity, beginning on the upper left of the diagram with the *initiatio secundi status* marked by the reign of Uzziah ('Ozias'), in which the prophet Isaiah appeared, and characterized by the clergy. Mankind is on the eve of the dawning of the third age, characterized by a new order of monks – the words *presens tempus* can be seen below the bell-joint of the trumpet, still in the age of the clarification of the Son (*clarificatio filii* in the diagram). The *status* are not rigidly divided; they are seen by Joachim rather as relay runners in a race: at one point the runner gets ready to hand over the baton and the two runners run along side by side before finally making the change-over.[18] A herald, as it were, of the third age had already appeared in St Benedict of Nursia, founder of monasticism; a new order of monks, yet to come, would characterize the third age, and would be agents of the new spiritual understanding.

Joachim did not exactly know what this order would be: in the phrase of his modern interpreter Marjorie Reeves, like Moses he viewed the promised land, but could not enter it himself.[19] To be a member of that new order had a powerful attraction, and it is little surprise that religious of various kinds after

---

[15] I follow here Reeves, *Prophecy* (with full literature, cited above, p. 99, n. 28), and *MRS* II (1950), pp. 57–81, work which I admire. For the broad context, see R. W. Southern, 'Aspects of the European tradition of historical writing: 3 History as prophecy', *TRHS*, 5th ser. xxii (1972), pp. 159–80, esp. pp. 173–7; orientation in H. Grundmann, *Studien über Joachim von Floris* (Leipzig, 1927); *Neue Forschungen über Joachim von Floris* (Marburg, 1950); discussion in relation to heresy in Leff, *Heresy* i, pp. 68–83; reflections in F. Seibt, 'Utopie im Mittelalter', *HZ* ccviii (1969), pp. 555–94; B. McGinn, 'Symbolism in the thought of Joachim of Fiore', in *Prophecy*, ed. Williams, pp. 143–64 (notes originality in development of symbols of growth and the role assigned to papacy); extracts on angelic pope and from Bonaventure, Spirituals, in McGinn, *Visions*, pp. 186–238.

[16] *Il libro delle figure dell' Abate Gioacchino da Fiore*, ed L. Tondelli, M. Reeves and B. Hirsch-Reich, 2nd edn (Turin, 1953), ii tavola 18ab; M. Reeves and B. Hirsch-Reich, *The Figurae of Joachim of Fiore* (Oxford, 1972), pl. 9, and discussion (note two versions), pp. 120–9; authenticity of *Liber figurarum*: pp. 75–98.

[17] Rev. i: 10–11.

[18] See introduction to *Il libro* i by L. Tondelli, pp. 86–9; Reeves, *Prophecy*, p. 138; Reeves and Hirsch-Reich, *Figurae*, pp. 122–3. Note Reeves's summary (*MRS* ii, p. 77), 'The third *status* describes the emergence of a new plane of spiritual existence rather than the appearance of a new set of institutions.'

[19] *Prophecy*, p. 146.

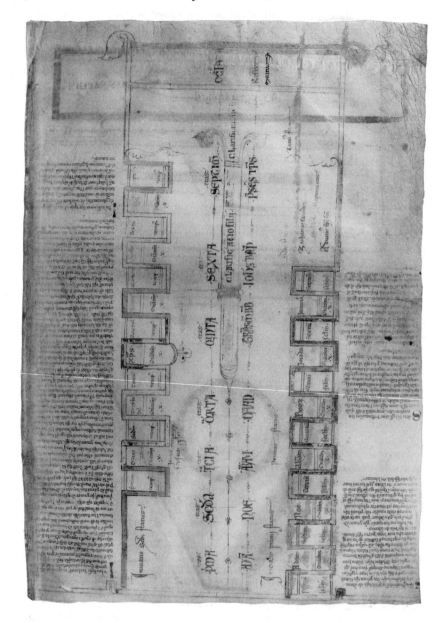

FIGURE 5   The third age of the Spirit: the seven *etates* of the world; Oxford MS 255A
fol. 8v.
Reproduced by permission of the President and Fellows of Corpus Christi College, Oxford.

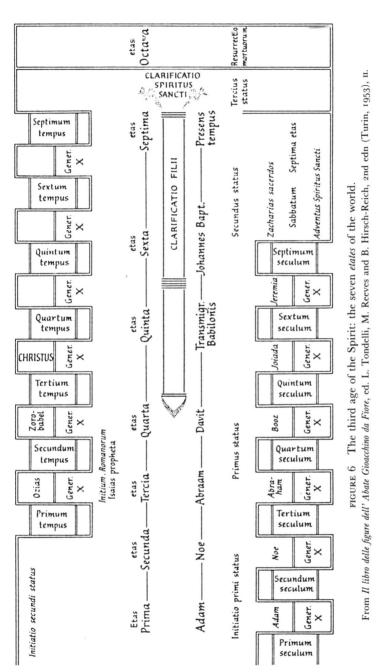

FIGURE 6   The third age of the Spirit: the seven *états* of the world.

From *Il libro delle figure dell' Abate Gioacchino da Fiore*, ed. L. Tondelli, M. Reeves and B. Hirsch-Reich, 2nd edn (Turin, 1953), II.

Joachim's day believed that the spiritual understanding of the new age was to
be bestowed on their institution. The friars, with their consciousness of
innovation were natural candidates, and the legend grew that Joachim had in
fact forecast not one order but two, and that he had sketched the habits of the
two major orders, the Dominicans and the Franciscans.[20] But of all the groups
to whom Joachim appealed, the Franciscans were affected most deeply.[21]

Some of the reasons for the attraction of Joachim's ideas can be glimpsed
from the diagram. One is the perennial attraction of the approaching end,
seen in the proximity of the bell of the trumpet to the culmination of history, to
be seen beyond the line on the right of the trumpet. To the ever-fascinating
task of attempting to calculate the time of the Last Things, Joachim brought
distinction of mind and a method familiar to all Scripture students of the day.
That the Old Testament provided parallels and prophecies of the New was a
commonplace; Joachim's method involved extending this use of parallels,
natural in a time in which the inner meaning, as opposed to the literal sense,
of Scripture was of such dominant importance, to provide a key to the time
after the New Testament. As there was a concordance between the pattern of
events in the Old and New Testaments, so there would be a concordance
between the events described in Scripture and those that took place after
the writing of the New Testament, and Joachim worked indefatigably on
traditional exegetical principles[22] to solve the riddle of the future.

The essence of the technique lay in recognizing the key events and
personalities, in their numerical sequence, which provided the parallels,
mapped out time and marked the approach to the end of the world. As is
familiar in such speculations, each disappointment in forecasting can readily
be overcome; the basis of calculation may be altered, while the principle
remains intact, and the reader of prophecies prepared for some new date.[23] So
one such date, 1260, marked by an extraordinary outburst of flagellating
penitential processions in Italy, spreading over the Alps to Germany and
Poland, passed by with no supernatural event.[24] The focus of expectation
moved on, and 1290 became the date, with subsequent transferences right
through the Middle Ages, so long as Joachimite techniques remained as basis
for prophecy.

The Franciscans' scriptural training and their preaching, with its taste for
vivid symbolism and anecdote, opened the way for interest in Joachim's rich
store of parallels and symbols; the high importance that all friars attached
to Francis, and the early sense that something new, blessed by God, had
appeared in the order, contributed to the spread of Joachimism in various
forms and to the loose assimilation of the Franciscans by some writers to the

---

[20] Ibid., pp. 72–3.

[21] Ibid., pp. 135–292.

[22] Reeves stresses the basis of Joachim's thought in traditional exegesis; see e.g. *Prophecy*, pp. 10, 16–17.

[23] Southern, *TRHS*, 5th ser. XXII, p. 177.

[24] Reeves, *Prophecy*, pp. 54–5; R. Manselli, 'L'Anno 1260 fu Anno Gioachimito?', in *Il Movimento dei
disciplinati nel settimo centenario dal suo inizio* (Perugia, 1962), pp. 99–108 (composite work, fundamental on
Flagellants); G. Dickson, 'The flagellants of 1260 and the crusades', *Journal of Medieval History* XV (1989),
pp. 227–67 at pp. 233–5, demonstrates that the Flagellants in this episode were accused of heresy at a late
stage, outside Italy when clerical participation fell away. They were originally vigorously orthodox and
hostile to the Cathars; note up-to-date bibliography, pp. 261–7. I owe help to the author.

role of the new order of the third age. An identification of Francis with the angel of the sixth seal in the Apocalypse, who in the Joachimite hypothesis was the herald of the new age, became a commonplace among Franciscan writers.[25] Attachment to Joachimism stretched all the way from a loose use of his symbols, as a kind of decorative *jeu d'esprit*, to a profound involvement in versions of his ideas which acted as a mainspring to religious life.

In the process Joachim's own views were remodelled. He had said very little about poverty for his new order in the third age; that aspect of religious life was crucial for Franciscans, and in their versions it became the decisive mark of the new order. Joachim had anticipated an intensification of persecutions as an immediate prelude to the dawning of the third age. There were to be two Antichrists, one shortly before the third age, the other at its end, as part of the persecutions which would herald the second coming and the end of human history.[26] The success of Islam under Saladin gave him one clue that his third age was not far off: it represented the requisite increase of pressure on the Church. But it was a characteristic of Joachim as an apocalyptic writer that he set the events of his own time in the full context of history, and so in the diagram of the dragon of the Apocalypse in the *Liber figurarum* (Figure 7) Saladin features as one head in a sequence going back to Herod; the other, pseudo-Joachimite diagram (Figure 8) demonstrates both the process of adaptation and the diminishing of Joachimite prophecy to serve the preoccupations of one context in time.[27] The dragon in this example has turned into a bird of prey; the Holy Roman emperors assume a more important place on the side of evil, with both Henry I and Frederick II among the heads, the seventh, larger than all the rest, being that of Frederick. The text refers plainly to Frederick II and his heirs (*cum successione sua*) as Antichrist; the great struggle of the papacy with the Hohenstaufen is thus seen as the prelude to the coming of the third age. By contrast, the genuine Joachimite drawing leaves the last head anonymous – this is the Antichrist of Joachim's writings, yet to appear in history. The diagram gives only one mild form of adaptation – it may be allowed to stand for a wide variety of use and abuse of Joachimite ideas.

Guglielma and Dolcino

Worse distortions of Joachim appeared outside the Franciscan order, in unlearned milieux where ideas were passed on from original Joachimite and pseudo-Joachimite texts, it would seem, by oral transmission. In Milan the bones of a certain Guglielma, who had died in 1281, were dug up and burned

[25] Reeves, *Prophecy*, p. 176; S. Bihel, 'S. Franciscus, fuitne angelus sexti sigilli (Apoc. 7:2)?', *Antonianum* II (1927), pp. 59–90; for changing patterns of pseudo-Joachimite literature and emergence of angelic pope, see H. E. Lee and M. Reeves, 'The School of Joachim of Fiore', in Lee *et al.*, ed., *Western Mediterranean Prophecy*, pp. 3–15; B. McGinn, *The Calabrian Abbot: Joachim of Fiore in the History of Western Thought* (London, 1985) ch. 7 (relates Joachim to Aquinas and Bonaventure).

[26] Reeves, *Prophecy*, pp. 295–392; H. M. Schaller, 'Endzeiterwartung und Antichrist Vorstellungen im 13 Jahrhundert', in *Festschrift für Hermann Heimpel* (ed. Mitarbeitern des Max-Planck-Instituts für Geschichte) II (Göttingen, 1972), pp. 924–47.

[27] *Il libro*, ed. Tondelli *et al.*, II, tavola 26, fig. 2; analysis in Reeves and Hirsch-Reich, *Figurae*, pp. 269, 274 (p. 147, for manifestation of Antichrist; index, for discussion of Antichrist and Gog and Magog).

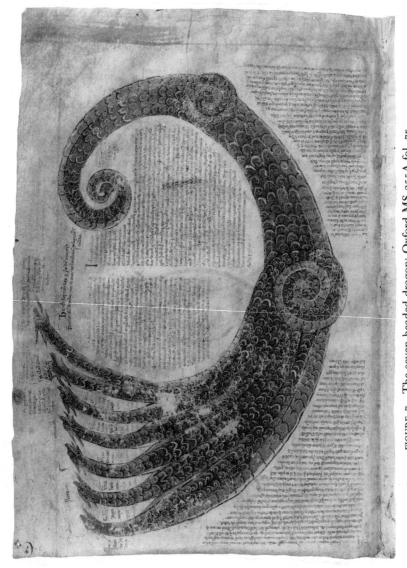

FIGURE 7 The seven-headed dragon; Oxford MS 255A fol. 7r.
Reproduced by permission of the President and Fellows of Corpus Christi College, Oxford.

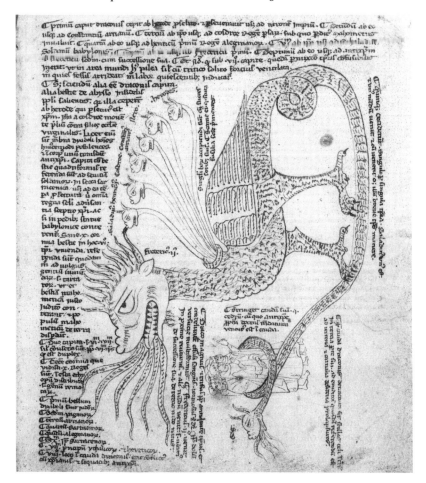

FIGURE 8 A debased dragon; MS Vat. Lat. 3822 fol. 5r.
Reproduced by permission of the Vatican Library.

by the inquisition in 1300, when it appeared that a circle of her initiates in Milan revered her as an incarnation of the Holy Spirit.[28] The relatively harmless but simplistic idea of the angelic pope,[29] shortly to come to cleanse the Church, took on an unusual guise in the hands of this circle, who had come to believe that a woman from their midst, Manfreda de Pirovano, would be the pope, who would convert the Jews and Saracens and usher in a new age. She would be accompanied by women cardinals: all higher offices in the

[28] Reeves, *Prophecy*, pp. 248–50; S. Wessley, 'The thirteenth-century Guglielmites: salvation through women', *SCH* Subsidia 1, pp. 289–303.

[29] Ibid. (see index); F. Baethgen, *Der Engelpapst* (Halle, 1933); see B. Töpfer, *Das kommende Reich des Friedens* (Berlin, 1964) (survey of prophecies, esp. in twelfth and thirteenth centuries, subtly related to economic and political background; Marxist assumptions).

Church would be held by women. The existing gospels would be superseded by four new ones, written under the guidance of the Holy Spirit. Joachimite ideas an interpretation of apostolic life and the effect of interdict and dispute in the Milanese Church on the administration of the sacraments, all fostered the growth of the movement.

Guglielma's heirs were not difficult to uproot; the Apostolic Brethren, however, founded by Gerard Segarelli in Parma in 1260, the year of the Flagellant outbreak and one of the key dates of Joachimite prophecy, were more resilient and had a surprisingly wide circle of influence.[30] Segarelli, according to Salimbene the chronicler, had been refused admission to the Franciscans at Parma; a simple, unlearned man who must nevertheless have had some force of personality, he gathered a group who, like him, practised the most direct and literal imitation of the life of the apostles, to the embarrassment of the Franciscans, as Salimbene's hostility reveals. Quite literally, they lived for the day, begged only necessities of life which were consumed on the spot, had only one habit where the Franciscan rule allowed two, engaged in demonstrations whereby they stripped off their clothing and divided it afresh amongst themselves, so as to show their utter detachment from individual ownership, and called themselves, not *minores*, as the official order did, but *minimi*.[31] They lasted, and gained popular approbation, because they followed the Franciscan ideal with a rigour, even to excess and fetishism, in a way that the majority of the friars of the later thirteenth century did not. Parma supported them; the bishop in early years did not move against them. But the Council of Lyons in 1274 banned unauthorized orders; in 1285 Honorius IV banned them explicitly; in the 1290s proceedings for heresy were taken against some members. Segarelli, first condemned to imprisonment, was burned in 1300. Inquisition proceedings of 1299 in Bologna give us a glimpse of a group, not as yet violently opposed to the Church[32] but justifying disobedience through their own attainment of the state of perfection of the primitive Church by the practice of poverty. Popes of the post-Constantinian Church (that had abandoned the poverty of the primitive Church), they argued, had no right to force them to give up their way of life.

With the replacement of Segarelli in the leadership by Dolcino, the bastard son of a priest from the diocese of Novara, who had picked up some learning, the sect grew more strongly heretical, and responded with violence to the pressures of the inquisition. Dolcino issued a manifesto in 1300, in which he claimed direct inspiration by the Holy Spirit for himself and a crucial role in the imminent coming of a new age for the Apostolics he led. Instead of the three *status* of the Joachimites he postulated four – one, of the patriarchs and prophets of the Old Testament, a second, initiated by Christ and the apostles and lasting till the time of Constantine, a third, just nearing its close, from Constantine, and a fourth, about to come, in which the true apostolic life of his

---

[30] Reeves, *Prophecy*, pp. 242–8, with sources; Leff, *Heresy* I, pp. 191–5; I have made greatest use of Töpfer, *Reich*, pp. 280–324, illuminating in its comparisons of Dolcino's views with other prophecies.

[31] Ibid., pp. 284–6, 292. Töpfer notes that the term *apostoli* was used rather by outsiders than the group itself.

[32] Töpfer's interpretation.

group would prevail, and, side by side with the *status*, four *mutationes*, of which the fourth had been initiated by Gerard Segarelli. The conviction of the overriding value of the apostolic life, as observed by Dolcino's group in contrast to all others, led logically to the insertion in Joachim's scheme of a fourth *status* to accommodate it.[33] Even Francis's position is dimmed in comparison with that of the leaders of the Apostolics. He is not actually given the place of a 'forerunner' of the new *status*, shortly to come, and the way of life of the Apostolics, because of its stricter poverty, is taken as superior to that of St Francis and St Dominic. The fate foretold for the existing Church at the coming of the new age was dramatic: pope, prelates, clergy and monks, except for a repentant remnant, were to be exterminated within three years by a new emperor, Frederick, the king of Sicily, who had successfully defied papal and Angevin expeditions against him; then the holy pope would appear, and all the benefits of the new age would follow. This extravagant picture was rounded off by a passage in which Dolcino described a pattern of history in terms of the seven angels and seven Churches of the Apocalypse, in which Segarelli was the angel of Smyrna and he was the angel of Thyatira. In a second manifesto of December 1303 prophecies, unfulfilled, were brought up to date, and again in a manifesto at the end of 1304 which has not come down to us.

But there was no waning of confidence; some even alleged that Dolcino himself was to be the pope of the new age. He took to the mountains between Vercelli and Novara in 1304, and recruits followed him, both local peasants and Apostolics from farther afield, who supported him in plundering raids and violent resistance of Church forces. Ghibelline leaders, with whom he had mysterious contacts,[34] may have emboldened him, and no doubt the inquisition's repression stimulated a violent response; the poverty of peasants near his mountain refuge made them susceptible to his teaching. But the rapid development under Dolcino of an extravagant but not profoundly dangerous movement[35] into a violent rebellion is pre-eminently a tribute to the heady influence, in appropriate hands, of pseudo-Joachimite ideas of the new age. It took more than one expedition and an application of the crusading indulgence before Dolcino was taken and burnt in 1307 and his following destroyed; even then adherents outlasted the leader and the failure of his prophecies.

In the Franciscan order itself, well before these events, one scandal, that of the Eternal Gospel in 1254, served to reveal the dangers of the third *status*. The question about Joachim's construction always was: What was the significance of the transition between the second and third *status*? Did it imply supersession of the present hierarchy and sacraments, in the same fashion as the coming of Christ and his founding of the Christian Church superseded the Synagogue and the Old Law? For Joachim this was never so. With talents rather poetic and artistic than dialectical, he saw the scriptural parallels and precedents in terms of a constantly moving kaleidoscope of images. The patterns of three,

---

[33] Töpfer, *Reich*, p. 299, following R. Kestenberg-Gladstein, 'The "Third Reich": a fifteenth-century polemic against Joachimism and its background', *JWCI* XVIII (1955), pp. 242–95 at p. 251.

[34] Töpfer, *Reich*, pp. 314–16.

[35] I have not been able to examine evidence of aberrant views on sexual activities; they are discussed by Töpfer (*Reich*, pp. 292–3).

with their dangers, were always accompanied by patterns of two, standing for the two dispensations of the Law and Grace, of the two eons, before and after Christ, which would last to the end of time.[36] In the *Liber figurarum*, the words 'end of the New Testament in diagrams are never associated with the transition from the second to the third *status*, only with the consummation of the orthodox patterns of twos. The changed conditions of life in the third *status* represented a fructification of trends in the second *status*, but not revolutionary institutional change. And yet, whatever Joachim's intentions, the whole tenor of his treatment of the third *status*, with its emphasis on 'spiritual men' and new spiritual understanding, tended easily to subvert faith in the present, visible order, with its hierarchy, laws and sacraments.

In 1254 a crude adaptation of Joachim by Gerard of Borgo San Donnino, who taught that Joachim's three principal works were the gospel of a new age, superseding the Old and New Testaments, revealed to all just what the dangers were.[37] His condemnation ended the phase of relatively carefree use of Joachim, and was followed by refutations of the three-age theory, but not the complete jettisoning of Joachimism. There was much more in Joachim than the three *status*, whose sinister potential had often not been recognized in early years, and various quite orthodox writers continued to make discriminating use of his symbols and categories. The Spirituals, however, held firmly to him, and wedded their doctrine of poverty to a version of Joachim's apocalyptic speculations, more subtle than that of the simple-minded Gerard, but still tending ultimately to the subversion of the contemporary Church.

No authentic text of Joachimite work has come down to us from the Spiritual Franciscans' leaders in mid-century, John of Parma and Hugues de Digne, but in Olivi's *Lectura super Apocalipsim* we have a major Joachimite text that gives us a clue to the nature of his influence in the south of France.[38] The work, completed late in life and, no doubt, the fruit of reflection on his sufferings and that of the Spirituals, adapts Joachim wholeheartedly to his own time. As in Joachim's own work, mankind was on the eve of great events, but they were seen pre-eminently in terms of current Franciscan history. It was St Francis who was the initiator of a new age, and his rule was its gospel; full spiritual understanding would come to Francis's true disciples (i.e. the Spirituals), but only after the persecutions of the carnal Church, made up of all the evil forces in the visible Church, and especially the enemies of poverty and the advocates of pagan learning, the false doctors. A deepening of suffering, and the falling away of many in the Church, would be followed by the joys of the new age, described in terms very like Joachim's. So the struggle

---

[36] Reeves, in *MRS* II, pp. 74–6. I find the description of Joachim as a poet helpful. See discussion of Joachim's orthodoxy by Reeves (*Prophecy*, pp. 126–32).

[37] Lambert, *Poverty*, pp. 107–9; Reeves, *Prophecy*, pp. 59–70; B. Töpfer, 'Eine Handschrift des Evangelium aeternum des Gerardino von Borgo San Donnino', *ZG* VII (1960), pp. 156–63.

[38] Manselli, *Lectura*; criticism in Leff, *Heresy* I, pp. 122–39, esp. p. 139. See E. Pásztor, 'Le polemiche sulla "Lectura super Apocalipsim" di Pietro di Giovanni Olivi fino all sua condanna', *BISIAM* LXX (1958), pp. 365–424; Cazenave, in *Christianisme*, ed. Brenon and Gouzy, p. 34, on Olivi's reference to sack of Béziers by crusaders as an event accompanying opening of sixth seal; see also p. 60. Survey by Lee and Reeves, 'Petrus Johannis Olivi', in *Prophecy*, ed. Lee *et al.*, pp. 17–26, stresses, against Manselli, *Lectura*, force of Joachimist influence on him (p. 19), notes he never equates Babylon and the Roman Church (p. 23) and calls his work 'the first major revision of Joachim's system' (p. 26).

between Spirituals and Conventuals in the south of France was invested with a cosmic significance. Joachim gave the groundwork for this scheme, but his fluctuating symbolisms had been given a precise, historical meaning. The dangers implicit in a third age were still there and intensified by being given a more definite historical setting. The problem, as with other Joachimites, lay in the relationship between a hypothetical new epoch shortly to dawn, and the institutions and laws of the contemporary Church and, although on this issue Olivi was careful, in controversy with his own sympathizers, to urge adherence to the commands of lawful authority in the Church and to distinguish in the *Lectura* between the carnal Church as a set of evil forces inside the Church and the visible Church as a whole, his teaching in the work very easily gave rise to revolt and heresy.

A similar subversive effect followed from the transposition of the Franciscan crisis, apparent here and elsewhere, into Joachimite terms. Spirituals, anxious about the undermining of the observance in the order through papal bulls and the glossing of the rule, harked back to Francis's Testament, called for literal observance and looked askance at papal 'clarification'. But what if the rule was the gospel of a new epoch, and if Francis and his disciples, with the rule and the Testament, had taken the mantle of Christ as at the beginning of the Christian epoch? Was the rule in fact above all papal clarification and glossing? What if the persecutors of the Spirituals, their superiors and the false doctors were followers of Antichrist? Might not resistance *à l'outrance* to them be justifiable? Thoughts of this kind helped to raise a disciplinary dispute inside a religious order to the plane of doctrinal conflict. Moreover, Joachimism gave a purpose to the Spirituals' troubled lives. The sense of certainty of their victory gave them both courage and obstinacy, and helps to account for a certain extravagance and recklessness in their actions which tended to make the split between Spirituals and many of their superiors irreconcilable. So with the development from Joachim to Olivi: though heresy proper has not been reached, we stand on its verge. With the development of Joachimism and Spiritual ideas on poverty amongst simpler friars and Midi tertiaries behind Olivi we do reach heresy.

The Beguins and popular heresy

In his *Lectura* Olivi inferred nothing more from the prophecies of approaching persecution than the necessity for the Spirituals to show patience in their sufferings. His comments on the Apocalypse were presented with caution, as possible but not certain interpretations of the future and, though he strongly developed Joachim's sentiment that the mystical Antichrist would be found within the Church and referred to the coming of a pseudo-pope, he never identified the carnal Church or Whore of Babylon with the Roman Church. In his popular works of edification, edited by Manselli,[39] he exhorts his followers to virtuous life on traditional lines of Franciscan piety; only

---

[39] *Spirituali*, pp. 267–90. B. Tierney, *Origins of Papal Infallibility, 1150–1350* (Leiden, 1972), ch. 3, argues that Olivi's doctrine of infallibility was developed in order to meet the utterances of a pseudo-pope. His concern was to buttress the papal decrees already issued on the Franciscan way of life. For Olivi's views on the Apocalypse, see Burr, *Olivi*, pp. 173–83.

mentions of the need for vigilance as the Last Times approach betray his special interests.

When a local adherent, the friar Matthew de Bosicis, who went to Rome in 1299 with five Beguins and unlettered women taking with him the works of Olivi, made a confession of faith at a date between 1299 and 1304, no doubt in consequence of the suspicion then spreading of the Spiritual movement, his words showed a simple adherence both to Olivi and his teaching and to wholly orthodox tenets on the need for obedience and the nature of the visible Church.[40] But was Matthew exercising 'economy' in his confession, and not revealing all his thoughts?[41] That there were grounds for disquiet in Olivi's oral contacts with his followers emerges from the ostensibly trivial point of the moment at which the spear pierced Christ on the cross. This occurred, Olivi said, before rather than after death; but that was not what the Vulgate text said. Olivi's ground for change, amongst other things, was the vision of a contemporary, which he alleged against Scripture. With the *usus pauper*, the spear-wound tenet was treated by followers as the teaching of a master, to be received with veneration. The affair gives us a glimpse of another more cloudy and visionary Olivi, not usually revealed in his writings.[42]

Authorities believed that his popular influence was baleful. Preoccupied with the prime battle over Olivi's scholastic views and the *usus pauper*, they did nevertheless periodically advert to the popular background in the province. In 1285 he was accused of being the head of a 'superstitious sect'; in 1290 Nicholas IV called for investigation of certain brothers 'who seemed to introduce schism into the province of Provence'; in 1299 a provincial council warned against extravagances; there was an investigation of his work on the Apocalypse, and a complaint about it in 1311.

The tragedy of the Spiritual movement was that its settlement was so long delayed. Treatment by the usual procedures of disciplinary action within the order could not work, because superiors who attempted to carry them out were self-interested and stained with abuses, especially in the Midi. There was yet too much idealism amongst the friars, and too much sympathy among outside sympathizers, churchmen and laymen, for a local repression to be carried out without complaint or publicity. The Spirituals, for all their faults, carried the authentic note of the passion for poverty; and this both united them to St Francis, and ever won them some hearts. At the same time, grounds for disquiet on doctrinal grounds did exist, both in Italy and in the Midi, in the influence of Joachimite thought, the rigidity and lack of balance of Spiritual views on poverty, and the exaggerated place that the rigorists gave to their heroes, above all to Olivi. So neither side could achieve victory for

[40] Tierney, *Origins*, pp. 42–6.

[41] Compare the declaration of Cathars at Lombers 1165, above, p. 59; see M. D. Lambert, 'The Franciscan crisis under John XXII', *FS* XXXII (1972), pp. 123–43 at p. 131n. Manselli, in the tradition of Morghen, tends to stress the importance of the actions of ecclesiastical authority in 'creating' heresy in the province of Provence, especially after the burnings of 1318. To demonstrate this he must argue for the orthodoxy of Spirituals and Beguins there before the major persecutions of 1318 and the following years, when documentation is sparser and the point is very difficult to prove. Burr, *Kingdom* reassesses Olivi's work and explains why he alarmed authority.

[42] Lambert, *Poverty*, pp. 172–3; for all controversies, see chs 7, 8; fuller account, esp. valuable on Olivi's treatises and thought, Leff, *Heresy* I, pp. 100–63.

their views, which tended through combat to become more extreme; and as the disputes dragged on, first inside the order, then at the papal court and at the Council of Vienne, patience waned, and the Spirituals and Beguins became more deeply involved in Joachimite extravagance. Clement v, sympathetic but weak, never grasped the nettle: he removed some of the worst superiors from office, and stopped persecution, but did not make a viable settlement.[43] Then the whole landscape darkened for the Spirituals, as the chance of a double vacancy in both the papacy and the generalate from 1314 to 1316 removed central control, and allowed a resumption of persecution. The raising, then the dashing of hopes, and the renewal of persecution, was the stimulus to rank heresy; the identification of the carnal Church with the whole visible Church, that seemed to have turned against them, transformed individual popes and churchmen into the evil figures of Joachimite prophecy.

The distinctions in Olivi's work on the Apocalypse were finely drawn: it was not to be expected that untrained tertiaries would go on making them and stay within orthodoxy as they found Olivi's reputation attacked and heard of the cruelties of Conventual superiors. Olivi's death in 1298 did not help; equivocal as his teaching was, he did restrain the wilder spirits. Dead, his tenets became the centre for the *cultus* of an unauthorized saint, his death-day celebrated as a feast, pilgrimage to his tomb stimulating conversions to the Spiritual way, Joachimite interpretation turning him into the angel of the seventh seal, whose face shone as the sun.[44] Joachimism heightened expectations and stimulated a sense of crisis. Extravagance reached great heights: at the end of the chain of persecution, in 1325, a weaver, William Ademarii, a Beguin from Narbonne, told an inquisitor that Olivi had made a work on the Apocalypse that was admirable, and such that, if all the heads of men were reunited into one sole head, it could not have composed such a work if it had not been made by the Holy Ghost, and that it would convert the Saracens to the faith of the Roman Church – one of the events, in fact, that was to mark the start of a new epoch.[45]

Thus a popular heresy was in the process of formation in the Midi in the first two decades of the fourteenth century, fanning out from Spiritual friars to tertiaries under their influence to sympathetic secular clergy and lay patrons in the towns. The area affected abutted on, and to some degree corresponded with, old Cathar-infected regions, but the inspiration was quite different. Olivi and his followers were firm in their opposition to both the Cathars and the Waldensians, whom they saw as members of Antichrist, and there are hardly any signs of interpenetration of doctrine between Catharism and the Spiritual heresy.[46] Furthermore, the old centres of Catharism lay farther to the east, whereas the Spiritual heresy had its centres in two towns less

---

[43] Leff, *Heresy* I, pp. 155–6, Lambert, *Poverty*, pp. 198–201; Manselli, *Spirituali*, p. 109, is interesting; comment, Burr, *Olivi*, pp. 193–4.

[44] Rev. 10: 1, from Catalan *De statibus ecclesie*, dated by Manselli to 1318 (*Spirituali*, pp. 164–7). It is fair to add that the general trend of Manselli's exposition (chs 2–4) differs from mine and, using esp. minor works of the Spirituals and supporters, stresses their relative orthodoxy before 1318 and the arbitrary nature of persecution. I have not been able to use *Franciscains d'Oc: Les Spirituels ca. 1208–1324, CF* x (1975).

[45] Manselli, *Spirituali*, pp. 181–2; on literacy see R. E. Lerner, 'Writing and resistance among Beguins', Biller, Hudson, *Literacy*, pp. 186–204.

[46] Ibid., p. 264; for a possible exception, see p. 221.

important in Catharism and nearer the coast: Narbonne because of Olivi's memory, and Béziers because of the patronage of the devoted lay supporter Pierre Trancavel, and also because the two convents had been taken over by Spirituals during the interregnum in the papacy and generalate. The area of diffusion stretched at its maximum extent from the coastal line of Perpignan to Nice and, inland, from Toulouse to Avignon.[47] There was a thinner band of support over the Pyrenees, in more developed regions of the kingdom of Aragon. The core lay in the towns: workers in the country were not affected and neither was the layer of immigrant northern Frenchmen, lay or clerical.[48] It was a Languedocian heresy, and may even have owed something to local feeling against authority. Towns backed the Spirituals and appealed on their behalf partly because they were opposed to the activity of the inquisition and its implications in secular politics, and adherents may well have been attracted by a movement which came to denounce wealthy upper clergy, because of their own experience of the clergy in Languedoc.

The Cathar crisis does not seem to have brought a major change in spiritual quality in the higher clergy; a more effective juridical activity can be observed, and the restoration of tithes opened the way to a major church-building programme in the century between 1250 and 1350 but this was not the same as spiritual revival.[49] Franciscan rigorists, in their obvious destitution, were not, in externals, wholly unlike the perfect; and the interrogations of the inquisition show how Beguins were attracted by the poor life of their leaders.[50] In each case, it was the ethics of the dedicated individual which formed a major appeal. Rich as well as poor laymen were involved but there were numbers of poor tradesmen of modest culture, butchers, weavers and the like, whose attitudes to the rich and powerful who, they believed, formed the carnal Church, were surely in part shaped by their social position and the gulf which separated them from the wealthy. Nevertheless the heresy sprang mainly from a religious motive: it was the belief of elite groups, devoted if unsubtle rank and file Franciscans, and dedicated laity. Numbers were fairly small – 120 members of the first order who took over the convents of Narbonne and Béziers, smaller numbers of friars in Italian provinces. When the inquisition set about destroying the popular base of the heresy in the Midi, they were working on groups linked by geography, family or individual personalities that did not usually number more than twenty and were often less. There was no popular involvement in terms of adherents or patrons on anything like the scale of Catharism.

Paradoxically, John xxii,[51] the dynamic administrator whose election in

---

[47] Ibid, p. 256; for Cathars' sites, see above, p. 115.

[48] Ibid., pp. 258–63.

[49] See J. H. Mundy, 'Charity and social work in Toulouse, 1100–1250', *Traditio* xxii (1966), pp. 203–87, esp. p. 206; Wakefield, *Heresy, Crusade*, p. 130 and n. For a case of the Church benefiting from an individual accused of heresy, see Wakefield, in *Names* xviii (1970), pp. 294–5. I owe references to Professor W. L. Wakefield.

[50] See Manselli's comments (*Spirituali*, chs 7, 8, *passim* (most valuable section)), and Leff, *Heresy* i, pp. 212–30.

[51] For John and the Franciscans, see Leff, *Heresy* i, pp. 157–66, 206–11, 230–3, 238–55 (see characterization of John (pp. 206–7) and analysis of his terminology, using *Quia vir reprobus*); Lambert,

1316 ended the long vacancy after Clement v, was at one and the same time responsible for cutting short the movement of Spirituals and Beguins and so safeguarding orthodoxy and for putting the finishing touches to the development of full-blown heresy within the movement. One hardly knows whether to wonder more at the energy and efficiency which John brought to the task of repression or the recklessness and haste which he demonstrated in his handling of the doctrinal problems of the Franciscans.

For him, a native of Cahors, who had worked in regions neighbour to the Spirituals' catchment area in the south and came informed to the problem, the question was not whether the movement was dangerous or unorthodox but how it might most effectively be put down. Leading Spirituals who had patrons were removed from the scene without punishment, the rebellion in Narbonne and Béziers ended, Olivi's teaching on the Apocalypse again subjected to academic examination, recalcitrant Italians pursued. His neatest stroke was to take down the previous bull of clarification on the rule, Clement v's *Exivi de Paradiso*, extract two clauses, on the wearing of poor clothing and the prohibition of granaries and cellars, which Clement had concluded were points of obligation for the friars yet should be subject to the individual discretion of superiors, and to reiterate them in a bull of his own, *Quorumdam exigit*, insisting on the power of superiors to decide what was poverty (*vilitas*) in clothing and when it was right to have the security of food storage through using cellars and granaries.[52]

Quorumdam was used to sort sheep from goats. An inquisitor presented it to suspect friars and put to them two questions. Would they obey the precepts contained in *Quorumdam exigit*? Did they believe that the pope had the power to make such precepts as were contained in *Quorumdam exigit*? The questions touched on a nerve-centre, for to say 'yes' meant giving up the patched, dramatically poor habits that recalled Francis's dying words about his early life in the Testament, and served as a party badge and, against the tenor of the rule, allowing the foresight for the morrow, implied in the keeping of cellars and granaries. To return to obedience to superiors on these issues meant giving up the distinctive Spiritual position and admitting that, as John said, poverty was great but 'unity was greater';[53] to admit the pope's power of dispensation over the rule was to abandon the view, forged by the Spirituals in the battle over the observance, that the Franciscan rule, written under divine inspiration, was like the gospel and not subject to alteration by any human hand.

Four friars were obdurate in refusing assent and, after a high-ranking commission had reported that to refuse the papal right to make the precepts contained in *Quorumdam exigit* was tantamount to heresy, were burnt at Marseilles in May 1318.[54] Armed with *Quorumdam* and his decision, plus a bull which condemned unauthorized groups of friars and tertiaries (*fraticelli, fratres*

Poverty, ch. 10, and in *FS* xxxii, pp. 123–43; Tierney, *Origins*, ch. 5, is illuminating on the theory of papal power. Note his correction (p. 188) of Leff, *Heresy* i, pp. 241, 246, 249, on John and the key of knowledge.

[52] *BF* v (Rome, 1898), no. 289, pp. 128–30.

[53] Ibid., p. 130b.

[54] For event and significance, see Manselli, *Spirituali*, pp. 150–78, 190.

de paupere vita, bizzochi or *beghini*),[55] the inquisition was equipped to roll up the movement in the south of France. Another bull, with a somewhat arbitrary list of errors, was issued primarily against Spirituals in Tuscany.[56] Meanwhile, a commission reported adversely – and with some injustice – on Olivi's work on the Apocalypse, and theologians condemned a more definitely heretical Catalan work on the ages of the Church. Olivi's *Lectura* was not definitively condemned until 1326; but his tomb was destroyed early in the pontificate, and possession of his books was treated as incriminating.

Over some seven or eight years inquisitors destroyed the core of the heresy, catching the members of the first order who escaped the net spread by John and the Conventuals in 1317, moving against the patrons who helped fugitives and the Beguins who were the chief lay supporters. Condemnation to crosses, pilgrimages and burnings, and the usual pressures to produce recantations whittled support away, providing occasional small batches for the pyre, beside the Cathars and Waldensians, who still required attention in this region.[57] By 1326–7, when the inquisition laid by the heels Pierre Trancavel of Béziers and his daughter, who used his resources to aid refugees, and Bernardo Maurini, the secular priest of Narbonne who gave valuable exhortation and encouragement to the cause, the back of the movement was broken.[58] Thereafter, although there was still an aftermath in Languedoc, Catalonia, Majorca and the western Mediterranean,[59] the Spirituals had lost their most significant territorial base.

So the crisis in the south ended. Yet John, who did most to destroy the movement, also played a part in pushing it deeper into heresy. The four friars who stood firm at Marseilles were regarded as martyrs, and interrogations after 1318 tell us of the shock that the news of the deaths gave to the fugitive friars and Beguins. Surely this blow was one of the persecutions that heralded the opening of the seventh seal of the Apocalypse and the new epoch in history? The decision against the rule, as they saw it, helped to confirm identification of John XXII with the mystical Antichrist who, it was prophesied, would strike against Francis and his true followers. When John, nothing if not thorough, turned his attention in 1322–3 to the contemporary doctrine of poverty of the whole Franciscan order, and made a dogmatic decision on the poverty of Christ and the apostles in an anti-Franciscan sense,[60] that only strengthened their conviction of his true position, as the enemy of the elect. Was not persecution the mark of those who would enter on the Sabbath age of quiet and contemplation? The ashes of those who burned were gathered up and venerated as relics. Gagliarda, wife of the notary Bernardo Fabri,

---

[55] *Sancta Romana* (*BF* v, no. 297, pp. 134–5).

[56] *Gloriosam ecclesiam* (ibid., no. 302, pp. 137–42).

[57] See Bernard Gui's first-hand account in *Practica inquisitionis heretice pravitatis, auctore Bernadone Guidonis*, ed. C. Douais (Paris, 1886); G. Mollat, *Manuel de l'inquisiteur* (Paris, 1926) (abridged, with Fr. tr.); further materials in P. Limborch, *Historia Inquisitionis* (Amsterdam, 1692); account of sources in Manselli, *Spirituali*, ch. 1.

[58] Manselli, *Spirituali*, pp. 234–7.

[59] See D. Douie, *The Nature and the Effect of the Heresy of the Fraticelli* (Manchester, 1932); for a discussion of Arnold of Vilanova, his influence, Beguins in Aragon and Catalonia, see Lee and Reeves, in *Prophecy*, ed. Lee *et al.*, pp. 27–88.

[60] *Cum inter nonnullos* (*BF* v, no. 518, pp. 256–9).

confessed in a human touch that she had said over such relics kept at their home, 'If you are the bones of saints, help me.'[61] Others were firmer in their convictions. The *sermo generalis* before burning, at which the errors of the heretic were described and denounced, and the actual execution could and did have the effect sometimes of actually spreading heresy. At times of burnings the priest Peirotas was busy in the localities, using the occasion to exhort fellow believers, by the example of courage in martyrdom, to persevere in belief.[62] There was a chain-reaction, stiffening Beguins and others in their beliefs. The decisions of John strengthened the view that he was Antichrist, and precipitated discussion of the place of present events in the approach to the seventh age of the Church. Eschatological hopes made adherents more determined to be faithful to their beliefs; *Quorumdam exigit* decided them not to yield on habits and granaries; burnings provided more saints, nucleus of a spiritual Church opposed to the carnal Church of pope and prelates. But the effects could not last; the persistence of the inquisition soon swept the recalcitrant few away, and forced the others into recantation.

John's settlement was effective but undiscriminating.[63] An artificiality hangs round the decisions in *Quorumdam exigit*, leaving the impression that heresy had come to consist in opposition to the orders of the pope. The authoritarian approach to problems of doctrine was characteristic of John. An impatient administrator, he produced a decision that provided a convenient basis for inquisition action. Later, when involved in controversy with the whole Franciscan order, he produced decisions about poverty that were careless, easily open to attack and which failed to grapple with the real issue – the place of poverty in the religious life and its relation to Christian perfection. His lack of care helped to cause another revolt of Franciscans, so that by the end of his reign there were not only *fraticelli de paupere vita*, the first-order heirs of the old Spirituals, but also *fraticelli de opinione*, former members of the official order, who opposed his decisions on the poverty of Christ.

Yet heresy there was, 'uncreated' as well as created, for a long incubation lay behind the views of the Beguins. John unwittingly stimulated certain excesses; but he did not bring the heresy as a whole into being.[64] Its essence lay in exaggeration. From earliest days poverty had been a prime occupation of the Franciscans, but it was transmuted by the simpler Spiritual friars and Beguins into the one crucial issue before the Church – a very different position from that of St Francis. The cumulative effect of the disputes, the repressions and the anxieties of rigorists about their views was to go far towards overturning the basis of Christian ethics,[65] and making it consist simply in renunciation of goods and destitution in daily living. Joachimism and the imminent expectation of cosmic change heightened the distortion. The intensified struggle between good and evil on the eve of the end of the world

[61] Manselli, *Spirituali*, p. 221, n. 3.
[62] Ibid., pp. 218, 315–18.
[63] Contrast John's handling of the Dominicans; see E. Hillebrand, 'Kurie und Generalkapitel des Predigerordens unter Johannes xxii', in *Adel und Kirche: Festschrift für G. Tellenbach* (Freiburg, 1968), pp. 499–515. I owe the reference to Mr A. Murray.
[64] There is a difference of emphasis between my judgement and that of Manselli and Leff.
[65] Knowles, *Religious Orders* ii, p. 93.

(or, as in Joachim's view, of the present epoch) tended to narrow down to the battle over the observance of poverty. A sectarianism made the writings of one devoted friar with a talent for speculative thinking and a taste for the Apocalypse into a teacher on a par with Paul, or with the Four Doctors of the Church; and turned the Franciscan rule, on which a divine inspiration had played, into a writing that stood on a level with the gospels themselves. The battle over obedience, first in the order, then with the ecclesiastical superiors at large, led on to a viewpoint which rejected the whole visible Church, equated the pope with the mystical Antichrist, and waited confidently for the supersession of the hierarchy.

Earlier generations were inclined to shrug off dangers in prophecy. If they were false, events would prove them so.[66] The Midi heresy showed again the flaws in this view. Exaggerations of poverty showed up elements of unhealthy thinking in the whole Franciscan order, and through the Johannine crisis brought the Franciscans to their lowest ebb in the fourteenth century. It was a tragedy for the Church. The events of the early fourteenth century revealed how a popular heresy could emerge within the very citadel of the Church. It was the enemy within.

By the end of John xxii's pontificate in 1334 the roll-call of popular heresies and movements of religious dissent had swelled – the Apostolics, Dolcino's rebels, the extremist Spiritual Franciscans, and their outflow in the tertiaries and Beguins of southern France and the *fraticelli* of Italy, the heretical mystics, and the adherents of the Free Spirit in Germany, Silesia and Bohemia. The combative old man was busy to the last with the aftermath of his settlement of the problems of the Franciscans, writing at length in 1329 to refute the members of the order under the former minister-general Michael of Cesena, who could not accept his decisions on the poverty of Christ and had broken into revolt in the previous year,[67] then embroiling himself in his last years in a controversy over his own doctrine of the Beatific Vision,[68] first evolved in reaction against Olivi's treatment of the issue. The Vision affair, however, remained personal: no theological judgement was issued and John's successor, Benedict xii, sensibly regulated the matter in his bull *Benedictus Deus* of 1336.

Under Benedict the pace of activity died down. Time and periodic persecutions whittled away the heretics. Dolcino and the Apostolics had been a once-for-all outbreak. The Beguins of southern France had been exposed to intensive inquisition activity in the 1320s; they gave scant trouble afterwards. The intellectual Franciscans under Michael of Cesena, secure in their refuge

[66] This explains the long toleration of doubtful pseudo-Joachimite speculation. For normal use of prophecy in Middle Ages, see R. E. Lerner, *The Powers of Prophecy* (Berkeley, Los Angeles and London, 1983), summary: pp. 183–97; note comment, p. 194, on chiliastic beliefs as 'commonplace aids in coping with reality'. See also R. K. Emmerson, *Antichrist in the Middle Ages* (Manchester, 1981).

[67] *Quia vir reprobus* (*BF* v, no. 820, pp. 408–49); Leff, *Heresy* i, pp. 238–55; B. Töpfer, 'Die Anschauungen des Papstes Johannes xxii über das Dominium in der Bulle "Quia Vir Reprobus"', in *Folia Diplomatica* (Brno, 1971), pp. 295–306.

[68] Knowles, *Religious Orders* i, pp. 248–52; Pásztor, in *BISIAM* lxx, pp. 365–424 and 'Una raccolta di sermoni di Giovanni xxii', *Bulletino dell' Archivio Paleografico Italiano*, n.s. ii–iii (1956–7), pp. 265–89; D. L. Douie, 'John xxii and the beatific vision', *Dominican Studies* iii (1950), pp. 154–74; M. Dykmans, *Les Sermons de Jean xxii sur la vision béatifique* (Rome, 1973); review: B. Smalley, *MA* xliii (1974), pp. 52–3.

with Lewis of Bavaria in Munich, having only an intellectual challenge and no popular appeal through austerity of life, faded with the deaths of their founders about mid-century. In Italy, especially in the south, and in tiny groups elsewhere, the *fraticelli* who would not accept John's settlement and regarded him as a heretic continued an existence in the half-light.[69] Sectarian to the last, they disputed among themselves as to who would be the Saviour to usher in a new age. Most commonly, they unchurched all who gave obedience to John XXII and his successors, on the grounds that his decisions on poverty were heretical and the practices of the Church and Franciscan order unfaithful to Christ's precepts. But they advanced no new arguments, living on with the themes of their attack on John XXII unchanged, supported by a popular reverence for the austerities of their life. In Florence they had a particularly long influence.[70] It took the determination of the saints of the Franciscan Observance in the fifteenth century, Capistrano and James of the March, who blended a life of true poverty with orthodoxy, to roll up the last remnants of the rebellion. The last of them disappear from recorded history with a trial at Rome in 1466.

Prosecutions of supposed adherents of the Free Spirit fluctuated according to individual interests, and tended to run down as the vitality of the mystical movement in the beguinages faded. At Strasburg repeated persecutions are recorded, in 1317–19, 1365, 1368–9, 1374 and 1404.[71] In the first instance, in 1317, bishop John I was pursuing heresy, pre-eminently among the males, the beghards;[72] later, probably from the pontificate of Urban V in the sixth decade of the century, the curia, rather than the bishop, seems to have provided the major impetus; later still, an individual inquisitor had greatest weight. A strand of genuine heresy and disobedience cannot be discounted as a factor behind these persecutions, but one major recurring source of trouble lay in the resentments of the secular clergy in the city against the popular influence of mendicants who were intimately linked with the beguine movement.[73] Targets of the persecutions varied, including beghards, anticlericals and individualists, deviant mystics, beguines in convents, pious women, tertiaries: the effects of the troubles were to drive the beguine movement more than ever towards the mendicants, obviously for protection. Prejudice played a considerable role, and later persecutions produce less good evidence for doctrinal deviations.

In Germany, Silesia and Bohemia prosecutions were affected by the will of the ruler, being inhibited in Germany for the duration of the contest between John and Lewis of Bavaria, but supported in Silesia and Bohemia by the

[69] Leff, *Heresy* I, pp. 230–8, Douie, *Fraticelli*, pp. 209–47, documents ed. F. Ehrle, in *ALKG* IV, pp. 63–180, with discussion of term *fraticelli* (pp. 138–80) (see esp. remarks on *fraticelli* unconnected with Spirituals (pp. 168–78)). Summary by Oliger in *DTC* XIV, cols 2522–49; F. Vernet, ibid., VI, cols 770–84, s.v.

[70] Stephens, in *PP* LIV (1972), pp. 36–53.

[71] Patschovsky, in *DA* XXX (1974), pp. 56–198. Not all persecutions are well recorded; date of 1365 is a hypothesis (ibid., p. 113). Summary (partially modified by Patschovsky) by Lerner (*Free Spirit*, pp. 85–105); see case of Małkaw (ibid., pp. 101–3) for a classic case of slander.

[72] Lerner, *Free Spirit*, p. 96; on decision of Council of Mainz 1310, see ibid., pp. 141–2. On name of John I (incorrectly given as 'of Dürbheim' in Lerner, *Free Spirit*), see Patschovsky, *DA* XXX, p. 94, n. 82.

[73] See Patschovsky's summary (*DA* XXX, pp. 116–18). Breaches of discipline play an important role, and the terms beguine and beghard are loose ones.

Margrave Charles, later king, and again given free scope in Germany when the pro-Church Charles reigned as Emperor Charles IV.[74] They revealed numbers of individual enthusiasts of varying orthodoxy, not necessarily adherents of the Free Spirit, together with Waldensians, the most resilient heretics of these regions. In an interesting case at Schweidnitz in Silesia the inhabitants of a beguinage were shown to be followers of a fiercely ascetic life, with much flagellation, fasting and hard work, believers in their superiority, despite outward humility, and despising church attendance, for which they were inclined to substitute their own prayers. Free Spirit beliefs in union with God did exist among them, but not libertinism, though they were accused of it.[75] The wave of persecution in the Empire led by Martin of Prague, Peter Zwicker and Eylard Schoenveld towards the end of the fourteenth century and in the early years of the fifteenth,[76] though mainly directed against the Waldensians, carried beguines, beghards and supposed heretical mystics into the inquisition's net, but by the time of the Council of Constance in 1414–18 the stream ran thinly. At the council, the beguines, shrunken in number, were defended against attack: *Ad nostrum*'s influence had waned: few more cases turned up in the fifteenth century, although the pursuit of the mystical way still had its hazards. The last well-recorded case of Free Spirit heresy north of the Alps is that of Hans Becker of Mainz, burned in 1458.[77]

The heresies that emanated from the Franciscans, the mystics and the imaginations of churchmen were disquieting, not so much because they represented *per se* an important direct threat, but because they were symptomatic of failings in the late medieval Church.

Though the Spiritual Franciscans had some powerful patrons, notably in southern royal houses, their case was not one that of its nature would stimulate a serious revolt against the Church. The practice of poverty, rather than the whole structure of belief woven round the Spirituals' protest, formed the basis of their popularity. *Fraticelli* met a real need which orthodoxy did not. The tragedy of the disputes, so trenchantly resolved after 1316, was that they lost to the sects idealists who were sorely needed. Probably the heresy of the Languedocian Beguins and the *fraticelli* would not have come into existence if the order before the fourteenth century had been able to contain and give outlets to its zealots; after they had gone and the controversies had had their enervating effect, the order was the weaker, and the way to needful reform made harder by being associated with heresy.

Still less than the Franciscans were the adherents of the Free Spirit capable of mounting an assault on the established system. At worst, they were isolated, individual deviants: moreover, as we have seen, there was a great deal of artificiality about this heresy. What the Free Spirit episode did show was the inability of authority at the time of Vienne and afterwards to come to terms with the beguine movement and to provide guidelines for its life, satisfactory to all parties in the Church. The cases after *Ad nostrum* also show us evidence of an anticlericalism both more widespread and more significant in the history of the Church than the Free Spirit.

[74] Lerner, *Free Spirit*, pp. 107, 131.
[75] Ibid., pp. 112–19.
[76] Ibid., pp. 145–6; for proceedings of Zwicker in Brandenburg and Pomerania, above, p. 158, n. 33.
[77] Lerner, *Free Spirit*, pp. 177–81.

Part IV

Evangelical heresy in the late
Middle Ages

Church and society: Benedict XII to Eugenius IV

With the death of John XXII the most sustained effort of the popes at Avignon to recover their erstwhile power and independence came to an end; John's successors lacked his exceptional talents, and their problems grew.[1] The most significant legacy from John lay in the development of administration and the increased sophistication of papal fiscal machinery; under his successors the process of reserving benefices for papal provision went on developing, primarily for fiscal reasons; the volume of papal business grew, and itself created a demand for more finance. The popes, whether efficient or not, austere or luxurious, were caught in an inflationary spiral[2] in which their real power was in no way increased, while the activity of their officials grew and the opportunities for true reform, if anything, diminished. There was a quantity of self-interested protest at a high level about the growth of papal intervention and the 'sinful city' of Avignon, coexisting with what could fairly be called informal concordats[3] between the papacy and secular governments, with growing bureaucracies that needed rewards, hard-pressed for resources at a time of economic regression, and anxious to benefit from the treasures of the Church. A system had come into being, based on detailed compromises, which met the needs of various interests in Church and State, however much complaint was made about it; in practice, in the underlying alliance between Church and State, it was the State's power which was now uppermost.

At the same time, papal centralization and defects in its administration excited popular disapproval, reinforced by the feeling of the devout that the proper place for the popes was at the tombs of Peter and Paul. Within the college of cardinals there were signs of the growth of an oligarchy, seeking to assert the powers of electors and put shackles on individual popes. Much

---

[1] See above, p. 172, n. 1; also M. E. Aston, *The Fifteenth Century: The Prospect of Europe* (London, 1968).

[2] Southern, *Western Society*, p. 133.

[3] I owe the phrase to Dr A. V. Antonovics.

valuable day-to-day business transacted at the curia, and a certain sophistication within the bureaucracy could not weigh in the scales against the general loss of prestige and leadership suffered at Avignon.

In 1378, shortly after the return from Avignon to Rome, disaster occurred. The conclave elected an unsuitable candidate, the aggressive and wilful Urban VI. A genuine reaction against the man they had chosen, combined with divisions among the cardinals, oligarchical sentiment and national feeling, created a schism. All existing problems were vastly accentuated. Thenceforward two popes existed, one with a seat at Avignon under Clement VII and his successors, and the other at Rome under Urban VI and his successors, excommunicating each other and their rivals' supporters, and deploying all available resources to unseat their opponents. Conflicts between states had helped to create the Great Schism, and now kept it in being; all the abuses for which the papacy had been held responsible in the past were sharply increased, as electors on the rival sides chose men of war and diplomacy rather than reformers, and the popes sacrificed all higher considerations to the search for victory.

Need stimulated response, and a conciliar movement developed, primarily in order to end the Great Schism, but secondarily, however, to reform papacy and Church, and in some cases to check a papal headship that appeared unworthy by leadership through general councils. The way to these objectives proved hard. At the Council of Pisa in 1409, the adherents of the conciliar party introduced a third claimant to the tiara, reigning as Alexander V, who was intended to end the conflict, but failed to obtain the withdrawal of his rivals. His existence only made matters worse, as did that of his successor, John XXIII, elected in 1410. Not till 1417 at the Council of Constance did one man, Martin V, emerge as a generally acceptable candidate. Weakened by the schism and by the advantages the kingdoms had gained during it, the papacy under Martin V trod warily and slowly regained ground. Both Martin and his successor, Eugenius IV, had to face tenacious resistance from supporters of the conciliar party, who wanted reform on their own terms, and they could only be said to have effectively outridden opposition from this quarter by about 1439, after Eugenius had succeeded in splitting the movement by transferring the Council of Basle first to Ferrara and then to Florence, and scoring the triumph of securing union between the Greek and Latin Churches.

Throughout the fourteenth century, the schism and the days of vitality of the conciliar movement, reform was constantly discussed, proposals put forward, and sermons preached, often in the most violent terms and by holders of high clerical office, denouncing abuses without bringing about any major reforming action. The need for reform tended to become a cliché. Naturally circumstances, especially after 1378, focused attention on the need for reform at the head. But how was it to be effected? Different voices recommended different means, and wished to carry measures of varying degrees of vigour. If there was to be reform in the head, should it not be in the members also? And yet bishops and cardinals were in various ways beneficiaries of the system to be reformed, and there were secular interests to be considered also. Meanwhile, the immediate need was to end the schism. After it was over, more profound reform remained on the agenda, as it had done on so many occasions in the past, but it tended to be driven into the background by the struggle between papalists and conciliarists, and so was never realized.

A concomitant, and to some degree a result, of these events, was a feeling of mistrust towards ecclesiastical institutions, especially those on a large scale; it was reinforced by the Great Schism, but is discernible earlier. It underlies the loss of vitality of the major orders, and helps to explain the earlier success of the beguine movement, till it was checked by official disapproval and the heresy accusations. While all the high-level disturbances in the leadership of the international Church continued, a popular religion blossomed in the towns, in the parish churches, and in the confraternities which became so popular, and which assembled various social groups for the practice of their religion. A great vogue existed for works of popular devotion in the vernacular, and there was some dissemination of scriptural versions in the form, not of the bare text of the original, but in compilations and meditations linked predominantly to the mystical movement of the late Middle Ages. The practice of pilgrimage flourished and the cult of saints developed, sometimes to extravagance. In the wealthy towns a merchant class spent heavily on the building and decoration of churches; preachers readily drew large crowds, and the individual prophetic figure characteristic of the time, the mystic or the reformer, attracted reverence.

Anticlericalism was the natural accompaniment to the major failures in leadership and to the abuses. It was not always the case that the state of the clergy was worse in the fourteenth and fifteenth centuries than it had been earlier, but their deficiencies were attracting a more impatient response from the laity.[4] The relationship between clergy and laity had undergone a change, due to the widening horizons, the spread of lay education and an increasing lay self-consciousness and independence which become apparent at about the turn of the thirteenth and fourteenth centuries north of the Alps. Italy had long been a special case because of the higher standards of education attained by the laity there in an earlier age. Congregations were less ready to accept a clerical leadership *per se*; they were more questioning, and their expectations were higher. A low opinion of the clergy was fostered in this period by elements in the clergy themselves, through denunciatory sermons; though one has to note the existence of a literary, satirical anticlerical tradition, of clerks making jokes about clerks, which is as old as Walter Map in the twelfth century.[5]

One difference between the late Middle Ages and earlier centuries was that anticlerical ideas were more likely to be put into effect in the latter period, and Erastianism was both more possible and more widespread. The clerical profession had always been a net holding all manner of fish, and it continued to be so; ordinations were on a considerable scale, and investigation of suitability merely formal; the bishop was generally a remote figure, appointed for political or social rather than religious reasons, unable, even if he willed, to break through the barriers of custom effectively to discipline or unite the clergy of his

---

[4] See Rapp, *L'Eglise*, ch. 9, and on Italy, D. Hay, *Italian Clergy and Italian Culture in the Fifteenth Century* (London, 1973); on German anticlericalism, see W. Eberhard in *Historisches Jahrbuch* CXIV (1994), pp. 349–80.

[5] I owe comment to Professor C. N. L. Brooke.

diocese; there were many avenues of promotion open to the talented priest, and a parochial post was not necessarily rewarding or attractive. It was at the level of the parish clergy, despite effort at reform and some improvements, that the late medieval Church proved least effective, and it was here that some of the greatest stimuli to anticlericalism existed.

Extremism was a characteristic of the time. It links to political events and to economic troubles. The Hundred Years' War between England and France, which broke out in 1337, initiated a long sequence of conflicts, produced devastation over wide areas of France, and had a baleful effect on Church life; we have seen the part it played in the outbreak and continuation of the Great Schism. Secular governments had their own problems of authority, made worse by economic pressures and the effects of warfare. The Black Death in 1348–51 was a catastrophic event, removing more than a third of the population, and sparking off a great outburst of penitential flagellation, intended to assuage God's wrath and expiate the sins of the individual penitent; renewed visitations, though less disastrous, had important demographic effects and elicited similar, if not so violent, emotional responses.[6]

Processions of men, initially well organized, walking two by two, with a precise ritual to follow, of the saying of *Pater Nosters* and *Aves* and of flagellation accompanied by chants and songs, passed through Austria (probably their place of origin), Hungary, Germany, Bohemia, the Low Countries and Picardy, summoning the citizens of the towns to which they came to join them and scourging themselves in some public spot, generally the market-place.

The most striking feature lies in the strength of the emotions which lay behind these painful and repeated self-chosen penances, a reminder of the violence of feeling still latent in popular spirituality, comparable to the early crusade impulse, the Alleluia preachings in thirteenth-century Italy, or the outbreak of flagellation in 1260, coupled with the self-control often apparent in a movement that appears to be quite spontaneous, uncontrolled by any existing authority, and in the hands of the laity. The would-be flagellant took an oath to carry out his flagellation for thirty-three and a half days, recalling the years of Christ's earthly life, confessed to the masters of the movement, and undertook to pay his debts or make restitution for past wrongs. Within the procession he followed a strict ritual and obeyed the masters, flagellating twice a day in public and once at night; after the conclusion of the pilgrimage he promised to flagellate on Good Fridays for the rest of his life. Unbeneficed clergy joined, but the great bulk of penitents were laymen.

The attitudes of ecclesiastical authority varied. In the Low Countries, for example, the bishop of Thérouanne formally authorized them; at Tournai a

<hr/>

[6] E. Delaruelle, 'Les grands processions de pénitents de 1349 et 1399', *Il Movimento dei disciplinati nel settimo centenario del suo inizio* (Perugia, 1962), pp. 109–45 (on Netherlands, but with general references); G. Székely, 'Le mouvement des Flagellants au 14e siècle, son caractère et ses causes', in *HS*, pp. 229–38, Erbstösser, *Strömungen*, pp. 10–69 (Marxist analysis, with hypothesis of penetration of the movement in Thuringia by Free Spirit), R. Kieckhefer, 'Radical tendencies in the Flagellant movement of the mid-fourteenth century', *JMRS* IV (1974), pp. 157–76 (re-examination of sources, with critique of Erbstösser); English account in Leff, *Heresy* II, pp. 485–93. See J. V. Fearns's map and notes (*Atlas zur Kirchengeschichte*, ed. Jedin et al., pp. 48, 65). For general comment, see R. E. Lerner, 'The Black Death and Western European eschatological mentalities', *American Historical Review* LXXXV (1981), pp. 533–52; F. Graus, *Pest-Geissler-Judenmorde. Das 14. Jahrhundert als Krisenzeit*, Göttingen, 1987; review, A. Patschovsky, *DA* XLIII (1987), pp. 284–5.

rule which the Bruges flagellants had adopted was presented to the chapter; but the author of the *Annales Flandriae* thought that they were beghards, and attacked their belief that all sins would be remitted after their penance. The fear was of a lay movement without clerical control that had undertaken mass penance without authorization and without receiving the sacrament of penance from the priesthood. Moreover, there were extravagances. A Dominican preacher, for example, said that the blood of the flagellants was more precious than any since Christ's. In certain areas, notably Thuringia and Franconia, they tended to become more violent and anticlerical. Conceivably this was the case more often when their arrival preceded, rather than followed, the plague. Before the arrival of the Death, flagellation was one of the few outlets open to a fear-ridden population; after it had arrived, the worst could be seen, and there were practical tasks, such as burying the dead, available to dampen emotions.[7]

In the end, Clement VI condemned them in 1349. As the stimulus of mass mortality faded, so the movement waned, although there were recrudescences, in some cases associated with much more overt antisacerdotalism and heresy proper. The use of the scourge, long a traditional monastic discipline, had been taken up by the laity in a crisis on a mass scale, quite independently of the hierarchy, and by some of them turned into a kind of supreme sacrament.

The Death, a unique catastrophe for contemporaries, sparked off a religious response of unusual intensity; other long-term changes in the economy and society, still imperfectly understood, and the effects of warfare produced tensions and uprisings in town and country. The roots of these disturbances lay in the major changes in the Western economy which made themselves felt from almost the beginning of the fourteenth century in certain regions, affecting class relationships, the internal life of towns, and the condition of peasants. In towns a major factor lay in the rigidity of government by closed circles of wealthy bourgeois, directing affairs to their own profit, and arousing the hostility of artisans eager to share in the new wealth. Before the Death, the increase in town populations in advanced areas to an unprecedented size accentuated this hostility, as small groups of families were seen to regulate the destinies of so many; after the massive fall in population tension continued, as the rich in a contracted economy attempted to hold on to every source of wealth.

Troubles had begun in the late thirteenth century in the Low Countries, and continued during the following century; there were sporadic crises elsewhere and widespread disorder in Western Europe at various times between the spring of 1378 and the early months of 1383.[8] In France anger was turned against royal officials, tax collectors and moneyers; generally at the time of the Black Death the fear of mortality issued in pogroms of Jews, who were accused of responsibility for the epidemic; in England there were periodic xenophobic outbreaks.

In the countryside lords who were under heavy economic pressure attempted to enforce ancient rights over the peasants and, after the fall in population, to prevent free movement for better wages or conditions at a time

---

[7] Kieckhefer's hypothesis.
[8] M. Mollat and P. Wolff, *The Popular Revolutions of the Late Middle Ages* (London, 1973).

of labour shortage. In France, one of the most violent peasant uprisings, the Jacquerie, took place in 1358; in England, the Peasants' Revolt of 1981 led to the death of Simon of Sudbury, archbishop of Canterbury; the mob attacked officials and destroyed records, and briefly held the south-east of the country in fear. A combination of grievances came to a head with the imposition of a poll tax for an unsuccessful war; the underlying factor was the irritation of a comparatively prosperous peasantry with out-of-date restrictions which lords were attempting to impose on them. Further visitations of the plague, on a smaller scale, in the later fourteenth century and in the fifteenth added to the tension of life, sometimes inducing flight to penance, as in the Flagellant episode. Man's mortality was unusually vivid in the years following 1348.

Thought was marked by a tendency to take issues to extremes, and by a mistrust of reason.[9] The great system-building of the thirteenth century was over. The synthesis between faith and reason of St Thomas Aquinas had fallen under heavy attack almost as soon as it was launched. The wholesale condemnation of theses, some of St Thomas, some of others, by Bishop Etienne Tempier of Paris in 1277 marked the turning-point; thereafter different groups of scholastics separated, debating among one another individual issues; the effect of the Tempier condemnations was first to create confusion, and, then, in the long run, to facilitate a division between the spheres of faith and reason.

New ideas appeared with great rapidity; Duns Scotus, the Scottish Franciscan who died in 1308, both subjected traditional Aristotelian and Augustinian views to effective criticism and launched forth on a structure of thought of his own, inventing novel technical terms to do so. William of Ockham, an English Franciscan who had his career in a university cut short when he joined Michael of Cesena's revolt against John XXII's decisions on poverty, was the fountain-head of a powerful current of thought often referred to, somewhat inaccurately, as nominalism. This school had in common with some thinkers of the eleventh and twelfth centuries a stress on the particular in the traditional debate about universals.[10] But discussion was being carried on in the fourteenth century in a quite different atmosphere from that of earlier centuries. Where Aquinas and other thirteenth-century thinkers had been concerned to demonstrate how far natural reason supported the truths of faith, the trend in Scotus, Ockham and other contemporaries was to stress the contingent and limited nature of man's knowledge. Ockham went farther than Scotus on this road; moreover, his expositions on the absolute freedom and overriding power of God, buttressed by a series of brilliant paradoxes, set a gulf between man and the unknowable God and appeared to sap the traditional bases of moral theology. Reason could not support faith, which rested on revelation and authority.

The separation thus effected had beneficial effects in one sphere, for it opened the way to advances in natural science; on the other hand, it

---

[9] G. Leff, *Medieval Thought from St Augustine to Ockham* (Harmondsworth, 1958), pt 3; for debate on Ockhamism and its effects (with recent literature), see Rapp, *L'Eglise*, pp. 332–46, and for more recent work by Leff, below, p. 270, n. 4.

[10] For explanation, see Leff, *Thought*, pp. 104–14, 259–60; and on terminology, Rapp, *L'Eglise*, p. 337 and my comment below (p. 228, n. 8).

undermined traditional supports for faith and moral behaviour, and issued in a fashion both for scepticism and for fideism; if reason could not support faith, it could be argued, then neither could it disprove it, and beliefs, even if they seemed improbable, could be accepted on external authority alone. How far Ockham has been adequately understood by modern writers, and how far he was responsible for some of the effects attributed to his teaching, is still the subject of debate; responsibility for some of the more extreme positions of fourteenth-century intellectuals may well lie with other, lesser contemporaries or successors of his. Whatever the ultimate origins of Ockhamism and the so-called nominalist school, it provoked a reaction against this *via moderna*, notably by Thomas Bradwardine, archbishop of Canterbury, who died in 1349, during the Black Death, reasserting traditional doctrine and in metaphysics taking up the opposite position to the Ockhamists, that of realism.[11] Characteristically, however, this reaction too was often marked by the extremism that we must expect of the age.

The more critical climate of opinion, the currents of thought stemming from Ockhamism in the earlier fourteenth century, and the weakening of clerical authority and prestige in the age of the Avignonese papacy and the Great Schism are essential background for the study of the evangelical heresies of the late Middle Ages, stemming from Wyclif, the English Lollards[12] and the Bohemian Hussites. The existence of so much high-level dissent, the reiteration at all levels of the need for reform, and the widespread doubt and uncertainty about the true nature of the Church and the authority of the pope gave opportunities and stimuli unknown to the heresies of the past. Wyclif, co-founder with his early preachers of the English Lollards and part-inspiration of the Bohemian Hussites, was one of the leading academic figures of his day; his progress into heresy in his last years, ignoring the verdict of authority, then deliberately disseminating his views, was something novel in a scholastic of his eminence. An academic could speak to academics, and sparks of Wyclifite heresy blew about in the university world, taking fire here and there among scholars, and passing from them more widely into society.

The widespread criticism of authority, the consciousness of abuse and the scandals of the schism both gave cover to and stimulated Wyclif's attacks. So his heresy gained, for a little time, a base in the university of Oxford, and, because of Wyclif's academic reputation, found its way to the university of Prague. Certain ideas of Wyclif on disendowment and clerical jurisdiction had a natural appeal to rulers and nobility – the potential was there to build upper-class patronage on a scale not achieved by any previous heresy. Heretical doctrine and practical politics could work together. Moreover, the heresies of Wyclif, the Lollards and the Bohemian preachers all lay within the main stream of Christian doctrine and appealed to discontents which were of

---

[11] Leff, *Thought*, pp. 296–9; for explanation of realism and the reaction against scepticism, see literature below (p. 228, n. 7; p. 229, n. 13).

[12] The best explanation of the origin of the name is in D. Kurze, 'Die festländischen Lollarden', *AKG* xlvii (1965), pp. 48–76; for first official use of it against English heresy by Bishop Wakefield in August 1387, see *A Calendar of Henry Wakefield Bishop of Worcester 1375–95*, ed. W. P. Marett, Worcester Historical Society, n.s. vii (1972), pp. 150–2, a reference I owe to Professor R. M. Haines. The term was used in Oxford against academics by Henry Crumpe in 1382.

common concern; the ground for support was wider than the appeal of the Spiritual Franciscans could be, and lacked the alien, exotic quality in Catharism, ultimately repugnant to informed Western Christians. Three factors – the initial base in universities, the potential for gaining upper-class support and the wide appeal of their teachings – made the new evangelical heretics more dangerous to the papacy and hierarchy than any earlier movement.

And yet, although Wyclif and his fellows gave expression, often in radical form, to widespread discontents, and worked within an existing intellectual and spiritual tradition, to which they were deeply indebted, their teachings and heresies only struck deep root in two countries, England and Bohemia. Wyclifite and Hussite heresies of various kinds were disseminated, and found some echoes, in Scotland, France, Poland, Hungary, Austria and other German-speaking lands, even in Dalmatia, but provoked no long-lasting response. Lands earlier moved by heresy were, on this occasion, not especially fertile. The machinery of repression moved against the heretics; Wyclif, Hus and the rest formed only a section amongst the many voices raised in favour of reform; there were still deep reserves of feeling behind orthodox doctrine and traditional practice; there was no printing to spread heresy rapidly from one country to the next; precisely the factors which built up Hussitism in the lands of the Bohemian crown acted to cut back support in neighbouring countries. So there was no breakthrough for the new heresies. But still the Wyclif affair and the rise of Lollardy was a major event in English Church history, and the long Hussite crisis formed a turning-point in the Bohemian lands.

13

John Wyclif

England produced no significant heresy before the late fourteenth century. Orthodox movements, whether it was the developing interest in the canon law, the new monasticism of the twelfth century, or the orders of friars in the thirteenth, passed into England. Contacts with Europe culturally and ecclesiastically remained close. Commercial and economic links with the towns of Flanders, once a fertile ground for religious dissidence, remained active through the wool trade. Yet heresy from the Continent made no impact, and there was no native growth of it[1] before Wyclif fired an old store of combustible anticlericalism and untapped religious zeal in the late fourteenth century.

One reason for this lay in the tight-knit, close-governed nature of the English Church. By continental standards, the control of the ruler over the Church remained very close. The investiture controversy in England was a very brief one, and ended in a compromise that left the substance of power in the matter of appointment to high ecclesiastical office in the hands of the crown.

England was never the scene of the most spectacular scandals in appointments, which on the Continent were most often associated with areas of aristocratic dominance. Royal influence over episcopal appointments tended to be consistent with a fair standard, sometimes, indeed, a distinguished one, as the episcopate of the thirteenth century shows. Ecclesiastical abuse, that first stimulus to heresy, was not notably apparent in England before the fourteenth century. The Franciscans, whose decline on the Continent brought a new heresy to birth in the sect of the *fraticelli*, kept their

---

[1] For the rare exceptions, see below, p. 282.

purity and combined good life and learning longer in England than perhaps in any other province. Finally, the effective administration of the country kept a check on the ports, and care was taken to filter the ideas which might pass into the country. Cathars who came in from the Continent under Henry II were swiftly rounded up and sentenced.[2] In 1224 the first Franciscan missionaries were kept in Dover castle until they were able to prove their innocence of unorthodoxy.[3] Through the thirteenth century there is evident a care to supervise merchants from France and elsewhere who might be tainted with heresy.

By the latter half of the fourteenth century, the position of the Church had quietly and undramatically worsened. The episcopate was not unworthy, but it generally lacked the exceptional quality of the previous century. As in Europe generally, no new movement of note had arisen to fill the gap left by the decline of the friars as a source of the most disinterested zeal. There was still vitality in the religious scene, but it was a vitality that could easily lead away from orthodoxy. The English mystics, writing their treatises in the vernacular, making their own direct ascent to God, were no doubt read by few, but they may well be symptomatic of a wider feeling that was not fully content with the official channels of worship and organization. By the end of the century official sources were taking note of the existence of a new man, the literate layman; some action was taken to make a place for him, but not enough. The sermon literature of the time reveals the readiness of the churchmen to denounce abuses; it also reveals, by its repeated mention of abuses over the years, a failure to uproot them. Certain old failings remained throughout the later Middle Ages: an excess overall of clergy, an excess of ill-paid unbeneficed clergy who formed a reservoir of discontent, a monasticism that could not be fairly called decadent but had ceased to be a motive force, a certain canonists' petrefaction in the machinery of the Church, too formal in its procedures easily to allow reform to be effective.

Against this background the period of war strain and ineffectual government which followed on the renewal of the Hundred Years' War in 1369 becomes significant. The failures in the French war and the taxation necessary to pursue campaigns that were in fact beyond the powers of the English kingdom created a cry for disendowment. The size of ecclesiastical endowments gave obvious occasion to this agitation; it was made popular by the desire of the Commons to do something to shift a burden of taxation that, ineptly imposed, helped to spark off the Peasants' Revolt in 1381. Unconnected with reforms as it was, the agitation against the Church gave special opportunities to radical preachers. It favoured the mendicants, with their old complaints against the endowed possessioners, and it gave a brief popular platform to John Wyclif. It favoured anticlericalism, not specially strong in England, but at this time given an exceptional outlet by John of Gaunt and other soldiers and politicians. Ineffectual government in the dotage of Edward III and the minority of Richard II facilitated the rise of extremism and the struggles of factions, some of whom turned to attack the Church as part of their internal struggles.

[2] Above, p. 60.
[3] *Chronica de Lanercost*, ed. J. Stevenson (Edinburgh, 1839), p. 30. I owe the reference to Dr R. B. Brooke.

When a native heresy appeared and was carried rapidly about England, the Church was unprepared. Lack of familiarity with heresy inside the country cut off English churchmen from the developments that had led to the rise of the papal inquisition on the Continent. The inquisition came to England only in the one exceptional case of the Templars, and, once the alarm was raised, the episcopate adopted cumbersome procedures in an attempt to stamp out the infection. Though they achieved the essential task of preventing Lollardy from coming to power, they had neither the experience nor the personnel to prevent a rapid expansion of adherents on the eve of the Peasant's Revolt, or to cut the movement off totally in the aftermath of Oldcastle's revolt early in the fifteenth century. Orthodoxy was never able fully to erase the effects of the agitation of the 1370s and the years immediately following, in which Wyclif's heretical ideas were formulated and the first Lollard preachers began to spread their message along the roads of England. But, before we examine the origins of Lollardy proper, it will be necessary first of all to outline Wyclif's career, and attempt some answer to the long controversial question: why and how did Wyclif come to hold his heretical views?

THE DEVELOPMENT OF WYCLIF'S HERESY

Early career

No exact parallel to Wyclif's career can be found in the history of medieval heresies. His is a unique case of a university master turned heresiarch, who inspired a popular movement against the Church. A heresy charge was a recognized hazard in the intellectual contests of the Schools, and not necessarily of great import; deliberate defiance of the Church, such as Wyclif came to make in his last years, was another matter altogether. Two thinkers in the fourteenth century, Marsiglio of Padua and William of Ockham, had made such a defiance and developed lines of thought which show affinities to Wyclif's;[4] but neither is truly comparable. Ockham founded no movement – he joined the schism of Michael of Cesena and developed his views of the Church from the safety of Lewis of Bavaria's court at Munich, and his influence remained intellectual. The same is true of Marsiglio, an astonishingly secular-minded writer but a lone voice, political theorist rather than theologian, without a reputation or depth of learning like that of Wyclif. He too inspired no popular movement.

On the other side, the leaders or founders of popular heresies had not hitherto been men of intellectual standing. They had most frequently been preachers and agitators like Henry the Monk, Valdes or the dualist preachers of the twelfth century. Arnold of Brescia had an intellectual training, but his heresy owed all to his eloquence and powers of personal leadership.[5] Even Petrus Johannis Olivi offers no clear parallel, for, although he was of intellectual calibre to be mentioned in company with Wyclif and was

---

[4] Leff, *Heresy* II, pp. 411–44 *passim*, and 'The changing pattern of thought in the earlier fourteenth century', *BJRL* XLIII (1961), pp. 354–72; see Offler's comment on Leff's treatment of Ockham (*EHR* LXXXIV (1969), p. 574).

[5] Above, pp. 52–4.

the major inspiration of a popular heretical movement, he was in no sense the founder of the Spiritual Franciscans, which without him would certainly have existed, though they would have been less dangerous.[6]

Wyclif's heresy owed nothing to any pre-existing heretical movement. Its popular adherents, the English Lollards, came in the end to resemble the Waldensians, but they did so quite independently of any continental influence. They owed the germ of their beliefs, simplified and adapted as they were, to Wyclif himself. Wyclif's radical ideas were powerful enough to inspire a movement which outlasted persecution for over a hundred years, produced a literature of its own and a line of martyrs and devoted missionaries right up to the time of the Reformation, without their originator ever apparently having displayed any outstanding powers of personal leadership or even any very direct interest in the practicalities of building up a new religious group. The spontaneous incubation of so dangerous a heresy in intellectual authority, and the ambiguities of his relationship as a scholar with a movement of popular preachers, all lend special interest to the study of his life.

Wyclif was a product of the intellectual environment of Oxford, where by far the greater part of his life was passed, from the time of his entry to the university as a young man to his enforced departure at roughly fifty years of age in 1380.[7] His dabbling in politics in the 1370s took him away on occasional missions, and the last years of his life (after 1380) were spent in retirement in the rectory at Lutterworth. Otherwise he remained, in the usual and necessary fashion of the day, an absentee from the benefices whose revenues made possible his academic work at Oxford. His experience was very largely academic, and much less either pastoral or political.

Oxford marked him deeply, whether by direct influence or by provoking violent reactions. As a young man, he fell under the influence of the nominalism then fashionable, which had developed from the writings of William of Ockham and his school, and was marked by a mistrust of the power of reason to demonstrate the truths of faith.[8] Nominalism, and the scepticism and fideism which accompanied it, are fundamental for the understanding of the fourteenth-century intellectual scene, arousing deep conflicts, and opening the way for a series of radical or extremist thinkers to put forward their views. The anti-intellectual tone of moralists of the time and the development of the English school of mystics represent one kind of hostile reaction to this prevailing mode of thought;[9] the maturer Wyclif represents

[6] Above, pp. 192–3.

[7] H. B. Workman, *John Wyclif: A Study of the English Medieval Church* 1–11 (Oxford, 1926) is an old-style compendium still valuable for facts. A helpful survey of thought is in Leff, *Heresy* 11, pp. 494–558; a vital corrective to Workman on political side, frailer on religious aspect, is K. B. McFarlane, *John Wycliffe and the Beginnings of English Nonconformity* (London, 1952); see also M. J. Wilks, '*Reformatio regni*: Wyclif and Hus as leaders of religious protest movements', in *SCH* IX, pp. 109–30. I am indebted for the account of Wyclif here to Leff and, above all, to the illuminating article of B. Smalley, 'The Bible and eternity: John Wyclif's dilemma', *JWCI* xxvII (1964), pp. 73–89. I have also benefited from attendance at her unpublished lectures on Wyclif.

[8] 'Terminism' is felt by some historians to be a more accurate label. I have here used 'nominalism' simply because it is more familiar.

[9] Smalley, *JWCI* xxvII, p. 73.

another reaction. In place of the distrust of reason introduced by the nominalists, he put forward, as Beryl Smalley shows, what he saw as a better way of reasoning.[10]

A strong reaction against nominalism at Oxford was, in itself, nothing new. Both Bradwardine and Fitzralph, for example, had earlier written against this school.[11] Like Wyclif they were Augustinians. The major thinker, Bradwardine, attacked the Ockhamist school not without effect, and probably some of the philosophical realism he had defended survived in the background. He and Fitzralph provide occasional parallels to Wyclif, who came to admire them; he adapted one of his best known theses, on dominion and grace, from Fitzralph.[12] The work of Thomas Buckingham *c.*1350 shows that Bradwardine's great work against the nominalists, the *De causa Dei*, was still being discussed; this would make it natural for Wyclif to develop an interest in analogous problems. But when Wyclif's own metaphysical position had been fully formed and came under hostile criticism, no-one suggested that anyone else was responsible for it. His final position was too individual and idiosyncratic to have been borrowed: he had worked out an answer for himself, which differed drastically from the ideas of his youth.

From nominalism he swung round to the opposite extreme – to ultrarealism. Research has shown scattered through his writings, phrases in which he looks back on his past 'sophistries' in something of the same manner and tone that a spiritual writer might use in bewailing the sins of his youth.[13] The violence of the reaction was something analogous to a conversion, and he plainly had quasi-religious feelings about the philosophical position that he had come to adopt. Speaking of realism ('the knowledge of universals') he once said, 'A knowledge of universals is the pre-eminent step on the ladder of wisdom by which we search out hidden truth; and this, I believe, is the reason why God does not permit the school of universals utterly to fail.'[14] The element of personal conversion involved in the adoption of realism helps to explain the obstinacy with which he later clung to his metaphysics.

The intellectual environment of the Oxford in which he grew to maturity is a necessary background both for the high reputation he came to hold and for some of the idiosyncratic features of his thought. It is generally agreed that between *c.* 1350 and 1370, the time of his initiation into academic studies, there was a lack of outstanding thinkers.[15] Wyclif spoke contemptuously of the thinkers of his age, and looked back behind them to Bradwardine and Fitzralph, as we have seen, and still further to Grosseteste in the thirteenth century.[16] At the time his metaphysic was formed, he needed the discipline of

[10] Ibid.; note comparison between Plotinus and Wyclif. For summary of background, see pp. 73–7.

[11] J. A. Robson, *Wyclif and the Oxford Schools* (Cambridge, 1961), chs 2 and 3 (graceful introduction, fundamental for Wyclif's early philosophy); Fitzralph: below, p. 233, n. 37.

[12] A. Gwynn, *The English Austin Friars in the Time of Wyclif* (Oxford, 1940), pp. 35–59.

[13] Robson, *Wyclif*, p. 145, more forcefully by B. Smalley reviewing Robson (*MA* xxx (1961), p. 202) and *JWCI* xxvii, pp. 77–81; another view in M. J. Wilks, 'The early Oxford Wyclif: papalist or nominalist', *SCH* v, pp. 69–98.

[14] Smalley's translation (*JWCI* xxvii, p. 81); for text, see Robson, *Wyclif*, p. 154, n. 1.

[15] Robson, *Wyclif*, pp. 97–112, S. H. Thomson, in *Speculum* xxxviii (1963), pp. 497–9, J. M. Fletcher, in *HJ* lxi (1962–3), pp. 179–80.

[16] B. Smalley, 'The biblical scholar', in *Robert Grosseteste, Scholar and Bishop*, ed. D. A. Callus (Oxford, 1955), esp. pp. 70, 83, 95–7; Robson, *Wyclif*, pp. 26–9, 186, Smalley, in *MA* xxx, pp. 202–3.

effective controversy to check the extremism to which he was naturally prone[17] and he did not get it. Because of this relative vacuum of leading figures, he seemed to overpower his contemporaries. Those who later became his enemies witness to the great effect he had. Thomas Netter of Walden, whose *Doctrinale* was the most effective reply to Wyclif's academic supporters, said that at first he was 'astounded by his sweeping assertions, by the authorities cited, and by the vehemence of his reasoning'.[18]

But most of all, he influenced contemporaries because, in contrast to the sceptics, he offered certainty of knowledge. The example of Scripture may be taken to illustrate this. Wyclif was troubled that the sceptics were criticizing Scripture. An important quotation came from Augustine's *De doctrina Christiana*, 'Faith will waver if the authority of Holy Scripture should fail. If faith wavers, then charity weakens.'[19] It was nominalism which he felt was undermining faith in Scripture; already, he believed, the supporters of nominalism were leading the laity into error.[20] His answer flowed from a metaphysic based on the indestructibility of universals. Scripture became a divine exemplar conceived in the mind of God before creation, and before the material Scriptures were written down. Because it was a divine idea, every word of it was true, and every part as authoritative as the other.[21]

It was a bold thesis, which at first might seem to bowl over the opposition. Yet the certainty was purchased at a high price, and the philosophical position Wyclif adopted had unorthodox implications, notably on the eucharist. John Kenningham, who was in debate with Wyclif in 1372–4, had seen that Wyclif's ultrarealism made impossible an acceptance of the orthodox doctrine of transubstantiation, with its concomitant annihilation of substance. As Wyclif moved from philosophical to doctrinal works, the awkward consequences of his metaphysics became ever more apparent. William Woodford, the Franciscan, early perceived his problem on the eucharist.[22]

At an early phase of the development of his thought, Wyclif became involved in politics. His entry into royal service took place probably in either 1371 or 1372. In 1374 he was describing himself as 'in a special sense the king's clerk'.[23] The invitation came either from the Black Prince or John of Gaunt; in either case the motive was plain. Wyclif was already known for his anticlerical views, and he was being engaged because it was felt that his opinions on disendowment and the necessity of reform of the Church by the

---

[17] Leff, *Heresy* II, p. 500.

[18] Robson's translation (*Wyclif*, pp. 203–4).

[19] Smalley's translation, *JWCI* XXVII, p. 75; the original, ibid., n. 10, and in Wyclif's *De veritate sacrae scripturae*, ed. R. Buddensieg (WS), I, pp. 157–389.

[20] Smalley, *JWCI* XXVII, p. 77; the Middle English poem *Pearl* makes significant assumptions about the laity's interest in theology (Robson, *Wyclif*, p. 33).

[21] Robson, *Wyclif*, pp. 163–4. I am indebted to Professor M. Deanesly for showing me the importance of this.

[22] Leff, *Heresy* II, pp. 500–12, making the Kenningham affair basis for analysis. Note comment on Wyclif (p. 505): 'he had an inexhaustible supply of logical devices which hid an impoverished and inflexible mode of thought.' See Robson, *Wyclif*, pp. 162–70, Smalley, *JWCI* XXVII, pp. 86–7. For Wyclif on Scripture, see Leff, *Heresy* II, pp. 511–45. Leff, in 'The place of metaphysics in Wyclif's theology', *SCH* Subsidia V, p. 223, notes that the problem of Wyclif's philosophical position for transubstantiation is already apparent in the *De Universalibus*.

[23] Workman, *Wyclif* I, pp. 231–9; dating approximate.

State could be a useful counterweight to the more traditional views of clerical speakers.[24] Wyclif's known service was relatively limited. In 1371 he may have sat silent in parliament, while two Augustinian friars were arguing for the legitimacy of taxing the Church's wealth in time of war – the evidence is uncertain;[25] in 1374 he was a diplomatic agent in negotiations with the papacy; in 1377 he gave an opinion in the government interest on the export of bullion to Avignon; and in 1378 he defended, in effect, the actions of royal servants in a *cause célèbre* on the violation of sanctuary.[26] But these episodes had an importance out of proportion to their intrinsic weight, for they secured to Wyclif the protection of great men, who headed off ecclesiastical authority's attempts to silence him. In two hearings, one in St Paul's in 1377, the other in Lambeth palace chapel in 1378, when the bishops tried to take action, the protection, first of John of Gaunt, then of the Black Prince's widow, was decisive.[27]

The residual loyalty of Wyclif's former employers, together with the effect of the Great Schism on the freedom of papal action, preserved Wyclif from any personal judicial proceedings in the last years of his life, thus enabling him to produce his most radical treatises. Royal service coincided roughly with the time in which his interests turned to the doctrine of the Church. In the *Postilla super totam bibliam* (finished 1375–6), he can be seen stressing the poverty and humility of the early Church, and beginning to use Scripture as a standard of criticism for the Church of his own time.[28] The need for poverty is again stressed, though still with moderation, in the *De civili dominio* (1376–8).[29] By the time we reach the *De ecclesia* (1378) Wyclif is defending a quite revolutionary doctrine of the Church which would overturn the established order.[30] This was the year of decision in his work as well as the year of the Great Schism.

It is difficult to think that there was no interaction between the two sides of his career. When Wyclif put himself in the service of anticlerical politicians,[31] he could think, however unrealistically, that he was helping to hasten the time when the State would bring about the reform of the Church by force according to his own prescriptions. At the same time, the effects of this experience

[24] McFarlane, *Wycliffe*, pp. 58–60.

[25] The late Mr J. W. Sherborne drew my attention to an ambiguity on this point.

[26] Workman, *Wyclif* I, pp. 240–6, 302–4, 313–24; perspective in McFarlane, *Wycliffe*, chs 2 and 3; see esp. his summary on Wyclif's motives, pp. 84–5.

[27] Workman, *Wyclif* I, pp. 284–8, 307–9.

[28] B. Smalley, 'Wyclif's Postilla on the Old Testament and his Principium', in *Oxford Studies presented to Daniel Callus* (Oxford, 1964) Oxford Historical Society, n.s. XVI, for 1959–60, pp. 253–97, and analysis in G. A. Benrath, *Wyclifs Bibelkommentar* (Berlin, 1966); review: J. Crompton, in *JEH* XVIII (1967), pp. 263–6.

[29] Workman, *Wyclif* I, pp. 257–66; Leff, *Heresy* II, pp. 529–30. See below, p. 237, n. 52.

[30] Workman, *Wyclif* I pp. 6–20; challenge of his ecclesiology best seen in Leff, *Heresy* II, 516–45.

[31] His biographers deprecate this, Workman mildly (*Wyclif* I, p. 279; cf. p. 282), McFarlane more fiercely (*Wycliffe*, p. 70). Both quote the chronicler's phrase, 'running about from church to church', on his preaching in the London diocese in the autumn of 1376 (see T. Walsingham, *Chronicon Angliae*, ed. E. M. Thompson (RS, London, 1876), pp. 115–16; McFarlane's dating); McFarlane believes that in this he was acting the part of Gaunt's 'clerical hireling', by stirring up public opinion against his enemy William of Wykeham, then bishop of London. Benrath (*Bibelkommentar*, p. 336, n. 137) sounds a warning against this interpretation. The chronicler is not favourable to Wyclif. If W. Mallard's dating is correct (*MH* XVII (1966), p. 99), we have six examples of sermons from the autumn of 1376, concerned with moral and spiritual instruction or a movement of renewal in the Church. They are not aimed at Wykeham.

together with the increasing pressure of controversy as the true nature of his views became apparent, helped to make him more bitter and violent. From 1378, the tone of his works tended to change for the worse; he was inclined to quote himself more, and abuse his enemies more violently; his theology becomes more radical, and his denunciations more repetitive. Personal disappointment may have played a part in the sharpening of his attacks on the Church and contemporary churchmen. Certainly he could have hoped for more than he got from his high patrons, and we can readily understand the violence of his attacks on the endowed monastic orders when we examine the case of Canterbury Hall, intended to put monks and seculars into one foundation of which he was appointed warden. He actually occupied the post for two years, only to find himself turned out by a monk archbishop of Canterbury in 1367.[32]

Yet personal experience was no more than a contributory factor. His doctrine of the Church was closely allied to his metaphysics. An early citation may suggest how his view of the Church was influenced by his ultrarealism. He wrote, 'I consider that the Church ordains nothing, unless there is an underlying reason; on account of which there is rational cause that it *is* so before it be ordained by man.'[33] So clearly did he have the archetypal reality of the Church before his eyes that he came to reject in its favour the visible Church of the fourteenth century.[34] Just as in the case of Scripture, the Church had existed from eternity; Wyclif denied the doctrine that it had come into being with the incarnation. In comparison with this eternal Church, the visible Church steadily lost authority in Wyclif's writings till it became in the end simply the dwelling of Antichrist. An adaptation of the Augustinian doctrine of predestination had the effect of voiding the visible Church of authority. Elect and foreknown were rigidly divided in this world. The elect were immune from the consequences of mortal sin: their grace of predestination stood, even with mortal sin. Conversely, the ministrations of the foreknown, however high they stood in the ecclesiastical hierarchy, were void of effect. The result was to remove the necessity of a priesthood, since every one of the elect was necessarily more priest than layman as a member of the Church.[35]

The heretical implications of Wyclif's doctrine need no underlining. Nor does the breach with traditional teaching in his doctrine of Scripture. He never made the text of the Bible alone the standard of judgement for all

---

[32] Workman, *Wyclif* I, pp. 171–94; McFarlane, *Wycliffe*, pp. 27–30. The decision against Wyclif was taken in 1367; he was finally deprived by 1371.

[33] Smalley's translation is in *JWCI* XXVII, p. 83; text, amended by her, in footnote.

[34] See esp. Leff, *Heresy* II, pp. 515–16; on the external factors in Wyclif's progression to heresy, see p. 499.

[35] On the vital importance of metaphysics for Wyclif's view of the Church, see Leff, *Heresy* II, p. 511; analogous stress for doctrine of Scripture is in Benrath, *Bibelkommentar*, ch. 5; Leff, *SCH* Subsidia V, pp. 217–32, notes that 'there is an undeniable discontinuity in his intellectual development which cannot be explained simply by an appeal to intellectual criteria' and refers to the censure of articles from *De civili dominio* by the pope in 1377 as the 'immediately obvious candidate' among non-intellectual factors influencing the discontinuity (p. 218). He withdraws some earlier views in the light of the publication of Wyclif's *De Universalibus* but observes (p. 232) that while each of his positions was founded 'in contemporary attitudes or traditional doctrine', their ultimate effect was the 'rejection of traditional doctrine over the central truths concerning the nature of the Church, the role of the Bible, and the eucharist'.

doctrine and conduct, for he always retained the need for an established interpreter – the Fathers – as a shield against heresy, above all Augustine.[36] But towards the end of his life, he did come to say that everything that was not in Scripture directly or by implication was Antichrist, and in practice Scripture more and more came to be an exclusive measuring-rod.

This attitude amounted to a radical innovation, for fourteenth-century theologians had not made a distinction between Scripture, tradition and the laws of the Church, which were understood to harmonize. Thomas Netter of Walden perceived this when he said, 'What chiefly fills me with dismay is that Wyclif in all his proofs halves the Christian faith: he accepts, so he pretends, the faith of Scripture; but beyond the written faith he disregards and sets aside that faith of the whole church which Christ and also Paul the Apostle handed down, though not in writing.'[37]

As for the Church of Wyclif's day, by his death it had been stripped in his writings of all claim to belief. It had been stigmatized as the Church of Antichrist; the hierarchy had been rejected; the papacy, subjected to an historical analysis, had been shown to have no justification. In detail, Scripture properly interpreted and described as 'God's law', had replaced canon law. Monastic life of every kind had been rejected as unfruitful: disendowment was to provide a basis for reforms, a class of preaching clergy. In an extraordinary demolition of the assumptions of the medieval Church, Wyclif took away the functions of monks and friars; the contemplative life and the monastic liturgy was useless.[38]

The indestructibility of universals and the consequences which Wyclif drew from it also involved him from early days in an inconsistency – he could not both accept transubstantiation and maintain his metaphysics. In Kenningham's time he had evaded the issue; it remained an unsolved question till 1379, when, with the publication of *De apostasia* and *De eucharistia*, he denied the doctrine held by the Church. It was a deeply emotional issue, one on which, it has been lately argued, Wyclif was influenced as much or more by scandal at contemporary eucharistic practice and its consequences as by his awkward philosophical position. He was not at ease in his teaching. He disliked what he interpreted as idolatry in the reaction to the elevation of the Host at mass or to the Corpus Christi processions, and he came to refer to transubstantiation as a 'harmful transaction'. It involved a doctrine marked by hypocrisy, postulating appearance without reality. He made clear his

[36] On Wyclif's use of Scripture as an authority, M. Deanesly, *The Significance of the Lollard Bible* (London, 1951); P. De Vooght, *Les Sources de la doctrine chrétienne d'après les théologiens du xive siècle et du debut du xve* (Paris, 1954) (a defence of Wyclif); M. Hurley, '"Scriptura Sola": Wyclif and his critics', *Traditio* xvi (1960), pp. 275–352; reissued separately (New York, 1960) (corrects De Vooght); review by B. Smalley, in *EHR* lxxviii (1963), pp. 161–2 (best short summary).

[37] Quoted by Hurley, in *Traditio* xvi (1960), p. 329. Note comment on Fitzralph and *sola scriptura* in K. Walsh, 'Preaching, pastoral care and *sola scriptura* in later medieval Ireland: Richard Fitzralph and the use of the Bible', *SCH* Subsidia iv, pp. 251–68. See also on the role of Fitzralph, K. Walsh, 'Wyclif's legacy in Central Europe in the late fourteenth and early fifteenth centuries', *SCH* Subsidia v, pp. 397–417 at pp. 398–9.

[38] Leff, *Heresy* ii, pp. 534–41; Workman, *Wyclif* ii, pp. 73–82 (stresses effects of schism and Spenser's crusade); McFarlane, *Wycliffe*, p. 95; for monasticism, see T. Renna, 'Wyclif's attacks on monks', *SCH* Subsidia v, pp. 267–80.

opposition to the annihilation of substance, but he arrived at no final definition of his own, even, it seems, altering his position in the very last years of his life. It was an emotional topic because he cared deeply about the sacrament.[39]

The eucharistic heresy had great historical importance because it led to the parting of the ways with the last of the Oxford supporters outside his own proto-Lollard group, and to his departure from Oxford. In mid-winter 1380–1, the chancellor, William Barton, one of Wyclif's opponents, summoned a commission of twelve doctors, which by a narrow majority condemned his eucharistic views. There is no ground for thinking that the commission was packed or manipulated by outside ecclesiastical authority: it fairly represented a growing disquiet within the university about the development of Wyclif's views.[40] It mattered more than the condemnation of the theses on dominion and disendowment sent to Gregory XI at Avignon in 1377, for the beginning of the Great Schism in the following year eliminated the papacy's further interest, and on these issues Wyclif knew he could count on the support of his lay patrons as well as some academics. On the eucharist he lacked support. Disquiet about his eucharistic beliefs affected the Commons in the parliament of 1381 and alienated John of Gaunt. When in the *Confession* of May 1381 he reiterated his denial of transubstantiation he was defying both his fellows and some supporters. In the same year he withdrew from the university and retired to the rectory at Lutterworth. The eucharist controversy was not dampened; tension rose as Wyclif's views were promulgated in the vernacular by his followers to a wider audience. The doctrine of the mass was especially sensitive; orthodox vernacular instruction on the eucharist eschewed any resort to detailed explanation; the philosophical terms of scholastic debate on the subject, *transubstancio, substancia, accidens*, had not been translated. The convention was that such matters were not to be ventilated before the laity. Netter summed up the traditional view when he said, 'In the affairs of the faith, skilled spiritual men are said to understand: the rest of the people only simply to believe.' The alarm and hostility of authority was demonstrated by their moves to give publicity to the repudiation of Wyclif and confirmation of the doctrine of transubstantiation.[41]

Wyclif and Lollardy

Wyclif had kept university supporters surprisingly late. There were a number of reasons why he should have had a strong influence. The most important has

[39] Robson, *Wyclif*, pp. 187–95; Leff, *Heresy* II, pp. 549–57; M. E. Aston, 'John Wycliffe's Reformation reputation', *PP* xxx (1965), pp. 40–1, for contrast between Wyclif's views on the eucharist and the Reformers' notion of them; Crompton's summary in *JEH* XVIII (1967) p. 263–6; important discussion by Catto in *SCH* Subsidia IV, pp. 269–86. A. Kenny, 'Wyclif', *PBA* LXXVI (1990), pp. 91–113, discusses Wyclif's philosophy and the eucharist at pp. 102–4 (helpful quotations).

[40] McFarlane, *Wycliffe*, pp. 97–9, corrects Workman, *Wyclif* II, pp. 140–8; note also Leff's summary (*Heresy* II, p. 554, n. 8) on Workman's treatment earlier (pp. 30–41) of Wyclif's eucharistic doctrine.

[41] On the role of dominion theory, see Workman, *Wyclif* II, pp. 292–9; McFarlane, *Wycliffe*, pp. 79–81; for place of English Benedictines in stimulating papal intervention, see D. Knowles, *Religious Orders* II, pp. 98ff.; on eucharist and vernacular, see M. E. Aston, 'Wyclif and the vernacular', *SCH* Subsidia V, pp. 281–330; quotation from Netter, p. 302 (*Doctrinale* II, cap. 44, col. 277); penetrating comments: pp. 299–300; publicity of followers in London: below, p. 246.

already been mentioned: in an age when the fashion in theology was doubt, he offered certainties. He was a bold dialectician and an able debater. His use of Scripture and the completion of his *Postilla super totam bibliam* in 1375-6 helped to bring back the Bible to the centre of studies. His anti-intellectual and Christocentric piety, the appeal for reform and the denunciation of abuses, all corresponded to strands of contemporary thinking, and could call forth suitable echoes.[42] For the arts faculty, in their conflicts with law, he would gain popularity by his trenchant attacks on canon law.[43] His stress on the need for poverty in the Church and his attacks on the possessioner orders made him a natural ally of the friars, above all the Augustinians, who kept on terms with him longer than any other group. In 1377 four doctors from the mendicant friars were ready to defend Wyclif in St Paul's.[44] An Augustinian, Adam Stocton, described Wyclif on his copy of the *De potestate papae* as *venerabilis doctor*; only later was this crossed off in favour of *execrabilis seductor*.[45] It was only with the eucharistic heresy that he was abandoned by the friars.

Finally, Wyclif in his ultrarealism was in the van of a European movement of reaction against early fourteenth-century nominalism. This kept alive a respect for him independent of his late heresies, evidenced for us, for instance, in the acephalous and anonymous manuscripts in which his philosophical works were being collected in Oxford in the fifteenth century, or the reaction by university masters to Arundel's heavy-handed visitation in 1411; they were clearly not Wyclifites, but nevertheless valued university independence and thought Wyclif's views might still be at least the subject of argument.[46] The reputation of Wyclif was accepted in some surprising quarters. Archbishop Arundel himself acknowledged the justice of the Lollard William Thorpe's remarks when he was standing trial in 1407. 'Sir,' Thorpe said, 'Master John Wycliffe was holden of full many men the greatest Clerk that they knew then living; and therewith he was named a passing ruely [virtuous] man, and an innocent in his living.' Arundel acknowledged that, 'Wyclif your author [founder] was a great Clerk', and that 'many men held him a perfect liver.'[47]

This reputation drew essential support for the heresy. As the condemnations of Wyclif's work became effective, particularly after the Blackfriars Council of 1382 and Courtenay's visitation of Oxford, the more superficial supporters in the

---

[42] Benrath, *Bibelkommentar*; Crompton in *JEH* XVIII (1967), pp. 263–6; De Vooght (*Sources*) notices how much more Wyclif quotes Scripture than was usual among contemporary commentators; see the discussion (favourable to Wyclif) on pp. 168–200.

[43] J. Fines, 'Studies in the Lollard heresy' (unpublished Ph.D. thesis, University of Sheffield, 1964), pp. 18–19. I am indebted to the author for generously allowing me to use his thesis.

[44] Workman, *Wyclif* I, p. 286; McFarlane, *Wycliffe*, pp. 74–5.

[45] Gwynn, *Austin Friars*, pp. 238–9. J. E. Crompton (*JEH* XII (1961), p. 163) warns against considering the Carmelites generally as *quondam* allies.

[46] Robson, *Wyclif*, pp. 240–6; review by J. M. Fletcher in *HJ* LXI (1962–3), pp. 179–80; E. F. Jacob, 'Reynold Pecock, Bishop of Chichester', *PBA* XXXVII (1951), pp. 121–53; J. Catto, 'Some English manuscripts of Wyclif's Latin works', *SCH* Subsidia V, pp. 353–9, discusses the existence of scholars, not necessarily linked to Lollardy or Hussitism, who continued to be interested in Wyclif's logical, philosophical or polemical works.

[47] Quoted by McFarlane, *Wycliffe*, p. 35, from Thorpe's *Examinacion* (*STC* 24045); modern edn by H. Christmas for Parker Soc. (Cambridge, 1849); see A. W. Pollard, *Fifteenth-Century Prose and Verse* (London, 1903), pp. 118–20, and J. Fines, 'William Thorpe: an early Lollard', *History Today* XVIII (1968), pp. 495–503.

university fell away.[48] But a distinguished and controversial career had gathered enough varied strands of patronage and interest for a residue of scholars to remain committed supporters. The existence of this circle was vital to the development of English Lollardy, for it provided the popularizers who mediated Wyclif's thought to a wider public.

Vital, too, were Wyclif's views on the relations between Church and State and the necessity for some measure of ecclesiastical disendowment, for it was obviously these which attracted the attention of great men, involved him in politics and gave him a wider public notoriety. Wyclif's remedy for the abuses of the Church lay in forcible reform by the secular power. The low moral standards of the Church were, he believed, caused by an excess of property – the State would help to bring about change by some measure of disappropriation. The clergy would be left a sufficiency. Tithes they might have, since they were permitted by the Old Testament; but even this concession was subject to good behaviour – they could be withheld by parishioners from a sinful clergy.[49]

As early as 1370–1 Wyclif had been expressing his ideas on possession; but it was not until the *De civili dominio* of 1376–8 that he put them in written form.[50] A doctrine of dominion and grace such as he developed there had a considerable lineage. It had once been used in an ultramontane sense by the Augustinian Giles of Rome, who had argued that dominion could only be justly held through the Roman Church; all outside it, heathen or excommunicate, forfeited thereby lawful rights of possession and authority. Fitzralph turned the argument against the friars, his *bêtes noires*, by arguing more generally that all rights of authority and possession derived from God, and were thus dependent on the holder being in a state of grace; the friars, who were not, thus did not justly exercise the rights which they held within the Church. Wyclif simply took over this argument, and developed it to cover the whole Church. It linked, of course, with his fierce attacks on clerical abuses: plainly many of the clergy were not in a state of grace, could not justly hold dominion, and might be deprived of their possessions. As a theory, it obviously commended itself to lay lords who, in a time of unsuccessful war and weak government finance, were seeking for some new means of financing the war effort. Wyclif attracted interest because of the virtually uninhibited place he gave to the secular power as disappropriators and reformers of the Church.

At first sight the theory of dominion and grace might seem to have dangerous and anarchical implications for lay lords as well as churchmen. Might they not also fail to be in the state of grace necessary to hold lawful dominion, and might they not also be open to disappropriation? In practice, that awkward conclusion did not have to be drawn: in the *De officio regis* (1379)

---

[48] McFarlane, *Wycliffe*, pp. 106–15; Workman, *Wyclif* II, pp. 246–93.

[49] For Wyclif's attitude to property and government, see M. E. Aston, 'Lollardy and sedition, 1381–1431', *PP* XVII (1960), pp. 1–44; Leff, *Heresy* II, pp. 527–31; Smalley, *JWCI* XXVII, pp. 87–9. Wyclif's doctrine on the conditional nature of the clergy's right to tithes was among the Twenty-four Conclusions condemned in 1382; see Leff's comment (*Heresy* II, p. 529). I am indebted to Mrs Aston for answering my queries.

[50] McFarlane, *Wycliffe*, p. 60; relation to predecessors in Gwynn, *Austin Friars*, pp. 59–73.

Wyclif provided an answer in his thorough-going Erastianism. The king was God's vicar. He and secular lords could not lawfully be resisted. Even tyrants must be accepted. Sin did not invalidate their authority – only that of churchmen.[51]

It is now becoming clearer that the doctrine of dominion and grace, which became so famous in Wyclifian historiography, never had the importance that older writers tended to give it in the structure of Wyclif's thought. It was overshadowed by the much more fundamental attack on the authority of the visible Church contained in Wyclif's predestinarian views and in the consequences he drew from them.[52] Yet its historical importance was considerable.

One of the first to be alarmed by Wyclif's views were the monks, a prime target in the attack on Church wealth. It was they who early engaged Wyclif in controversy on this subject, and it was they who sent propositions from the *De civili dominio* to Avignon to be censored by the pope in 1377.[53] Amongst the views which Gregory XI condemned were opinions which appeared to put all civil dominion into uncertainty, and thus affected lay lords as well.[54] When other controversialists took up their pen against Wyclif and the Lollards, they were naturally not slow to point out the dangers of anarchy for the secular power, which, as they saw it, were embedded in the doctrine of dominion and grace; William Woodford the Franciscan, for example, argued that the upshot of Wyclif's views on dominion was that he legitimized a popular disappropriation of 'kings, dukes and their lay superiors whenever they habitually offended'.[55]

This was to misunderstand Wyclif. When the peasants in 1381 did engage in forcible disappropriation, they earned Wyclif's firm condemnation in the *De blasphemia*, together with a note that the overtaxing which had caused the revolt would not have been necessary if his remedy of a measure of ecclesiastical disendowment by the State had been put into practice.[56] Wyclif never lost faith in lay lords as potential reformers and thus, somewhat oddly, at the end of his life combined a stark ecclesiastical egalitarianism with a profound belief in the just authority of the civil power. In his scheme of things, a sinful pope might be deposed, a sinful or tyrannous king not; the orders of society remained sacrosanct. In secular politics, Wyclif remained profoundly conservative; in ecclesiastical matters he became a near anarchist. This juxtaposition of viewpoints might well be criticized as unrealistic, for few would agree that the abuses of the late fourteenth century sprang so exclusively from the ecclesiastical side.[57]

---

[51] Description of *De officio regis* in Workman, *Wyclif* II, pp. 20–30; on significance, see Leff, *Heresy* II, pp. 543–5.

[52] I follow Leff, *Heresy* II, pp. 546–9. He differs from M. J. Wilks, 'Predestination, property and power: Wyclif's theory of dominion and grace', in *SCH* II, pp. 220–36 (see Leff, II, p. 546, n. 2). Yet both dethrone the doctrine of dominion from its former position within the totality of Wyclif's beliefs. Contrast Workman, *Wyclif* I, pp. 262–3.

[53] Above, p. 234, n. 41.

[54] Texts in Workman, *Wyclif* I, p. 293, n. 5. For Lollard sources generally, see *FZ*; and for account of origins, J. Crompton, 'Fasciculi Zizaniorum', *JEH* XII (1961), pp. 35–45, 155–66.

[55] Aston, *PP* XVII, p. 9.

[56] Ibid., pp. 3, 36, n. 5.

[57] See Smalley's comment, in *JWCI* XXVII, p. 88.

Wyclif's ideas on disendowment drew him into political affairs, and seemed for a moment to open the way to reform on the lines he desired: in the event, the checks in Wyclif's writings against civil anarchy tended to be forgotten, as circumstances, the actions of some of his followers, the fortuitous event of the Peasants' Revolt, and the skill of his opponents all combined to give him and the movement he inspired the reputation of being political anarchists [58]

Yet while Wyclif was losing support among the upper classes and in the universities, the movement of preachers was already getting under way; this carried his beliefs to a wider public, and partially compensated for these losses by embedding Lollardy among a section of the artisan class. Wyclif's connection with this process of evangelization is not well recorded. We know relatively little of his life once the breach with Oxford had been made. At Lutterworth he had as companion his secretary, John Purvey.[59] We can infer from the unbroken flow of controversial Latin treatises in his last years that he spent much of his time writing. These works break no new ground: they continue to spell out, with increasing acrimony and radicalism after he had lost all official support including that of the friars, the implications of his doctrines of Scripture, the Church and the eucharist.[60]

A host of vernacular treatises was once attributed to him,[61] and, although the majority must stem from the hands of his followers, a case still remains for some being written by him personally. A vernacular literature was a natural outflow from his ideas on the supremacy of Scripture, the necessity for the laity to set in hand reform, and his long-term pastoral concern. When wrestling with the grave problem of the eucharist, he showed a repeated concern for the way in which the laity regarded the mystery of the mass, and an impatience with the use of Latin terms which had no scriptural warrant to explain it. He threatened to publish his views to the people as early as 1380, and it is likely that he did so. Together with his followers, he broke a barrier on discussion of theology in the vernacular; Wyclifites, it has been pointed out, were responsible for an injection into the English language of technical terms hitherto unknown so as to deal with the doctrine of transubstantiation.

[58] Aston, *PP* XVII, p. 5.

[59] M. Deanesly, *The Lollard Bible and Other Medieval Biblical Versions* (Cambridge, 1920) (still best general survey on popular attitudes to Bible reading; ch. 9, pp. 225–51, on Wyclif as instigator of a vernacular Bible; value also for Lollard history (1384–1408), if read beside McFarlane); see esp. her reflections on his recantation, pp. 283–5; pungent comment in McFarlane, *Wycliffe*, pp. 119–20, 152–3; correction is needed of Deanesly on treatises attributed to Purvey (see below, p. 246, n. 7); for Purvey's apparently quite radical views, see A. Hudson, *The Premature Reformation* (Oxford, 1988), pp. 159, 174, 242, 292, 301, 325, 327, 333, 340, 353, 355, 364, 385.

[60] McFarlane, *Wycliffe*, p. 118; Workman, *Wyclif* II, p. 307; Smalley, *JWCI* XXVII, pp. 73–89.

[61] *Select English Works of Wyclif*, ed. R. Arnold, I–III (Oxford, 1869–71); *The English Works of Wyclif hitherto unprinted*, ed. F. D. Matthew (London, 1880) EETS, o.s. LXXIV; *Wyclif: Select English Writings*, ed. H. E. Winn (Oxford, 1929); attributions: M. Aston, '"Caim's Castles": poverty, politics and disendowment', *The Church, Politics and Patronage in the Fifteenth Century*, ed. R. B. Dobson (Gloucester, 1984), pp. 45–81; 'Wyclif and the vernacular', *SCH* Subsidia V, pp. 281–330, at pp. 320–6; Aston on the *Wicket*, *PP* XXX (1965), p. 40 and n. 40, shows how one Lollard work, which differs in its thinking from Wyclif, may yet have 'parallels from Wyclif's Latin works for certain of its arguments'. A major work of research on the interrelations between Latin works, and between Latin and the vernacular, remains to be done (Aston in *SCH* Subsidia V, pp. 284–5). See comments by A. Hudson, 'A Lollard compilation and the dissemination of Wyclifite thought', *JTS* XXIII (1972), pp. 65–81.

He was not wholly consistent; in one of his last works, the *Opus evangelicum*, he issued a caveat against the ventilation of theological problems before the common people;[62] there is even a whisper of some kind of mild accommodation with authority at the end of his life. He repeatedly submitted his works to correction, more as a challenge to his opponents to pick holes if they could; at the end there was less defiance.[63] It did not matter: the crucial opening to the vernacular had been made. The greatest achievement of these years was the vernacular translation of the Bible. That, too, was a natural outcome of Wyclif's doctrinal position. If the visible Church had lost its authority to mediate salvation to the people, then the word of God, properly interpreted, was the one remaining certainty.[64] The novel relationship set up by Wyclif between Bible and Church demanded wider access to the Scriptures. If it was God's law, which should be asserted over the accretions of canon law that had usurped its place, then it should be known to those, clergy or laity, who had the duty of seeing that it was observed in England. The reform Wyclif envisaged was to take place on the basis of Scripture; it should then be known to the secular powers, who were to compel the clergy to reform, and to those elements among the existing clergy who were ready to heed the call to repent. Hence the phrases which occur in the *Opus evangelicum*, arguing that there was 'no man so rude a scholar but that he may learn the words of the gospel according to his simplicity';[65] or earlier, in the *De veritate sacrae scripturae*, that 'all Christians, especially secular lords, ought to know and defend the holy scriptures'.[66] He stresses the guidance of the Holy Spirit on those of good life, but not necessarily of much learning, who seek to understand.[67] In thoughts such as these lay a starting-point for later Lollard thinking.

The first translation, however, did not go so far. It was a painfully literal crib of the Vulgate, with past participles rendered direct into English and a

[62] Smalley, in *MA* xxx (1961), p. 203, comparing *Johannis Wyclif De ente: librorum duorum excerpta*, ed. M. H. Dziewicki (WS, London, 1909), p. 131, with *Opus evangelicum*, ed. J. Loserth, I (WS, London, 1895), p. 367; original phraseology in Robson, *Wyclif*, p. 217; contrasted with Valdes in Deanesly, *Lollard Bible*, p. 245. On the practicability of Wyclif's position in his last year, note Smalley's comment: 'By that time he resembled a man who sets fire to a skyscraper and hopes that only the right people will notice.'

[63] Aston in *SCH* Subsidia v, pp. 325–8; on eucharist and vernacular, ibid., pp. 291–330; note illuminating comment on authority's lack of comprehension of the menace of vernacular writings, as opposed to preaching, pp. 288–9; Hudson's view: p. 290, n. 22.

[64] Leff, *Heresy* II, ch. 7; see esp. p. 524. A. Kenny, 'Wyclif', *PBA* LXXVI (1990), pp. 91–113, argues at p. 106 for Wyclif's direct participation in translation; Aston, in *SCH* Subsidia v, p. 284, is cautious on Wyclif's responsibility.

[65] Ed. J. Loserth, I, p. 92; tr. Deanesly, *Lollard Bible*, p. 246. Other work on the Lollard Bible is in S. L. Fristedt, *The Wycliffe Bible* I (Stockholm, 1953); review: L. Muir in *Speculum* XXXIII (1958); comments: C. Lindberg in *MS Bodley 959: Genesis–Baruch 3.20 in the Earlier Version of the Wycliffite Bible* (Stockholm, 1959–73), 6 vols. Developing hypotheses are in the introductory notes to each of Lindberg's volumes, with conclusions in the fifth (1969): authorship: pp. 90–7; summary: pp. 97–8. A further summary is given in the final volume (pp. 66–70). I am indebted to Dr A. B. Cottle for drawing my attention to this work. On commentaries, there is H. Hargreaves, 'The marginal glosses to the Wycliffite New Testament', *Studia Neophilologica* XXIII (1961), pp. 285–300. Fristedt, *Wycliffe Bible* II (1969), edits the Latin text and English translation of a treatise by Augustine of Hippo (*De salutaribus documentis*) to demonstrate the principles of translation adopted in revising the EV and argues vigorously for Wyclif's participation; see I and II, bibliography.

[66] Ed. R. Buddensieg, I (WS, London, 1905), p. 136; tr. Deanesly, *Lollard Bible*, p. 243.

[67] See esp. tr. from *De veritate sacrae scripturae* (Workman, *Wyclif* II, p. 151).

Latin word-order imposed rigidly on the English sentence.[68] It was not intended for indiscriminate dissemination; one purpose may well have been to aid preachers who, basing themselves on the scriptural text on Wyclifite principles, would need to read out translations in their sermons. A translation of the whole Bible would give them a work of reference. Elements of Latin they might already possess; a crib to the Vulgate would be an ideal aid for them. More ambitiously, the translation could serve in a lord's household, where the newly literate upper-class laity might read the text and expound it to their subordinates.[69] The literalness of the version expressed a continuing reverence for the Vulgate; if the written Scripture expressed God's Word, then it might be dangerous to make free with the word sequence. Moreover, a rigid following of the Latin word-order facilitated the insertion of glosses phrase by phrase in a similar fashion to Richard Rolle's orthodox translation of the Psalter.[70]

Versions of the Bible for the laity were not wholly unprecedented. Certain vernacular versions existed in orthodox circles in various European countries, intended for the use only of rulers and the highest nobility. Wyclif cited them in defence of English translations. If Anne of Bohemia could have versions in Czech and German, he argued, then why were English versions to be judged heretical?[71] The precedent was only a partial one, for these Bibles circulated in a highly restricted milieu, where every check existed against misunderstandings of the text. They were expensive devotional toys. Even the first Wyclifite version would have had a wider diffusion. Copies were multiplied, and could be expected to pass freely into the hands of well-disposed laity at a level below that of the court circle. Moreover the Early Version was gradually modified in the direction of a greater fluency. The translators worked methodically on, it seems, from Old Testament to New, and even the Early Version had gained in

---

[68] Compare the Vulgate of Gen. 1:3 ('Dixitque deus, fiat lux, et facta est lux') with the translation in MS Bodley 959 ('And God said/be made light/And made is light') (spelling modernized) (Lindberg, *MS Bodley 959*; see p. 74). For this early version, see *The Holy Bible . . . in the Earliest English Versions*, ed. J. Forshall and F. Madden (Oxford, 1850); the edn is criticized by Fristedt (*Wycliffe Bible* I), who notes that they left over eighty MSS uncollated, and argues that they have not arrived at the ultimate originals of either EV or LV. His work is followed up by Lindberg in his edn of MS Bodley 959, the incomplete copy of the OT in the EV which ends at Baruch 3: 20, and argues that this MS of *c.*1400 represents the earliest extant version, in fact an original copy of an English prototype, both being revised and corrected. Fristedt suggested that the regular use of northern and north-west midland dialect in some of the earliest MSS, and especially the treatment of the Yorkshire 'and(e)', revealed Wyclif's hand in correction, and possibly also in tr. of EV. Lindberg rejects this, believing that, though Wyclif, with or without helpers, did translate the NT, the dialect mixture in MS Bodley 959 points to Nicholas of Hereford as the supervisor of the OT translation, and its crudities of translation exclude the possibility of Wyclif's direct participation. S. L. Fristedt, 'The dating of the earliest manuscript of the Wycliffite Bible', in *Stockholm Studies in Modern Philology*, n.s. 1 (Stockholm, 1960), pp. 79–85 at p. 80, suggests that Hereford's origins were in Yorkshire. The same writer gives a polemical discussion at pp. xlvii–lxvii of volume two of his *Wycliffe Bible*; Hudson, *Premature Reformation*, p. 242, with more Lindberg references, rejects attempts to allocate authorship.

[69] Deanesly, *Lollard Bible*, p. 245.

[70] Ibid., pp. 144–7.

[71] *De triplici vinculo amoris*, in *Polemical Works in Latin*, ed. R. Buddensieg, 1 (WS, London, 1883), p. 168; Deanesly, *Lollard Bible*, p. 248. See also M. J. Wilks, 'Misleading manuscripts: Wyclif and the non-Wycliffite Bible', *SCH* XI, pp. 147–61 at p. 155, n. 34; on the German Bible commissioned by Anne's brother Wenceslas, see F. Unterkircher, *König Wenzels Bibelbilder* (Graz, 1983). The use of the vernacular, Czech or German, for Scripture translation did not become controversial in Bohemia as it did in England.

impact by the time that the New Testament was reached by a prolonged process of development as translators felt their way towards a more idiomatic rendering.[72]

In contrast to Rolle's Psalter, the Wyclifite version presented all who cared to read with a bare text, not merely of the psalms, which because of their use in worship presented a special case, but also of those parts of the Bible which contained the most abstruse expositions of doctrine. Even in its clumsy early version, the Wyclifite translation had begun to break with medieval tradition which saw Scripture as a whole as a difficult text, to be assimilated by a trained clergy through the means of handbooks and expositions, and mediated to the faithful perhaps by gospel harmonies, but not under any circumstances to be placed raw in their hands without check and supervision.[73] The translation made vivid indeed Wyclif's innovation of separating Scripture from the whole body of tradition and the deposit of faith and making it stand starkly on its own. The early literal version was, of course, only a beginning: it had none of the driving force of the free translation which came out after Wyclif's death. But it was Wyclif's most important bequest to the Lollard movement.

On preaching, Wyclif's contribution to the rise of Lollardy is most ambiguous. Certainly the duty of preaching had a high place in his revolutionary concept of Church life, for it was the principal means of conveying the truths of Scripture to ordinary men. His late works are scattered with references to 'poor priests' who were to hear and spread true doctrine, and in one of his *Sermones quadraginta* we note Wyclif's feeling that he is speaking to members of a 'recognizable movement'.[74] But there is no evidence that Wyclif sent out priests himself. If he had been active in the development of preaching campaigns, then one would have expected Lutterworth to have been a centre of popular Lollardy. Yet it produced no single Lollard in all the record of heresy trials. Walsingham's picture of Wyclif sending out preachers in russet mantles is not confirmed by the other chronicler of early Lollardy, Henry Knighton, who shows Wyclif in a passive role, attracting acolytes by his academic reputation and his skill in disputation.[75] William Thorpe's account in the record of his trial conveys a similar picture when he speaks of those who 'commoned [communed] oft with him, and . . . loved so much his learning that they writ it, and busily enforced them to rule themselves thereafter'.[76] Walsingham wrote of ordinations of Lollards in Salisbury diocese, and there was indeed a case of a William Ramsbury being tonsured by a certain Thomas Fishburn, and invested with a russet habit to go and preach the heresy.[77] The chronicler assumed that Wyclif did the same. In fact, Wyclif was not the organizer of the heresy: his legacy to his followers lay in the realm of ideas.

[72] Hudson, *Premature Reformation*, pp. 238–40.

[73] Deanesly, *Lollard Bible*, p. 239.

[74] Mallard, in *MH* xvii (1966), p. 99.

[75] *Chronicon Henrici Knighton*, ed. J. R. Lumby (RS, 1895), ii, p. 186; Workman (*Wyclif* ii, pp. 201ff.) needs correction on the sending out of poor priests. McFarlane (*Wycliffe*, p. 101) brings good sense to bear.

[76] Pollard, *Fifteenth-Century Prose*, p. 119.

[77] Aston, *PP* xvii, p. 13. See below, p. 251, n. 23.

That it was an explosive legacy will be apparent if one considers the doctrinal positions which Wyclif had reached in the course of his intellectual odyssey. He left the Lollards a set of ideas with all the potential to build an effective movement. His predestinarianism did away with the authority of the visible Church; his doctrine of Scripture armed his followers with an inexhaustible arsenal of criticism against it. He came near to a doctrine of the priesthood of all believers; he did away with a hierarchy in the Church and, by his stress on the poor priests against the Caesarean clergy, appealed to a pre-existing cleft within the Church of his day. Finally, the literal translation of the Bible took the first step towards putting the bare text, with all its dangerous heresy-making potential, into the hands of any man who cared to read for himself or attend a Lollard conventicle.

14

The English Lollards

The early evangelists

The reactions in Oxford to Wyclif's eucharistic heresy, the Peasants' Revolt and Courtenay's purge were all in their different ways blows to Wyclif's ideas and following, yet they were not fatal. Religious feeling, leaning in Wyclif's direction, obviously lay close to the surface and could easily be mobilized, while counteractions came a little too late, when Wyclif's following was already at work. So Lollardy spread quickly, in Knighton's view, 'like the overwhelming multiplication of seedlings'.[1]

A small group of academically trained men – we may call them proto-Lollards – mediated the master's late, radical ideas to the priesthood and to a wider, popular audience. Of these the best known are Nicholas Hereford, Philip Repton, John Aston and John Purvey. The first three had been attracted to Wyclif's ideas in Oxford; the fourth was evidently a man of education and, one assumes, of university training, but details are lacking. Repton was an Austin canon; the others were secular clerks. Their position was a little equivocal, for all at one time recanted or submitted to ecclesiastical censure, and two (Hereford and Repton) finally abandoned support of Lollardy for ever. No doubt their academic standing is relevant: they were men who desired reform and had been swept away by Wyclifite ideas; counter-argument, more mature reflection and, perhaps, realization of the

---

[1] *Knighton*, ed. Lumby, II, p. 183; Fines, *Studies*, p. 33 ('quasi germinantes multiplicati sunt nimis'); C. Cross, *Church and People 1450–1660: The Triumph of the Laity in the English Church* (Hassocks, 1976) esp. chs 1 and 2 (penetrating survey on Lollardy); A. Hudson, 'Wycliffism in Oxford 1381–1411', *Wyclif in his Times*, ed. A. Kenny (Oxford, 1986), pp. 67–84, and *Premature Reformation*, ch. 2, illuminate the role of Oxford.

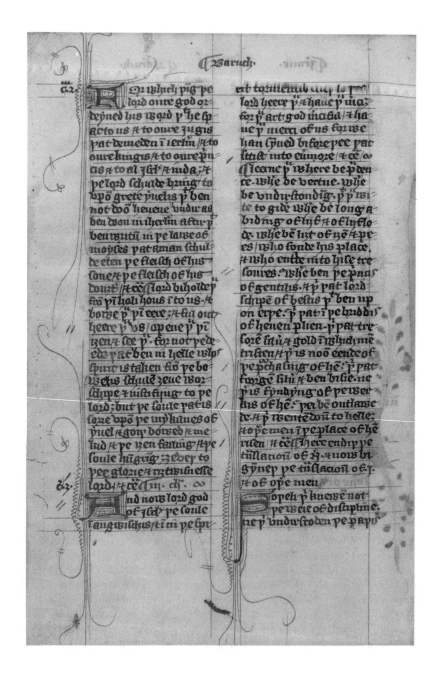

FIGURE 9   The Lollard Bible: the Early Version breaking off at Baruch 3: 20 (cf. p. 245, n. 3, with the note of the break, 'Here endith . . .' seven lines from the bottom in the right-hand column in the illustration). CUL MS Ee. i. 10 fol. 61v.

Reproduced by permission of the Syndics of Cambridge University Library.

consequences of persistence in heresy detached them from their new beliefs. Even so, the first enthusiasm had kept its hold for one, perhaps, two of them, who returned to Lollardy; and in any case submission came too late to obviate the effects of their work. Martyrdom was not essential for the growth of Lollardy.

Hereford,[2] a man of academic calibre, an Oxford master of arts, was believed by Knighton to have been the first leader of Lollardy, and there is evidence that he played a significant part in the writing of the first Bible.[3] It was he who preached the inflammatory sermon on Ascension Day 1382 at Oxford in the vernacular, openly advocating disendowment by the laity. He was a natural radical, who supposedly once preached a sermon arguing that Archbishop Sudbury, who was lynched in the Peasants' Revolt, had deserved his fate, and a man of curious optimism, who responded to Courtenay's excommunication of him by travelling to Rome to appeal to Urban VI in person. After escape from Rome and a period underground, he was arrested. Eventually he recanted some time before 1391, and not only recanted, but spoke against Lollardy.

Repton, the Austin canon of St-Mary-in-the-Fields, Leicester, recanted before Hereford, and rose to be abbot of his house and finally bishop of Lincoln, where he had to pursue 'Lollards. As bishop he worked hard as a reformer within the Church.[4] Lollardy for a time had seemed to him a key to reform; then he dropped it. But an underlying zeal remained.

Aston was originally of the diocese of Worcester. Like the rest, he recanted; but later he returned to Lollard evangelism, and seems to have died in the heresy about 1388.[5]

John Purvey,[6] probably of Lincoln diocese, was described by Knighton as the 'fourth heresiarch': he lived in the same house as Wyclif, he said, was intoxicated by his views and laboured to forward them. Netter, who refuted two of his works, called him the librarian of the Lollards, the disciple and the glossator of Wyclif, epithets compatible with a work of assemblage and propaganda rather than creativity. He appears later than the rest in the records of pursuit by the bishops and lasted longer in the movement. When he

---

[2] Workman, *Wyclif* II, pp. 131–7, Deanesly, *Lollard Bible*, pp. 232–6, 276, 377 (but with no sound evidence of Leicester canonry), McFarlane, *Wycliffe*, pp. 102, 107–12, 115, 118, 126–9, 137; Hudson, *Premature Reformation*, pp. 70–3, 81, 111, 122, 161, 176–8, 200–1, 241–2, 283–4, 337–8, 365, 509–10.

[3] Certain MSS of EV break off at Baruch 3:20; Bodl. MS Douce 369, part 1, gives Hereford as translator to that point; Cambr. Univ. Lib. MS Ee. i. 10 (opposite) notes, 'Here endith the translacioun of Her. and now bigynneth the translacioun of J. and of othere men' (spelling slightly modernized). See Lindberg, *MS Bodley 959* V, pp. 90–7, who argues that the break was caused by Hereford's final recantation, not by his flight to Rome in 1382; contrast Deanesly, *Lollard Bible*, p. 254. MS Bodley 959 breaks off at the same point without comment. Fristedt (*Wycliffe Bible* II, p. xlvii) observes that the break 'simply marks the point at the bottom of the last recto column . . . where the scribe waited for the ink to dry'. Hudson, *Premature Reformation*, pp. 241–2, sees the evidence as weak and rejects attribution to Hereford as 'misguided'.

[4] Workman, *Wyclif* II, pp. 138, 162–3, 252, 282–9, 335–6; Deanesly, *Lollard Bible*, pp. 121–3; McFarlane, *Wycliffe*, pp. 102–3, 108–15; M. Archer, 'Philip Repington, bishop of Lincoln, and his cathedral chapter', *UBHJ* IV (1954), pp. 81–97; Hudson, *Premature Reformation*, pp. 43–4 (Knighton's handling of the Repton affair), 70–3, 77, 79, 200–1, 283–4.

[5] Workman, *Wyclif* II, pp. 138, 162–3, 252, 282–9, 335–6; Deanesly, *Lollard Bible*, pp. 135–6, 276, 445; McFarlane, *Wycliffe*, pp. 102, 109–11, 113–14, 122, 126–8; Hudson, *Premature Reformation*, pp. 66, 70, 73, 77–8, 122, 200–1, 283–4.

[6] Academic in contrast to the simpler Lollards: there is still no evidence that Purvey was at Oxford.

was finally laid by the heels and recanted in 1401, it was a heavy blow; put on probation by being given the benefice of West Hythe, conveniently near Archbishop Arundel's castle of Saltwood, he held it for only three years before he resigned, driven back, it would seem, by his true feelings toward Lollard evangelism. There is evidence that he continued in the heresy for years afterwards.

Recantations could not break the movement. Hereford had a career as an evangelist before and after the abortive journey to Rome. Repton had time to introduce Lollardy to Leicester and Brackley on the road between Oxford and Northampton. Aston preached in Bristol and Leicester. Hereford, Repton and Aston challenged Courtenay in 1382 by making public their eucharistic views in London by means of vernacular handbills and posters. Purvey was hardly molested in his long career as Lollard before trial and recantation. Enough was done to embed Lollardy in some key centres and to scatter converts and writings. Some places were likely to be unreceptive: Lincolnshire, for example, was too backward and conservative, but Leicester had major advantages for incipient Lollardy. It lay at a distance from the episcopal manors of the bishop of Lincoln, John Buckingham, who, conscientious and resident as he was, seems not to have entered Leicestershire at all after 1366. John of Gaunt had authority there and exercised local patronage in the Lollard interest; it had a superfluity of unbeneficed chaplains, who caused trouble; and it contained St Mary's Abbey, whose benefices gave ample scope for the preaching of Philip Repton.[7]

In addition to the principal academic Lollards, there were others, less notable but still academically trained, who took to evangelizing. The two best known are Richard Wyche, a priest of the diocese of Hereford, who was active during the late fourteenth century in the north, had contacts with Sir John Oldcastle, and was burnt in London in 1440 after a long and indefatigable career as an evangelist.[8] He would have been too young to know Wyclif personally, but he argued so skilfully with the assessors of the bishop of Durham, and was so familiar with Wyclif's views that he must have had an academic background. William Thorpe, who travelled round England in a threadbare blue gown, preaching and talking with well-disposed clergy for nearly twenty years before he was brought before Archbishop Arundel in 1407, claimed to have known Wyclif personally, and talked of the

[7] All previous work on Purvey is superseded by A. Hudson, 'John Purvey: a reconsideration of the evidence', *Lollards and their Books* (London, 1985), pp. 85–110, with its devastating revelation, pp. 102–3, of the manner in which a mere guess at his authorship of LV and General Prologue passed into academic currency. Leff, *Heresy* II, pp. 578–83, analyses Lavenham's compilation of his heretical theses. For Leicester's role and the effects of college patronage see A. K. McHardy, 'The dissemination of Wyclif's ideas', *SCH* Subsidia v, pp. 361–8.

[8] F. D. Matthew, 'The trial of Richard Wyche', *EHR* v (1890), pp. 530–44; M. G. Snape, 'Some evidence of Lollard activity in the diocese of Durham in the early fifteenth century', *Archaeologia Aeliana*, 4th ser. XXXIX (1961), pp. 355–61; J. A. F. Thomson, *The Later Lollards, 1414–1520* (Oxford, 1965) (standard account of Lollard trials, see below p. 266, n. 89), pp. 15, 148–50, 177, 192; McFarlane, *Wycliffe*, p. 162; letter to Hus in *The Letters of John Hus*, tr. H. B. Workman and R. M. Pope (London, 1904), pp. 30–4; *Responsio*, in *FZ*, pp. 370–82; Hudson, *Premature Reformation*, pp. 127, 160–1 (Wyche's trial and attitude to martyrdom), 164, 172, 190, 221–2 (trial evidence), 244, 274, 276, 284, 325, 341, 345, 357, 370, 373, 376, 378, 381–2.

master's career as an academic;[9] it seems likely that he also had had academic training.

Others still, like Thomas Brightwell, an Oxford man with prebends in Leicester, once associated with Wyclif's heresy but an early backslider, Thomas Hulman, rector of Kibworth Harcourt between 1380 and 1385, William James, a marginal figure in the outbursts of Oxford Lollards in 1382, pursued and captured outside Oxford for heresy in a time of anti-Lollard scare in 1395, are examples of lesser-known men who, without the *éclat* of the leading evangelists, spread the word by the ordinary casual mechanisms of preaching or parochial life.[10]

Behind the named individuals lies a penumbra of committed Oxford academics, whose existence is demonstrable by the mute evidence of a substantial class of scholarly vernacular material, designed to spread Lollardy outside the university through an instructed clergy, creating a revolution in doctrine and in Church–State relations by means of the written and spoken word.[11] As more is edited and analysed, it becomes clear that Courtenay's counter-measures of 1382 cut off some of the heads of heresy in Oxford and checked its open development but left many roots, which continued to be productive well into the archiepiscopate of his successor Arundel.

The translation of the Bible, in a set of versions stretching from the crudely literal crib for the Vulgate to an eloquent and idiomatic rendering, commanded the services of a whole sequence of scholars over years in what can only have been a tedious and demanding labour. There was an early work of removing the corruptions from versions of the Vulgate; a need to elucidate the text by using patristic commentary from the *Glossa Ordinaria*; creative work to be done in bending the vernacular for use in a biblical translation; finally, an immense task of writing, correcting and rewriting the translation. The academic conscience can be seen at work in the mass of corrections in the text of the Early Version, MS Bodley 959. The time-scale was considerable. The Early Version was in existence in Wyclif's lifetime, since he wrote of the utility of the translation of the gospels for the instruction of secular lords; the developments which came to term in the Late Version might well have been completed by 1395–7. Amongst the hidden group of scholars responsible for the translating were some capable of breaking the psychological barrier imposed by the literal text of the Vulgate as the word of God – a barrier never breached by Wyclif himself.

An individual voice of academic Lollardy in the period from Christmas 1389 to Easter 1390 was that of the author of the *Opus Arduum*, a Latin exposition on the Apocalypse, written by a man lying in prison for his views, who used scriptural exposition to denounce the evils of the friars and the persecution of the Lollards. He knew of the Lollard machinery of book

[9] Text of Thorpe's account of his trial in Pollard, *Fifteenth-Century Prose*, pp. 107–67; J. Fines in *History Today* XVIII (1968), pp. 495–503, esp. p. 497; Hudson, *Premature Reformation*, pp. 220–1, in her analysis calls it 'faction'.

[10] Hudson, *Premature Reformation*, pp. 77, 78, 88–9.

[11] It is Professor A. Hudson's achievement to have demonstrated this. For early popularization, see *Premature Reformation*, pp. 103–10; Wycliffite Bible: pp. 108–9, 231–47; *Opus Arduum*: pp. 264–6, authorship: p. 266, n. 189; A. Hudson, 'A neglected Wycliffite text', *Lollards and their Books*, pp. 43–65.

production and wrote confidently of the replacement of works which the bishops had destroyed by others which were 'much stronger'; strangely, though he wrote from prison, he had access to the full apparatus of biblical academic commentary. The vigour of the denunciation of Urban VI and the oddity of a man condemned for heresy having facilities to write a heretical treatise make Nicholas Hereford, perhaps merely technically under restraint in the care of a pro-Lollard magnate, a possible author; an alternative candidate may have been an academic detained in the Franciscan house at Oxford, who would thereby have a library to use. Yet, whatever hypothesis is correct, the writer remains simply in the text the 'faithful preacher' and in this is characteristic of the majority of Lollard writers, who were determined on anonymity, and consciously so, for they were the elect, subsumed as individuals in the movement for reform. Under pressure, fearing introduction of the death penalty on the continental model and enjoining on himself and others the need for patience under persecution, the author was still, since he wrote in Latin, confident enough of his ability to appeal to an academic audience.

The persecution of which the author of the *Opus Arduum* spoke was still a long way from destroying the intellectual leadership in Oxford and its writing-office. Between 1384 and 1396 it produced a working dictionary of theological, ethical and ecclesiastical learning arranged alphabetically under headings, forming a guide to Wyclifite thought. It is a substantial work – some 509 entries in the fullest version, the *Floretum*,[12] comprising approximately 3,000 pages of modern print – and makes full use of patristic and traditional commentary and of the canon law, subtly deployed so that it can be turned against the canon lawyers, the enemies of the Lollards. There are 180 passages of quotation from Wyclif's pastoral work. The appropriate entries are clearly heterodox; but much is not, and the whole is not notably polemical. It is designed to provide a preaching clergy without access to a major library with an adequate apparatus of learning. An intermediate version, with the same number of entries but reduced content, and a shorter one called the *Rosarium*, with 303 entries, together with one extant text of the early fifteenth century, Trinity College, Cambridge B14.50, combining the *Rosarium* in the vernacular with other Lollard material, including sermon notes, shows both how the authors adapted their material for different readers and how the working dictionary might be used in the field by a Lollard preacher. The *Floretum* was an academic project and its derivative commentary material implies use of a major library.

Much the same might be said of the Glossed Gospels, vernacular commentaries, generally drawn directly from the standard, orthodox compilation, the *Catena Aurea* of Aquinas, but also implying consultation of original authorities.[13] The complexities of the MS tradition, comprehending long and

[12] A. Hudson, 'A Lollard compilation and the dissemination of Wycliffite thought', *Lollards and their Books*, pp. 13–29; 'A Lollard compilation in England and Bohemia', pp. 32–42; partial summary, *Premature Reformation*, pp. 106–8, including changed estimate of length, p. 107, in contrast to *Lollards and their Books*, p. 14.

[13] Hudson, *Premature Reformation*, pp. 108, 248–59 ('part of an attempt to build up a library of materials ... an effort ... worthy of Oxford Wycliffism in the 1390s', pp. 148–9); extracts in A. Hudson, *Selections from English Wycliffite Writings* (Cambridge, 1978), pp. 49–52, 60–4.

short commentaries on different gospels and the lack of a uniform system of citation are indications of multiple authorship, albeit, probably, under one directing mind. Groups of verses from the Early Version of the Wycliffe Bible are followed by a sequence of commentaries on them. Again, the reader is struck by the academic care given to production, the labour involved and the likelihood that an extensive library had been used for the citations.

Yet another academic production of the years before 1400 – and one which exceeds all others bar the Wyclifite Bible – is the Lollard sermon-cycle,[14] a vernacular collection amounting in its fullest version to 294 sermons, designed for use in association with the liturgy and providing a complete set of sermons for epistle and gospel respectively on Sundays, for named saints (expurgated on Lollard principles, for the movement was very wary of post-biblical saints), for other unspecified saints and martyrs and for other weekdays. In all, there was provision for 120 weekday sermons. There were two major rearrangements of parts of the cycle, every sign of professionalism in rubrication and correction, and evidence that over forty different hands had been at work on the collection.

Translation was not simply drawn from the Wyclifite Bible, nor was exegesis derived from the Glossed Gospels, though there may be fortuitous likenesses. We have yet another substantial and independent academic work, based on a professional writing-office and meeting substantial production costs. Of the thirty-one extant MSS, about twenty are of such a size as to require a lectern to read from.

The content is demanding and allusive. Much is conventional and orthodox, but passages of fierce, anticlerical denunciation, especially of the religious orders, are also included. The authors appear not to have felt the need for the anecdotal aids characteristic of the orthodox preaching, which they denounced, and the collection lacks conspicuous literary skills. Their assumption seems to have been that the Bible would speak for itself and that a sustained, rational exposition, without artifice, would carry the day with lay congregations.

Together, Wyclifite Bible, the Latin *Floretum*, the Glossed Gospels and the sermon-cycle provided the apparatus for a take-over of the English priesthood from within for Lollard, reform ideas – all carefully assembled by an industrious and capable academic leadership, confident that they could persuade their fellow clergy to open their churches to the vernacular Scriptures and to Lollard sermons, preached extensively, and on weekdays as well as Sundays.

It was not to be. One of the reasons why the Lollard leadership failed to make a breakthrough in their battle against the hierarchy of the day lay precisely in the uncompromising academic quality of their major productions.

[14] *English Wycliffite Sermons*, ed. A. Hudson, I (Oxford, 1983), ed. P. Gradon, II (Oxford, 1988); review of I by R. B. Dobson, *JEH* xxxv (1984), pp. 271–4; Hudson, *Premature Reformation*, pp. 25–6, 197–9; debate on aims of sermon-cycle: p. 199 – 'Church use, or use modelled on church reading? . . . It will be best at this point to keep an open mind.' I believe the nature of the MSS, as demonstrated by the author, to be such as to presuppose a production for use in existing churches. Joan Baker's statement (ibid., pp. 199–200) on Lollard sermons in 1511 represents a supporter's hyperbole; for extracts and notes, see Hudson, *Selections*, pp. 52–4, 64–6, 168–70, 172–3.

One is entitled to ask: how much use was ever made of the massive sermon collection, for example? And yet the existence of this quality of academic leadership, and of its learned propaganda which the bishops were not at first able fully to suppress helps to explain their alarms. Authority, aware of this shadowy and often anonymous academic threat to their position, lingering into the fifteenth century, had justification for its timidities.

A second category of early Lollard evangelists consisted of chaplains, unbeneficed priests and lower clergy generally. Here Lollard tenets fell on fertile soil. The proportion of beneficed to unbeneficed clergy seems to have risen in the later Middle Ages. They had little in common with a wealthy upper clergy.[15] In the Peasants' Revolt the lower clergy were active as agitators and sometimes associated with the most violent episodes. Some may indeed already have been wandering anticlerical agitators, as John Ball had been for years before the revolt broke out. Doctrines which rejected a hierarchy in the Church, wished to redistribute Church wealth and sharply criticized the religious orders and the upper clergy, would find willing hearers in this category. Often such clergy were close to the laity and would make some common cause with them. Chaplains were frequently the sons of craftsmen. As Lollardy put down roots among the craftsmen, so chaplains and the unbeneficed clergy would find themselves talking to their own kind. Their class and their economic background made them more effective and dangerous evangelists. Training was hardly thorough. They were thus open to the influence of new doctrines and, by lack of education, shielded from the academic treatises in which Wyclif's opponents sought to refute his views.[16] In their hands, together with lay helpers, Lollardy both spread widely in the country and began to lose its academic basis.

The case of Swinderby at Leicester is a good example of the way in which this happened.[17] The first seed was most likely planted by Philip Repton, with his strong local connections. It flowered in a nucleus round the chapel of St John the Baptist outside the walls of the town, where a chaplain called Waytestathe and a craftsman, William Smith, became active in preaching and the production of tracts. The most notable member of the group, however, was William Swinderby, who had had a career as a revivalist before Lollardy appeared on the scene, travelling round the country from a base in a cell at the abbey of St-Mary-in-the-Fields, or living as a hermit in the woods outside the town. Lollardy gave him a congenial set of tenets to preach; to Lollardy he

[15] A straw in the wind is the drawing apart of higher and lower clergy in convocation during the second half of the fourteenth century. Attitudes to taxation differed. Dr J. R. L. Highfield, to whom I am indebted, tells me that 'usually the hierarchy joined the king in bullying the lower clergy', and that Courtenay's intervention as bishop of London on behalf of lower clergy was exceptional.

[16] Convocation was using the vernacular in the 1470s (J. R. L. Highfield, 'A note on the introduction of English into the proceedings of the Convocation of Canterbury', *MA* xlix (1950), pp. 60–3). Were clergy who had to be addressed in English more likely to accept a sect stressing the vernacular? (Dr Highfield in a private letter.) Anti-Lollard academic work is discussed in Hudson, *Premature Reformation*, pp. 45–58, 430–40. Popular antidotes are rarer; see Fines, *Studies*, p. 41, n. 3, p. 119; for anti-Lollard sermons of Henry v's reign, R. M. Haines, '"Wild Wittes and Wilfulness": John Swetstock's attack on those "Poyswunmogeres", the Lollards', in *SCH* viii, pp. 143–53; for parentage of chaplains, see Deanesly, *Lollard Bible*, p. 189.

[17] McFarlane, *Wycliffe*, pp. 103–5, 121–5, 127–36, 150, 174.

brought gifts of denunciation and rhetoric that remind us of Henry the Monk in the twelfth century, who, like Swinderby, came to heresy only after a previous career as an orthodox preacher.[18] Like him, he could rouse a town, using popular support at Easter 1382 to defy the bishop's inhibition against preaching and getting the mayor and twelve leading citizens to put their seals to a letter supporting his denials of heterodoxy. There is no doubt, however, of his Lollard commitment, despite the tendency of his accusers to attribute to him, ready made, the opinions condemned at the Blackfriars Council. Aston's appearance in the town may have been a spur to his heresy. The errors which he abjured before the bishop of Lincoln illustrate some of the tenets which appealed to Leicester citizens. He had taught, among other things, the rightfulness of parishioners withholding tithes from an incontinent parish priest, the illegitimacy of imprisonment for debt, or of a prelate excommunicating except where he knows the sinner to be already excommunicate by God. The priest in mortal sin who says mass 'rather commits idolatry than makes the body of God'.[19]

Swinderby was one of the most effective of all the evangelists. He planted heresy in Leicester and some of the market towns round about, then in Coventry, and finally in western Herefordshire, where the gentry gave him protection against the bishop. He almost certainly converted the young Oldcastle, the future military leader of Lollardy. Only in 1392 did his career come to an end, when he disappeared with a faithful companion into Wales.

Others, too, had considerable achievements. In the early fifteenth century William, the parish priest of Thaxted, nurtured a whole series of Lollard groups in Essex. In one circle at Colchester a Franciscan, John Brettenham, joined in the reading of tracts and translations.[20] Similarly, heresy in the north Midlands owed much to the chaplain William Ederick from Aston-on-Trent.[21] William Sawtry, the first Lollard to be burnt, had been a chaplain in Norfolk and had an unknown period of Lollard preaching behind him when he was first apprehended in 1399.[22] William Ramsbury is an interesting case of a Lollard layman being ordained by one of the sect and then wandering for four years before 1389, spreading his beliefs in the Salisbury diocese. He held some radical views, notably on marriage, with sentiments that sound oddly like that attributed to the adherents of the Free Spirit; yet he had not emancipated himself from the mass, which he said according to the Sarum use with vestments, allowing himself a few omissions.[23]

---

[18] Above, p. 44.

[19] Swinderby's abjuration is in *FZ*, pp. 337–9; Hudson, *Premature Reformation*, pp. 73–7, analyses accusations and abjuration, rejecting McFarlane's description (*Wycliffe*, p. 104) of Swinderby's teaching as 'a very watery and simplified version of Wycliffe's novel doctrines'; influence of Aston, p. 77.

[20] McFarlane, *Wycliffe*, pp. 173, 178.

[21] Ibid., pp. 174–5, 178.

[22] Ibid., pp. 150–2.

[23] A. Hudson, 'A Lollard mass', *JTS* XXIII (1972), pp. 407–19; on the Free Spirit, see esp. article 14 alleged against Ramsbury and the writer's argument from the conjunction of articles 7, 10, 13, 14, of influence on Ramsbury of the 'contemporary sect' of the Free Spirit. I do not believe this sect existed (see above, pp. 188–8), though aberrant inferences from mystical experience were made by individuals (as this article observes, on the basis of English texts); and I suggest the starting-point for Ramsbury's views lay in dislike of clerical and monastic celibacy (note article 9), and had a practical rather than mystical

The laity

A heresy which preached the equality of laity and priesthood might be expected to find lay evangelists also. William Smith was an example, often to be repeated in fifteenth-century Lollardy, of the self-taught craftsman disseminating heresy. A conversion to vegetarianism and teetotalism after he had been jilted was in turn followed by service to the Lollard group. He taught himself to read and, when Swinderby had left the scene, continued with the activity of producing works based on Scripture and the Fathers, possibly copies of the Glossed Gospels. Practical issues of worship and religious practice rather than highly academic heresy took chief place: when he and his fellow Lollards of Leicester were denounced in 1389, the accusations related to lay preaching, indulgences, auricular confession, tithes and the veneration of images.[24] Doubtful views on transubstantiation may have been unjustly attributed to the Leicester group.[25] Smith's career was cut short by a visitation in 1389 from Courtenay, who saw to it that his Lollard works were surrendered and he did penance.

In Herefordshire, Walter Brute, an esquire of very small landed resources, of Welsh background and some dialectical and rhetorical gifts, with a bias towards the Apocalypse, was aide to Swinderby.[26] He taught that a layman held the keys of absolution as much as a priest and that women had the power to preach, to consecrate the eucharist and to absolve. Northampton harboured a Lollard group in 1392–3; Anna Palmer, an anchorite at St Peter's church, was described as principal receiver of Lollards, associated with six others including priests and laity. A major role seems to have been played by John Fox, the mayor. Here vanity and self-display were as much in evidence as righteous living, with William Northwold 'in Northampton amongst the Lollards and misbelievers reputed a prophet speaking with the tongue of an angel', laying false claim to a doctorate of divinity, and preachers dressing themselves in hoods and gowns to which they had no right.[27]

Thomas Compworth, an esquire of Kidlington in Oxfordshire, is an uncommon example of a follower higher in society who was more than a mere fautor of heresy, having indulged in lay preaching and got himself into trouble by refusing tithes to the abbot of Osney.[28] In general, however, the laity were not public preachers. Their role was that of a supporting layer, encouraging their clergy and forming reading circles. Claydon, the prosperous tanner from London burnt in 1415, invited friends to join him in readings and brought his servants into the heresy.[29] Adherents in the stationers' trade were especially

keynote (note stress on procreation in article 10). There may have been actual promiscuity (article 14), or accusations may have slandered him, working a heresy out of a preacher's denunciatory hyperbole.

[24] McFarlane, *Wycliffe*, p. 140; Hudson, *Premature Reformation*, pp. 74–7, hypothesis on Glossed Gospels, p. 76, n. 100.

[25] McFarlane, *Wycliffe*, pp. 124, 131, 133.

[26] Ibid., pp. 136–8; Hudson, *Premature Reformation*, pp. 47–8, 99, 274, 291, 295, 298–9, 326–7 (opinions and rebuttals); see her 'Laicus litteratus: the paradox of Lollardy', Biller, Hudson, *Literacy*, pp. 222–36.

[27] McFarlane, *Wycliffe*, pp. 140–4, quotation from McFarlane's version of the original; Hudson, *Premature Reformation*, pp. 78–80, noting some discrepancies between the two major sources.

[28] McFarlane, *Wycliffe*, pp. 141, 143, 178.

[29] Thomson, *Later Lollards*, pp. 140–2.

useful for the distribution of tracts. Included among the heretics denounced at Leicester in 1389 were a parchmener and a scrivener. Oldcastle had connections with the stationers' trade in London: heretical tracts of his were discovered in an illuminator's shop in Paternoster Row in 1413, and after his rescue from the Tower his refuge was in the house of a London stationer, William Fisher.[30]

An appeal to the individual to search out the truths of Scripture for himself was part of the drawing power of Lollardy: it was most effective for the self-taught, for those who had lately become literate and for those in a trade which required literacy.[31] The craftsmen and bourgeoisie who in Leicester, Northampton, London and elsewhere took to Lollard doctrines were not necessarily poor men; through their skills they often finally acquired a competence, or sometimes even more. The successful among them would be aware that they had succeeded largely by their own efforts. For most of them the late fourteenth century was a period of prosperity. In Bristol and its hinterland, where the efforts of early preachers, Hereford, Aston and Purvey, bedded down Lollardy in the class of skilled artisans, the textile industry which supported many of them was doing well. Such people would not have taken to a faith which preached wild millenarianism; this was more likely to appeal to the genuine poor.

Craftsmen and lower clergy predominate among the Lollards; but there were exceptions. Swinderby in the Welsh March touched the gentry class; they protected him against the bishop of Hereford. From this area came Sir John Oldcastle, one of the converts of high rank, being a baron through marriage. There are other isolated examples.

The most interesting of all is the group known as the Lollard knights.[32] Differing lists of names of men of gentle birth involved with heresy are given for us independently by two chroniclers, Knighton and Walsingham,[33] amounting to ten names in all. Further research confirms that something genuine lay behind the accusations. Walsingham called them 'the hooded knights' because they would not uncover in the presence of the Host. K. B. McFarlane, giving a verdict of 'not proven' on three of the ten cases, provides a detailed analysis of the lives of seven, all professional soldiers, all in the court circle, all in service to Richard II by the early 1380s. Several were linked either to the Black Prince or his widow. One knight of Lollard sympathies, Sir John Cheyne, may have been a lapsed priest. They were all known to each other, and the chance that the chroniclers, with the mass of gentry and aristocracy of England to choose from, should have picked on a group of men with lands in different parts of England, but none the less linked by personal ties, has long appeared to be an *a priori* argument in favour of their accusations.

[30] McFarlane, *Wycliffe*, pp. 163, 166.

[31] Ibid., p. 180.

[32] W. T. Waugh, 'The Lollard knights', *SHR* xi (1913), pp. 55–92 (pioneer study); K. B. McFarlane, *Lancastrian Kings and Lollard Knights* (Oxford, 1972), pp. 139–232 (lectures, ed. J. R. L. Highfield, superseding all previous work.) Note contrast in tone (esp. pp. 139, 221–6) to *Wycliffe* on Lollardy's potential; Hudson, *Premature Reformation*, pp. 90, 112–14, 119, 214–17, 430.

[33] *Knighton*, ed. Lumby, II, p. 181; *Thomae Walsingham historia Anglicana*, ed. H. T. Riley, II (RS, 1864), pp. 159, 216; see also *Chronicon Angliae*, RS, p. 377.

The Lollard knights included three who demonstrably gave help to the movement. Sir John Montagu was sufficiently committed to remove the images from his chapel at Shenley and to harbour Lollard preachers. Sir Thomas Latimer made his seat at Braybrooke in Northamptonshire, a Lollard centre, and was summoned before the council in 1388 at the time of the Merciless Parliament to answer for the possession of heretical books. That was a party move by the Appellants' faction, striking at a king's man by means of the heresy accusation. Latimer felt sufficiently secure, however, to continue to back heresy. At Chipping Warden, a small market town in the same county of which he was lord, the bishop of Lincoln had extreme difficulty in getting a writ served in 1388–9 on a chaplain accused of Lollard preaching. Latimer even brought a suit before the king's justices against the bishop's summoner. At the time of Hereford's arrest in 1387, Sir William Nevill petitioned for the prisoner to be delivered to his keeping as constable of Nottingham castle, 'because of the honesty of his person' – a strange description of a Lollard preacher on the run and betraying Nevill's sympathies, as McFarlane observes.[34] A sudden glimpse such as this in the records reveals attachments hitherto unproved; it is fair to surmise that some other cases of high-born sympathy never reached our records.

Sir John Clanvow, a great friend of Nevill, who died on an expedition with him near Constantinople, wrote in the last year of his life (1391) a vernacular religious treatise on the broad and narrow way, which reveals an ardent piety, nourished by a contemplation of the sufferings of Christ and marked by a concern for preserving an ethical life amongst the temptations of the world.[35] There is no breath of overt heresy in it, and it lacks the astringent criticisms of the Church to be found in Lollard work; yet it is easy to see a platform for some interest in Lollardy in the direct and practical tone of this work, its scriptural basis and its moral earnestness. If Clanvow ever had a connection with Lollardy, he entered into it, we may say from this evidence, out of religious faith. So too, we may surmise, did Sir John Cheyne, whose name, partially erased, has been found in a French Bible now in the Bibliothèque Nationale in Paris, and Sir Thomas Latimer and his wife, who in 1366 obtained permission for a portable altar and other religious practices, presupposing an active and traditional piety.

For others among the knights, we have no such direct evidence of their mind. Some may have been anticlericals; certainly the proportion of professional soldiers among them, and links with the Black Prince, have led to conjectures that it was a liking for disendowment proposals as a means of raising war finance that led them to flirt with the heresy, and the interest of some members of the group in the lands of alien priories, taken into the king's hands during the wars with France, may be a pointer in this direction.[36] But the group included some whose interests were not confined to war: Montagu

[34] *Lancastrian Kings*, p. 199.

[35] V. J. Scattergood, ' "The two ways": an unpublished religious treatise by Sir John Clanvowe', *English Philological Studies* x (1967), pp. 33–56; see passage on Christ's sufferings (pp. 53–4). I am indebted to Dr V. J. Scattergood and Dr A. B. Cottle for information. Contrast McFarlane's characterization (*Lancastrian Kings*, pp. 200–6, esp. p. 201); comment in Hudson, *Premature Reformation*, pp. 422–3.

[36] McFarlane, *Lancastrian Kings*, pp. 190–2.

was a man of cultivated taste; Sir Richard Sturry had a copy of the *Roman de la Rose*, and was acquainted with Chaucer and Froissart; Clanvow and Sir Lewis Clifford both knew Chaucer, and Clifford bought ballads from Deschamps; V. J. Scattergood has given reasons for identifying Clanvow as the author of the poem *The Boke of Cupide*.[37] If Lollardy could find adherents such as these, we should be wary of underestimating the danger presented to the Church. No bishop could act uninhibitedly against these men when they were of such rank and stood so high in royal favour. They, and probably some others like them, formed small bulwarks of protection for Lollard evangelists in the twilight period after 1382.

Yet the group did not develop. No great issue comparable in its effect to the breach of Hus's safe conduct to Constance for Bohemian nobility emerged to swing noble opinion behind heresy.[38] It has even been suggested on the evidence of the wills of Latimer, Clifford and Cheyne, where they describe themselves as 'false' or 'traitor' to God, that they abandoned any attachment to heresy they may have had before their deaths.[39] Apparent acceptance of the doctrine of purgatory or going on crusade were actions of some members of the group that argue in the same direction. The wills, however, may easily mislead, and their language reveal a religious sentiment shared by some Lollards and other wholly orthodox contemporaries. Lollard beliefs are too fluid at this stage and Lollards too often inconsistent for their support of crusades or belief in purgatory to be taken as indicating abandonment of all patronage of heresy. Even if the Lollard knights never wholly gave up their interest – and we shall probably never know with certainty – on the other hand they do not seem directly to have won many more recruits, or to have succeeded in changing the climate after 1382 in Lollardy's favour.

The appeal of Lollardy

Lollard tracts invited their readers, as it were, to teach themselves; implicit in the process was the direct relationship between the reader and the Holy Spirit, who would inspire those of good life.[40] Preaching remained the first means of gathering converts; the tracts and the vernacular Scriptures came second. They provided ammunition for the preachers, and confirmed the converts in their beliefs after they had joined the reading circles. After preaching came the informal dissemination of beliefs, at work, in taverns, in the family circle, through trade connections.

From an early period the Lollards were reproducing parts of the Bible in translation for instructional purposes: we have a glimpse of the process at

---

[37] 'The authorship of "The Boke of Cupide"', *Anglia* LXXXII (1964), pp. 137–49. On Clanvow, Clifford and Sturry, cf. *Chaucer Life-Records*, ed. M. M. Crow and C. C. Olson (Oxford, 1966), index, s.v. J. A. F. Thomson, 'Orthodox religion and the origins of Lollardy', *History* LXXIV (1989), pp. 39–55 (argues against an over-rigid view of Lollardy in the fourteenth century; Chaucer's parson: pp. 42–4; Latimer's altar: p. 47; Cheyne's book: p. 48).

[38] Below, pp. 311–13.

[39] Originally Waugh's suggestion (*SHR* XI, pp. 63, 72, 86, 88); more subtle analysis by McFarlane (*Lancastrian Kings*, pp. 207–20); Hudson, *Premature Reformation*, p. 430, notes that Sir William Beauchamp, patron of the Lollard Robert Lychlade, was 'an early advocate of devotion to the Holy name of Jesus'.

[40] Deanesly, *Lollard Bible*, p. 269; see transcript of Lollard tract (p. 452).

Leicester in 1384, when William Smith was at work copying scriptural material.[41] But the Early Version, pedantic and unlovely, was an imperfect instrument for a popular movement. With the development from it of the graceful and free-flowing translation known as the Late Version the situation began to change. It was completed by about 1395–7,[42] and the fact that many manuscripts of it are extant, especially from the first forty years of its existence, shows that it met a real need in the population. Viewed through the eyes of Lollard clergy or lay evangelists, the text could point the way to heresy; the epistles and gospels, for example, could be used to stress the contrast between the simplicity of the early Church and the formalism of the contemporary ecclesiastical scene,[43] and the readings which came to form the staple activity of the sect, could draw out the absence of overt warrant in the scriptural text for such doctrines as purgatory or transubstantiation.

Lollardy's appeal to independent judgement has to be set against the background of ordinary Church life, where laity and clergy were set apart, and the laity still had a relatively passive role. Books of devotion, like the *Lay Folk's Mass Book*, assume that two sets of devotions will be proceeding simultaneously, one for priest, one for laity. The laity hearing the gospel in Latin was compared in a contemporary judgement to an adder which is affected by a charm said over it, even though it cannot understand the words.[44] In fact orthodoxy, despite the issue of vernacular works of instruction and the development of a literature of devotion, had not fully adapted itself to the needs of an age of increasing literacy. This gave a heresy based so much on the written text its great opportunity.

One of the most vital features of late medieval English religious life was its devotional movement. It is enshrined permanently for us in the apparatus of worship of the late medieval English parish church. This movement was not imposed from above – the records of the time allow us to see that the adornment of the parish church, using every device of the craftsman to heighten the sense of the numinous, was a popular matter, and that ordinary parishioners readily subscribed. The Lollards had no sympathy for this; Smith and Waytestathe at Leicester were accused of chopping up an image for firewood, and Smith of calling images of Our Lady at Walsingham and Lincoln 'the witch of Walsingham' and 'the witch of Lincoln'. St Catherine in the hands of Smith underwent a second martyrdom in a curious parody of the judicial ordeal: were she a true saint she would bleed, if not she would make an excellent fire.[45] Thorpe represents himself in his trial by Arundel as attacking all paintings and images in church, pleading against this the second

[41] Ibid., p. 278.

[42] Deanesly, *Lollard Bible*, pp. 252–67; Hudson, *Premature Reformation*, pp. 242–7.

[43] See J. Fines, in *JEH* xiv (1963), p. 165.

[44] B. L.Manning, *The People's Faith in the Time of Wyclif* (Cambridge, 1919), pp. 7–9 (outdated on preaching and biblical translations, but retains value for citations from contemporary edifying texts). See C. Wordsworth and H. Littlehales, *The Old Service-Books of the English Church* (London, 1904), pp. 284–6; and the fine chapter in Hudson, *Premature Reformation*, pp. 390–445.

[45] McFarlane, *Wycliffe*, p. 140, on the accusations; for the parody of the ordeal and the rest of the sentence, I quote the unpublished survey by R. M. Haines, 'The changing face of Lollardy', in Dalhousie History Seminar, Oct. 1986. I am indebted to Professor Haines.

commandment.[46] The Lollards disliked symbolism and mystery – it seemed to them merely to obscure essential truths. In this way, on a lower level, they were following the lines of Wyclif himself, who laid such stress on the rational approach to faith.

The rational approach in their hands often came to mean a minimal approach to credal statements. Wyclif's consubstantiation, based as it was on a philosophical realism, came to be accepted by them on the basis of mere common sense. The bread could still be seen after the words of consecration; therefore it was plain that the substance of bread still remained. Sometimes, we may deduce, Lollard preachers appealed to a pre-existing doubt about the more difficult doctrinal demands of the Church. Richard Wyche before the bishop of Durham represented himself as appealing to the laity who were onlookers to confirm his own 'minimal' approach to transubstantiation – he was too honest not to admit that in this instance they did not support him, but one sees the way in which he would as a preacher have approached the laity in this matter.[47] Lollardy provided an outlet for certain kinds of scepticism, about saints and their miracles, pilgrimages, wonder-working images and, above all, the central miracle of the mass.

Anticlericalism played a strong part. It must have been the most usual springboard into heresy, which commonly began in an alienation from the Church, caused by dissatisfaction with the clergy. The frequently expressed Donatist view that a state of sin in the celebrant invalidated the sacrament, or the plan of reform that would turn the clergy into salaried officials would have had little point if there had not been a dissatisfaction with the state of life of the clergy. When an approach was made to secular authority, Lollards were always ready to play their anticlerical card, appealing to the layman's suspicion of Church wealth, or, as in the Twelve Conclusions of 1395, attacking clerical celibacy.[48]

Lollardy often issued from an outraged Puritan conscience. Lollard writers and preachers could denounce the failings of the visible Church, often with considerable literary skill, because they had themselves felt them so deeply. We may consider Purvey's tract as a case in point, where a faint-hearted adherent is brought to full conversion by a sarcastic narration of the easygoing ways of the ordinary parishioner, enjoying his 'theatres, wrestlers, buckler-players . . . dancers and singers', dining and drinking by night and going to church afterwards, with the good ale rising into his brain and preventing him from noticing the false doctrine of the sermon.[49]

Lollards had a sharp consciousness of sin. Swinderby's appeal to the king's justices in parliament, with its references to the ghostly enemy and the approaching end, gives us some inkling of whence this preacher drew his power.[50] The *Lantern of Light* gives much space to a stern warning against sin

---

[46] Pollard, *Fifteenth-Century Prose*, pp. 133–7; general comment in E. F. Jacob, *The Fifteenth Century* (Oxford, 1961), pp. 282–3.

[47] *EHR* v (1890), p. 532.

[48] *FZ*, pp. 360–9; on unchastity, no. 3 (p. 361).

[49] Deanesly, *Lollard Bible*, p. 274.

[50] McFarlane, *Wycliffe*, p. 133.

in general. It is in the first instance a call to repentance.[51] The revivalist element in Lollardy could readily deceive the unequipped parishioner. Owst has long shown us how fiercely the sermon and devotional literature of the time could attack clerical abuses.[52] Lollard denunciation might at first sight be believed to correspond with the sermons of orthodoxy, and there is some evidence that this is what happened. Thomas Beeby, a Leicester mercer, in 1382 left money in his will both to Swinderby and to the Franciscans, who were then the firm enemies of Lollardy.[53] Thomas Netter noticed how the audiences of the Lollards were liable to doubt whether they really were heretics.[54]

The entry of Lollard ideas was the easier because of the existence of a desire for quite radical reform within orthodoxy. Chaucer, when he described the Parson in the General Prologue to the *Canterbury Tales*, making him so like Wyclif's blueprint and omitting (perhaps fortuitously, perhaps not) any mention of his saying mass or hearing confessions and drawing so black a picture of the monk, the friar and other ecclesiastical personalities, witnesses not so much to his own positive Lollardy as to the degree to which Lollard ideas in the years after the founder's death ran parallel to some widespread concerns about Church life.[55] *Dives and Pauper*, a popular manual for the laity, at least opened the question of the potential ill-effects of some popular devotions and admitted, for example, that men might use images simply to win money.[56] Lollards were aware of these tendencies within orthodoxy and they were also anxious to link themselves with pre-existing popular religious literature. Certain MSS of the English Psalter and the *Ancren Riwle*, which were ascribed to the orthodox mystic Richard Rolle, have been subjected to Lollard interpolations, no doubt with the aim of suggesting that Lollardy was not a novelty, but that such views had earlier had the support of an accepted devotional author who himself wrote in the vernacular.[57] The interpolated English version of the orthodox *Lay Folk's Catechism* served a straightforward propagandizing purpose, and did it rather crudely, for the Lollard sections exist in strange proximity to Archbishop Thoresby's offer of indulgences to

[51] *The Lantern of Light*, ed. L. M. Swinburne (London, 1917) (*EETS*, O.S. CLI). Ch. 13 is repr. from 1831 edn in *Medieval Culture and Society*, ed. D. Herlihy (New York and London, 1968), pp. 404–10. Heresy lies in rejection of papacy and hierarchy for the company of the elect and in attitude to Scripture (pp. 15, 16, 25, 31); the author shares the Lollard rejection of images and pilgrimages (pp. 37–8, 84–5) and claims right of free preaching (pp. 11–12). But he accepts priesthood (p. 34) and has reverence for sacraments (p. 59), and there is no Donatism or rejection of transubstantiation in his work. For ethical concern, note denunciation of oppression of rich (pp. 69–71), Sabbatarianism (p. 91), attitudes to bribery (pp. 112–14) and selling suffrages (as he sees it) for money (p. 93). Ch. 12 is a commentary on the Ten Commandments; see Hudson, *Premature Reformation*, pp. 211–14.

[52] E.g. G. R. Owst, *Preaching in Medieval England* (Cambridge, 1926), pp. 292–4; Fines, *Studies*, p. 21.

[53] McFarlane, *Wycliffe*, pp. 124–5.

[54] *Thomae Waldensis Carmelitae Anglici doctrinale fidei catholicae ecclesiae*, ed. F. Bonaventura Blanciotti, I (Venice, 1757), cols 20–1; Fines, *Studies*, p. 34, n. 2.

[55] Hudson, *Premature Reformation*, pp. 390–4.

[56] Manning, *People's Faith*, p. 101. *Dives and Pauper* (*STC* 19212–14) was completed between 1405 and 1410. See P. H. Barnum's edn, *EETS* CCLXXV (1976), CCLXXX (1980); Hudson, *Premature Reformation*, pp. 417–21.

[57] Deanesly, *Lollard Bible*, p. 304; E. Colledge, '"The Recluse" – a Lollard interpolated version of the "Ancren Riwle"', *Review of English Studies* XV (1939), pp. 1–15, 129–45; H. E. Allen, *Writings ascribed to Richard Rolle* (New York and London, 1927).

readers – something wholly against Lollard views, which the interpolators had nevertheless not removed.[58] The sermon-cycle combined orthodox with Lollard instruction in the framework of the Church's liturgy.[59] As late as 1401 biblical translation had not been condemned.

The strands of belief

Variety of belief in the early days was a consequence of the development of the preaching strata in the movement from the proto-Lollards of academic circles to the simpler chaplains and laymen, and it was implicit in a theology which urged every man to seek his own guidance in the open Scriptures. Gradually a more academic Lollardy faded, as it was no longer reinforced by graduate recruits, and the simpler Donatism and anticlericalism of the less-educated preachers took its place. Fundamental to the movement were the ideas of the relationship between Scripture and the Church which went back to Wyclif; inevitably, even among the proto-Lollards, the initial nuances were lost. The need to do battle with opponents and press on with an aggressive missionizing may also have helped to radicalize Lollard thinking; this, Deanesly suggests, was the effect on the naturally scholarly and moderate Purvey, which helps to explain the discrepancies between his pre-1401 treatises[60] and the errors he abjured in 1401,[61] and the tract *Sixteen points putten by bishops ordinarily upon men which they clepen Lollards*, written after 1401, when he was no longer under the same pressures.[62] Direct contradictions between different Lollard authors are not lacking. The Twelve Conclusions of 1395 was pacifist,[63] the *Lantern of Light* of 1409–15 accepted the necessity of 'righteous smiting'.[64] The *Lantern* contained no eucharistic heresy, and was altogether moderate on the sacraments;[65] yet both Sawtry (burned in 1401) and the tailor Badby (burned in 1410) went to the stake in part because of their rejection of transubstantiation.[66] The *Lantern* expressed no Donatist views; yet the evidence of enquiries of the period shows that this was a relatively frequent heresy.[67] Lollardy was

[58] Ed. T. F. Simmons and H. E. Nolloth (London, 1901) (*EETS*, o.s. cxviii) (see esp. pp. 102, 103, 106); Workman, *Wyclif* ii, pp. 158–60, correcting Nolloth. See Wordsworth and Littlehales, *Service-Books*, p. 262.

[59] Above, 249, n. 14. Debate in 1401: Hudson, *Premature Reformation*, p. 417.

[60] Theses extracted therefrom by the Carmelite Lavenham in *FZ*, pp. 383–99; see Workman, *Wyclif* ii, pp. 165–7, Leff, *Heresy* ii, pp. 578–83, for analysis of relation to Wyclif's thought. But note that Leff is using Lavenham, not Purvey's confession.

[61] *FZ*, pp. 400–7; the first five topics of Lavenham's compilation appear as topics of the abjuration.

[62] Text in Deanesly, *Lollard Bible*, pp. 462–7; dating follows Deanesly's hypothesis (pp. 461–2; discussion on pp. 284–5). Note difference between views on priesthood in Lavenham's treatise, pp. 387–9 (distinguished from Wyclif's by Leff, *Heresy* ii, p. 580) and those in the Sixteen Points (Deanesly, p. 465).

[63] See *FZ*, pp. 366–7; discussion of texts in Workman, *Wyclif* ii, p. 391, n. 2; H. S. Cronin, 'The Twelve Conclusions of the Lollards', *EHR* xxii (1907), pp. 292–304.

[64] Ed. Swinburne, p. 99.

[65] Ibid., pp. xv (introduction), 59.

[66] *FZ*, pp. 410, 411; Foxe, *Acts and Monuments*, ed. S. R. Cattley, iii (London, 1837), pp. 221–9, esp. p. 222 (Sawtry); pp. 235–9 (Badby); McFarlane, *Wycliffe*, pp. 150–2, 154–5. On Foxe, see below, p. 380, n. 66. On the Badby case, P. McNiven, *Heresy and Politics in the Reign of Henry IV: The Burning of John Badby* (Woodbridge, 1987). A Bristol link, fear of eucharistic heresy, and tension springing from the preparations for holding a Parliament in 1410 at Bristol are suggested as factors in the trial of Badby in M. Aston's review, *EHR* cv (1990), pp. 451–2.

[67] Above, n. 51.

as much a mood as a formal body of doctrines, and for a long time distinct strands of belief co-existed.

The doctrinal relation of Lollardy to Wyclif is complicated. The exigencies of evangelization meant that Wyclif's conclusions were adopted without the arguments that he used to reach them.[68] For many the philosophical background to his thinking soon faded, and the moral stress of Wyclif tended to assume the centre of the stage. No major Lollard treatise, it would seem, took up the implications of dominion by grace for civil possession, though it was treated in the sermon-cycle and occasional suspects had firm views on the point.[69] Most revealing of all is the change which Wyclif's eucharistic beliefs underwent in the hands of the Lollards. His positive views, as we have seen, can most fairly be said to have corresponded at the end of his life with consubstantiation; but the *Wicket*, put out under his name, much later, preached that the eucharist was a simple commemoration meal.[70] In this way Wyclif was simplified and at times distorted, detached from his contemporary academic setting and used as figurehead for a movement that had grown away from him. Yet he could certainly have recognized some of the tenets of late Lollardy. The effect of his explosive ideas on Scripture and the body of the elect are traceable throughout Lollard history.

The actions of authority

From one point of view, the reactions of Church leaders were eminently successful. By sounding the alarm, achieving a clear condemnation of some Wyclifite tenets, and purging Oxford in 1382, Courtenay checked the heresy's potential for rising in society and maintaining its intellectual base.[71] The Peasants' Revolt in the previous year was a stroke of luck. Wyclif's own reactions to it were plainly hostile;[72] nevertheless, it was widely believed that Lollards had some responsibility, and the belief influenced authority's reactions.[73] Its immediate sequel was a statute restraining the activities of preachers. Already eucharistic heresy was beginning to frighten away the more opportunistic anticlerical supporters; the belief that Lollardy meant sedition helped the process on. When Hereford and Repton sought out Gaunt as a shield in 1382, after coming under fire from Courtenay, they met with a refusal, symptomatic of the change in atmosphere that had taken place.[74]

On the other hand, the failure of bishops to follow Courtenay's vigorous lead and the absence of a fully co-ordinated machinery of repression was equally decisive for the continued existence of Lollardy. The preachers were not adequately checked; bishops did not react quickly; Buckingham was not

---

[68] See Leff's comment on the Twenty-five Points: *Heresy* II, p. 576.

[69] See Thomson, *Later Lollards*, pp. 29, 145; Hudson, *Premature Reformation*, pp. 360–2.

[70] Aston, in *PP* xxx (1965), pp. 37–8; also her 'Lollardy and the Reformation: survival or revival', *History* xlix (1964), pp. 149–70.

[71] Courtenay's vital role was first noticed by McFarlane in his *Wycliffe*: Courtenay, not Wyclif, is the true hero of the book.

[72] Above, p. 237.

[73] The most helpful article on this is Aston, 'Lollardy and sedition', *PP* xvii. I am much indebted to it. See also H. G. Richardson, 'Heresy and the lay power under Richard II', *EHR* li (1936), pp. 1–28.

[74] Workman, *Wyclif* II, p. 282; McFarlane, *Wycliffe*, p. 110.

notably speedy in dealing with the Leicester outbreak; Trefnant, bishop of Hereford, was slow and, in his action against Walter Brute, somewhat easily satisfied by a generalized confession of orthodoxy.[75] Erastian bishops tended not to be keen heresy-hunters; it has been suggested that they were aware of some sympathy in high places.[76] Concern for justice and for the soul of the Lollard also tended to outweigh the practical merits of draconian measures. The long delays allowed to Oldcastle before condemnation were, admittedly, due to the personal wishes of the young Henry v; but the reluctance to burn in the case of the insignificant tailor Badby can only have sprung from humanity and a care for souls.

England was slow to follow continental example, and in some matters retained her individual customs. Torture was not used; time for reflection in an episcopal prison was usually effective enough in inducing confessions. Great stress was laid on the need to convert the prisoner from his heresy. Richard Wyche spent some three months in the bishop of Durham's prison, during which time he was subjected to six hearings before the bishop or his advisers, as well as two visits to him by individuals seeking to influence his mind, before the two formal sessions in which he was excommunicated and sent back to prison.[77] The rewards for recantation were generous: Purvey received a benefice after he had given in, and the anchoress Matilda at Leicester found that after she had been brought back to orthodoxy the archbishop offered indulgences to those who gave her gifts.[78]

This restraint helped to keep preachers in the field after they could have been laid by the heels. William Taylor, the academic Lollard, is the classic example. He was cited twice by Arundel, in 1406 and 1410, and on both occasions did not appear. He was taken to court in the Worcester diocese in 1417, and in 1420 came before Archbishop Chichele, when he recanted. Six months later he was arrested in Bristol and sentenced to life imprisonment, but he was released, and only burnt when he had been caught yet again.[79] Wyche is a similar example; his career as a missionary could have been brought to an end long before 1440 by keeping him under some surveillance.

The laity were most moved by the fear of rebellion, and action was most likely when their political interests were involved. Thus Courtenay pressed home his attack on Lollardy in the period of reaction which followed the Peasants' Revolt of 1381; the action of the Cambridge parliament of 1388, setting up new commissions of laymen as well as churchmen to deal with Lollardy, was in part an outcome of the Appellants' wish to maintain order in the secular as much as in the ecclesiastical sphere; when burning was introduced by the statute *De heretico comburendo* in 1401, the Church had been able to take advantage of political events. A usurper king needed all the help

[75] McFarlane, *Wycliffe*, pp. 121–4, 135–7. For lack of zeal by Wakefield of Worcester, see *SCH* xi, pp. 143–4.

[76] McFarlane, *Lancastrian Kings*, pp. 225–6. For Buckingham, see *SCH* ix, pp. 131–45.

[77] Wyche's own account is in *EHR* v (1890), pp. 530–44; on torture, note the dark phrase about Hereford and Purvey attributed to Arundel in Pollard, *Fifteenth-Century Prose*, p. 165. But there is no general evidence for torture; see Thomson, *Later Lollards*, p. 230.

[78] Fines, *Studies*, p. 40.

[79] Thomson, *Later Lollards*, pp. 24–6.

he could get from the clergy, and he may well have thought that the measures intended to deal with unauthorized preachers could also be useful in checking the growth of political conspiracies and conventicles.[80]

At other times the attitude of the laity was somewhat changeable. In 1384 Nassington's translation of the *Speculum vitae*, an entirely orthodox work of piety, was submitted to the chancellor of Cambridge for a learned judgement for fear that it was heretical.[81] Yet the careers of the great evangelists, such as Thorpe, Wyche and Purvey, would have been quite impossible if the overwhelming majority of their hearers had not declined to betray them to authority. In the Commons conflicting emotions decided the approach to heresy; on the one side, the laity were unwilling to put more power into the hands of churchmen; on the other, they could be spurred on by the belief that State and property were being threatened by Lollardy. Anticlerical sentiment, a taste for the vernacular, and an unwillingness to be ruled overmuch by ecclesiastics accounts for some of the unwillingness to press home the repression of Lollardy.

Finally, Lollard attitudes to the secular power were affected by the course of events. They had inherited from Wyclif the belief that the secular authorities should be the instrument to reform the Church,[82] and the last two decades of the fourteenth century saw a series of attempts to persuade the State to take action. Only after long disappointment did a section abandon persuasion in favour of a *coup d'état*. After the *coup* failed, the general tendency was to leave the reform of the Church in the hands of God, and wait quietly for better times. Wyclif himself constantly appealed to the State; Swinderby to the justices in parliament. Tracts were written with an eye to influencing the upper classes, and in 1395 a Lollard bill demanding reform was put on the doors of Westminster Hall and St Paul's when parliament was in session.[83] As late as 1410 a proposal came before parliament to disendow the possessioners; but it gained no support at all in the quarters where it mattered most – with the king and the prince of Wales.[84]

Oldcastle's revolt

The immediate occasion for the resort to force by Lollardy was the imprisonment of their most distinguished secular leader, Sir John Oldcastle.[85] Oldcastle was, like some of the Lollard knights, a man who made his way through the profession of arms, rising from a modest family background in Herefordshire: there is a parallel between his military service to the future Henry V when prince of Wales and the service of some Lollard knights to the Black Prince.[86] But times had changed. Henry V was a man of devout

[80] Aston, *PP* XVII, pp. 32–3.
[81] Deanesly, *Lollard Bible*, pp. 215–16.
[82] For Wyclif's attitudes, see Leff, *Heresy* II, pp. 543–5.
[83] Correction of Deanesly (*Lollard Bible*, p. 283) on 1395 episode in McFarlane, *Wycliffe*, p. 147; see Aston, *PP* XVII, p. 17.
[84] Ibid. It should be noted that it is not necessarily of direct Lollard inspiration.
[85] For what follows, see W. T. Waugh, 'Sir John Oldcastle', *EHR* XX (1905), pp. 434–56, 637–58; and succinctly, with additional evidence on Oldcastle's rebellion, in McFarlane, *Wycliffe*, pp. 160–83.
[86] Above, p. 253; McFarlane, 'The origins of the Lollard movement', in *Relazioni* VII, pp. 216–17

character, and a determined opponent of heresy; Oldcastle was a fully committed Lollard. The only wonder is that he should have been left at liberty for so long. Probably a principal reason was his station in society. Though a clear abetter of Lollardy, twice brought before the council to answer charges relating to heresy, he was subjected to no punishment. In the end, however, he was unable to withstand the evidence of association with Lollard chaplains and the distribution of their tracts. In 1413 he was arrested. At his trial in St Paul's he defied Arundel, declared his heresy on the eucharist and the Church, and was condemned. During the forty days respite which he was allowed by special grace of the king to reconsider his position, he was rescued from the Tower, and he proceeded to raise his followers in rebellion. The aim has never been clarified; the royal view expressed in proclamations was that Oldcastle intended to kill the royal family, nobility and upper clergy, and to dispossess the Church. We may assume that Oldcastle intended to enforce a Lollard reform. It was a wild scheme. The revolt should be seen as a gambler's throw that never had any realistic chances of success. The plot was betrayed, and the rebels rounded up before they could inflict damage.

It should impress us that a prisoner on the run could rouse rebellion from scattered Lollard congregations and self-seekers scattered as far west as Bristol and as far north as Derby. Map 6 plots the results of McFarlane's researches into the judicial records of the investigations into the revolt.[87] A shrewd judge, he estimated that our picture of the extent of the rebellion may not be far from the truth, for the attempt at revolution, even including the assassination of the king, plainly roused both officials and the populace to counteraction.

Rebellion was one result of the Lollard missionizing of the previous decades. Areas where the bishops had found Lollards to prosecute tend to coincide with those which sent men to join Oldcastle's last throw. Bristol, the old Lollard centre, sent the largest contingent, some forty craftsmen setting out under the leadership of six chaplains; the Leicestershire villages' participation reveals that, even if Leicester itself was not so deeply involved, the heresy was still embedded in the surrounding countryside. Yet some Lollard-influenced areas were mute on this occasion – Swinderby's old preaching-ground in Herefordshire and on the Welsh border generally, East Anglia, that we know to have given evidence of heretical activity, Oldcastle's area of influence in Kent.

Sometimes the depositions enable us to pick out a decisive leader who has roused a region. Such were William the chaplain of Thaxted, the evangelist of Essex; Walter Gilbert alias Kibworth, who had influenced both the Leicestershire villages near Kibworth Harcourt and the Derby area; and, in Derby and its surrounds, another chaplain, William Ederick; in Oxfordshire William Brown alias Davy, a glover of Woodstock. The patrons of heresy in higher classes also had their part to play – at Drayton Beauchamp in Buckinghamshire, the Cheynes; at Smeeton Westerby, among the Leicestershire villages, the most committed of the Lollard knights, Sir Thomas

(earlier stage of his research into Lollard knights); for academic influences, see Hudson, *Premature Reformation*, p. 89.

[87] It follows closely McFarlane, *Wycliffe*, pp. 172–80.

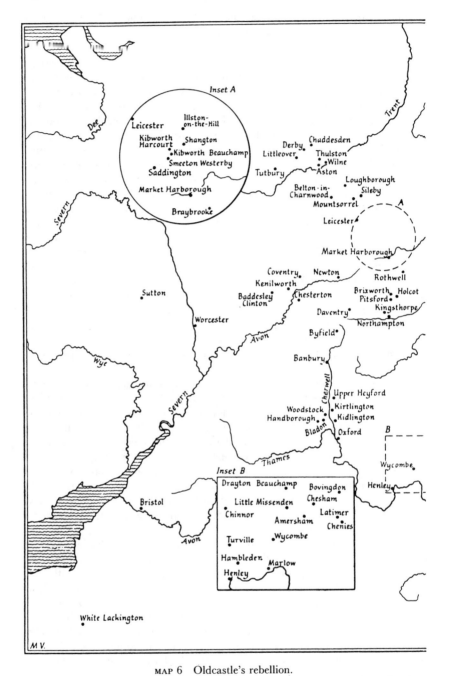

MAP 6   Oldcastle's rebellion.

Source: From K. B. McFarlane, *John Wycliffe and the Beginnings of English Nonconformity* (London, 1952).

0   50 Miles

0   80 Km

Witham

Welland

Nene

Gt. Ouse

Cam

Lark

Mildenhall

Yare

Waveney

Hitchin

Thaxted

Halstead

Stanbridge

Dunstable

Gt. Gaddesden

Pattiswick

Coggeshall

Colchester

Kelvedon

Lea

Chesham

Amersham

Maldon

Thames

Wey

Davington

Stour

Medway

Dover

Latimer, its lord; in the lower valley of the Cherwell in Oxfordshire, Thomas Compworth.

Yet the map only presents a partial picture of the extent of Lollard sympathies in Henry v's reign, despite the energy of the commissioners in collecting evidence. The total numbers involved were very small. Three hundred is a maximum. Some may well have declined Oldcastle's call on principle; others may not have been able to come in time, because of their geographical isolation from London. The rebellion attracted the seditious and adventurers who had no unorthodox religious affiliations, but were merely out for the tangible rewards of a successful rebellion, as in the case of the rich brewer of Dunstable who bought gilt spurs in anticipation of the knighthood that was to reward his participation. The proof of the participation of non-Lollards lies in the actions of the government. Of those sentenced to be executed, a majority was condemned to be hanged. The bodies of the genuine Lollards were burnt after they had been hanged; this was an action adopted only in a small proportion of the total cases. Numbers of rebels and sympathizers were treated mercifully, and in these cases many were released after a term of imprisonment without being handed over to an ecclesiastical court – another indication that opportunists predominated over those of religious conviction.

The revolt marked a turning-point in the relation between Lollardy and the State. It finally demonstrated to the country that the suspicion that heresy and sedition went together had good grounds.[88] Little hope as Lollardy had of gaining wide support before 1414, the revolt finally condemned it to the underground existence of a small minority.

LOLLARDY UNDERGROUND

The prosecutions after 1414[89]

In the surge of anxiety following the revolt plots were discovered linking Lollards with England's enemies – the Scots, the Welsh, the false Richard II – and emotions against the sectaries ran high.[90] The somewhat eccentric but orthodox English mystic, Margery Kempe, being taken through Beverley under arrest, was confronted by local housewives, who ran out of their houses

---

[88] See Aston, *PP* XVII, p. 35.

[89] For comprehensive survey based on episcopal registers and other evidence, see Thomson, *Later Lollards*, maps pp. 52, 118, 172; reviews: M. Deanesly, in *JEH* XVII (1966), pp. 265–6; S. H. Thomson, in *Speculum* XLI (1966), pp. 774–5; M. McKisack, in *JTS* XVII (1966), pp. 505–6; R. B. Dobson, in *SHR* XLVI (1967), pp. 63–4. For intensive study of select dioceses, exploiting esp. Westminster Catheral MS on Norwich prosecutions 1428, Lichfield heresy court book (discovered by Fines) for Lichfield prosecutions 1511–12, see Fines, *Studies*; maps pp. 60, 167; analysis of Westminster Cathedral MS in appendix 2; insights in ch. of conclusions. Best short account of Lollard trial is J. Fines, 'Heresy trials in the diocese of Coventry and Lichfield, 1511–12', *JEH* XIV (1963), pp. 160–74; for prosecution records also his 'The post-mortem condemnation for heresy of Richard Hunne', *EHR* LXXVIII (1963), pp. 528–31, and Thomson, *Later Lollards*, pp. 223–4. Documents are in *EHD* IV, ed. A. R. Myers (London, 1969), pp. 837–78. I am indebted for generous help to Dr Thomson and Dr Fines.

[90] Thomson, *Later Lollards*, pp. 8–18, Aston, *PP* XVII, pp. 20–3.

shaking their distaffs and crying out, 'Brennith this fals heretyk'.[91] Because of
the revolt, public opinion turned decisively against the Lollards; there was
natural indignation at the bloody details of the plot, and all the warnings of
the bishops in the earlier decades seemed amply confirmed. In this phase of
high emotion, detection and prosecution had every assistance. Oldcastle,
hidden by sympathizers, was none the less rounded up and executed.
Through the effects of the revolt and the state of opinion, the limited support
of those of gentle birth for Lollardy faded out, and the congregations lower
down the social scale were put under heavy pressure.

Yet such intensity of feeling could not last. Groups of Lollards, the majority
quite unconnected with the revolt, rode out the storm. Surviving pro-Lollard
clergy and other evangelists helped to keep the movement in being. Secular
interest waned; the impetus to detection passed back again to ecclesiastical
authorities. In 1428 Archbishop Chichele was apparently calling for fair
copies of prosecution records to be deposited at Lambeth, with a view to
making persecution more effective by co-ordinating information.[92] Stiff drives
against heresy launched in Canterbury and Norwich dioceses showed that the
Lollards were still in existence, and in considerable numbers;[93] in the Norwich
diocese 101 came before the courts between 1424 and 1431.[94]

Then in 1431 another revolt was launched, but feebly, in circumstances that
made it almost a caricature of that in 1414; though it resembled the Oldcastle
rebellion in aiming at disendowment and the removal of the king and
aristocracy, its leaders, William Perkins, a former bailiff of Abingdon with a
record of conviction for non-religious offences, and John Russell, former
associate of Richard Gurmyn the Lollard baker, in the London textile
industry, once engaged in false moneying, were a far cry from Oldcastle, and
the action fizzled out in the scattering of handbills in London, an assembly at
East Hendred to march on Abingdon abbey, and a similar abortive attempt
on Salisbury cathedral.[95] Only in Coventry, where there were executions, and
in Leicester did something more serious occur. The link with Lollardy was
tenuous – Perkins and Russell seem more like opportunists than members of
Scripture-reading circles. Clergy had hardly any share, and we hear nothing
of the doctrinal unorthodoxy of participants.

Thereafter no violent movement labelled as Lollard again gathered support
over even as wide an area as the 1431 plot had done. *Pari passu*, as far as our
records are concerned, incidence of prosecutions drops away in the following
decades. Apart from an action under Bishop Chedworth in the Chilterns in
1462–4, we meet few cases about mid-century.

91 Thomson, *Later Lollards*, p. 195.
92 Fines, *Studies*, appendix 2, and *EHR* LXXVIII, pp. 528–31.
93 For incidence of prosecutions, see table in Thomson, *Later Lollards*, pp. 237–8.
94 Fines, *Studies*, p. 245.
95 Fullest account by Aston, *PP* XVII, pp. 24–30 (note valuable footnotes); Mrs Aston kindly informs
me she would now modify some of the views in her article. I have followed the approach of Thomson (*Later
Lollards*, pp. 58–62, 102, 146–8), minimizing the seriousness of the affair. Note doubts on Lollard
participation (p. 61), and see his 'A Lollard rising in Kent, 1431 or 1438', *BIHR* XXXVII (1964), pp. 100–2.
Humphrey, duke of Gloucester, made enquiries after the rising in Leicester and Coventry. There were also
enquiries of various kinds in Wiltshire, Somerset, Cambridgeshire, Kent and in Hertford, and Sir John
Cheyne, of Drayton Beauchamp (Buckinghamshire), and his brother Thomas were arrested.

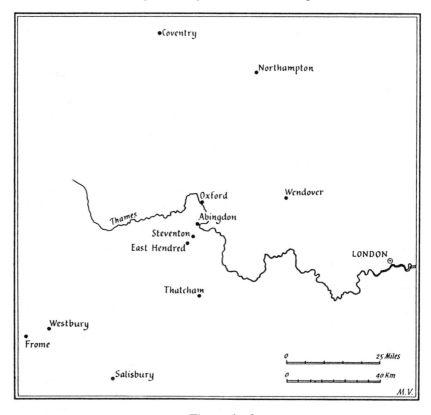

MAP 7   The revolt of 1431.

Recorded prosecutions form a kind of parabola over the course of the
fifteenth-century – higher in number in the earlier decades, descending in the
centre of the period, then rising again in a curve from 1486, when there was an
important action in Coventry and Lichfield diocese, to the eve of the
Reformation, when Protestantism from the Continent comes in to add another
dimension to local heresy, and to complicate the task of the historian of
Lollardy.

From 1486 prosecutions started to occur more frequently, and in certain
areas they involved a greater number of abjurations – 74 in Coventry and
Lichfield in 1511–12,[96] 96 in Salisbury diocese between 1491 and 1521, 300 in
Lincoln between 1511 and 1521. The diocese of London, which included
Essex as well as the capital, was strongly affected: a high figure may be given
for the prosecution there in 1511,[97] 50 for the prosecutions of Fitzjames in
1518, over 200 (when Protestantism from abroad was already in the field)

---

[96] Fines, in *JEH* xiv, p. 161.
[97] For this estimate and the other figures, see Fines, *Studies*, p. 245. On episcopal approaches, see
M. E. Aston, 'Bishops and heresy: the defence of the faith', Id., *Faith and Fire*, London, Rio Grande, 1993 (coll.
articles).

between 1527 and 1532.[98] If the mid-century lull in our records corresponds to a real lull in prosecutions, we can reconstruct what happened. Pressure from the bishops lessened in the middle years, so Lollardy revived and made more converts; an increased tempo of prosecution was the response, which none the less failed to stamp out the heresy.[99] Still a small minority, Lollardy was a tough one. It survived to merge with the new Protestantism.

The reasons for survival

Two reasons may be given for this survival, one linked to the interests of the English episcopate, the other to the indigenous qualities of the heresy and the nature of its adherents. Bishops, as we have seen on the Continent, tended to have a less sustained interest in the pursuit of heresy than inquisitors had; in England at this time they had multifarious duties and political commitments; some were absentees. It is therefore not surprising that only a proportion of them took active steps against Lollardy. Moreover, the proceedings that they did take were not of the drastically efficient, repeated kind that could uproot a heretical group altogether, without leaving a remnant that would start to evangelize once the pressure was lifted.

The individual, truly thorough investigations occasionally recorded throw into relief the deficiencies of the majority of episcopal prosecutions. At Norwich Bishop Alnwick kept at his task from 1428 to 1431, ensured that the forceful leader of the Norwich heresy, William White, was captured and burnt, and saw to it that eighteen of those who abjured were each given a copy of their abjuration to take home with them as a reminder of penalties that might occur for relapse. The Alnwick prosecutions formed part of a wider drive, involving Kent, Essex and Suffolk as well, spurred on by fears of England's heresy being reinforced by the Hussite movement in Bohemia. In 1427 Martin v had asked for the sentence of the Council of Constance to be carried out: the exhumation of Wyclif's bones in the following year was the response of the English episcopate to his request, and when, in 1428, convocation discussed procedures against heretics they also in the same session considered a subsidy for the crusade against Bohemia. Urgency was given to the moves against Lollards by the betrayal of preparations for a rebellion, nipped in the bud by Archbishop Chichele, Alnwick and other bishops.[100]

Other members of the episcopate did not proceed with the same thoroughness. One wonders whether the efficiency at Norwich is responsible for the fact that we hear no more of heresy there after Alnwick's action. In

---

[98] A. G. Dickens, *Lollards and Protestants in the Diocese of York* (Oxford, 1959), p. 8, and his survey, 'Heresy and the origins of English Protestantism', in *Britain and the Netherlands* II, ed. J. S. Bromley and E. H. Kossman (Groningen, 1964), pp. 55–6; cf. Thomson, *Later Lollards*, pp. 137–8, 170–1.

[99] Fines's hypothesis (*JEH* XIV (1963), p. 160); support for a comparable view in J. F. Davis, 'Lollards, reformers and St Thomas of Canterbury', *UBHJ* IX (1963), pp. 1–15 at p. 6; verdict of 'not proven' by Thomson, *Later Lollards*, p. 3; discussion in Hudson, *Premature Reformation*, pp. 447–50.

[100] Fines, *Studies*, pp. 74–9, 83–6, Thomson, *Later Lollards*, pp. 131–2; M. E. Aston, 'William White's Lollard followers', *CHR* LXVIII (1982), pp. 469–97 (shrewd analysis of teaching and structure of White's group), commenting on *Heresy Trials in Diocese of Norwich 1428–31*, ed. N. Tanner, Camden, 4th ser. XX (London, 1977) (definitive edn, see review: M. D. Lambert, in *JEH* XXXII (1981), p. 118); on Lollard geography, see R. G. Davies, 'Lollardy and locality', *TRHS* 6th ser.

Coventry the well-conducted investigation of 1511–12 brought seventy-four before the court, of whom only forty-five were sufficiently deeply involved to be mentioned by name.[101] Coventry was a strong centre; but it also looks as if a thorough drive was uncovering the connections of heresy in a way that was not usual elsewhere.

For a series of prosecutions in England, our records give us only a trickle of abjurations, probably pruning some, but never all, of the branches of a local grouping, and so leaving a residue to grow again. Mercy as well as inefficiency kept heresy alive, maintaining an English distinction between relapse *vere* and *ficte*, which put off the final penalty and helped to keep missionaries in the field.[102] Heresy tended to be uncovered by chance. The routine of archidiaconal visitations of Kentish textile villages in the years before 1511 give no hint that there was heresy there at all; yet, when a drive was launched in 1511, it became clear that it was rife among them.[103] Perhaps the inclusion of heresy among the commissions of vicars-general at the end of the fifteenth century improved the situation; in general, however, the launching of prosecutions remained quite fitful and spasmodic for most of the period.

The other factor preserving Lollardy was its appeal to the craftsman, the skilled artisan and his family who, the residual upper class support cut off, became the carrying class of the sect in its terminal phase. A Lollard community was above all a reading community, basing its common life on the public and private reading of the Scriptures and of Lollard tracts. At Coventry the sect came together for readings, either in twos, with a teacher helping a new convert, or in small groups.[104] In the Norwich group Margery Baxter had her husband read aloud to her in bed at night 'from a book of the law of Christ'.[105] Lollard schools gave specific instruction, perhaps inculcating the aphorisms which conveyed beliefs to neophytes and illiterates.[106] The effects of the Lollard scares were to inhibit internal reform. Fear of the vernacular tended to check rather than foster the struggles of the medieval Church to raise the standards of the humble parish clergy. There is no evidence that Pecock's attempt at the use of reason in counter-argument had any effect. The answers of the Church to Lollardy tended to be the heating up 'of the fires of devotion'. Those features of the English Church to which the Lollard temperament objected were not changed, and it was never likely that they would be.[107] Copying and distribution kept the Scriptures and the heretical literature in being, a jump ahead of authority, which tried but never

---

[101] Fines, in *JEH* XIV, p. 161; Thomson (*Later Lollards*, p. 109) shows there were more guilty than this; on the episcopate, a balanced statement by R. G. Davies, 'The episcopate', in *Profession, Vocation and Culture in Later Medieval England*, ed. C . H. Clough (Liverpool, 1982), pp. 51–89.

[102] Davis, *UBHJ* IX, p. 6.

[103] Thomson, *Later Lollards*, p. 190; on vicars-general and heresy, see Davis, *UBHJ* IX, p. 3. *Kent Heresy Proceedings 1511–12*, ed. N. Tanner, Littlehampton, 1997.

[104] Fines, *JEH* XIV, p. 166.

[105] Thomson, *Later Lollards*, p. 130.

[106] Fines's hypothesis (*JEH* XIV, p. 167).

[107] See review of Hudson, *Premature Reformation*, by R. M. Haines in *Canadian Journal of History* XXIV (1989), pp. 221–2; note the comment, p. 222, 'The author censures the negativism of Lollardy's critics, yet on the basis of the picture she has painted accommodation was inconceivable.' On the fires of devotion, see E. F. Jacob, 'Reynold Pecock, bishop of Chichester', *PBA* XXXVII (1951), pp. 121–53; on Pecock, see also R. M. Haines, 'Reginald Pecock: a tolerant man in an age of intolerance', *SCH* XXI (1984), pp. 125–37; aphorisms, sardonic on Church life: Fines, *JEH* XIV, p. 163.

succeeded in gathering it all in. The inner membership conducted their activities in an atmosphere of earnest study – which was exactly what would attract a type of recruit frequent among the skilled artisans. A reading sect had a natural appeal to a class in which literacy was incipient, and which included hard-working, independent people anxious to learn and to form judgements for themselves.

Conditions of work for the skilled man, who in order to gain an apprenticeship and earn a living was forced to move about, helped evangelization by person-to-person contact and kept loose links between the major Lollard areas; for example, John Jonson, the Birmingham cutler caught in 1511 in the ordinary course of pursuing his craft, had moved from his birthplace near York to London to be apprenticed, then migrated in turn to Coventry, Gloucester, Bristol, Taunton and other places, then to London, Maidstone and finally back to Coventry and Birmingham. Lollard meetings could easily be disguised as trade contacts.[108] In one interesting example, industry itself formed the matrix of heresy, when Thomas Moon of Loddon, a glover, used his workplace to influence employees. There Lollardy passed from the laity to the clergy, as John Pert, a reader in the school built up at Loddon under Moon's influence, in turn initiated Hugh Pye, chaplain at Loddon.[109] Mobility imposed itself on a veteran evangelist, helping him to keep ahead of persecution, while at the same time possession of a skill helped him to move round the country. So James Willis the weaver, burnt in 1462, long eluded capture by changing his residence from one Lollard centre to another, from Bristol to London and finally to the Chilterns, confessing in Lent and taking communion at Easter, all the while instructing followers and keeping his copies of Lollard literature.[110] A few dedicated men of this kind were a mainstay of the movement at the end, whose vitality rested on the determined missionary.

Lollard beliefs might descend in great secrecy, as in the Morden family at Chesham in the Chilterns, where Richard Ashford, son-in-law of John Morden, knew nothing of his father-in-law's hidden beliefs till the old man opened his heart to him on his deathbed, initiating Ashford in a heresy he retained till his capture in 1521.[111] In another case in Coventry, a daughter was brought by her mother to the heretical household of the Laudesdales to be read to from a large book; years later she brought her husband to the same house to receive instruction.[112] Such family affiliations might keep the heresy going. Leading personalities, however, were needed to make converts in larger numbers and to efface the effects of anti-heresy drives. Occasionally we catch glimpses of these key men in action: for example, William White in East Anglia, instructing by vivid demonstration, employing a layman to celebrate

[108] Does this explain the prominence of skilled men in underground movements? See J. F. Davis, 'Lollard survival and the textile industry in the south-east of England', in *SCH* III, pp. 191–201 at p. 196, citing analogy of skilled men in popular radicalism in eighteenth-century Austria. For Jonson, see Fines, *JEH* xiv, p. 163.

[109] Fines, *Studies*, p. 54.

[110] Thomson, *Later Lollards*, pp. 34, 68–71, 152, 236n, 242. He abjured at the end, when he could not have hoped this would save his life.

[111] Ibid., pp. 90–1.

[112] Ibid., p. 110, Fines, *JEH* xiv, pp. 165–7, 171.

the eucharist at Easter in place of himself, despite the fact that he was in orders, or quasi-ceremonially eating cold sausages with his followers on Good Friday to defy the Church's ordinance on fasting.

White's distinctive views can be traced repeatedly in the confessions of his followers. Even an individual turn of phrase, contrasting the dead wood in the making of images with the strength of the growing tree, recurs in the confessions. White's personality gave a special cast to the East Anglian group. Teaching travelled down from layer to layer, sometimes given a particular twist by the more independent-minded, even eccentric members. One theme did not survive the transition from teachers to lesser fry. White's doctrine that the eucharist was 'corpus Christi in memoria' did not take root: John Reve, glover of Beccles, for example, believed that it was simply material bread.

The number of cases in the ensemble of the trials in which an individual is mentioned provides a working guide to his or her importance in the diffusion of heresy. So the leading teachers emerge, as we might expect, as White himself, mentioned sixteen times, flanked by Hugh Pye, twelve times. Both were in orders. White had been a leader in Tenterden and he was aided by others who had also once been active in Kent. Below White and Pye came a class of missionaries and teachers in schools, some lay, some in orders, mentioned six times or less, shading down to three in the case of John Waddon, once in Kent, who was executed. Below this category came local supporters and those who gave hospitality to Lollards in their homes, mentioned between one and five times, including the redoubtable Margery Baxter with her pungent housewife's sayings.

Authority in the Alnwick prosecutions took care to preserve individual statements and did not force them into the mould of pre-existing interrogations; suspects, for their part, were, it has been suggested, astute enough in some cases to feign illiteracy in the hope of mitigating their guilt. White's sphere of influence seems to have lain outside Norwich itself, which as far as extant and exploited records are concerned, remained remarkably untouched by heresy, its population faithfully supporting its numerous parish churches in traditional ways up to the Reformation.[113] What must have been a personal charisma is now lost to us but implicit in results, in the case of Thomas Man, long resident in the Chilterns, who claimed that he and his wife had converted between 500 and 700 followers. No doubt he exaggerated, but there was a core of truth, for a witness at his second trial in 1518 said that he had instructed followers at Amersham, Billericay, Chelmsford, Stratford Langthorne, Uxbridge, Burnley, Burnham, Henley, Newbury and London, as well as in Suffolk and Norfolk.[114]

[113] For Norwich, see N. Tanner, *The Church in Late Medieval Norwich* (Toronto, 1984) reviewed by N. Orme, *JEH* xxxvi (1985), pp. 312–13, remarking that Tanner's sources may lead to an underestimate of the 'less successful sides of religious life'; note also comment by R. B. Dobson in *EHR* cii (1987), p. 478: 'the Reformation was possible in 1530 and not in 1370 because the late medieval Church had succeeded in stimulating the religious aspirations of its parishioners not too little, but too well'. The problem is twofold. (1) Norwich seems strangely immune from Lollardy. (2) It moved rapidly from a rich traditional Church life to Protestantism. On White and his following, see Aston, in *CHR* lxviii (1982), pp. 469–97 (note tabular analysis of structure, p. 481); 'cold sausages': Fines, *Studies*, p. 54; aphorisms as teaching aid: *JEH* xiv, pp. 166–7.
[114] Thomson, *Later Lollards*, pp. 170–1, Dickens, 'Heresy and origins', p. 58.

Whether the psychology of the convert was affected by the circumstances of his work it is now impossible to say. Where the records allow us to check occupations, they lie most frequently in the textile industry, this being the biggest employer of skilled workers in England.[115] Weavers as such are not specially prominent. As the master clothier emerged, employing his own labour and depressing the status of the once-independent worker to that of a wage-earner subject to dismissal, so circumstances of work for many deteriorated. The sources do not allow us to say whether many Lollards were seeking a psychological refuge from a disadvantageous economic position in an underground religion preaching religious equality;[116] we have no positive hint that this was so, though the possibility cannot be excluded. The number of prominent Lollards who had servants points against this view; more significant is the evidence that, broadly speaking, Lollardy survived in regions where it had already laid down support before 1414, at a time of greater prosperity for textile workers. A living tradition of Lollardy went on attracting recruits, whether work circumstances changed or not. The assumptions and outlook of the craftsman,[117] which made a minority susceptible to the Lollard mission, were what counted.

Class structure and distribution

The attractions of Lollardy to the artisan class worked in two ways. On the one hand, they gave it endurance within the Scripture-reading circle after the disaster of 1414; on the other, they made it more difficult for the heresy ever again to climb higher in the social scale. Adaptation to the needs of artisan circles accompanied, and was a consequence of, the diminution of the academic leadership. Oxford had been purged originally by Courtenay, then again by Archbishop Arundel in 1411, and the doors to academic recruitment thereby closed. Academically trained men of an older generation who stayed in the field were whittled away in time. Peter Payne, an academic latecomer of considerable talents, left for Bohemia after he had been cited for heresy in the reaction after Oldcastle;[118] his logic pupil, Ralph Mungyn, worked on till he was condemned to life imprisonment in 1428;[119] the veteran Wyche was burnt in 1440.[120] By mid-century, though occasional conversion from within the religious orders brought in trained men, leadership was in the hands of unbeneficed clergy, generally of limited learning, and laymen, self-taught or instructed in Lollard schools. These could speak to their own kind; but they

[115] The most determined attempt at statistics by Davis in *SCH* III, pp. 191–201. I owe advice to Mr H. B. Clark. Skilled artisans in East Anglia 1428–31 in Fines, *Studies*, p. 60; in Coventry 1511–12, Fines, *JEH* XIV, p. 162. Occupations are not necessarily given in sources.

[116] This forms one of the explanations of Lollard survival discussed by Davis, *SCH* III: see esp. pp. 198–201.

[117] Dickens brings out the significance of artisan membership: see introduction to his *Lollards and Protestants*. In 'Heresy and origins' he comments on 'cranks and individualists' (p. 48), artisan mobility (p. 57), 'increasing . . . mental independence' (p. 64).

[118] Below, p. 344, Emden, *Biographical Register, Oxford*; R. R. Betts, *Essays in Czech History* (London, 1969), pp. 236–46.

[119] Thomson, *Later Lollards*, pp. 143–5.

[120] Ibid., pp. 148–50.

could not compose, and so new Lollard texts did not emerge, the only exceptions in the present state of knowledge being the lost tracts of William White from the 1420s and Wyclif's *Wicket*, of uncertain, but possibly late fifteenth-century date.[121] Nor could they easily carry the heresy higher in the social scale. The association between Lollardy and sedition kept those of gentle blood away, and fresh recruits in that class were not made.[122] Wealthier business circles were touched in London, and the number of Lollards in this category had grown by the sixteenth century. The rich might help the poor through their common bond of belief: so the illiterate water-carrier, Robert Benet, who kept in his belt a translation of the Four Evangelists which he could not read, went for shelter in 1497 to the house of John Barret, a goldsmith of Cheapside. Richard Hunne, whose mysterious death after arrest for heresy in 1514 created an outcry, was of the Merchant Taylors: his conflicts with the Church may have owed something to his marriage to Anne Vincent. The connection is not quite clear, but if Anne's father was Thomas Vincent, then Hunne was the son-in-law of the devoted evangelist who taught Hacker his beliefs. In London the wealth and privileges of sections of the clergy were peculiarly obvious, and gave a hold to Lollardy. Most wanted to reform rather than undermine the position of the clergy, but there were perennial financial quarrels between the Church and the city, an ambience in which the religious dissidence could grow. On the eve of the Reformation there was 'a distinct heretical community' in the capital.[123] To a lesser degree the upper echelons of Coventry society were involved in heresy: richer men's interest can be glimpsed about the time of the 1511–12 trials.[124] The overall picture is of a sect able both to survive and to grow at a certain level of society, but not able to break much fresh ground, socially or intellectually.

Map 8, which plots prosecutions for heresy between 1414 and 1522, illustrates this underground phase of Lollard history. Three inferences may be made from it. One is that Lollardy survived, broadly, in the same regions where it had lodged before 1414, and did not, it would seem, open up new ones. As Thomson has shown, Lollardy after 1414 was to be found in seven regional groupings, based in Kent, London, the Chilterns and the mid-

---

[121] Perspective given in Aston, *History* XLIX, and on *Wicket*, see her remarks in *PP* xxx (1965), pp. 37–8; Hudson, *Premature Reformation*, pp. 11, 203–4, 289, 451–2 (on content); on White's tracts, see Fines, *Studies*, p. 52.

[122] That is, in England. Some thirty persons in the late fifteenth century in Kyle and Cunningham, Ayrshire, including gentry and members of the court circle, were accused of Lollardy (Thomson, *Later Lollards*, pp. 204–7). Scotland did not undergo the experience of Oldcastle's revolt. But were the accusations justified? Early Lollard history in Scotland is obscure. Linguistic barriers existed, but there would have been points of entry for influences from England in the ports of the east coast and the universities. I owe information to Mr D. V. Murdoch; discussion of Scotland and north of England: Hudson, *Premature Reformation*, pp. 126–7.

[123] S. Brigden, *London and the Reformation* (Oxford, 1989), pp. 66–7; the will to reform rather than undermine: p. 67; the distinct heretical community: p. 84; Dickens, 'Heresy and origins', pp. 54–6; for earlier cases in London, see Thomson, *Later Lollards*, pp. 85–6, 156–7 (I prefer 'rich' as translation of *locupletes* (p. 85n.); background given in J. A. F. Thomson, 'Tithe disputes in later medieval London', *EHR* LXXVII (1963), pp. 1–17.

[124] I. Luxton, 'The Lichfield court book: a postscript', *BIHR* XLIV (1971), pp. 120–5. I owe this reference to Dr J. A. F. Thomson. See also C. Cross 'Popular piety and the records of the unestablished Churches 1460–1660', *SCH* XI, pp. 269–92; for Buckinghamshire, see below, p. 371.

Thames Valley, Bristol and the West Country, the Midlands, especially Coventry, Essex and East Anglia, with lesser clusters in Hampshire, and the Forest of Dean. As far as we can see, it was a southern survival. We know that at the time of Richard Wyche's trial in 1403 a community existed in the Newcastle area.[125] So many northern registers for the period have disappeared that it is impossible to say whether it lived on or not, and whether heresy was so exclusively a southern phenomenon. Oldcastle's revolt, for reasons of geography if nothing else, had no northern participants; it too was a southern phenomenon, and its rebel-bearing regions correspond fairly to those of Lollard survival after 1414: London, the Chilterns and mid-Thames Valley, Bristol, the Midlands and Essex all sent rebels to Oldcastle and produced heretics after that date. One oddity is Kent, almost blank for the rebellion, although Oldcastle should have had a local following through the Cobham estates he held there, and it was fertile for heresy later. The other is East Anglia, which contained heresy on some scale in the 1420s; it may be blank for the rebellion merely because of its isolation from London.[126] In sum, however, there is a geographical correspondence between the rebellion and the post-1414 heresy.

Within the seven regions prosecutions continued to be launched at varying intervals through the period; only in East Anglia do they come more or less to a stop. Persecution, in other words, was ineffective in eliminating heresy from at any rate six of the seven major regions.

Sometimes there are long periods between drives; the area of the Chilterns was only investigated vigorously on three occasions, by Chedworth in 1462–4, Smith in 1511, and Longland in 1521–2, yet it produced substantial hauls of heretics every time; from the well-documented prosecutions of 1462–4 and 1521–2 we can distinguish a number of places as fertile in heresy in the last prosecution as in the first, despite the intervening lapse of time.[127] Often individual towns and villages have but one or two prosecutions recorded. This, however, can be somewhat deceptive. Episcopal registers, the staple source of evidence, tend to give places of origin less profusely than the rarer heresy court books. So if we must use registers alone, our source may give us, for example, only a selection of principal places and omit to mention lesser villages. The evidence, dependent as it is on the chances of detection and the survival of judicial records, is fragmentary and discontinuous.

Certain notorious centres of heresy emerge none the less from the evidence we have: London at the top of the list, partly because it was the focal point of a large diocese and refugees from elsewhere fled to anonymity there;[128] Bristol, with a striking continuity and evidence of survival in certain districts, especially the Redcliffe area;[129] Tenterden, the Kentish textile village where

---

[125] M. G. Snape, 'Some evidence of Lollard activity in the diocese of Durham in the early fifteenth century', *Archaeologia Aeliana*, 4th ser. xxxix (1961), pp. 355–61.

[126] McFarlane, *Wycliffe*, p. 173.

[127] Fines, *Studies*, pp. 102–9, 157–205; Thomson, *Later Lollards*, ch. 3.

[128] Thomson, *Later Lollards*, pp. 139, 155, 236.

[129] Ibid., pp. 22, 25, 26, 28, 33, 34 (see also 35), 39, 44, 46, 47; compare entries for 1448 and 1511–12 (a group active c. 1505–6) and note evidence of a continuity over half a century in the Redcliffe area; note also that the longest gap in prosecutions lies between 1457 and 1476, a time of general slackening of prosecution in England. Social composition in Bristol (according to Thomson) is as follows. 1420 two

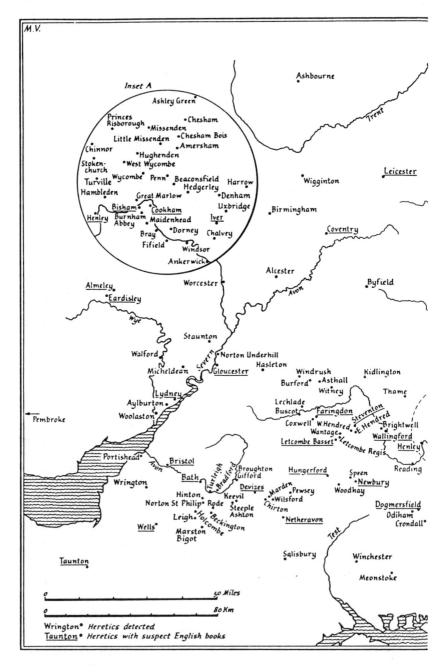

MAP 8 Lollardy underground.

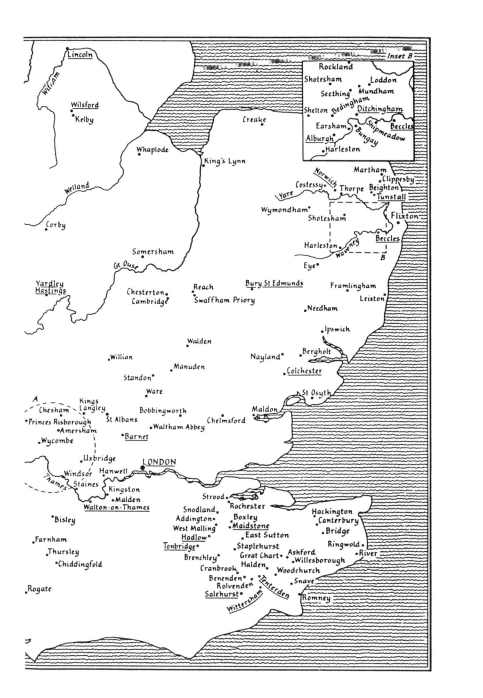

Inset B

Rockland
Shotesham
Seething
Shelton Bedingham
Earsham
Alburgh
Harleston

Loddon
Mundham
Ditchingham
Shipmeadow
Bungay
Beccles

Lincoln

Witham

Wilsford
Kelby

Creake

Whaplode

King's Lynn

Welland

Corby

Somersham

Gt. Ouse

Yardley
Hastings

Chesterton
Cambridge

Reach
Swaffham Priory

Bury St Edmunds

Framlingham
Leiston

Needham

Martham
Norwich
Costessy
Thorpe
Wymondham
Shotesham

Clippesby
Beighton
Tunstall

Flixton

Yare

Harleston

Eye

Waveney

Beccles

B

Ipswich
Bergholt
Nayland
Colchester

Walden

Willian
Manuden
Standon
Ware

St Osyth

Maldon

A
Chesham
Kings
Langley
Princes Risborough
Amersham
St Albans
Bobbingworth
Waltham Abbey
Chelmsford
Wycombe
Barnet

Uxbridge
LONDON
Windsor
Hanwell
Staines
Thames
Kingston
Malden
Walton-on-Thames

Bisley

Farnham
Thursley
Chiddingfold

Rogate

Strood
Snodland
Addington
West Malling
Hadlow
Tonbridge
Brenchley
Cranbrook
Benenden
Rolvenden
Salehurst
Wittersham

Rochester
Boxley
Maidstone
East Sutton
Staplehurst
Great Chart
Halden
Woodchurch
Snave
Tenterden
Romney

Hackington
Canterbury
Bridge
Ringwold
Ashford
Willesborough
River

White probably laid down a tradition;[130] Coventry, active in heresy and in the revolt of 1431.[131]

Another inference to be drawn from the map is that prosecutions in the seven regions of survival were generally launched against individuals or groups involved in Lollardy rather than against anticlericals or isolated heretics unconnected with the movement.[132] Heresy drives give us for a moment, it is true, a glimpse of the religious sentiments in an area, not all of which fall neatly into the rival categories of Lollardy or orthodoxy. Endemic anticlericalism was the milieu in which Lollardy floated and a convert passed through personal contact with a committed member from anti-Church views of an uncoordinated kind into a deeper involvement. The laconic entries of the episcopal register do not always enable us to draw this line, which in reality must often have been ambiguous.

One criterion of high reliability does exist, however, and has been noticed on the map. When prosecutions record the presence of suspect vernacular books in a locality, we can feel a measure of confidence that we are on the trail of a Lollard reading-circle, for these books were most commonly the tracts and Scriptures of the heretics rather than innocent vernacular works of piety such as *Nicodemus* or *Dives and Pauper*. Records of the presence of these books are to be found in every one of the seven major regions in which Lollardy survived; in some they lie thickly, and prosecutions of suspects with books occur repeatedly over the years in the same places. True Lollardy formed the core of the cases in these regions up to the eve of the Reformation.

One further inference may be that Lollardy, by and large, survived in artisan circles, for the map demonstrates that the clusters of heresy-bearing localities lie in the areas of high population where industry had been developed. Only two regions significant in the development of the textile industry, York and the south Cotswolds, are either omitted or scantily represented; the gap in the former region may be due to *lacunae* in the surviving records, and in the latter to the lack of prosecuting zeal of the bishops of Worcester.

The map tends to underestimate the extent of the Lollard survival. No doubt, despite some sifting of the sources, the prosecutions still include some of mere sceptics, anticlericals and idiosyncratic heretics, but the exaggeration of the survival of true Lollardy which ensues must be more than offset by the contrary effects of defective source material. Many episcopal registers have been lost; others list no heresy, not because it did not exist, but because bishops and their officers did not detect, and perhaps were uninterested in pursuing it. There are curious blanks. Wales, into which Swinderby and Brute disappeared, has but two cases: of a priest and a layman at Pembroke in 1486

priests; 1423 one of the same priests (William Taylor); 1448 weaver (unnamed), smith; 1476 three men (no details); 1511–12 (a group active *c.* 1505–6) carpetmaker, wiredrawer and others, no information for 1429, 1441, 1448 (case of William Fuer of Gloucester), 1457, 1499.

[130] Ibid., pp. 173, 174, 175–6, 178 (somewhat tentatively), 180, 187–9.

[131] Ibid., pp. 101 (John Grace, called a 'false prophet', but not a Lollard): see Aston, *PP* xvii, p. 14 and n. 70, 104–6, 107–16, for 1489 prosecution, see Fines, *Studies*, p. 129, and for 1511–12, *JEH* xiv, pp. 160–74.

[132] For cases of individual heresy in the fourteenth century, see below, p. 282.

and 1488.[133] Was this due to absence of heresy, aided by the linguistic barrier over part of the region, or to ecclesiastical disorganization? One cannot say. The Welsh March is another puzzling area, for the region that included Oldcastle's seat and had once been Swinderby's campaigning ground might have been expected to have a later history of Lollardy, yet it is mute in the revolt of 1414 and has evidence of only two subsequent prosecutions: one at Almeley in Oldcastle's estates in 1433, and another at Eardisley in 1505,[134] both revealing the presence of suspect books. The border area was later of importance in the history of Nonconformity,[135] and registers for crucial periods are missing: there is a presumption that there was more Lollardy in the March than the map reveals.

It must be emphasized that the map is simply a pictorial record of the evidence of prosecutions of Lollards and other religious dissidents in the extant registers and court books; used with care, it gives us a blurred outline of the heresy underground, but never the complete picture.

Late Lollard beliefs

Life underground and the disillusionment of 1414, perhaps of 1431 also, largely stripped the sedition from Lollardy. Willy nilly, Lollards found themselves in some opposition to the State as it backed the demands on them of the Church, but they mostly gave up conspiracy. An apocalyptic tradition, one strand among the beliefs, though not a dominant one,[136] comforted some with the expectation of change in their favour; this was especially the case in a group at Newbury, uncovered in 1490–1.[137] In 1448 William Fuer of Gloucester expected war with the Catholics but, being pacifist, would not participate himself.[138] Lollards no longer planned to bring about conflict on behalf of their faith. There was no one left to call the regional groupings together, which existed without much knowledge of each other; individual contacts there were, and an evangelist might keep in contact with two, even three, regions, but nobody any longer knew them all. Survival, rather than military or political victory, was the immediate concern.

Late Lollards were not very conscious of Wyclif; his distinctive ideas on dominion or predestination or the role of the secular ruler were generally lost to view;[139] but his legacy still helped them.[140] The concept of the Scriptures as a divine exemplar, existing before the creation, had worked on the minds of

---

[133] Thomson, *Later Lollards*, pp. 44–5. The priest was Irish.

[134] Ibid., pp. 31–2, 48.

[135] W. T. Morgan, 'The prosecution of Nonconformists in the consistory courts of St Davids, 1661–88', *Journal of the Historical Society of the Church in Wales* XII (1962), pp. 28–53; on Herefordshire parishes, pp. 30–1; note how Nonconformists, like Lollards earlier (Thomson, *Later Lollards*, pp. 1–2), tended to live near boundaries of jurisdiction. I owe information to Mr W. T. Morgan.

[136] Cf. Davis, in *SCH* III, p. 200; Thomson, *Later Lollards*, pp. 240–1.

[137] Thomson, *Later Lollards*, p. 78; note reference to prophecy of Lollard victory in a book known in East Anglia, p. 131.

[138] Ibid., p. 36.

[139] Comment of Hudson in *Premature Reformation*, pp. 269–70.

[140] For interesting notes on the reverse side of the picture – continuity in Lollardy from Wyclif – see ibid., p. 472.

the early Lollards and clerical missionaries;[141] the effect of this belief in the final phase, however little ordinary followers could have grappled with the earlier philosophy which underlay it, was to provide comfort in persecution. Its effect was to substitute for the authority of the Church the infallibility of Scripture;[142] Wyclif's doctrine of the Church acted in a similar fashion. The visible and hierarchical Church which persecuted the Lollards was the Church of Antichrist; the true Church became the congregation of true believers.

Investigatory procedure made Lollardy sound very negative. An interrogator subjected the suspect to a series of standard questions, negative replies on orthodox points being recorded to be used as the basis for convictions.[143] Three denials of Catholic belief and practice recur: on the veneration of images, on pilgrimages, and on the mass.[144] The basis for the denials often lay in a simple logic. John Morden of Chesham in Buckinghamshire, explaining his beliefs about the mass to his still orthodox son-in-law, said, 'Thou art deceived, for it can nothing profit thee; for it is but bread and wine; and so it is when the priest began with it at mass, and so it is when the mass is ended.'[145] Alice Rowley at Coventry seized on the priests' gain from mass offerings to call the service a 'pretty falsehood' of the priests which enabled them to buy the bread for the Hosts and then to sell it at a higher price.[146] In East Anglia Margery Baxter resorted to a coarse *reductio ad absurdum* to attack transubstantiation.[147]

Morden's statement on images was similar to his view of the mass. 'They are but stocks and stones', he said, 'for they cannot help themselves, how can they help thee? And the worshipping of them is but idolatry.'[148] On images the appeal to the unvarnished text of Scripture was potent. John Burell, of the East Anglian Lollards, appealed to the decalogue to dismiss the medieval practice of veneration.[149] Dislike of pilgrimages was bound up with the attack on this veneration, since representations and relics of the saints were the customary goal of the pilgrim's journey. In East Anglia the crucifix was attacked in terms oddly reminiscent of the Bogomils; 'no more credence should be done to the crucifix', it was said, 'than to the gallows which thieves be hanged on.'[150] At Coventry the focus for discontent lay in a particular image of Our Lady.[151] Pilgrimage centres received sarcastic names: among the

---

[141] I am indebted to Professor M. Deanesly for this comment in a private letter; see also her view in *JEH* xvii (1966), p. 266.

[142] Note Hudson's comment, *Premature Reformation*, p. 510: 'The Bible was the central pivot of the whole.'

[143] Thomson, *Later Lollards*, pp. 224–6, 228–9; on Coventry, a typical case, see Fines, *JEH*, xiv, pp. 169–71. For trial records, see A. Hudson, 'The examination of Lollards', *BIHR* xlvi (1973), pp. 145–59.

[144] Thomson, *Later Lollards*, p. 91 (note comment, p. 126).

[145] Ibid., p. 91, spelling modernized, as in later quotations.

[146] Fines, *JEH* xiv, p. 166.

[147] False gods eaten by the priests, who later 'emittunt eosdem per posteriores in sepibus turpibus sedentes' (Fines, *Studies*, p. 67, n. 3).

[148] Thomson, *Later Lollards*, p. 91.

[149] Ibid., p. 126.

[150] Fines, *Studies*, p. 63; Lambert, *Medieval Heresy*, 1st edn, p. 17.

[151] Thomson, *Later Lollards*, pp. 104, 112.

East Anglian group Canterbury became 'Cankerbury'.[152] James Willis disapproved of church music and bellringing; in East Anglia church bells were described as 'Antichrist's horns'.[153] There is a recurrent feeling that the Church's demands on the faithful were unnecessary, a mumbo jumbo dictated by the desire of priests to get money or gain their own ends. Pilgrimages were rejected on the grounds that they involved waste of money.[154]

Beyond the three best-known denials, different Lollards attacked various other sacraments. In East Anglia during Alnwick's prosecutions, and again in London in 1499, marriage as a ceremony was rejected as superfluous: the basis lay in the belief that the will of the two parties was sufficient, without the presence of priest or any formal ceremony.[155] Dislike of ceremonies and mortuary fees lay behind the rejection of the need for burial in consecrated ground, implicit in the statement of Thomas Whyte of Ringwold in Kent in 1473, that it was as good for his soul if his body were buried in a marsh as in a cemetery.[156] Objections to the practice of baptism by a priest in church were expressed by two men from Lydney in 1470, who said it could be done as well in a ditch as in a font.[157] This was an aphorism with a long history, for it is met in the confession of James Willis at his last trial in 1462, and in the confession of William Bull, the Dewsbury shearman, in 1543.[158] In a sense this was not heresy, but rather an objection to a canonical practice. A rejection of baptism altogether occurs in the East Anglian group, always one of the most radical, on the grounds that a child was redeemed in any case by Christ's blood;[159] rejection of sacraments or ceremonies of the Church was the message of the aphorisms of the sect, couched in terms that would be familiar to workers, in towns or on the land. For a Dewsbury shearman the font was a 'stinking tarn';[160] for a Lollard at Steeple Ashton in Wiltshire in 1488 it would be better to be sprinkled with lake water than holy water if the priest was a sinner;[161] for another at Kevill (Keevil) in 1506, Ball the carpenter could make as good images as those which were worshipped.[162] The 'better than' or 'as good as' of these comparisons is characteristic of the wry, sardonic religious egalitarianism of the typical heretic.

The appeal to reason could have odd results. Beside the standard views, we meet now and again quite idiosyncratic beliefs, such as that of John Edward in the Newbury area, who believed that Our Lady conceived and bore another son after Christ's ascension; or that of John Wodeward of Wigginton, near Tamworth, who was against baptism because there was no baptism before the

[152] Ibid., p. 126.
[153] Ibid., p. 69; Fines, *Studies*, p. 63.
[154] See Fines's comment (*Studies*, p. 250).
[155] Thomson, *Later Lollards*, pp. 127, 159. Is there any analogy to this in the case of Ramsbury (above, p. 251)?
[156] Ibid., p. 183.
[157] Ibid., p. 41.
[158] Ibid., p. 69; Dickens, *Lollards and Protestants*, p. 48.
[159] Thomson, *Later Lollards*, p. 127; Fines, *Studies*, p. 66.
[160] Dickens, *Lollards and Protestants*, p. 69.
[161] Thomson, *Later Lollards*, p. 45.
[162] Ibid., p. 83.

time of Christ.[163] Such ideas can hardly have been inculcated in the reading sessions of the movement. Sometimes the opening of the Scriptures led to the development of odd personal views; sometimes an eccentric parishioner was attracted to the Lollard circle. Or concern with heresy alerted authority to doctrinal deviations unconnected with Lollardy which existed under the surface. Heresy did exist in England before Lollardy and some twelve cases, of scepticism, idiosyncratic belief, perhaps mental unbalance, not connected with any organization, have been uncovered in published records between 1300 and 1370.[164] Then there was no need for a doctrinal alert; after Wyclif and the turn to active persecution, more of such casual cases might come to light.

The tone of Lollardy, sceptical, ironical, highly suspicious of emotion, kept the members of congregations from exaggerated eschatological views.[165] Unlike the frontier Protestants of the American Mid-west, the Lollards read their Scriptures within an orthodox ambience, however much they kicked against it; they did not have the Bible and no other culture or background at all, as did the American pioneers, and so were not inclined, as they were, to arrogate to themselves the rights and obligations of Moses and the Old Testament prophets.[166] There is no sign of the gathering of artisans round a teacher claiming special divine inspiration,[167] or of the wildness, springing from an obsessive concern for the biblical text, such as apparently led the Presbyterians of Halmadary near Strathnaver in the Scottish highlands close to performing human sacrifice about 1740 in imitation of Abraham and Isaac.[168] Persecution did not produce the state of exaltation which Manselli rightly distinguishes in the later stages of the proceedings against Olivi's followers.[169] Accusations of sexual immorality, frequently launched against continental heretics, were hardly ever made in England.

Pushed up against orthodox parish life and its ceremonies, which many of them dare not evade, and lacking strong intellectual leadership, it was natural that fifteenth-century Lollards should express their religious feelings in explosive negatives. We hear very little of rites of their own: occasional celebrations of the eucharist, some confessing to each other. Perhaps a ceremony lies behind the Coventry password, 'For we shall all drink of a cuppe'.[170] Whatever Lollard rites did exist, they were not important. The

---

[163] Ibid., pp. 76–7, 104. Comment in K. Thomas, *Religion and the Decline of Magic* (London, 1961), p. 168.

[164] J. Fines's calculation (*Studies*, pp. 8–16). F. Makower, *The Constitutional History and Constitution of the Church of England* (London, 1895), pp. 183–94. See cases of Margaret Syward in I. J. Churchill, *Canterbury Administration* (London, 1933), I, pp. 313–14; Ralph Tremur, in *Exeter Episcopal Registers: Register John de Grandisson*, ed. F. C. Hingeston-Randolph, II (London, 1897), pp. 1147–9, 1179–81; summary in Manning, *People's Faith*, p. 70.

[165] Thomson, *Later Lollards*, p. 249. It is one of Thomson's services to have clarified this point.

[166] I owe this comparison to Professor M. Deanesly. Note, however, the contrast between the stable Scripture-reading Lollard circles and the effects of Scripture within the Taborite movement (below, pp. 323–6, 328–31, 333–41).

[167] See above, p. 50.

[168] J. MacInnes, *The Evangelical Movement in the Highlands of Scotland, 1688 to 1800* (Aberdeen, 1951), pp. 103–4. I owe the reference to Mrs T. Maley.

[169] Above, pp. 210–11.

[170] Aston, *PP* xvii, p. 13 and notes; Fines (*Studies*, p. 251) argues that most believed in the priesthood of

strongest positive part of their life was the reading, the mutual exhortation and the earnest practice of the virtues. The core of their belief lay in the direct contact of the praying, reading adherent with God, based on Scripture and unencumbered by any sort of intermediaries. It was a simple, radical sort of belief, with a spiritualizing view of the sacraments.

Anticlericalism grew stronger. Recourse to the Fathers became less and less feasible; they may even be attacked. The more strictly academic and doctrinal concerns faded. *Scriptura sola* became the norm; the ethical concern, always important, became dominant. Lollardy had adapted to the circumstances of its followers. The swing in Lollard opinion, moving farther away from its founder as time went on, made similarities to Waldensians, especially of the more radical kind, ever more apparent, despite the lack of contact with them and the different origins of English Lollardy. Though Lollards had less explicit doctrine of their own than any other movement to set against the Church, and they lacked any formal distinction between preacher and rank and file, with the special obligations and celibacy of the preachers, yet they had in common with the Waldensians an ethical stress, an emphasis on word rather than sacrament, biblical translation, and an appeal to artisan membership. Both movements had the power to inspire a line of dedicated evangelists and pastors, more inclined to bow to persecution, so that they might live to fight another day, than many of the Cathar perfect, but quite as tenacious. On these few men both movements to a large degree rested. Other contributory factors in the survival are the relative leniency of the English tradition of persecution after the reaction to the Oldcastle revolt was spent, and the sporadic character of Waldensian persecution. Possibly, too, the fact that Waldensians rejected the oath and the shedding of blood, and thus were prohibited from entry to the leading classes of medieval society, meant that nobility had no reason to be jealous of them or to covet the lands which could be taken from them after conviction for heresy.

There is much to be said, however, for the view that both late Lollardy and Waldensianism of the Poor Lombard variety were the heresies of the Middle Ages *par excellence*, the perennial religion of the layman from lower classes, who painfully acquired some booklearning or learnt by rote passages of Scripture and passed on by word of mouth his anticlerical, Donatist views, mixed with an earthy scepticism about facets of Catholicism. Even in radical Hussitism, whose history, as we shall see, was so much briefer and more dynamic than that of the Lollards or Waldensians, we meet similar wry aphorisms. Perhaps the durability of both the English and the continental heresy was due in the last resort to its appeal to this submerged reasoning piety, the beliefs of laymen who had their own devotional life and their own doubts about individual points of doctrine. A Valdes or a Wyclif and his followers could appeal to these sentiments. But they did not call them into being, and, among the multifarious causes of heresy, this body of largely hidden sentiment has been one of the underestimated forces in medieval Church history.

all believers. For eucharistic beliefs, see Thomson, *Later Lollards*, pp. 82n., 112, 246–7; Fines, in *JEH* xiv, p. 167.

15

The Bohemian reform movement

Introduction

At almost the same time that English Lollardy as a political force went down
to defeat in Oldcastle's rebellion, a comparable movement of religious dissent,
in part stimulated by Wyclif's writings, was shaking the bonds of the distant
kingdom of Bohemia. The dramatic but desperate revolt of Oldcastle was the
last throw of the native English movement; after it, as we have seen, a residue
of Lollards lived on underground by dint of their own tenacity and by courtesy
of the lack of determination in persecution of some members of the episcopate.
In the sixteenth century they showed some fresh vitality. But as a political
force, even in potential, they ceased to exist after Oldcastle's revolt. In
Bohemia reform and heresy went a great deal farther. Disputes, in which
Wyclif's name figures prominently, shook the university of Prague; agitation
reached the Bohemian court and the international Church assembled at the
Council of Constance. At the moment when Henry v's soldiers were hunting
down Oldcastle's conspirators, many of the Bohemian nobles were displaying
their solidarity with the cause of their native reform leader, Jan Hus. Four or
five years later, when Lollardy was reduced to a few of the clergy and some
hardy artisan circles in England, its basis in the nobility and merchant classes
almost wholly vanished, Hussite supporters were intimidating their opponents
and preparing to do battle for their beliefs.

All was not Wyclif in the Bohemian movement – indeed it would be a
misnomer to describe Hussitism *tout court* as his child. Nevertheless his ideas
played a significant part in the complex of factors underlying the Hussite
movement, and some of the religious enthusiasts given free play by the events
leading to the revolution shared the ideas of the English Lollards.

The most remarkable feature of Hussitism was its repudiation of the close
control of the papacy in doctrinal matters, and its establishment, however
briefly and imperfectly, of a measure of religious toleration.

For some seventeen years, between the Defenestration of Prague in 1419 and the acceptance of Sigismund at Jihlava in 1436, and to a lesser degree in the years of struggle before 1419, the older unity of doctrine and canon law in the West under the papacy was, first in practice, then in open defiance, broken in pieces in this one country, and a remarkable range of belief unfolded. The Hussites and their supporters went farther than any other popular religious movement labelled as heresy before the Reformation in shaking the old order, and for this reason demanded extended study. The history of their struggle, a failure in the end yet, relatively speaking, the most successful of them all, forms a natural conclusion to a study of the major heretical movements of the Middle Ages.

The setting[1]

Bohemia was a latecomer to the circle of advanced nations. Under the first Přemyslid rulers it had been hardly more than a frontier province, on the fringe of the Holy Roman Empire; then under the last rulers of the dynasty it advanced more rapidly, aided by the influx of colonists and the growth of the indigenous population, to achieve under the Luxemburgs, above all Charles IV (king, 1346–78), a remarkable flowering of economic, cultural and political life. Charles had been administrator of the country on behalf of his absentee father John; then from 1346 he ruled both as king in Bohemia and as Holy Roman emperor till his death in 1378, and sought to make the country a focal point in his revised conception of the old Empire. With his father, he succeeded in securing the elevation of the see of Prague to metropolitical status; in 1348 he founded the university of Prague as an intellectual centre and training ground for administrators within the Empire; by his addition of the New Town he added greatly to the size and economic significance of his capital; finally, by his summons to the Austrian Augustinian canon Waldhauser to come and preach in his lands, he gave impetus to an indigenous movement of Church reform, the platform from which emerged, after decades of agitation, the Hussite revolution of the fifteenth century.[2]

---

[1] F. Seibt, 'Die Zeit der Luxemburger und der hussitischen Revolution', in *Handbuch der Geschichte der böhmischen Länder*, ed. K. Bosl, I (Stuttgart, 1967), pp. 351–536 (comprehensive, with bibliography; insufficiently known in England); F. Seibt, 'Bohemica, Probleme und Literatur seit 1945', in *HZ*, Sonderheft IV (1970), esp. pp. 49–99 (introduction to post-war work on Bohemia, with comments; valuable for Czech literature). I am indebted to Professor F. Seibt for comment and information. In English, K. Krofta, 'Bohemia in the fourteenth century', in *CMH* VII, pp. 155–181 (now old); S. H. Thomson, 'Learning at the court of Charles IV', *Speculum* XXV (1950), pp. 1–20; R. R. Betts, *Essays in Czech History* (London, 1969), omitting ch. 3 (pp. 29–41) (on this, cf. Leff, *Heresy* II, p. 632n.); H. Kaminsky, *A History of the Hussite Revolution* (Berkeley and Los Angeles, 1967) (fundamental and detailed study of history of ideas in relation to politics up to 1424, with distinguished knowledge of doctrinal sources); bibliography: pp. 551–3; on Charles IV: pp. 7–8. J. K. Zeman, *The Hussite Movement and the Reformation in Bohemia, Moravia and Slovakia (1350–1650)* (Ann Arbor, 1977) (bibliography); F. Seibt, *Hussitenstudien, Personen, Ereignisse, Ideen einer frühen Revolution* (Munich, 1987) (collection of articles published elsewhere, distinguished by understanding of personal motives). Background in E. Werner, *Jan Hus* (Weimar, 1991), chs 1 and 2. Names are given in the Czech forms here, except where a German or anglicized form is likely to be more familiar to the English reader.

[2] F. Seibt, *Karl IV: Ein Kaiser in Europa 1346 bis 1378* (Munich, 1978), pp. 367–97 (classic, wide-ranging account); full bibliography: K. Walsh, in *SCH* Subsidia V, p. 401, n. 14

His own part in sponsoring reform and opening the way for Hussitism is equivocal. On the one hand, many features in Bohemian Church and intellectual life which aided the progress of the movement had their roots in, or were affected by, the policies of his brilliant reign; on the other, his own piety, sincere as it was, remained relatively conventional. He, and the forerunners of Hussitism, whom he sometimes sponsored, did not favour heresy: he was the author of stern decrees against beghards and in favour of the inquisition. Religious feeling and economic interest combined to make him one of the great relic-collectors, and Prague a centre for saint cults and rich churches – features vividly attacked for their associated abuses by early preachers of the reform. The opening of Bohemia as a centre for the Empire involved also the opening of the Bohemian Church to the inroads of Avignonese fiscality, and appointment to high office became a matter of agreement between him and the popes.[3] His appointments to episcopal sees were generally wise, but biased in favour of his friends and servants; he secured the persons he wished, while the papacy was given exceptional opportunities to obtain cash and benefits from the kingdom.

The nobility were the losers by such arrangements. They were beneficiaries from the traditional *Eigenkirche*, with its heavy lay control, and in this distant area the *Eigenkirche* style of Church government lasted on well after its supersession in more advanced lands. Reform ideas on Gregorian lines were only beginning to make their impact in the thirteenth century, when free election was secured for the sees of Prague and Olomouc, and Andrew of Prague led his campaign for freedom from lay control. For a long time papal intervention was slight and hesitant: for the whole period 1221–1316 Jaroslav Eršil has uncovered only twelve papal provisions relating to Bohemia.[4]

It was the absence at the curia of the bishop of Prague, John of Dražice, between 1318 and 1329 that opened the way for the introduction of papal provisions on an extensive scale; when it came, it came with a rush. Under Charles, all bishoprics and an increasing number of abbacies fell within papal rights of provision – at least theoretically – while in ten years of Clement VI's pontificate 300 bulls sent to Bohemia were concerned with lesser benefices.[5] Many of these provisions concerned appointments of foreigners, especially Germans. There was a comparatively small gap in time between the old lay-controlled *Eigenkirche* and the late medieval type of informal concordat between pope and ruler for the distribution of office. This had important consequences, for the nobility retained a strong memory of their rights under the *Eigenkirche* and were, not wholly unjustly, inclined to see papal provisions as a system for rewarding foreigners. The course of events created a natural

---

[3] J. Eršil, 'Les rapports administratifs et financiers de la papauté avignonaise avec les pays de la couronne de Bohême entre 1352 et 1378', *Rozpravy československá Akademie Věd* LXIX (1959), p. 130 (summary of Czech article); R. E. Weltsch, *Archbishop John of Jenstein (1348-1400)* (The Hague and Paris, 1968), pp. 40–9; role of nobility and patronage in J. M. Klassen, *The Nobility and the Making of the Hussite Revolution* (Boulder, 1978), pp. 27–34.

[4] Eršil, 'Rapports', p. 131; for general background, see F. Mildenberger, 'Die böhmischen Länder im Früh-und Hochmittelalter', Bosl, *Handbuch* I, pp. 165–347. The background to the problems of John of Dražice is clarified in Patschovsky, *Anfänge*, pp. 30–43.

[5] Eršil, 'Rapports', p. 132. Dr A. V. Antonovics in a private letter notes that there are problems of evidence.

interest group, stronger than its opposite numbers in England, that had in practice seen rather more of late medieval papalism at work at the financial level and rather less of reforming Gregorianism, and was ready to swing its support behind a movement which advocated disappropriation and an implicit return to the rights of lay patrons.[6] The whole issue, like most others in Bohemia, was complicated by the existence of an incipient division in language and culture between German and Czech peoples.[7]

Much of the early development of Bohemia was due to the entry of German colonists. The early Bohemian towns tended to be German-dominated, and the mining areas, especially centring on Kutná Hora (Kuttenberg) and Jihlava (Iglau), which brought so much wealth to the Bohemian crown, were largely in the hands of German immigrants. The indigenous Slav peoples at first followed a German lead, their peasants adopting the settlement rights of the Germans because they were so successful, and their nobility, through the clergy, adopting the knightly culture of the German-speaking lands. But by the turn of the fourteenth century the flow of German immigration had passed its peak,[8] and signs appeared of an increasing self-consciousness in the Czechs of the Bohemian lands, with a greater interest in their language. The number of translations begins sharply to increase: the knightly literature of the preceding era is translated from German, by the end of the thirteenth century a complete Czech psalter is in existence, there are creeds and prayers in Czech, and in the course of the fourteenth century a Czech translation of the *Historia scholastica* of Peter Comestor and a Czech life of Christ put together by a Dominican from the *Meditationes vitae Christi*.[9] First awareness of national and linguistic difference appeared among the clergy; it was complicated by the development of a local patriotism, supporting inhabitants of the kingdom, Czech or German, against inroads of foreigners.

Yet, wherever social tensions existed in fourteenth-century Bohemia, they could readily become associated with the linguistic distinction between Czech and German speakers, as in the case of the slow Czech penetration of towns, where Czech speakers might come to resent the dominance in local government of the wealthier Germans, or in the relations of Czech nobles with towns in their neighbourhood, where the national difference served to heighten class antagonism. In Church life the rising standards of the lower Czech nobility in education carried them more frequently into the ranks of the clergy, and caused resentment of the entrenchment of the Germans in high positions, the inevitable consequence of their earlier cultural lead. Under the Luxemburgs there were attempts to redress the balance, as in the founding of Roudnice (Raudnitz), a house of Augustinian canons for the sons of Czech-speaking parents, which became a centre for the vernacular religious tradition, or Charles IV's foundation of a house for Czech canons in the old imperial palace at Ingelheim, in the middle of a German cultural area.[10] What

---

[6] Seibt, 'Die Zeit', p. 440.

[7] K. Bittner, *Deutsche und Tschechen: Zur Geistesgeschichte des böhmischen Raumes* (Brünn, 1936).

[8] Seibt, 'Die Zeit', p. 416.

[9] Ibid., pp. 458–60, E. Winter, *Frühhumanismus: Seine Entwicklung in Böhmen* (Berlin, 1964).

[10] F. Seibt, *Hussitica: Zur Struktur einer Revolution* (Cologne, 1965) (essays often subtle and stimulating, based on textual analyses), see on nationalist issue: p. 62 (Roudnice), pp. 63–4 (Ingelheim); reviews:

Charles wanted in Bohemia was a balance between races and languages; but he did not wholly succeed in getting it, and underlying antagonisms continued, witnessed for us by the abbot Ludolf of Sagan, who studied in Prague in the 1370s and spoke of the hostility of German and Czech as comparable to that between Jew and Samaritan.[11] Balance was harder to maintain after 1378, when the strong central direction of Charles was replaced by that of his son, Wenceslas IV (1378–1419), who, surrounded by grave political difficulties, was incapable of emulating his father's mastery of this problem, or indeed any other.

A third characteristic feature of the Bohemian kingdom lay in the existence from about 1350 of a movement described by Eduard Winter, its principal historian, as 'early humanism'. Its most striking, but also more superficial, feature was letter-writing in the new humanistic style and the literary contacts with Prague of Petrarch, who stayed in the capital, and of Cola di Rienzo. Of more lasting significance was the new piety referred to by Winter as a parallel and even forerunner of the better-known Netherlands *devotio moderna*. In Bohemia it was associated pre-eminently with the spread of houses of Augustinian canons, who arrived in Bohemia in 1350, and were favoured by two archbishops of Prague, by Charles IV and by a number of noble patrons. Their spirituality stressed the study of books, notably by Augustine and the Fathers, the inner religious life of the individual, typified for example in the influential constitutions of Roudnice by the division of the *dormitorium* into individual cells, and had a strong pastoral concern. Other religious houses contributed; the Cistercian Königsaal produced the devotional masterwork, the *Malogranatum*, translated during the century into both German and Czech, and the Premonstratensian house of Tepl played a part in biblical translation. As Seibt has warned us,[12] the influence of these new ideas affected only a thin upper layer of society; the Augustinian canons were no direct protagonists of the Hussite movement, but rather its opponents and, after the revolution, often its victims. Yet at least the *devotio moderna* of Bohemia helped to create in some influential circles the atmosphere of moral earnestness and a certain caution towards the formal and external machinery of traditional religious life that made a propitious climate of opinion for Hussitism.

Conflicts over the arbitrary and dangerous procedures of the inquisition, introduced as a permanent institution by John XXII in 1318, probably in the first instance through the fear of the heresy of the Free Spirit, contributed to instability in Church life. The strange affair of the Italian doctor and philosopher, Richardin of Pavia, whose book was condemned for Averroistic views, led to the suspension of bishop John of Dražice in 1315. Colda of Colditz, the Dominican who took office in 1318, clashed with secular

A. Borst, *ZFK* I/II (1967), pp. 176–7; R. Kalivoda, 'Seibt's "Hussitica" und die hussitische Revolution', *Historica* XIV (1967), pp. 225–46; E. Lemberg, *Geschichte des Nationalismus in Europa* (Stuttgart, 1950), p. 135–44.

[11] Bittner, *Deutsche und Tschechen*, p. 11; see *Speculum* XLIV (1969), pp. 310–11.

[12] Seibt, 'Die Zeit', p. 447; note section on monasteries, pp. 444–9. I am indebted esp. to Seibt's survey for Bohemian background. On the Bible generally, see J. Kadlec, 'Die Bibel in mittelalterlichen Böhmen', *AHDLMA* XXXVI (1964), pp. 89–109, a study comparable to Deanesly, *Lollard Bible*; but see, on the effects of Scripture within Tabor, below, pp. 323–4, 329–31, 335–7.

authorities in Prague and with the Prague canon, Michael Folclini; he was threatened with death and twice had to leave the city. Gallus of Neuhaus interpreted his duties with a remarkable freedom; clashes took place over issues that could only in an arbitrary and artificial fashion be called heresy. Pope and bishop, apart from the early episode with John of Dražice, worked well enough together: it was the fear of an inquisitor's wide powers, the secrecy of witnesses and arbitrary condemnations, and anxiety for the security of traditional jurisdictions which threw up *ad hoc* alliances of judges, town governments and the secular clergy against the quasi-political activities of certain inquisitors, and created a ferment of opinion, damaging to Church authority.[13]

The beginnings of the Bohemian reform movement

Some of these characteristics may be seen in the preaching of Conrad Waldhauser,[14] who from 1363 worked as a freelance preacher supported by a benefice in Leitmeritz, then operated from the chief church of the Old Town of Prague. Charles's invitation to him to preach, and his position as his confessor and court chaplain, gave him official status from the outset. A keynote of his preaching was the denunciation of the abuses of the clergy, especially of simony. Religious orders were a special target because of their avarice and laxity; parents were even warned against putting their children into the novitiates of the mendicant orders because of their failings. Waldhauser disliked the abuse of relics: he attacked the passing off of a relic of St Barbara carried in procession in Prague as the saint's own, when its original, as he believed, could only be in Prussia. Denunciation of clerical abuse, a strong ethical stress, and radical social criticism were mingled with apocalyptic denunciations of the pseudo-prophets that deceived the people. Soon clerical opponents complained of him, and he was forced to go to answer them at Avignon, where he died in 1369. But before his career thus ended, he had established a circle of hearers among the Prague townspeople and students, and helped to set the tone for what was to follow.

His successor and convert, Jan Milič of Kroměříž, once a notary in the imperial chancellery, then a canon at the cathedral, had been led by Bible-reading and the preaching of Waldhauser to turn his back on his old life. After a year of solitude he became a poor preacher of repentance in 1364, based on the parish church of St Giles in Prague.[15] The style was reminiscent of the orthodox wandering preachers of the twelfth century: we recognize the same fiery asceticism, the refusal of meat and wine, sleeping on the hard ground, long prayers and lack of rest, combined with a certain vein of eccentricity, demonstrated in his obsessive interest in the coming of Antichrist and his

---

[13] Patschovsky, *Anfänge*, pp. 15–65, 78–80.

[14] Leff, *Heresy* II, pp. 610–11; Seibt, 'Die Zeit', pp. 466–8.

[15] P. De Vooght, *L'Hérésie de Jean Huss* (Louvain, 1960) (fundamental for theology of Hussites and opponents to 1415); see also his more detailed *Hussiana* (Louvain, 1960), pp. 7–21 (both reviewed by G. Miccoli, *SM*, 3 sér. III (1962), pp. 189–96). Kaminsky, *Revolution*, pp. 5–55, repays study; J. M. Clifton-Everest, 'The eucharist in the Czech and German prayers of Milič z Kroměříže', *Bohemia* XXIII (1982), pp. 1–15.

extraordinary denunciation of Charles IV, his journeyings to convince the pope of the evils confronting the Church, and finally his strong moral concern and his interest in the conversion of prostitutes, reminiscent of the activities of Henry the Monk. Success with his hearers gave him the opportunity to take over twenty-nine houses in the prostitutes' quarter of the city, which he renamed Jerusalem and turned into a house for reclaimed prostitutes together with a community of preachers living a common apostolic life. Success in preaching, the institution of a new kind of parish in Prague, fiery denunciation of the sins of the clergy on the lines of Waldhauser, perhaps the hint of the suspect beguine style of life being fostered in Jerusalem, led to his being compelled to answer accusations launched against him in 1373, and to go to Avignon to do so. After justifying himself, he died before he could return to Prague, and his enemies combined to destroy the experiment of Jerusalem.

De Vooght, with justice, calls him the father of the Czech reform,[16] for in him the movement took root in a native Bohemian. His preaching at St Giles, then at the Týn church in Prague, was in Latin and Czech – German he had to learn in order to reach another category of hearers. By the foundation of Jerusalem, however short-lived, he began the process of gathering a nucleus of the reform-minded around an institution within the capital, and, to judge by the twelve articles of complaint against him, such as the charge that he recommended daily communion to inmates at Jerusalem, and used the phrase *Sanctus est sacerdos*,[17] he pointed the way to future developments.

The third in the line of reformers in Prague was Matthias of Janov, the theoretician of the movement.[18] Milič had been no intellectual, but Matthias, his disciple, had studied in Paris (1375–81), to leave as a *magister artium*. In Prague he lived as a titular member of the cathedral chapter, supported by his patron Adalbertus Ranconis, then for the last five years of his life from 1389 with the aid of a benefice in Nova Ves outside Prague. With Matthias the reform movement gained its major written work, the *Regulae veteris et novi testamenti*, a set of twelve rules of conduct, four derived from the Old Testament and eight from the New, intended to defend the faithful from the insidious attacks of Antichrist, whose members Matthias saw as omnipresent in the body of the visible Church. The work was a loosely articulated set of treatises, designed to meet the emergency in which he believed the Church lay. By a return to the evangelical law found *par excellence* in Scripture and by the adoption of frequent communion, the Christian would be armed spiritually against the hypocrisy and formalism of existing Church life. Matthias continued the tradition of castigating the sins of the clergy and the religious orders while reinforcing the apocalyptic consciousness of his predecessors.

The work is overshadowed by the developments subsequent to the outbreak of the Great Schism, which seemed to be bringing the scourges of Antichrist within the Church to a climax. Attacks on clerical disorders had been common enough in Western Europe; in other countries, as in Bohemia,

[16] *Hérésie*: cf. pp. 14, 20–1.
[17] Seibt, 'Die Zeit', p. 468, noting controversy on what he did in fact say.
[18] Leff, *Heresy* II, pp. 612–19 is helpful; see De Vooght, *Hérésie*, pp. 21–35, Kaminsky, *Revolution*, pp. 14–23 (quotations but frail psychological interpretation).

congregations who heard these attacks believed them, but did not act; then the shocking spectacle of two rival popes, at Rome and Avignon, excommunicating each other and their rival's supporters – with Christendom divided into two camps because of the papal schism, exacerbated by national disputes – gave a new urgency to consideration of the state of the Church. As the schism dragged on, its obvious damage to the Church greater than in earlier papal disputes of the kind, men became convinced of the need, not only to stop the conflict by restoring unity to the papacy, but also to see that abuses in the Church were ended. Circumstances focused attention on the popes as the source of troubles, for, in the need to get and keep supporters and money, both sides positively fostered abuse.

The outbreak and continuance of the schism is essential background for the understanding of the development of the Bohemian reform, for it stimulated the fight for change, and forced churchmen to think more about the nature of the Church and the papacy's place in it. It also weakened the authority of the papacy for dealing with doctrinal dissent, as the reform in Bohemia began to pass into heresy.

The situation was made more difficult after 1378 by the problems of Wenceslas as ruler.[19] His accession coincided with the outbreak of the schism; his character and circumstances meant that he could never be relied on to back the suppression of heresy (or what was labelled as heresy) in his kingdom. Charles had divided the Luxemburg inheritance among six relatives and, though Wenceslas had the lion's share in the kingdom of Bohemia, and was simultaneously king of the Romans, he was frequently troubled by the disputes and needs of the Luxemburg heirs, and unable either to use Bohemia as a firm support-point to develop his policies in the Empire or to rely on his powers in Germany, enfeebled by a long course of development outside his control, to aid him in Bohemia. In his kingdom he faced many troubles with his nobility, exacerbated by his relatives, especially by his brother Sigismund, and even had to endure imprisonment at the hands of his own subjects. He never secured coronation as emperor, and in 1400 he was deposed as king of the Romans and replaced by his rival Rupert of the Palatinate. All this, together with the complexities of the politics of the Great Schism, distracted him from Church affairs in Bohemia, leaving neither time nor inclination either to co-operate with reform or to help other churchmen put down the Bohemian movement. Wenceslas's problems had not fully unfolded at the time of Matthias's writing of his *Regulae*, but they are not irrelevant to it. Both the Church and Bohemia had entered on a time of troubles, and Matthias's work reflects this in the urgency of its writing.

A number of features were, admittedly, not wholly novel: his attack on the proliferation of regulations in canon law, and his yearning for a new simplicity, the implied appeal to an earlier, more primitive Church, the interest in distinguishing the true Christians from the members of Antichrist within the visible Church – all have parallels in a century of Church life confronted with problems calculated to stimulate theological thinking of this type. What, however, is most striking in Matthias of Janov is his insistence on

---

[19] Seibt, 'Die Zeit', pp. 473–94.

the value of the eucharist. To it he devotes the great part of the first two and all of the fifth of a massive five-book work, and it inspires some of his most eloquent passages.[20] Just as the return to the Bible enables the faithful to find their way through the suffocating mass of regulations of human invention, so the practice of frequent, and preferably daily, communion enables them to avoid the distractions of needless formalism in worship, of false relics and miracles. It is this which sets off Matthias from other reformers of the time.[21]

The advocacy of frequent communion for the laity was the issue which attracted the hostile attention of authority. In 1388 and 1389 the decrees of the Prague synod against attacks on the veneration of images and against the receiving of communion more than once a month by the laity were aimed, among others, at Matthias's teaching. On both issues he recanted; but he was again in trouble in 1392, two years before his death. Such harassments hardly affected his influence, and, though, disciplined by loss of his functions for six months, he suffered no major disabilities. His work was not heretical, but nevertheless, it enshrined in written form some of the essential views of Bohemian reformers. · It was a preacher's exercise, and concerned with Christian practice rather than dogma; if the theology was correct, the whole trend was towards criticism of the actions of churchmen, and in the stress on the personal spiritual probity of the individual lay raw material for attacks on the Church and its leadership. The vehement attacks on abuses were now available in written form, and influential after Matthias's death, as well as in his lifetime.

Each of the major figures, Waldhauser, Milič and Matthias of Janov, had had to meet entrenched clerical opposition; none of them had allowed their course of action to be deflected by it. A proof of their influence with some of the laity lies in the case of Thomas of Štítné, the south Bohemian country gentleman who attended lectures at Prague university and issued a series of handbooks for family religion in the vernacular, quite orthodox and unoriginal, but inculcating the same wariness towards formalities and superstitions in popular religious life, the same caution about the calibre of life in the monastery, and the same stress on the Bible and frequent communion for the laity.[22]

The influence of the new ideas was reinforced by the foundation of the Bethlehem chapel in Prague, opened for sermons in the Czech vernacular in 1394 and seating 3,000 people.[23] Among the patrons was a German knight, Johannes von Mühleim, but it was predominantly a Czech enterprise: together with the burgomaster of the Old Town, three masters of the Bohemian nation at the university were to fill the preacher's benefice. Bethlehem was thus the successor to Milič's Jerusalem as a focal point for reform; the vernacular preaching for which it was founded helped to stress the Czech aspect of the movement.

[20] Leff, *Heresy* II, p. 616.
[21] As Kaminsky observes (*Revolution*, pp. 21–2).
[22] M. Spinka, *John Hus: A Biography* (Princeton, 1968), pp. 19–20 (by enthusiastic supporter of Hus, valuable for factual detail), review: P. De Vooght, in *RHE* LXV (1970), pp. 183–5.
[23] Spinka, *Hus*, pp. 47–51; Seibt, 'Die Zeit', p. 501; see his whole summary on Hus (pp. 500–6).

Reform ideas were not confined to Bethlehem and the audiences of the popular preachers. They also made their way at university level[24] in the complaints of John of Dambach, a Dominican, pupil of Eckhart and teacher of theology in the early days of Prague, who contrasted the baleful effect of the interdict on Church life in Germany with Charles's relic-collecting at home – a theme characteristic of the dislike of Bohemian reformers of formalism at the expense of true pastoral care – and later in the theses of Henry Totting of Oyta and of his pupil Conrad of Soltau, who in 1377 expressed doubt about the administration of the sacraments by concubinaries. Henry of Bitterfeld, the German Dominican who held a chair at Prague, spoke for frequent communion, and expressed his unease about indulgences, helping to form a Prague tradition on which Hussites proper were to build.

Thus by the end of the century there was a breadth of base to the reform movement of the preachers in Prague, aided by the existence of the Bethlehem chapel and the popular support it brought, and some dissemination of innovating ideas in the university. Yet no parallel success was being achieved in the prime aim of the movement, the reform of the body of clergy in Bohemia.[25]

The wealth of the Bohemian Church fostered abuse. Superfluity in endowments attracted unworthy candidates for ordination, and inspired an unhealthy interest in Church goods on the part of the laity. It would also seem that there were simply too many clergy: Tomek calculated that in Prague towards the end of the century, a city of 35,000 to 40,000, there were 1,200 clergy, 200 of them at the cathedral.[26] There was not work enough for them to do, and a contemporary treatise complains of the plight of clergy who did not know how to live from the daily mass-stipend of a Prague *groschen*. So, added to the dangers of overendowment, Bohemia was saddled with a clerical proletariat, a source of dissension within the clerical body and of scandal to the laity. Surviving aristocratic influence had something to do with this: John IV of Dražice, bishop of Prague, the founder of Roudnice, struggled against the abuse of the *mercenarii*, priests paid only a portion of their stipend by aristocratic patrons who confiscated the remainder to their own use. Both the first archbishop of Prague, Ernest of Pardubice, John's successor and then, after him, Archbishop John Očko of Vlaším were able to carry out administrative reforms in co-operation with the lay ruler; neither was able to make a substantial change in the situation. Between Avignonese centralism and the control of the royal power, the ecclesiastical head of the Bohemian Church had little room for manoeuvre and, although Charles IV was sympathetic to reform, he was not prepared to push it on to the detriment of a system of royal patronage that benefited his bureaucracy rather than Church interests.

Under Wenceslas hopes diminished. His archbishop, John of Jenstein, had a strong personal piety and an interest in reform, but lacked political finesse; under his regime friendly relations with the ruler broke down in the pressure of schism politics, as John remained firm on the Roman side, while Wenceslas

---

[24] Seibt, 'Die Zeit', pp. 462–5.
[25] Ibid., pp. 436–44; Weltsch, *Jenstein*.
[26] Cited by Seibt, 'Die Zeit', p. 439; see De Vooght, *Hérésie*, pp. 99–101.

veered, for his own ends, towards Avignonese interest. The archiepiscopate was disturbed by disputes, with Wenceslas in 1393 claiming what a modern Wilici has described as a return to the old proprietary system.[27] Personal conflict culminated in the same year in the murder of John of Pomuk, the archbishop's official; finally, John resigned. It was the tragedy of his generation that John of Jenstein could not make his way through these conflicts, for he had some contact with Matthias of Janov, wrote treatises himself, and was in touch with devotional currents of the time.[28] In the event, perhaps not wholly willingly, by supporting the attack on Matthias's advocacy of frequent lay communion, he ranged himself with the opposition and his own attempt at administrative reform, in the visitation of Prague in 1379–80, was checked by legal action and not resumed. Jenstein claimed that it was the first such major visitation, and it revealed that in no less than sixteen out of thirty-nine churches the incumbents gave cause for scandal.[29] After Jenstein, neither of his successors, his nephew Olbram ze Škworce (1396–1402) and Zbyněk Zajíc of Hasenburg (1402–11), showed themselves equal to the demands of their position.

Abuse thus continued, intensified by such scandalous arrangements as that arrived at between Wenceslas and the Roman pope, Boniface IX, in 1393 whereby a jubilee indulgence was granted to pilgrims visiting four churches in Prague as if they had visited Rome, and a half of their offerings at the church of St Peter on Vyšehrad were granted to the king.[30] The result of the failure to reform was an impatience in some sections of the population with churchmen, and a new stridency among the reformers. Earlier preachers stressed individual piety and the Second Coming; reform was to come through spiritual renewal by holy men. Matthias lamented the schism, but did not propose constitutional mechanisms to end it, as members of the conciliar movement did.[31] Now that was beginning to change; the element of popular demonstration against ecclesiastical failings intensified; the use of force to institute necessary reform was becoming more prominent.

The influence of Wyclif

A further novel factor was introduced by the appearance of Wycliffite ideas at the Charles University in Prague. Although his theology was not wholly unknown in early days – for Nicholas Biceps, a Prague professor, was arguing against Wyclif's eucharistic beliefs while Wyclif was still alive,[32] it was the philosophical works which first attracted attention. Marginal comments in manuscripts of Wyclif's philosophical works, which by a coincidence were copied by the young Hus, earning to help his keep as a student, convey the

[27] Weltsch, *Jenstein*, p. 72; see his ch. 2 generally (pp. 40–78).
[28] Ibid., pp. 154–79.
[29] Ibid., p. 162.
[30] Ibid., p. 71.
[31] I am indebted to Professor Seibt for discussion on this point.
[32] D. Trapp, 'Clm 27034: unchristened nominalism and Wycliffite realism at Prague in 1381', *RTAM* XXIV (1957), pp. 320–60; background in F. Šmahel, '"Doctor evangelicus super omnes evangelistas": Wyclif's fortune in Hussite Bohemia', *BIHR* XLIII (1970), pp. 16–34 (succinct and illuminating). I owe this reference to the late Professor C. D. Ross.

atmosphere in which this interest in Wyclifite philosophy sprang up. One warns the reader that the treatise *De ideis* should not be recommended to *non intelligentibus*; another sounds a note of uneasy admiration. 'O Wycleff, Wycleff, more than one head you have turned.'[33] These two comments show members of the university reacting in a similar manner to the Oxford scholars who first heard Wyclif's ultrarealist philosophy. It was difficult, sometimes alarming, and it could bowl men over with its bold propositions.

Interest in the philosophical treatises soon led on to an interest in the theological; and in stages, aided by the visits of Bohemian scholars to England, Wyclif's more dangerous works arrived in Bohemia. Two of these scholars, bachelors of the university, seem to have established direct contact with English Lollards and to have stayed at Latimer's manor at Braybrooke. Together with the treatises, they took back with them a fragment of Wyclif's tomb. Thereafter, until Lollardy was forced irretrievably underground, the two movements in England and Bohemia remained in contact.[34]

Wyclif brought complications.[35] On the one hand, his works gave a much stronger intellectual framework to the ideas of reform that had long circulated in Bohemia, and, for those who accepted Wyclif's inspiration, it imparted a new aggressiveness to the drive for reform. At the university the entry of his thought ended the phase of disparate, even somewhat opportunistic, reform thinking, which coexisted in the last three decades of the century with the predominantly moral revivalist preaching associated with Waldhauser, Milič, Matthias of Janov and the priests at the Bethlehem chapel. On the other hand, it repelled some intellectuals who had been sympathetic to reform, and gave a new handle to its opponents inside Bohemia, who were able to tar reformers with Wyclif's heresy.

In contrast to England, local circumstances in Bohemia provided an additional reason for the popularity of Wyclif's writings. It lay in the hostility, mingled with envy, of the Czech masters for the Germans at the university of Prague. One of these manuscripts of Wyclif has in the margin the gloss, in another hand: 'Haha, Germans, haha, out, out.'[36] The manuscript is of a philosophical work: the comment expresses the pleasure of a Czech at finding a philosophical weapon against the prevailing nominalism of the German masters. Ultrarealism could bloom in Prague because it seemed to be an answer to the Ockhamist views of, probably, a majority of the teachers in the theological faculty, who hailed from German-speaking lands or sprang from the Germans within Bohemia.

In the first years of the university Czech students had been few in number. By Charles IV's foundation the university was divided, on the Parisian model, into four nations, described according to the points of the compass, as Bohemian, Polish (which in practice often meant German), Saxon, Bavarian.[37]

---

[33] Šmahel, *BIHR* XLIII, pp. 18–19 and 19, n. 2; incorrect attribution by Spinka (*Hus*, p. 38).

[34] Šmahel, *BIHR* XLIII, pp. 20, 25, for scholars' visits; Betts, *Essays*, pp. 132–59, for English–Bohemian contacts generally.

[35] Seibt, 'Die Zeit', pp. 501–2; intellectual landscape in Šmahel, *BIHR* XLIII.

[36] Cited by Šmahel (*BIHR* XLIII, p. 20).

[37] For these and following details, see Seibt, 'Die Zeit', pp. 449–57; also Bittner, *Deutsche und Tschechen*, pp. 102–6; on the university with bibliography, see Betts, *Essays*, pp. 13–28.

At the outset the Czechs (who would be only a part of the Bohemian 'nation') formed an insignificant proportion. In time, internecine university disputes and the founding of new universities in German-speaking lands led to a fall in the proportions of Germans to Czechs overall. In the arts faculty during the 1380s 25 per cent of all graduates came from the Bohemian nation, by about 1400 the proportion had risen to 36 per cent. Where the Bohemian nation in early years had provided some 10 per cent of the deans in the faculty – an elective office – they were providing almost 40 per cent by the years 1391 to 1408. In theology their masters had not earlier been leading lights. As a body, they tended to adhere to a somewhat conservative Augustinian realist tradition, and to have some feelings of inferiority: to such Wyclif's ultrarealism, with its bold answers to Ockhamism, would appeal as a means of exalting their own intellectual position *vis-à-vis* the Germans. By reaction against this, Germans tended to be the initiators in attacks on the orthodoxy of Wyclif and those who defended him – though not exclusively, for there were cross-currents, not all Germans being nominalists, and some Czechs of a moderate realist position opposing the ultrarealism of the Wyclifites. Nevertheless, the Czech–German division added a new dimension to the study of Wyclif and controversy about him.

Jan Hus

Just as Wyclif's teaching had begun seriously to affect the university, Jan Hus was appointed rector of the Bethlehem chapel. The new strands now discernible in the Bohemian reform movement all met in him: Wyclif, the stress on a Czech reform, the new urgency against abuse. His academic training brought him to Wyclif: he was a member, though not the most prominent, of the new radical generation of Czech masters to whom Wyclif initially appealed.[38] Other Czech masters made the pace, and were deeper thinkers. Hus, in this resembling the older tradition of the fourteenth-century reformers, was first and foremost a preacher, agitator and spiritual writer. Some time before his ordination as priest in 1400, he underwent conversion and ceased to be, as he later confessed, a conventional clerical careerist.[39] He found himself at the Bethlehem chapel. Flajšhans, the editor of his sermons, estimates that he preached some 3,000 sermons during the twelve years of his service at Bethlehem, normally twice on every Sunday and saint's day, to overflowing congregations. Under him the Bethlehem chapel became the centre of the popular movement, as it had not been under his two predecessors, who had been distracted by other duties. By combining his preaching at the chapel with his position at the university he brought together the popular reform movement in the capital and the critical university masters.[40] The situation can be vividly reconstructed, for we have

[38] Early university career in Spinka, *Hus*, pp. 24–53; early theological work in De Vooght, *Hérésie*, pp. 54–64; note contrast of latter's judgement (*CV* VIII (1965), p. 236) and that of F. M. Bartoš (*CV* IX (1966), pp. 176–7); on his audience, F. Šmahel, 'Literacy and heresy in Hussite Bohemia', Biller, Hudson, *Literacy*, pp. 237–54 at p. 245; proceedings of the Bayreuth Conference on Hus, to be ed. F. Seibt, will add an international dimension.

[39] Spinka, *Hus*, pp. 28, 43–6.

[40] Ibid., p. 51; F. Seibt, 'Die Hussitische Revolution', *Hussitenstudien*, pp. 79–96 (reflections of 1963, still helpful) at p. 81.

texts of his sermons, even down to notes for his own delivery, showing immediate emotional rapport with his audience,[41] 'and then, as the audience responds, speak against idolatry'; 'this is the judgement of the letter. And then amplify if the attitude of the people justifies it.'

The chapel was a large, plain building, a preaching-church somewhat in the style of the churches of the Franciscans. On the walls were pairs of pictures: the pope on horseback and in pomp, contrasted with Christ in poverty, carrying his cross; Constantine making his donation to the pope, contrasted with Christ, wearing a crown of thorns, before Pilate.[42] Sermons corresponded to the pictures – orthodox, but fiercely attacking the abuses of the modern Church, and repeating the contrast with the poverty and simplicity of the primitive Church. Hus never fell into the Donatist view, impugning the validity of the sacraments administered by the unworthy priest,[43] but, a deeply emotional man and a committed reformer, he was touched to the heart by the abuses that he saw around him, and he communicated this indignation to his congregation.[44] The effect of his preaching was enhanced by his own good life and obvious lack of personal ambition – he never wished for higher office than that of rector of Bethlehem, and his sermons and letters have running through them a thread of pastoral concern for all ranks of Prague society.[45]

The congregations at the Bethlehem chapel were Czech-speaking. Hus did not continue the practice of the earlier reformers, of speaking in both the Czech and the German vernacular; he spoke only Czech. He had been born among free peasants in an area of rich German settlement in southern Bohemia, and was conscious of the national and linguistic differences, so apparent in a nationally mixed area. He believed that the Czechs should be first in the offices of the kingdom of Bohemia, 'as are the French in the kingdom of France and the Germans in their own lands'. With the elements of Czech nationalism came also a consciousness of their special religious responsibility. He derived Bohemia from the Slav *Bóh* ('God'), called the kingdom *christianissimum*, and wrote of the *verny Chechy*, the faithful Czechs.[46] At Bethlehem he extended the range of his congregation, appealing to some artisans as well as the Czech-speaking middle class. A prominent part was

---

[41] Kaminsky, *Revolution*, p. 40, n. 124.

[42] Spinka, *Hus*, pp. 48–9.

[43] Leff, *Heresy* II, pp. 659–62; also his 'Wyclif and Hus: a doctrinal comparison', *BJRL* LX (1968), pp. 387–410.

[44] See De Vooght's comment (*Hérésie*, pp. 71–4); also Kaminsky, *Revolution*, p. 40, and comment on De Vooght (ibid., pp. 35–7).

[45] *The Letters of John Hus*, tr. M. Spinka (Manchester, 1972), and *John Hus at the Council of Constance* (New York and London, 1965), Spinka's tr. of Peter of Mladoňovice's account of Hus's trial, with introduction (letters of Hus, pp. 237–98); for background on churchmen and social conditions, see P. Brock, *The Political and Social Doctrines of the Unity of Czech Brethren in the Fifteenth and Sixteenth Centuries* (The Hague, 1957), pp. 11–34; Weltsch, *Jenstein*, pp. 130–40.

[46] On Hussitism and nationalism, there is a subtle chapter in Seibt, *Hussitica*, pp. 58–124; on Hus, see pp. 87–9, 100. For Hus's stress on preaching rather than liturgy at Bethlehem, see interesting passages in E. Werner, 'Wort und Sakrament im Identitätsbewusstsein des tschechischen Frühreformators Jan Hus (um 1370–1415)', *Sitzungsberichte der Akademie der Wissenschaften der DDR, Gesellschaftswissenschaften* (1989), no. 13, pp. 3–26. I owe help to the author. His biography, *Jan Hus*, investigates Hus's thought and emotions.

played by Czech hymns. But he did not reach the German-speaking middle class of the capital, and his tenure of the rectorate of Bethlehem tended to aid the polarization, gradually taking place in the early fifteenth century, between Czech reformers and German opposition.

The attack on Wyclifites

This polarization was accelerated by the development of an attack on supporters of Wyclif by German masters, which began in 1403 with an appeal for action against Wyclif's works to the Prague diocesan authorities by Elias Hübner,[47] a Silesian Dominican from the university, continued with an attack on the Czech Wyclifite Stanislav of Znojmo's writing by John Štěkna, an *emigré* from Prague, and culminated in 1408 with an appeal to the curia by Ludolf Meistermann, a Saxon also from the university. Interest in Wyclif's philosophy often coexisted with membership of the reform movement, and attacks on him tended to be seen by reformers as covert attempts to stifle their movement. The fact that Germans were responsible for these attacks drew the Czechs together in defence, not necessarily of the substance of Wyclif's teaching, but of the right to read and teach him, whether or not they all as individuals shared Wyclif's views. In fact some certainly did not, and there was a spread of views from very moderate teachers who thought Wyclif could be used, to Stephen Páleč and to Stanislav of Znojmo, who actually taught the Wyclifite eucharistic doctrine of remanentism, thus denying transubstantiation, in his *De corpore Christi*. Both of these produced works so influenced by Wyclif that the Wyclif Society in the nineteenth century thought that they were Wyclif's own.[48] Jerome of Prague was a passionate supporter who brought back from Oxford copies of Wyclif's *Dialogus* and *Trialogus* and engaged in an international agitation against abuses of the Church. But controversy should not be seen solely and crudely in terms of battle between German nominalists and Czech realists and there were Czechs such as Andrew of Brod, who did not defend the teaching of Wyclif in his last phase, and disliked the idea of remanentism spreading in Bohemia.[49]

The pro-Wyclif Czech party were lucky in that the archiepiscopate was then held by Zbyněk, a former soldier of high family, ill-equipped theologically yet sympathetic to reform, who was lenient to the Wyclifites, and took till 1408 to make up his mind that firm action against the spread of Wyclif's views was necessary. The contrast to Courtenay's resolution against Lollardy is obvious.[50] Zbyněk's benevolence delayed condemnation, for though the German masters were strong enough to secure a university decision against Wyclif, they needed the archbishop's backing to bring the Wyclifites down, and the prolonged debate on the issue, mediated to the populace by Czech

[47] For doctrinal disputes, see De Vooght, *Hérésie*, pp. 75–118; Spinka, *Hus*, pp. 47–85.

[48] On varying influence of Wyclif, see De Vooght, *Hérésie*, pp. 85–92; on the sincerity of Hus's rejection of remanentism, ibid., pp. 60–3, 96–7, 365–6, 473–4; *Hussiana*, pp. 263–91.

[49] Kaminsky, *Revolution*, pp. 38, 113, n. 54; Spinka, *Hus*, p. 71; on Jerome of Prague, see Walsh, in *SCH* Subsidia v, p. 406; on the nominalist–realist division, see ibid., p. 405.

[50] Above, p. 260.

students at the university, popularized radical tenets of Wyclif (or alleged tenets) in a way that nothing else could have done.

Hübner's original list of excerpts was an old one – the forty-five items included twenty-four from the English condemnation made at the Blackfriars Council of 1382, and the remaining twenty-one probably came from an earlier condemnation[51] – and he was attempting to argue that Wyclif had already been officially condemned, and that such condemnations should automatically be given effect in Bohemia. At the time this did not make much of an impression; but the excerpts were disseminated over the years in a way that Hübner and his colleagues never expected. They were cited out of their contexts, in short and pungent sentences that could not have been better adapted to act as the slogans of a popular movement.[52] They solved the problem of conveying ideas of Wyclif from the difficult setting of the master's prolix Latin treatises.

Such sentences are article 10 ('It is contrary to Scripture that churchmen should have possessions'), article 16 ('Temporal lords can at will take away temporal goods from the Church and possessioners who habitually offend') or article 14 ('Any deacon or priest can preach the word of God without the authority of the apostolic see and the Catholic bishop') had an immediate and subversive significance. In effect, the excerpts thus collected were such as to void the hierarchical and sacramental system of the Church, open the way to a reduction to apostolic poverty, and put her in the hands of the royal power and the temporal lords. Powerful heresies were represented: article 4, denying sacramental validity to the acts of a bishop or priest in mortal sin, was pure Donatism; article 5 denied Christ's institution of the mass; article 37 said that the Roman Church was a synagogue of Satan. Two excerpts, articles 7 and 11, by undermining both absolution and excommunication, much weakened the position of priesthood and episcopate. Bandied to and fro, the articles containing such sentiments passed out of university circles.

Meanwhile, in the university Wyclif remained a centre of debate. The questions would always arise: How much of Wyclif was to be assimilated? Was it to be the philosophy only? The reforming sentiments and the political ideas? The remanentism and the doctrine of the Church? The Czechs at the university continued to maintain a common front despite their individual differences. When Zbyněk started to put real pressure on them in 1408, they responded by agreeing as a body to forbid any defence of the forty-five articles 'in their heretical, erroneous and objectionable sense',[53] an action which preserved by implication a right to read Wyclif, but explicitly condemned only these specific articles, leaving open the question of their rightful attribution to Wyclif.

Yet the writing was on the wall when, ten days earlier, the master Matthew of Knín was tried in the archbishop's court and subsequently had to abjure remanentism, and there is little doubt that a full uprooting of Wyclif in

---

[51] Kaminsky, *Revolution*, p. 24, n. 66.

[52] Šmahel, *BIHR* XLIII, p. 22, see also pp. 24–6. Text of 45 articles, M. Spinka, *John Hus' Concept of the Church* (Princeton, 1966) (useful summary, pro-Hus in tone; review: L. Nemek, in *CHR* LV (1969), pp. 78–80), pp. 397–400; analysis in De Vooght, *Hérésie*, pp. 80–3.

[53] Tr. Spinka, *Hus*, p. 83.

Bohemia would still have been possible if Zbyněk had been able to follow up his first actions of the spring of 1408. The curia had backed Meistermann when he made his appeal: this turned the affair into an issue of authority, and made up the archbishop's mind for him. Gone were the days of the synodal decrees against abuse and the invitations to Hus to preach, pressure from abroad took Stanislav of Znojmo and Páleč away from Bohemia, to abandon Wyclif and become enemies of the movement they had once supported.[55] Implicated as they were in late Wyclifism, the Czech masters, as these events show, could yet have been deflected from defence of Wyclif, and popular dissemination of heresy could have been checked if Zbyněk had been able to keep up his counteraction.

What intervened was politics and the interests of Wenceslas in an emotional cause, which made it possible to build a party round the defence of reform, Jan Hus and the radical tenets of Wyclif, and created a new situation, without parallel in the history of Lollardy in England.

---

[54] On Zbyněk's early favour to reformers and his change of mind, see Spinka, *Hus*, pp. 66–7, 69–71, 79, 83–7; and on his attitude to authority, De Vooght, *Hérésie*, pp. 95–6, 101; see below, p. 301.

[55] Events outlined in De Vooght, *Hérésie*, pp. 105–6; for subsequent views, see below, pp. 304–5, 307, 311, 316.

16

Politics and Hussitism, 1409–1419

The decree of Kutná Hora

Schism politics interrupted Zbyněk's proceedings, and finally brought the effectiveness of his archiepiscopate to an end. Tired of the contest between the rival popes, a group of cardinals renounced allegiance to their masters, and proposed the election of a compromise candidate who should rally churchmen of both sides to end the schism. But their candidate, the conciliar pope Alexander v, was unable to do this, and so the move merely created three popes instead of two.

At the time, however, the conciliar proposal drew Wenceslas's favour. An agile, wavering politician,[1] he saw a chance to regain the office of king of the Romans he had lost in 1400, and to confront his rival, Rupert of the Palatinate, by shifting from the Roman to the conciliar interest, demanding support for his claim against Rupert as his price for doing so. This affected the Wyclif case, for it created a rupture with Zybněk, who in his soldierly fashion declined to break his oath to the Roman pope,[2] and suddenly made the Czech element in the Bohemian nation at the university seem a valuable source of support. To make his move to the council's party, Wenceslas needed the university on his side, and found that the German-dominated nations, Bavaria, Saxony, Poland, at the Charles University, obedient to Zybněk and mindful of the benefices they might one day wish to have in German-speaking lands of the Roman obedience, declined to change allegiance, while the Czechs generally, hoping for conciliar support for their reform and less interested in the lands following Rome outside Bohemia, were ready to follow

---

[1] Characterization, with reassessment, in Seibt, 'Die Zeit', p. 477.

[2] The oath is fundamental for Zbyněk's opposition to Wenceslas's decision for the conciliar party in January 1409; it is a good hypothesis that it also mattered in Zbyněk's turn against the reformers in 1408. See above, pp. 298–9.

their king's plan. To get the university's vote, despite the hostile nations, Wenceslas simply changed the voting system of the nations by the decree of Kutná Hora (Kuttenberg) on 18 January 1409, which henceforth allowed the Bohemian nation three votes instead of one, and reduced the three foreign nations to one vote overall.[3] The Czechs were the majority in the Bohemian nation by that time, so Wenceslas got the change of allegiance he wanted. Kutná Hora and the secession of foreign masters and students to the number of seven or eight hundred, which followed their failure to reverse Wenceslas's decision, while it incidentally spread opposition to reform and to Wyclifism more widely in foreign universities, turned the Charles University into a regional university of a new pattern, and altered the balance of power broadly to the advantage of the reform party. Though not yet overall victors, the reformers had less opposition to conquer than before, since they no longer had to reckon with a concentration of opposition in the foreign nations. In the arts faculty Wyclif supporters now appeared to have a majority; in theology the situation was more complicated, since the philosophical ground of Wyclif's thinking was resisted by some Czech masters of the older tradition;[4] in any case the Bohemian nation included still the indigenous German masters, inclined against the reform party. Yet ground had been gained.

Most important was the realignment of political forces accompanying Kutná Hora. It had been won, in part, by skilful agitation under the direction of the lawyer John Jesenic[5] and the 'political intellectual' Jerome of Prague, the strange, stormy figure of the movement, a layman who was a theological teacher and a heavily committed realist.[6] Under their direction a link was forged between the ideas of the reform and the superior rights of the indigenous inhabitants of the kingdom. The association of this incipient feeling with Wyclif and reform was the distinctive feature of the Bohemian situation, which continued, despite vicissitudes, to hold and to grow in strength till older authorities broke down before it. The need to push Kutná Hora through helped the Bohemian reformers to become a political as well as an ecclesiastical party, allying with forces in the capital, and devising a propaganda that would appeal to native leaders. John Jesenic helped by creating a structure of theory, in part derived from Wyclif, justifying the supreme rights of the royal power in Bohemia in his work, the *Defensio mandatii*, thus influencing the king when he was uncertain whether to hold to his decision.[7] The notion of the Bohemian nation, chosen of God, faithful to its ideals, was launched by the Kutná Hora agitation.

In immediate terms, there was now a working alliance between king and reformers sufficient to prevent any legal action against the advocates of

[3] Seibt, 'Die Zeit', pp. 490–1; Kaminsky, *Revolution*, pp. 56–75 (Kutná Hora and sequel, with insight into political motives); F. Seibt, 'Johannes Hus und der Abzug der deutschen Studenten aus Prag 1409', *AKG* XXXIX (1957), pp. 63–80; analysis of decree in Seibt, *Hussitica*, pp. 65–7; *Hussitenstudien*, pp. 1–15.

[4] See case of Blasius Vlk (Spinka, *Hus*, pp. 92–3).

[5] Kaminsky, *Revolution*, illuminates this.

[6] Betts, *Essays*, pp. 195–235; interesting investigation of nationalism in Seibt, *Hussitica*, pp. 77–86; note summary on p. 86. See F. Šmahel, 'The idea of the "nation" in Hussite Bohemia', *Historica* XVI (1969), pp. 143–247; XVII (1969), pp. 93–197; F. Šmahel, 'Jan Hus – heretic or patriot', *History Today* XX (1990), pp. 27–33.

[7] Kaminsky, *Revolution*, pp. 67–70. Leff, *Heresy* II, pp. 628–9, on Kutná Hora, requires amplification.

Wyclif, initiated abroad, from taking effect. The king hardly cared seriously one way or another about the cause of reform, but he was interested in scotching any foreign moves on doctrine that might disturb the peace of his kingdom, and he was inclined for the moment to see Zbyněk as the source of these disturbances. He and his magnates found useful the pleas made for apostolic poverty and against ecclesiastical authority, but this was about as far as his positive interest in the reform cause went; nevertheless, uncertain as he was as a long term Hussite ally, his attitude, coupled with the development of popular feeling, was quite sufficient to undermine Zbyněk's continued action against Wyclif supporters.

The archbishop called in Wyclif's works, excommunicated those who had held them, and proclaimed an interdict, without fundamentally altering the situation.[8] When he tried to bring the affair to a summary end by burning Wyclif's works in 1410, he encountered a popular agitation of university students and Prague citizens, who disrupted services, threatened priests, and invented a sarcastic ditty about the burning and Zbyněk's lack of theology. Popular opinion was influenced both ways, and the old theological battle over Wyclif came into the streets, with the opposition to Wyclif also taking to the pulpits, labelling the reform party Wyclifite,[9] and performing its parody of a reformer's mass. On the one hand, a party blocking the heresy case against Wyclif came into existence, blending learned university judgement, with its plea for free study of Wyclif and its varying mixtures of Wyclifite teaching and native reform, with political forces interested in Bohemian independence and royal power, supported at a much more uncivilized level by street agitation; on the other side were opponents, Czech and German, also capable of mounting popular agitation, with some strength in the capital but rather stronger in the provinces.

Hostility to his interdict finally forced Zbyněk out of office in July 1410; not long afterwards he died in exile. He was the last archbishop prepared to use all the canonical machinery to put down Wyclif's supporters. The king's physician, Albík of Uničov, his immediate successor, showed no eagerness in pursuit; Conrad of Vechta, archbishop from 1413, was equivocal in his attitude. In practice, a kind of Gallicanism,[10] facilitated by Wenceslas's policies, the enfeeblement of central authority in the Church, and Hussite pleas for the right of the kingdom to deal with its own affairs, was shielding Bohemia from the traditional pursuit of heresy. The tricky task of the pro-Wyclif party was to keep the king to this Gallican line.

Jan Hus and Nicholas of Dresden

In the aftermath of the Kutná Hora affair Hus rose to the position which he held until his death as the principal symbolic figure at the head of the

---

[8] Events to death of Zbyněk described in Spinka, *Hus*, pp. 100–20, 122–9; De Vooght, *Hérésie*, pp. 115–23, 128–43, 148–51; and motives in Kaminsky, *Revolution*, pp. 70–5.

[9] Seibt, *Hussitica*, pp. 10–14. *Hussitae* was first used at time of Council of Constance (ibid., p. 11, n. 23). It was a term of abuse.

[10] See Kaminsky, *Revolution*, p. 74; for Conrad, see F. Seibt, 'Konrad von Vechta', *Hussitenstudien*, pp. 241–52.

movement.[11] He had not at first been a leader, but he had already become a target of the legal action against Wyclif's supporters; he was notorious to the conservatives because of the sharpness of his attacks on clerical abuse and, though his fame was most due to his popular oratory, he rose in intellectual pro-Wyclif circles as Páleč and Stanislav of Znojmő defected, and the departure of the foreign Germans gave chances for Czech scholars. In 1409 he was elected rector of the university. In 1410 he gained greater prominence through protesting against Zbyněk's burning of the books.

He was still not the most radical of the reform theologians; part of the case against him was that he provided a shield for preachers and agitators more clearly heretical than he was. This radical wing had certainly been in existence for some years; but its presence was felt more deeply because of the events of 1412.[12] In May an agent of John XXIII began to preach in Prague the crusade against Ladislas of Naples, and to offer indulgences to those who took the cross. The crusade was a mere instrument of schism politics, and the use of indulgences unusually cynical. The king, however, was in favour of the crusade and gained some of the proceeds. Hus's denunciation of the practices employed in the indulgences trade offended him and broke the alliance with the royal power.

The year 1412, however, both coincided with the emergence of more Waldensian-type popular heresy among the reforming party and gave new chances for radicalism. Typical of the popular demonstrations was the procession led by Voksa of Valdštejn, in which a student, dressed as a prostitute with bare breasts hung with a mock papal bull, mimicked the hawking of indulgences. Chests intended for indulgence money were smeared with mud; at the cathedral the treasure chest received a pronouncement addressed sardonically to the disciples of the evil demon Asmodeus, Belial and Mammon. Jerome of Prague found himself in his element, composing, if we may believe his enemies, popular Czech songs, slapping a Franciscan who disagreed with him, intervening in a quarrel between an exhibitor of relics at St Mary of the Snows and a Hussite bystander, and snatching a sword to put friars to flight.[13] In July preachers of the indulgences were interrupted by young men in their sermons at the cathedral, Týn and St James's churches. The royal wrath was aroused by the indulgence agitation, and the magistrates ordered three offenders to be beheaded. Crowds followed their corpses to the Bethlehem chapel, and clothes were dipped in their blood. The Hussite movement had gained its first martyrs.

Increasing violence on the Hussite side touched off counter violence from the conservatives. In the cathedral, priests beat protesters in the sanctuary; a crowd from neighbouring parishes assembled to storm the Bethlehem chapel;

[11] Perspective by Seibt, 'Die Zeit', pp. 500–6. See text of complaints against him by Prague clergy in F. Palacký, *Documenta J. Hus vitam illustrantia* (Prague, 1869), pp. 153–5; interesting comment in Leff, *Heresy* II, p. 627.

[12] Events described in Spinka, *Hus*, pp. 130–64, and theology of Hus and opponents in De Vooght, *Hérésie*, pp. 183–204; *Hussiana*, pp. 303–62; Walsh, in *SCH* Subsidia v, pp. 400–1, notes widespread conviction inside and outside Bohemia, including the reformer Dietrich of Niem, that the crucial influence behind the movement was Wyclif.

[13] Betts, *Essays*, pp. 216–18; Kaminsky, *Revolution*, pp. 88–9, esp. n. 129.

Páleč preached in Czech at the St Gall church, denouncing Wyclif as the greatest and most astute of heretics.[14]

Naturally, at a time of bitter feelings, the pressures of academic politics and of mass audiences gave prominence to the most exaggerated opinions among the debaters Znjomo and Páleč evolved the notion of the *ecclesiasticum et misticum compositum*, with the pope its head and the cardinals its body, which appeared to shrink the Church to pope and cardinals only. The phrase used for the description of Scripture, a *res inanimata*, till it was vivified by the decisions of the Church, so defined, particularly distressed Hus. Hussite views on the Church were a ·response, in part, to an extremist doctrine of their opponents. Both sides reacted to each other.

Late in 1411 or early in 1412 the Hussite radicals were reinforced by the arrival in Prague of a party of Germans from Dresden, former teachers who had mingled a radical theology with the normal grammar and the arts; the later confession of a pupil reveals that in their Dresden school they had taught the rejection of oaths, the right of all priests to preach freely without further authorization, the disendowment of the Church, the rejection of obedience to the Roman hierarchy and of the papal headship, and the inclusion of all necessary belief within the Bible.[15] It sounds Waldensian, and it remains controversial whether the beliefs of this group represent an autonomous outgrowth of Waldensianism in an intellectual environment, or merely a case of German Wyclifism, possibly formed initially among students at Prague who left after Kutná Hora.

Installed in Prague, the Dresden group were a radical influence. Most important was the master Nicholas of Dresden, who composed the *Tabule veteris et novi coloris* some time before October 1412. They can most naturally be associated with the phase of street agitation in the time of the indulgences crisis, for their natural setting was plainly processional placards, conveying in a striking visual form the contrast between the Churches of the popes and of the apostles. Collections of authorities confront each other: on one side, the tables of the Old Colour, of the early Church; on the other, the tables of the New Colour, being texts and authorities which demonstrated the realities of the life of the papal Church as interpreted by Nicholas, forming a vivid and uninhibited attack on the whole apparatus of the law, hierarchy and endowment.

On the Prague streets the identification would have been plainer. A late Czech version of the *Tabule* illustrates the texts with pictures, and there is a high probability that the original was intended to be learned apparatus for a sequence of propaganda paintings, stretching from an early pattern of twos, contrasting Christ bearing his cross with the pope riding on a horse,[16] or Christ washing the feet of the disciples with the pope having his feet washed in the curia,[17] to the climax in which the Antichrist of Revelation is depicted in

[14] De Vooght, *Hérésie*, p. 219.

[15] H. Kaminsky, 'Nicholas of Dresden and the Dresden School in Hussite Prague', in *Master Nicholas of Dresden: The Old Color and the New*, ed. H. Kaminsky and others (*TAPS*, n.s. LV, i) (Philadelphia, 1965), pp. 5–28, esp. pp. 6–7.

[16] Table 1 (ibid., p. 38); Kaminsky, *Revolution*, p. 40–9.

[17] Table 8 (ibid., pp. 60–1).

papal regalia surrounded by whores.[18] In Nicholas, we can see, the Hussite movement was passing from the theme of reform, however radical, within the existing framework of the Church, to an explicit rejection of it as the work of Antichrist.

Prague at this time gave special opportunities for men with a talent for street agitation. Before the end of the century it had attained the highest population figure for any city in central Europe.[19] Moreover, in the New Town of Charles IV there was an unusual concentration of manual workers: it was these men who formed the audiences for agitators such as Nicholas of Dresden and, later, Jan Želivský. F. Graus has produced calculations which suggest a high degree of poverty in Prague: 40 per cent of the population are classified by him as indigent.[20] Peasant immigration continually reinforced the *chudina*, the town poor dependent on casual labour; poverty coexisted with great wealth in the nobility and the patriciate, and class divisions reinforced the radical preachers' appeal. For the hungry and the underemployed, reiterated denunciations of an over-endowed Church and simoniacal benefice-holders from the ranks of the patriciate held a special appeal. For the preachers the issues doubtless remained theological; for their hearers social and economic factors came powerfully into play.

The New Town was also unusual because of its governmental position. The struggle of the artisans against the patriciate for a place in town governments, a general feature in Bohemian towns in the second half of the fourteenth century, could most easily be won by the workers in their guilds in the New Town because of their strong numerical position. These guilds gave support to the Hussite movement; the German chronicler Andrew of Ratisbon noticed their importance. Yet the guilds of the New Town could hold together only so long as the conflict with the patriciate demanded unity. An earlier united adherence to reform broke down and, as revolutionary doctrine emerged from what had been initially a more moderate movement, part of the New Town support went over to the conservatives.[21] There remained as a rank and file for radical preachers the less established middle class and the true poor.

Meanwhile, news from Prague as it reached the curia painted the situation in the darkest colours and led to further action. In July 1412, as part of the case launched against the best-known reform supporter, a major excommunication was pronounced against Hus by Cardinal Stefaneschi, technically for non-appearance. An interdict on Prague forced Hus out of the city.

Exile from Prague, which lasted till Hus finally left Bohemia for Constance, gave Hus the opportunity to put his thinking on to a firmer theoretical basis. Controversy over Wyclifite issues with his opponents tended to cohere round the fundamental question of the nature of the Church. Politically, the cause of

---

[18] Table 9 (ibid., p. 62); see heading ('What is said of the Antichrist applies to the Pope').

[19] Seibt 'Die Zeit', p. 431.

[20] Czech work, cited in J. Macek, 'Villes et campagnes dans le Hussitisme', *HS*, pp. 243–56 at pp. 245, 250, nn. 12, 13; F. Seibt, in *HZ*, Sonderheft IV, ed. W. Kienast, pp. 65–7; general background, M. Małowist, 'The problems of the inequality of economic development in Europe and the later Middle Ages', *Ec.HR*, 2nd ser. XIX (1966), pp. 15–28, esp. p. 21. I owe this reference to Dr A. V. Antonovics.

[21] F. G. Heymann, *John Žižka and the Hussite Revolution* (Princeton, 1955) (detailed pro-Czech narrative from 1419), pp. 47–8.

Bohemian reform tended to move into a dangerous impasse,[22] with intransigent conservatives and reformers still locked in conflict, foreign churchmen anxious over Bohemian heresy, and the king, who summoned in vain a commission to reconcile differences, unable to bridge the gap between the parties. Hus's appeal to Christ from the Church was effective writing, but made no change in the situation.[23] Meanwhile, the rival protagonists – Stanislav of Znjomo and Páleč on the one side, Hus on the other – continued a passionate debate about the Church, to which Hus's *De ecclesia*, published by being read in the Bethlehem chapel early in June 1413, was the most significant contribution.[24] It was a full-scale answer to the doctrine of the Church implicit in the *consilium* of the conservative theologians at the synod of February. In contradiction to Páleč and Znjomo's notion of the *ecclesiasticum et misticum compositum*, Hus took as his starting-point the definition of the Church by Wyclif as 'the congregation of the predestinate'. Loserth long ago shook the early romantic tradition of Czech scholarship by demonstrating through simple textual comparison how deeply Hus plagiarized from Wyclif's writings;[25] his conclusion was that Hus was a puppet of Wyclif. Today, with a better understanding of the methods of scholasticism and a more realistic appreciation of Hus's intellectual powers, the discovery of widespread borrowing no longer shocks. Hus's relation to Wyclif was subtle. Wyclifian terminology was skilfully redeployed in the interests of a moderate and very largely orthodox theology.[26] Wyclif was valued as a reformer, while the full implications of his thought were not drawn out.[27]

Of course, such a proceeding was undertaken at the expense of fully systematic thought; but Hus was not a theological luminary of the first rank.[28] The structure of the *De ecclesia* makes this apparent. Part one was concerned with the nature of the Church, and discusses Wyclif's definition; part two deals with practical issues. In the first part Hus commits himself to the Wyclifite definition of the Church as the body of all the predestined, which, understood as Wyclif intended it, was heresy; yet in the second he fails to draw

---

[22] Seibt, 'Die Zeit', p. 503.

[23] De Vooght, *Hérésie*, pp. 224–9, discussion of appeal at Constance, p. 395, text tr. in Spinka, *John Hus at the Council*, pp. 237–40.

[24] Context in De Vooght, *Hérésie*, pp. 245–88; on Hus's doctrine of the Church, see *Hussiana*, pp. 124–69; most detailed account in Spinka, *Hus's Concept*; on Hus as thinker and his fate, see Leff, *Heresy* ii, pp. 657–85, and his acute observation in *BJRL* l (1968), pp. 387–410, stressing moral and practical character of his work. For the text, see *Magistri Johannis Hus tractatus De Ecclesia*, ed. S. H. Thomson (Cambridge, 1956). A still usable translation is that of D. S. Schaff, *De Ecclesia: The Church, by John Huss* (Westport, Conn., 1915). Proceedings of the Bayreuth conference of 1993 on Hus are in the press (ed. F. Seibt).

[25] J. Loserth, *Huss und Wiclif* (Munich and Berlin, 1884; 2nd edn, 1925. Engl. tr., London, 1884), written in six weeks (Thomson, in *Speculum* xxxviii (1963), p. 118); see Kaminsky, *Revolution*, pp. 36–7; Šmahel, in *BIHR* xliii, pp. 26–7.

[26] A major theme of De Vooght, *Hérésie*: see esp. ch. 12 (review by S. H. Thomson, *Speculum* xxxviii (1963), pp. 116–21); F. M. Bartoš, 'Apologie de M. Jean Huss contre son Apologiste', *CV* viii (1965), pp. 65–74, controversy, ibid., pp. 235–8, ix (1966), pp. 175–80; E. Werner, 'Der Kirchenbegriff bei Jan Hus, Jakoubek von Mies, Jan Želivský und den linken Taboriten', *SDAB, Klasse für Philosophie*, Jhrg. 1967, x, pp. 5–73; on Hus, pp. 9–26; comment: Walsh, in *SCH* Subsidia v, p. 400 – 'it is arguable that this intellectual sustenance was less essential for Hus himself than it was for Jerome of Prague'.

[27] Leff (*BJRL* l (1968), pp. 387–410) brings a clear mind to bear.

[28] Leff and De Vooght have been preferred on this to F. M. Bartoš (as revealed in *CV* viii (1965), pp. 65–74).

out the implications of the definition. In Wyclif's writings his concept of the Church, with its vital distinction between the *presciti*,[29] foreknown to damnation and the elect, logically led him to a denial of orthodox belief on the priesthood: no-one who was of the ranks of the *presciti* could be a true priest. In practice, priesthood in Wyclif's late writings has no obvious place. When we turn to part two of Hus's *De ecclesia*, we find he is ceasing to follow Wyclif: more at home in discussion of the practical issues confronting the Church, he veers towards the older and orthodox tradition in Matthias of Janov, of a distinction within the Church between the communion of the elect and the body of the faithful. The priesthood remains, even at the cost of logic. The turning back to Matthias is characteristic: it shows Hus in the last resort more the heir of the earlier Czech reformers than of the Wyclif he so venerated.[30]

In one issue his thought had moved during his career. In the *De ecclesia* he rejected the papacy as an institution of divine origin. The Petrine text referred only to Peter's confession of belief in the Son of God. The papacy, he believed, had originated with Constantine, and was dispensable. In his doctrine of the Church, therefore, Hus was unable to achieve the feat to which he attained elsewhere, of preserving Wyclif's words within a frame of orthodoxy: there, driven by his contemporary experience of the schism, he broke quite clearly with orthodoxy.[31]

Meanwhile, secure in aristocratic protection during his exile, he preached widely from his base in southern Bohemia, building up noble support in the countryside. When, in 1415, 452 of the nobility and gentry of Bohemia and Moravia put their seals to a protest to the Council of Constance against Hus's execution, a significant proportion of them, according to T. Č. Zelinka's calculations, sprang from this region, where Hus was active during his exile.[32] In this period he was at his most radical: 'he performed divine services, and preached at Kozí Hradek in a barn . . . he inveighed against the pope, bishops and canons, and constantly heaped abuse on the spiritual order'. The Czech chronicler goes on to describe activities at Kozí Hradek (sited immediately south of Tabor on map 9) of a more violent character. 'Here', he said, 'the priest Věněk began to baptize children in a fishpond, and to slander the chrism and holy oil and holy water.'[33] He was describing the beginning of Taborite radicalism in the countryside, a movement of which Hus could not have approved, but which he may have helped to stimulate by his rural sermons.

The emergence of the radicals

In the second decade of the fifteenth century the movement in the countryside rapidly took on a radical tinge: especially after the death of Hus and the introduction of Utraquism in 1415 as a Hussite Church began to form,

[29] See Thomson's criticism of De Vooght's use of the term (*Speculum* XXXVIII, pp. 116–21).
[30] Leff, in *BJRL* L, p. 406.
[31] De Vooght, *Hérésie*, pp. 466–8.
[32] Spinka, *Hus*, p. 180.
[33] Tr. by Kaminsky, *Revolution*, p. 165; on chronicler, see ibid., n. 78.

parishes in the country were taken over by adherents of the reform, and radical priests inspired by the Hussite reform in Prague came out to conduct missions in the country. Some did not take benefices at all, and denounced those who did as 'priests of Pharaoh'.[34] These priests ostentatiously spurned all the apparatus of the late medieval Church, destroyed images, baptized, like Věněk, in ponds and streams, and celebrated mass in a 'purer', truncated liturgy in stables and barns. Their views were Donatist and anti-sacerdotal.

Spontaneously, this radical movement came to resemble post-1414 Lollardy, especially of the school of William White of Norwich,[35] or the Poor Lombard wing of the Waldensians.[36] To what extent the Hussite radicals were reinforced by a pre-existing underground Waldensianism in the countryside of southern Bohemia, finding an outlet as authority and the bonds of society were shaken by the Hussite movement, is uncertain.[37] The Waldensianism uncovered by the persecutions in fourteenth-century Bohemia and Moravia had in some instances a profound inner resilience, which enabled its determined members to survive persecution and the death of loved ones at the hands of inquisitors, to recover fully from the domestic disaster of confiscation of goods and still to continue evangelizing. Such members of the movement would have been receptive to radical Hussitism; but how far Waldensianism would have been able to leap the linguistic barrier between Czech and German remains uncertain.[38]

During Hus's exile, controversy made clear the impossibility of finding a formula to reconcile Hus with his opponents; Hus had become isolated from the king. In the capital the situation grew less favourable. The interdict imposed in 1412 represented perhaps the first success which the conservatives had had with public opinion since 1403. When in April 1413 Hus still lingered in Prague on one of his visits, and the parish clergy observed the interdict, there were disquieting signs that public opinion was being mobilized against him.[39] The king requested Hus to leave to avoid disturbances. His physical safety was still not in question, but the kingdom remained under pressure from abroad.

[34] Ibid., p. 201; narration generally on pp. 132, 141–70 (clarification of radicals' origins is a major ~vice of Kaminsky; see also his 'Hussite radicalism and the origins of Tabor, 1415–1418', *MH* x (1956), ˙02–30).

˙ompare the radicals' sayings (Kaminsky, *Revolution*, pp. 166–7) with the Lollard aphorisms (above, pp. . ˙ ·1).

[36] ˙ ˙ ˙e, pp. 74–6, 92–5.

[37] A. ˙nár, 'Les Vaudois en Bohême avant la révolution hussite', *CV* lxxxv (1964), cxvi, pp. 3–17, supersede˙ ˙ H. Thomson, 'Pre-Hussite heresy in Bohemia', *EHR* xlviii (1933), pp. 23–42. See discussion, more positive on Waldensianism than Molnár, in Kaminsky, *Revolution*, pp. 171–9; Gonnet and Molnár, *Les Vaudois*, ch. 5; the crucial account, based on new evidence is in Patschovsky, *Quellen zur Inquisition* (above, p. 153, n. 20–2), pp. 120–3.

[38] Patschovsky, *Quellen zur Inquisition*, pp. 35–6, discussing relatives of the smith, Henry of Jarosov nad Nezárkou, in southern Bohemia; discussion of the possible relevance of the search for a deeper, inner spiritual life, discernible in inquisition sources, p. 120. Jerome of Prague said early in 1409 that heretics had been burnt in Prague within living memory – but not pure Bohemians (Seibt, *Hussitica*, p. 80). Were they Germans? Kaminsky discusses bilingualism, in *Revolution*, p. 178, n. 114.

[39] De Vooght, *Hérésie*, pp. 262–3

Hus at Constance

An initiative, born of Luxemburg family affairs, seemed to break the impasse. Sigismund, the brother of Wenceslas and often his enemy, had in 1410 been elected king of the Romans, by implication in rivalry to Wenceslas who would not accept that he had been deposed from this position. In 1411 the two brothers sank their differences. Sigismund promised not to have himself crowned emperor so long as Wenceslas was alive. Then in 1414, if we can accept Bartoš's interpretation, the brothers struck another bargain.[40] Wenceslas agreed to the coronation of Sigismund on condition that Sigismund managed a settlement of his problem with Hus. The council which, largely through the initiative of Sigismund, had been summoned at Constance to settle the schism, offered a way out of the Hus issue. Hus should leave Bohemia to appear before the fathers of the council, thereby relieving Wenceslas of the external pressure on the kingdom, which he so much disliked.[41]

Probably neither of these lay rulers understood the intensity of feeling about Wyclifism. Hus hoped for more from the council than from the pope, and in optimistic moments believed that its members would join with him in reform. At Constance he had a sermon ready written but never delivered, calling on the council to put an end to the abuses.[42] He never completely trusted the safe conduct Sigismund offered – he wrote of the danger of death, and made his will before he left – but at the same time he was aware of the dangers to Bohemia if he stayed away from Constance. To go offered the chance of legitimizing the Bohemian movement and spreading it to the whole Church: bravely, and a little optimistically, he finally took the chance.[43]

When in October 1414 Hus left Bohemia on his journey to Constance, the movement for reform entered on a new phase. Long years of controversy within the kingdom had the effect that Hus, leaving for judgement at the curia, like Waldhauser and Milič before him, had behind him a much wider range of supporters and a much more thoroughly aroused public opinion.[44] A party that included clergy, skilful organizers, court officials and nobility followed with a passionate attention the twists and turns of a theological investigation which lasted from the end of the year, when Hus appeared first as an independent theologian freely come for learned discussion, to July 1415, when he was burnt as a heretic.[45] Stage by stage Hus's position worsened as, despite the initial compromise when John XXIII left him freedom of movement in return for the promise not to preach or appear at the formal ceremonies of the council, he was arrested and the safe conduct disregarded. Then in March, after John had fled from Constance, he was taken to be held incommunicado in the castle of the bishop of Constance at Gottlieben and

---

[40] For all the complications, see Seibt, 'Die Zeit', pp. 476–93.

[41] *CV* VIII (1965), pp. 69–70; Spinka, *Hus*, p. 222.

[42] Spinka, *Hus*, p. 226.

[43] Seibt, 'Die Zeit', pp. 505–6, on safe conduct, p. 504 and n. 40; will in *Letters of John Hus*, tr. H. B. Workman and R. M. Pope (London, 1904), pp. 149–51; see De Vooght, *Hérésie*, p. 316.

[44] Seibt's comment ('Die Zeit', p. 504).

[45] The best modern account is De Vooght, *Hérésie*, pp. 325–459; see also Spinka, *Hus*, pp. 219–90, comments in Kaminsky, *Revolution*, pp. 52–5, 125, 133, 136–61; correction in P. De Vooght, 'Jean Huss et ses juges', in *Das Konzil von Konstanz*, ed. A. Franzen and W. Müller (Freiburg, 1964), pp. 152–73.

finally brought back to be exposed to tumultuous public hearings and condemned. Weeks of well-meaning pressure to secure recantation, always firmly refused, ended in the ceremonies of degradation and public burning.

This dark story was described in the *Relatio* of Peter of Mladoňovice, secretary to Hus's noble supporter, John of Chlum, who observed the course of events in Constance.[46] His work was the Passion of a martyr, forming the classic picture for public opinion in Bohemia, its story of the death in chapter 5 becoming a set text for reading on the national day of Hus's suffering, 6 July. Sigismund, failing to stand by his safe conduct, was overheard acceding to Hus's burning, and thus played Judas; a party of native Bohemians, headed by the inveterate Czech enemy Páleč, the legal expert Michael de Causis, John Nas, the Prague canon of a German family, and Bishop John the Iron of Litomyšl, stood in the place of the Scribes and Pharisees at the trial of Jesus, and called for a hostile judgement. Hus, referred to as 'the Master', bore his martyrdom with patient dignity. The story, if written with *parti pris* by one of his supporters, followed the facts of the case, reproducing documents and quoting the participants with the pungency of an eye-witness. Hus himself, apart from the stay at Gottlieben, was never held so close that he could not receive visitors and write letters. The simple letters of exhortation to his friends written at Constance came to form a part of the devotional literature of a saint, suited to strengthen the faith of simpler followers who could not follow the complexities of the debates during the trial. For the nobles, and for humbler followers, the issue of honour, centring on the safe conduct Sigismund had given, became a key factor; for it was something instantly comprehended by them, when theological complexities passed them by. Hus and his followers believed their master was to have the chance to explain the principles of the Bohemian reform at the council; the fathers at Constance had no such idea, and intended to investigate Hus like any other heretic. When it became clear that Hus was not going to receive anything other than the normal treatment of a heretic, the sense of shock and betrayal in Bohemia grew.

In October 1414 some leading nobles had written to Sigismund, drawing attention to Conrad of Vechta's certificate of Hus's orthodoxy, and urging him to ensure that Hus was not 'furtively abused, to the dishonour of our nationality and of the Bohemian land'.[47] That note, of the dishonouring of Bohemia by the council, continued to be struck. The nobles at home, informed by John of Chlum and his party and stimulated by a nucleus of committed Hussites, wrote letters of protest to Sigismund.[48] Sigismund had to consider Bohemian opinion; the childlessness of Wenceslas made it virtually certain that he would be the heir if anything occurred to remove Wenceslas from the throne. He was not prepared to commit himself *à l'outrance* to defend Hus from a council bent on prosecution of heresy; he did, however, use his influence to

[46] Text in Spinka, *John Hus at the Council*, pp. 89–234.

[47] Tr. Kaminsky, *Revolution*, p. 138; on term tr. as 'nationality', see Seibt, *Hussitica*, pp. 102–17.

[48] Spinka, *John Hus at the Council*, pp. 153–4, 158–61; on feeling behind letters, see Seibt, *Hussitica*, pp. 102–17; on party organization, pp. 138–40; Klassen, *Nobility*, pp. 92–9; chs 7–8 give analysis of noble attitudes to Hussitism. For survey, with penetrating comment, on Hussitism, see F. Šmahel, *La Revolution Hussite: Une anomalie historique* (Paris, 1985).

FIGURE 10   Hus led to execution, from a contemporary woodcut.

Photograph: Bildarchiv der Österreichischen Nationalbibliothek. Reproduced by permission of Weidenfeld and Nicholson.

ensure that Hus was given a public hearing,[49] and d'Ailly and the directing forces of the council allowed Hus such hearings in order to satisfy Sigismund, despite the fact that by 7 June their own minds were made up against Hus.

The hearings gained virtually nothing for Hus and his cause – the hearing of 7 June had to be adjourned because of disorder, and in two subsequent hearings Hus was interrupted too constantly to enable him to make an effective plea. Instead, they formed a part of the martyrdom: Peter headed his chapter on them in the *Relatio*, 'Here follow the so-called Hearings, but in Truth not Hearings but Jeerings and Vilifications.'[50] Towards the end, Sigismund became convinced that Hus was a heretic. Without following the theology with any attention, his interest then lay in urging Hus to recantation. Hus's scruples and his unwillingness to recant what he had not written Sigismund plainly did not understand. Then, when the final tragedy occurred and Hus was burnt, the resultant emotions in Bohemia blackened the council as an acceptable doctrinal authority, together with Sigismund as a ruler of honour, and fatally discredited the party of native Bohemians under Bishop John of Litomyšl, who had pressed for a condemnation and expected to go on to break the Hussites at home.

The protests of the nobility culminated in the letter of 2 September 1415 to the council, which baldly asserted that Hus was falsely burnt,[51] and amounted to a direct defiance of the proceedings of the council. In the eight copies which reached the council, 452 nobles of Bohemia and Moravia had put their seals to this defiance.[52] Such a rejection of an ecclesiastical decision on a matter of faith has no earlier parallel, certainly not in the patriotic support of an old Church, said to have been infected by heresy, in backward Bosnia,[53] or the mobilization of Languedocian patriotism and some religious feeling, part patronage, part true adherence, for the Cathars among the southern French baronage.[54] The actions of the council in 1415 had resulted in something new in the history of medieval heresy. A deeply emotional issue, rapidly comprehensible to all, in which religious sentiment blended with the defence of the honour of Bohemia, had assembled a wide segment of the nobility in the defence of a cause now branded as heresy.

Such a mobilization of opinion at home, it will be noticed, would not have been possible if Hus had been induced to abjure. The protesters were aware that Hus died *non convictus et non confessus*;[55] had this not been the case, many who were not directly committed to the cause of reform would not have been brought to join the protest of 2 September, and Hus's own party would have been left in disarray.

To Cardinal d'Ailly, Hus was just another case of heresy.[56] A nominalist, he believed that realism had the eucharistic heresy of remanentism as a

---

[49] De Vooght, *Hérésie*, pp. 335, 385–6.
[50] Spinka, *John Hus at the Council*, p. 163.
[51] Kaminsky, *Revolution*, pp. 143, 144 n. 9.
[52] See the distribution of protesters in map 9, pp. 314–15. For text and list of names, see Palacký, *Documenta*, pp. 580–90.
[53] Above, p. 98.
[54] Above, pp. 97–8.
[55] Seibt, 'Die Zeit', pp. 505–6.
[56] Bartoš, in *CV* ix (1966), pp. 175–6; see also *CV* viii (1965), pp. 72, 236; De Vooght, *Hérésie*, p. 389.

MAP 9   The Hussite movement in Bohemia and Moravia.
Source: Adapted from *Atlas Československých Dějin* (Prague, 1965), no. 6B.

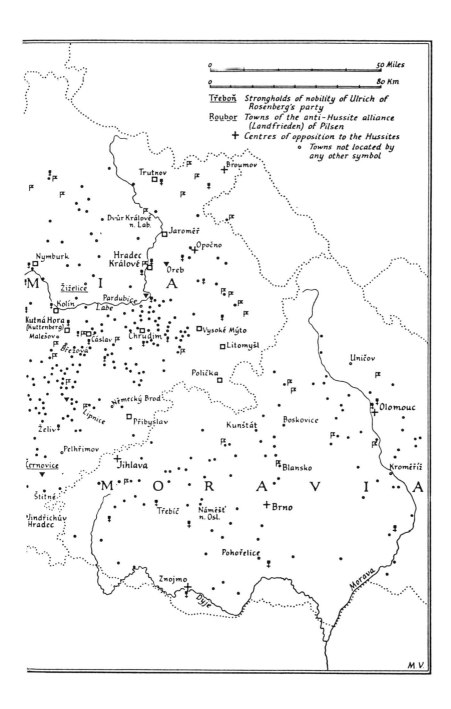

0   50 Miles

0   80 Km

Třeboň   Strongholds of nobility of Ulrich of
              Rosenberg's party

Roubor   Towns of the anti-Hussite alliance
              (Landfrieden) of Pilsen

✝   Centres of opposition to the Hussites

○   Towns not located by
              any other symbol

Trutnov

Broumov

Dvůr Králové
n. Lab.

Jaroměř

Opočno

Nymburk

Hradec
Králové

Oreb

'M   I   A

Žiželice

Kolín

Pardubice

Labe

Kutná Hora
(Kuttenberg)

Malešov

Březová

Čáslav

Chrudim

Vysoké Mýto

Litomyšl

Uničov

Polička

Německý Brod

Lipnice

Přibyslav

Kunštát

Boskovice

Olomouc

Želiv

Pelhřimov

Černovice

Jihlava

Blansko

Kroměříž

'M   O   R   A   V   I   A

Štítné

Třebíč

Náměšť
n. Osl.

Brno

Jindřichův
Hradec

Pohořelice

Morava

Znojmo

Dyje

M.V.

consequence, and was not impressed by Hus's denials. For the body of the council, the reputation of Hus in Bohemia was decisive; if they wavered in that view Páleč, John of Litomyšl and the rest were there to assure them.[57] Thus Hus's series of negative *diminfo nec tenui nec teneo* to the old Wyclifite forty-five articles made an impression, and his efforts at clarification had the result that the distorting forty-two articles of Páleč were finally whittled down to eleven; nevertheless, his own past defence of Wyclif dogged him. In part, the feeling of the council was comparable to that of inquisitors facing a simple heretic, who took the accused's denials for cunning evasions: repeatedly members of the council expressed the view that, though Hus might make sophistical denials, he continued to believe heresy with his heart. He was not allowed to examine the witnesses against him. While the extracting of articles from his works was supervised by the investigating commission with care, and did contain just, as well as unjust, attributions of doctrine, it was the testimony of witnesses that most obviously distorted Hus's views;[58] too many arrived at the council believing in Hus's guilt and the complexity of the evidence did not help them to shed their prejudice.

At the end, Hus refused to abjure, though to do so would have saved his life. He refused because of his utter unwillingness to abjure articles extracted from his works that he did believe and to recant articles that he claimed were not his own.[59] His courage helped to preserve the Bohemian movement. When on 31 August John of Litomyšl, following up the burning, received authorization to act against Hussites, he found a great barrier of sentiment interposed between Bohemia and the council decrees.

The lay chalice

Almost simultaneously the movement had acquired a symbol of its breach with the hierarchy assembled at Constance.[60] In the autumn of 1414 certain Hussites began to administer the chalice to the laity, and the practice spread. John complained to the council of irregularities accompanying the lay chalice; consecrated wine was carried about the country in flasks, and a woman who claimed the right of the laity to impose Utraquism snatched the chalice from the hands of a priest.[61] On 15 June 1415 the council prohibited the administration of the chalice to the laity. They admitted the facts of Christ's institution of the eucharist in both kinds and the precedent of the primitive Church, but argued that both the lay chalice and the reception of the eucharist after dinner had been discontinued for good reasons.[62] Hus had not initiated the chalice – 'Go slow, Kubo', he was supposed to have said to his

[57] Kaminsky, *Revolution*, pp. 37–40, 52, Leff, *Heresy* II, p. 648.

[58] De Vooght, *Hérésie*, pp. 334, 363, 388–90, 394, 410–11, 420–2.

[59] See comments in M. Creighton, *A History of the Papacy from the Great Schism to the Sack of Rome* II (London, 1899), ch. 5. Tr. of thirty articles on which Hus was condemned in Spinka, *John Hus at the Council*; comment: F. Seibt, 'Hus in Constanz', *Hussitenstudien*, pp. 229–40.

[60] On introduction of chalice and controversy on it, see Kaminsky, *Revolution*, pp. 98–126; F. Seibt, 'Die *Revelatio* des Jacobellus von Mies über die Kelchkommunion', *DA* XXII (1967), pp. 618–24. On Jakoubek generally, see P. De Vooght, *Jacobellus de Stříbro († 1429), premier Théologien du Hussitisme* (Louvain, 1972).

[61] Kaminsky, *Revolution*, p. 132, and his section on 'The Utraquist victory' (pp. 126–36).

[62] Ibid., p. 116.

friend Jakoubek before he left – realizing that it would complicate the situation for him at Constance. It was preaching that for him had the greatest significance; in the past he had not given close adherence to Matthias of Janov's teaching on the frequent communion of the laity; he observed that Jesus had begun to preach at the age of twelve, and at the age of thirty preached three years and several months long until his death, while he celebrated mass but once at the end of his time on earth. In the past he had noted, against the lay chalice, that the laity would not know how to communicate *pulchre*. None the less, when his own situation had darkened at the council and he had little to hope for, he rejected the council's decree because it was a decision which went against Scripture.[63]

Jakoubek, early defender of the lay chalice, spoke of the idea coming to him by *revelatio*, by which he meant the illumination which comes after prolonged consideration and study. Who exactly first raised the issue is still not clear. But it was a natural project to spring out of study of Matthias of Janov, who laid such stress on the importance of frequent communion, and to whom Jakoubek and others were so indebted. Over the centuries the laity had been excluded from the reception of the consecrated wine by a spontaneous development of the liturgy without any protest being made or the exclusion even being noticed: lack of interest in the issue was a natural concomitant of a situation in which the laity did not receive communion more than once a year.[64] Elsewhere in the fourteenth century, as in the case of the German mystical movement, stress on frequent communion did not lead to agitation for the restoration of the lay chalice. The Bohemian reform, however, was floated in an atmosphere of anticlericalism, which grew more intense in the early fifteenth century: in that atmosphere it is explicable that the withdrawal of the chalice should eventually have been seen as an unjust deprivation for which the clergy were responsible.

Paradoxically the council's decree against the chalice actually fostered its spread. The decree of 15 June was followed by Hus's burning on 6 July: the two decisions tended to be lumped together in the minds of the Bohemians and Moravians, and the emotional reaction against the one buttressed the other.

Once the idea was launched, pre-existing Hussite thinking about the Church was brought into play in its defence. The chalice, at first sight a minor issue of eucharistic practice, renewed the debate over the whole nature of the Church and its *magisterium*, which had developed over Hus's *De ecclesia* and had been important at Constance.[65] Both sides were agreed that the body and blood of Christ were contained wholly in either the wine or the bread after consecration, yet the withdrawal by custom, despite the words of institution by Christ in the Last Supper, raised the question: what were the limits of the Church's power of decision over scriptural precedents? The conservatives argued that the Church, having seen the benefits of communion in one kind,

---

[63] Ibid., pp. 133–4; Werner in *Sitzungsberichte AWD* (1989) at p. 9; note Hus's treatment of eucharistic abuses, discussed pp. 6–8, and compare Catto on Wyclif's attitudes, *SCH* Subsidia IV, pp. 269–86.

[64] D. Girgensohn, *Peter von Pulkau und die Wiedereinführung des Laienkelches* (Göttingen, 1964); review: H. Kaminsky, *Speculum* XLI (1966), pp. 132–4.

[65] Kaminsky, *Revolution*, pp. 108–26 *passim*.

could rightly decide against the earlier precedents. For the Hussites that view was impossible, for the Church which decreed such alterations in early practice was the stained Church responsible for such evils in contemporary Christian life. They took their stand on such texts as John's, 'Except ye eat the flesh of the Son of Man and drink his blood, ye have no life in you.'[66]

The introduction of the chalice gained momentum as humbler members of the Hussite party among the clergy followed Jakoubek's lead, Hussite aristocrats sponsored the chalice, and local congregations eagerly responded. Passions were aroused. Prague, where the movement began, split into reformed congregations where the chalice was given, and traditional ones where it was not. In April 1415 the town councillors prohibited either side calling each other heretics.[67] Utraquism touched every attender at mass in an immediate fashion; it forced the ordinary man to think out his relation to the Hussite movement before he took the step of going over to a congregation where the chalice was administered. The erosion of discipline brought about by the earlier conflicts over Wyclifism now enfeebled attempts to suppress the movement.

In November 1415 a further attempt to use coercion had the effect of bringing the victory of Utraquism. Conrad of Vechta, the cautious and opportunist royal servant, was induced to impose an interdict on Prague on the grounds that it gave residence to John Jesenic, who had long been excommunicate. As the support for the lay chalice, apart from Christian of Prachatice, lay among the unbeneficed clergy, the interdict made possible a takeover on a revolutionary scale.[68] Those who refused the chalice found themselves restricted to the suburban churches, where the interdict had not been imposed. A lifting of the interdict only brought the archbishop into difficulties with the council, still sitting at Constance; when it was reimposed in 1416 lasting damage had already been done to the conservative position.

Giving the chalice to the laity involved more than a mere liturgical change. Where, as in Prague, the crowd pressed for the lay chalice, or, as elsewhere in the country, the noble patrons of livings wanted it, benefice-holders were presented with an ultimatum: in the last resort, to accept the chalice or to leave.[69] The same process operated in Moravia, where the canons of Olomouc complained to the council of the barons who maintained Utraquist priests.[70] Such actions necessarily involved a breach of the legal structure which gave the clergy tenure of their livings and rights to tithes and alms, and left decisions over their discipline to the bishops and the procedures of the canon law. Introducing the lay chalice by force was an actual demonstration of the superior powers of the laity over their clergy, whether it was exercised in the name of the lay patrons or of a local congregation, perhaps loosely represented by a Utraquist crowd. Utraquism could thus appeal to patrons among the nobility who hoped to recover the wider powers of patrons that they had held

[66] John 6: 53.
[67] Kaminsky, *Revolution*, pp. 156–7.
[68] Ibid., pp. 157–61; note general comment by Seibt (*Hussitica*, p. 129).
[69] Kaminsky, *Revolution*, p. 160.
[70] Ibid., p. 163.

under the *Eigenkirche* system.[71] Wyclif, Hus and the Czech reforming party had taught the need for a poor Church, and Hus in his Czech work on simony had spoken of the rights of lay patrons and their duties to ensure spiritual care of a benefice:[72] Utraquism offered the opportunity to secure all these things.

Failure of Utraquists to impose their will in the parish churches also affected the situation. It tended to result in the formation of *ad hoc* congregations, for whom Hussite priests celebrated mass, in the words of one complaint, 'in fields and on casks, in barns on no consecrated altar'.[73] Such arrangements might begin, *faute de mieux*, because a consecrated altar for Utraquist masses had been denied; they became demonstrations by the radical wing of the movement of their rejection of the apparatus of material aids to devotion and of the traditional ceremonial of the medieval Church. In congregations, Utraquism was one of a number of rejections, of the need for confession, for set forms of service, for law, even for priesthood with special powers.

Not all of these concomitants of Utraquism were desired by the nobility *en masse*; indeed, the Hussite league formed to defend Hussitism on 5 September 1415 by almost the same group of fifty-eight nobles who had sent the initial letter of protest about Hus's burning, never mentioned the lay chalice at all among the articles of their agreement.[74] The league stood for free preaching on Hussite lines without consideration for any technical issues of provision and appointment. The authority of bishops was not *per se* excluded: if accusations of error were made, the compact provided that a priest should be taken to his bishop for judgement, but that clause was subject to the important proviso that the error must be demonstrable by Holy Scripture and that, if the bishop attempted to punish a priest 'improperly, privately and without demonstration on the basis of Holy Scripture' the decision should be left in the hands of the university.

In effect, the league interposed a barrier between the kingdom and the operations of either the council or ecclesiastical authorities obedient to the council within the kingdom. The doctrinal authority of the international Church was replaced by that of the university,[75] and the jurisdiction of bishops made subject, in a way now characteristic of Hussite proceedings, to the private conscience of members of the league.

Nevertheless the league acted as a shield for the spread of the chalice, and inhibited the carrying out of hostile decrees of Constance through the vital years 1415–16. Citations to the council of all the 452 nobles who had put their names to the protest of September 1415 and proceedings against the magistrates and courtiers held responsible for allowing the spread of

---

[71] Seibt, 'Die Zeit', pp. 512–13, early geographical distribution of Utraquists, p. 514; Kaminsky, *Revolution*, pp. 151–6.

[72] Ibid., pp. 152–3.

[73] Tr. from letter of canons of Olomouc (ibid., p. 163).

[74] Tr. ibid., pp. 144–5; on background, pp. 141–61; see still E. Denis, *Huss et la guerre des Hussites* (Paris, 1878, 1930) (based on pioneer work of the great F. Palacký, yet has charm and perspective, and grows in value post 1415), pp. 177–9; J. Kejř, 'Zur Entstehungsgeschichte des Hussitentums', in *Die Welt zur Zeit des Konstanzer Konzils. Reichenau-Vorträge im Herbst 1964: Vorträge und Forschungen* IX (Constance and Stuttgart, 1965), pp. 147–61.

[75] See Kejř, *Die Welt*, p. 53.

Utraquism were of no effect, since the league's membership was so weighty as to inhibit any Catholic reaction inside Bohemia from compelling obedience to these summons.[76]

The king remained passive. He carried neutrality towards the council almost beyond the limits of the possible. Alone of the kings of Western Europe, he sent no ambassadors to Constance. Probably his queen was more affected by the death of Hus than he was; his prevailing emotions seem to have been one of pique at the insult to his power, and suspicion of his brother's plans. Although he made no protest himself, he did nothing to prevent the protest letters of his nobility from being despatched. His whole position with regard to his nobility was weak. Aristocratic powers in Bohemia were a problem of long standing.[77]

Seen from one point of view the division of the country into factions based on religious differences was nothing more than a continuation of earlier baronial dissidence[78] and Wenceslas's response, doing nothing and declaring that there was no heresy in Bohemia, a natural course of action for a ruler who lacked effective weapons against his nobles. The council, however, was not sympathetic to Wenceslas's difficulties, and had in their hands the threat of a crusade, a fact which probably influenced Wenceslas to attempt to act against the Hussites late in 1416. The reaction did not achieve very much;[79] it neither diminished the use of the lay chalice, nor brought about a return of the ecclesiastical property that had been seized in previous years, and the king soon gave it up.

In the country, Čeněk of Vartemberk, meeting the threat of a stifling of the Utraquist priesthood in the long run by the refusal of the hierarchy to ordain men of Utraquist views, compelled a suffragan bishop in the Prague diocese to ordain at his castle of Lipnic his own candidates, all Hussite and tending to be radical in their theology.[80] The university, threatened in the winter, emerged from stress as the active doctrinal authority of a Hussite Church which the league of September 1415 had envisaged.[81] They settled their internal disputes by declaring on 10 March 1417 that the chalice was beneficial to the salvation of all.

Radicals and moderates within the Hussite movement

Early in 1417 the university was engaged in defining its position towards its own Hussite radicals just as much as towards the council and its Catholic opponents. The gulf between the moderates of the stamp of Christian or Jesenic and the provincial radicals was already wide. The extremists, especially in the provinces, wanted drastic changes that entailed upsetting customary services. Rejecting purgatory involved the abolition of the

---

[76] Kaminsky, *Revolution*, pp. 149, 222–3; Denis, *Hus*, pp. 184–5.

[77] Seibt, 'Die Zeit', pp. 476–7, Heymann, *Žižka*, pp. 24–8, 37; Klassen, *Nobility*, pp. 47–74.

[78] Kaminsky, *Revolution*, pp. 147–8. Sigismund, who hoped to inherit Bohemia, was probably sincere in his appeals for unity at this time.

[79] Ibid., pp. 223–7.

[80] Ibid., p. 242; Klassen, *Nobility*, ch. 6.

[81] Full context, ibid., ch. 5, an account which supersedes earlier narratives of events in 1417–18.

chantries and the traditional masses for relatives and ancestors. Already a Czech version of the mass was in circulation, sponsored by Jakoubek;[82] provincial radicals wished to go beyond this and truncate the mass, turning it into a simple communion service with preaching closely based on the words of Scripture. They wanted to reject the intercession of saints. The radicals discussed in a letter of Christian of Prachatice to Wenceslas Koranda, a provincial preacher, advocated that 'dubious relics of the saints should be thrown out on dung heaps'.[83] Koranda was actively destroying images. If the radicals had their way, the moderate Utraquists would find customary patterns of Church life turned upside down. Moreover, there was an element of opposition to authority in the movement in the provinces: the driving-force came from certain lower clergy, but Christian also referred to unlearned laymen and women who were asserting their opinions.

The radicals were rejecting authority in the Church, whether of the bishop or of the university masters, in favour of the appeal to the text of Scripture. Their ideal was that of the gathered community centred on the chalice, using the power of magistrates to make the law of God prevail. From an attack on Hussite Church authority, there was an easy transition to the attack on secular authority, the rights of property, and the position of the nobility. Moderate Hussites, whose aims might be summed up in the desire for a measure of autonomy from the Roman Church and for the lay chalice, had every reason to be perturbed. The problem was not new in 1417. It followed from the cast of Hussite preaching before 1415, with its appeal to the law of Christ as overriding unjust decrees of the Church.[84]

Hussite theses opened the way to private judgement as the norm; the problem as the movement began to move sections of the populace was to know where to stop. At first the radicals, Nicholas of Dresden and Jakoubek, had worked together for the introduction of the lay chalice; probably in the autumn of 1415 they split, initially over the existence of purgatory. In the following year Nicholas left Prague and went to Meissen, where he was executed: Želivský, who took his place in 1418–19 as the radical preacher of the movement in Prague, believed that he had been pushed out by the university masters. Nicholas, in his sermon collection *Querite primum regnum*, was defending, in effect, Waldensian theses: he was rejecting all killing and oath-taking, and his discussion of the powers of the priesthood virtually eliminated the bishop. This was too much for the main body of Hussite masters, and for Jakoubek.[85]

Jakoubek's own position was unusual. As a leading radical among the masters and as the originator of the lay chalice, he held a certain responsibility

---

[82] Ibid., pp. 198, 257; cf. p. 194.

[83] Tr. ibid., p. 169. Note Kaminsky's reconstruction of the probable attitudes of Hussite lords to such actions (ibid., pp. 228–9).

[84] See Werner, 'Der Kirchenbegriff', pp. 14–15, 21; A. Molnár, 'Hus et son appel à Jésus-Christ', *CV* VIII (1965), pp. 95–104; De Vooght, *Hérésie*, pp. 151–3, 173, 176, 208–9, 226–7, 395; *lex Christi* in Prague 1408: see pp. 89–92; for Jesenic on this issue, see Kaminsky, *Revolution*, pp. 63–4. On the use of the term *lex evangelica* in pre-Hussite Bohemia, see S. H. Thomson in *Speculum* XXXVIII (1963), pp. 116–21.

[85] Želivský's evidence: Kaminsky, *Revolution*, p. 219; *Querite*: ibid., pp. 207–13; death at Meissen: Kaminsky, 'Nicholas of Dresden', p. 12.

for the extreme positions which were emerging in the provinces.[86] Clergy influenced by him went from Prague to preach in the country. Their violent destruction of images, so dangerous to unity, could find support in his writings; in 1414 in his *Sermo de confessione* he had rejected confession to a priest as inessential. A puritanical strain in his character, which led him to condemn singing and dancing, brought him closer to the radicals than to the moderate Prague leadership.

At the same time Jakoubek formed a part of the body of masters that were engaged in discussions intended to hold the often contradictory wings of the movement together. Because of his popularizing of the lay chalice, his simple and unworldly life, and his long connection with the reform party in the university, he occupied a position of leadership, and perhaps more than anyone helped to keep the wings together at a crucial stage.

The St Wenceslas synod of 28 September 1418 represented another attempt at a formula for unity, this time both more far-reaching and more inclined towards radicalism.[87] An assembly of masters and priests agreed on twenty-three articles, and laid down that in future no-one was to teach any novelty without first submitting it for examination 'by the community of the brethren'. The articles rejected some key Waldensian-type theses, on the denial of purgatory, the refusal of the death penalty, Donatism and the right of laymen to consecrate at mass. The underlying principle of the extremists, that the explicit statements of Scripture constitute all that may be believed, was not allowed; yet, at the same time, the principle of the appeal to the primitive Church was preserved and, while a number of traditional Roman practices were allowed, they were suffered only under such qualifications as would still in fact allow for their abolition if the congregation so wished. The use of images, for example, was tolerated only if they were 'not wantonly or falsely adorned, in such a way as to seduce the eyes of communicants'[88] and provided it was not accompanied by outward acts of devotion, such as kneeling or the burning of candles. Latin was kept for the mass, but Czech was prescribed for the epistle and gospel, and all was subject to future change; ceremonies helpful to the law of God were to be kept 'unless something better is found'.[89] Infant communion, strongly disputed by John Jesenic and Simon of Tišnov, was allowed. The intention was to brake development on some issues, and to bring extremists under a Hussite synodal authority.

Unity among the Hussites from 1415 to 1418 was made easier by the rigid attitudes of the council. Having committed themselves in *Cum in nonnullis*, the fathers gave no sign thereafter till the end of the council in April 1418 that they were ready to negotiate the kind of compromise on the chalice that might

---

[86] For this and Jakoubek generally, Kaminsky, *Revolution*, is fundamental: see esp. pp. 180–204, synopsis in his 'Hussite radicalism and the origins of Tabor, 1415–1418', *MH* x (1956), pp. 102–30; comments by De Vooght, in *RHE* LXIII (1968), pp. 543–7, with deserved praise, but with some doubt whether Kaminsky sometimes explains theological opinion too much by the background of events and politics.

[87] Kaminsky, *Revolution*, pp. 259–64.

[88] Kaminsky's tr. (ibid., p. 261).

[89] From Kaminsky's summary (ibid., p. 260).

have split moderate Hussites from extremists.[90] Those like Simon of Tišnov, who found the pace too hot, were offered no kind of halfway house between Hussitism as it was developing and complete submission to the other side. The election of Martin V as pope in November 1417, who had had earlier, hostile experience of the Hus case,[91] ensured the continuance of a firm line towards Bohemia. The project of a crusade was taken up again.[92] Early in 1419 the king determined on the only possible answer – the suppression of Hussitism. This, the last Catholic reaction of the reign, sparked off revolution.

Tabor and revolution

The king's major action was to decree the suppression of Utraquism in Prague and in the royal towns controlled by his officials. In the capital he yielded sufficiently to the entreaties of the magistrates and the burgomaster to allow three monastery churches to be left for the administration of the lay chalice. But all the others, apart from Christian of Prachatice's church, were reoccupied by Catholic incumbents.

The Catholics celebrated their victory provocatively. Churches and altars were ceremoniously reconsecrated, Hussite clergy forbidden to use the side altars of churches, Utraquists thrust out of office, and absolution refused to the sick who would not renounce the chalice. Parish schools provided a point of conflict within the capital. The Utraquists did not give them up; the returned incumbents opposed to the chalice thereupon established their own in bell-towers and in buildings belonging to their parish. Pupils of the rival schools exchanged blows and, as adults joined in, affrays developed in which men were killed. The forces of moderate Hussitism felt unable to react against their king in his desperation. It was left to the radicals to fight the repression, and thus to save the whole movement from oblivion.

In the provinces, the sudden prohibition of Utraquism in the churches drove out the zealous congregations wherever the royal order was obeyed. Automatically, initiative passed to the radical clergy. In southern Bohemia, the traditional radical area, chronicles describe the assembling of deprived Utraquists at about Easter time, when under the old order the annual communion of the laity was due.[93] A hill, probably Nemějice near the castle of Bechyně, became a gathering point at which Utraquist congregations received the chalice and listened to sermons, and was renamed Tabor after the site in Galilee where Christ took his disciples for the transfiguration;[94] it soon became the centre for a dramatic development of radical Hussitism. Persecution at this late stage fused scattered congregations and precipitated change. Tabor, from being an occasional meeting-place, became a settlement,

[90] For conciliar attitudes, see Kejř, *Die Welt*, p. 60.

[91] Spinka, *Hus*, p. 114.

[92] For these and subsequent events, Denis, *Huss*, pp. 198–209 is still serviceable. Kaminsky, *Revolution*, pp. 266–96, blends narrative with analysis of motives of Želivský and incipient Taborites; his 'The Prague insurrection of 30 July 1419', *MH* XVII (1966), pp. 106–26, is the best account of the defenestration.

[93] Tr. of sources in Kaminsky, *Revolution*, pp. 278–80.

[94] Kaminsky, *Revolution*, pp. 280–3 and notes. Fundamental Czech work on Tabor by J. Macek (Marxist) (reviewed, Seibt, 'Bohemica', p. 96 (and index s.v. Macek); discussed in Kaminsky, *Revolution*, pp. 149n., 172n., 285n., 287–8, 320n., 341–2, 352n., 393, 398, 403–4, 422).

with peasants from a distance abandoning their goods and setting off to the mountain for the services and the preaching; attempts by lords to prohibit their peasantry from attending helped to precipitate their flight. Other hills in southern Bohemia were taken as sites and given biblical names such as Horeb[95] and Olivet.[96] Congregations came together in great numbers in a kind of cycle of liturgical celebrations and open-air preaching missions, culminating in a meeting of 22 July which deeply impressed the chroniclers. They estimated the numbers present variously at forty and fifty thousand, and described contingents derived from the areas of Pilsen, Domažlice, Hradec Králové, Moravia and Prague.[97]

Preaching under the shadow of the imminent end of the lay chalice, a persecution which to the crowds at this time seemed to resemble those that presage the Last Things, aided the spread of chiliastic expectations. The renaming of Bohemian hills after the mountains in Scripture, as Molnár points out, would set up powerful echoes in the minds of the congregations – of the delivery of the Law to Moses on a mountain, of Christ's Sermon on the Mount, of the meeting of God and man in the transfiguration at Tabor.[98] Preaching and communion was followed by a meal, resembling the *agape* of the early Christians. Collections were taken to meet the costs of owners of fields damaged by the assemblies.[99] Food was shared equally, even to eggs and crusts of bread. Sermons were fiercely denunciatory of the clergy.[100] The climb up the hills intensified the feeling of withdrawal from a wicked world; a Taborite song stressed flight into mountains: 'Therefore do not resist evil,' it ran, 'but go out to the mountain, and here learn Truth; for so Christ commanded when he prophesied on the mountain and preached of the destruction of the temple.'[101] In a similar fashion the simple communism of the eating arrangements for poor peasants would mark the contrast between the charity of the mountain and the duties and obligations to their lords of the manorial world below from which they had come.[102]

In Prague the Taborite demonstrations in the countryside were paralleled by long processions of Utraquists to the churches where the lay chalice was still allowed. The king, on his way to mass, found himself surrounded by a crowd under the leadership of Nicholas of Hus, a petty nobleman of the radical party, demanding the re-granting of general permission for the lay chalice and infant communion;[103] he had Nicholas arrested. When the Utraquist councillors of the New Town intervened, he consented to banish him. Nicholas seems to have gone to agitate among the Taborites. Wenceslas dismissed the Utraquist councillors of the New Town on 6 July, replacing

[95] Heymann, *Žižka*, pp. 131–3.

[96] Kaminsky, *Revolution*, p. 288, n. 84.

[97] Ibid., pp. 290–2.

[98] Tr. from Czech, ibid., p. 283, n. 63. For A. Molnár's work, see Seibt, 'Bohemica', pp. 86, 91, 96, 97, 105. Original Czech form is Tábor.

[99] Denis, *Huss*, p. 203.

[100] Evidence of Lawrence of Březová (Kaminsky, *Revolution*, p. 284).

[101] Tr. in Kaminsky, *Revolution*, p. 286.

[102] Macek's reflection cited ibid., p. 285.

[103] Denis, *Huss*, pp. 203–4; for development of opinion on Nicholas, cf. ibid., p. 224, Kaminsky, *Revolution*, pp. 410–12, Heymann, *Žižka*, p. 198; M. Polívka, 'Nicholas of Hus', *Historica* XXVIII (1988), pp. 75–121. I owe the reference to Mr T. A. Fudge.

them by Catholics, who forcibly took over the remaining Utraquist parish schools, prohibited their processions, and probably imprisoned Utraquists.

At this juncture Jan Želivský, a former Premonstratensian who had abandoned his order and taken on the mantle of Nicholas of Dresden in Prague, took a hand in events.[104] There was much tension in the city as the king, characteristically moved by a personal episode in which he detected an insult to his power, seemed at long last to have decided to crush the Utraquists' movement. He was fearful of the Taborites: reports circulated that they were planning to depose him in favour of Nicholas of Hus. Želivský had arrived in Prague in about 1418, and had begun a career as a radical preacher based, in the days when Utraquism still flourished, on the church of St Stephen in the New Town. In the Catholic reaction early in 1419 he lost St Stephen; but was a preacher in one of the churches reserved for the Utraquists, Our Lady of the Snows. A large building, it housed a congregation of small artisans and poor people from the New Town. Želivský saw himself as their representative, describing himself in copies of his sermons there as 'Ž, preacher of the poor, unfortunate, miserable, oppressed'.[105] Powerful and eloquent preaching linked him intimately to his poor audiences. The Latin outlines for his vernacular sermons over a period from April to November 1419 survive, placing him in the radical tradition of Jakoubek, vividly contrasting Roman practice and the primitive Church, forceful in denunciation. A natural extremist, he was contemptuous of the university masters who had bowed to the king's will. The poor of his congregations helped to form the demonstrative processions of Utraquists in the capital; no doubt they sang the abusive songs about the rich lords and the clergy which have come down to us. The sermons dwell on the suffering of the true Christian, but not in any passive sense: suffering is linked with struggle.

On 30 July he used his congregation for a violent demonstration intended to destroy the new royal policy of suppressing the Utraquists.[106] After a sermon at Our Lady of the Snows, he took the consecrated Host in a monstrance, and led out his followers, some armed with pikes, swords and clubs, to his former church of St Stephen. Finding the Catholic priest had locked the doors against them, the congregation smashed them down and took over the building, which immediately was used for an Utraquist communion. From St Stephen, Želivský and the rest moved to the New Town hall, where they found a number of the Catholic Czech councillors of the king's appointment. They demanded from them the release of the Utraquists held by them in prison. When the councillors refused, the angry crowd broke in, and threw some thirteen of them from the windows into the street below, where those who survived the fall were killed. Želivský's men then took over the New Town hall, and summoned the residents to arms, electing four military captains and, later, new councillors to replace their victims. A force under the

[104] For Želivský as theologian, see Molnár, in *CV* II (1959), pp. 324–34; as politician and military leader, see Kaminsky, *Revolution*, Heymann, *Žižka* (see index). Kaminsky uses Molnár's edition of sermons to reconstruct events of 1419.
[105] Molnár, in *CV* II, p. 327.
[106] Kaminsky, *MH* x, pp. 106–26; *Revolution*, pp. 289–96. Seibt ('Die Zeit', p. 515) notes that it was a conflict between Czechs, Hussite and Catholic.

sub-chamberlain arrived at the town hall, but was too outnumbered to be able to restore the situation. The king, inflamed, yet persuaded of the need to compromise, was forced to confirm in office the New Town magistrates who had been thus intruded. Just over a fortnight later he died of apoplexy.

Inflammatory sermons, working on the imaginations of the poorest sections of the Prague population, had done their work. Želivský, however, was not only a scriptural preacher of great power, but was also a practical organizer and a politician. Kaminsky has given us attractive grounds for believing that the revolution of 30 July was a planned affair. Želivský planned a coup that would destroy the king's policy. His followers, if they broke out spontaneously against the councillors who shilly-shallied over delivering up the prisoners, were not so out of control as to loot the bodies of their victims;[107] the chains of office remained untouched on their corpses. The insurrectionaries proceeded at once to the business of electing captains and taking over control of the New Town. It is likely that Želivský did not stand alone but formed part of a conspiracy with members among the leaders of the Taborites.[108]

In a morning's action the radicals had gone far towards capturing Prague for their ideal. The death of Wenceslas spoiled the plan, but could not put back their cause. With the defenestration they had brought off a successful rebellion against their king, and had wrecked the Catholic reaction most dangerous to them. Reform in Bohemia, which entered on a new phase with the enactment of the decree of Kutná Hora in 1409, culminated in 1419 in a revolution against the established order in the name of religion.

---

[107] Kaminsky, *MH* x, p. 113.

[108] Kaminsky's major hypothesis, attractive, not proved to the hilt. See also his attempt to relate the defenestration to Želivský's sermon (ibid., pp. 120–6; *Revolution*, pp. 292–3).

Success and failure: from the defenestration to the agreement at Jihlava

The aftermath of Želivský's coup

Wenceslas's death put the future of Hussitism into the melting-pot.[1] Sigismund, his brother, was the lawful heir, unacceptable to the radicals because of his record of complicity with the decisions of Constance, but still not wholly to be ruled out by the moderates. Moderate Hussites included in their ranks many attached to the principle of legitimacy, such as the university masters and the nobility, who would have found it difficult to reject Sigismund if only he had given some guarantees for a continued authorization of the lay chalice. Probably Ernest Denis was not wrong when he said that he could have taken the kingdom if he had moved at once. But he had other preoccupations, and the moment passed.

The Hussites united on a programme. At an assembly in late August or September, the barons and the towns set out their requirements.[2] They were,

---

[1] F. M. Bartoš, *The Hussite Revolution 1424–37*, ed. J. M. Klassen, East European Monographs CCIII (Boulder, 1986) (abridged, poor tr. of *Husitská revoluce* I (last chapter) (Prague, 1965) and II (Prague, 1966); narrative by master of Hussite history, sympathetic to Taborites and Orebites); Denis, *Huss*, p. 212; still well-balanced narrative of events, 1419–36; ibid., pp. 211–454; to death of Žižka (1424), esp. for political and military aspects, cf. Heymann, *Žižka* (with final survey, 1424–36, pp. 456–83); lucid summaries in Creighton, *Papacy* II. Seibt, 'Die Zeit', pp. 494–536, gives outline to 1436 with full literature. Kaminsky, *Revolution*, pp. 296–494 (often used here), is esp. valuable on Tabor and ideology, but stops in 1424; for brief analysis, see his 'The religion of Hussite Tabor', in *The Czechoslovak Contribution to World Culture*, ed. M. Reichigl (The Hague, 1964), pp. 210–23. For concepts and nomenclature, see Seibt, *Hussitica* (sections on just war, *jiazyk-linguagium, obec-communitas*); survey with perspective in F. Seibt, 'Die Hussitenzeit als Kulturepoche', *HZ* CXCVI (1962), pp. 21–62, sources tr. (esp. on radicals, Taborites) pp. 253–329; Peter Chelčický's teaching (pp. 333–443) in *Das hussitische Denken im Lichte seiner Quellen*, ed. R. Kalivoda and A. Kolesnyk (Berlin, 1969), introduction by Kalivoda, with up-to-date Marxist interpretation and literature; broad comparison, F. G. Heymann, 'The Hussite revolution and the German Peasants' War: an historical comparison', *MH*, n.s. 1 (1971), pp. 141–59.

[2] Kaminsky, *Revolution*, pp. 296–8; for general problem of communities, Estates, see Seibt, *Hussitica*, pp. 125–82, and cf. K. Hrubý, 'Senior Communitas – eine revolutionäre Institution der prager hussitischen Bürgershaft', *Bohemia* XIII (1972), pp. 19–43 (sociological approach).

in effect, the conditions of acceptance for Sigismund. Though Utraquism was not treated as a necessity for all, the lay chalice was to be authorized, the traditional reservation of the chalice to the priest and Utraquism coexisting, if necessary, in the same church. Simony, widely interpreted, was to be put down, and priests were not to hold civil office. Bishops were to ordain candidates for orders without discriminating between Catholics and Utraquists and neither side was to call the other heretics. Utraquists were asking, not for victory, but for peaceful coexistence. They intended to hold on to the gains of the past: the university was to remain the doctrinal authority; there was to be free preaching; papal decisions were to take effect in Bohemia only at the will of the king, council and barons. Yet there was still a desire for recognition within the international Church.

The nationalist demands were more far-reaching. The Czechs were to have the first voice in the kingdom. Judicial proceedings were to be held in the Czech language. Foreigners were not to take either civil or ecclesiastical office if capable Czechs were to be found to fill them. Thus, at the moment of crisis, the nationalist demands in Bohemia, which had grown contemporaneously with the religious, each supporting the other, reached their fullest expression. Other clauses reflected the interests of smaller groups. Prague had a special section of its own. The nobles had their particular interests; royal rights of taking escheats were to be restricted, Wenceslas's treasure was to be used in the interests of the kingdom, a hint that it should not be used to reward foreigners, such as the Germans and Hungarians of Sigismund's entourage, in preference to natives. The towns wanted an amnesty, the confirmation of their liberties, and laws against usurers and Jews.

The rise of the military Tabor

One group was hardly catered for: the radicals. The death of Wenceslas had been followed by disturbances in Prague and other towns where they had a strong following. A crowd led by Jan Žižka, a professional soldier in the royal service, sacked the Carthusian house at Smíchov outside the capital;[3] the inmates, largely Germans, had to be put in custody at the Old Town hall for their own safety. Inside Prague brothels were destroyed by zealots. In the provinces the great assemblies on the hills for communion and preaching continued unabated. Unaided, the New Town radicals under Žižka and Želivský took the fortress of Vyšehrad; in November a group which included pilgrims from the provinces took royalist positions in the Small Side.

Despite their protestations, the assemblies were a political force, and were undergoing a transformation into a fighting one. Queen Sophie and Čeněk of Vartemberk at the head of the council of regency saw the danger, and took counter-measures. In November the first pitched battle between the rival sides took place near Živhošť,[4] when a force of royalist nobility cut off a group from the south making their way to the November demonstration in Prague. In the capital the danger of a takeover by the radicals was more acute; but the combined forces of the New Town and the provincial zealots were unable to

---

[3] Heymann, *Žižka*, p. 69; background, ch. 4 generally.
[4] Kaminsky, *Revolution*, p. 307.

hold opinion on their side. The Vyšehrad was given up again to royalist troops, and the men from the provinces left Prague in disappointment, a mood which facilitated the swing to force.[5] Already at the 30 September assembly outside Prague, Wenceslas Koranda, leader of the Pilsen contingent, had said, 'The time to wander with the pilgrim's staff is over. Now we shall have to march, sword in hand.'[6] Koranda, with Nicholas of Hus, formed part of a small leading group engaged in the direction of the mass of pilgrims towards specific objectives, in the first instance political, then military.

Like the Waldensians, the radicals were initially believers in literal observance of the texts of the gospels prohibiting the shedding of blood; but even the Waldensians took up the sword in special circumstances, as for example, when their mountain refuges were attacked by troops under the inquisition.[7] There was an easy psychological transition from violent demonstrations, the image-breaking long usual in radical circles, the destruction of monasteries and brothels, on to the actual shedding of blood.

Preaching facilitated the process. In the winter of 1419–20, their leaders comforted the disillusioned with the prospect of the imminent end of the world. In a new coming of Christ their enemies would be destroyed; the remnant to be saved – which would come, of course, from the ranks of the radicals – were to flee to five cities in Bohemia,[8] where they would be saved from the wrath to come. Jakoubek and the main body of university masters reasoned against the radicals' use of texts and, in particular, against the necessity to flee to the cities of protection. On another side of the movement, Peter Chelčický, the yeoman of Waldensian views, stood apart from this development, and later wrote that he believed that the devil had deceived them into thinking that they were 'angels who had to eliminate all scandals from Christ's kingdom'.[9] Through all vicissitudes he clung to literal pacifism, and refused to have any contact with secular power. None the less, the prophets had their way. Lawrence of Březová describes how peasants sold up their holdings, even at a low price, and with their wives and families came to the radicals' centres, throwing their money into a common fund.[10] The end did not come, and the mood of imminent expectation passed, but not before it had played its part in setting up a confederation of like-minded radical communities.

The five cities of the prophecy were all places where the radicals had made an early impact, and lay in western Bohemia: Pilsen, Saaz (Žatec), Louny, Slaný, Klatovy. Pilsen lay under the command of the fighting priest, Koranda, and was soon reinforced by Žižka, who brought a remarkable military expertise to canalize the energies of the dedicated men. Another area of refuge lay in south Bohemia, where Písek had a long tradition of extremism. Hradec Králové was yet another centre: here lay the rechristened Mount

---

[5] Best described, ibid., ch. 7.

[6] Heymann, *Žižka*, p. 80; for analysis of political situation in September–October 1419, see Kaminsky, *Revolution*, pp. 301–6.

[7] Lea, *Inquisition* II, pp. 259–60, 267.

[8] Kaminsky, *Revolution*, p. 311ff.; Isa. 19: 18.

[9] Ibid., p. 321 (tr. Kaminsky); for literature on Chelčický, see below, p. 352, n. 13.

[10] Ibid., p. 331.

Horeb, with the Orebites under the priest Ambrose.[11] Both the southern and western centres were soon under attack. This intensified the religious emotions amongst the radical elect, but also led to losses. In a skirmish, Žižka for the first time demonstrated his skill in the use of artillery and war-wagons; but there was resistance to Koranda inside Pilsen, and disillusion when the projected date for an end of the world in mid-February 1420 passed. In March, after an armistice, Žižka and a party of the most determined followers left Pilsen to join the south Bohemian centre of resistance. There Písek seems to have fallen to the royalists, probably in February; but the zealots who had had to leave the town made a surprise attack before dawn on Ash Wednesday on another nearby town, Ústi-nad-Lužnicí, which they took.[12]

Finally, moved by the needs of defence, they left Ústi for the abandoned fortress of Hradiště, on a near-impregnable site formed by a peninsula, with water defences on three sides from the rivers Lužnice and Tismenice. Ústi was burnt, and contact with the old and normal life was cut off. A rigorous communism was set up, with the holding of private property being taken as a mortal sin. Fortifications were put up at great speed, and the population divided into four groups for military and political purposes under captains. From the fortress parties went out to subdue the surrounding countryside. To this society Žižka brought his soldiers and his military genius. The fortress was renamed Tabor. To the old pilgrimage Tabor near Bechyně, there had succeeded a new military Tabor.

Much as Cromwell was able to develop his military innovations in the intense religious atmosphere of the New Model Army, so Žižka used the religious exaltation of the inmates of Tabor to mould them into an unusually well disciplined fighting force. Among the Taborites the failure of the end of the world to occur as anticipated did not lead to a slackening of zeal: to the prediction of the imminent and catastrophic end there succeeded the notion that Christ had already come, but secretly as a thief in the night;[13] his public advent was yet to be. Meanwhile, it was a time of vengeance. After fighting would come the reward: the elect who had fled to the mountains would possess the goods of the wicked. The nature of Tabor inevitably drew only the most dedicated of radicals from their homes and normal way of life. In an atmosphere of feverish religious activity, novel ideas were thrown up very rapidly. A hostile witness describes the priests telling their followers of the wealth they would have when the millenium dawned: they would have an abundance of everything and would no longer have to pay rents to their lords.[14]

The violence of Tabor had religious roots; it also had a more practical cause, in the difficulties of supporting the zealots and their families; they needed the booty to be won in expeditions against their enemies. As the financial pressures made themselves felt, they were forced to impose the traditional lords' exaction of *holdy* on neighbouring peasants. This created

---

[11] On these and all Hussite groupings against geographical background, Seibt, 'Die Zeit', pp. 518–27.

[12] Events in Kaminsky, *Revolution*, pp. 329–36; military aspect in Heymann, *Žižka*, ch. 6.

[13] Kaminsky, *Revolution*, p. 345.

[14] Tr. ibid., p. 340 – surely significant for economic motivation. I owe to Mr T. A. Fudge reference to M. Polívka, 'Popular movement as an agent of the Hussite revolution in late medieval Bohemia', *History and Society*, ed. J. Purs and K. Herman (Prague, 1985), pp. 261–85.

disillusion; but the feeling of membership of the elect, the inspiration produced by the community in the fortress, the preachings, and the simple celebrations of the Utraquist communion, without regular altar, vestments or mass ritual, created a long-lasting momentum for Tabor that could ride out minor setbacks.[15]

Žižka's task was to improvise an army from the materials available to peasants.[16] Threshing-flails, consisting of swipples studded with iron spikes, initially had to serve in place of conventional weapons; as their worth became apparent, they were deliberately manufactured. Peasant carts made do as transport: soon Žižka adapted them as war-wagons. They were improved for defence purposes by adding boards to protect both their occupants and the wheels, and places were made for hand-guns. Shields were developed to close gaps between wagons. Žižka had had experience of warfare against the Teutonic Knights in a campaign on behalf of the king of Poland, and may there have learnt something of the use of wagons; but the extension of their use from transport to a whole system of mobile defence seems to have been his innovation. The great virtue of Žižka's war-wagons was that they enabled mobile columns to switch rapidly and effectively to defence against cavalry attack.

Sigismund and the battle of Vitkov Hill

Meanwhile negotiations continued, spurred by the moderate Utraquists' fear of the excesses of the Taborites.[17] At a diet at Brno in December 1419 the Estates swore obedience to Sigismund, and Prague asked for forgiveness for its rebelliousness. It seemed as if he would allow a policy of toleration for the lay chalice, provided that his wishes were respected on other matters. Quietly he appointed two Catholic nobles as steward and chamberlain, with control of royal castles and towns, to outflank Čeněk of Vartemberk. Again a successful entry as ruler to Bohemia seemed eminently possible. But Sigismund spoiled his chances by dropping the mask of compromise.

Another diet at Breslau assembled the magnates of the Empire; in the atmosphere of power there, the direct military solution of the Bohemian problem seemed attractive. There were still centres of Catholic dominance in the country. At Kutná Hora the German population was engaged in a wholesale elimination of Hussites who, as the town's executioner became overburdened, were thrown into the abandoned shafts of silver mines. In south Bohemia the Hussites had been unable to eliminate the opposition of Ulrich of Rosenberg (Rožmberk). In February Sigismund decided for an expedition, declared a crusade by Martin v. In Breslau he demonstrated his new attitude to Bohemian heresy by assenting to the burning of a Hussite merchant from Prague. As far as recalcitrant towns were concerned, he

---

[15] The atmosphere is reconstructed by Kaminsky in *The Czechoslovak Contribution*, ed. Reichigl, pp. 210–23; for the composite work on Tabor up to 1421, see F. Šmahel *et al.*, *Dějiny Tábora* I, pt 1 (České Budějovice, 1988), review: E. Werner, in *ZG* XXXVIII (1990), pp. 457–9; wide-ranging discussion of the degree to which one may speak of revolution at Tabor and after by Šmahel, *Anomalie*.

[16] Heymann, *Žižka*, pp. 97–101.

[17] Ibid., ch. 7; Denis, *Huss*, p. 233–7; Kaminsky, *Revolution*, pp. 361–5.

marked the contrast between him and his vacillating brother by quashing Wenceslas's mild response to a revolt of workers' corporations against the town council in Breslau.

In the winter and spring 1419 on the university masters debated the issues of war and peace.[18] In February Žižka submitted this theme to the university – an interesting demonstration of links, however frail, which still held between different wings of the movement. A little earlier two priests, one in favour of the radicals, the other more conservative, debated publicly the righteousness of war; the dispute was referred to Jakoubek and Christian of Prachatice for judgement. They disliked the deductions being made by the provincial radicals from the imminence of the end of the world, but they allowed a right of resistance by Utraquist communities even against the will of the lords.

The necessities of the time were drawing university masters, as well as the Taborites, into the justification of revolution against the established order. In their discussions they moved, stage by stage, away from the traditional and much qualified support for Christian warfare to be found in Wyclif, and derived by him from Aquinas, to an acceptance of holy war, and even obligatory war, for the Bohemians who held to the cause of the chalice. Wyclif's exposition left no place for resistance against a lawful ruler; the Prague masters in their need boldly left him behind. As Seibt explains, their achievement was considerable.[19]

The crusade did what nothing else could do; it pushed into temporary unity the disparate forces of Hussitism.[20] In Prague, Old and New Town came together on 3 April 1420, and made an agreement setting up a form of military government under captains, with temporary powers overriding, though not superseding, those of the magistrates.[21] Želivský, who had been somewhat isolated during the phase of negotiation with Sigismund, regained influence. The citizens sent out a manifesto which struck the nationalist chord. Sigismund was to be repelled, as he had summoned a crusade and had called in the Germans, 'our natural enemies'. Responsibility for schism did not lie with the Czechs: the Church, a malicious stepmother to them, had repelled them, despite the fact that they had only wanted to follow Christian law.[22] Čeněk, the weathercock of Hussitism, returning from Sigismund, joined the Prague citizens in their defiance, took over the Hradčany castle, and rallied the nobility. On 20 April the lords issued their manifesto, a formal *diffidatio* directed against Sigismund which enumerated his faults, from his complicity in the burning of Hus to the alienation of the Margravate of Brandenburg and the naming as bishop of Moravia of an 'enemy of the Slav race'.[23]

In both manifestos there was a similar theme of honour and nationality, defined in terms of language. The Czech keyword was *jazyk*, best translated as

---

[18] Kaminsky, *Revolution*, pp. 317–29; Seibt, *Hussitica*, ch. 2 (valuable for the intellectual origins of discussion).

[19] Seibt, *Hussitica*, p. 55; note comment: pp. 53, 57.

[20] Ibid., p. 17; note discussion of Hussites' lack of any self-devised term for all members of the reform movement, p. 14.

[21] Kaminsky, *Revolution*, p. 368.

[22] Denis, *Huss*, pp. 238–9.

[23] Ibid., p. 239.

'tongue'.[24] It use links the manifestos of 1420 with the protests of the Bohemian and Moravian nobility in 1415. The later ones, which form a sequence of high rhetoric through the 1420s, almost certainly are the work of one hand, and reflect the interest of the Prague patriciate, university-educated, touched by humanism, and less orientated towards religion than secular concerns. Linguistic nationalism was a relatively sophisticated notion, but it was calculated to stir the emotions of Czechs far from university circles.[25]

As the crusaders made their way into the country, national feeling was reinforced by stories of martyrdom, the *passiones* of humble Hussites, of which the best-known is the burning together of parish priest, peasants and children who refused to recant at Arnoštovice in July 1420 by the troops of the duke of Austria.[26]

The manifesto of 3 April also included a formula for religious unity among the rival Hussite groups; modified, it reappeared on 20 April, and again on 27 May; decked with texts and authorities, it was translated and transmitted to Sigismund's army and to other towns. The formula became known as the Four Articles of Prague;[27] it was the minimum platform of Hussitism. The articles proclaimed Utraquism; the 'proper and free preaching of the word of God'; the necessity for all priests, from the pope downwards, to 'give up their pomp, avarice and improper lordship'; and for the Bohemian realm and nation to be cleansed both from public mortal sins and from slander. Different groups could read into it different meanings. The nobility on 20 April omitted the reference to public mortal sins; the radicals on the contrary, saw the same fourth article as an invitation to a revolutionary upheaval in the country. But the lay chalice united all.

Yet for many radicals it formed only a preliminary to a wholesale revision of the mass, which stripped it down to the decisive scriptural texts, all translated into Czech, and it turned into a communion service bereft of traditional vestments and ceremonial.[28] Where the most moderate were satisfied with the concession of the lay chalice, and perhaps the translation of epistle and gospel into the vernacular, others went further, and treated the first article as giving them the right also to administer the chalice to infants. Modifications of the articles in different versions reflected the tensions beneath the surface. But the articles served their purpose: evolved under the pressure of invasion, they held together moderates and radicals for a common defence. They represented a minimum of what all would accept. They lasted long because no better formula could be found to reconcile the irreconcilable.

In the city of Prague the new common actions of April and May and the stress on the national interests of the Czechs in the manifestos led to a major emigration of Germans and Catholics, not to be reversed.[29] Houses, gardens

[24] Seibt, *Hussitica*, pp. 102–9.
[25] In this and earlier sentences, I follow Seibt's research (*Hussitica*, ch. 3 (see p. 117); *HZ* CXCVI (1962), pp. 21–62).
[26] Denis, *Huss*, p. 248.
[27] Kaminsky, *Revolution*, pp. 369–75, Heymann, *Žižka*, ch. 10.
[28] Discussed, Kaminsky, *Revolution*, pp. 375–83.
[29] Denis, *Huss*, p. 261.

and possessions were confiscated and redistributed, the community thus claiming a wholly revolutionary right of disposal. In this way the appeal of the manifestos to a linguistic nationalism issued speedily in action, and the flight of the Germans and the ruin of the German-Catholic patriciate with the takeover by Czechs created interest-groups inextricably committed to resistance. The emigration of the late spring and early summer could be paralleled elsewhere. The reform still retained a supra-racial significance, and a line-up of German Catholics inside and outside the kingdom versus Hussite Czechs was still far from automatic. Among the towns Pilsen, which unlike many Bohemian towns was exclusively administered in the Czech language, after a brief episode of radical dominance under Wenceslas Koranda, stayed faithful to the conservative side, while on the other side Saaz, a town of mixed linguistic usage with a strong German population, stayed with the Taborites.[30] Nevertheless, the events of 1420 had gone far to unite Czech interests with the chalice. Even at this late stage, moderate Hussites and nobility again tried to treat with Sigismund; but, being rejected, reunited with the Taborites, who entered Prague in May.

The city's chances of surviving siege were not high, for Sigismund commanded a great force, and royalists held the fortresses of the Hradčany and Vyšehrad on two sides of Prague.[31] The weakness of the royalist position lay in the difficulty of supplying such an army, and, more than all else, the problem of morale, with native Bohemian Catholics fighting uneasily at the side of Sigismund's foreign subjects from Germany and Hungary. The battle of Vitkov Hill decided the issue. It was not a full-scale engagement, and the losses to Sigismund's army were not high; his troops failed by the narrowest of margins to secure the ridge of the Vitkov in a strategic position on the northeast of the city. The balance was turned by Žižka's eye for crucial ground and the fighting qualities of his Taborites.

In defeat, Sigismund listened to the advice of his Bohemian nobility, had himself crowned in the cathedral, then moved away from the city to the security of the Kutná Hora region, where he delayed through the rest of the summer and early autumn. Never wholehearted in military plans for long, he seems to have believed that his presence alone in the kingdom would in the end rally support for him as lawful ruler, and that the Hussites' unity would break down in internecine strife. But this was sadly to underestimate both the general suspicion of him as the betrayer of Hus, and the Czech national feeling against the Germans and Hungarians in his entourage. In November he came back too late to save the Vyšehrad fortress from going down to the assault of the Praguers, and in March 1421, after other conflicts, left Bohemia altogether with little accomplished. His hesitation and final departure were valuable to the Hussite cause, for they gave Žižka the chance later in 1420 and in 1421 to reduce towns and fortresses on the Catholic and royalist side, till Bohemia, though never wholly won for the chalice, formed a substantial bastion of Hussitism.[32]

---

[30] Seibt, in *HZ* CXCVI (1962), pp. 21–62; *Hussitica*, pp. 95–6.

[31] Heymann, *Žižka*, ch. 9, for military details.

[32] This point is clarified by Heymann (*Žižka*, pp. 170–2, 174–5, 181–2, 199–208, 217–19); on the significance of the events of 1420, see F. Seibt, 'Vom Vitkov bis zum Vyšehrad', *Hussitenstudien*, pp. 185–

Húska, the Adamites and the end of Želivský

Military success formed a shield for debate and organizational moves in which the Hussite parties defined their positions and eliminated their extremists. In the flush of victory after Vitkov, the Taborites attempted to swing Prague to their views, presenting a programme of Twelve Points to the community, demanding either instant action on clauses of the Four Articles, such as the disappropriation of priests or an interpretation of the clause on 'public sins', which would have imposed a puritanical regime on the city.[33] Their call for university masters to be subject to the 'divine law', which for the Taborites meant Scripture alone, would have destroyed the position of the university as the doctrinal authority of the Utraquists, and their demand that monasteries, 'unnecessary' churches, vestments and gold and silver chalices should be destroyed went far beyond the views of the moderate majority in the city. Destruction of the monastery at Zbraslav south of the city and desecration of the royal graves by a drunken contingent added disgust to the fear of Tabor of the moderates.[34] Repudiated, the Taborites left, and in September marked the doctrinal breach with Prague Hussitism by electing one of their preachers, Nicholas of Pelhřimov, as bishop. He was needed to ordain priests, to give status to Taborite preaching, and to organize it; the election marked a stage of definition within Tabor as well as against Prague, as the informal processes of the chiliast past gave way to more settled arrangements natural to a city-state, with dependent towns, craft industries developing, and peasants paying dues; by its disregard of apostolic succession, it also closed a door to reconciliation with the Utraquists.[35]

As a settled church developed in the towns of the Taborite lordship and their dependent populations, so problems of discipline arose. Martin Húska, one of the most eloquent Taborites and an 'ordainer' of Nicholas as bishop, led a party within Tabor that denied a real presence in the eucharist, and taught that the bread and wine should not be received kneeling but informally, in quantity rather than sacramentally, in love-feasts reminiscent of the early Church.[36] The eucharist turned into a commemoration meal. Ardent as the Taborites were to strip down the mass to its scriptural components, abolishing all pomp, vestments and accretions to the liturgy, pleading against their moderate Utraquist opponents that Christ did not dress in a chasuble, they were not prepared to follow Húska's inferences from Scripture and reason. The eucharist was a highly sensitive issue among all Hussites, and the Taborites, radical as they were, were yet the heirs of Matthias of Janov and the fourteenth-century reform; although they had moved from transubstantiation, none the less they were believers in a real presence, and the belief was of great emotional importance. Martin deployed the rationalist argument that

207 (note comment on Kaminsky, *Revolution*, at p. 197); on the literature of the Taborites, see A. Molnár, 'La letteratura Taborita', *RSLR* XVIII (1982), pp. 3–23; T. A. Fudge, 'The magnificent ride: myth, heresy and propaganda in the radical Hussite movement' (Cambridge PhD, forthcoming) (full bibliography *c.* 1370–*c.* 1450).

[33] See tr. in Kaminsky, *Revolution*, pp. 376–7.
[34] Heymann, *Žižka*, p. 168.
[35] Kaminsky, *Revolution*, pp. 385–91.
[36] Subtle account, with full tr. of sources, ibid., pp. 397–433.

the physical body of Christ was in heaven, and could not be in the eucharist,[37] and, pleading the scriptural analogy of the Feeding of the Five Thousand, the people receiving seated on the ground, he contrasted the sacramental doses of wine and bread to the full banquet of the love-feast that he wished to introduce, while followers in the passionate fashion characteristic of Tabor proceeded to empty monstrances and trample on Hosts as a demonstration against traditional sacramental doctrine and practice.

Then Tabor exercised its authority to put down Húska's followers by force. As the new views evolved, Taborite leaders were engaged in discussion, centring on liturgical practice, with the moderate Utraquists of Prague, who had to be warned of the spread of the heresy, referred to as Pikartism, from Pikart, a corruption of Beghard, and a loose term of abuse for a heretic.[38] Húska, imprisoned, then released, finally taken in the summer of 1421, was burnt in August with the concurrence of both wings of Hussitism.

The Húska heresy has been plausibly explained by Kaminsky as a development from the chiliast phase of the whole Taborite movement; Húska's group moved on from the point where their former fellows called a halt. The immediate issue of the laity's right to divide consecrated Hosts among themselves, on which Húska was first imprisoned early in 1421, was but the tip of a whole interpretation of Christian life that was out of accord with Tabor, and came to involve heresy still more profound than the eucharistic tenets. Fragmentary references make possible a reconstruction of Húska's teaching as based on a belief in the realization of the kingdom among his Taborite group, in a way that made the law of Grace unnecessary. Paul's strictures on the Corinthians' confusion of the eucharist with indulgent feasts did not apply in Húska's view; his group believed it was right to make the eucharist a love-feast, in Peter Chelčický's description, 'meeting in love on the holy day, being diligent in the word of God, feasting and filling themselves up . . . and not growing thin on the little piece of bread of the popish and heretical supper'.[39] Chelčický found Húska's views drastic and disconcerting. Martin, he said, was 'not humble or at all willing to suffer for Christ'.[40] He quotes him as believing in a new kingdom of the saints on earth, in which the good would not suffer, and saying, 'If Christians were always to have to suffer so, I would not want to be a servant of God.'

It seems that some of the group came to believe that, because the kingdom had been realized in them, ordinary laws no longer applied. A heretical opening for the Lord's prayer, 'Our Father who art in us', was attributed to them by their opponents;[41] a section of Húska's followers, it was said, went so far as to act as if they were in the state of innocence before the Fall, men and women going naked, on the argument that clothes were a consequence of the Fall, and having sexual intercourse if they willed, and saying that it was no

---

[37] Jakoubek's version (ibid., p. 424). Compare rationalist arguments on transubstantiation (above, pp. 58, 257, 280).

[38] Kaminsky, *Revolution*, pp. 407–18. On beghards, see above, pp. 181–8; Lerner, *Free Spirit*, pp. 36–44.

[39] Tr. in Kaminsky, *Revolution*, p. 424. I follow Kaminsky's reconstruction of the development of Húska's views. Note criticism of Macek (ibid., pp. 403–4). On Chelčický, below, p. 352.

[40] Ibid., p. 400.

[41] Ibid., p. 427. Note the curious parallel with the Amalriciani (see above, pp. 99–100).

sin.[42] This extreme development followed on ejection from Tabor – the Adamites, as they were called, formed a strange community, defending themselves against attack from the main body, and having to be crushed by Žižka in battle, who had numbers of them burnt. Húska himself rejected the views of this group. Žižka, who sent a list of their evil doings to Prague,[43] believed that the community committed still worse acts, murder and sodomy included.

There is now no sure means of getting behind this testimony; one can only note the possibility of slander, the undeniable fact that the group had aroused Žižka's ferocious anger, and the extraordinary hot-house atmosphere of Tabor in its early years, still, despite its greater anchoring in the economic world, relatively detached from ordinary living and dominated by the intense preaching of its priests and tireless discussion of Scripture. It was a setting in which every kind of dissident and novel belief was liable to come rapidly to life. Lawrence of Březová, the chronicler, attributed the start of the well-attested eucharistic heresy of Húska to the influence of a party of Pikarts and their families, possibly in fact Waldensians, who first came to Prague as refugees in 1418.[44] The fact may be relevant, but it is not a necessary postulate for the emergence of fresh heresy on the radical side in 1420–1. Taboritism itself was the great incubator of heresy.[45]

Prague came to the fore in the months after the fall of the Vyšehrad in November 1420.[46] The original centre for reform and revolution, it gained prestige from the military success won by its own forces, Tabor being sparsely represented at the assault; and in the spring it gathered under its hegemony a league of cities in mid- and western Bohemia. The adherence of Conrad of Vechta to the Four Articles in April 1421, after long wavering, was also a gain for Prague as well as for the cause of Hussitism generally.[47] His adherence ensured that there would be a sufficient flow of ordinations to eliminate the risk of priesthood in Bohemia gradually dying out, and it gave a cover of legitimacy to Hussitism, however much this was repudiated by Sigismund and the ecclesiastics in the outside world. But at Čáslav, where in June 1421 a diet declared its adherence to the Four Articles, again rejected Sigismund, and attempted to gain Silesia and Lusatia for the movement, the composition of the government of twenty members, set up as a kind of oligarchic substitute for a ruler, showed by the limited place it gave to Prague's representatives that the capital's bid for leadership would not succeed.[48] Nevertheless, its capture by the radical forces would still have meant a fundamental change in the balance within Bohemia, and the year of Prague's bid for hegemony as a city

[42] Report of Lawrence of Březová, tr. Kaminsky, *Revolution*, p. 430; *FRB* v, p. 475.

[43] *FRB* v, pp. 517–20; tr. Kalivoda, *Das hussitische Denken*, pp. 327–9. Episode discussed by Lerner (*Free Spirit*, pp. 119–24).

[44] *FRB* v, p. 431; discussed, Lerner, *Free Spirit*, pp. 121–3.

[45] My view. Lerner (*Free Spirit*) is more sceptical about sexual excesses; I think they may have developed spontaneously; see now criticism of Lerner by Werner in *Sitzungsberichte AWD* xiii (1989), pp. 3–26 at p. 23, n. 63.

[46] F. Seibt, 'Communitas primogenita: zur Prager Hegemonialpolitik in der hussitischen Revolution', *HJB* lxxxi (1962), pp. 80–100.

[47] Heymann, *Žižka*, pp. 220–1.

[48] Ibid., ch. 14; Heymann, 'The national assembly of Čáslav', *MH* viii (1954), pp. 32–55.

MAP 10   Hussite town leagues in 1421 and 1427.

Source: Map by H. Rüthing, from Herder's *Atlas zur Kirchengeschichte* (Freiburg-im-Breisgau, 1970), no. 69A.

was also the year of Želivský's boldest attempt to bring both Old and New Town under his dictatorship.[49]

The accidental death of Nicholas of Hus late in 1420 gave an opening for leadership, and the takeover of German and Catholic houses by Želivský's adherents in the aftermath of the emigration of spring 1421 strengthened the radicals' voting power. After Čáslav he felt strong enough to sack the administrators of the Old Town and declare the union of New and Old. For some months the city was ruled under the dictatorship of one of his radical supporters. But it was an uneasy success; Želivský always had the crowd with him to push forward his measures, but also the long-term opposition of the propertied classes, the moderate Utraquists and the Prague patriciate against him working on his administrators, so that political radicals appointed by him lost the edge of their zeal in face of conservative pressure. What finally broke him was the defeat of the Prague forces at Most and his failure to bring victory

---

[49] Kaminsky, *Revolution*, pp. 451–60; Heymann, *Žižka*, pp. 241–53, 266–7, 272–3, 278–80, 307–18.

in the field to the city's forces in the way that Žižka had done for the Taborites. In February 1422 John Hvězda, his dictator, lost office; in March Hvězda's more conservative successor had him executed. His courageous death brought a reaction from the manual workers that formed his support, yet fatally weakened his party: Prague thereafter could be usually reckoned as a pillar of the moderate party, in religion and politics.

The clash of classes and the inability of the artisans and poor to prevail against the wealthier in Prague were the main reasons for Želivský's fall. Religion also played a part, for Želivský believed in *scriptura sola* as the authority for Hussitism, and was constantly attempting to upset the doctrinal position of the university masters and subject it to the 'divine law', as the Taborites did, while his party came to treat the mass as a bare communion service, in the manner of Tabor. Jakoubek and the university masters were firm against Želivský. 'Be diligent. Stop him,'[50] were Jakoubek's words to the magistrates, two days before Želivský's murder.

The major parties

As Prague and Tabor thus cut down their dissidents, debate still continued between the moderate centre of Utraquism, based in the capital, and the radical force of Taboritism. While they talked, searching for a way to unity, their own differences tended to clarify.[51] Tabor's supporters debated their eucharistic beliefs, and settled on a common doctrine, that Christ's body and blood were contained in the bread and wine 'in a sacramental or figurative sense'.[52] This divided Tabor from the believers in transubstantiation or consubstantiation on the moderate Utraquist side. Controversy over mass vestments continued; as usual in such conflicts, it was the visible sign of difference that attracted most attention, intensified by the focus of all Hussites on the eucharist, the natural consequence of their tradition and of the adoption of the lay chalice. Taborite ritual was now of the simplest – consisting of a common recitation of the Lord's Prayer, then the words of Christ at the Last Supper, pronounced in the vernacular on an unconsecrated altar, perhaps a table, the eucharistic vessels being ordinary cups and plates, and the church being bare of adornment. Priests wore no vestments, and were not distinguished from the laity. All received communion. Sermons, vernacular singing, and gospel-reading formed a part of what was a congregational service, with an emphasis very different from that of the traditional mass. When Taborites discussed the eucharistic celebrations of the Utraquist party, they attacked features of it as being useless to the people. The utility to the congregation is foremost. Fixed forms were inimical to the Taborite mode of life – readings of set portions of Scripture, for example, were dismissed because they would prevent the clergy from exposition 'according to the needs of the people and the time'.[53]

---

[50] Kaminsky, *Revolution*, p. 460.

[51] Kaminsky, *Revolution*, pp. 436–52, 460–81. For Tabor, I found his discussion in *The Czechoslovak Contribution*, pp. 210–23, esp. helpful.

[52] Kaminsky, *Revolution*, p. 455.

[53] Ibid., p. 470. See description of Taborite eucharist (ibid., pp. 444–5).

Divergences thus went so far between Utraquist and Taborite practice that it was difficult to see how any compromise formula could be worked out, though their representatives tried hard to do so. Moreover, beneath the liturgical differences lay a fundamental distinction of outlook which ran through all the issues dividing the parties. The Utraquists were reformers who desired changes where they saw a necessity for them; if there was not a positive reason for change in existing structures, on the whole they preferred to keep them. The Taborites were revolutionaries who insisted that all belief and practice must be brought to the touchstone of Scripture, the practice of the primitive Church, and common utility. It was *scriptura sola* at its starkest, set in the context of independent communities of peasants and artisans, wielding political and military power. Under its impetus, a series of components of traditional Catholicism, purgatory, the intercessory role of the saints and of Mary, the sacrifice of the mass, went down to destruction, leaving a religion of stark contrasts, between heaven and hell, God and Antichrist, Scripture and the Babylon of Rome.

One other feature of Tabor, which sprang from the residue of the eschatological expectation in which it was born, was the belief, helpfully expounded by Kaminsky, that they were, not merely the imitators of the primitive Church, but that they in some way reincarnated that Church and possessed all its powers. This acceptance of a sovereign power of decision over all precedent and tradition emerges from Nicholas of Pelhřimov's discussion of the reliance to be placed on the Four Doctors and the Four Councils, a norm for the Utraquists. 'If by revelation . . . of Scripture', he said, 'God should today grant a more potent understanding to someone, that man would be more to be believed than those Doctors.'[54] *Scriptura sola*, the political independence and military power of the Taborite communities, and their belief in God's direct guidance on them, together made the Taborites one of the most dynamic movements of the Middle Ages. But it also made any form of accommodation with them extraordinarily hard.

Through the debates the two major parties were in fact drawing apart, for all the efforts at compromise. The effects of definition can be seen in the decisions of two synods, one held after the diet of Čáslav in 1421, the other almost a year later in 1422. The first, defining eucharistic belief in terms of the real presence, left open the way to compromise with Tabor; the second, by using the term 'corporeal substance', excluded their beliefs.[55] Within Tabor the departure of Žižka to join the Orebites removed an influence tending to restraint in religious matters; Tabor was allowed to become more radical, and compromise became yet more difficult.[56] Among the Utraquists the rise of John Příbram, a former adherent of Jakoubek, who still wanted the lay chalice, but in the context of reconciliation with Rome, and was prepared to cut away the other innovations of Hussitism to get an accommodation with the Church, sharpened the division with Tabor.[57] In 1422 and 1423 there were episodes of actual fighting between the two sides. The search for a substitute

[54] Ibid., p. 469.
[55] Ibid., pp. 462–3.
[56] Heymann, *Žižka*, pp. 354–6, 361–73.
[57] Kaminsky, *Revolution*, p. 461.

for Sigismund tended to weigh on the conservative side, for the candidate who arrived in Bohemia, Sigismund Korybut, nephew of Witold of Lithuania, first as governor-general for his uncle, then later as a claimant in his own right, favoured moderation in the reform.[58] His only chance, he came to see, of achieving acceptance in Europe as king in place of Sigismund was by making a reconciliation with the papacy, and so his influence was all on the side of Přibram's party. In any case, he was the candidate of the moderates, the nobles and bourgeois, who were uneasy at having no monarch. On the other side, Žižka originally tolerated Korybut. Tabor and the other radicals as a whole were indifferent, if not hostile, to monarchy.

It can be seen that almost every factor, the religious division, the conflict of class implicit behind it, and the differences in national policy, tended to keep Utraquists and Taborites apart. In favour of unity was the sense of common origin in the Bohemian reform, the symbol of the lay chalice, and the belief of many in both parties in the value of discussion. Tabor had a learned leadership, able and willing to engage in debate. There were experiments in toleration, but the Utraquists, though open to considerable deviation, were in the last resort unable to accept two such distinct sets of belief in Bohemia, while in Tabor there was too much that was irreconcilable. The gulf yawned.

One factor above all kept the two parties from civil war: the continuing pressure from the outside world. Sigismund had not given up the struggle when he withdrew in March 1421; he came again towards the end of the year with a formidable force, missed his chance of co-ordinating a two-pronged attack on the kingdom, but still had a numerical superiority over his opponents when Žižka soundly defeated him at Německý Brod early in 1422.[59] Vanquished, still attempting diplomatic moves against the Hussites, then distracted by his oriental schemes and the problem of the Turks, and not always on good terms with the imperial princes, he did not return for fourteen years to Bohemia. Nevertheless, there were other expeditions and pressures still, if not so formidable, Martin v remained an unyielding opponent and Ulrich of Rosenberg's party among the nobility supported conservatism.[60]

Every crusade – and there were such expeditions, given the crusade indulgence, in 1420, 1421, 1422, 1427 and 1431, as well as lesser forays – pushed the parties into unity to repel the invader. Bohemia was a beleaguered country; alone, the moderates could not be sure of defending it; they had to sink their differences with the radicals to keep native independence and the lay chalice in being. And yet military action, decisive as it was, only staved off

---

[58] Heymann, *Žižka*, ch. 20, Kaminsky, *Revolution*, pp. 460–2; below, p. 342; on the Slav background, see Denis, *Huss*, pp. 308–25; later career of Korybut in Heymann and Denis; Bartoš, *Revolution*, pp. 5–24.

[59] Heymann, *Žižka*, pp. 302–3; see Heymann, 'The crusades against the Hussites', *A History of the Crusades* III, ed. A. Hazard (Madison, 1975), pp. 586–646.

[60] On Hussite wars and military techniques, I owe to Professor W. Eberhard the following references: B. S. Hall, *The Technological Illustrations of the so-called 'Anonymous of the Hussite Wars'* (Wiesbaden, 1979); C. Grünhagen, *Hussitenkämpfe der Schlesier* (Breslau, 1872); V. Schmidtchen, 'Volker, Karrenbüchse und Wagenburg: Hussitische Innovationen zur Technik und Taktik des Kriegswesens des späten Mittelalters', *Wirtschaft, Technik und Geschichte, Festschrift für Albrecht Timm* (Berlin, 1980), pp. 83–108; S. Petrin, *Der Österreichische Hussitenkrieg, 1420–1434* (Vienna, 1982). Seibt, 'Die Zeit', pp. 518–31, describes this period; list of crusades: p. 525; see map 9 for Ulrich of Rosenberg's party. The classic, aged work is F. von Bezold, *König Sigismund und die Reichskriege gegen die Hussiten* (Munich, 1872–8).

the problem of the future of Hussitism. What was to happen next? Both Tabor and the moderates wanted in their different ways to spread their views to the outside world; they could, together, defend the bastion of Bohemia against any army that the Catholics, often ill led, were able to put against them, earning in the process such a reputation for Hussite troops that opposing forces sometimes dissolved at the mere sight of them; but they did not have anything like the same success in the peaceful process of disseminating their beliefs. From about 1423 at latest the support of Bohemia for Hussitism could be expected to hold; but there was no major fresh advance made after that date for the chalice, or for either of the two parties.

Attempts at spreading Hussitism

One plan that foundered sprang from the moderates, aiming at a reconciliation with the Church on terms that would preserve the chalice and their reform. Alliance with Slav powers to the east on a platform of resistance to Germans seemed to offer the chance of replacing Sigismund, bringing in a diplomatic counterweight to the emperor, and perhaps spreading Hussitism. Hence embassies offered the crown to the Slav rulers, Wladislav Jagiello, king of Poland, and his cousin Witold, grand duke of Lithuania. There were factors for the scheme in the Slav resurgence, which had led to the defeat of the Teutonic order at Tannenberg in 1410. Czechs had aided Poles on that occasion, and there was some common Slav feeling to build on. Sparks of Hussitism had reached Poland through native students attending the Charles University; Jerome of Prague had once stayed at the court of Witold; the reactions of Sigismund and the fears of Polish bishops suggest that a field for missionary activity did exist in these Slav lands.[61] Wladislav, however, though he would have welcomed a chance to strike at Sigismund, had too much to lose by acceptance. Witold, more committed against Sigismund, eager to win a crown, and at times enticed by the vision of a grand pan-Slav realm, maintained his interest longer; but the papacy's influence was insistent, and he fell away in 1423. His nephew Sigismund Korybut, originally his emissary, offered himself as candidate in 1424, and in effect, became leader after the death of Žižka. But he brought only himself and a few followers, not the support of another State, for Witold disowned him; when in power the military success of a Žižka generally eluded him, and he entered on secret negotiations with Martin v. When discovered, he was imprisoned in 1427, and sent home in 1428.[62] The affair discredited for the time John Příbram and his party. The plans for Slav alliance had not worked.

Peaceful missionizing in German-speaking lands was another means of spreading Hussitism; it produced sparks of response but no conflagration, and did not change the outlook for the Bohemian cause. There were no major conversions to swing a ruler or a whole region to the chalice, only quiet underground missionizing on the pattern of the Waldensians by individuals who become known to us when they eventually fall into the hands of the

---

[61] Heymann, *Žižka*, pp. 30–1, Seibt, 'Die Zeit', p. 532; Betts, *Essays*, pp. 219–20; Denis, *Huss*, p. 309. Seibt, *Hussitica*, pp. 82–3 is interesting.

[62] Heymann, *Žižka*, pp. 456–7, 460–1.

inquisition.[63] Perhaps the most notable of them was Friedrich Reiser of Donauwörth, who received episcopal consecration at Tabor and was active for a long period in south Germany and Alsace till his burning in 1458; he was succeeded in office by Stephen of Basle for a further ten years. But nothing of great significance came of this work. The Hussites worked to spread their views in popular propaganda: the Four Articles were speedily translated and spread, and vernacular manifestos were dispatched to explain their movement. Saaz, the German-speaking area attached to Hussitism in northern Bohemia, was especially active in the field of written propaganda. But, without the rapid and effective dissemination of views made possible by the printing-press in the sixteenth century, the whole enterprise remained necessarily small-scale. Luther sold some 30,000 copies of his early works between 1517 and 1520; no comparable opportunity was available to the Hussites. Moreover, peaceful missionizing did not consort easily with military power, and the very success of the movement in Bohemia tended to work against its influence outside.[64] The decree of Kutná Hora, leading to the flight of German masters, created an interest block against Hussite theses in neighbouring universities; the flight of German Catholics later worked in the same direction. The association between the reform and Czech linguistic nationalism naturally weakened the international potential of Hussitism.

The offensive expeditions

Peaceful missionary work then, did not, perhaps could not, be expected to bring victory to the cause. There remained military power and negotiation at the highest level with ecclesiastical authority, to secure recognition for the Bohemian movement that would give it immediate security from attack in its own lands, with the possibility of spreading in Europe later. From 1426 to 1433 Procop the Shaven, the Taborite priest from southern Bohemia, heir in military skills to Žižka, though not quite his equal, led expeditions into neighbouring lands, with the aim of extorting by force from the Church this official recognition.[65] 'We truly bear the burden of the war,' he said, 'only in order to bring about the recognition of these holy truths by the Church of God, and to live and see the blessing of peace and good days from which unity, brotherly love, moral reform and everything else will come.' Procop led radical forces, and a secondary aim was to maintain *élan* in groups, still radical in religion, that had lost their revolutionary zeal in social matters, and were in danger of earning the hatred of the peasants for their exactions. Action abroad brought booty and prestige without damaging Bohemia. The old magic in fighting still worked, and Procop won great victories, conquering Silesia, winning tribute from the Germans round about, and taking his army to the

---

[63] Seibt, 'Die Zeit', p. 532; *Hussitica*, pp. 94–5; H. Köpstein, 'Zu den Auswirkungen der hussitische-revolutionären Bewegung in Franken', *Aus 500 Jahren deutsch-tschechoslowakische Geschichte*, ed. K. Obermann and J. Polisensky (Berlin, 1958), pp. 16–20; H. Köpstein, 'Über den deutschen Hussiten Friedrich Reiser', *ZG* VII (1959), pp. 1068–82. I owe these references to Professor R. E. Lerner.

[64] This still seems a fair generalization, despite the evidence for German Hussitism given by Seibt, 'Die Zeit', pp. 524–4, 529–30 (with full references).

[65] Heymann, *Žižka*, pp. 457–63; Bartoš, *Revolution*, chs 3–8; speech of Procop on war and peace: p. 101.

Baltic in support of Poland. His actions, the expeditions of the Orphans, and the sufferings of the lands round Bohemia, coupled with the fears of churchmen that Hussitism might spread if the situation were not defused, led to negotiation.

Negotiation and settlement

One more crusade was mounted, then repulsed at Domažlice in 1431. In 1433 long preliminary negotiation ended in the entry of a party of Bohemians on reasonable terms to Basle to treat with the fathers of the council. This included all the major groups, Procop himself, John Rokycana, the skilful and learned representative of what might be called the middle Utraquist group, anxious for acceptance by the Church, but only in a manner that would preserve the substance of their wishes; Nicholas of Pelhřimov for the Taborites, and Peter Payne for the Orphans.[66] Thus unity held as far as the negotiating table. On the other side, the leading spirit at the council, Cardinal Cesarini, who barely saved his life at Domažlice, had seen in practice the threat which Hussite power presented, and was convinced of the necessity to negotiate and to make reforms in the Church, more so than the hesitant pope, Eugenius IV, with whom the council was at odds.

Yet neither Cesarini nor his fellow members of the council intended that changes, even such as moderate Hussites wanted, should be imposed in the West; they desired to carry out reforms, indeed, on their own lines, but, most of all, to lead back the erring flock in Bohemia to the Church by gentle but temporary compromise and conciliation. Hussites cherished still the illusion that, if they were allowed to speak, the reasonableness of their case and the necessity for the lay chalice would be seen by ecclesiastical authority. It was an idea that reached back to Hus, in his undelivered sermon on the evils in the Church for the fathers at Constance; and it was still held at Basle, remarkably enough, by Procop the Shaven. That illusion was broken; still, the negotiators were realistic enough to insist on a foolproof safe conduct for their party, and they tried hard to secure an imposition of the lay chalice on all in Bohemia, Catholics as well as Utraquists, and so obviate the dangers of civil war.

Jakoubek, the finest of bridge-builders between the parties because of his personality and his role as the initiator of the chalice, had died in 1429: no-one could replace him. The economic decline of the Charles University had long dimmed the ardour of some university masters. The nobles mistrusted the military forces of the radicals, who had fought too long and now had too many mercenaries in their ranks. The negotiations did not stop their expeditions, still winning victories in 1431, 1432 and 1433, yet showing signs of indiscipline.[67]

In 1433 the radicals tried to eliminate Pilsen and its region of south-west

---

[66] Denis, *Huss*, ch. 11; E. F. Jacob, 'The Bohemians at the Council of Basel, 1433', in *Prague Essays*, ed. R. W. Seton-Watson (Oxford, 1948), pp. 81–123; Creighton, *Papacy* II, chs 5 and 6; on Rokycana, see Heymann, 'John Rokycana: church reformer between Hus and Luther', *CH* XXVIII (1959), pp. 3–43; on Payne, see above, p. 273; Betts, *Essays*, pp. 236–46; Bartoš, *Revolution*, pp. 73–98.

[67] For this phase, see Bartoš, *Hussite Revolution*, ed. Klassen (clear narrative by master of Hussite history, but with some lack of perspective on opponents of Hussitism), pp. 73–105.

Bohemia. Siege was opened in July.[68] The target was tempting because Pilsen and its *Landfriede* formed the last major support for Catholicism at a time when a series of other, external objectives had been closed to Hussite offensives by truce agreements, yet the decision to attack was fateful. It meant bringing the sufferings of war back again to Bohemia, and it exceeded the armies' powers. Opinion, influenced on the one side by the effect of army requisitions and on the other by the vision of peace aroused, yet not fulfilled, by the Basle negotiations, began to move against the fighting brotherhoods. The blockade, weakened by the introduction of provisions by the Taborite traitor Přibík of Klenové, dragged on; troubles broke out and Procop, removed from command by his captains, was replaced after a time by the unsatisfactory Čapek of Sány. While the brotherhoods were preoccupied in Pilsen, a conspiracy was hatched. The siege was broken off and on 30 May 1434 a confederation of conservative forces, including Hussite, Moravian and Catholic nobility and the Old Town of Prague, met the radicals, Taborites, Orphans and New Town under Procop in battle at Lipany and utterly defeated them.[69]

Curiously, smoke and wagon formation that had been so potent for the defeat of the crusading army at Ústí on the Elbe in 1425, was here cunningly turned against the Taborites and Orphans, who were lured out of their secure encampment and destroyed. Procop, who had so notably combined military leadership with the gifts of a statesman, was among the dead.

The battle marked the end of the military power of the radicals and opened the way to the acceptance of the Church's terms. The legates of the council had reported back that the lay chalice was one issue which would command wide support in the country; the council would have to make a concession of substance. In a confused scene in November 1433 at Prague, representatives of both sides accepted a version of the Four Articles known as the Compactata of Basle.[70] Lipany enabled this to become the basis of a final settlement, after yet more negotiation, at Jihlava, when in 1436 the Bohemians promised peace and were reconciled to the Church.

The settlement allowed the lay chalice for all who wished it, but did not declare it to be holy and salutary and did not impose it on the country. Division in Bohemia between Utraquists and Catholics thus remained. The council had merely granted permission for the chalice but had not encouraged it and had given no opening for the spread of the practice in the Church. The communion of infants, a valued Hussite practice, was not dealt with. The punishment of mortal sin was reserved to those 'whose office it is'; preaching was to be conducted by 'the priests of the Lord and by worthy deacons'.[71] Little here was to be seen of the radicals' zeal for righteousness in the kingdom, and the free preaching of lay men and women that they permitted.

[68] Ibid., pp. 105–11.
[69] Ibid., pp. 112–18.
[70] Partial text in Denis, *Huss*, pp. 495–8; analysis: W. Eberhard, *Konfessionsbildung und Stände in Böhmen, 1478–1530* (Munich and Vienna, 1981), pp. 41–3; review article: R. Kalivoda, 'A new approach to the post Hussite development of Hussitism', *CV* XXVII (1984), pp. 73–90; see also D. Daniel, in *Speculum* LXII (1987), pp. 412–14.
[71] Heymann, *Žižka*, p. 471; on infant communion, see D. R. Holeton, *La Communion des tout-petits enfants: Etude du mouvement eucharistique en Bohème vers la fin du Moyen-Age* (Rome, 1989).

FIGURE 11   The Emperor Sigismund, *c.*1430; attributed to Konrad Laib, Kunsthistor-
isches Museum, Vienna.
Photograph: Archiv für Kunst und Geschichte, Berlin.

Priests were not to be owners of estates and they were to administer faithfully
the property of the Church. The last clause came nearest to the most
substantial effect of the Hussite revolution: the widespread transfer of Church
and monastic lands to the laity, whose secure ownership was guaranteed by
Sigismund fifteen days after the ceremony at Jihlava.

With the reconciliation with the Church came also the return of the legitimate ruler. In the last years of the negotiations Sigismund had played a skilful role, promising more privately to the Hussites than the representatives of Basle would concede, until in the end they accepted a weak settlement on the security of Sigismund's word. They were deceived; once back in power, Sigismund, in the short period before his death in 1437, initiated a Catholic reaction. Rokycana, elected archbishop of Prague by the Estates in 1437 with an eye to thus providing a Utraquist whose presence in the archiepiscopate should act as a guarantee of the security of the Compactata, was never confirmed in his office, and the province was ruled administratively into the sixteenth century.[72] The cathedral, on the castle side of the Vltava, occupied by a Catholic chapter, never received him; in the eyes of the papacy the see had remained vacant from the death of Conrad of Vechta.

The return of Sigismund marked the end of the classic phase of Hussite history. Between 1415 and 1436 the Hussites defied the Church and were the first declared heretics to beat off a Catholic crusade. In these years they changed entirely the basis of the economic life of the Church in Bohemia, produced a new kind of clergy, and forced high ecclesiastical authority to treat with them on equal terms. Inside their country they undermined the centralized power of the Luxemburg monarchy and produced a fighting force to terrorize Europe. Though they had no-one to match the powerful, if flawed, intellect of Wyclif, they mobilized a remarkable variety of interest and talent before 1419, and threw up a series of notable personalities, from Hus himself to Jakoubek, with his advocacy of the chalice and his leadership in the university, Nicholas of Dresden as a popular agitator, Želivský as priest-politician, Žižka and Procop as field commanders. Their fatal weakness lay in the cleft dividing the radical from the moderate wing of Hussitism. Radicals, through Želivský, made the revolution, and, through Žižka and the Taborites, defended it. Moderates could not do without them, yet could not in the long run live with them. Beside the fighting, there were also quite novel episodes of toleration, a will on both sides to widen the bounds of discussion, and a perennial, sometimes naïve yet refreshing belief in the potency of discussion in religious affairs.[73] In the end, the division of parties destroyed the pristine aims of the movement; war-weariness combined with the skills of Catholic representatives and of Sigismund to bring about a settlement unsatisfactory and insecure to the Bohemians.

At Jihlava the Hussites were given a promise that future bishops would be ready to ordain Utraquist candidates to the priesthood. It was said that the Council of Basle would be sending letters to all Christian princes requiring them to accept the Utraquist Bohemians as good sons of the Church.[74] These steps were never taken, and the Hussites were not given the secure and lasting

[72] G. H. Williams, *The Radical Reformation* (London, 1962), pp. 209–10.
[73] See Seibt, in *HZ* cxcvi (1962), pp. 21–62; for effects of Hussite revolution (esp. disendowment of Church), see E. Werner, 'Die hussitische Revolution: Revolutionsbegriff und Revolutionsergebnis im Spiegel marxistischer, insonderheit tschechoslovakischer Forschungen', *SSAWL* Phil-hist. Klasse cxxix (1989), pp. 5–38.
[74] Eberhard, *Konfessionsbildung*, p. 43.

recognition for which they had fought and negotiated. Nor had they succeeded in spreading their reform outside the lands of the Bohemian crown.

And yet a letter of majesty issued by Sigismund early in 1436, a part of the price paid by him for his return to power, made arrangements to provide security for Utraquist priests and their parishes. Catholics, communicating under one kind, were confined to parishes where the practice of Utraquism had never existed. Parishes where communion had been given under both kinds were to continue their Utraquist tradition – in other words the decisive issue was not the will of the king, or the beliefs and practice of the priest, but the will of the congregation in the parish.[75] Amidst much that proved disappointing to the Utraquist cause, these decisions of Sigismund, forging a base for religious freedom and for the coexistence of Catholics and Utraquists, were potent for the future. They opened the way to a new phase of Utraquist history, in which the Bohemians fought, not so much for the right to spread, or even impose Utraquism in the Church at large, but for a measure of religious independence in their own country.

[75] Ibid., p. 44.

18

The *Unitas Fratrum* and the development of confessions

The emergence of George of Poděbrady

Rokycana's failure to achieve recognition was symbolic of the changes occurring within the Hussite movement. Tenacious, personally humble, capable of fiery preaching, he was a reformer rather than a confessional leader or a theologian of high calibre and to the end of his days looked for a reconciliation with the papacy which never came.[1] Utraquism had an emotional significance, a history and link to fighting Czech nationalism sufficient to maintain it in being, but its earlier supporters had never wished for a break with the Church and as they waited and manoeuvred for acceptance by a pope on terms acceptable to their tradition, something of the inner vitality of their movement began to fade.

The disorder in the country and the emergence of regional Landpeace associations facilitated the rise of a shrewd Czech nobleman, George of Poděbrady, who after the death of Albert of Austria, Sigismund's Habsburg son-in-law, succeeded in becoming governor of Bohemia, then regent to Albert's son Wladislav Posthumous and, finally, after Wladislav's premature death, king of Bohemia in 1458.[2] At the coronation the awkward problem of the status of Rokycana, unrecognized as archbishop of Prague, and his sacramental role, was resolved by securing the services of two Hungarian bishops who provided the vital episcopal presence while Catholic lords placed the crown on George's head and he swore an oath in secret to maintain obedience to the Roman Church and lead his people 'from errors, sects and heresies'. Fortunately, Charles iv's coronation *ordo*, which George followed,

---

[1] F. G. Heymann, 'John Rokycana – church reformer between Hus and Luther', *CH* xxviii (1959), pp. 240–80; F. Seibt, 'Das Zeitalter Georgs von Podiebrady', in *Handbuch der Geschichte der böhmischen Länder*, ed. K. Bosl, i (Stuttgart, 1967), pp. 537–68 at pp. 555–6.

[2] F. G. Heymann, *George of Bohemia, King of Heretics* (Princeton, 1965); Klassen, *Nobility*, p. 143, contrasts his fate with that of Čeněk of Vartemberk's dynasty.

prescribed that the royal candidate should receive communion from the chalice, and the act satisfied the Utraquists. Thus, diplomatically, with mental reservations about the significance of the secret oath (for George maintained that Utraquism, accepted by the Compactata, could not be regarded as heresy), a Hussite ruler, not even from the blood royal in descent from the Luxemburg dynasty, was accepted as king.[3]

George's native wit brought him recognition by Pius II and the Emperor Frederick III and enabled him at first to neutralize the persistent opposition of Catholic Breslau as a prelude to a blunt request to Pius for a permanent recognition of the chalice in 1462. It failed utterly, leading to a sentence against George personally by Paul II in 1465, a fostering of the rise of the Catholic League of the Green Mountain of opposition aristocrats within his lands and a struggle against his rule under a Catholic banner by Matthias of Hungary. George's qualities as a ruler, the papacy's wish to organize resistance to the Turks, used by George's diplomats to elaborate a scheme for international peace amongst princes (which would incidentally have preserved George's lands from ecclesiastical sanctions) and a subtle blend of force and diplomacy preserved his rule in all dangers.[4] But at his death in 1471 he did not feel strong enough to bequeath his kingdom to his son. Instead he passed the inheritance to the Catholic Wladislav II of Poland of the Jagiellon dynasty. The status of Utraquism within the kingdom was preserved but the opportunities for the spread of the chalice that had once appeared open through the election of a Hussite ruler passed away.

Utraquist attitudes to the papacy were marked by a strange blend of suspicion and optimism. Mistrust flared up, no doubt reinforced by the memories of years of battling against papal armies, when Cardinal Carvajal, entrusted with a mission of enquiry by Nicholas V in 1448, attempted to leave Prague in secrecy after he had encountered Hussite opposition to his views. He took with him – possibly accidentally – the original copy of the Compactata of Basle which he had been studying in his lodgings. A detachment of cavalry ensured that it was taken from him before he reached the frontier.[5] Much faith was placed in the Compactata, negotiated at a time when the pope had not finally broken with the council, and in certain ambiguous phrases about it contained in letters of Eugenius IV. It was not realized how much the fact that it was negotiated with the council in the first instance rather than the papacy weakened its effect, and how determined the post-Basle papacy was to liquidate the effects of conciliarism, including the agreement with the Utraquists.

As Aeneas Sylvius Piccolomini, Pius II in his younger days in 1451 had visited Bohemia on behalf of Frederick III and had talked sympathetically with George: it led George to hope for too much from Aeneas when he attained office. The trip to and from Bohemia included a detour to Tabor on the way home, where Aeneas looked on the gate with its shields, one of an angel carrying a chalice and the other of Jan Žižka, and debated theology with

---

[3] Heymann, *George*, pp. 160–72.

[4] Analysis of policy in Seibt, 'Das Zeitalter', pp. 539–52; see also Heymann, *George*, pp. 586–611, for survey, interesting on relationship between George's policy, Utraquism and the *Unitas*.

[5] Heymann, *George*, pp. 36–40.

veteran Taborites and a Polish refugee theologian, John Gałka. The biblical knowledge of some Taborite women impressed him and he contrasted it to that of contemporary Italian priests, to their detriment. But his strongest impression was of the depth and variety of heresies which he encountered, and of the boldness of their defenders.[6] Behind the movement for the chalice lay a more profound doctrinal challenge to the Church. The most that he was prepared to allow for the Utraquists was a temporary concession of the chalice for those who had been accustomed to it, a concession which would be extinguished as an older generation died out. This was not what the Hussite armies had battled for.

Illusions about the possibilities of a papal acceptance were favoured by a certain intellectual isolation of the Utraquist leadership. George had scant formal education, no Latin and limited German: he and his servants, capable enough in their dealings with neighbouring princes, lacked insight into the papal curia and its assumptions. Rokycana's international contacts were restricted by his anomalous position. He tended to share the view of other Utraquist churchmen that, because the lay chalice was rightful, Church authority was in the end bound to concede it. The Compactata had demonstrated that concessions could be won from authority: it was a matter of time, patience and determination before permanent recognition was obtained. They did not see the truth, that though individual popes differed in the means which they favoured in dealing with the problem of Bohemia, all were set on the ultimate elimination of the lay chalice.

Reaction against the long wars and the casual violence associated with the breakdown of the brotherhoods, as well as George's need to establish his orthodoxy in the diplomatic struggle for his own recognition, created a pressure for order and respectability. As governor of Bohemia in 1452 he secured the surrender of Tabor, now a shadow of its former self, and imprisoned a recalcitrant few, including their bishop Nicholas of Pelhřimov. In 1461 he renewed the decree of Charles IV against heresy. In 1462 he put pressure on a convocation of clergy, both Catholic and Utraquist, to cease wrangling – a measure that was prudent in view of the political implications of religious tension within his lands, but marked a contrast with the early Hussite decades of vivid and informed debate among theologians.[7]

Circumstances, and George's policy, were combining to confirm the continuing existence of two recognized confessions, Catholic and Utraquist. George worked hard to see that they lived in peace with each other. A Hussite Latin gradual from the years 1450–60, commemorating the martyrdoms of Hus and of Jerome of Prague on Hus's death-day of 6 July, set in a liturgical context quite Roman and conservative, with a word-play on *constancia*, linking the site of the council which condemned Hus to his own fidelity to death, reflects the attitude of Utraquism of the time, cautious yet firm, waiting for recognition.[8] On the other side, as Seibt has observed, the Catholic Church in Bohemia and Moravia about this time took on some of the

---

[6] H. Kaminsky, 'Pius Aeneas among the Taborites', *CH* XXVIII (1959), pp. 281–309.

[7] Heymann, *George*, pp. 60–3, 238–44, 290–1.

[8] T. J. Talley, 'A Hussite Latin gradual of the XV century', *Bulletin of the General Theological Seminary* XLVIII (1962), pp. 8–13. I am indebted to the author for advice.

attributes of a Counter-Reformation, in Moravia organized round the bishopric of Olomouc and in Prague, in the absence of a recognized archbishop, led by the cathedral chapter and dean. In Moravia elements of a traditional structure of churches and monasteries survived and there were even new monastic foundations.[9] St John Capistrano's violent preaching against Utraquism in journeys between 1451 and 1454 had little effect in the heartlands of the movement but helped to renew Catholic support in Silesia, uneasy with the compromises of its leading class.[10]

Stability rather than mission was the keynote of Utraquism – a stability that was made more difficult by the effects of the non-recognition of Rokycana in a shortage of fresh ordinations to a priesthood serving those who accepted communion in both kinds. For Rokycana to ordain would weaken the Utraquists' case for papal recognition. Contact with the Greek Church to secure valid ordinations was not fruitful and the expedient use of Polish clergy, who were willing to leave their country and accept Utraquism for the sake of higher living standards, weakened fervour.[11] The royal subchamberlain, Vaněk Valečovsky, a moderate Utraquist, troubled by the politicization and deteriorating standards of the clergy of his confession, agitated in 1457 against their weaknesses.[12] On the wall of his house in the Old Town he had an allegory of the churches painted, reproaching the clergy on both sides. Horses were attached to both ends of a wagon, with rival coachmen, symbolizing the clergy both Catholic and Utraquist, whipping them up to pull in rival directions, while the passengers, frustrated in their search for salvation, fought among themselves.

The rise of the Unitas Fratrum

Dissatisfaction with the Utraquists led directly to the rise of a third religious force in Bohemia and Moravia. Peter Chelčický, identified by Bartoš as a yeoman farmer called Peter of Záhorka who had at first been attracted to the Taborites, separated himself from them because of their acceptance of the rightfulness of shedding blood. 'If power were supposed to be administered through Christ's faith by means of battles and punishments', he asked, 'why would Christ have abolished the Jewish Law and established a different, spiritual one?'[13] Chelčický was uncompromising, even rejecting the Hussite

[9] Seibt, 'Das Zeitalter', pp. 554–5.
[10] Ibid., p. 555; Heymann, *George*, pp. 69–80, 119–20; criticism of J. Hofer: p. 69, n. 9; R. Rýšavý, 'Die erste Hussiten-mission des heiligen Johannes v. Capestrano in Mähren (1451)', *FS* XIX (1932), p. 225–55.
[11] For the problems of the Church, see E. Denis, *Fin de l'indépendance Bohème* I: *Georges de Podiebrad. Les Jagellons* (Paris, 1890) still has value; for its historiographical significance, see Eberhard, *Konfessionsbildung*, p. 19; the 1930 reissue of Denis: p. 21, n. 50; illuminating assessment, Eberhard, 'Ernest Denis, Konzeption der böhmischen Geschichte und ihre Funktion in der tschechischen Geschichtswissenschaft', *Frankreich und die böhmischen Länder im 19 und 20 Jahrhundert*, ed. F. Seibt and M. Neumüller (Munich, 1990), pp. 49–66.
[12] Heymann, *George*, pp. 100–2.
[13] Kaminsky, *Revolution*, p. 322; his relation to Tabor and the Waldensians, pp. 391–7; F. Seibt, 'Peter Chelčický', *Lebensbilder zur Geschichte der böhmischen Länder* I (Munich and Vienna, 1974), pp. 49–61, repr. *Hussitenstudien*, pp. 209–16; Brock, *Czech Brethren*, ch. 1; M. L. Wagner, *Petr Chelčický* (Scottdale, Penn. and Kitchener, Ontario, 1983); A. Molnár, 'Bekenntnisse der böhmischen Reformation', *Jahrbuch für die Geschichte des Protestantismus in Österreich* XCVI (1980), pp. 310–32; H. Kaminsky, 'Peter Chelčický: treatises

victory at the Vyšehrad over Sigismund in 1420 as a breach of the commandment against killing. He rejected life in towns and lived quietly on his estate, working with his hands and writing a series of ethical treatises in the vernacular, marked by colourful rustic metaphor, in which he denounced evils in Church and State with unswerving idealism, insisting on the duty of the Christian to have nothing to do with the exercise of political authority. Clergy and nobles alike were 'fat and gluttonous Baals'.[14] Observance of the exhortations of Christ in the Sermon on the Mount was a direct obligation. Like the Waldensians, he believed that poison entered the Church with Constantine; like them also, he rejected the use of oaths. Pope and emperor he compared in his best-known work, *The Net of Faith*, written about 1440, to great whales ripping through the net of faith spread by the apostolic fishermen in the fifth chapter of Luke to gather the elect, and so mangling it that only barely visible shreds of that original net, the primitive Church, remained. Withdrawal, humility, prayer, refusal of all power, judicial and military authority, and restoration of the way of life of the apostles was the only way open to the true Christian.

After so much warfare, diplomatic and high State action in the name of religion, it was little wonder that this ideal of radical separatism came to draw support. Chelčický stood apart from all the great events but maintained contacts with Hussite leaders. Despite a fundamental difference of views, Rokycana admired him, corresponded with him during his own exile from Prague, borrowed from one of his treatises in his eucharistic work and recommended him to his nephew Gregory and other devout men influenced by Chelčický's writings, who came together at the remote village of Kunwald in north-eastern Bohemia in 1457–8.[15] Close by, at the town of Žamberk, they found a Utraquist priest called Michael exhibiting the purity of life for which Gregory and his friends had searched for so long. Protection was given by Poděbrady who owned the estate of Litice where Kunwald lay. They called the members of the group brothers and sisters, practised community of goods on the apostolic pattern for priests and teachers, and some laymen, and attracted to their number peasants and simple craftsmen, working with their hands. The oath was utterly rejected, thus making it impossible to participate in judicial proceedings. Priests and lay preachers had no private property. The group followed Chelčický's stress on the sufficiency of Scripture and instructed the illiterate so as to make Scripture accessible to them.

Under Gregory's leadership communities formed elsewhere in rural isolation where the tenets of the movement with its utter rejection of civil obligations could more easily be observed. A high moral life was a prerequisite, with stiff penances for those who fell, and an ultimate penalty of

on Christianity and the social order', *Studies in Medieval and Renaissance History* I, ed. W. Bowsky (Lincoln, Nebr., 1964), pp. 106–79; analysis: pp. 107–36. I owe references and gifts to Professor Kaminsky and the late Professor Molnár.

[14] Wagner, *Chelčický*, p. 137; analysis of *Net of Faith*: pp. 132–47.

[15] For further history of this group, see Brock, *Czech Brethren*; Wagner, *Chelčický*; R. Říčan, *Die Böhmischen Brüder: Ihr Ursprung und ihre Geschichte*, tr. B. Popelář (Berlin, 1961); note ch. 23 by A. Molnár on theology; J. T. Müller, *Geschichte der Böhmischen Brüder* I–III (Herrnhut, 1922–31) (standard work); Zeman, *Hussite Movement*, pp. 97–111; Denis, *Fin* I, pp. 281–366 (still a moving account despite its age and its underestimate of Utraquism).

expulsion, and so numbers remained low. Persecution, brought on by Poděbrady's need to ensure his position in relation to the papacy and ward off accusations of complacency to heresy, led to Gregory's imprisonment in Prague and some recantations. But Rokycana's sympathetic handling and the group's manifest lack of concern with politics helped to preserve them. The group, known as the Brethren of Christ's Gospel, later as the Unity of Brethren (*Unitas Fratrum*), began to define its position and in 1464 in a meeting in the Rychnov mountains worked out a set of distinctions important in subsequent history between the *substantialia* of the movement in belief, hope and love, the *ministerialia*, consisting in the word of God, the sacraments, the power of the keys, and the *accidentalia*, consisting in Church ordinances.

Gregory, disappointed in his search for a pure priesthood amongst the Armenians, the Greek Orthodox and the Waldensians, decided to provide them directly for his communities. In 1467, while the kingdom was distracted by the aftermath of Paul II's action against the king, the leadership came together secretly at Lhotka near Rychnov. On 26 March after prayer and fasting the sixty members of the assembly chose nine as suitable for ordination, prepared twelve pieces of paper, nine of them blank and three with the word *jest* ('he is'), on them and gave nine of the twelve, arbitrarily chosen, to the nine candidates. They wanted three to be ordained priest. Gregory, conscious of the importance of the decision, looked for an indication of God's will. Were they to have a priesthood of their own? The chance of the lots could have left all nine with blank slips in their hand; as it was three candidates unfolded slips with *jest* on them. 'God showed His wisdom and power in us', Gregory wrote.[16]

Michael the Utraquist priest then went to the oldest Waldensian *barba* in Bohemia and received ordination from him, on the supposition that the Waldensians had a fount of orders going back to the uncorrupted Church before Constantine. Finally Michael ordained the three himself, renounced his own orders, both Catholic and Waldensian, and asked for a new confirmation from Matthias, chosen on grounds of moral excellence as the chief of the three. When Gregory informed Rokycana, he condemned these moves.

There followed from 1468 to the death of Poděbrady a period of sharp persecution, even of executions, which did not break the movement. They were not economically vulnerable since most members supported themselves. Numbers were small and their lives simple. Gatherings for prayer took place in houses. It was easy to disperse and re-form. The *Unitas* members were tolerated by lords who valued their conscientious work on their estates: when, later, in 1481, Matthias of Hungary exiled them because they had given refuge to Waldensians fleeing from persecution in Brandenburg, and brothers fled to Moldavia, a petition from Moravian lords persuaded Matthias to bring them back again. Others, touched by their simplicity and sincerity, gave them protection out of sympathy. A flow of pungent vernacular treatises defended their position and exposed failings among the Utraquists. A residual relationship subsisted with the official Utraquist Church: while Rokycana lived, Gregory did not wholly despair of a change of heart and in a seventh

---

[16] Müller, *Brüder* I, p. 127; Říčan, *Brüder*, p. 29; note comment on implications for the future of the community and the concept of the episcopate.

and last letter appealed to the archbishop to join them. In 1473 and 1478 the Brethren were allowed hearings by the Prague masters.

Recurrently, idealists brought up as Utraquists threw in their lot with them. When, for example, the priest Michael Polak, preaching in the Prague Old Town against laxities in his own Church, was imprisoned and died of torture in 1480, his suffering sparked off a reaction among students and teachers in Prague which carried them into the *Unitas*. The most distinguished of them, Luke of Prague, wrote later that Polak first made him feel 'the burdensome hunger after truth'; he read Chelčický, was moved by his uncompromising adherence to Scripture and finally joined the Brethren.[17] Luke, scholastically trained at the Charles University, with a knowledge of the classics and the Fathers, brought a depth of learning to the *Unitas* and, first as a junior to others, participated in major changes and then later as *de facto* leader and the *Unitas*'s principal theologian, buttressed and defended them.

By the 1480s tensions over justification by faith or by works had arisen, which had to be settled by a decision of the Inner Council: some feared an 'overgreat straitness', leading to the 'great evil of a vain religion . . . of trust in oneself'. Brethren entered towns and were embarrassed by the reproach of townsmen that they avoided civil obligations out of idleness. Some felt needlessly restricted by the *Unitas*'s regulations about commerce. In Litomyšl a growth in the number of adherents, facilitated by Bohus Kostka, member of a noble family early drawn to the *Unitas*, created special problems. Nobility, with rare exceptions such as the Kostka family, generally felt excluded from membership by the rigorous rejection of the oath and began to wish for entrance. At a synod at Brandýs in 1490 two such candidates participated in proceedings. The assembly, although recommending that members should not accept office as an alderman, judge or grand master of a guild or become a tavernkeeper or go to the wars, or take part in judicial proceedings involving judgements of blood, none the less permitted such things. 'If', they said, 'a Brother should be forced by the civil authority, against his conscience . . . he should submit . . . in whatever is not against God.'[18]

The ambiguous statement did not succeed in holding rival views in check; most moved on to dilute the inheritance of Chelčický and became known as the Major Party; a minority, often known as the Amosites from their leader Amos, a trader in wax, dissented and held to the old ways. In 1495 it was agreed by a majority that the writings of Chelčický and Gregory were of no absolute validity and should be disregarded if they did not correspond to the needs of the times. At Chlumec the split between the Brothers became final.[19] Luke altered the balance in the *Unitas*'s theology between works and faith. The egalitarianism of Chelčický disappeared, as did outright prohibition of the oath, judicial office, certain forms of commerce. The *Unitas* forfeited something of its distinction. Yet it entered the sixteenth century a growing

---

[17] See Říčan, *Brüder*, for a sympathetic account of Luke; in addition to A. Molnár's chapter in Říčan on theology: Gonnet and Molnár, *Les Vaudois*, pp. 276–80, on Luke and the Waldensians.

[18] Brock, *Czech Brethren*, p. 128.

[19] Discussion of theological issues in A. Molnár, 'Die kleine und die grosse Partei der Brüderunität', *CV* XXII (1979), pp. 239–48.

force, still earning admiration for its humility and ethical concern, and capable of riding out sporadic waves of slander and persecution.

The development of a Utraquist party and the agreement of Kutná Hora

The succession of the Catholic Jagiellon Prince Wladislav II in 1471 did not work to the benefit either of the kingdom or of Utraquism.[20] The damaging effects of the civil war and the battle against the claims of Matthias of Hungary continued until 1478, and were only brought to an end at the price of massive concessions to Matthias, and a settlement which roused the suspicions of the Utraquists. Former Catholic rebels were again taken into favour. Wladislav, leaning on their support rather than that of the Utraquists, looking for a reconciliation with the papacy and anxious to maintain his position in Hungary, showed himself hostile to the Utraquists. Some of the parishes, where the chalice had been guaranteed, slipped away from them under the pressure of the Catholic nobility.

In response the Utraquists organized and formed a party within the State as compensation for the loss of power at the centre of politics which they had enjoyed through the years of Poděbrady's rule, setting up a consistory of eight priests and four laymen with Wenceslas Koranda, the successor of Rokycana, at its head, forming a committee of three nobles, later called Defensores, to represent the Utraquist interest, reinforced by three further nobles and also creating an organization of deans to call decanal synods, oversee the affairs of the Utraquists in the localities and keep a wary eye on the activities of the *Unitas* and the Catholics.[21] Lamed as they were by the inability of Wenceslas Koranda to ordain priests, the consequence of the continuing failure of papal recognition, the Utraquists were in practice building a separate Church organization, carrying political power because of its ability to call crowds into action, to agitate and to move both towns and Utraquist nobility in a power complex against the king. These forces protected an Italian bishop who was brought into the country in 1482 to break the logjam of unfulfilled ordinations.

Prague, as before, was a keypoint. The king had used opportunities to put councillors in office who worked for a policy of Catholic restoration and declined to bring Prague into the Utraquist alliances which had sprung up to resist him. When these councillors went a step further and asked the Catholic party for protection for the capital, it was too much for the Utraquists, who rose in 1483, drove out or killed the councillors, even in some cases repeating the defenestration of 1419, and forbade communion in one kind altogether in Prague, thus actually prohibiting the dissemination of the agreed theological standpoint of the Compactata of Basle, that grace was conveyed as fully in

---

[20] For this phase of Hussite history, Eberhard, *Konfessionsbildung*, is preferred to K. Richter, 'Die böhmischen Länder von 1471–1740', *Handbuch der Geschichte der böhmischen Länder* II (Stuttgart, 1974), pp. 99–143; see Eberhard, pp. 9–40, for historiography and Czech literature; p. 37 for judgement on Richter (still a valuable quarry for facts); survey, with positive assessment of Utraquism, in F. G. Heymann, 'The Hussite – Utraquist Church in the fifteenth and sixteenth centuries', *ARG* LII (1961), pp. 1–26.

[21] Eberhard, *Konfessionsbildung*, p. 50; for note of reassessment of Koranda by K. Krofta, see p. 21.

communion under one kind as it was in both.[22] The Catholics were driven out, monasteries stormed and the death penalty decreed for any who engaged in secret negotiations with the king or the Catholic party in the kingdom. Wladislav, turning to the Catholic nobility for support, found they had no taste for a conflict with such determined opponents.

He was forced to negotiate. Prague assumed the leading role which it had held once before in the Hussite revolution. The king had to guarantee the freedom of the Utraquists' Italian bishop to exercise his office and to accept leaders of the rebellion as Prague councillors. At Kutná Hora in 1485 the two major religious forces in the kingdom, Catholics and Utraquists, united in a form of toleration.[23] It was agreed in an assembly of that year, confirming a decision of 1484, that both groups should keep the parishes which they held in Bohemia, those with the lay chalice, and those without, and should respect that dualism in peace for thirty-one years.

Neither side obtained all that they wanted. The Catholics had never given up the hope of restoring the religious status quo as it had been before Constance and the revolution of 1419, and so would have preferred but a short period of stabilization. Utraquists had wished for a permanent settlement, guaranteeing stability and equal treatment for them beside the Catholics for an indefinite period. Thirty-one years was a compromise between views that could not in the long run be reconciled. At the heart of the agreement lay the Compactata of Basle and the letter of majesty of Sigismund. These were again accepted. The rights of patrons were, however, effectively set aside by a decision of Kutná Hora, that the confessional affiliation of each community or parish church should remain undisturbed, irrespective of the views of the local lord. Conflict and fluctuation of confessional adherence through alienation of land was thus avoided. The individual gained his freedom: he was not to be compelled to follow the religion of his lord. The decree of toleration was a major achievement of the Hussite revolution, based in the last resort on a return to the dynamism of the years before the Compactata. Saaz (Žatec) bluntly asked three of its fellow towns which were they going to stand with, king or country?[24] Prague demanded the chalice as a necessity for the faithful and not merely as a tolerated ritual idiosyncracy.[25] In face of this, the king and the conservative forces yielded, not least because some of the Catholic nobility had come to believe that the repression of heresy could not be allowed to take precedence over the interests of the country, and others, especially the most

[22] Eberhard's comment, *Konfessionsbildung*, p. 55; compare his note, p. 52, on the statement of the Utraquists earlier to the king, on papal confirmation of the Compactata, that it had already been confirmed by the higher power of the Basle Council and the Emperor Sigismund – a sign, he believes, of a greater intransigence and independence within Utraquism.

[23] On Kutná Hora and its immediate consequences, see ibid., pp. 56–73; W. Eberhard, 'Toleranz als historischer Lernprozess der europäischen Kulture', *Akademische Monatsblätten, Zeitschrift des Kartellverbandes katholischen deutscher Studentenvereine* c (1988), pp. 2–7; general survey: J. K. Zeman, 'The rise of religious liberty in the Czech reformation', *Central European History* VI (1973), pp. 128–47; for an original survey of the Hussite revolution as a whole, see R. Kalivoda, *Revolution und Ideologie: Der Hussitismus* (Cologne and Vienna, 1976); review, H. Kaminsky, in *Speculum* LIII (1978), pp. 386–9; I owe offprints to Dr Zeman and Professor Eberhard, to whom I am indebted also for advice; the latter tells me that a work is to be expected on the Jagiellon period by J. Macek.

[24] Eberhard, *Konfessionsbildung*, p. 58.

[25] Ibid., p. 59.

powerful, saw, via a settlement of the religious issue, an opening to a peaceful
increase of their power within Bohemia.[26] Kutná Hora was accepted because
of the exigencies of politics and the solidarity of the Utraquist Estates.

The Utraquists and the Unitas *in the late fifteenth and early sixteenth centuries*

One group, however, was excluded: toleration did not extend to the *Unitas*,
and they remained subject to periodical persecution, which was sometimes
aided by the Utraquists. They remained excluded when the decision of Kutná
Hora was renewed in perpetuity in 1512. Utraquists were ambivalent about
the Brethren; sensitive about accusations of heresy, they at times denounced
and persecuted them, making clear to the outside world the gulf between
them; at other times Utraquist lords quietly protected them, while some who
had grown disillusioned with the long wait for papal recognition, were
inclined to make common cause with them and adopt some of their views.
Wencelas Koranda denounced both the Brethren and the supporters of Rome
on various occasions, but in the 1490s, roused by fears of the activities of a
wing of conservative Utraquists willing to move towards an accommodation
with Rome, he directed his fire chiefly against the papal Church, sharpening
criticism of their errors and stressing the issues on which the Utraquists
differed, such as the lay chalice, the practice of infant communion and the use
of Czech in the liturgy.[27] Voices were raised in favour of coming to agreement
with the curia: the humanist Bohuslav Hassenstein of Lobkowitz argued that
agreement could end Bohemia's isolation and improve its economic and
cultural situation and Wladislav favoured an ending of the conflict over
Utraquism if it would bring aid for him from the curia against the Turkish
threat to Hungary.[28] In reaction against such views, what has been described
as a Left-Utraquist wing of the Church began to emerge.

The curia did not intend to make concessions of any importance: it
continued a policy of stifling the Church by cutting off the opportunities to
obtain episcopal ordination. Somehow the Utraquists none the less sustained
their priesthood and their claim to the apostolic succession through bishops
recognized by Rome. Yet there were strains. Partly because of this, the quality
of the priests was uneven and there were abuses. The ecclesiastical position of
Bohemia isolated the Charles University and, although it continued to train
administrators and priests, a tendency grew for the best students to go abroad.
It became provincial.[29] No first-class theologian on the Utraquist side came
on the scene after the death of Koranda in 1519.

The more radical Utraquists were disinclined to wait for papal recognition
and tended to abandon interest in the Compactata. Humanist and Utraquist
Gregor Hrubý of Jelení translated Lorenzo Valla's exposure of the Donation

[26] W. Eberhard, 'Interessengegensätze und Landesgemeinde: die böhmischen Stände im nachrevolutionären Stabilisierungskonflikt', *Europa 1500*, ed. F. Seibt and W. Eberhard (Stuttgart, 1987), pp. 330–48 at pp. 335–6.
[27] Eberhard, *Konfessionsbildung*, pp. 63–4; on Koranda's pluralist attitudes, see F. G. Heymann, 'The Hussite–Utraquist Church in the fifteenth and sixteenth centuries', *ARG* LII (1961), pp. 1–16 at p. 9.
[28] Eberhard, *Konfessionsbildung*, p. 67 (Bohuslav), p. 64 (Wladislav).
[29] Ibid., p. 102; Heymann, *ARG* LII, pp. 11–12.

of Constantine and Erasmus's *Encomium Moriae*. Wenceslas Písecký, formerly a master at the Charles University, defended Utraquism in Italy in 1510 and attacked Aeneas Sylvius Piccolomini's *History of Bohemia* as a source for the erroneous judgements passed on Bohemia as a place of heresy. The failure of yet further negotiations about the renewal of the archbishopric of Prague in 1512–13 led to a flurry of literary activity, within which a growing tendency to stress the foundation of Utraquism in Scripture was evident. From 1513 Jan Miruš was a parish priest in Prague, an effective preacher and a supporter of views that appear to have stood close to those once held by the priests of Tabor and by the *Unitas*.[30] The influence of the *Unitas* on the Utraquists grew as the Brethren attracted members higher in society.

Kutná Hora put the seal on the policy long followed by George of Poděbrady of achieving unity through the acceptance of two confessions, exercising mutual toleration, under the leadership of the monarchy. But it did not end the tensions within Bohemia. The Hussite revolution had changed the political and economic landscape. A massive disendowment of the Church had taken place.[31] The role of the clergy had changed and their authority and wealth had diminished. The monarchy had forfeited much of its economic power, which had passed to the nobility, and it had been forced into financial dependence on the Estates. Town leagues had played an important part in the revolution: towns now formed one of the Estates and were eager to sustain a political as well as an economic role. The Estates were capable of unified action; most often, they disputed or formed varied alliances according to shifting needs and policies, knights and towns tending to stand together against the nobility. The Estates in the fifteenth century had established their power, but it was necessarily an unstable authority which they wielded.[32]

The reigns of the two Jagiellon monarchs, Wladislav II and Lewis, who succeeded him in 1516, were marked by a weakness of central authority and by conflicts, both between the Estates and within them. Often these were primarily based on political and economic issues, but religious ones recurred and intertwined with the others. In the conflicts it was the Left-Utraquist wing, ingeniously and pertinaciously using political skills, who demonstrated that an inner vitality had still not left the Hussite movement.[33] The Left-Utraquists carried on their political struggle about office, decisions about parishes and representation of their viewpoint in external negotiations because they cared about the reform and the future of their Church. It was they above all who prevented the Catholicizing tendencies of the Jagiellons, the increasing political authority of the most powerful of the Catholic lords, and the minimalizing attitudes to the Compactata of the pro-Rome group within Utraquism from undermining the achievements of the past and ending the independence of their Church. When the teachings of Luther began to

---

[30] Eberhard, *Konfessionsbildung*, pp. 103–5.

[31] On its significance, see E. Werner, *SSAWL* Phil-hist-Klasse cxxix (1989), pp. 5–38; Seibt, *Hussitenstudien*, p. 30; Šmahel, *Anomalie*.

[32] Summary, Eberhard, *Konfessionsbildung*, pp. 113–16; discussion of positive features of Jagiellon epoch: Eberhard, in *Europa 1500*, ed. Seibt and Eberhard, pp. 345–8.

[33] It is the principal service of Eberhard to have brought out the importance of Left-Utraquism.

touch Bohemia, it was the *Unitas*, emancipating itself from a position at the margin of society, and the Left-Utraquists, looking behind 1433 and the attempt to accommodate with ecclesiastical authority to the independency of the Taborites, who were the most vital religious forces in the land.

19

Medieval heresy and the Reformation

Introduction

Politics, force and the power of new ideas in varying combinations in the sixteenth century created the Reformation. The unity of doctrine under the papacy for which medieval churchmen and laymen sacrificed so much, in time, labour and lives, broke down and Europe divided into Catholic and Protestant states, cities and regions, battling against each other in speech, writing and arms. The intentions of some of the groups condemned as heretics in the Middle Ages, Waldensians, Lollards and Hussites, appeared to have been achieved, at least in part, but by the hands of others. The power of the State, repeatedly used against dissidents by churchmen in the Middle Ages, was now used by Protestants in authority in their turn against the heirs of those churchmen. The easygoing religion of the majority in the medieval age gave way to a more disciplined and often more aggressive Catholicism, organizing its membership more coherently, attempting to put down the remnants of pagan folk religion and bringing new religious orders to birth.

The world changed. The heretics of the past disappeared, their remnants absorbed into the new Reformed Churches. Utraquism in Bohemia held for a time but faded out. The *Unitas Fratrum* lost its austerity and individuality.

The new Reformers looked on the religious dissidents of the past with mixed feelings. They recognized many affinities between their doctrines and their own, saw them as fellow warriors for the truth and valued them as courageous witnesses to the evangelical cause in earlier centuries. But they had reservations. Lollards and Waldensians, for example, were marked by their long underground existence and lacked an intellectually trained leading class. The Reformers, keen university minds, conscious of the rectitude of their message, did not feel that they had anything to learn from the heretics of the past. The heretics themselves were proud of their traditions and understandably reluctant to shed them at the requirement of their new and powerful cousins in belief. Hussites declined to be absorbed into the Lutheran Churches. In the Waldensian Valleys deep emotions were stirred, between a conservative and resilient peasant population of the mountains and freshly trained Calvinist pastors from the outside world with the pastors feeling impatient with slow minds and with customs which seemed to them to be undesirable remnants of the medieval past.[1]

THE WALDENSIANS

The Italian Alps and the mission of Farel

News of the Swiss Reformation, of Berne and the charismatic preacher Guillaume Farel seems first to have stirred the Italian Valleys. The book always played a major role.[2] In 1526 one of the *barbi* called Martin, possibly Martin Gonin, came back from Switzerland and German-speaking lands bringing Reformation literature. Initiatives came from *barbi* who had international horizons, such as Georges Morel, probably originally from Embrun, fluent in Latin as well as French and Provençal, and Martin Gonin, linked to the printing trade.

Morel and another *barba*, Pierre Masson from Burgundy, went to question Reformers in 1530 on their beliefs. In Basle Oecolampadius commented on Waldensian beliefs and practices set out by Morel in a Latin letter.[3] Morel, well read in Luther and Erasmus, spoke none the less with enthusiasm of the simple Christocentric piety of his Waldensians and of the itinerant, disciplined life of the *barbi*, celibate and practising manual labour. He wrote: 'We are in agreement with you in everything. From the time of the apostles we have had in essentials an understanding of the faith which is yours. The only difference is that, through our own fault and through intellectual laziness, we have not grasped the sense of Scripture as correctly as you. That is why we have come to you for you to direct, instruct, edify and teach us.'[4] For Morel the driving force was respect for a superior scriptural learning. Oecolampadius's reply, based partly on Morel's description of Waldensian belief and practice, partly on his knowledge of the *Unitas*, whose views he assimilated to the Waldensians, was welcoming but lacking in understanding of their clandestine tradition and the outward conformity with Catholic practice, born of centuries of persecution. His ideal was of a settled Protestant parish system, manned by a residential married pastorate, supervising the faith and practice of their flock on the spot, and he looked askance at the wandering *barbi* with their underground instruction.[5]

[1] E. Cameron, *The Reformation of the Heretics: The Waldensians of the Alps 1480–1580* (Oxford, 1984); reviews: P. Biller, in *EHR* CII (1987), M. D. Lambert, in *JTS* XXXVII (1986), pp. 256–9, preferred to R. Mackenzie, in *JEH* XXXVIII (1987), pp. 126–8; discussions by G. Audisio and E. Cameron, 'Les Vaudois des Alpes: débat sur un ouvrage récent', *RHR* CCIII (1986), pp. 395–405, 405–9; J. F. Gilmont, 'Les Vaudois des Alpes: mythes et realités', *RHE* LXXXIII (1988), pp. 69–89.

[2] Cameron, *Reformation*, pp. 129–66; interpretation in the light of Biller's criticisms.

[3] Gonnet and Molnár, *Les Vaudois*, pp. 298–304.

[4] Ibid., p. 299; G. Gonnet, 'I rapporti tra i Valdesi franco-italiani e i riformatori d'oltralpe prima di Calvino', *Ginevra e l'Italia* (Florence, 1959), pp. 1–63 at pp. 20–44.

[5] Gonnet and Molnár, *Les Vaudois*, pp. 300–1.

Bucer, whom the two *barbi* consulted at Strasburg, rejected this nicodemism on similar grounds, although with more understanding of the manner in which it had evolved and of the dangers inherent in suddenly jettisoning it. He called the reception of the sacraments of the Catholics 'great infirmity' and rejected aspects of the disciplined practice of the Waldensians as savouring too much of a legalistic attitude, overly based on works rather than faith.[6]

Such a conflict of views was inevitable, given the origin of the Waldensians as a movement of ethical reform. They came to exclude a number of Catholic beliefs and practices, such as the doctrine of purgatory, the invocation of Our Lady and the saints, yet retained in their leadership a kind of reformed priesthood, celibate like the Catholics, laying great stress on certain defined practices. No doubt the emphasis placed on the Scriptures, memorized in the vernacular, opened the way to the reception of new translations and Protestant interpretations, but there was much that was unfamiliar in the Reformed tradition, to be assimilated by their congregations only after prolonged discussion and instruction.

Bucer was unhappy about the Waldensian attitude to secular authority, and their rejection of oaths: his attitude to the Waldensian rejection of the Constantinian Church was on all fours with that which he proclaimed eleven years later to the *Unitas*: 'Religion is always built by the power of the Holy Spirit alone, and not by that of any creature. But the institutions and governments of cities are no less the work of this same Spirit which governs ecclesiastical institutions and ministries.' Part of this conflict arose from a difference of scriptural emphasis. The community of goods among the *barbi* was inspired, as was the community in a Catholic monastery, by the primitive Church described in the fourth chapter of Acts, while Bucer preferred to lay stress on the early Christian communities who were the recipients of St Paul's epistles and on Paul in the thirteenth chapter of Romans, with his insistence on obedience to terrestrial authority. 'If God wishes', Bucer wrote, 'he will raise the temporal power to be the minister of his flock, even against its will.'[7]

The mission of 1530 bore fruit and in a series of discussions and meetings the Valleys moved towards reception of the Reform, with the year 1532 marking a decisive stage in the turn towards sixteenth-century Protestantism. Farel dominated the events of that year, which committed the Waldensians to reform: the rank and file followed the lead of the *barbi*, without clearly understanding what they were doing. Two worlds collided. Farel was nearer to Calvin, whom he had brought in to reform Geneva, than he was to Luther. There was much in the Waldensian practice which he rejected. The *barbi* abandoned the fixed fasts, private confession, the laying-on of hands, the system of common property and the celibacy, Donatism, the stress on works and the literal interpretation of Scripture.[8] Not all agreed: some *barbi* wished simply to stay with their ancient customs, others were mindful of the long contacts with the Hussite movement and the *Unitas*. Nevertheless, the attraction of the Reform carried the day against uncertainty and opposition.

---

[6] Ibid., pp. 301–4.   [7] For this and the preceding quotation, see ibid., p. 304.

[8] G. Audisio, 'Pourquoi une Bible en Français pour les Vaudois?' in *Olivétan, traducteur de la Bible*, ed. G. Casalis and B. Roussel (Paris, 1987), pp. 117–34; Audisio, *Luberon*, pp. 181–2. I owe information to Dr C. Trueman.

Behind Farel, a typical French Protestant leader with his driving energy and clarity of mind, lay the emotional force of the Calvinist type of dogmatic system built on Scripture, seductive for men whose lives had been devoted to the learning and exposition of Scripture. Farel, moreover, who sprang from Gap in Dauphiné, seems to have been able to speak to the Waldensians in their own language.[9]

He also persuaded the Waldensian leadership to subscribe the massive sum of 800 écus d'or to a new vernacular translation of the Bible – a historical curiosity, for the Picard Pierre Robert Olivétan, whom Farel sponsored and who came into the Valleys in the autumn of 1532, partly to spread the Reform, translated the Scriptures into French, a language not well known to the *barbi* or their people, their linguistic bond being an Alpine variant of the language of oc, not North French oeil. Olivétan's Bible was designed to have parallel translation into French, then being diffused under official auspices as a lingua franca in Provence, and into Latin, the language of the medieval Church and of a minority of *barbi*.[10]

Farel seems to have seen in the Waldensians an ideal instrument for making reality of his dream of a new standard translation underpinning the orthodoxy of the growing Protestant circles of French-speaking lands, based on the Hebrew and Greek and superseding the older work of Jacques Lefèvre of Etaples, which had been a translation of the Vulgate.[11] He had long been interested in a Protestant press, and from 1529 had been in collaboration with Pierre de Wingle, a Lyons printer who moved for security to Geneva, and then to Neuchâtel, won by Farel for the Reform in 1530. There in the Swiss Reformed stronghold Pierre de Wingle printed Olivétan's version in June 1535.

Farel's plan did not work out as he had hoped. Olivétan's massive folio was suited to public, formal meeting to hear the Word in a Protestant assembly rather than the secret consultation and undercover reading of the *barbi* in the house of an adherent, and the Waldensians were unsuited to providing a nucleus of reliable distributors. Selling a Bible was a task of a different order to the distribution of the tracts in the Protestant interest in which Farel and Pierre de Wingle had hitherto been engaged. Olivétan himself, a reticent man who habitually used a pseudonym, a translator rather than an exegete, who saw himself simply as an instrument for the communication of God's word, was moved by his experience of the Waldensians, with whom he lived for much of the time between the autumn of 1532 and February 1535, when he dated his preface 'from the Alps' before leaving to oversee the work at Neuchâtel. In the preface he makes fun of the practice of writing elaborate, flattering dedications to influential patrons; instead he dedicates his work to

---

[9] For Farel see Audisio, *Luberon*, esp. ch. 5; Cameron, *Reformation*, pp. 168–70; G. Audisio, 'La fin des vaudois (XVIe siècle)?', in *Vaudois*, ed. Audisio, pp. 77–99 at p. 90 (see also note on place and date of decision to accept the Reform, p. 91).

[10] Audisio in *Olivétan*, ed. Casalis and Roussel, pp. 122–8; on the size of subscription, see Cameron, *Reformation*, pp. 208–9; Audisio, in *Vaudois*, ed. Audisio, p. 92, comments on the purpose of it.

[11] J. F. Gilmont, 'La publication de la Bible d'Olivétan: audaces et limites d'une enterprise de precurseurs', in *Olivétan*, ed. Casalis and Roussel, pp. 31–7; also p. 137; on Lefèvre generally, see J. Jordan, 'Jacques Lefèvre d'Etaples: principles and practice of reform at Meaux', *Contemporary Reflections on the Medieval Christian Tradition*, ed. G. H. Shriver (Durham, NC, 1974), pp. 95–115. Olivétan translated the Old Testament from the Hebrew; his New Testament version was a revision of Lefèvre's, using the Greek.

'the poor little Church of Jesus Christ', and writes with emphasis about the sufferings of the Waldensian communities.[12]

He was meeting the wishes of the Waldensians by providing them with a printed version, eliminating the scribal errors of MS production, and, again, as they wished, unlocking the treasures of Hebrew and Greek; they received from him a push in the direction of Protestantism through his marginal comments. No doubt some bought the costly folio: Audisio has uncovered a case in 1540 of a family near Apt in Provence who had come originally from Piedmont and presumably took the translation with them when they migrated over the Alps.[13] As a whole, it did not sell well, and for the rank and file little immediately changed. The *barbi* had their ancient Vaudois translations, minuscule in size, *aides-mémoire* for a text which through rote learning in their long training had already sunk into their minds.[14] The Olivétan text, like the decisions of 1532, was a portent of a new age, which many Waldensians were not yet ready to enter.

The growth of Calvinist influence

A generation was needed before the Waldensian communities on both sides of the Alps could be grappled to the Reform. Two *barbi*, Daniel de Valence and Jean de Molines, struck out against the trend and set off in 1532 to Mladá Boleslav to alert the *Unitas* to what had been happening and to find out from personal contact whether they had sacrificed their earlier moral fervour, and their preachers had abandoned celibacy.[15] On the latter they satisfied themselves. Perhaps they had hoped to enlist the authority of Luke of Prague in resistance to rapprochement with Farel and the Swiss, but he had been dead four years. Instead, the leaders of the *Unitas* wrote a letter to the Waldensians of the Valleys, advising them to be less precipitate and to prove the spirits, and recalling their long fidelity to their traditions. Dialogue was not prohibited – the *Unitas* itself under John Roh had been attentive to the new teachings – but the *Unitas*'s ancient confrères were reminded of the long-lasting links between the movements and warned that consolation was to be found 'in Jesus Christ alone'. But the Valleys in 1533 repudiated the initiative of the *barbi*. The decision marked the end of the years of sporadic contact and co-operation between Hussites and Waldensians: the Valleys lost their ecumenical links, and turned in more on themselves, a process which was accentuated when their Italian co-religionists in Calabria and Apulia were decimated in the persecutions of 1560. Swiss influence came to predominate.

In 1555 Calvin was fully in charge in Geneva. He valued the personal qualities of the Waldensians, but seems never to have wavered from the view that false doctrines were present among them, and that their teaching, especially on works, needed to be brought into accord with his own. In time

---

[12] Text in *Olivétan*, ed. Casalis and Roussel, pp. 169–76.

[13] Ibid., pp. 136–7.

[14] G. Tourn, 'Sans nom ni lieu', ibid., pp. 21–9, also pp. 135–6.

[15] Gonnet and Molnár, *Les Vaudois*, pp. 311–18; Cameron, *Reformation*, p. 191, for a revision on Calvin's attitude. Earlier contacts: A. Molnár, 'Luc de Prague et les Vaudois d'Italie', *BSSV* LXX (1949), pp. 40–64.

Geneva-directed pastors came to displace the *barbi* altogether, and the process of thus uniting the Valleys to the Calvinist system began in 1555.[16] Thereafter a series of pastors was introduced, often at risk of their lives, to instruct, to diffuse literacy, to deal with idiosyncratic and undesirable local customs. It was recognized that the bringing in of the Protestant harvest in Piedmont was the most dangerous task a minister could undertake; there was also an inevitable gulf between such men as Scipione Lentolo, Neapolitan, trained in Venice, the product of the college at Geneva, minister at Angrogna from 1559, and his simple congregations of mountain people, whom he accused of 'excessive avarice and dedication to the things of this world' – probably a townsman's criticism of the cautious attitudes formed by the grinding poverty of many in these localities. Lentolo in his *History of the Great and Cruel Persecutions* began to write up Waldensian history. His work, and that of others, such as Girolamo Miolo, probably an ex-Dominican, linked by birth to the community of Waldensian exiles in Geneva, who wrote a subtle *Brief History* about 1587, steering a middle course between the crudities of inquisitorial propaganda and Calvinist unease about facets of old Waldensian belief and practice, demonstrated how times were changing, for histories are commonly written just as the phenomena they record are passing away.[17]

In the later sixteenth century the Valleys abandoned their distinctive traits. They retained proudly their name, and their claim to a great antiquity of dissent from Catholicism, but in most other respects became indistinguishable from the expanding circle of Calvinist Churches.

The Waldensians in the French Alps

In the Luberon, on the French side of the Alps, much the same process was at work. Here Lutherans and others began to penetrate the countryside and to alarm authority. The Waldensians, immigrants from the Italian side of the Alps, had lived for decades in a near-impenetrable nicodemism with their Catholic neighbours, outwardly conforming, albeit with reservations, carefully intermarrying and transmitting their religion secretly through households. Though they were in touch with their co-religionists and often still had lands for renting in the Waldensian mountains, they did nothing to excite persecution. Lutheran missionizing, the work of Farel, and the fear that both excited in ecclesiastical authority, coupled with the effects of a general impoverishment of the region, isolating the Waldensians, making them disliked as foreigners, undermined the atmosphere of discreet toleration. Quite suddenly, they came under heavy pressure. Jean de Roma, a Dominican from Bourges, noted by Farel as early as 1523 for his ferocious diligence against heretics, initiated proceedings against Lutherans in 1532 and 1533 which revealed the secret presence of Waldensians. The inquisitor through his interrogations came to believe in the existence of a conspiracy of Waldensian heretics, both structured and international, separate from the Lutherans, and dangerous.[18] Economic tensions and a growing suspicion of

---

[16] Cameron, *Reformation*, pp. 155–66.

[17] G. Miolo, *Historia breve e vera de gl'affari dei Valdesi delle Valli*, ed. E. Balmas (Turin, 1971).

[18] Audisio, *Luberon*, p. 90; for a description of Jean de Roma, see Cameron, *Reformation*, pp. 149–50.

the aliens from Piedmont led local witnesses to denounce, where earlier they had remained silent. Jean was checked, and died of plague in the summer of 1533. But it was too late. The incoming of the Reform, Lutheran, Farellian, Calvinist, had changed the climate beyond recall; Waldensians, faced with the new beliefs, suffered, as in Piedmont, a crisis of identity and, after the massacre of Mérindol of 1545, when a French royal army devastated villages of the Waldensians and engaged in wholesale killing at Mérindol, came to make common cause with the new Protestants.

Religious fervour from the Catholics, passive suffering for their faith from the Waldensians, cannot provide us with a complete explanation of the tragedy of Mérindol. Waldensians fought. Attacks from Catholics brought reprisals; in Labrières the Waldensians fortified themselves and men of Mérindol pillaged a neighbouring abbey. Fear of breakdown of public order helped to unleash an army in 1545; pillaging by Catholics, quondam neighbours of the victims, can be explained less by hostility to heresy than by their will to recover the costs of maintaining a royal army in their midst.[19] But Mérindol and the other repressions achieved wide publicity and were a turning-point. After an uncertain intermediate phase, the underground Waldensians, pushed towards Protestantism by persecution, became Huguenots. Jean Rouet of Lourmarin married in a Catholic church in 1553 at Mérindol; in 1564 he had his son Joseph baptised in the Calvinist church at Lourmarin.[20] Those who had married and had their children baptised in Catholic churches ceased to preserve the precarious symbiosis of the past: they turned instead to Calvin's congregations. Despite the years of persecution and silent protest, Waldensianism yet had something of compromise about it – part of the movement still looked back to the medieval past, whereas such an approach in the stern climate of the sixteenth century seemed wholly inappropriate. Perhaps, too, Audisio's theory has something to commend it – that the Waldensian attitude to poverty smelled of the thirteenth century, and the epoch of the mendicants. It was not compatible with the changing attitudes of the Reformation epoch, much more inclined to give a positive valuation to riches and see the hand of God in the work of the prospering Protestant tradesman.[21] The leadership of the movement lacked the training and equipment to take part in the great debates about doctrine characteristic of the new age. So Waldensianism disappeared in the Luberon as a separate entity, just as it did in Piedmont, but without even leaving its name behind. It was absorbed, traceable only in the unusual number of countrydwellers who were Huguenot in the lands in Provence where the Piedmontese Waldensian immigration had taken hold, an exception to the general rule that labourers on the land were Catholics, industrial workers Huguenots, in the Protestant nucleus in the massacre village of Mérindol, and in the survival of clusters of old Waldensian family names.

---

[19] Cameron, *Reformation*, pp. 151–4; review of Audisio, *Luberon*, in *JEH* xxxvii (1986), pp. 336–9; Audisio, *Luberon*, p. 370; on Dauphiné, P. Paravy in Biller, Hudson, *Literacy*, pp. 160–75.

[20] Audisio, *Luberon*, p. 426.

[21] Ibid., pp. 438–9; for a survey of the transition to Protestantism, see Audisio, in *Vaudois*, ed. Audisio, pp. 77–99, esp. pp. 95–6.

Survivals outside the Alps

As in the Luberon, so in the other regions of Waldensian survival in France –
the minorities disappear into the more powerful and numerous Reform
movements. In Apulia and Calabria, sometimes described as a kind of 'India'
of sixteenth-century Catholicism, a remote quasi-missionary province, where
Waldensian communities long survived, Tridentine Catholicism put forth its
powers in 1560 and launched a crusade in 1561. War, interrogations,
confiscations and burnings decimated the Waldensians, and a successful
Jesuit mission, following on the heels of persecution, reconverted the region.
Waldensianism ceased to be a force in southern Italy.[22]

No consistent resistance was put up against Catholic revival in Italy.
Gonnet, musing in 1983 on the reasons for the failure of the Reform to capture
Italy, listed, together with the resurgent Catholicism of the Council of Trent,
the work of the Holy Office from 1542, the setting up of the *Index librorum
prohibitorum* in 1559, Paul VI's iron resolution, the Bull *Licet ab initio* of 1562 and
the tribunal of the inquisition which it put into action, a failure of will on the part
of the supporters of Reformation in Italy, disorganized, over-individualistic,
inclined to a pot-pourri of religion, philosophy and magic, and irresolute
before persecution.[23] Italian Reformers, many of whom fled before the forces
of repression, mattered more outside than inside Italy. The political confusion
favoured the cause of the papacy: it was not in the interest of princes to
support Protestantism. Gonnet wrote of an 'exhaustion of Reform', of a
movement unquiet, even tumultuous and anarchistic which spoiled the
opportunities which might otherwise have been open to intelligent, serious-
minded groups (among whom he included the Waldensians) to change the
course of Italian history. More recently, Welti confirms Gonnet's view of the
lack of a geographical or doctrinal nucleus for the opposition to the Italian
Church, and of the efficiency of its repression of dissent, notably of the
potential of merchants carrying disturbing influences over trade-routes.[24]
Menchi has written of the influence of Erasmus, who stirred a whole
generation of young Italians with his educational works. Controversialists
attacking Erasmus's religious teaching paradoxically roused a new interest in
his works on this theme, hitherto neglected. A movement for change came into
being, based initially on Erasmus's high educational reputation, widely
diffusing his writings on religious freedom. The *De immensa misericordia Dei* was
translated three times in the 1540s and 1550s. But the inquisition intervened,

[22] An account of the Jesuit mission is given by M. Scaduto, in *Archivum Historicum Societas Jesu* (1946), pp. 1–76 (Audisio, *Luberon*, bibliography). Merlo, *Valdesi*, pp. 109–13, reviewing G. Audisio, *Le barbe et l'inquisiteur: Procès du barbe vaudois Pierre Griot par l'inquisiteur Jean de Roma (Apt, 1532)* (Aix en Provence, 1979), notes how Griot saw Puglia and Calabria as a land of freedom. See Audisio, *Les Vaudois*, pp. 207–10.

[23] G. Gonnet, 'Sur les causes de la faillite en Italie des mouvements d'opposition à l'église officielle au moyen âge et au seizième siècle', *CV* xxxvi (1983), pp. 177–93.

[24] Review of M. Welti, *Breve storia della riforma italiana* (Casale Monferrato, 1985), by R. Mackenzie in *JEH* xxxviii (1987), pp. 126–7. The classic account of the Italian Reform is in Delio Cantimori, 'The problem of heresy', in *The Late Italian Renaissance, 1525–1630*, ed. E. Cochrane (London, 1970), pp. 211–25 (tr. of article in *BSSV* lxxvi (1957), pp. 29–38).

sharply checking this diffusion of subversive Erasmian views; here again, repression reigned.[25]

What is significant is that no modern writer on the Reformation has felt that Waldensianism had any noteworthy part to play in the success or otherwise of Reform in the peninsula; only Gonnet speaks a word of the 'might have been' of Waldensians, amongst other, quiet Protestant-orientated groups. Earlier persecution had pushed them to the margins.

The same generalization can be made about the French Reformation. Waldensians in France had been much reduced over the centuries. In Dauphiné they outlived a crusade. They continued in secrecy in Provence and the Comtat Venaissin. Immigration from Piedmont reinforced the numbers but did not modify their passive role, imposed by persecution. They transmitted their faith with resolution, but they did not missionize, or change the views of their Catholic neighbours.

Only in Germany does a question-mark about the deeper influence of Waldensianism remain. Böhmer long ago concluded from a dogmatic comparison that surviving congregations in Germany and Austria acted as a stimulus for the development of the Anabaptist groups well known in the early sixteenth century.[26] They had a considerable number of traits in common – the rejection of the oath, of war, of the holding of civic office. They shared an uncompromising rejection of the world. The rejection of infant baptism or the practice of ordaining the preacher may, it is said, have acted as a first step towards the rebaptizing characteristic of the movement. But these are only hypotheses still,[27] and there is too much uncertainty about the early Anabaptists to come to firm conclusions about their connection with the Waldensians, significant as they were in German-speaking lands.

THE LOLLARDS

The sixteenth-century movement

Unlike the Waldensians of France and Italy, the Lollards of England had not been pushed to the margins of society, and into mountain and frontier lands. The prosecutions of the sixteenth century show that they still existed in the regions singled out in Thomson's survey and were strong in the capital.[28] Persecution had lopped out a quondam leading class of trained clergy and eliminated the possibility of working a major change in England's religious beliefs by a process of academic-based education from above, using the

---

[25] Review by P. G. Bietenholz of S. S. Menchi, *Erasmo in Italia 1520–1580* (Turin, 1987), in *ARG* LXXX (1989), pp. 315–18.

[26] *RPTK* xx, col. 832.

[27] J. K. Zeman, 'Anabaptism: a replay of medieval themes or a prelude to the modern age?', *Mennonite Quarterly Review* (1976), pp. 259–71, puts weight on a spontaneous birth. I owe comment to the Reverend G. Chatfield. Audisio, in *Vaudois*, ed. Audisio, pp. 81, 89, 96–7, notes our ignorance of the fate of the eastern wing of the Waldensians in Austria, Bohemia and lands further east in the sixteenth century and inclines to think that the Waldensian movement before the age of the Reformation had *de facto* divided into two, based on the barrier between the vernacular of the Alps and of the German-speaking lands, *barbi* and *Brüder*.

[28] Above, pp. 274–9.

vernacular, as Wyclif and the early founders had wished, but it had not destroyed the vitality of the movement.

The evidence of the courts suggests that recruitment was on the increase on the eve of the Reformation. Homespun evangelists in the Lollard style, repeatedly on the move, converting, carrying books, outwardly conforming, ready to recant, then slipping away to carry out what had plainly become for some a consuming task, helped to keep Bible-reading groups in being and gathered new recruits. John Hacker, the water-carrier, was known first in Hampshire and probably in Berkshire, and then resided in the Lollard locality of Coleman Street in London, making forays to the Chilterns, to Burford and the North Downs; subsequently he lived in Essex while keeping in touch with his fellow believers in London. Prosecution would not silence him: he abjured in 1521, but continued unabashed with his evangelizing until he was caught again in 1528. Hacker spoke effectively to his own kind: in London, for example, he was in contact with a bricklayer, a tallow-chandler, a saddler's wife, a haberdasher, a pointmaker and some tailors.[29] A summary of the judgement on James Brewster, who was burnt at Smithfield in 1511, conveys the atmosphere in which a humble, grassroots movement both retained and increased its adherents.

> First, That he had been five times with William Sweeting in the fields keeping beasts, hearing him read many good things out of a certain book, at which reading were also present at one time Woodrof or Woodbinde, a netmaker with his wife . . . Item, For having a certain little book of Scripture in English, of an old writing almost worn for age, whose name is not there expressed . . . Item, Because he, hearing upon a time one Master Bardfield, of Colchester, thus say: 'he that will not worship the Maozim in heart and thought shall die in sight', he asked afterwards of William Man, what that word Maozim should mean, who told him, that it signified as much as the masing God, to wit, the sacrament of the altar.[30]

The Lollard movement in its last phase adapted to its general loss of a clerical, trained leading class, and succeeded in putting the reading community in the centre of its life, with laymen and laywomen instructing, discussing, learning and evangelizing in different ways according to talent and opportunity, thus giving an impetus to small-scale growth. The movement had a deep suspicion of any form of clericalism; as, through circumstances of persecution, it became more and more heavily a lay movement, so its doctrine of the priesthood of all believers was lived out in practice within a web of house-churches and by casual, everyday occupational meetings.[31] The lay teacher, supporter and missionary came into the forefront. He or she was naturally less vulnerable than the *barbi* of Waldensianism, leaders who made the decision in the interest of their own survival to maintain rather than to missionize, working through

[29] Hudson, *Premature Reformation*, pp. 474–9. Hudson's whole chapter, 'The re-emergence of Reform', pp. 446–507, repays study, together with reference back to Aston, in *History* XLIX (1964), pp. 149–70.
[30] Foxe, *Acts and Monuments* III, p. 216.
[31] Hudson, *Premature Reformation*, pp. 449–51.

families in deep secrecy, keeping their movement alive in hard times but not expanding it. Lollardy, in its last phase, unlike Waldensianism, was not dependent on the ministrations of a select, trained few.

Though the vernacular mattered for the Waldensians, as it did for the Lollards, the scriptural and other texts were not at the centre in quite the same way. Lollardy was a religion of the book, and it had the resilience of a movement based on an underground literature, no longer growing, but copied, concealed, read out, and passed from hand to hand, still well able to stir the imagination, to console in adversity and to open simultaneously a world of literacy and of novel religious ideas. The records show its continuing potency.

A group of Buckinghamshire Lollards in the prosecutions of 1521–2 were described as sitting in Iver Court, the farm of a substantial Lollard, Robert Durdant, 'reading all the night in a book of scriptures'. Durdant invited guests to his daughter's wedding from Windsor, Amersham and London, who used the occasion to meet in a barn and listen to readings 'which they liked well'.

Buckinghamshire, an ancient Lollard site, gives proof that not all the heretics were of humble rank. John Phip of Hughenden was said to have burnt suspect books worth 100 marks to ward off prosecution.[32] Recent scrutiny of the Subsidy Rolls reveals that in Amersham, Great Marlow, Denham and Hughenden, Lollards were spread through the structure of society and by no means confined to the poorer levels.[33] Nor, in these few favoured localities, were they so small a minority. Over one quarter of those eligible to pay taxes in 1524–5 have been calculated to be Lollards, and of the total of Lollards that with good probability can be so labelled approximately 40 per cent were in the category paying from £4 to £9 and no less than 37 per cent in the category paying £10 and over. Men in these classes would hold authority, employ servants, bequeath inheritances by will and were able to exert pressure on dependants.

The state of Lollardy in Amersham showed what could be done by using wealth. Alice Saunders threatened a waverer with penalties if he left Lollardy, and when Thomas Houre abandoned his beliefs, saw to it that her husband dismissed him from his job, and that he even forfeited his post as holy-water clerk.[34] Lollards did not often wield that kind of influence, but research on adherents elsewhere, in Coventry and in Colchester,[35] demonstrate the existence of more patches of wealth among the membership than has hitherto been supposed. Further work may reveal more still.

Ecclesiastical authority, sweeping into its net larger batches of suspects on the eve of the Reformation, occasionally burning, was not getting on top of the movement. The distribution of persecutions makes it highly probable that repression never eliminated nuclei in Lollard-influenced localities: even in East Anglia, so silent after the thorough persecution of Alnwick, it now seems

---

[32] Cross, *Church and People* (sympathetic and imaginative account of late Lollardy), p. 35.

[33] D. Plumb, 'The social and economic spread of rural Lollardy: a reappraisal', *Voluntary Religion*, ed. W. J. Sheils and Diana Wood, *SCH* 23 (1986), pp. 111–29.

[34] Ibid., p. 121; for a characterization of the Buckinghamshire group, see Cross, *Church and People*, pp. 34–5.

[35] For Coventry, see above, p. 270; for Colchester, J. C. Ward, 'The Reformation in Colchester, 1528–1558', *Essex Archaeology and History* xv (1983), pp. 84–95; Hudson, *Premature Reformation*, p. 479.

that some at least lived on. The characteristics of English Lollardy, the ease of communications, the mobility and resilience of some missionaries and the special opportunities of the capital allowed it to survive and to some degree expand in London and in a swathe of localities in the south.[36]

Lollardy and Protestantism

The coming of continental Protestantism to England initially affected clergy and graduates primarily, and did so on a small scale, touching the universities, London and the east coast. Bishop Tunstall in a letter to Erasmus dismissed it as a reinforcement of Lollardy. 'It is no question of pernicious novelty,' he wrote, 'it is only that new arms are being added to the great crowd of Wycliffite heresies.'[37] Lutheran success in Germany could encourage the old Scripture-reading circles. Nicholas Field from London, presiding at a reading amongst Lollards in the Chilterns, was able to reinforce his point about the needlessness of the many traditional fasting days by referring to their elimination in Germany.[38] In an interesting case from Chesham an old Lollard, Thomas Harding, first convicted about 1506, prosecuted again after being informed on in 1532, was found to have under his floorboards such works of Tyndale as *The Obedience of a Christian Man* and *The Practice of Prelates*: at his trial he was convicted of a series of customary Lollard heretical beliefs, with a small admixture that was unquestionably Lutheran, derived, no doubt, from his reading of Tyndale. He had remained what he had for so long been – a determined Lollard, with views on images that were Lollard rather than Lutheran, for example, but quiet study had begun to carry him on in the direction of continental Protestantism.[39]

The old form of dissent could open the way to the new, and can be seen doing this in the case of John Tyball, of Steeple Bumstead in Essex, the articulate and persuasive lay convert to Lollardy, who succeeded in drawing Richard Fox, the incumbent of his parish, over to his opinions. Fox worked on the Augustinian friars of Clare in Suffolk. When one of their number, Thomas Topley, came into Fox's room, and found Wyclif's *Wicket* lying there, he read it and was moved by its exposition on the eucharist. 'I felt in my conscience a great wavering for the time that I did read upon it,' he said in his confession, 'and afterwards also, when I remembered it, it wounded my conscience very sore.'[40] Conversion was carried further by the preaching of Miles Coverdale,

[36] Cross, *Church and People*, pp. 36–7; Hudson, *Premature Reformation*, pp. 446–7; on East Anglia, see D. MacCulloch, *Suffolk and the Tudors* (Oxford, 1986), pp. 148–9.

[37] A. G. Dickens, *The English Reformation*, 2nd edn (London, 1989), p. 59. I am indebted to Professor Dickens for his comments on the first edition of *Medieval Heresy*, printed in its German translation, *Ketzerei im Mittelalter: Häresien von Bogomil bis Hus* (Munich, 1981), pp. 494–5, with my own reflections, ibid., p. 495, and for valuable references. Note Dickens's new chapter, pp. 13–24, and his survey of Lollardy, pp. 46–60.

[38] A. G. Dickens and Dorothy Carr, *The Reformation in England to the Accession of Elizabeth I* (London, 1967), pp. 38–9.

[39] Hudson, *Premature Reformation*, pp. 505–7.

[40] Foxe, *Acts and Monuments* V, pp. 39–40; Hudson, *Premature Reformation*, p. 480; Cross, *Church and People*, pp. 40–1; comment by Aston, in *History* XLIX, p. 162: 'Lollards might not actually make Protestants, but they could sow fertile seeds of doubt.'

and the *Wicket*'s influence was accompanied and reinforced by Erasmus. Old Lollardy in this instance was a part of a complex of influences carrying some English circles into Protestantism and creating vital centres for the popular support of a Reform movement imposed, in stages, from above.

Tyball was unusual, consciously setting himself to make inroads into the clergy; the gulf, social and intellectual, between old Lollardy and new Lutheranism is manifest in the story of his journey to London with another Lollard to see Robert Barnes, Lutheran, one-time prior of the Augustinian house in Cambridge and member of the White Horse circle of early Protestants. Tyball showed Barnes 'of certain old books that they had; as of Four Evangelists, and certain Epistles of Peter and Paul in English'. Barnes made little of Tyball's Lollard translations, which were, he said, not to be compared with Tyndale's New Testament, 'of more cleaner English', which he promptly sold to them for 3s 2d. He also met Tyball's request to write a letter to Richard Fox to confirm him in his views.[41]

The Late Version of the Lollard Bible, in its time a massive work of scholarship, was bound, as a translation of the Vulgate, to yield place to Tyndale, as a translator from the original languages – and, into the bargain, a master of English, the ultimate source of the literary triumph of the Authorized Version.[42]

Lutheranism did not always cohere with Lollardy. Luther disliked the moralism of the Epistle of James, the 'epistle of straw', to which the Lollards were drawn, and he did not share the Lollard hostility to the devotional apparatus of the late medieval Church, *tout court*, for all his attacks on abuses. His eucharistic beliefs were incompatible with those of the later Lollards.[43]

Ecclesiastical judges did not always know what to make of the differences between the two sets of beliefs. In the case of Thomas Bilney, who was made to recant by Tunstall in 1527, two interrogatories were available, one which was designed for a Lutheran offender, and was written in Latin, and another, written in English, designed for a Lollard and entered in the margin of the register. Against Bilney the Latin and Lutheran questions were used, and they may well have made him sound much more Lutheran than he was. The implicit assumption was that learned heresy would be Lutheran and that of the rank and file Lollard.

Bilney explained the development of his views in a letter to Tunstall as based on his personal experience of reading Erasmus's Latin version of the New Testament, probably soon after its publication in 1516, and especially of the sentence from 1 Timothy, 'It is a true saying and worthy of all men to be embraced, that Christ Jesus came into the world to save sinners.' This one sentence, he said, 'did so exhilarate my heart that immediately I felt a marvellous comfort and quietness'. He went on to say that he read Scripture anew, 'wherein I learned that all my travails, all my fasting and watching, all the redemption of masses and pardons, being done without trust in Christ . . .

[41] Dickens and Carr, *Reformation*, pp. 35–6; J. Strype, *Ecclesiastical Memorials* (Oxford, 1822), i, pt 2, pp. 54–5.
[42] *Tyndale's New Testament*, ed. D. Daniell (New Haven and London, 1989). I am indebted for loan to Mr A. Johnson.
[43] D. MacCulloch, *The Later Reformation in England, 1547–1603* (Basingstoke, 1990), pp. 67–8.

these, I say, I learned to be nothing else but even . . . a hasty and swift running out of the right way'.[44] Remorse at his recantation drove him out to preach again without authorization in Norwich Diocese, distributing Tyndale's New Testament. He was burnt in 1531. Bilney was certainly not an orthodox Lutheran and J. F. Davis has given good reason for assuming that his judges in 1527 got it wrong; in fact his views then formed a personal amalgam of Lollard teaching, with its violent rejection of images and pilgrimages, and a reforming Cambridge Erasmianism.

Lollards, with their experience of underground book smuggling, aided the entry of Protestant books from abroad: Robert Necton, an importer of Tyndale's New Testament, was yet another of Hacker's contacts.[45] John Tewkesbury, a London haberdasher, burnt for heresy in 1531, also in Hacker's circle, read and sold both Wyclif's *Wicket* and Tyndale's *Obedience of a Christian Man* and *Wicked Mammon*.[46] Printing resurrected old Lollard texts, and gave them a wider audience; perhaps significantly, evidence suggests that the texts were being put out by publishers in a time-scale a little after the original continental works – and naturally the Lollards' texts are only a small proportion of the total flowing in from abroad. But they were there: Wyclif's *Wicket*, the General Prologue to the Late Version, Thorpe's *Trial*, the *Lantern of Light*, the *ABC Against the Clergy*. No doubt they were convenient material to feed a Protestant press, requiring neither translation for the English market or any special preparation, and they served a Protestant purpose without mention of the name of Luther.[47] But they also met an ideological need. They demonstrated to the reading public that the battle against the conservative clergy was not a new one and that arguments like Purvey's on the rightfulness of biblical translation and that of the *ABC* on the evils of ecclesiastical lordship, had all been rehearsed before.

A twilight world was developing in the 1520s and 1530s in which Lollardy and Lutheranism, despite their differences, met and mingled. In London, certain wards and districts had a continuity of Lollard occupation; here, in the parish of St Sepulchre's, Oldcastle was concealed for a time after the failure of his rebellion in 1414, and in the same district John Claydon held his readings of the *Lantern of Light*. Hacker long had his base in Coleman Street, and one of his followers, John Stacy, a warden of the Bricklayers' Company, had a scriptorium there. A vicar of All Saints, Honey Lane, was a distributor of Protestant literature, and the pulpits of such churches as St Vedast, St Mary Woolchurch and St Mary Abchurch gave willing congregations to Reformed preachers.[48] Old and new supported each other. When the teaching of Zwingli

---

[44] Dickens and Carr, *Reformation*, pp. 28–9; comment: Cross, *Church and People*, pp. 54–5; MacCulloch, *Suffolk*, p. 150, based on arguments of J. F. Davis, 'The trials of Thomas Bylney and the English Reformation', *Historical Journal* XXIV (1981), pp. 775–90; J. F. Davis, *Heresy and Reformation in the Southeast of England* (London and New Jersey, 1983), pp. 9–10; Hudson, *Premature Reformation*, pp. 496–8.

[45] Hudson, *Premature Reformation*, pp. 481–2.

[46] Ibid., p. 477.

[47] Ibid., pp. 491–2; perspective by Aston in her article on Lollardy and the Reformation in *History* XLIX (1964), pp. 149–70. A. Hudson, '"No Newe Thyng": the printing of medieval texts in the early Reformation period', *Lollards and their Books*, pp. 227–48.

[48] J. F. Davis, 'Lollardy and the Reformation in England', *ARG* LXXIII (1982), pp. 217–36 at pp. 224–5; Brigden, *London* (analysis of Londoners' reaction to Reformation, with sensitive re-creation of contemporary emotions); vivid depiction of Lollardy, pp. 86–106, see also pp. 411, 416–17; Stacy, p. 106.

reached England it is natural to assume that that, too, would combine with Lollardy and more easily and effectively, because Zwingli, like the Lollards, taught that the eucharist was a commemoration meal.[49]

What can be assumed is that Lollards would merge most naturally with teaching more radical than that of Luther, and that their affinities might be expected to lie with the Puritans rather than with the ultimate victor in the struggles about the English Reformation, the Church of England. So in Kent it can be no surprise to find a continuity of radical dissent in the same textile villages that had once been the haunt of William White in the fifteenth century. In 1511 Lollards were prosecuted in Benenden, Tenterden and Cranbrook; in 1539 a letter from Thomas Cromwell to Cranmer complained about the presence of sacramentaries in a number of localities, including Cranbrook; in 1556 John Philpot of Tenterden was tried for views which coincide with Lollardy rather than Lutheranism; under Elizabeth, Cranbrook became a well-known Puritan centre.[50]

The role of Lollardy

Lollardy disappeared; but it did so by merger and osmosis, in ways that can now only be guessed at. An older view, that Lollardy played no part at all in the coming of the Reformation, which was brought about by the interplay of politics and the inflow of Protestantism from the Continent, is untenable;[51] no-one would now argue that late Lollardy had lost all its capacity to move men, or that the success of Protestant enactments under Henry VIII and Edward VI was unrelated to the development of some public opinion in a Reform direction. What will long remain controversial is the degree to which popular views so moved, and the exact role of Lollardy in this peaceful change of opinion.[52]

The leading authority, A. G. Dickens, has described the heartland of the English Reformation before Elizabeth, where Protestant communities were most strongly developed, as 'a great crescent running from Norwich down to Hove and beyond'. Within that area there was a most intensive development

[49] MacCulloch, *Later Reformation*, gives a warning about the absence of evidence for contact between intellectuals of the Zwingli tradition and Lollards; on the accurate understanding of what Zwingli's views were, see now A. E. McGrath, 'The eucharist: reassessing Zwingli', *Theology* XCIII (1990), pp. 13–19.

[50] Davis, in *ARG* LXXIII (1982), pp. 222–3.

[51] G. R. Elton, in *New Cambridge Modern History* II: *The Reformation 1520–59* (Cambridge, 1958), p. 227: 'Lollardy played no part in the Reformation', a view superseded the following year by A. G. Dickens's pioneering *Lollards and Protestants in the Diocese of York* (above, p. 269, n. 98) and its implications: see esp. pp. 243–5, and M. McKisack's review in *PP* XVII (1960), pp. 93–5; comment by Dickens in corrected reprint of 1982; Elton makes a retreat in *NCMH*, 2nd edn (Cambridge, 1990), p. 263.

[52] Debate on the role of Lollardy in the English Reformation forms part of a wider controversy over the part played by Protestant ideals in shaping opinion. A. G. Dickens, *The English Reformation* (London, 1964), following on the views in his *Lollards and Protestants*, long held the field. It has been challenged by C. Haigh, 'The recent historiography of the English Reformation', *The English Reformation Revisited*, ed. C. Haigh (Cambridge, 1987), pp. 19–33 (see also introduction); for a powerful reply, see A. G. Dickens, 'The early expansion of Protestantism in England', *ARG* LXXVIII (1987), pp. 187–222; survey: R. O'Day, *The Debate on the English Reformation* (London and New York, 1986), esp. pp. 102–200; wise comment in M. E. Aston, *England's Iconoclasts* I (Oxford, 1988), p. 158: 'No adequate method has yet been found to test the plausible hypothesis that there was some continuity between pre- and post-Reformation dissent.'

in Suffolk, Essex, London and Kent; a western offshoot ran up the Thames Valley into Oxfordshire and Berkshire, and thence into Gloucestershire and Wiltshire. The swathe of territory, although it includes the capital and east-coast ports, with Kent, which one would expect to be most readily open to continental influence, embraces, though it does not precisely comprehend, the traditional areas of Lollardy. It creates a presumption that there has been an interaction between the two. London, the underground capital of Lollardy, where authority found the maintenance of control particularly hard, was also a centre for Protestantism: here there was a long tradition of copying, and then of printing. Secret congregations could readily exist. St Nicholas, Cole Abbey and All Hallows, Honey Lane, were for example, utterly diverse in attitudes, but they could quietly survive in close proximity.[53] This aided both old Lollardy and new Protestantism.

A comparison of Lollardy underground and of the burnings of the martyrs under Mary gives a broad but not very exact correspondence of areas of origin. The maps have a very different time-scale, the Lollard one, based on prosecutions, plotting the recorded incidence of Lollardy between 1414 and 1522, and the map of the Marian martyrs that of the place of origin and place of burning of those who suffered for their religious opinions in Mary's short rule; in fact in the three years and nine months from 3 February 1555 to the end of the reign.[54] The situation is confused by the differing attitudes of the gentry in various localities. There is, for example, a strong tally of martyrs in Sussex, but this may owe as much to the persecuting zeal of its gentry as to the depth of Protestant feeling.[55] Some turned a blind eye to the opinions of those in their area of authority, and were either sympathetic, or wanted no trouble; others responded earnestly to the policies of the government.

What must strike the observer is the new steadfastness of the victims of the burnings, and the rigour of the judges. Authority in England burnt but rarely before Mary's age. A figure has been cited of 544 trials between 1423 and 1522, issuing in only twenty-nine, possibly thirty-four, burnings.[56] Mary's judges burnt over 300 in a remarkably short space of time. The Protestant hagiographer, John Foxe, a generally careful recorder, listed 285 victims.[57] The Elizabethan historian John Strype gives figures for burning comparable to Foxe, ranged under counties, to a total of 288; A. G. Dickens has noted that a few cases are neither in Foxe nor Strype.[58]

Mary and her clerical advisers, reared in the traditions of the Spanish Counter-Reformation, were determined to extirpate heresy utterly. The

[53] Brigden, *London*, p. 417; on the geographical distribution, see Dickens, *ARG* LXXVIII, p. 211.

[54] For Lollardy underground, above pp. 274–9. For distribution of burnings and social analysis of victims, Lambert, *Medieval Heresy*, 1st edn, pp. 371–3; analysis: J. H. Blunt, *The Reformation of the Church of England 1547–1662* II (London, 1882), ch. 5. I am indebted to my wife for analysing Foxe and making the map, to the late Mr D. Bethell for suggesting its making and Professor D. M. Loades for information.

[55] M. J. Kitch, 'The Reformation in Sussex', *Studies in Sussex Church History*, ed. M. J. Kitch (Hassocks, 1981), p. 94; see discussion in O'Day, *Debate*, p. 154.

[56] J. A. Guy, *Tudor England* (Oxford, 1988), p. 26 and reference given.

[57] References in Lambert, as above, n. 54.

[58] J. Strype, *Ecclesiastical Memorials* III, ii (Oxford, 1822), pp. 554–6; Dickens, *English Reformation* (1964 edn), pp. 264–72.

bishops, faced with offenders whose youth meant that their religious opinions had been formed after Henry's break with Rome, failed to notice an opportunity to allow mercy. These accused had been brought up when the Scriptures were freely available in the vernacular and Protestant views had begun to circulate. It could not be said that they had been instructed in the old faith, and then had wittingly turned their back on it – the assumption of medieval prosecutions.[59] This was a far cry from the slow-moving English bishops of the past, with their readiness to accept, and repeatedly accept abjuration. Before their judges the accused, gathered in organized churches of their own,[60] often humble men and women, resisted and defied their judges, where the Lollards of the past had preferred to suppress damaging evidence, to feign repentance and live to fight another day. Even those whose views suggest that they were in fact Lollards shared in the new attitudes, and went unhesitatingly to their deaths.

The impact on public opinion was all the greater because of the concentration of prosecutions and burnings within a small geographical area: 85 per cent of the burnings took place in London, south-east England and East Anglia.[61] Before the end there were signs of a stirring of opinion against authority. Restrictions were placed on those who could attend these spectacles – in itself a negation of the assumptions behind burning, that it should deter, and that it should be a public repudiation of heresy. Together with the unpopularity of Mary's Spanish marriage, and the failure of Pole and the government to revitalize the priesthood and, with rare exceptions, to counter Protestant propaganda, the burnings were a landmark in the slow change of sentiment amongst the mass of people who were neither zealous Catholics nor members of the new-formed Protestant communities.

Foxe, in his *Acts and Monuments*, popularly known as the *Book of Martyrs* by recording the sufferings of Mary's victims, gave a vital emotional underpinning to the Elizabethan Church.[62] In his first, English, edition of 1563 and in subsequent, improved versions published in his own lifetime, in 1570, 1576 and 1583, he showed himself scholarly and conscientious. Deeply committed to the Protestant cause, he none the less knew how a painstaking accumulation of detail carried conviction. The stories he related were of a type that all could understand and appreciate, of the courage of the humble before an unjust authority. The version of 1563 ran to over 1,800 pages, with more than fifty woodcuts and a calendar of martyrs and confessors. A truly Protestant history of the Church was in being, and capable of reaching a wide audience, through sales, only exceeded by the Bible, through readings, and through its use in the pulpit. It was the inevitable companion to the English Bible, and helped to secure the English Reformation.

Lollardy had a part to play. Foxe was influenced by the pioneer of Lollard

---

[59] P. Hughes, *Reformation in England* (London, 1953), II, pp. 275–7; on the martyrs, see Dickens, *English Reformation*, pp. 293–301; sympathy for them: p. 297; role of women: p. 300; on a persecutor, see G. Alexander, 'Bonner and the Marian persecutions', *English Reformation Revisited*, ed. Haigh, pp. 157–75.

[60] P. Collinson, *The Elizabethan Puritan Movement* (London, 1967), p. 24; see Cross, *Church and People*, p. 113.

[61] Guy, *Tudor England*, p. 238.

[62] Analysis in O'Day, *Debate*, pp. 16–30.

MAP 11A   The Marian martyrs in England.

history, John Bale, with whom he once shared lodgings. Bale, who published
an account of Arundel's investigation of Oldcastle at Antwerp in 1544, saw
the need to rewrite the history of the Church, and to displace in the public
mind the Catholic martyr Becket by the Lollard Oldcastle. Foxe built on
Bale's ideas.[63] He emphasized the Lollards from an early stage in the
compiling of the *Martyrs* and its Latin forerunner, because their history was
the answer to the gibe of the Catholic controversialist, where were you before
Luther?

His was a providential history. For the first 300 years after the apostles,
Foxe believed, the Church suffered; for another three it flourished; then
declined for 300 until about the year 1000. There followed the time of
Antichrist, then in the sixteenth century the 'purging of the Church of God'.[64]

---

[63] L. P. Fairfield, 'John Bale and the development of Protestant hagiography in England', *JEH* xxiv
(1973), pp. 146–60.

[64] O'Day, *Debate*, p. 17.

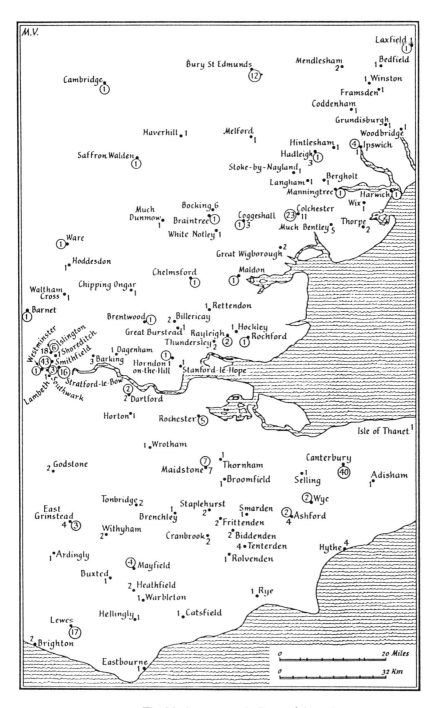

M.V.

Laxfield 1

Mendlesham 2 · Bedfield
Bury St Edmunds · 1 · Winston
12 Framsden · 1
Coddenham · 1
Cambridge · 1 Grundisburgh · 1 · 1
Woodbridge
Haverhill · 1 Melford · 1 Hintlesham · 1 4 · Ipswich
Saffron Walden · Hadleigh 1
Stoke-by-Nayland 1 Langham · 1 · 1 Bergholt
Manningtree 1 · Harwich 1
Wix · 1
Much Bocking · 6 Coggeshall Colchester
Dunmow · Braintree 1 1 3 23 11 Thorpe
White Notley · 1 Much Bentley 5 · 2
Ware Great Wigborough · 2
1
Hoddesdon
Chipping Ongar Chelmsford Maldon
Waltham Brentwood 1 1 Rettendon
Cross · 1
Barnet 1 Great Burstead 2 Billericay
1 Thundersley Rayleigh 1 Hockley
Westminster Islington Shoreditch 2 2 1 Rochford
18 6 Dagenham
43 Smithfield 1
1 3 16 3 Barking Horndon 1
Lambeth Southwark on-the-Hill 1
Stratford-le-Bow Stanford-le-Hope
2
2 Dartford
Horton · 1 Rochester 5
Isle of Thanet 1
Wrotham
1
Godstone Thornham
2 Maidstone 7 1 Canterbury
7 Broomfield Selling 40 Adisham
1 1 1
Tonbridge 2 Staplehurst Wye
East 1 2 Smarden 2
Grinstead Brenchley 1 Ashford
4 3 Frittenden 2
Withyham Cranbrook Biddenden 4
2 2 Tenterden Hythe 4
Ardingly Rolvenden
1 Mayfield 1
4
Buxted
1 Heathfield
2 Warbleton
1 Rye
Hellingly 1 Catsfield 1
Lewes 1
17
Brighton
2
Eastbourne
1

0   20 Miles

0   32 Km

MAP 11B   The Marian martyrs in England (detail).

The Lollards were witnesses for truth in England who grappled with Antichrist; the martyrs of Mary's reign were continuing the same struggle; Elizabeth was a second Deborah, called to battle for the truth. Foxe had borrowed from Wyclif and the Lollards the assumption of a golden age of the Church, brought to an end by Rome and its clergy.

The reader who followed the story of Wyclif, his translation of the Bible, the attempted and failed reform, the persecution of the Lollards, then the intensity of Mary's attack across the pages of Foxe might not have realized, for all the detail which Foxe gives about their lives and beliefs, that Lollards were radical dissenters in a number of ways different from the adherents of Elizabeth's national Church. Foxe suppressed a little when he worked on the Waldensians for he glided over their rejection of all but two sacraments;[65] his account of the Marian martyrs omits reference to the separatists among them.[66] He wrote with a purpose, to defend an embattled English Church against its enemies, and to encourage its supporters, and presented the pre-history of Protestantism as a simple and unified whole.

The most signal service of Lollardy, it may be, was to provide Tudor and subsequent Protestants with a pre-history of heroes and martyrs before Luther. But they also had a more humdrum role, in preparing public opinion for the changes that they were no longer able to bring about themselves. They 'lacked the power of regeneration'[67] in consequence of long repression, but they could provide a secondary service, assisting the entry of Protestant ideas, and softening attitudes. Richard Flynte of Topcliffe in North Yorkshire, brought before the court in 1542 for failing to make his Easter confession, excused himself on the grounds that 'there was a saying in the country that a man might lift up his heart to God Almighty and need not be confessed at a priest'. When he was asked where he had heard this opinion, Flynte answered, perhaps honestly, that he did not know.[68]

The episode is a reminder that there was a diffused Lollardy, propagated outside the strict Scripture-reading circles, closely analogous to anticlericalism and sometimes fed from it, that sapped the foundations of traditional Catholicism. Flynte's sentiment, like that of the minority of Lollards within the country, was fundamentally subversive of medieval religion, and was a part of the ensemble of ideas blowing to and fro, casually diffused, that helped to create the climate in which Reform ideas could grow and flourish. It is not easy to define, but the evidence for these views lies in the whole sequence of pithy and earthy Lollard aphorisms and negatives, displayed at trials, diffused in the readings of the movement, and quietly spread in society. They helped,

---

[65] Cameron, *Reformation*, p. 246.

[66] J. W. Martin, *Religious Radicals in Tudor England* (London, 1989), pp. 171–8; for Foxe's qualities as a historian, see J. F. Mozley, *John Foxe and his Book* (London, 1940), J. A. F. Thomson in *SCH* II, pp. 251–7; P. Collinson, 'Truth and legend: the veracity of John Foxe's Book of Martyrs', *Clio's Mirror: Historiography in Britain and the Netherlands*, ed. A. G. Duke and C. A. Tamse (Zutphen, 1985), pp. 31–54, who comments (p. 35) that Foxe 'worked only a little more carelessly and a few shades more partially than would be tolerable in a modern doctoral thesis'. Note comments on style, pp. 48–9, and the intriguing transmutation of the contemporary Lollard view of William White as a saint into conventional sixteenth-century terms (such as a 'good and godly man').

[67] Aston, in *History* XLIX, p. 169.

[68] Dickens, *Lollards and Protestants*, p. 48.

with many other factors,[69] to bring down in England the medieval Church, which had persecuted the Lollards.

Luther's encounters with Utraquism[70]

The young Luther shared the views of his German contemporaries on the dissidents in Bohemia. He rejected those who broke the unity of the Church and referred to the *Unitas Fratrum* as Pikhards. A volte-face over the Bohemians followed from his volte-face over the medieval Church. In the disputations at Leipzig in July 1519, Eck reproached him with defending the heretical views of Hus on the papacy, for which he was condemned at Constance. Luther at that time still rejected the Hussite movement as a schism but acknowledged the rightfulness of some of Hus's teaching. Then, when he read Hus's *De Ecclesia*, he wrote: 'We are all Hussites without knowing it, and Paul and Augustine.'[71] As he was brought to a firm opposition to the papacy, so reservations about the Bohemians were dropped. In 1520 he had the *De Ecclesia* printed and early in 1521 began to refer to Hus as a saint.[72]

Luther was welcome to Utraquists who were disillusioned with the attempts at reunion with Rome. They valued him, not so much because of his doctrines *per se*, as because of his effective opposition to the papacy.[73] They do not seem at first to have differentiated clearly between him and Erasmus. The appearance of a protest movement in Germany, which had in consequence of

---

[69] O'Day, *Debate*, pp. 137–40; W. J. Sheils, *The English Reformation 1530–1570* (London and New York, 1989), pp. 7–9; R. Whiting, *The Blind Devotion of the People: Popular Religion and the English Reformation* (Cambridge, 1989), though concentrating on the south-west, has comments of wider application – see esp. pp. 256, 266; and note p. 268, where he speaks of 'a Catholic collapse', but 'not necessarily or immediately a Protestant enthusiasm'. On the nature of late medieval piety, see C. Richmond, 'Religion and the fifteenth century English gentleman', *The Church, Politics and Patronage*, ed. R. B. Dobson (Gloucester, 1984), p. 193–208, P. Heath, 'Urban piety in the later middle ages: the evidence of Hull wills', ibid., pp. 209–34; interesting note on the evidence on survival of belief in purgatory, C. Burgess, ' "By Quick and by Dead": wills and pious provision in late medieval Bristol', *EHR* cii (1987), pp. 837–58. D. MacCulloch, reviewing Davis, *Lollardy*, in *JEH* xxxv (1984), pp. 483–6, notes a piety 'vigorous and demonstrative but largely untouched by the austerity of the continental *devotio moderna*', which 'expressed itself in a highly materialistic form', and argues that the piety itself 'provoked a peculiarly English variety of reforming reaction just as much as the ideas of Wycliffe'.

[70] W. Eberhard had originally thought of working on the theme of Luther in Bohemia 1520–1620 (*Konfessionsbildung*, p. 7), but discovered that: (a) basic groundwork had not been undertaken; (b) it was not easy to avoid analysing the theme one-sidedly, in terms of the one-way influence of the German Reformation on Bohemian neighbours. His two books, *Konfessionsbildung* and *Monarchie und Widerstand: Zur ständischen Oppositionsbildung im Herrschaftssytem Ferdinands i in Böhmen* (Munich, 1985), concentrate on the development of the attitudes of the Bohemian Estates, parties within them and the interaction of politics and religion in the Bohemian confessions. They are concerned primarily with the political history of Utraquism, but none the less provide much information on religious history of Utraquists and *Unitas* and on the influx of Lutheranism. See also survey, F. G. Heymann, 'The Hussite–Utraquist Church in the fifteenth and sixteenth centuries', *ARG* lii (1961), pp. 1–16. I owe a copy of this to Dr M. Polock.

[71] *Les Vaudois*, ed. Gonnet.and Molnár, pp. 284–90; citation: reference on p. 289.

[72] S. H. Thomson, 'Luther and Bohemia', *ARG* xliv (1953), pp. 160–81 at p. 176; for Erasmus's influence, see A. Molnár, 'Erasmus und das Hussitentum', *CV* xxx (1987), pp. 185–97.

[73] Eberhard, *Konfessionsbildung*, pp. 129, 147.

the crusades in the fifteenth century for so long been the seat of the greatest hostility to the Hussite movement, was all the more poignant and exhilarating. It offered the opportunity to break out of the long isolation that had afflicted the Utraquist Church; contacts with Luther were thus speedily taken up by individual adherents of the Left-Utraquism which, on quite other grounds, had come into increasing prominence in Bohemian politics and in the churches of Prague before Luther's fateful change of heart. Such radicals as Jan Poduška, priest of the Tyn church, Wenceslas Roždalovský and, from 1522, Martin Hánek praised Luther, as did the popular lay preacher, the hermit Brother Matthew; the fact that such men obtained places in Prague and were tolerated is to be attributed to a growing strength of Left-Utraquism. The language barrier operated against a full and direct overspill from Lutheran strongpoints into Czech-speaking lands, such as occurred in northern and north-western Bohemia where inroads were made in the ranks of German-speaking Catholics. Knowledge of, and enthusiasm for Luther was at first mediated to Czech areas by individual preachers, influenced more profoundly in their beliefs by the tenets of the _Unitas_ and recurrent Taborite-type attitudes to Scripture and the mass, but excited by a new star in the firmament of dissidence against Rome.[74]

Both sides were moved. Luther, when he got wind in 1522 of an attempt by Catholic clergy and conservative Utraquists to negotiate with Rome, come to an accommodation over the lay chalice and sacrifice the distinctive role of Utraquism, wrote a letter to the Estates designed to influence opinion against such a move, in which he praised Hus and Jerome of Prague and suggested a union of sentiment between like-minded Bohemians and Germans. The letter was successful – a tribute both to his reputation and to the growing force of the Left-Utraquist wing, who had been making progress since the removal of the conservative Administrator, Korambus, early in 1520. Politics aided confessional interests. The towns' representatives had long been drawn towards Left-Utraquism as part of their reaction against the policy of the Catholic higher nobility, bent on cutting back the towns' economic and constitutional gains.[75]

Gallus Cahera, a priest from Litoměřice, succeeded Poduška and Roždalovský, who died young of plague, as principal supporter of Luther in Bohemia after he had spent time with the master in Wittenberg. Luther formed a high opinion of him. It was his great error, for Cahera was an unstable egoist. When the Prague Council asked Luther in 1523 for his judgement on the thorny subject of maintaining the Utraquist priesthood, he replied in his _De instituendis ministris_ recommending that a bishop be chosen from among the existing Utraquist priests who had been ordained under the Roman rite, to carry out the necessary ordinations, and gave Cahera's name as a suitable candidate. The Church shrank from the explicit breach involved in choosing their own bishop, although Cahera was made solitary Utraquist Administrator with wide powers, a quasi-bishop.[76]

---

[74] Ibid., pp. 127–31; Hánek: pp. 136–7.

[75] Ibid., pp. 134–5; Korambus: p. 131; for general basis of development of parties, confessions, pp. 74–119 are illuminating; Thomson, _ARG_ XLIV, pp. 176–7.

[76] Eberhard, _Konfessionsbildung_, pp. 140–1, 165–71, supersedes all earlier work on Cahera.

How far radical views had spread among the Left-Utraquists is shown by the Candlemas Articles of January 1524 evolved by the Utraquists of Bohemia and Moravia, stressing the pure word of the law of Christ, its intelligibility and its precedence over all authorities, whether Church Fathers or Hussite teachers of the past.[77] The focus was on the two sacraments, holy communion and baptism, and there was a curious avoidance of the term 'sacerdos'. The articles spoke of servants, not priests, or of the 'clerus', and stressed the need for examination of conscience before reception of communion. The echo of Luther's voice was to be found in an article recommending the repression of Church feast days in the interest of putting down idleness, and in another on the role of the paterfamilias proclaiming the gospel within the family circle. The Candlemas Articles reveal the degree of influence being exerted on traditional Utraquism by the forces of the *Unitas* or of individual priests, such as Martin Hánek of Bethlehem, with Taborite-type views and by Luther himself; and the existence, beside these strands, of a perennial Hussite concern for toleration of differing views within the Church. A clear division between Lutheranism and Utraquism lay in the Church's rejection of Luther's views on the marriage of the clergy and its lack of understanding of Lutheran solafideism.

In the same year as the Candlemas Articles, a reaction in Prague was initiated by the conservative master Pašek, exploiting the views of conservative food guilds and manipulating the organs of government, which lasted till 1528. Right-Utraquists and Catholics again co-operated and yet another initiative was launched for a reunion with Rome. Pressure was put on Hánek and the Utraquist radicals, and there were bannings and imprisonments as well as burnings of a Lutheran, an Anabaptist and supporters of a fringe group of the *Unitas*. Cahera, perhaps mindful of Luther's action against his own extremist Karlstadt, fell in with the reaction. Luther, who vainly appealed to him, was bitterly disappointed; the conservative Utraquists turned against Lutheranism and thereafter Luther grew more cautious in his dealings with the Utraquists.[78]

In 1526 the last of the Jagiellon rulers, King Lewis, drowned at the battle of Mohacs against the Turks. The Estates and the parties united on a candidate, Ferdinand I of the Habsburg dynasty. The decision was a tribute to the will of the parties, determined to avoid civil war and a crisis with neighbouring lands and to put the interests of the community first.

The fact that there was tension between the pope and the Habsburgs encouraged some Hussites to be more willing to accept him; in doing so, they overlooked the warning implicit in Ferdinand's record of repression of Lutherans. Each party hoped for different concessions from the new monarch. Those who opposed the Regents, for example, who stood for the enlargement of the power of great nobles at the expense of monarchy, looked to a revival of central authority. It was another sign of the Hussite preoccupation with their own history and traditions and the secondary role played in their mind by Luther and his teaching.[79]

[77] Ibid., pp. 139–44 (fresh analysis).
[78] Ibid., pp. 150–81; comment, Thomson, *ARG* XLIV, pp. 160–81 at p. 178.
[79] Richter, in *Handbuch*, ed. Bosl, II, pp. 147–50; on issues in choice of Ferdinand, Eberhard,

Ferdinand, an energetic ruler brought up in the world of Spanish Catholicism alien to the Bohemian tradition of liberty, gave sincere acceptance of the Compactata, but only in a narrow sense. Influenced by his confessor Fabri, subsequently bishop of Vienna, who stayed with him in Prague in 1528 and wrote a work pointing out the contradictions between Luther's teaching and the Hussite position and expressing a preference for the latter, Ferdinand followed a long-term policy of building an alliance between Catholics and conservative Utraquists so as to erect a barrier against the inroads of more radical dissidents, Lutherans, Left-Utraquists, members of the *Unitas*, Anabaptists.[80] By a skilled balancing policy he aimed to integrate the quarrelling parties and recover monarchical authority; in this he had a great measure of success over time and began the process of building the Habsburg absolutism which destroyed Hussitism in Bohemia.

Luther and the Unitas

Luther as a young friar almost certainly gained his knowledge of the *Unitas* from the *Apologia* made in their defence by Luke of Prague to King Wladislav and printed in Latin at Nuremberg in 1511, and from the controversy which this unleashed with Jerome Dungersheim, professor at Leipzig. The detail of Luther's lectures on the Epistle to the Romans in 1516 make plain that he was, in his own mind, continuing a debate with the views of Luke.[81] When the decisive change in his attitude came after the clash with Eck, he felt the need for reconciliation. 'It is high time', he said in his appeal *An den christlichen Adel der deutschen Nation* of 1520, 'that we quite honestly and sincerely consider the case of the Bohemians, to unite them with us and us with them'.[82]

Relations with the *Unitas* were more difficult than with the Utraquists because of Luther's unease about their eucharistic teaching. Members of the *Unitas*, espcially John Roh from Litomyšl who had been impressed by a reading of Luther's writings, took the initiative. Roh and a companion, Weisse, visited Luther in Wittenberg in 1522; Luke took up correspondence; Luther clarified his own position in his *Vom Anbeten des Sacraments* of 1523; further exchanges took place between Luke and Luther marked by a will to mutual understanding and by Luke's joy at the recognition of common ground. None the less, Luke was a theologian of calibre, not ready to give up the distinctive doctrines of the *Unitas*, long established, for which they had suffered persecution, and it was he who broke off the correspondence in 1523. Doctrines of the eucharist and justification divided them and contact had not been renewed when Luke died in 1528.[83]

Konfessionsbildung, pp. 203–13, is helpful; Ferdinand did not stand on a right of inheritance and his succession was agreed in Bohemia.

[80] Ibid., pp. 245–8, noting, p. 246, the earlier existence of such a policy; for Ferdinand's brother, see now F. Seibt, *Kaiser Karl v und die Reformation* (Berlin, 1990); on religion and the development of Estates, W. Eberhard, in *Crown, Church and Estates*, ed. R. J. W. Evans and T. V. Thomas (London, 1991), pp. 23–47.

[81] Thomson, *ARG* xliv, p. 166.

[82] Ibid., p. 172.

[83] Ibid., pp. 174–6; Richter, in *Handbuch*, ed. Bosl, ii, p. 123; J. T. Müller, *Geschichte der böhmischen Brüder* i (Herrnhut, 1922), pp. 389–417 (classic account of *Unitas*); A. Molnár, 'Luther und die böhmischen Brüder', *CV* xxiv (1981), pp. 47–67; see also W. Eberhard, 'Bohemia, Moravia and Austria', *The early Reformation in Europe*, ed. A. Pettegree, Cambridge, 1992, pp. 23–48.

The years 1530 to 1532 marked a turning-point in the history of the *Unitas*, as in the Synods a party of younger clergy, anxious to widen the appeal of the *Unitas* and open it to external influences, broke through the resistance of their elders.[84] In 1530 a number of nobles, who had been protectors, took the decision to accept baptism; the social and political significance of the *Unitas* began to increase. In 1525 it has been calculated that the numbers of adherents had climbed to about 150,000;[85] advance continued and recruits were won at the expense of the Utraquists. The appeal of Brother Vavřinec Krasonický was heard and the *Unitas* began to send candidates to university at Wittenberg. It was decided that the writings of Luke of Prague should have authority only in so far as they reflected that of Scripture. The views of John Roh on the desirability of opening contacts with Luther and the German Reformation prevailed. In 1532 the Synod chose John Augusta as one of the bishops; he was very young and had only been made priest the year before; he was a fine polemicist, a party chief, a preacher and man of both brilliant and dangerous qualities;[86] his powerful personality exerted a sway over the *Unitas* until his death in 1572. He believed in closer links with Lutheranism. At the time of the Synod, the leadership was asked for a written statement of belief to be shown to Margrave George of Brandenburg; written in Czech, it was translated by Weisse, the quondam companion of Roh in visits to Luther, into German with the title *Rechenschaft des Glaubens*. It showed very plainly the symbolic character of the *Unitas*'s belief on the eucharist, which clashed with Luther's doctrine of the Real Presence. The translation fell into the hands of the Zwinglians, who were delighted with a statement in accord with their own views, and had it printed in Zurich as a means of reinforcing their own position *vis-à-vis* the Lutherans. A new German translation was made and sent to Luther who gave it a foreword and had it printed in Wittenberg. Luther at this time wanted a united front against the Papists and valued the support of the Brothers. The *Rechenschaft* had many affinities with Luther; there was some movement in eucharistic doctrine towards the Lutheran position. A decision of 1532 had diminished the importance of the second baptism on entry to the *Unitas* and asserted the full validity of baptism of infants.[87]

But a gap between Luther and the *Unitas* remained; the *Unitas* had not accepted Lutheran justification theology. They retained a more explicitly ethical stress and a disciplinary mechanism within the Church, and they were unwilling to abandon celibacy. Luther went on publishing works of Hus and in 1538 issued a Latin version of the *Confessio* of the *Unitas*. He seemed, however, content to stop short of a formal link. He once said to representatives of the *Unitas*: 'Let us both, you Czechs and we Germans, be apostles. You labour there, as conditions demand and we will strive here as we are impelled.'[88]

[84] Eberhard, *Monarchie*, pp. 97–112.

[85] Richter, in *Handbuch*, ed. Bosl, II, p. 117. For development of *Unitas*, see Eberhard, *Monarchie*, pp. 97–112.

[86] Judgement of E. Denis, *Fin de l'indépendance bohême* II: *Les Premiers Habsbourgs* (Paris, 1890) (the least durable part of his narrative, but still a vivid account), p. 100; see O. Odložilík, 'The Reformation leaders of the Unitas Fratrum', *CH* IX (1940), pp. 253–63.

[87] Thomson, in *ARG* XLIV, pp. 178–9; Eberhard, *Monarchie*, pp. 113–30.

[88] Thomson, *ARG* XLIV, p. 179.

The opening of links with Wittenberg and the German Reformation had its effects on Wenceslas Mitmánek.[89] Sent to Wittenberg in 1530 by the *Unitas*, he travelled widely was influenced by Melanchthon and his concept of a True Church, invisible and not precisely delimited in its organization. On his return, he left the *Unitas* for Utraquism, soon rose to a position of influence, and argued more decisively than other Left-Utraquists for creating links with the *Unitas*, a policy which failed to win lasting support. The ferment of the German Reformation worked among the Utraquists in general, helping to induce among the Left wing an emphasis on the gospel, derived ultimately from German lands, which pushed into the background the earlier Taborite-type views of these circles on the eucharist, but never going so far as to create a unified Protestant Church in Bohemia.[90]

Augusta, child of pious Utraquist parents, retained links with Utraquist churchmen and was prepared to engage in vigorous polemic. He dreamed of a unity of church members, bringing together Utraquists, Lutherans and the *Unitas*. He spoke from a position of strength, for the *Unitas* was growing and was literarily active, unoppressed, as a select minority, with the problems of political and ecclesiastical management which fell on the Utraquists. But Augusta's efforts brought no wider union; they publicized the *Unitas* but also irritated the Left-Utraquists, whose position he criticized as illogical. In effect, the wider publicity given to the *Unitas*, its efforts at establishing contacts with the German Reformation and the crystallizing of its doctrines in a *Confessio* brought members to the status of being, in practice, a third confession within Bohemia, beside Rome and the Utraquists.

It was, however, a confession that had been given no legitimacy. The decree of toleration of Kutná Hora excluded them, and juridically if not in practice they remained in a state of exclusion. The aftermath of the Catholic victory over the Schmalkaldic League at Mühlberg in 1547,[91] from which Ferdinand returned in anger to punish the Bohemians who had failed to follow his summons to the campaign brought a sharp persecution on the *Unitas*. Augusta was put in prison for sixteen years. The Moravian lords, however, despite their religious allegiance, had generally not declined to obey Ferdinand's summons and his wrath did not fall on Moravia. There persecution was relatively ineffective; in consequence many of the Bohemian *Unitas* fled to Moravia, where the centre of gravity of the movement thereafter lay; others concealed themselves in Utraquism; others again moved farther afield into Poland; here and elsewhere the diaspora set in motion by Ferdinand gave the *Unitas* an international following.

The policies of the Habsburgs

Meanwhile Ferdinand continued to strive to create a union between Rome and the conservative Utraquists and to bring vitality into his own Church in Bohemia, which had suffered, just as Utraquism had, from long conflicts,

[89] Eberhard, *Monarchie*, pp. 257–63.
[90] Ibid., p. 310.
[91] For build-up of tension, Mühlberg and its aftermath, see Eberhard, *Monarchie*, pt III, pp. 335–501; effects on *Unitas*: Müller, *Brüder* II, pp. 199–238; Richter, in *Handbuch*, ed. Bosl, II, pp. 152–7.

massive disendowment and shortage of priests. He had hopes that the Council of Trent would help in building a bridge between Utraquism and Catholicism but the definitions of Trent, fencing off Catholicism, worked rather in the opposite direction. Peace, he believed, would come to his realms if once the dissidents, Lutheran, *Unitas*, Anabaptists, could be excluded or driven into renunciation of their beliefs, and the Utraquists who stood close to Rome given the essential recognition of the lay chalice. An effective revival of Catholicism would have to wait, it was apparent, on the emergence of a new generation of clergy.

Ferdinand's invitation to Petrus Canisius and the Jesuits to settle in Prague led to the development of the Collegium Clementinum and the foundation of a new and more effective system of Catholic education which put up some bulwarks against the growth of Lutheranism and began to stem the outflow of the sons of nobles and wealthy bourgeois to German Protestant universities. But the Jesuits were more interested in the maintenance and deepening of Church life than in opening lines of communication with the Utraquists.

In the last decade of his reign, Ferdinand succeeded in gaining greater control over the official organs of the Utraquists – a facet of his will to develop the power of the monarch, and of his plan to ward off the influence of Left-Utraquists and bring the Right wing into a working union with Rome. However, he failed repeatedly in his attempts to persuade the papacy to permit the lay chalice. Finally, in 1564 Pius IV allowed it under conditions in the newly revived Archbishopric of Prague, in Olomouc and in some other dioceses. It was the last year of Ferdinand's life, and the measure should have crowned his endeavours to remove dissident Utraquism from his realms.[92]

In fact, it did not. It had come too late and what would have been a measure of prime importance in the fifteenth century had no significant effect in the conditions of 1564. Luther had followed Hussite precedent in adopting the lay chalice: old-style Utraquism was being outflanked.

Another link with the past disappeared as the Compactata was abandoned by general agreement under Maximilian in 1567.[93] It had come to be seen as no more than an instrument employed by the monarch to restrict the activities of Utraquists. It had never concerned the *Unitas*, and the inner development and radicalization of Left-Utraquism had outpaced it. In the third quarter of the century, Lutheranism grew apace despite the repressive policies of the Habsburgs, repeatedly moderated in practice by political necessity and pressures from abroad.

Lutheranism and the precedent of the Confession of Augsburg facilitated the agreement on doctrine enshrined in the Bohemian Confession of 1575.[94] It sprang from an initiative of the Estates, where the nobility of the *Unitas* and of the Utraquist allegiances could come to agreement more easily than their clergy. Maximilian and the Catholics opposed it, and that fact assisted the confessions in coming to agreement. The Augsburg Confession provided a basis, albeit modified by the tenets of Utraquists and the *Unitas*. The latter could hope for a measure of recognition, but they did not intend to give up

---

[92] For Ferdinand's policy and the response, see Richter, in *Handbuch*, ed. Bosl, II, pp. 158–61, 176–80.

[93] Heymann, *ARG* LII, p. 14; Richter, in *Handbuch*, ed. Bosl, II, p. 172.

[94] Richter, in *Handbuch*, ed. Bosl, II, pp. 172–3.

their independent Church order. Maximilian was only willing to give oral approval; little in practice was gained.

Utraquism sank. It lost its popular links; clergy became demoralized; there were losses to Lutheranism; others, closer to Rome, took the final step and surrendered to the papacy. In 1587 and in 1591 groups of clergy, some of note with two Administrators among them, took an oath of obedience to the pope and the archbishop of Prague and renounced the distinctive practices and tenets of Hussitism.[95] A majority of Utraquist clergy continued their independence and the evangelical wing succeeded in making some improvements.[96] But the Church was not what it had been.

The sixteenth century was the epoch in which the *Unitas* flowered, overcoming the schism of the Amosites, gaining ground at the expense of Utraquism and responding to persecution by flight and fresh missionizing. With the aid of their protectors they made excellent use of the printing press.[97] A powerful vernacular hymnology emerged. It was decided that some control should be exerted over the hymns used by various congregations which circulated in hand-written versions and in 1561 an official hymnbook was printed, with a foreword noting how the writing of hymns had been stimulated by the age of persecution.

John Blahoslav, who battled with Augusta over the rightfulness of pursuing learning within the *Unitas*, translated the New Testament into Czech from the Greek and was a mainspring behind the collective effort to produce the monument to original work with the Czech vernacular, the six-volume Kralice Bible with commentary, completed in 1588. Blahoslav contributed to the language itself: his Czech grammar was designed to purify the language rather than to serve the schools of the Brothers. He justified the project as a recreation for times when he was too tired to pursue theology. His disciple Orlik called him a 'precious jewel' of the *Unitas*.[98] With his death in 1571, and that of Augusta not long afterwards, there passed the generation of great bishops.

Successors were unable to resist decline. The practice of sending the most promising clergy for training at universities outside Bohemia exposed them certainly to wider horizons, but also to novel influences. At first they went to Lutheran universities, then, after Melancthonian teachings had been eliminated, to Calvinist centres in Germany or in Switzerland.[99] Calvin's influence grew at the expense of their own independent tradition. Celibacy ceased to be obligatory for the clergy. The practice of private confesson was eroded. Its part had been vital in sustaining the ethical calibre of the *Unitas* from the time of Luke of Prague's *Directives to Priests*. For a time after his death, the authority of the *Directives* was weakened because of synodal decisions of 1531 and the impact of Lutheran ideas, but after a period of uncertainty both Augusta and

---

[95] Ibid., p. 174.

[96] M. S. Fousek, 'Spiritual direction and discipline: a key to the flowering and decay of the 16th century *Unitas Fratrum*', *ARG* LXII (1961), pp. 207–25 at p. 208.

[97] For inner history of *Unitas* and Blahoslav, see Müller, *Brüder* II, pp. 344–68; hymns and dating of Kralice Bible, Richter, in *Handbuch*, ed. Bosl, II, pp. 198–9.

[98] Denis, *Fin* II, p. 257.

[99] Fousek, *ARG* LXII, p. 209.

Blahoslav recalled their followers to the heritage of Luke. Augusta's *Art of the Work of the Lord's Ministry*, written during his imprisonment, revived Luke's concept, albeit with warnings against overscrupulousness. A structure of probation, confession and examination of new members, with a catechumenate and a sequence of steps to be taken before admission to full membership maintained an exclusive Church on the principles of Peter Chelčický.[100] Its fruit in the standards of conduct of the members had been the major appeal of the *Unitas*. The practice of private confession was being vigorously defended against Calvinist objections in 1558; later however, it faded out as the *Unitas* lost its sense of identity. Members, deprived of the rigour of the old discipline, went over to other Churches, in Poland to the Calvinists, in Bohemia and Moravia to the Utraquists.[101] The clergy, without the tool of confession, ceased to have an insight into the needs of the souls committed to them. Comenius, bishop in exile, mourning over the near-extinction of his Church, concluded in 1649 that the cause of it was not the enemies of the *Unitas*, the persecuting forces of the Habsburgs unleashed after the victory of the Catholics at the battle of the White Mountain in 1620, but the Brethren themselves. By abandoning the inner Church discipline bequeathed to them by Luke of Prague, they had destroyed themselves.[102] Certainly a 'hidden seed' survived as he had hoped it would, in Moravia, and crossed the borders to Herrnhut in Saxony, where under the leadership of Count Zinzendorf in the eighteenth century, the Moravian Brethren entered on a new and yet more striking phase of their history. Yet in the late sixteenth and early seventeenth centuries they had come within a hair's breadth of foundering altogether.

In this it was like the other movements condemned as heretical by the medieval popes. Lollards, Waldensians, Utraquists, *Unitas* survived all manner of pressures to live on into the Reformation epoch. The Lollards contributed to the success of the English Reformation; but then they and the Waldensians were absorbed into sixteenth-century Protestantism. The Utraquists in the fifteenth century had achieved a measure of public recognition. They had become a force to be reckoned with for kings, popes and governments and continued to play a major role in the history of Bohemia and Moravia in the sixteenth century. But in time they changed character; the Compactata were abandoned and the lay chalice ceased to have its traditional importance; its most conservative clergy submitted to the papacy; Left-Utraquists both lost ground to Lutheranism and were, in the end, themselves profoundly influenced by Luther. Their independent existence ceased in the seventeenth century.

Thus medieval heresy merged into the Protestant Reformation.

---

[100] The central theme of Fousek's article.
[101] Fousek, *ARG* LXII, p. 208.
[102] Ibid., pp. 207–8, 222, 224.

20

Heresy and reform

Reform and heresy were twins. The Dark Ages and its fissiparous Churches, dominated by kings and aristocrats, repeatedly threatened by inner anarchy and external pressure of barbarians, produced very little heresy. The Christianity of the epoch gave security: it protected its adherents in life and offered them hope at death. This pre-Gregorian world 'enjoyed a secure understanding of the holy. It resided not in men but in places, objects and rituals under the custody of a priesthood whose value resided not in the ephemeral acknowledgement of personal virtue, but in the general recognition that it held the keys.'[1] Reform, and the stirrings of fresh intellectual life in the eleventh century, began to change those assumptions, and thus the rebirth of popular heresy took place just as new life emerged within orthodoxy. A revival in the schools of France, the reading of John Scotus Eriguena, a backlash from the tide of monastic renewal, the beginnings of lay literacy and the formation of new groupings in society are all variously responsible for short-lived incidents of heresy in the eleventh century.

On a small scale the Peace of God movement, fuelled by the will of both clergy and laity to escape the consequences of the breakdown of order in parts of France, roused a febrile enthusiasm, with high expectations of its leaders; disappointed, supporters readily turned to heresy.

On a much wider scale, the orthodox Gregorian reform of the eleventh century captured the energies of enthusiasts and engaged them in the struggle against abuses in monastic and ecclesiastical life. As these movements gained impetus, the incidents of heresy appeared to dry up for a time. But Leo IX, Gregory VII and the other heroes of the reform had let a genie out of its bottle. They had insisted on the sacred character of the priesthood and the necessity of lives matching the vocation of the clergy, and thus had put before the

[1] Moore, *Origins*, p. 277.

membership of the Church the notion of individual responsibility. They had demanded high ethical standards. These were ideals which inevitably could not be realized as a whole in the circumstances of the time and as something of the first impetus of reform faded in the twelfth century, heretical groups reappeared, led by fiery, dissenting preachers of the calibre of Henry the Monk.

Reform within orthodoxy and heretical movements outside it interacted with each other. So the notion of individual responsibility touched the monks, turning them against the practice of accepting oblates, which in the Dark Ages had seemed wholly unexceptionable, and at the same time influenced the heretics against infant baptism. The most common heresies of the century shared by various groups were, firstly, that the unworthiness of the priest made the sacraments which he administered invalid and, secondly, that the baptism of infants, being administered before they could make any conscious decisions of their own, was worthless: these views had their starting-point in the general preoccupations of Church and society of the time.

Waldensianism became an international heretical movement but its lay founder never intended to break with the Church. Valdes showed his originality when he commissioned translations of Scripture and the Fathers. Refused the right to preach, he preferred in the last resort to follow the mission he believed he had received from God, rather than obey ecclesiastical authority. His movement was the only one condemned as heretical by the papacy to survive from the twelfth century into the age of the Reformation, mainly because of the courage and high ethical standards of its celibate leaders, the *barbi*, and of the manner in which they adapted to a life of secrecy and to the needs of a peasant following.

Catharism, by contrast, was the exotic intruder in the Western tradition, the child of Bulgarian and Byzantine Bogomilism, carrying into Latin Christendom the dualist doctrine that all matter is evil, with its destructive consequences for central doctrines of orthodoxy. It made its landfall in the West for reasons connected with the preoccupations of the Western Church, their adepts making an initial impact because their poor, wandering and hunted life so well reflected the life of the apostles sent out to preach, two by two, by Jesus in the gospels. An interpretation of the apostolic life, not as the settled life of the early Christian community in Jerusalem, but as poor wanderers on the lines of the sending of the Seventy, had not hitherto found a secure home within orthodoxy. Cathar preachers filled a gap.

Western churchmen were more hostile to Catharism than to any other heresy because it offered so profound a doctrinal challenge to Catholicism, was a complete counter-Church with distinct hierarchy and rites, and in some sense clearly represented a recrudescence of an ancient heresy. Manichaean in strict terms it was not, for Bogomil was not the heir of Mani, but churchmen were perfectly right none the less to see in it a dualist sect, whose inspiration had much in common with the heresy which had once attracted Augustine and had then been denounced by him.

Hostility was compounded by the West's lack of experience of heresy. The *tabula rasa* of the Dark Ages had left them ill-equipped to deal with it, and a sense of powerlessness persisted through the twelfth century as the menace of heresy increased. It only began to dissipate as Innocent III took measures against it, as the mendicant orders began their work and as Gregory IX began to issue wide ranging commissions to investigate and condemn heretics. Dominic had been inspired by an encounter with a Cathar heretic in Languedoc to follow a vocation to preach against heresy and meet its appeal by counter-reason, and both his order and the sister order of the Franciscans provided dedicated men to serve as inquisitors. Preaching became more frequent and more effective. Catholic fraternities and Third Orders developed. Innocent's decree on annual confession began to bear fruit. In consequence, the weaknesses of Catharism were exposed and its heroic but vulnerable leading class, the *perfecti*, were hunted down. It disappeared, leaving not a wraith behind of its own influence and teaching.

It is hard to imagine Catharism establishing itself at any later stage in the history of the Western Church. It made converts when it did, above all, because of a lack of instruction of the laity, who had no adequate defence against eloquent and determined preachers using the texts of Scripture and the incidents of the gospels in the interest of a core of teaching that was profoundly heretical but not understood to be so by innocent auditors.

The records of investigation of heresy from the thirteenth century onwards provide us for the first time with something approaching an informal religious survey. We learn from them the opinions of many humble people, and can see how thin the veneer of Christianity could be, and how much doubt, materialism and paganism existed in the age of faith – the raw material for the detaching of Church members from a superficial Catholicism as a preliminary to entry to heresy. The positive achievements of the Latin Church in the epoch of the Cathars were real enough, but they affected in the main the upper layers of society, ever the best recorded. Moreover, achievement was patchy and regional, and frictions associated with the new relationship of clergy and laity that flowed from the reforms and with the wealth and privilege of individual clergy provided occasion for many disputes, feeding anticlericalism and creating a class of fautors, not heretics themselves, but willing to give protection to heretics as a stick to beat the churchmen with.

The Cathar experience left its legacy in a set of mechanisms designed to meet the problem of heresy, which remained in being for the rest of the Middle Ages. Legislation to enforce the backing of the secular power for repression was accepted by rulers. Capital punishment as the ultimate penalty for the obdurate became the norm. Most significantly, confiscation of goods, as Henry C. Lea long ago observed, was a penalty which provided a continued incentive to potential beneficiaries to pursue heretics and provide backing for their condemnation.

Alone, however, it does not explain the repeated successes of repressive action, which sprang from an underlying and commonly underestimated commitment to orthodoxy, based, it may be, on the recognition that authority was indivisible and that in the last resort the lay and ecclesiastical powers, despite their family quarrels, must support each other. Support might also spring from indignation at what was seen as an irreverent assault on the mystery of the mass, as in the case of Lollardy: when Wyclif crossed the Rubicon and rejected transubstantiation, much support fell away. It might be felt that churchmen had their own hobbyhorses, were over-privileged and over-wealthy and that they made free with accusations of heresy for their own ends; yet denials of the core of Christian belief stirred opinion in most places and at most times. No doubt public opinion and clerical propaganda demonized heretics; in the late Middle Ages the Waldensians in particular were crudely caricatured, but the identification of heresy as the work of the devil made acceptance of such caricaturing easier and fostered the view that toleration of heresy would bring down the wrath of God on a locality.

The heretics of the late Middle Ages were more intimately associated with elite groups than Catharism had ever been, with its lack of substantial clerical support and its paucity of intellectuals. The heresy of the Beguins in the Franciscan province of Provence and the *fraticelli* in Italy in the early fourteenth century sprang out of the internal struggles of the Franciscan order over their observance of poverty, fanning out into the lay world through the institution of the Third Order, aided by the powerful and enigmatic personality of Petrus Johannis Olivi, a Janus figure looking, on the one hand, to the orthodox Franciscan tradition, an academic teacher of high quality, and on the other to cloudy, mystical circles of excitable laymen and women. Working on the mind of Olivi was the magnetic concept of a third *status* in history, shortly to open, bringing after tribulation a time of new happiness and blessing for mankind, the fruit of the meditations of Joachim of Fiore in the second half of the twelfth century. He released an idea of great potency in the Church, which, when mishandled and misunderstood, gave a spur to heresy and rebellion.

Crisis in the Beguin affair was induced by the intensity of the struggle over poverty among Franciscans and their followers, in which the whole balance of Christian ethics was threatened by an extravagant stress on voluntary poverty; John XXII, who had the shrewdness to see this, attempted to settle a theological conflict by essentially administrative means, so creating more storms. His Bulls give colour to the view that popes in the later Middle Ages by defining and condemning created 'new' heresies, giving fresh work to inquisitors and bishops' officers and ever diminishing the indeterminate territory in which differing views could be held without incurring condemnation.[2]

The heresy stirring among tertiaries and enthusiasts and put down by John was no artificial construct. The heresy of the Free Spirit, on the other hand, was. Misunderstanding, prejudice born of tensions in towns between secular and regular clergy, unpopularity of the unprotected women of the beguinages, and certain potentially perilous teaching about the mystical way stimulated authority to define a heresy and sect which, as a coherent and organized whole, never existed; the belief that it did cost innocent lives. Worse still, the bishops of France and the officers of Philip the Fair, using inquisition and torture, falsely imputed gross errors and blasphemies to the order of Templars, apparently for the sake of their money, and destroyed them. The mechanisms of repression and the fear of the enemy within put potent weapons into the hands of the ruthless.

[2] A principal theme of Leff, *Heresy*

With the partial exception of Olivi and perhaps Amaury of Bène no leading academic ever became involved in popular heresy. Accusations of heresy and error were records of debate in the schools and were settled within the schools. Only John Wyclif, a first-rate intellectual, launched a popular heresy and that in the last six years of his life. His motives, and the thinking behind his decisions may never be wholly clarified. The effects were remarkable. His followers translated the whole Bible into the vernacular, launched a rebellion designed to depose and kill the king, and contrived to put into action a movement which, despite some heavy persecutions, lasted into the Reformation epoch and played some part in bringing about religious change in England.

In the lands of the Bohemian crown his ideas fermented within an existing reform movement; suspicion of complicity with them led to the burning of Hus; that act, coupled with the passion for reform, Hus's own preaching, Czech patriotism and enthusiasm for the lay chalice sparked a rebellion against the Council of Constance, then the king, finally the pope, and a series of Rome-inspired crusades, which were all brought to nought.

For the first time the mechanisms of repression were rendered ineffective. State power and the support of a substantial body of aristocrats, moved by patriotism and indignation at Hus's fate, were mobilized. Forces were unleashed at Tabor and Horeb, where peasants and their families, climbing the hills, left behind in the plains below the divisions of society between lord and peasant, priest and layman, the world of lordship, private property and clericalism. Together, until 1434 and the decisive clash at Lipany, Tabor and nobles, in uneasy alliance, formed a shield which could not be turned aside.

In the end, the concessions wrung from authority by the success of Hussite arms proved unstable; though as late as 1485 the resilience and powers of organization of Hussites were sufficient to force from their Catholic enemies and a reluctant king an extraordinary agreement on mutual tolerance, and Utraquists even in the sixteenth century showed a dour political skill in maintaining their cause, the movement at last faded. Times changed. Ferdinand I, the Habsburg ruler of Bohemia, had dreamed that the concession of the lay chalice by the papacy would reconcile at least moderate Utraquists to his rule. It was not to be; when Pius IV made the concession in 1564, there was no major response. Other ideas occupied the central stage.

In the Reformation epoch the unity of belief of the medieval Church broke down and Europe was divided – as it has been until the present day. Research has undermined an older, simplistic interpretation that saw in the victory of the Reformers the fruit of an ever-increasing incidence of abuse and disorder in the late medieval clerical establishment. True, the papacy was unable to provide any lead, for reasons which Mandell Creighton long ago gave us;[3] yet, below that level and a 'calcified' Church leadership,[4] there was still much vitality, a profound piety, and a series of small-scale reforms and developments.

Luther, it has been pointed out, was himself the child of one such late medieval monastic reform.[5] What distinguished the Reformation epoch was

---

[3] See his own summary of intentions in his classic *History of the Papacy* (above, p. 316, n. 59) in L. Creighton, *Life and Letters of Mandell Creighton D.D.* II (London, 1904), pp. 231–2.

[4] F. Oakley, *The Western Church in the Later Middle Ages* (Ithaca, NY, and London, 1979), p. 315.

[5] Ibid., p. 318.

the quality of mind of Luther himself and his successors, that fused older grievances and anticlericalisms and the regional patriotisms so vividly represented in the events of the Hussite revolution, with a doctrinal challenge more profound and far-reaching than any which emerged in the history of medieval heresy.

So old heresies were left behind. The lay chalice ceased to matter. The Waldensians, still despite heavy persecution nobly incarnating the medieval ideal of the poor wandering preacher in an age in which it was no longer greatly valued, yielded place to settled, Geneva-trained Calvinist pastors; Waldensians kept their name with its heroic associations, but in reality surrendered to Calvin. Lollards, the least organized of the movements condemned as heretical by the papacy, after playing a background part in the movement of the English towards Protestantism, lost their separate identity.

While so much else changed in the sixteenth century, the medieval concept of heresy and the overriding duty to repress it by force remained in being. Definitions of orthodoxy changed profoundly, but both Catholics and Protestants were agreed in asserting its importance and in using the power of the State to impose their versions on the recalcitrant. Friar John Forest was burnt under Henry VIII for fidelity to the medieval doctrine of the papacy; Calvin's Geneva declared itself the legitimate heir to the authority of the now discredited medieval Church by burning Servetus for his anti-Trinitarian views; in the seventeenth century Episcopalians in Scotland executed Covenanters; as late as 1697 a medical student was put to death in Edinburgh for denying the Trinity, while the reputation of the Catholic Church was long blackened by the attempts of the inquisition to repress Protestantism over centuries and by the barbaric ritual of the auto-da-fé. Perhaps this was the most baleful and lasting result of the struggles of the medieval Church with heresy.

The Christian Church in the East as well as the West was the heir to the assumptions of the pagan Roman Empire and of the whole ancient world, of the duty of the ruler to enforce right belief, and, with some hesitation, its leaders came to act on those assumptions. None the less, repression of wrongful belief in the West came during the Middle Ages to take on a dynamic quality which it did not have in the East.

Byzantine churchmen shared the horror of heresy and emperors took a direct part in the pursuit of heretics. Burning was a penalty imposed on the obdurate in the Byzantine Church as well – we have a vivid description by Anna Comnena of the burning of the Bogomil leader Basil in Constantinople – but it was less frequently used. Police action in the Byzantine world was more sporadic and less organized. The Byzantines were used to heresy. Western writers were aware of this. Guibert de Nogent atributed the higher incidence of heresy there to the fact that the air was lighter and purer, which gave the Greeks thinner bodies and more volatile minds and made them more liable to neglect the authority of their elders and so fall into heresies. Byzantium was the heir to the speculations of the Greeks and the proliferation of belief in the early Christian centuries. Heresy had often in the past allied with nationalist movements against the supremacy of Constantinople, and the emperor and patriarch had had to live with the consequences of past doctrinal disputes.

The West, with its experience in the Dark Ages of a comparative absence of heresy, was more crudely impatient, and, as Catharism in the late twelfth century showed its power over minds, suffered an intense feeling of fear and powerlessness. A ferocious response followed, issuing in the use of the secular weapon against heresy, and the development of inquisitorial procedures. How those procedures, and the attitude of mind fostered by them, contributed to the witch mania and the persecution, above all, of innocent women is becoming ever more plain through modern research.[6] The persecution of the witch spanned the Reformation and afflicted both Catholics and Protestants.

Did Western churchmen of the thirteenth century and afterwards believe that if they were vigilant and energetic enough, a time would come when the Church would be entirely cleansed and there would be purity of faith? Perhaps they did. Certainly both sides in the wars of religion and in the long battle between Reformation and Counter-Reformation worked on the assumption that the use of force, deployed with adequate efficiency, could have this effect. When long before, in the 1040s, Wazo of Liège was asked for advice on the treatment of heretics, he had pleaded Scripture and argued that wheat and tares should grow together till harvest. Many lives and much suffering would have been saved had his voice been heard.

---

[6] Cohn, *Inner Demons, passim*; D. Müller, 'Hexenprozess und Frauenrepression', *Heresis* XII (1989), pp. 33–51.

Glossary of heretics

Adamites. A heretical sect imitating nakedness of Adam, described first by Epiphanius and Augustine, then by Isidore of Seville; possibly originally to be identified with licentious Gnostic sect, the Carpocratians, but as organized, persisting sect in Middle Ages, wholly imaginary. Abusive term for a Hussite group. (pp. 335–7)

Albigenses, Albigensians. The term for Cathars in south of France, originally referring to adherents in the region of Albi.

Amalriciani. Pantheists; followers of Amaury of Bène (condemned 1210).

Apostolics, Apostolic Brethren. Exaggerated imitation of the Franciscans, with heresies on poverty and perfection, founded by Gerard Segarelli in Parma 1260; broke into rebellion under Dolcino di Novara (burnt 1307). (pp. 202–3)

Arnoldists. Followers of Arnold of Brescia (executed 1155), of Donatist and anticlerical views, attempting to impose apostolic poverty on the Church as an obligation; a north Italian movement or strand of thought. (pp. 52–4)

beghards. Men leading a religious life without rule or vows, similarly to the female equivalent, the beguines, but more mobile, sometimes gaining a living by begging; accused of Free Spirit heresy in early fourteenth century. See beguines, Beguins, Free Spirit. (ch. 10, s. 2)

beguines. Pious women leading a religious life without rule or vows, singly or in convents, often linked to the mendicant orders; popular from the early thirteenth century, but inhibited by prejudice and accusations of Free Spirit heresy in the fourteenth century. Name originally popular and pejorative, from Albigensis. (ch. 10, s. 2) See also beghards, Beguins, Free Spirit.

Beguins. A pejorative term from the same root as beguine; applied to tertiaries and others of either sex associated with Olivi and other Spiritual Franciscans, chiefly in the Franciscan province of Provence, with exaggerated views on the place of poverty; suppressed after issue of *Quorumdam exigit* by John XXII in 1318; spelling with capital and no 'e' adopted for convenience in this book to mark distinction from the beguines. (ch. 11) See also beguines, *fraticelli*, Spiritual Franciscans.

Bogomils. A heretical movement, so called from the name (possibly a pseudonym) of a tenth-century Bulgarian village priest, preaching opposition to the Greek Church and teaching that all matter is evil; active in Byzantium and the Balkans; spread into Western Europe to form Cathar sect. (pp. 55–7)

Bohemian Brethren. See Unitas Fratrum.

Calixtines. See Utraquists.

Cathars. Dualist heretics, teaching that all matter is evil. Derived originally from Bogomil influence and (possibly) Paulicians in Western Europe; active from twelfth to late thirteenth or early fourteenth centuries, esp. in parts of Lombardy and southern France. Term (Greek, 'pure ones') should properly be restricted to their leading class, the *perfecti*, but is commonly applied to the whole movement. (chs 4, 6, 7)

Flagellants. Movements, most commonly of laymen, engaging in mass flagellation in public as a form of penance; orthodox in origin; in 1260 stimulated in Italy by diffused Joachimite expectation of the end of the world; in 1349, by Black Death (term most commonly applied to participants in this episode), esp. in the kingdom of Germany and neighbouring lands; condemned by Clement VI. (pp. 220–1)

fraticelli (also **fratricelli, fraterculi**). Spiritual Franciscans in Italy who broke away from the order to follow a literal observance; exaggerated place of poverty in religious life; condemned by John XXII in 1317; term (from the Italian *frate*) may also be used loosely for orthodox members of orders or hermits. (ch. 11)

Free Spirit. Adherents of supposed sect of deviant mystics, esp. among beguines and beghards, accused of libertinism and autotheism after issue of *Ad nostrum* by Clement V in 1312; no organized heretical group in fact existed, and accusations were often imaginary, particularly when levelled against beguines. (ch. 10, s. 2)

Henricians. Followers of Henry the Monk, preacher of penance, then heretic, influenced by Peter of Bruis, active in the first half of the twelfth century in French-speaking lands, who rejected the sacraments and the doctrine of original sin. (pp. 44–8)

Horebites. See Orebites.

Humiliati. Loosely organized congregations in northern Italian towns leading a penitential life with manual labour and preaching; refusal to laymen among them by Alexander III of the right to preach led to heresy, as in the case of the Waldensians; Innocent III gave regulations to Humiliati willing to return to the Church in 1201. (pp. 65–8, 92, 95) See Poor Lombards.

Hussites. Generic term for Bohemian reform movement which challenged the papacy in the fifteenth century; originally a term of abuse; may be used in practice for the more moderate members of the movement. (chs 16–19) See also Taborites, Unitas Fratrum, Utraquists.

Joachimites. The term used in this book for writers and others, both orthodox and heretical, seriously influenced by ideas and symbols emanating ultimately (but often in false and distorted versions) from the exegetical, prophetic works of Joachim of Fiore. (chs 6, 11)

Lollards. (i) Imprecise popular term current in German-speaking lands, pejorative in origin and derived from *lollen, lullen* ('to sing'), applied to men leading a religious life without rule or vows; synonym of beghard.

(ii) In England relates to adherents of a popular evangelical heresy, given initial stimulus by teaching of John Wyclif, based on individual faith and supremacy of Scripture; apparently first applied in 1380 to followers of Wyclif's teaching (late in his life) in Oxford. (chs 13, 14) See Beghards.

Lyonists, Leonists. The moderate wing of the Waldensian movement, so called after the original centre at Lyons, that remained faithful to the tradition of Valdes and his early followers; separated from Poor Lombards from 1205; survived in France and its borderlands. (chs 5, 6, 8)

Orebites. Radical Hussites from Hradec Králové (Königgrätz) in eastern Bohemia who formed a community and military force comparable to Tabor under the priest Ambrose, renaming their town after the Mount Horeb of Scripture. (pp. 330, 340, 343–4)

Passagians. A small group, possibly only found in Lombardy, who observed to the letter OT precepts, including circumcision; condemned by Lucius III in 1184. (pp. 68)

Pataria. An eleventh-century reform movement in Milan, supported by the papacy. (pp. 36–7)

Patarene. An Italian term for heretics, especially Cathars, current from third Lateran Council of 1179.

Paulicians. A heretical sect dating back to the early centuries; dualist by the ninth century and opposed by the Byzantine Church; a possible factor in the rise of Bogomilism and Catharism.

Petrobrusians. Adherents of Peter of Bruis, village priest originally from the Embrun region who preached in south-west France c. 1119–c. 1140, rejecting all external forms of worship. (pp. 47–9)

Pikarts. A loose term of abuse for heretics, derived from beghard. (p. 336)

Poor Lombards. Waldensians, based initially in northern Italy, influenced by the Lombard climate of opinion to a more radical and anti-Church attitude; formed congregations supported by manual labour under influence of Humiliati, split from the Lyonists in 1205; active missionaries, esp. in German-speaking lands. (chs 5, 6, 8)

Runcarii. A synonym for Poor Lombards, derived from John de Ronco, leader in the Waldensian split of 1205; used by the Passau Anonymous about heretics prosecuted in 1266. (chs 6, 8)

Speronists. A minor sect, followers of Ugo Speroni of Piacenza, who disseminated a heretical predestinarian doctrine, and rejected the sacraments and belief in original sin; condemned by Lucius III in 1184. (pp. 77–8)

Spiritual Franciscans. Rigorist members of the Franciscan order who struggled for a strict observance of the rule, esp. in poverty, and appealed to Francis's Testament; extremists among them provided the starting-point for *fraticelli* and other heretics condemned by John XXII in 1317 and subsequent years. (ch. 11)

Taborites. Radical Hussites who began as a religious movement with eschatological expectations, later developing into a military and political organization, whose fighting powers were vital to Hussite success; major support for drastic religious changes in lands controlled by the Hussites; name of Tabor, with scriptural echoes, given to fortress south of Prague in 1420, thereafter their base. (chs 16–18)

Unitas Fratrum (or **Bohemian Brethren**). A small, rigorist group within the Hussite movement influenced by pacifist ideas of Peter Chelčický, formally separated from Utraquist Church in 1467; ancestors of Moravian Brethren. (chs 18, 19)

Utraquists. Supporters of the lay chalice, who insisted that communion should be given to the laity in both kinds (*sub utraque specie*), i.e. bread and wine; the usage, initiated in Prague in 1414, was condemned by the Council of Constance in 1415. The lay chalice became a symbol to the Hussite movement. (chs 17–19)

Vaudois. See Waldensians.

Waldensians (or **Waldenses**). An evangelical heresy of the late twelfth century, springing from an orthodox poverty and preaching movement launched by Valdes, a former businessman of Lyons; fell into heresy following refusal of the right to preach and subsequent condemnation by Lucius III in 1184; split into a Lyonist and Poor Lombard wing, but continued in France, Germany, parts of Eastern Europe and Italy and survived into modern times. (chs 5, 6, 8, 19)

'Waldo, Peter'. Form for Valdes (Lat. Valdesius) employed esp. by older historians; Peter, though used by Waldensian controversialists in the fourteenth century, was not historically Valdes's name. See Waldensians. (chs 5, 6, 8)

Abbreviations

ABAW	*Abhandlungen der königlichen bayerischen Akademie der Wissenschaften (Historische Klasse)*
Act. Fel.	*Les Actes du Concile Albigeoise de Saint Félix de Caraman*, ed. A. Dondaine, *Miscellanea Giovanni Mercati* v (*Studi e Testi* cxxv) (Rome, 1946), pp. 324–55.
ADRSP	*Archivio della deputazione Romana di storia patria*
AFH	*Archivum Franciscanum Historicum*
AFP	*Archivum Fratrum Praedicatorum*
AHDLMA	*Archives d'histoire doctrinale et littéraire du Moyen Age*
AKG	*Archiv für Kulturgeschichte*
ALKG	*Archiv für Literatur- und Kirchengeschichte des Mittelalters*, ed. H. Denifle and F. Ehrle
AM	*Annales du Midi*
ARBB	Académie royale de Belgique, *Bulletin de la classe des lettres et des sciences morales et politiques*
ARG	*Archiv für Reformationgeschichte*
ASI	*Archivio storico Lombardico*
BF	*Bullarium Franciscanum* v, ed. C. Eubel (Rome, 1898). *Epitome*, ed. C. Eubel (Ad Claras Aquas, 1908)
BIHR	*Bulletin of the Institute of Historical Resarch*
BISIAM	*Bollettino dell'istituto storico Italiano per il Medio Evo e archivio Muratoriano*
BJRL	*Bulletin of the John Rylands Library*
Bouquet	*Recueil des historiens des Gaules et de la France*, ed. M. Bouquet
BS	*Balkan Studies*
BSAHDL	*Bulletin de la société d'art et d'histoire du diocèse de Liège*
BSRS	*Bulletin of the Society for Renaissance Studies*
BSSV	*Bollettino della società di studi Valdesi*
CCM	*Cahiers de civilisation médiévale*
CEC	*Cahiers des études Cathares*
CF	*Cahiers de Fanjeaux* (Toulouse):
	I *Saint Dominique en Languedoc* (1966)
	II *Vaudois Languedociens et Pauvres Catholiques* (1967)

CF	III *Cathares en Languedoc* (1968)
	IV *Paix de Dieu et guerre sainte en Languedoc au XIII siècle* (1969)
	V *Les Universités du Languedoc au XIII siècle* (1970)
	VI *Le Credo, la morale et l'inquisition* (1971)
	VII *Les Evêques, les clercs et le roi (1250–1300)*
CH	*Church History*
CHR	*Catholic Historical Review*
CMH	*Cambridge Medieval History*, ed. J. R. Tanner, C. W. Previté-Orton and Z. N. Brooke (Cambridge, 1911–36), 8 vols
CV	*Communio Viatorum*
DA	*Deutsches Archiv*
DHC	*De Heresi Catharorum in Lombardia*, ed. A. Dondaine, in 'La Hiérachie Cathare en Italie', *AFP* XIX (1949), pp. 280–312
DHGE	*Dictionnaire d'histoire et de géographie ecclésiastiques*
DLZ	*Deutsche Literaturzeitung*
DTC	*Dictionnaire de théologie Catholique*
DZG	*Deutsche Zeitschrift für Geschichtswissenschaft*
EC	*Etudes Carmelitaines*
EcHR	*Economic History Review*
EEQ	*Eastern European Quarterly*
EETS	*Early English Text Society* (London, 1864–). Original series (o.s.)
EFV	*Enchiridion Fontium Valdensium* I, ed. G. Gonnet (Torre Pellice, 1958)
EHD	*English Historical Documents*, ed. D. C. Douglas (London, 1953–). 13 vols
EHR	*English Historical Review*
EV	Early Version of Wyclif Bible (see pp. 239–40)
FF	*Forschungen und Fortschritte*
FFor	*Franziskanische Forschungen*
FRB	*Fontes Rerum Bohemicarum*, ed. J. Goll, V (Prague, 1893)
FS	*Franciscan Studies*
FZ	*Fasciculi Zizaniorum*, ed. W. W. Shirley (RS, 1858)
HJ	*Hibbert Journal*
HJB	*Historisches Jahrbuch*
HS	*Hérésies et sociétés dans l'Europe pré-industrielle, 11e–18e siècles*, ed. J. Le Goff (Paris and The Hague, 1968)
HZ	*Historische Zeitschrift*
IP	*Istoričeski Pregled*
JEH	*Journal of Ecclesiastical History*
JGMO	*Jahrbuch für die Geschichte Mittel- und Ostdeutschlands*
JMH	*Journal of Modern History*
JMRS	*Journal of Medieval and Renaissance Studies*
JTS	*Journal of Theological Studies*
JWCI	*Journal of the Warburg and Courtauld Institutes*
LMA	*Le Moyen Age*
LV	Late Version of Wyclif Bible (see p. 256)
MA	*Medium Aevum*
Mansi	J. D. Mansi, *Sacrorum conciliorum nova et amplissima collectio* (Florence and Venice, 1759–98), 31 vols
MBPH	R. I. Moore, *The Birth of Popular Heresy* (London, 1975)
MGH	*Monumenta Germaniae Historica*
MH	*Medievalia et Humanistica*
MOPH	*Monumenta Ordinis Praedicatorum Historica*
MRS	*Medieval and Renaissance Studies*
MS	*Mediaeval Studies*

NMS	*Nottingham Medieval Studies*
NT	New Testament
OT	Old Testament
PBA	*Proceedings of the British Academy*
PL	J. P. Migne, *Patrologia Latina* (Paris, 1844–64)
PP	*Past and Present*
RB	H. Grundmann, *Religiöse Bewegungen*, 2nd edn (Hildesheim, 1961) (1st edn, 1935)
RBPH	*Revue belge de philologie et d'histoire*
Relazioni	*Relazioni del x congresso internazionale di scienze storiche* (Florence, 1955)
RES	*Revue des études slaves*
RHE	*Revue d'histoire ecclésiastique*
RHL	*Revue historique et littéraire du Languedoc*
RHPR	*Revue d'histoire et de philosophie religieuse*
RHR	*Revue de l'histoire des religions*
RPTK	*Realencyklopädie für protestantische Theologie und Kirche*, 3rd edn (Leipzig, 1908)
RQH	*Revue des questions historiques*
RR	*Ricerche religiose*
RS	*Chronicles and Memorials of Great Britain and Ireland during the Middle Ages* (London, 1858–97) (The Rolls Series)
RSCI	*Rivista di storia della chiesa in Italia*
RSI	*Rivista storica Italiana*
RSLR	*Rivista di storia e letteratura religiosa*
RSPT	*Revue des sciences philosophiques et théologiques*
RTAM	*Recherches de théologie ancienne et médiévale*
SCH	*Studies in Church History*

    i Ed. C. W. Dugmore and C. Duggan (London, 1964)

    ii Ed. G. J. Cuming (London, 1965)

    iii Ed. G. J. Cuming (Leiden, 1966)

    iv *The Province of York*, ed. G. J. Cuming (Leiden, 1967)

    v Ed. G. J. Cuming (Leiden, 1969)

    vi *The Mission of the Church and the Propagation of the Faith*, ed. G. J. Cuming (Cambridge, 1970)

    vii *Councils and Assemblies*, ed. G. J. Cuming and D. Baker (Cambridge, 1971)

    viii *Popular Belief and Practice*, ed. G. J. Cuming and D. Baker (Cambridge, 1972)

    ix *Schism, Heresy and Religious Protest*, ed. D. Baker (Cambridge, 1972)

    x *Sanctity and Secularity: The Church and the World*, ed. D. Baker (Oxford, 1973)

    xi *The Materials, Sources and Methods of Ecclesiastical History*, ed. D. Baker (Oxford, 1975)

    xii *Church, Society and Politics*, ed. D. Baker (Oxford, 1975)

    xiii *The Orthodox Churches and the West*, ed. D. Baker (Oxford, 1976)

    xiv *Renaissance and Renewal in Christian History*, ed. D. Baker (Oxford, 1977)

    xv *Religious Motivation: Biographical and Sociological Problems for the Church Historian*, ed. D. Baker (Oxford, 1978)

    xvi *The Church in Town and Countryside*, ed. D. Baker (Oxford, 1979)

    xvii *Religion and Humanism*, ed. D. Baker (Oxford, 1981)

    xviii *Religion and National Identity*, ed. Stuart Mews (Oxford, 1982)

    xix *The Church and Healing*, ed. W. J. Sheils (Oxford, 1982)

    xx *The Church and War*, ed. W. J. Sheils (Oxford, 1983)

xxi *Persecution and Toleration*, ed. W. J. Sheils (Oxford, 1984)
xxii *Monks, Hermits and the Ascetic Tradition*, ed. W. J. Sheils (Oxford, 1985)
xxiii *Voluntary Religion*, ed. W. J. Sheils and D. Wood (Oxford, 1986)
xxiv *The Church and Wealth*, ed. W. J. Sheils and D. Wood (Oxford, 1987)
xxv *The Churches, Ireland and the Irish*, ed. W. J. Sheils and D. Wood (Oxford, 1989)
xxvi *The Ministry, Clerical and Lay*, ed. W. J. Sheils and D. Wood (Oxford, 1989)
Subsidia i *Medieval Women*, ed. D. Baker (Oxford, 1978)
Subsidia iv *The Bible in the Medieval World*, ed. K. Walsh and D. Wood (Oxford, 1985)
Subsidia v *From Ockham to Wyclif*, ed. A. Hudson and M. Wilks (Oxford, 1987)

SDAB	*Sitzungsberichte der deutschen Akademie der Wissenschaften zu Berlin*
SHF	*Société de l'histoire de France*
SHR	*Scottish Historical Review*
SM	*Studi medievali*
SSAWL	*Sitzungsberichte der sächsischen Akademie der Wissenschaften zu Leipzig*
STC	A. W. Pollard and G. R. Redgrave, *A Short-title Catalogue of Books printed in England, Scotland and Ireland, 1475–1640* (London, 1926)
TAPS	*Transactions of the American Philosophical Society*
TDH	*Tractatus de hereticis*, ed. A. Dondaine, in 'La Hiérarchie Cathare en Italie', *AFP* xx (1950), pp. 234–324
TR	*Theologische Rundschau*
TRE	*Theologische Realenzyklopädie* (Berlin and New York, 1987–)
TRHS	*Transactions of the Royal Historical Society*
TLZ	*Theologische Literaturzeitung*
UBHJ	*University of Birmingham Historical Journal*
WEH	W. L. Wakefield and A. P. Evans (ed.), *Heresies of the High Middle Ages* (New York and London, 1969)
WS	Wyclif Society
ZFB	*Zbornik Filozofskog fakulteta u Beogradu*
ZFK	*Zeitschrift für Kirchengeschichte*
ZFZ	*Zbornik Filozofskog fakulteta u Zagrebu*
ZG	*Zeitschrift für Geschichtswissenschaft*
ZRG	*Zeitschrift für Religions- und Geistesgeschichte*

Reading list

This list is confined to bibliographies and to suggested English literature for introductory reading.

BIBLIOGRAPHIES

P. Biller, 'Les Vaudois aux xive et xve siècles: le point', *Bibliographie Sommaire*, in *Les Vaudois des origines à leur fin (xiie–xvie siècles)*, ed. G. Audisio (Turin, 1990), pp. 65–75.

G. Gonnet, 'Bibliographical appendix: recent European historiography on the medieval inquisition', in *The Inquisition in Early Modern Europe*, ed. G. Henningsen and J. Tedeschi (Dekalb, Ill., 1986), pp. 199–223.

H. Grundmann, *Bibliographie zur Ketzergeschichte des Mittelalters*, in *Sussidi eruditi* xx (Rome, 1967; repr. in *Hérésies et sociétés dans l'Europe pré-industrielle, 11e–18e siècles*, ed. J. Le Goff (Paris and The Hague, 1968), pp. 411–67.

H. Grundmann, *Ketzergeschichte des Mittelalters*, *Die Kirche in ihrer Geschichte: Ein Handbuch*, ed. K. D. Schmidt and E. Wolf, ii, G.i (Göttingen, 1963) (short analysis with extensive bibliography).

A. Hudson, *The Premature Reformation* (Oxford, 1988), pp. 520–37.

Z. Kulcsár, *Eretnekmozgalmak a xi–xiv században* (Budapest, 1964).

G. Leff, *Heresy in the Later Middle Ages: The Relation of Heterodoxy to Dissent c. 1250–c. 1450* (Manchester, 1967), ii, pp. 741–77.

B. McGinn, *Visions of the End: Apocalyptic Traditions in the Middle Ages* (New York, 1979), pp. 347–63.

G. G. Merlo, *Eretici ed Eresie Medievali nella Storiografia Contemporanea* (Torre Pellice, 1994).

J. B. Russell and C. T. Berkhout, *Medieval Heresies: A Bibliography, 1960–1979* (Toronto, 1981).

P. Segl, *Ketzer in Österreich: Untersuchungen über Häresie und Inquisition im Herzogtum Österreich im 13. und beginnenden 14. Jahrhundert* (Paderborn, 1984), pp. xvi–cxxi.

E. van der Vekené, *Bibliographie der Inquisition: Ein Versuch* (Hildesheim, 1963).

WEH, pp. 820–46.

J. K. Zeman, *The Hussite Movement: A Bibliographical Study Guide* (Ann Arbor, 1977).

INTRODUCTORY WORK IN ENGLISH

Texts in translation

R. B. Brooke, *The Coming of the Friars* (London, 1975), pp. 140–59 (see also introduction, chs 3, 4, 5).

A. Hudson, *Select English Wycliffite Writings* (Cambridge, 1978).

B. McGinn, *Visions of the End: Apocalyptic Traditions in the Middle Ages* (New York, 1979).

R. I. Moore, *The Birth of Popular Heresy* (London, 1975).

E. Peters, *Heresy and Authority in Medieval Europe* (London, 1980).

J. B. Russell, *Religious Dissent in the Middle Ages* (New York and London, 1971). (Brief extracts.)

WEH. (The most extensive and varied collection in existence.)

General

T. Asad, 'Medieval heresy: an anthropological view', *Social History* XI (1986), pp. 354–62.

P. Biller, A. Hudson, *Heresy and Literacy, 1000–1530* (Cambridge, 1994).

G. Leff, *Heresy in the Later Middle Ages: The Relation of Heterodoxy to Dissent c. 1250–c. 1450* (Manchester, 1967), I, prologue, pp. 1–47. (Supersedes his 'Heresy and the decline of the medieval Church', *PP* XX (1961), pp. 36–51.)

W. Lourdaux and D. Verhelst, ed., *The Concept of Heresy in the Middle Ages (11th–13th C.)* (Leuven and The Hague, 1976).

R. I. Moore, *The Birth of Popular Heresy* (London, 1975), introduction. (The contemporary analogy between heresy and illness should be noted.)

J. H. Mundy, *Europe in the High Middle Ages 1150–1309* (London, 1973), ch. 14. (Effective and interesting in relating heresy and society.)

J. L. Nelson, 'Society, theodicy and the origins of heresy; towards a reassessment of the medieval evidence', *SCH* IX, pp. 65–77.

J. B. Russell, 'Interpretations of the origins of medieval heresy', *MS* XXV (1963), pp. 26–53.

J. B. Russell, *Religious Dissent in the Middle Ages* (New York and London, 1971). (Includes material from modern historians.)

WEH, pp. 1–55. (A precise factual account by W. L. Wakefield.)

Eleventh-century Western heresy

C. N. L. Brooke, 'Heresy and religious sentiment, 1000–1250', *BIHR* XLI (1968), pp. 115–31; repr. in his *Medieval Church and Society* (London, 1971), pp. 139–61.

R. Landes, 'The dynamics of heresy and reform in Limoges: a study of popular participation in the "Peace of God" (994–1033)', in *Essays on the Peace of God: The Church and the People in Eleventh Century France*, ed. T. Head and R. Landes, *Historical Reflections* XIV (1987), pp. 467–511.

R. I. Moore, *The Origins of European Dissent*, 2nd edn (Oxford, 1985).

J. B. Russell, *Dissent and Reform in the Early Middle Ages* (Berkeley and Los Angeles, 1965).

Lesser heresies of the twelfth century

N. Cohn, *The Pursuit of the Millennium* (London, 1970). (This edition supersedes that of 1957, now only of historiographical significance. In neither edition does he discuss millenarianism or apocalyptic material supporting the existing order in Church or State.)

R. I. Moore, 'Some heretical attitudes to the renewal of the Church', *SCH* xiv, pp. 87–93. (Relates interpretation both to anthropology and Gregorian reforms.)

R. I. Moore, *The Origins of European Dissent*, 2nd edn (Oxford, 1985).

J. B. Russell, *Dissent and Reform in the Early Middle Ages* (Berkeley and Los Angeles, 1965).

WEH, pp. 1–55. (Historical sketch by W. L. Wakefield.)

Waldensians

P. Biller, 'Medieval Waldensian abhorrence of killing pre-1400', *SCH* xx, pp. 129–46.

P. Biller, '*Multum ieiunantes et se castigantes*: medieval Waldensian asceticism', *SCH* xxii, pp. 215–28.

P. Biller, '*Thesaurus absconditus*: the hidden treasure of the Waldensians', *SCH* xxiv, pp. 139–54.

P. Biller, 'The oral and the written: the case of the Alpine Waldensians', *BSRS* iv (1986), pp. 19–28.

M. Deanesly, *The Lollard Bible* (Cambridge, 1920), chs 1–3. (The Waldensian movement outlined in relation to its use of vernacular Scriptures.)

R. Kieckhefer, *The Repression of Heresy in Medieval Germany* (Pennsylvania, 1979), ch. 4.

G. Leff, *Heresy in the Later Middle Ages: The Relation of Heterodoxy to Dissent c. 1250–c. 1450* (Manchester, 1967), ii, pp. 448–71. (Survey introducing little-known foreign literature. The comparison of Waldensians and Cathars (pp. 453–4) does not take adequate account of the varying intensity of persecution mounted against them, and is misleading on the geographical extent of the Cathar movement.)

B. Marthaler, 'Forerunners of the Franciscans: the Waldenses', *FS*, n.s. xviii (1958), pp. 133–42.

WEH, pp. 1–55. (Historical sketch by W. L. Wakefield; see also original texts translated, pp. 200–13, 220–41.)

Cathars

B. Hamilton, *The Albigensian Crusade* (London, 1974) (Historical Association pamphlet, G 85).

E. Le Roy Ladurie, *Montaillou: Village occitan de 1294 à 1324* (Paris, 1975) tr. B. Bray, *Montaillou* (London, 1978). (Reconstruction of life in a mountain village implicated in Catharism; abridgement of French original.)

M. Loos, *Dualist Heresy in the Middle Ages* (Prague, 1974). (Wide-ranging exposition marred by blandness on Cathar internal history.)

R. I. Moore, *The Origins of European Dissent*, 2nd edn (Oxford, 1985), chs 6–8.

J. H. Mundy, *The Repression of Catharism at Toulouse: The Royal Diploma of 1279* (Toulouse, 1985), pp. 7–72. (Argues for an early breaking of heresy; includes survey on early Catharism.)

J. Sumption, *The Albigensian Crusade* (London, 1978). (Vivid narrative; ch. 2 on heresy should be avoided.)

J. N. Stephens, 'Heresy in Medieval and Renaissance Florence', *PP* liv (1972), pp. 25–60. (Interesting attempt to trace heresy, Cathar and other forms, in one city.)

W. L. Wakefield, *Heresy, Crusade and Inquisition in Southern France, 1100–1250* (London, 1974). (Succinct analysis with good bibliography.)

WEH is especially strong on Cathar texts (with introductions).

Persecution and the response of the Church

B. Bolton, 'Innocent III's treatment of the Humiliati', *SCH* VIII, pp. 73–82.

B. Bolton, 'Tradition and temerity: papal attitudes to deviants, 1159–1216', *SCH* IX, pp. 19–91.

B. Bolton, *The Medieval Reformation* (London, 1983).

B. Hamilton, *The Medieval Inquisition* (London, 1981).

R. Kieckhefer, *The Repression of Heresy in Medieval Germany* (Philadelphia, 1979).

H. C. Lea, *A History of the Inquisition of the Middle Ages* (New York, 1888); I, chs 7–14, repr. with introduction by W. Ullmann as *The Inquisition of the Middle Ages: Its Organization and Operation* (London, 1963). (This is an old classic, seriously outdated on heresy itself, but worth browsing in for many facts and for its account of the machinery of persecution. Protestant bias in Lea's reflections is obvious, but does not necessarily affect factual accuracy.)

R. I. Moore, 'Popular violence and popular heresy in Western Europe c.1000–1179', *SCH* XXI, pp. 43–50.

R. I. Moore, *The Formation of a Persecuting Society* (Oxford, 1987).

E. Peters, *Torture* (Oxford and New York, 1985), pp. 11–74.

E. Peters, *Inquisition* (New York and London, 1986), chs 1 and 2.

A. C. Shannon, *The Popes and Heresy in the Thirteenth Century* (Villanova, Pa., 1949).

D. Webb, 'The Pope and the cities: anticlericalism and heresy in Innocent III's Italy', *The Church and Sovereignty* ed., D. Wood, *SCH* Subsidia IX (Cambridge, 1991), pp. 135–52.

Free Spirit

B. Bolton, 'Mulieres sanctae', *SCH* x, pp. 77–95. (Background.)

R. E. Lerner, *The Heresy of the Free Spirit in the Later Middle Ages* (Berkeley, 1972). (Standard account for northern lands.)

R. W. Southern, *Western Society and the Church in the Middle Ages* (Harmondsworth, 1966), s.7: 'Fringe orders and anti-orders'. (For the background of the beguines.)

Joachim of Fiore and Joachimism

G. Dickson, 'The burning of the Amalriciani', *JEH* XI (1989), pp. 247–69.

B. McGinn, *The Calabrian Abbot: Joachim of Fiore in the History of Western Thought* (London, 1985). (Clear-headed assessment of Joachim as thinker.)

M. E. Reeves, 'The Liber Figurarum of Joachim of Fiore', *MRS* II (1950), pp. 57–81. (Uncommonly illuminating.)

M. E. Reeves, *The Influence of Prophecy in the Later Middle Ages: A Study in Joachimism* (Oxford, 1969). (Standard account and major work, best used for reference on Joachim or individual Joachimite episodes.)

M. E. Reeves, *Joachim of Fiore and the Prophetic Future* (London, 1976). (Concise survey.)

M. E. Reeves, 'The originality and the influence of Joachim of Fiore', *Traditio* XXXVI (1980), pp. 269–316.

R. W. Southern, 'Aspects of the European tradition of historical writing: 3 History as prophecy', *TRHS*, 5th ser. XXII (1972), pp. 159–80.

S. Wessley, 'The thirteenth-century Guglielmites: salvation through women', *SCH* Subsidia I, pp. 289–303.

Spiritual Franciscans

D. Burr, *Olivi and Franciscan Poverty: The Origins of the Usus Pauper Controversy* (Philadelphia, 1989).

D. Burr, *Olivi's Peacable Kingdom* (Philadelphia, 1993).

D. Knowles, *The Religious Orders in England* I (Cambridge, 1948), ch. 11. (A short introduction to Franciscan history.)

M. D. Lambert, *Franciscan Poverty* (London, 1961).

G. Leff, *Heresy in the Later Middle Ages: The Relation of Heterodoxy to Dissent c. 1250–c. 1450* (Manchester, 1967), II, pp. 485–93.

D. Nimmo, *Reform and Division in the Franciscan Order 1226–1538* (Rome, 1987), pp. 139–201, 240–79.

Flagellants

G. Dickson, 'The Flagellants of 1260 and the crusades', *Journal of Medieval History* XV (1989), pp. 227–67.

R. Kieckhefer, 'Radical tendencies in the Flagellant movement of the mid-fourteenth century', *JMRS* IV (1974), pp. 157–76.

G. Leff, *Heresy in the Later Middle Ages* (Manchester, 1967), II, pp. 485–93.

John Wyclif

J. I. Catto, 'Wyclif and the cult of the eucharist', *SCH* Subsidia IV, pp. 269–86. (Suggests major revision on the roots of Wyclif's thinking.)

A. Kenny, ed., *Wyclif* (London, 1986).

G. Leff, *Heresy in the Later Middle Ages: The Relation of Heterodoxy to Dissent c. 1250–c. 1450* (Manchester, 1967), II, ch. 7. (Illuminating survey of the bases of Wyclif's thinking, to be contrasted to Catto, above.)

K. B. McFarlane, *John Wycliffe and the Beginnings of English Nonconformity* (London, 1952); reissued as *The Origins of Religious Dissent in England* (New York, 1966). (The political Wyclif and his opponents.)

B. Smalley, 'The Bible and eternity: John Wyclif's dilemma', *JWCI* XXVII (1964), pp. 73–89. (Explains Wyclif's philosophical position and its emotional significance.)

The English Lollards

M. E. Aston, 'Lollardy and sedition', *PP* XVII (1960), pp. 1–44.

M. E. Aston, 'Lollardy and literacy', *History* LXII (1977), pp. 347–71. (Illuminates Lollard reading-circles via analysis of literacy and illiteracy in the modern world.)

M. E. Aston, 'William White's Lollard followers', *CHR* LXVIII (1982), pp. 469–97. For collected essays, including the above, see M. E. Aston, *Lollards and Reformers: Images and Literacy in Late Medieval Religion* (London, 1984).

C. Cross, *Church and People 1450–1660: The Triumph of the Laity in the English Church* (Hassocks, 1976). (Sensitive survey.)

M. Deanesly, *The Lollard Bible* (Cambridge, 1920). (Remarkably unaffected by its age and of value for Lollardy and heresy generally.)

A. G. Dickens, 'Heresy and the origins of English Protestantism', in *Britain and the Netherlands* II ed. J. S. Bromley and E. H. Kossmann (Groningen, 1964), pp. 47–66.

J. Fines, 'Heresy trials in the diocese of Coventry and Lichfield, 1511–12', *JEH* XIV (1963), pp. 160–74.

A. Hudson, *Selections from English Wycliffite Writings* (Cambridge, 1978). (Introduction provides concise, factual survey.)

K. B. McFarlane, *Lancastrian Kings and Lollard Knights* (Oxford, 1972). (Corrects Wyclif biography on lay support for Lollardy.)

J. A. F. Thomson, 'Orthodox religion and the origins of Lollardy', *History* LXXIV (1989), pp. 39–55.

Hussites

F. Šmahel, 'Literacy and Heresy in Hussite Bohemia', P. Biller, A. Hudson, *Heresy and Literacy, 1000–1350* (Cambridge, 1994), pp. 237–54.

F. M. Bartoš, *The Hussite Revolution, 1424–37* (New York, 1986). (Factual account, usable for events after Kaminsky (below) ends.)

F. G. Heymann, *George of Bohemia, King of Heretics* (Princeton, 1965), ch. 23.

F. G Heymann, 'John Rokycana – Church reformer between Hus and Luther', *CH* XXVIII (1959), pp. 240–80.

F. G. Heymann, 'The Hussite–Utraquist Church in the fifteenth and sixteenth centuries', *ARG* LII (1961), pp. 1–16. (Initiated revision on strength of late Utraquism.)

E. F. Jacob, 'The Bohemians at the Council of Basel, 1433', in *Prague Essays*, ed. R. W. Seton Watson (Oxford, 1948), pp. 81–123.

H. Kaminsky, 'The Prague insurrection of 30 July 1419', *MH* XVII (1966), pp. 102–26.

H. Kaminsky, 'The religion of Hussite Tabor', in *The Czechoslovak Contribution to World Culture*, ed. M. Reichigl (The Hague, 1964), pp. 210–23.

H. Kaminsky, *A History of the Hussite Revolution* (Berkeley and Los Angeles, 1967). (This detailed and profound book is far from introductory reading, nor does it cover the history of the whole movement. But see ch. 1 for introduction. It may be consulted throughout with profit.)

G. Leff, 'Wyclif and Hus: a doctrinal comparison', *BJRL* L (1968), pp. 387–410.

F. Šmahel, ' "Doctor Evangelicus super omnes Evangelistas": Wyclif's fortune in Hussite Bohemia', *BIHR* XLIII (1970), pp. 16–34.

M. Spinka, *John Hus: A Biography* (Princeton, 1968).

M. L. Wagner, *Petr Chelčický* (Scottdale, Penn., and Kitchener, Ont., 1983).

K. Walsh, 'Wyclif's legacy in Central Europe in the late fourteenth and early fifteenth centuries', *SCH* Subsidia V, pp. 397–417.

Medieval heresies and the Reformation

M. E. Aston, 'Lollardy and the Reformation: survival or revival', *History* XLIX (1964), pp. 149–70.

S. Brigden, *London and the Reformation* (Oxford, 1989), pp. 86–106.

E. Cameron, *The Reformation of the Heretics: The Waldenses of the Alps 1480–1580* (Oxford, 1984). (Underestimates role of *barbi* and of Waldensian literature; clarifies transition to Calvinism.)

C. Cross, *Church and People 1450–1660: The Triumph of the Laity in the English Church* (Hassocks, 1976). (Sensitive survey.)

J. F. Davis, *Heresy and the Reformation in the Southeast of England 1520–1559* (London, 1983).

A. G. Dickens, 'Heresy and the origins of English Protestantism', in *Britain and the Netherlands* II, ed. J. S. Bromley and E. H. Kossmann (Groningen, 1964), pp. 47–66.

W. Eberhard, 'Bohemia, Moravia and Austria', *The early Reformation in Europe* ed. A. Pettegree, (Cambridge, 1992), pp. 23–48.

M. S. Fousek, 'Spiritual direction and discipline: a key to the flowering and decay of the 16th century Unitas Fratrum', *ARG* LXII (1961), pp. 207–25.

F. G. Heymann, 'The Hussite–Utraquist Church in the fifteenth and sixteenth centuries', *ARG* LII (1961), pp. 1–16. (Initiated revision on strength of late Utraquism.)

A. Hudson, *The Premature Reformation* (Oxford, 1988), ch. 10.

Index

Books and articles are listed wherever possible under authors, the page reference indicating the point where full title and date of publication is given.